STAFFORD BEER

AND CONTROL

The meaning of Operational Research and Management Cybernetics

SONS · London · New York · Sydney · Toronto

Made and printed in Great Britain by Butler & Tanner Ltd, Frome and London

TO CYNTHIA

From women's eyes this doctrine I derive:
They sparkle still the right Promethean fire;
They are the books, the arts, the academes
That show, contain and nourish all the world.

SHAKESPEARE in *Love's Labour's Lost* (1593)

CONTENTS

Part IV—OUTCOMES

PREFACE

This book is about management, and the way in which it may invoke the use of science to help solve problems of decision and control. Just what that means will be explained in the next several hundred pages.

Who wants to know? It seems that many people are interested in these topics and would like to think them through. Most of them do not want to be blinded by science or, for that matter, assaulted by mathematics. On the other hand, those who would like to think seriously will not be satisfied with something condescendingly simple and didactic. Hence the book is written in a very definite order.

In the first part there is a general and I hope lively discussion of the possibilities for interaction between science and management. It is urged that management is not a scientific topic, just as science is not in essence managerial. But the area of overlap, where the manager may draw on science, is identified. Here lies the scope for operational research. How this activity ever came to begin, and what it is really like, are brought out. This sets the scene for an investigation of its work in the second part. Part III continues that story, drawing especially on the science of cybernetics. And in the final part there is a discussion of outcomes—for industry, for automation, for government and for the profession of management science itself.

This seems to offer a logical development, and I have tried to float on top of it a steady evolution of concepts and terms. Thus although the book gets increasingly difficult as it goes along, the reader is supposed to have every chance of keeping pace with these. The insights which I want to communicate are not trivial ones, and they have to be fabricated of sophisticated concepts and terms. It seems to me high time that management, which is now a profession on which turns the future of every company, every country, and indeed of the world itself, should accept the need for a more advanced language than basic English.

So the book is written for people who are prepared to make an attempt to follow this development, and they would be well advised not to plunge into it in the wrong order. I have tried to restrict the use of sheer jargon, and have relied rather heavily on some intricate diagrams to help out the verbal explanations, but no doubt many difficulties remain. Whether he be manager, or scientist, or someone else altogether, the reader will surely encounter ideas and words he has not met before. Whether he regards this as tedious or exciting is likely to depend on his own view of the state of the world and its need for better results. My view is this: the old ideas and words have proved inadequate for building new approaches, and without new approaches to our problems we are due to be overtaken by discomforting events.

The claim for novelty in this presentation of science in management, then, is gladly and recklessly advanced—although I know it to be tactic-ally unsound. The manager, it is often said, eschews novelty on purpose and on principle; the scientist, it is often noted, will never admit it.. Never mind. If my view of these things is idiosyncratic, at least it is co-herent. The main trouble with existing orthodoxy in this field is its fragmentary, partial character. We shall not be able to make a bold new stand against the troubles that beset us, armed to the teeth with one favourite sort of mathematical equation or with the solitary slogan 'cut the costs'. We need a larger and a rounder view. It is for those who recognize this, and who accept that thinking-time is needed to formulate such a view, that I have written at such length.

The book derives from over twenty years' work in this field—and all of it in active leadership of active operational research. It has taken four years to write the book itself, and every word has been written, rewritten and corrected in the hours after midnight. This circumstance is made public, not to excuse the faults it may help to explain, but to emphasize that this is not an ivory-tower composition. I earn my living thus; and what is written here was written in day-by-day interaction with its remunerated practice. This is how the text comes to be studded with a great many practical examples which really happened. All of them have been altered slightly, or compounded of two or more real-life cases, so that no-one will be embarrassed. But they are all otherwise genuine; and almost all refer to projects for which I personally have been immediately or ultimately responsible. Whenever this is not the case, the fact has been acknowledged.

And this brings me to acknowledgments proper. I have made refer-ences in the text to certain people and to certain books, but in neither case does this exhaust my infinite indebtedness to others. Especially do I salute many colleagues, past and present, alongside whom I have worked, and the few close personal and professional friends, whether colleagues or not, whose thinking has influenced mine. Clearly one never knows the full extent of this influence, but they should know that I am thankful for it. In particular, I am grateful to Professor Russell L. Ackoff of the University of Pennsylvania for his extensive comments on the manuscript. He bears no responsibility for anything here, but many points are the clearer because of his intervention.

When it comes to acknowledging books, the situation is yet more difficult. The present volume is in no sense at all a review of management science. I felt under no obligation, therefore, to provide that extensive bibliography which is available elsewhere in any case. This feeling led to the compilation of a select bibliography, consisting of a short list of books which I felt I should like to recommend. The outcome was invidious in the extreme; it looked like the work of a censor, which I have no desire at all to be. I have left it out. In fact, many of the books which delight me most are by authors long since dead. I have raided their works for the chapter headings used as texts on which to hang some thoughts. The English quotation is often my own translation, and when it is I have done the author the courtesy of quoting his original as well.

There is, finally, one other acknowledgment that must be made by name. Christine Lindsey has typed and retyped these long and difficult pages, and I thank her very much.

S.B.

PART I

The Nature of Operational Research

Connective Summary

In so far as the application of science to the process of management is an innovation, Chapter 1 considers the managerial approach to what is novel. It sounds a warning to those who have prejudged the possibilities without realizing the fact, and points to the changes that have made contemporary science a different thing, of different relevance, from its popular image. Thus not only have its potentialities in management been hitherto unrecognized; but what has passed for science in management hitherto, was not.

In fact, the taking of a decision is best described as the fixing of a belief. In Chapter 2 the ways in which belief is actually fixed are shown to be based on mechanisms which, though rational, are not logical. They derive from biological necessity, not from intellectual processes, and result in decisions which have more to do with learning to survive than with the objective analysis of profitability. Industrial examples are given of the way all this works.

Into this picture is now projected an account of the origins of operational research. How did it come about that real science penetrated the zone of managerial intuition? Chapter 3 answers this question, and develops from this wartime genesis an examination of the civil relevance of the work. It ends with a brief example of a famous and very early OR job. This job is then used to investigate, in Chapter 4 and with considerable detail, six major aspects of the operational research activity that are commonly misunderstood. It considers the stereotyped

1

notions of what the scientist is like, what is the nature of the problem to be solved, what science itself is like, what sort of solution counts as appropriate, what the pay-off of the study ought to be and what counts as success. It shows precisely how these stereotypes constitute major barriers to the proper understanding and utilization of this work by the manager.

Finally, in Chapter 5, some of the questions raised are answered to show what scientific research can really do for management, and how this is not dependent on having 'all the facts' available for analysis. A modern industrial OR study is expounded, and the six stereotypes are again identified and replaced with more useful notions. The part ends with a formal and official definition of operational research, and a commentary on it.

1

AN INITIAL POSTURE

> There is nothing more difficult to carry out, nor more
> doubtful of success, nor more dangerous to handle,
> than to initiate a new order of things. For the
> reformer has enemies in all who profit by the old
> order, and only luke-warm defenders in all those who
> would profit by the new order. This luke-warmness
> arises partly from fear of their adversaries, who have
> the law in their favour; and partly from the
> incredulity of mankind, who do not truly believe in
> anything new until they have had actual experience
> of it.
>
> MACHIAVELLI in *The Prince* (1513)

1   How to Neutralize a Revolution

Machiavelli was perhaps the best sixteenth-century writer on management topics. He knew a great deal about the ways in which a man in
authority could wield his power for the primary purpose of staying in
authority. The recommendations he made to his Prince were notoriously
unfeeling toward those who had to be manipulated, or degraded, or
indeed sacrificed in the process. But his methods were in use before his
time and have been since—and for the same purpose. Only the degree
to which it seems expedient that the motives and the methods should be
overt or covert seems to change.

When it comes to revolutions, the advice becomes especially amoral.
Neither the anarchist nor the established ruler can afford many scruples
when he is involved in a revolution, and there is likely to be a good deal
of blood-letting on both sides. Yet some reforms are not concerned with
the overthrow of power, but of ideas. Such revolutions, mounted on a
purely intellectual plane, are readily dealt with—as Machiavelli points
out above. They do not even have to be suppressed. The basic technique

is to pretend that they do not exist. As a refinement, it is more advantageous still for Authority to allege that it has encompassed these ideas all along.

In the sixty odd years of the present century, there has been a colossal intellectual revolution in the basic thinking of science. Basically, certainly chronologically, it began with the overthrow of classical physics. The universe of space, time and gravitation became a different universe for the scientist after the theory of relativity became known. The particles with measurable position and momentum which populated that universe took on a different meaning for the scientist after the discoveries of quantum mechanics. The intellectual revolution of twentieth-century science has been accepted by the scientist, for it is proper to his work to uncover the essential characteristics of things. From that revolution has stemmed a series of new discoveries, and indeed new sciences. Atomic physics, astrophysics, a new chemistry, a new genetics, biochemistry and biophysics are all children of a revolutionary régime.

For the man of affairs, however, the position is quite different. His job is not to seek the truth, but to be the Prince. He manages companies and industries, civil and military services, parties and policies, administrations and governments. He manipulates large systems of men, materials, machinery and money. The intellectual revolution of science has largely passed him by; it does not exist for him. For the man of affairs, in Britain at least, to know much about science at all is rather unfashionable. We have heard a British Prime Minister declare that when he sanctioned the use of the atomic bomb in Japan, he knew nothing whatever of its possible effects. We have heard company directors boast of their ignorance of science, as if this automatically conferred a certificate of preoccupation with the higher things of life. So far so good.

It happens, however, that during roughly the same period that we have been discussing, another intellectual revolution has occurred. This has concerned basic thinking about the nature of management and control. This particular revolution may at once be allied with the one earlier discussed. For one of the subsidiary features of the revolution in scientific thinking was the realization that science is basically concerned with investigating how and why things are as they are. Science, in fact, is organized knowledge about the world, not organized knowledge about itself. Of course, the historical origins of the subject make this clear. But it must be confessed that, to this day, the organization of our universities and scientific institutions does not make the fact quite so plain. They suffer, as it were, from a hardening of the faculties. So the man of affairs is not altogether to blame, if, when confronted with a scientist, his first question is: 'What is your subject?' It is not enough to reply: 'I investigate the world.' One has to be a chemist, or a physicist, or a biologist; one has to acknowledge a *slant*. All this adds up to a confusion in the public mind between science and technology. To get back firmly to science: its job *is* to investigate the world; then it may as well investigate the nature of management and control as of the structure of benzene, or the atomic nucleus.

Indeed, science has been doing just this. It has been investigating the processes of management. The movement began early in the century and made slow progress until the First World War, when military exigencies caused it momentarily to flare into activity. Between the wars it was quiescent. But twenty years ago it began a vast surge forward. Out of the work done since 1940 has emerged a corpus of scientific knowledge about management and its problems that is called operational research, and about the nature of control that is called cybernetics. Today it is a sober fact to state that the pursuit of these two topics has wrought an intellectual revolution in the very basis of the conduct of affairs. But remember what happens to reformers.

In the first place, the man of affairs is not, by nature or in fact, much concerned with science. His concept of the subject is probably fifty years out of date. This anachronistic outlook is at once reflected in a denial that his area of action is a fit and proper field for scientific investigation at all. People still write to the newspapers on these lines. Next, the obsession in the public mind with *topics* of science, especially with technology, prompts the man of affairs to say that even if his preserves are not forbidden territory, at least science has no means of entry to them. He thus ignores the fundamental motivation of science, which is not to apply techniques, nor to 'do chemistry' (for instance), but precisely to *find* an entry. And so it comes about that the intellectual revolution concerning the basis of management and control does not exist for the man of affairs. It is easy enough, and common enough, for such a man (particularly at the highest levels) to declare that scientific activity in this area does not and cannot exist. His motives are pure; he does not engage a Machiavelli to advise him to say this. But the ghost of Machiavelli is feeding him the ammunition just the same.

And suppose this man of affairs should meet the operational research scientist or the cybernetician one dark night. What shall the ghost of Machiavelli prescribe then? We saw the answer at the start of this chapter. The man of affairs should reply: 'There is nothing new about

DC—B

these subjects; we have been doing them all the time.' Seek out some of the employers of operational research scientists and they will tell you just this.

That ends our primer on how to neutralize a revolution. The question is whether it also ends the attempt to make a revolution effective. This book is about the intellectual revolution in management and control. It talks about reform compared with which 'there is nothing more difficult to carry out, nor more doubtful of success, nor more dangerous to handle'. For this reason, and unlike other books about operational research and cybernetics, it is concerned mainly with neither teaching techniques nor stating facts. Indeed, the first quarter of the book is concerned precisely with this question of management and science as *interacting* activities. A serious but not solemn attempt will be made to investigate the nature of the muddle so far uncovered, and to break through the grave misunderstandings that have arisen. Anyone who really wants to join in this enquiry with an open mind, suspending judgment on the nature and value of this intellectual revolution until the end, is most heartily welcome on the journey.

But here is some free advice for the real Prince, whose object is not to be disturbed in his seat of power, and who seeks no exorcism for the ghost of Machiavelli which comforts him. These pages are full of reasons why there has been no revolution, and full of demonstrations that science cannot handle management problems. It is guaranteed to convince you that it contains nothing new. Please do not bother to read further; to be proved right at such great length will be bad for your soul.

2   Science and Decision

The whole idea of using hard science as an intrinsic part of the managerial process is alien to many. It is a proposal often countered by such remarks as 'management cannot be reduced to a science', or even 'management is an art'. But neither of these replies is at all relevant to the issue.

The processes of management are complicated. They are complicated for the individual manager for whom insight, value judgment, flair, acumen, maturity and experience *count*. They are even more complicated for the social entity that is a management group. Inside this, the climate of opinion, fashion, reputation, maintenance of face, dominance and every kind of personal relationship also count. There is neither need nor intention to complain bitterly about all this, or to demand that frail humans be replaced by infallible electronic computers. It is only in the eyes of the layman that science imagines itself omnipotent, and the human brain is still the best computer we have.

Now the input to the brain consists exclusively of sensations which are arranged in meaningful patterns. The meaning starts as a raw awareness of our place in the world that lies outside us; thus the pattern may be passively received. Or it may trigger off a whole series of physiological reactions, leading to a physical or emotional response. Reflection on these patterns is an intellectual process that forms new patterns of a higher order; distinctions are drawn between facts and illusions, particular facts may be generalized, inferences of many kinds may be drawn.

Decisions are patterns of a still higher order. So for science to examine decision is itself a most complicated business. It cannot involve less than is involved within the managerial society and the brains of its individual managers; in fact it must involve a good deal more—or it has nothing new to contribute. Let us examine briefly how this fresh contribution may come about.

A decision has to be reached about a certain piece of plant. Fortunately enough, there are various *facts* about this plant—verifiable statements which are common ground between the manager and scientist. For example, the plant exists; it was put there eighteen years ago; the manager's name is Ponsonby. On the face of it, one might write down all the facts and then pass to a list of *opinions* about this plant. It is efficient; it is too expensive; it is out of gear with the market; and so forth. But a little reflection shows that the dividing line between these two lists is not quite clear. We may best exemplify this by observing that some propositions would be entered as facts by one lot of observers and as opinions by another, and vice versa.

Consider a simple illustration. Tests have been run in the works to see whether one kind of machine tool is better than another. The purchasing department says that *A* is better than *B* because it is cheaper to buy. The production engineers say that *B* is better than *A* because it produces a better job. The accountants prefer *A* because its product has the higher profit margin. The sales people none the less argue for *B* because, although its product has the lower profitability, it is easier to sell. The task of a manager with a decision to reach is the task of rolling up all such small and isolated verdicts into a ball to produce a consolidated verdict about the relative merits of *A* and *B* 'on the whole', 'in the long run'. All these viewpoints are really opinions, although those who express them probably call them facts because there is an allegedly factual basis for them. The basis of this allegation will be considered later. Plenty of judgment is needed here, and the weighing of evidence: it is almost a juridical proceeding.

But let us return to the scientist. What has he to say about or to contribute to this state of affairs? He might discover, by the use of statistics, that the various advantages of B over A and A over B are in no case big enough, when compared with the number of trials, for any conclusion to be validly drawn at all. That is, given the amount of experience so far accumulated, all the results could have been due to chance. In this way all the little 'facts', and especially the big composite 'fact', dissolve away. The only fact relevant to a decision available in this story is the fact that there is no logical basis for reaching one.

Of course a manager might think that if he submits to this kind of scientific advice, he will never be allowed to do anything. As situations become more complicated, so the problem of establishing an adequate scientific basis for decision becomes greater. But here comes the scientist again, this time trying, in view of all this, to organize the experiments in more subtle and sophisticated ways so that a decision may after all be reached on logical grounds. Then, if we are determined to get rid of this scientist fellow somehow, let us declare that the answer has to be given by this evening and that the proposed tests will take three months. Surely that is the end of scientific advice in this problem? Not so. The scientist is not the dedicated maniac that so many take him for; he lives in a real world of pressures like everyone else. And if time will not permit him to reach concrete scientific conclusions, he must use whatever information there is in an attempt to establish the *probabilities* that one is better than another. This is not unscientific. The *whole* truth about a matter is never known. Scientific answers are always relative; they hold under certain conditions. The condition now being introduced is a constraint of time.

Now suppose that the probabilities are equal, as they would be if, for example, the A's and the B's had exactly the same characteristics over the run of tests made. The manager at this point may be thinking of tossing a coin to decide between the two, and the scientist observes in passing that this is a very scientific outlook. For where there is no evidence, it is best to acknowledge the fact candidly, rather than invent reasons for choosing A above B. However, there is more to come. If there is nothing *within* the A/B situation to indicate which is the better choice, then we should look *outside* the situation. This means attending to the question of vulnerability. To put it simply: where there is nothing to choose between machine tool A and machine tool B in any of the ways relevant to the product, it may be that A is made by a firm with a better reputation for delivering its products on time than the firm producing B. And so on.

This example should not mislead anyone to imagine, this early in the story, that scientific enquiry is appropriate to production decisions alone. Indeed, when an argument of this kind is deployed in connection with a board-level problem it is even more cogent. For the 'facts' that are passed around the table are in this case even more suspect, because they are really verdicts built out of many less important verdicts themselves masquerading as facts. At this level, decisions are based on assurances made by people one trusts, which are in turn based on opinions expressed by subordinates one trusts, who are in turn assumed to have trustworthy information. If opinions, verdicts and assurances are loosely regarded as facts, and if the processes by which they are propagated and accepted are loosely regarded as rational, it is no wonder that the best decisions are not always taken. Management scientists have much advice to give about all this; but to understand it, one must first acknowledge that the present methods of decision-taking are precarious.

The picture now emerging seems to be this. The brain of the manager is capable of taking into account a large number of considerations, some of which may ramify a long way from the apparent situation. It is capable of weighting these considerations according to their importance and to the degree of reliability of the 'facts' which measure them. The manager knows he does all this, and when someone says to him that science can help him in his job, he at once imagines that a decision procedure of a much simpler kind is going to replace his own brain processes—a procedure that will be no good. Why he should think this, I do not know, unless it be because what most people are taught about science is badly done, and an oversimplified notion of the philosophy of science has been generally accepted. This is perhaps the case; for even when operational research is being used, one frequently hears it said: 'Whatever you chaps may say, there are many other factors that I will have to take into account in reaching a decision.' Now the whole point about doing science in the managerial sphere is that it should be *good* science. And what kind of science is it that omits to take account of *all* the relevant factors which encompass a problem? At the least, science can certainly take account of as many factors as anyone can think of, and ought to find a few more that have escaped notice too.

3 The Manager and Science

No; the capability of science when applied in this area is not a diminished one. Scientists are people who have been trained in ways of examining the world which offer the best known means of making our beliefs about the way that world behaves correspond to the facts. This may sound an odd description of science to someone who thinks of it in terms of Boyle's law and the Wheatstone bridge, but such is the real nature of the subject. Then let us go back to the criticism with which we started. There is no question of trying to 'reduce' the process of management to 'a science'. The intention is simply to *augment* by scientific method the processes of which brains are capable in making judgments and taking decisions. In this way, it is hoped to lift various decisions which might otherwise have to be considered by hunch (or in the last resort by the toss of a coin) out of the arena of argument. The more we can measure, the more we can quantify, the more we can establish genuine fact, the more we can demonstrate what follows and what does not follow, the more we can calculate chance and risk, the less vulnerable need the ultimate decision be.

The first insight to be attained, it seems, is that to say whether management is a science (or could be reduced to it) or an art (in which all true managers glory) is not to the point. What matters is that every relevant skill should be turned to the task of producing good decisions and more effective strategies. Science by its very nature is adequate to aid the manager in this. For science is not a thing done by physicists, nor a thing done by chemists: it is the establishment of knowledge about the world. And that part of the world in which the operational research scientist operates is the area of management decision. It has to be accepted, however, that the OR scientist works with true scientific comprehensiveness; he is not a pedlar of techniques. If this is not acknowledged, the manager will never make the scientist a true partner— because he will not be able to see how he can.

In parenthesis, it should particularly be acknowledged that certain scientists themselves are often slow to understand this point. In an age of ever-increasing specialization, comprehensiveness in scientists is as much frowned upon in academic circles as it is unexpected by business men. But the mark of the true scientist is precisely his breadth of outlook. Consider this comment by Sir Herbert Reed, writing about the death of the very great Swiss psychologist, C. G. Jung. Reed remarks that Jung's comprehensiveness 'was not only the distinctive mark of his genius, but also the explanation of the scepticism with which his work was sometimes received in academic circles'. Reed goes on to justify Jung as follows: 'But just as there are certain distortions of science which we call historicism, or certain distortions of artistic style which we call mannerism, so there is a distortion of science which we may call scientism; and it is so far removed from the true spirit of science, which, as Bacon said, takes all knowledge to be its province, that it has become the real obscurantism of our time, turning a blind eye on all phenomena that cannot be accommodated to its own myopic vision.' There are some managers, and some scientists, who share myopia of exactly this kind where operational research is concerned. If this book is to be understood at all, the reader must start with a willingness to grapple with the real nature of science.

To set down the undoubtedly controversial point at once: neither the manager nor the scientist can prejudge the best approach to a particular decision. If science is to be applied, then a scientific attack must be used from the start. This prohibits the manager from saying 90 per cent of the things he customarily does say in briefing the scientist.

To take a thoroughly basic example, the manager will speak of the 'facts'—those that are known, those that are required, those that he proposes to make available. Rude things were said about 'facts' in the last section, and it is time to consider what this criticism really amounts to. In books on the philosophy of science, it is usual to take an example from the most basic kind of scientific fact—a measurement. How do we know that this thing weighs a gram? A little reflection will show how the fact that it does weigh a gram must depend on a chain of comparisons linking this gramsworth with some ultimately standard gram, and how the concept of a standard must in turn be hedged in with many qualifications about how it is to be measured, to what accuracy, and in what conditions. But all this, though interesting, sounds like metaphysical speculation to a practical man. He is therefore invited to try his hand at uncovering a simple fact from the following account of a real-life situation.

A section of a machine shop contains six roughly similar but not identical machines. The output from these machines for a succession of twelve identical periods of time is given at Table 1. The double line dividing periods 1–6 from periods 7–12 is the moment at which an

TABLE 1. Number of items produced per period on six machines.

Periods		1	2	3	4	5	6	7	8	9	10	11	12
Machines	A	572	570	568	nil	574	570	572	nil	570	572	nil	572
	B	550	548	nil	552	nil	nil	550	554	554	nil	552	550
	C	606	598	600	612	nil	609	610	615	nil	nil	612	nil
	D	nil	588	586	588	586	590	nil	nil	588	592	nil	590
	E	543	nil	nil	nil	535	550	560	565	558	545	550	548
	F	548	546	545	540	nil	542	544	542	546	548	nil	548

important change was introduced. The question is, was the change a good one or not?

Here is a possible approach to this question. There was a uniform level of activity in this place in each of the epochs 1–6 and 7–12. Namely, there were twenty-six productive and ten unproductive periods. So there is no need for any confusing details. Kindly extend the table to show the total output before and after the change, and strike the averages in each case. The manager's clerks are competent, and extend the table as in Table 1*a*. Well, the answer is clear: production has

TABLE 1*a*. To complete Table 1.

Total output before $= 14,816$ Average $= 569 \cdot 8$	Total output after $= 14,707$ Average $= 565 \cdot 7$

fallen. Certainly, then, the change was a mistake. Whether the man who suggested the change should be sacked or not is a matter of opinion —a question for the manager's judgment. But the outcome itself is a *fact*.

But wait a minute. Here is another manager, who argues like this. There is no need, he says, for any confusing details. Kindly extend the table to show the total output before and after the change, and strike the averages in each case. This manager's clerks are competent too— they just have a slightly different idea of what the manager means by these words. They extend the table as in Table 1*b*. Again the answer is clear. Production has risen on every machine. So the change was certainly advantageous. The manager must decide whether to give the innovator a bonus—that is his prerogative. But no-one can argue about the improvement itself. That is a *fact*.

TABLE 1*b*. An alternative completion of Table 1.

Machine	Average before	Average after
A	570·8	571·5
B	550·0	552·0
C	605·0	612·3
D	587·6	590·0
E	542·7	554·3
F	544·2	545·6

The odd thing is that we cannot even say which, if either, of these conclusions is correct. Of course it is possible to see *why* the two answers are different. But the machine differences taken into account in the second case (which makes it look preferable) may not be relevant. The change of practice on which judgment is required may itself have induced the particular apportionment of unproductive time to each machine that makes the first case bad. Secondly, as in the earlier example, a statistician might determine that whatever has been happening here does not matter, in that the changes could all be accounted for by chance.

So much, then, for the 'sacred fact'. It would be interesting to hear these two managers arguing the outcome at a management meeting. But it would be better, surely, to let the scientist concerned with a problem in which this situation figured find out the facts himself. That kind of judgment is his business. By the way, it is to be hoped that no-one will discard this example on the ground that he would inevitably see through the dilemma. Perhaps he would—if he had access to the original table. But the odds are that some clerk will have opted for one of these forms of presentation, and used it. In this way, the manager thinks he has taken a decision (to sack or promote an innovator) on the basis of a fact. In reality, the manager of this example was a nonentity. The sacking or promotion was a decision made *by the clerk*.

4 The Degradation of Science

Well, it may be said, the point that it is the province of science to *investigate* the world is taken. It will not be supposed that a scientist operating in the managerial situation is a man committed in advance to timing jobs with a stop-watch, or a man dedicated to the hopeless task of transforming the manager's personal thinking into the language of electronic computers, or a man who is 'given the facts' and told to analyse them. Is that not insight enough to be going on with? The answer is yes, subject to one further proviso: it should not be imagined that any piece of coherent or useful thinking is inevitably scientific thinking.

The mistaken idea that must be dispatched at this point is almost the opposite fallacy to the one already discussed. Just as there are people who believe that the scientist is a man with a gimmick (it might be Ohm's law, which is rather obviously inappropriate as a tool for helping managing directors), so there are people who think that science is no more than a synonym for coherence. This is really to use 'science' as an O.K. word, meaning roughly the opposite of 'superstition'. It is one of life's dear ironies that these two extremely different views are often held by the same person, but we will deal with the second outlook as if it were entirely distinct from the first.

A senior industrialist was once heard to say: 'All our conclusions are scientific; the only question is whether operational research can make the science more sophisticated, and the conclusions therefore yet more exact.' If one could take an entirely rigorous and objective view of this apparently innocuous statement, it would surely seem to be insane. It is not really so, of course, because the speaker is trying to say something which in his own eyes seems eminently sensible. Man is a rational animal, he is saying, and so long as he is in control of himself his behaviour must be scientifically sound. Irrational behaviour is the mark of halfwits, drunkards and delinquents. Now, to that speaker, it is evident that rational behaviour is something that necessarily follows scientific investigation—and follows it alone. But to adopt this use of words and the ideas behind them debases the notion of 'science', and degrades the meaning of the word.

In fact, scientific reasoning is extremely rare, is not very often indulged in by anyone who is not a trained scientist, and is a very difficult subject demanding lengthy study. The processes by which man the rational animal normally thinks and comes to conclusions are not scientific, and this is not said disparagingly. The way man (and this term, happily, includes the scientist) normally thinks is determined by the physiology of his brain. We know a good deal about the way the process works, and ought to admire it for the reason that nature has produced machinery which is competent to survive in a hostile and competitive world. But unless we clearly comprehend that science is (neither better nor worse than, but) entirely distinct from rationality in the sense of coherent and useful behaviour, this book will be meaningless.

There is, unfortunately, a considerable background of nonsense to be ploughed up before the word 'science' acquires its proper meaning in the vocabulary of managers. Sixty years ago, men such as Taylor and Gilbreth began to attack production and other physical processes by a basically scientific method. They set out to measure and to record, to analyse and to improve. Measuring, recording and analysing are certainly acts that belong to scientific activity, and the contemporary topics of method study and work measurement (which together comprise work study as an industrial management tool) are scientific. But the other legacy inherited from these pioneers was the term 'scientific management', which has had a less felicitous development. People have come to believe that any sort of thinking that incorporates facts and figures constitutes some phase of the scientific management that starts on the shop floor with work study. But this is not true. The techniques of the stop-watch, the micromotion camera and the chronocyclegraph are of little use in the boardroom: they cannot be focused on management decision. What techniques should replace them? The arithmetic average and the simple chart? Certainly not. A more sophisticated kind of science is needed to aid the decision processes of top management than is necessary on the shop floor, not a total collapse into the trivial. Anyone who wishes to live up to the ideals of scientific management set by the pioneers at the turn of the century, and hopefully embraced by many young managers in the twenties and thirties, must today understand operational research.

A first step that must be advocated is to forswear attitudes that degrade the idea of science. We have already seen how the basic build-ing-block of science, the fact, has been degraded to mean a verdict. We have noted how the word 'scientific' is abused in the context of manage-ment. (Not that managers need accept any blame for a general social phenomenon: we live in a world of scientific toothpaste, we are told to wash our hair scientifically, and there is a science of washing-up.) In between the basic, particular and the generic terms is an assortment of pseudo-scientific phrases that people use to comfort themselves. In a scientific age, a masquerade of scientific terms keeps up the spirits. And so there is a 'law of averages'—a term used to imply that probabilities continuously adjust themselves to converge on a target balance of fre-quencies, which they do not. There is the 'calculated risk'—a term used to mean that a risk is recognized but has not been calculated. Perhaps the real nature of science, and the capabilities it has to offer in the service of management (such as calculating risks, for example), will only be under-stood when the masquerade is over, and the scientific-seeming masks are dropped to reveal the intuitions underneath.

Real science in the nineteen-sixties is complicated and demanding, as we see it in atomic physics, in genetics or in space research. When science is applied to management the complication and the demands are no less severe. The manager cannot be fobbed off with methods that were, scientifically speaking, old-hat when Archimedes did the first operational research by advising the King of Syracuse on his combat strategy. If he wants more than this, and there is a great deal more for the taking, the manager needs to start again. He needs to survey present advanced management methods, which have been labelled 'scientific' either falsely or trivially; to evaluate the processes by which decisions today are actually reached and in which scientific method has no part; and he needs then to consider what it would be like to use the methods of modern science that are in fact available.

If any sort of perspective is to be achieved in mastering these aims, some time must be devoted to considering what the rational processes of the brain are really like. In what ways are these natural processes effective, in what ways unhelpful, and in what ways are they distinguished from scientific processes (which are far from natural)?

In the first place, the whole topic of discussion here is not deduction, nor proof, nor the application of facts. When we speak of management and its decisions we are really speaking of the settling of opinion or belief. This is not a process to be oversimplified. As has just been said, it is not true that belief is settled either by rigorously scientific method on the one hand, or by erratic and emotional caprice on the other. To study what really happens we need to consider the account given of the process by men who have made a special study of how it works—the philosophers and psychologists.

Any such account is divided more or less arbitrarily in so far as there are many ways of analysing thought processes. For present purposes it does not matter much which analytic scheme is used, so long as it gives something like the right proportion of importance to the scientific method of fixing belief—which is not a very large proportion at all. The particular set of categories chosen comes from the analysis made by the American philosopher Charles Peirce, who distinguished four main methods, the last of which alone is the scientific. Not only is this in roughly the right proportion, but his account of the other three modes of thinking will be found extremely relevant to the modern industrial situation.

In the next chapter, then, are set out Peirce's four basic methods of settling belief, with a discussion about each from the point of view of contemporary society.

2

ON FIXING BELIEF

Just the place for a Snark! I have said it twice:
That alone should encourage the crew.
Just the place for a Snark! I have said it thrice:
What I tell you three times is true.

LEWIS CARROLL in *The Hunting of the Snark* (1876)

1   The Method of Tenacity

The first method of fixing belief isolated by Peirce might be called the method of tenacity. It begins with a viewpoint, capriciously formed. Perhaps this was something learned at mother's knee; it might have been revealed by a sailor in a pub; or it is an idea culled from this morning's newspaper. Typically, it is what 'they' are saying (and they ought to know). At this stage, the viewpoint has no special merit for the man who expresses it, for its casual origins are understood—it is not a belief.

However, it is brought out—and increasingly brought out—to be aired. Gradually it becomes inculcated as a habit of thought; eventually it is indeed fixed as a belief. Be it noted at once that this is *not* emotional, random or quixotic behaviour; it is opinion that is steadily and systematically evolved, although not in a strictly rational fashion. In fact we know a good deal about the mechanisms that underlie this way of thinking; they are biologically, if not logically, valid. They come about in the following way.

Biologically speaking, organisms manage to adapt and to survive by sifting their experience and learning from it. This is most notably what happens in the case of the brain. Every time a particular pathway is traced through a set of nerve cells, it seems, it becomes easier to trace that pathway again in future. This is rather like the situation on a network of snow-bound roads: every vehicle that passes makes it easier for the next to pass, until certain routes through the network of roads must

17

obviously be preferred to others. The brain acquires maturity in exactly this way; if it were not so we should be incapable of coherent behaviour at all. Unfortunately, there is a snag.

For this is the very 'conditioning' process by which men are indoctrinated, for political ends, with beliefs that would otherwise be unwholesome to them. And of course if this result can be achieved by cunning in an authoritarian state, it can also be achieved by accident in the normal social environment. For everyone knows how cliché-ridden is most of our small talk; how we repeat ourselves from one conversation to another; how we confirm and even embellish an anecdote as the literal truth which may simply have started as an amusing fabrication. It is this kind of thing that goes on, according to Peirce, when the method of tenacity is being employed. It is not a scientific mode of thinking. But it is not the irrationality of a madman either, for there certainly is a scientific basis for saying why we think in this way, how we think in this way, and also for saying that it is a sensible way (on the whole) for a creature whose survival depends upon his ability to profit by experience *to* think.

But, after that apologia, it is still fair to point out the dangers surrounding this method of fixing belief. It is likely to deaden the facility for entertaining new ideas and to produce the reaction (in Peirce's own words): 'I could not believe the contrary, because I should be so wretched if I did.' New thinking means broaching a new pathway, risking a snow-covered road when alternative routes have already been cleared. We say then that people prefer the familiar; in fact, their brains are constructed as machines for reinforcing successful combinations of neural events, and reducing the probabilities that alternative combinations will be tried. Incidentally, this is surely one of the reasons why people so readily claim that their judgments are more or less scientific. For if I count it wretched to be *un*scientific within the scientific milieu of these progressive days, then I am likely to allege that whatever belief I have come to hold must count as a scientific opinion. But let us go on exploring the nature of the method of tenacity itself, observing how it actually operates in our lives, so that we may more readily recognize what a threat it constitutes to the development of new ideas.

The best use of the whole process is indeed that of intellectual conditioning—but only in its more constructive sense. We may teach a child that seven times eight equals fifty-six, so that he becomes conditioned to feel wretched if someone (including himself) should propose an alternative answer. But if we use this same process to facilitate the wrong pathways in the brain we shall produce aberrant behaviour. If we teach a child that 'la chaise' means 'the roof', he will feel confounded in France when invited to sit on a chair. The status of these propositions, the one arithmetic and the other linguistic, is quite different in science. The first is true, the second false; and the scientific approach to the validation of either proposition is quite different from that which must be used in the case of the other. But the status of the two propositions in *nature*, considered as contents of the mind, is the same. Each uses the brain as a learning machine to produce a conditioned response to a repeated stimulus. Thus subjectively, and no wonder, they appear equally valid. So if we now apply the label 'scientific conclusion' to the first example, it is likely to become attached to the other, for the subjective experience of the trainee is identical.

Let us take as an example what is happening in British industry about the use of operational research. How is it that operational research began as a tool for devising important strategies, but is now mostly used in industry at the merely tactical level? Well, when we began we were advised to go carefully, to make as few demands as possible, and to get the work started at all costs. Therefore we did not worry very much about pitching the work at its most effective and relevant level. How does a scientist find words to say to a managing director that he needs a scientific plan for his whole capital development programme, or a scientifically designed control system to contain the company's vast and rapidly expanding expenditure on stocks? No; we allowed ourselves to think it the path of wisdom to move slowly, and to encourage our work to grow from small beginnings. We said: let us install scientific planning on the third bit of plant on the right as you go in number six gate. We said: let us calculate the right number of items to stock in this sample stock bin, thereby demonstrating in principle how to clap scientific controls on stocks that must be replenished continually.

Whether this was the path of wisdom after all, or not, is still not clear; at any rate, it was all that we could do. How have managers responded? They began by wondering precisely what sort of activity they were nurturing. They took up a consciously open-minded position about this work, and said to each other that it was their duty to find out exactly what it does. As study succeeded study, it became increasingly clear that what operational research does is . . . whatever it happened to be doing. It is almost a pity that those early jobs succeeded so well, for managers discussed them among themselves and gradually built up, by the method of tenacity, an account of what operational research 'really' is. It is what it has repeatedly demonstrated itself to be. How could it be anything else?

This is a good example of a piece of genuine, physiologically sound,

irrational thinking. It belongs to non-science in management. It cannot
be tetchily dismissed as absurd, nor called a species of scientific conclusion that has slightly misfired. When the OR man eventually comes to
his management and proposes to undertake a study of a really advanced
kind, the sort of thing he is trained and fitted to do, the very people
who began by acknowledging their own ignorance and an earnest desire
to learn about the nature of this activity, turn round and tell the OR
man that this kind of work is not his province. They proceed to explain
to him what his own subject is about.

This is of course the reason for the existence of this book. There is a
solemn need at this point in time to start again, and to ask what are the
real purposes and capabilities of operational research. It must by now
be clear why this early chapter of the book is devoted to so odd a topic
as a discussion of the way in which we all think, instead of plunging
straight into the nature and origins of operational research. Unless we
confront ourselves with what has been going on we shall be completely
incapable of assimilating a fresh exposition—even if it were twice as clear,
and twice as convincing, as I shall be able to make it.

We must warn ourselves first of all about the method of tenacity;
useful as it normally is, it will not serve our purposes now. As a footnote, let it be said that this admonition applies just as strongly to
scientists themselves as to managers, for scientists are only human too.
Once he has been employed on a number of trivial and more or less
irrelevant projects, the scientist gets used to it; the method of tenacity
conditions him to believe that he is not the sort of creature he is. That
endearing trait of the scientist, a due humility in the face of the infinitely
complex and marvellous nature of the world, leads him to interpret his
own conditioning wrongly. He may think that the degraded form of
operational research often met with today is no more than the original
conception of the subject shorn of its more grandiose delusions. Up to
a point, this is the sober truth; but let us more constructively agree to
entertain the opposite view, so that if indeed the national operational
research capability is not being properly exploited there will be more
chance of recognizing the fact.

The point of this section is to argue that the method of tenacity is
illogical, but not a process that should be vehemently decried. To say
that a belief has been fixed in this way is not rude nor is it an accusation
of sheer prejudice, since this is the way the machinery in the cranium
actually works. But the device that works so well in adapting the animal
to its environment is no blessing when an intellectual breakthrough is
required. The need for this in man the animal is rare; but man the

manager, man the conceiver of change, must needs disrupt the pattern and alter the rhythm of his brain. It is surely predictable that, in his animal role, he will be cautious about doing this. The system rebels, but in so doing there is also a predictable outcome to his failure.

When an animal species is confronted with a slowly changing environment that suits it well it becomes specialized. Giraffes have acquired long necks, and zebras stripes; fish have gills, and cannot breathe the air. This is what is meant by specialization in biology. The process is the genetic equivalent of the adaptation processes of the individual brain. Strong preferred patterns are formed that neatly match the environment. Now suppose that environment changes radically and rather fast. An animal species that cannot change itself quickly enough to cope is overwhelmed. Specialization has become *over*-specialized. This is what happened to the dinosaurs.

Man as a species has developed a large brain to meet this threat of extinction. With this weapon, mankind has (uniquely) acquired a faculty for forecasting the threat, and for changing its capacity to cope artificially. For instance, man can forecast that if he ventures to the South Pole he will be too cold to survive, and he makes provision to keep warm; he does not wait for his species, or the explorer sub-species, to grow fur. Even so, the brain is not always equal to the task. When a man is brain-washed, the technique is precisely to confuse his ability to forecast events and to be prepared to meet them. This is done by making a random, instead of a systematic, connection between stimuli and responses. A species confronted suddenly with a new environment, alternating between a polar and a tropical climate, would not adapt to it sufficiently quickly to survive. A brain confronted suddenly with brain-washing techniques is beaten.

The moral of all this is to suggest that so long as the social, economic and industrial environments change slowly, the method of tenacity that our brains employ works well. We adapt. Today, however, these environments are changing rapidly. The method of tenacity produces too slow an adaptation to cope with the revolutions that the world is undergoing in every sphere. Unless those responsible for policy-making abandon this method, and turn to other ways of exploiting their cerebral equipment, our society will not adapt sufficiently quickly, and we shall become economically extinct. Manifestly, the nation is moving towards this fate. Governments are selected by the method of tenacity (the class vote); they operate by this method too (the British way of life). Industry is managed by the method of tenacity (it was good enough for my grandfather). New thinking everywhere is blocked by the method of tenacity (this idea has not yet been tried out, let someone else make the mistakes). Conversely, when new ideas about management and control have been discussed for a sufficiently long time, they too will be generally adopted, not by logic, but by the method of tenacity. But this time, perhaps, it will be too late.

2   The Method of Authority

The second way of settling opinion without being scientific is by appeal to authority. In today's society, this mode of thinking is possibly the most important in fixing belief; it is the will of the institution. On the face of it, this is a simple matter, with no subtle undertones; after all, people usually know when they are 'playing politics'. But the question is really much more complicated and insidious than this. First of all, Charles Peirce put the naïve point of view with some charm: 'When complete agreement could not otherwise be reached, a general massacre of all who have not thought in a certain way has proved a very effective means of settling opinion.' That was written later than Machiavelli, but long before the emergence of the Organization Man.

However highly placed he may be organizationally, an individual is part of the social system which gives life to the institution of which he is a member. The question of the extent to which he will conform to accepted ideas and values is by no means simply a matter of his own strength of character on the one hand nor of his ability to compromise on the other. He is aware of a number of pressures which work upon him, but unaware of a great many more which operate in less obvious ways. These are the natural laws which govern (up to a point) the behaviour of any large system, and we can go some way towards offering a scientific explanation of the way in which they work.

Let us start by picturing a system, any kind of system, in which the interesting feature is the distribution of heat. One small zone of this system is hotter than the rest. Now we know full well that if this system is left alone for a time, without any further input of energy or contact with the outside world, the hot zone will certainly not get any hotter. In fact the hot zone will gradually get colder. The heat which has been concentrated in the one small zone will gradually dissipate right through the system, until the distribution of heat is uniform throughout. This state of affairs is an example of the second law of thermodynamics.

We have learnt enough from experience to recognize intuitively that the picture just painted is correct, but it takes a lot more thinking and research and mathematical insight to develop all the consequences for systems in general. However, scientists do know how to describe the general case of this natural phenomenon.

They know, for example, that any system will gradually run down if cut off from a source of outside energy, because the energy internally available for useful work will gradually even out until there is none left. A system in this state is best regarded, perhaps, as *dead*. They also know that any flow of information in the system is related to these energy changes. In fact, it is easiest to think of information as being news about the states of energy in the different zones of the system—news which is carried about by the energy shifts themselves. Now as the system runs down, there is ever less energy available to carry ever less information about ever less important differences in internal states. When the system has finally stopped operating, because there is no internal energy potential left, there is nothing to know about the system any more. Thus high information levels are exactly correlated with high differentials in internal energies. This connection, by the way, is not fanciful or literary; the mathematical equations describing these two aspects of a self-contained system (which can be developed independently) turn out to be the same as each other.

By these self-same equations it is possible to see how the high energy associated with a particular individual or group inside an institution tends to be absorbed and assimilated by the remainder, because the system is struggling by its very nature to even things out. If it succeeds, then it becomes defunct—it runs down—or, in the language of the example given, when the heat is evenly distributed there is no potential left for doing useful work. Of course this application of thermodynamic principles to social systems is made by analogy, and the conditions do not hold perfectly. The system is supposed to be entirely self-contained, sealed off from the rest of the world, and no human institution, such as a firm, is entirely isolated managerially. Yet this fact, interestingly enough, does not so much invalidate the analogy as indicate the precise way in which real-life organizations alone manage to survive. This is by an interchange of managerial energy with the world outside the system.

Here is another conclusion to be drawn from the picture that is emerging. If the system cannot, or at any rate does not, disseminate its pockets of high energy in the way described, there is one other alternative open to it which will still conform to the natural laws of thermodynamics. The system may declare the high-energy pocket contained within it to be an independent sub-system. A heat-proof (energy-proof) shell can be built around the high-energy zone which will then stabilize itself within the shell, while the main part of the system stabilizes itself regardless of the special zone. Perhaps this is a sensible way for a social system to deal with its awkward components, and surely we have all seen this happen—it certainly can happen to OR groups. Scientists are to be 'on tap, but not on top'—isolated in a special box.

But note what thermodynamics teaches about this; observe the inevitable consequence. If no energy is permitted to flow, no information can flow either; the two apparent aspects of the system are two ways of talking about the same thing. So the common notion that highly-qualified, lowly-paid 'boffins' can be kept at arm's length and used to give *advice* (that is passing information) without making any organizational *impact* at all (that is affecting other people's behaviour) is not feasible. There are plenty of managers who honestly believe that specialist advice should be handled in this way; they shrug off suggestions that the treatment is immoral or unfair or even unworkable ('I *make* it work'). How will they cope with a demonstration that their scheme is fundamentally impossible?

The analysis that has been undertaken here is an attempt to explain the mechanism underlying the method of authority. It is worth reading again, for it is not a piece of ingenious argument or special-case pleading; it could all be set out coldly, scientifically, with its equations, in a passage that would very properly be skipped. Instead, let us see how the mechanism produces the settling of opinion.

Sociologists and other perceptive observers (including some managers) have detected, simply by going around, a phenomenon named by William Whyte the Organization Man. He is a man in the big organization who conforms, often without knowing it, to the will of the institution. He thinks by the method of authority. The thermodynamic model sorts out the laws of systems that operate him. The Organization Man is a component of a large system which, corporately, knows that it must even out its energy. Information about other components of the system and their energies continually reaches this man, comparisons are drawn and adjustments made. The system itself intends, basically, neither to expel energy nor to acquire energy from outside itself. Its *mores*, its institutional conventions and acceptable ways of behaving, become adapted to this end. Thus other benefits in a firm are arranged (quite possibly without conscious intent) as ways of dissipating energy (in this case cash, or insurance) to components of low energy. The equivalent information that comes with this energy constitutes a pressure, for the components must (on the average) accept the benefits, and do nothing to resist the evening-out flow. That is, they must not generate original information, their capacity for doing which is in any case being steadily diminished.

This is fairly obvious; the other aspect of the matter is more interesting. What happens to the aberrant component, the Non-Organization Man? He, of course, is not conforming to the rules—apparently the institutional rules, in fact the rules of closed systems. Well, the system cannot acknowledge his existence. Remembering that a social system consists of human relationships rather than mere bodies, it is possible to de-create, to extinguish, a component man, although he still goes about his work. This is done by ignoring him. Extinction, not opposition, is the point. The sheer power of the remark: 'He is not a Bloggs man' as made by the Bloggs organization is otherwise hard to understand. Clearly this is an argument from authority, clearly damaging, clearly non-analytic. The mechanism we have traced adds to this an explanation why the none the less unemotional, almost amiable, comment in fact involves the general massacre of all who have not thought in the Bloggs way. For a man who is not a Bloggs man is not just irritating or lacking in value to the Bloggs organization—he simply does not exist. To deny a man existence in this way is the ultimate form of censorship.

And so we reach the final end of the method of authority—an irrational process, and one that already partly controls our advanced civilization. Attempts by well-meaning managements to thwart the running-down process in their own large firms are thwarted. Look at any management course, any foreign visit, any internal conference. The Organization Men are there, sent by managements who instinctively know that they must break down the isolation of their systems, and begin to import and export information and energy. But it may be too late. Their men may be physically outside the system; organizationally they are still part of it. They explain with civility and conviction to the management course that all these nice new ideas have either (*a*) been used in their companies for years, or (*b*) been shown appropriate to every type of business but their own—which is a special case. They report on their foreign visits that they saw nothing of value, but that the trip was worthwhile, since a famous company owes it to society to share its insights with others. At internal conferences they say nothing; this is by far the best way to get on: 'He is a Bloggs man: one of us.' There is no thermodynamic fault in any of this.

The symptom to be on the watch for is acquiescence: the sign that the energy flows are all working as the system requires—towards a cessation of activity. It is irrelevant to these purposes whether the firm is flourishing as a commercial enterprise—it may do this for many years by sheer

weight. Even a charging rhinoceros would drop dead in its tracks if its
internal arrangements could succeed in spreading all its energy and
information evenly. And when you and I are dead, the pathologist will
find our bodies in exactly that state. No; men are endowed with individual minds, acquire different experience, erect idiosyncratic prejudices and beliefs. They therefore squabble, disagree and push each
other around. Civilization teaches us to do all these things with due
decorum; the social graces can still be observed. But when men actually
stop doing these things, use civilization as a rationalization of sheer
inanition, and absorb their (physical, not organizational) energy in
artificial battles—ranging from over-much golf to petty personal politics
that have nothing to do with the company's real business—look out.
These are Organization Men; the institution has cancer.

No space is devoted to prescribing remedies. That is not the problem
at this stage. The difficulties are: (i) to recognize the disease, (ii) to
acknowledge it, (iii) to understand its basic nature. We have discussed
these matters. The therapy itself is not difficult.

3   The Method of Apriority

Recall that this chapter set out to examine the context of human thinking in which the method of science is set. To understand what is distinctive about scientific method, it is essential to give formal recognition to
the existence of other ways of settling belief, two of which have so far
been examined. It has already been urged that these strictly irrational
ways of thinking are far from being stupid. They are intelligent in so far
as they have an experimental validity; they fit in with the way nature in
general operates. In fact there is a biological justification here for the
taking, since the whole point of these irrational methods is that they are
evolutionary, competent to adaptation, and hence to survival.

Now the third and last category of non-science proposed by Charles
Peirce is particularly susceptible to misunderstanding. In a society where
any kind of thinking is alleged to be more or less scientific, the category
that is now to be discussed is particularly likely to be confused with
science itself, especially, as it happens, by scientists themselves. This is
the method of apriority. First of all, however, we must explain the use
of this fairly unusual word.

An *a priori* argument in logic is one which begins from a set of axioms
which are assumed to be true, rather than from experiences that have
been undergone. Some philosophers have argued that such axioms are
innate in the mind, that they existed *prior* to experience (hence the

name). The practice of this kind of reasoning is called apriority. An example of one such axiom with which it is very hard to argue is Aristotle's principle of non-contradiction: 'A thing cannot be both itself and not itself at the same time.' One may doubt whether one did know this from birth, and suspect that it was indeed a conclusion based on experience gained when one began learning how to use words as names of things. But whatever the philosophic issues, it is certainly the case that people do in real life produce all kinds of arguments which begin with unexpressed assumptions that they take to be self-evident.

Now why should any proposition appeal to us as self-evident? The answer is clear: it is, as we would say, 'agreeable to reason'. What we really mean is that it fits in with all our experience, whereas to contradict it would make our whole way of thinking about the world quite absurd. So again we find a basically biological justification for the method of apriority: it works. Unfortunately, of course, people often adopt assumptions that seem self-evident to them, but which are by no means so to other people. Then the trouble starts, because it is characteristic of this kind of discussion that the assumptions are not clearly stated and agreed in advance. But this is not a discussion of logic; the case is much more interesting where people *do* tacitly agree on a set of axioms, which are common to the whole society which uses them unthinkingly, but which are nevertheless just plain wrong. People drawn together into one political party, for example, express views which are often genuinely incomprehensible (rather than wicked or illogical) to their opponents for precisely this reason.

How does a closely knit society with such an agreed set of axioms behave in the face of a contradiction to one of them? That is to say, a view is to be expressed which is *not* 'agreeable to reason' as far as these people are concerned. The answer is that such a denial is simply taboo; it must not be mentioned. Peirce says: 'Let it be known that you seriously hold a tabooed belief, and you may be perfectly sure of being treated with a cruelty less brutal but more refined than hunting you like a wolf.' In other words, people who give expression to the tabooed belief are due to be run out of the society—by invoking the method of authority.

Examples of this irrational method of fixing belief, the method of apriority, are legion—and very scientific they look too. The reason for this particular susceptibility to confusion which was mentioned earlier, is that the most powerful language of science, mathematics, also proceeds on sets of axioms. Euclidian geometry, to take a familiar example, only works because of the apriority built into its fundamental definitions.

For instance, the parallel lines which 'never meet' in a space according to Euclid, may be described as eventually meeting in a space according to Einstein. In other words, it is possible in science to deny a set of axioms and to replace it with another set, in which case a new way of describing the world emerges. For example, non-Euclidian geometries have been constructed, and very useful they are too. Philosophers and scientists, who are professional 'thinkers', are in principle distinguished by their readiness to deny the assumptions of their arguments and to see what happens. In practice, of course, since they are human like everyone else, they cannot always rise to the psychological challenge involved in this procedure. Human argument, in general and in short, is in the clutch of apriority as a method of fixing belief. It is a short cut, on the whole it works, and above all it is psychologically satisfying because the axiom is by definition something 'agreeable to reason'. But look what happens.

'Our stocks are rising fast, but they are rising in proportion to our turnover, so that's all right.' This managerial remark is no trumped-up example: it is often heard. It *sounds* utterly rational. But the implicit axiom that stocks are things that *ought* (in some sense) to vary proportionally with turnover is simply not verifiable in most cases. Let us look at the scientific reasons for this.

The point to be made is fundamentally a mathematical one, but an attempt has to be made to express it in ordinary English if the agreement not to use algebra in this book is to be honoured. So consider the elements that go to make up a stockholding cost and the way they are arranged. Material that arrives in stock always has a 'batch size'; a dozen of these, a gross of those, fifty-seven of something else—even a solitary straggler has a batch size of one. The cost of holding stock must reflect actual batch sizes, for the reason that part of this cost is invariant with the number of items. That is, when a batch of identical items comes into a store it has to be transported, recorded, and so on; there are many procedures which occur at a uniform cost, regardless of whether the batch contains seven, seventeen or seventy items. The turnover of items in the stock will also affect the cost of stockholding. In fact, if we try to write down some kind of formula for the cost of holding stock it is most likely to contain, among other things, an expression of the rate of turnover divided by an expression for the sizes of batches.

This allegation is not put forward as an axiom, but reflection surely shows that it expresses one aspect of stockholding cost that has to be considered in the equation. If we have such an equation and ask a mathematician to determine the size of stock that will minimize cost, he will use the differential calculus. His procedure is to 'differentiate with respect to the ordered batch size'—an absolutely necessary mathematical trick for the purposes in mind. In carrying this out, he will be compelled to *square* the expression for batch size. This is because that expression is in the denominator, as we saw; the squaring is then inescapable because of basic mathematical laws. Next, when he is asked to turn the formula round so as to express everything else in terms of the best batch size, which is the figure management would like to know, he cannot help getting the *square* of the batch size instead. So, to quote the required figure, he has to take the square root of his answer.

It was agreed earlier that the turnover would have to be a factor in the numerator, and the mathematical rules being followed will not square this figure. In the upshot, the batch size of stock goes up as the *square root* of the turnover. So much for the managerial apriority argument, which said that the stock should increase *directly* as the turnover.

None of this is advanced as offering a universally valid law about stockholding. To assert that would be to be guilty of scientific apriority, for an operational research answer to this kind of question would certainly not be advanced without examining particular experience. Nevertheless, something fairly fundamental has emerged which is at least enough to justify our denouncing the original contention as quite possibly wrong, and gravely wrong at that. There is reason here, that is to say, to beg management to recognize its use of the method of apriority, and to try the method of science instead.

4 The Method of Science

It is only now that we reach Peirce's fourth method of settling opinion: the method of science. And firstly we ought to ask whether or not this differs in kind from the three modes of thinking we have already discussed.

It is tempting, perhaps, to say that the method of science is rational, whereas irrationality characterizes most human thinking, and yet one can be rational without being scientific. It is better to attend to a special feature of the method of science, which might be called *rigour*. Rigour is a precise formulation of method: something clear and definite, testable and repeatable. If we want to use words carefully, in fact, the method of science *is* method. It follows from this that we ought not to have called the three modes of thinking already described 'methods' at all. They are habits of thinking, and the most flattering word we can use to describe them is 'procedures'. Such is our confidence in our usual way of thinking, however, that it may be doubted whether anyone who is not a specialist will already have revolted at the use of the word 'method' to describe these habits of thought. Moreover, this same careful person may have wondered whether Peirce's classification is itself a scientific—or methodical—classification. In fact, it is not—because it has no rigour. Its terms are neither exclusive nor exhaustive. It was used because it offered a convenient set of pegs on which to hang some thoughts.

Now that attention has been drawn to these matters, the reader's thinking about the method of science may have got into its stride, and indeed have been leaping ahead. 'Yes,' he may be saying, 'I realize what the author is expecting me to acknowledge now. After all, I do know what science is about.' But stop. How do we know what science is about? We were taught about it in our formal education and we therefore accept a basic orientation from authority; we assume that we know, and this is apriority; our views have often been reiterated—an argument from tenacity. It is not good enough. And yet this is no place for a formal treatise on scientific method, which it is instead intended to exemplify during the rest of this book. At this point, and in the context of discussion of the way people actually think, we can do no more than pinpoint the method of science in terms of the way people seem to regard it. Try reading the next two paragraphs against the criterion of your own beliefs about the nature of science.

People think of scientists as remote and dedicated men who follow an inexorable chain of discovery. Their work is regarded as abstract, for the apparently good reason that it picks out coherent and objective facts from life. All this makes it seem remote from biological necessity, remote from social utility, remote from the satisfaction of psychological drives, and remote indeed from life itself. Yet people recognize that it is the most powerful way of thinking that mankind has yet evolved, possibly just because of these characteristics, which seem to disentangle it from emotion and ambition. So people may think, but they are wrong.

The way that science works is much admired too, but also for reasons which are just not valid. It is thought to begin with the collection of objective facts, and to sift these logically. It is known to set up hypotheses about the way things work, to test these hypotheses exhaustively, and to try and formulate 'laws'—which is to say propositions—about the way things behave in general that turn out to be useful in predicting particular consequences. These approaches to problems are seen to be wholesome and good and likely to succeed. Hence people try to imitate them. They dress up arguments derived from mental procedures, which are no more than habits of thought, to look like scientific arguments. Yet science does not in fact follow this serial development.

Although the practising scientist can recognize in these last two paragraphs scientific-sounding descriptions, he would be likely to quarrel with every single statement proposed. The method of science is not really much like this at all. So the degree to which anyone thinks that science is like this is a measure of his incapacity to understand the relevance of science to management.

The arguments of this section are negative, and may therefore seem unconstructive. But the point they seek to make is tremendously important. Managers do in practice offer scientists strangely irrelevant reasons for thinking that there cannot be such a topic as management science. Careful reflection suggests that this is because their view of science is based on over-simplifications of the kind just exemplified. The appeal for the moment, then, has to be simply this. Let us equate the method of science with a kind of rigour which our ordinary modes of thinking do not have. And let us beware of a bogus rigour, deriving from an admiration of the achievements of science, which cuts improvised footholes for our leaps of intuition.

A succinct recapitulation of the arguments of this chapter will provide a reasonable perspective for the next. The mechanics of fixing belief by three commonly used mental procedures have been examined. The method of tenacity uses the process of conditioning, first carefully investigated by Pavlov, in the most advanced and sophisticated kinds of thinking. The method of authority hinges on the fact that the believer finds himself inside a system of which he is an indivisible part, so that his behaviour is inescapably affected by the gross behaviour of the system itself. The method of apriority uses the fact that all communication, even with oneself, requires a language in which to communicate, and assumes its ostensibly scientific conclusions in the premises which underlie the axioms of that language. At these three levels—the biological, the anthropological and the semantic—man is almost powerless to exert his free will in *rigorous* choice.

Such rational arguments as are used to justify these procedures are based on their practical effectiveness. The choices that people make are usually fairly successful, for reasons other than the method of science itself could underwrite. Thus the sort of validity these arguments enjoy is pragmatic, that is, they provide solutions which fit into our experience, which therefore work, and which therefore comfort the opinion holder be he manager or scientist. They may all have genuine survival value in the evolutionary sense; after all, organisms using comparable strategies which are in fact quite irrational do survive, from the mighty business enterprise to the coelacanth it sometimes resembles. But we ought to note that adaptation by methods which, though justifiably called rational, rely not at all on rigour also leads on occasions to going out of business, or to becoming extinct.

So it is that at the very point when a man becomes distinguished from other beasts, he perceives and admires not only the rational but the rigorous. Thus it comes about that the common procedures for settling opinion among men rarely remain strictly irrational, even when they are not fully rational; but they rarely become rigorous. We acknowledge a process called 'rationalization'—a word that is clearly in place in this present context, and a word that is significantly enough a technical term in the vocabulary of psychiatrists. And if we can make the transition from irrational processes to apparently rational ones, which is what this term means, we may well deceive ourselves about the next stage by calling them rigorous too.

Very well; the method of science is intended to import rigour into the rationality of managers. Managers sometimes use irrational procedures for settling opinions that will determine decisions in their problems; sometimes they use rational procedures; sometimes they jump the gap between the two by rationalization. Scientists do exactly the same thing, all too often, in settling opinions that will determine their own decisions, for scientists are men. But in their professional capacity, scientists bring to managerial problems the expertise of rigour. This book says why and how.

3

SOME DANGEROUS
PRECEDENTS

The *Principle of the Dangerous Precedent* is that you
should not now do an admittedly right action for fear
you, or your equally timid successors, should not have
the courage to do right in some future case. . . .
Every public action which is not customary either is
wrong, or, if it is right, is a dangerous precedent. It
follows that nothing should ever be done for the first
time.

F. M. CORNFORD in *Microcosmographia Academica* (1908)

1 A History of Contemporary Relevance

In order to find out why operational research is of any use, it is as well
to recapitulate the reasons why it came into existence in the first place.
If these can be made clear, the highly tendentious questions that are
often asked about the subject nowadays (such as: 'How does OR differ
from work study?') could not possibly arise. Now to make such a
survey it is necessary to go back to the early days of the Second World
War. This will rile some readers. Many people seem to feel that Hitler's
war has nothing whatever to do with contemporary problems; they
suspect that mention of it exemplifies no more than a sentimental attach-
ment to a spirit of comradeship in long past days of high excitement,
and to forgotten glories. But this is the way the history of the subject
was written, and we cannot change it if we would. Even so, in deference
to these reactions, we shall not harp on bellicose matters. This is not a
history of operational research, but a search for its meaning in its origin
and early days. It quotes some Dangerous Precedents, for in war some
things actually do get done for the first time, and enquires whether they
seem sensible enough and profitable enough to be emulated today.

Any group of managers at any given time has some sort of corporate outlook; it has a morale, it has pet theories and aversions, and it has a climate of opinion. Perhaps it is not too difficult to enter into the state of mind of the community of military managers in Britain during the early days of the war. First of all, a large number of sacred cows had laid down and died. There had been no immediate air raids, no gas attacks, the invincible Maginot Line had collapsed and the continent of Europe had been occupied by the enemy. Perhaps this situation is paralleled today in terms of the government of this country, and of its industrial management problems. If the facts are squarely faced, the most cherished political beliefs about the way in which the economy should be controlled are seen to be ineffectual in practice. If so, then it is unfortunate that the kinds of pressure exerted on a nation at peace do not have the psychological impact of threatened defeat in war. The possibility of kidding oneself, the electorate, the employees, remains open today; but this possibility was not open when the country's enemies sat on the other side of the Channel and we knew ourselves to be virtually defenceless. Secondly, there were then whole areas of military management in which circumstances compelled those in command to acknowledge freely that they were guessing. When aeroplanes do not return to their bases, when convoys do not get through and when armies are routed from 'impregnable' positions, the commander who declares that all this is according to plan and fully understood is asking for his bowler hat. And so there were vulnerable areas of management in which people were guessing, in which they knew they were guessing and in which they had to acknowledge they were guessing. A generation later in this insecure peace the fact of guesswork remains; the knowledge is buried perhaps a little deeper, and the admission is largely unknown—naturally enough, for there seems to be no ready excuse that a man can offer himself, never mind his critics.

Why should this vulnerability exist and what is its peculiar nature? This question can be answered by eliminating firstly those aspects of management that are not prone to criticism. There is, for example, the area within a manager's responsibility in which his knowledge and experience are complete and adequate. No-one in his right mind can deny that a good manager is basically capable of managing affairs which are thus defined; the point is simply tautologous. 'I ask my chaps to do nothing that I cannot do myself' is an old cry, heard in civilian as well as in military life. Yet the cry, in this highly technological age, is somewhat out of date although nobody minds that either. A military commander can and does consult, without loss of face, specialist advice. If he wants to fire a gun, he will use ballistics experts; chemists will advise him on the use of gas, psychologists on the state of the enemy's morale, engineers on his equipment, and so on. In these matters, the excellence of the good manager resides in knowing when and how to use the scientists and other specialist advisers that are on call, and to be able to judge what credence to place in them. Similarly, in industry and in government, the manager may call on accountants to install and interpret his financial and cost controls, on engineers to design his plant, on physicists, chemists and biologists to examine the quality of his product and its purity, on economists to assess the movements of his market, on statisticians to handle his data in a sophisticated way, and so on. Here, you might argue, is the complete manager: competent and assured, knowing a great deal about his own affairs, selecting and applying scientific advice with wisdom whenever necessary. What is left?

The answer to this question is all too simple when one thinks about it. Firstly, although a large number of problems will yield to the formula just expressed, there is likely to be a residue in which a conscientious manager is not at all sure what he ought to do. He has run out of knowledge, experience *and* advice. Yet he has to decide. Secondly, it may be borne in upon him that the situation with which he is trying to deal is hopelessly obscured by factors right outside his own jurisdiction; he may consider that, although he has to take a decision, the right policy can be determined only after taking into account the judgments of everyone else in the managerial community of which he is a part. In a well-run organization, he will know the motions to go through to ensure that this second class of problem is treated at a higher level (that of general management). But in this case, the general management organization itself may be in the first situation—at the limit of its knowledge, with no particularly relevant experience, and having taken all the specialist advice that it can think of seeking.

These are the vulnerable areas of management. The first is tactical; the second is strategic. Now history, disguised in the form of publications by Her Majesty's Stationery Office, relates how the armed forces tackled this problem in the early nineteen-forties. It is interesting that no formal and general decision was taken; it seems that the answer was a natural one, which naturally emerged. It was to call in some of the country's best scientific intellects and ask them to help. This solution can be distinguished rapidly and clearly from the technique of using scientific advice in the ways enumerated above. For the men now called upon were not asked to apply their own limited expertise to problems already labelled with the words inscribed over their university chairs.

The respectable and generally acknowledged use of the scientist is to say to him: 'You are a palaeontologist; here is a fossil; tell me what you can about it.' The challenge now being issued is of *this* form: 'You are a scientist (of some sort), which means that you have a mind trained to investigate natural phenomena, logically to take them apart with a whole set of highly sophisticated techniques, to re-assemble them and to declare what makes them tick; I have here an operation which is certainly a natural phenomenon; go ahead.' And so the manager is not asking the physicist to research into the atomic structure of uranium in order to make a bomb, nor the chemist to analyse a new poison gas, nor the biologist to investigate fatigue on the battlefield. He is asking the scientist to research into operations. And this, not surprisingly, is operational research.

It should at once be clear, and it is certainly most important to appreciate, that this is not the same sort of activity as is traditionally allocated to scientists. This is what is new about operational research. If there were such a scientific discipline as 'operationalics', then there would be an 'operationalist'. He could investigate tactical and strategic problems as belonging to his own specialism, and he would fall into the pattern of advice with which we are most familiar. But there is no such science. To which particular branch of science, then, should the manager have recourse? The question is unanswerable. The intention is not to use the man's expert knowledge of a branch of science, but to use the fact that he *is* a scientist. But if the kind of science this man practises is irrelevant to the present matter, there is still one judgment the prudent manager can make. If he has to form a team to tackle his tactical and strategic problems, then he does *not* want the whole team to consist of physicists, nor of neurophysiologists, nor of specialists in any other single aspect of scientific enquiry. For obviously the specialist is a victim of his own training; he may be asked to forget it and to operate as a scientist pure and simple—but how completely can he do so? In short, if the whole team consists of the same sorts of people, a bias that has nothing to do with the work in hand will become evident. So that is how and why operational research came traditionally, powerfully, and per-haps necessarily, to be interdisciplinary.

A few paragraphs ago it was said that the emergence of operational research was natural and informal. But it is worth taking a quick look at what actually happened. The movement began embryonically before the war, in so far as a number of civilian scientists had been helping the military to evaluate the operational implications of a new discovery—radiolocation. The collaboration of the people who were to become the first OR scientists with the people who were to make such effective use of them was thus mediated by a technical innovation. There existed (what the official history calls) an 'informal arrangement' that on the outbreak of war this group should be attached to the headquarters of Fighter Command. There the members of the group won a quick and great success, a success 'achieved by junior scientists who had not yet received academic distinction or organizational recognition, but were men of high talent, zeal, initiative and imagination, working under the guidance of experienced scientists'. This is still the character of operational research. Obviously, their success could not have been achieved without support, and the personal interest of the Commander-in-Chief is recorded from the same period.

The next move, in 1940, derived from another technical innovation. Radar equipment at gun sites gave the slant range and bearing of an attacking bomber. New apparatus was devised for providing a reading for the bomber's elevation, but it did not perform in service as it did under test. So here was another *operational* problem, a matter involving both science and management, but lying outside the capabilities both of the specialists who built the equipment and of the commanders trying to co-ordinate its use. This seems to have been the first occasion when a noted scientist was asked to apply himself to operational research. As is well known, the man concerned was an eminent physicist (a Nobel laureate indeed), Professor Blackett. And again the character of OR as an interdisciplinary activity becomes clear. For 'Blackett's circus', which eventually became the Army Operational Research Group, included another physicist, two mathematicians, three physiologists, a surveyor, two mathematical physicists, an army officer and an astrophysicist. Again, too, is found the personal interest of the Commander-in-Chief—of Anti-Aircraft Command this time.

Thus, when highly successful operational research comes to be done in a context of change, and when the mixed scientific teams formed by OR are attended to at the highest level of management, results accrue. Small wonder, then, that the work took such a hold so quickly in military affairs. Two years after the war began there were formally established operational research groups in each of the three armed services.

2   The Strategic Issue

There may seem little enough to learn from all this for the enlightenment of the nineteen-sixties. Yet, in a fundamental sense, the story reveals everything. Suppose that a large industrial undertaking has a plant it proposes to expand. Capital is available to finance this expansion, and the management has a good idea of what it wants to do. Consider how this situation has come about.

The company's business is based on a technology of long-standing effectiveness, but over the years many improvements have been made. Most of these improvements have been incorporated, or at least tested, in works' practice. The time is coming when, partly because of the obsolescence of plant and partly because of an expanding market, a new plant must be built. Those who see this most clearly form a lobby within the management group; gradually they carry their colleagues with them. Eventually the climate of opinion is right for a decision, in which all concur, to go ahead.

The lobby has not been idle. The latest techniques and machinery have been studied; the advice of engineers has been obtained. There is already a clear idea of what this plant should be like. Technical experts of every kind have been called in to discuss every facet of performance, and to estimate possible output. With this brief, accountants have been asked to prepare costings which they have based on those from previous experience, modifying the existing data intelligently to predict the effects of whatever changes are contemplated. Market research has reviewed the state of demand, and considered the conditions in which a new element of the market can be captured; advertising has been planned. The key problem of where to site the new factory has been examined by a committee on which all these interests were represented. Everything is ready, the decision is taken, the expenditure is approved, and construction begins.

All this is highly reminiscent of the preparations for war. For in war, much the same issues arise and they are handled in much the same way. What happens when operations begin? In war, it turns out that nothing happens exactly as was expected. Intelligence was defective and conditions are not quite those anticipated. Planning goes slightly awry and the unfolding of the strategy gets out of joint, causing serious delays. On the technical side, rather too many equipments that worked perfectly well on their trials misfire in the field. On the human side, people mysteriously let down the management; they do not always do as they are told, they misunderstand instructions, they even refuse to operate some of the equipment. Because of all these differences between intentions and fulfilments, the costs that were envisaged are all wrong; far too many factors have changed. And the enemy? Well, he is the last of our worries; we have not even encountered him yet. There are plenty of battles to fight against nature and the cussedness of things first. Soon the commanders are wondering whether they have chosen the wrong battlefield even. . . .

Is this a description of what happens in war—or in that industrial undertaking? The situation is exactly the same. As soon as it starts operating, the new plant makes a loss. Teething troubles, they say, which will be overcome. But there are some beautiful new plants that are still being subsidized ten years later by the old plants they were meant to replace. This must be the equivalent of 'losing the battle', although (as was remarked earlier) in civil life the hard facts can often be dodged. One is not called upon to bury the dead and depart. On the contrary, one can usually gloss over the disaster.

By changing the internal costing conventions, for example, the loss can be assimilated into the profits of other departments. The manager down the line who finds himself paying more than the market price for his raw material, as the result of internal transfers from the new plant 'at cost', will be upset. But when he is replaced, his successor will know that there were originally policy reasons for this which no-one quite remembers. If the plant is sufficiently big, moreover, there are still smoother ways out of the difficulty. Disasters of sufficient magnitude can, like the charge of the Light Brigade, be turned into victories. For example, the new plant which contributes massively to the national output of the product *must* be a success. Everyone knows that it is the latest and best of its kind; therefore (method of apriority) its costs are 'realistic'; therefore (method of authority) its prices are generally regarded as a proper basis for computing nationally acceptable prices; therefore, after a time (method of tenacity), it makes a profit. Prices have gone up, of course; the increases are blamed on dearer coal, electricity or transport, on the weather, on demarcation disputes—it does not matter much. The nation, knowing nothing about it, pays the bill for bad management.

This illustration is not a phantasy. Examples of such procedures do occur and have been studied. It ought to be appreciated, in particular, that any organization which tends to monopoly *might* be conducting itself, on occasion and possibly unconsciously, in this way. The risk that such things will happen extends from large public companies, through national corporations and nationalized undertakings, to the services and other government departments. But that is a digression; the real point is to say where operational research fits into this picture.

The root cause of the troubles that have been described, whether civil or military, is a failure to predict the manifold interactions of many variables in practice. In the two examples quoted, there is much experience on which to draw, much theoretical work and plenty of realistic test-ing. Yet the new situation will be compounded of all these things, and it is the mode of synthesis that is at fault. To illustrate this simply: if ten small uncorrelated supply lines feed into one large supply line, it is not economic to fix the capacity of the main flow as the sum of the *maximal* flows of all ten tributaries. In theory, all ten supplies might achieve their top rate of flow together; in practice, this never happens. Conversely, it is no good specifying a completion date as calculated from a day when all of ten components are due to arrive; in practice, this never happens either.

No; new techniques are required in order to measure, compare and predict the practical outcomes of strategic plans. These techniques neces-sitate work which is beyond the best that a committee of all the inter-ested parties can achieve. This work is operational research. By now, it is used all over the world to help validate military defence strategies in advance of (one might hope in place of) actual war. But industry very often disregards this lesson. Industrial OR is not often called in until all the plans are fixed. It is then asked to assist at the tactical level by making parts of the intended system more efficient. This again is one of those misapprehensions and misapplications of science, for presumably the management does not intend the result. This is the use of science for ensuring the ruthlessly efficient implementation of thoroughly bad plans.

The risk of doing just this is implicit in any large-scale activity. To consider each part of a large system separately, to find a perfect solution to the problems of each part, and then to add the solution together and call the result a strategy, does not necessarily work. Almost certainly, it does not yield the best of the available strategies. This assertion can be examined in a small way on the rugby field. The individual trying to play a superb game from his own point of view, on the theory that if each player does this the side will win, may be a spectacular wing three-quarter, but he is dropped from the team because he is selfish. The strong pack of forwards playing in perfect harmony may nevertheless be stopped; the game is lost before the outsides are ever given an oppor-tunity to open it up. The same is true on the battlefield and in industry. But it is the function of the football captain, the military commander and the managing director to see that these things do not happen. These are the leaders who must see in the whole an entity greater than the sum of the parts.

The point is that the leader has no mechanism for doing this once the system he controls grows to larger dimensions than can be comprehended in one man's brain. To preside over a meeting of junior managers, each of whom commands a section of the system, and to add up and reconcile their recommendations, must fall short of the best that can be done. This is what was wrong with the industrial development plan just described. The same outcome, for the same reasons, is obtrusive in national policies—for transport, fuel, education, and so on. Prediction of the effects of change in one department considered *in vacuo* is fairly accurate, but the interaction of these effects with the effects of change in other departments creates a totally new kind of system out of the whole. And the reason why no one man can cope with the prediction of the macro-behaviour of the new system is not just lack of vision. It is, to be quite precise, that the kinds of measurements he has been using change their nature and let him down.

These are the circumstances in which operational research is most useful. It was argued in an earlier chapter that the scientist is not an analyst of facts, but a man who first of all determines what the facts really are. His is the responsibility for creating new measures of the system that will still be adequate to its changing state. He has to predict the macro-behaviour of the evolving and organic whole. He does this, essentially, as a service for the leader who is responsible for that whole. No-one else is in a position to do so.

It may now be clear why emphasis was placed on the role of major technical change in the excerpt from military history, for if there is a major breakthrough in any technology that is relevant to an enterprise, this changes the character of the whole system. It does not merely have 'far-reaching effects' but actually turns the old enterprise into a new one in which the old thinking, the old costings, the old methods of control may well have no place whatever. The scientific description of the whole situation has to be rewritten, which is a job for operational research.

There is a ready example to hand; one that affects every kind of activity today. This is the breakthrough in automation and computation. Given that these new facilities and capabilities exist, it is not an exaggeration to say that no enterprise is the same as it was ten years ago. For if it is using these facilities to the full, its mode of working is radically different, its limitations are different, its opportunities are different and its entire management problem is different. If it has ignored the new facilities, its productivity has fallen (because productivity is the ratio of what *is* done to what *could* be done), its costs have gone up (in terms of foregone opportunities), its employment policy has changed (it uses men to do things machines could do better), and so on. This proposition is not philosophical skullduggery but a fact.

It is very widely said, and fairly widely accepted, that there has been a mysterious lag in the exploitation of these technological advances. People mumble about the slow-but-sure ways of practical evolution; they hope this explains the lag, and excuses it too. But the reason is different in kind from this. Automation in the nineteen-sixties is like radiolocation in the nineteen-forties: once it exists, the situation is new. To set up a managerial committee, advised by technical experts, *inevitably* has little effect. This organization is committed by its structure to an attempt to dress up the old system in modern clothes. But the old system is no longer required, in the dress of any period.

The first plan for using radar was (as it were) to automate the Observer Corps. Fortunately, those responsible quickly saw that this would not provide much of an advance but would simply build the limitations of men into the machines, and hold them back. So those responsible invented operational research, made it study the new situation scientifically as a radically different whole, and *doubled* the effectiveness of radar as a strategic tool (according to a history written soon afterwards). This is the recommended treatment for automation and computation today. Instead, the technical breakthrough is used precisely to automate men: the payroll application, the stock-control application, the costing application, the programmed lathe, and so forth. All these developments are good enough in themselves, but the new, higher-order strategic plan that is now possible has been largely overlooked. It is a job for operational research.

Perhaps there is now less impatience with the 'out-of-date' military history of this chapter. It has much to tell about the meaning of OR which has not been transferred to civil life after a quarter of a century. What the work is really like, how it emerges, what it can (quite basically) do, are all made clear by the evidence of past events. Contrast the understanding that has now been reached with the following statement, made twenty-one years later, by a senior industrialist in charge of a large civil OR effort: 'There is nothing fundamentally new in operational research, but it does make available modern mathematical methods for analysing facts.' Every phrase, every notion, almost every word, is wrong; the remark betokens total incomprehension of the nature of this work.

We have considered the emergence of operational research in a general way, and at its strategic level. But it is time to get down to brass tacks and to gain some insight into how this work is done. It is tempting to discuss a large and complex strategic problem in detail, yet this would be a massive undertaking at this stage. It is proposed instead to describe and discuss a small (in the sense of self-contained) *tactical* study which has certainly become very famous in the annals of operational research. Let us adhere to the military history that has served the discussion well, and quote a last example from the war.

3 A Famous Tactical OR Problem

By the spring of 1941 the difficulty experienced by Coastal Command of the Royal Air Force in sinking enemy submarines was becoming far too obvious. The search for submarines in the coastal waters around the islands of Great Britain was successful, and depth charges were being dropped from the aircraft at a low height. Unfortunately, little success was obtained in sinking them, and it will not have been forgotten that vital supplies of food were seriously threatened as a result. What was the policy by which the attacks were being made?

A depth charge was exploded by a hydrostatic firing pistol, a device which responds to the pressure of water and detonates the charge at a given depth. The depth setting on these charges began at 35 feet, and the detonation could be arranged for any depth below this. Now the theory was as follows. When a submarine is attacked from the air, it will see the approaching aircraft and dive. By the time the attacker has had time to catch up with the submarine, it will have reached a depth of between 50 and 150 feet—a calculation made by computing the speed of approach, the rate of a crash dive and the trajectory of the falling depth charge. A setting of 100 feet was therefore the recommended practice, based on specialist advice.

The typical problem in operational research has indeed this general appearance. There is a technical competence, a well-founded policy for applying that competence to achieve results, a practical state of affairs to which this capability and practice appear appropriately to apply, sane specialist advice on the mode of application—and there is failure. More than twenty years after the events now being described, this prescription for failure is being followed somewhere in every government department and in every factory. How does the operational research team that is called in set about its task?

In the first place, it has to be recalled that this is not an exercise being carried out on a blackboard for a class studying ballistics. It is a practical operation of war, in which the actual facts can be investigated. They were. The facts uncovered revealed that the basic assumptions of the theory were being falsified. It is just not good enough to say that 'the submarine sees the aircraft coming'. Perhaps it does—but at what stage? This depends on the weather: on the visibility, the position of the sun and the roughness of the sea. It depends too on the alertness of both crews—which will see the other's craft first, and how soon afterwards can they mobilize themselves for action? In short, if one considers the real-life problem, and not an idealized classroom version of it, one immediately sees the need for tactics which are robust in quite a large variety of circumstances. All sorts of variables begin to affect the situation which would not at first sight appear relevant; and let us remember that even the list of variables just enumerated supports sets of more complicated causal influences that lie behind each variable. Fatigue, state of morale, even (possibly) whether the captain of the submarine enjoyed his breakfast, enter into the picture. So the *whole* problem, not just the *real* problem, must be studied—not indeed by examining and measuring every factor, but by using an approach of sufficient flexibility to incorporate the full range of possible variation which might be encountered.

What next emerges is the critical fact that *if* the submarine has indeed reached a depth of 100 feet when the depth charge explodes, it has had time to manœuvre below the surface in a way which makes an accurate prediction of its whereabouts almost impossible. In this case, even if the policy for attack is right in theory, it is simultaneously wrong in practice, for it cannot actually work. When the idealized problem is enlarged to real-life dimensions, the probability of not hitting the point aimed at must be multiplied by the probability that the submarine will not be in that location; and the product—which is the probability that the submarine will not be killed—becomes very high. Thus the only feasible solution is to catch the submarine nearer the surface which again the practical facts revealed was perfectly possible. For three-quarters of the time, the submarine simply did not manage to dive as quickly as had been expected. This is a very good example of how an attempt to contain the worst possible situation in fact invalidates the whole policy when this boundary condition is seldom met.

Through this examination of the actual facts, the measurement of the actual operations and the computation of real-life probabilities, it was shown that a practical policy should concentrate on hitting submarines still at the surface or submerged for less than fifteen seconds. The corresponding computation of the depth setting then showed that the charge should detonate at 25 feet. And here we have to note a remarkably characteristic feature of an operational research solution. It often lies outside the framework of possibilities ever contemplated by the managerial solution. This means that the mixture of experience, knowledge and straight thinking by which the management's policy has been reached, has managed to delineate a range within which the answer is expected to lie, and the answer chosen is roughly in the middle of this range. The inexplicable failure of the management's policy, which is normally the signal for introducing operational research, often means that the best answer has unfortunately been excluded from the collection of plausible policies that management is prepared to believe offer solutions that really count.

In this example, that state of affairs is exemplified for us by the scale on the side of the depth charge, which had a minimum value of 35 feet, and a range of plausible solutions between 50 and 150 feet. With this apparently flexible array of possible actions laid out, and in this case engraved on brass, how can anyone be blamed for not realizing that the answer is completely outside the possibilities envisaged? Returning to the history, we find the OR scientists advocating that, since it is impossible to set the charge at 25 feet, the minimum depth of 35 feet should be selected—a depth still much shallower than anything yet attempted. And we find the second recommendation being accepted: new gauges should be made to encompass the still shallower depth that is really required. The new policy is put into effect. At once the rate of sinkings rises dramatically and, by the time the new gauge is in action, Coastal Command is recording a 700 per cent rise in sinkings. Thus, without years of special research and development effort, but simply by breaking through a conceptual barrier in policy-making and by studying the operational facts, a tremendous success is achieved. The whole picture is changed from everyone's point of view. Prisoners taken from sunken submarines now tell their interrogators that the amount of explosive in British depth charges has been doubled.

Finally, life is also considerably changed for those whose job it is to advise management on the detailed methods of working within a particular managerial policy. Such specialists as accountants and engineers can fulfil their functions only within the ambience of the range of policies with which management has chosen to work, and their conclusions have no relevance to other policies which have never been formally envisaged. This point is exemplified in the present story by the engineers responsible for the hydrostatic firing pistol that detonated the depth charges. When they were asked to change the gauge so that it could be set at 25 feet, they were faced with a completely fresh problem. For this is not simply a matter of screwing on a new gauge to the side of the charge. As was said earlier, the firing mechanism is activated by water pressure. But, when a depth charge enters the water, an air cavity is created behind it and the firing pistol cannot be relied upon to come into contact with the water until the charge has been submerged to a depth greater than 25 feet. And so a new research problem is created. Historically, the shape of the depth charge had to be altered, so that the part of its case carrying the firing pistol would slap against the water itself and not be within the air cavity.

There is a simple and straightforward operational research story—a famous one too. The setting is not grandiose, but the results were of huge importance. It might be worth while to read the story through again, for in the next chapter six key thoughts about the nature and use of operational research will be developed at some length, and each one of them will be derived from the history of the submarines that would not sink.

4

THE WEDGED BEAR

Visne ergo mihi librum sustinentem praelegere, ad
ursum inter angusta arte infixum consolandum
idoneum.

A. LENARD *(trans.)* in *Winnie Ille Pu* (1958)

or, in the original:

Then would you read a Sustaining Book, such as
would help and comfort a Wedged Bear in Great
Tightness.

A. A. MILNE in *Winnie The Pooh* (1926)

1 The First Tightness: Stereotyped Scientists

The three chapters completed have doggedly pursued the theme that
operational research is a radically new kind of activity which cannot
be properly understood unless a radically new look is taken at both the
scientific and the managerial functions. Most of us work, that is to say,
on stereotyped notions of these things—notions held from tenacity,
authority or apriority. In general, as argued in Chapter 2, this is no bad
thing, but in following the story of operational research that is also being
unfolded, it is vital to escape from the grip of these stereotypes. The hero
of this chapter, Winnie the Pooh, consumed all the honey he could find
in the home of his friend Rabbit, and became firmly stuck in trying to
emerge. We have just burrowed into the origins of OR and found some
honey; but in climbing out of the past we may well become stuck in our
stereotypes and misinterpret all that has been said. A Wedged Bear in
Great Tightness, discovered Pooh, must be starved out; he should be
sustained during this process by literature. Let us then pause for a while,
and use this chapter as a Sustaining Book.

The stereotype of the scientist as a man who 'does physics' or 'knows chemistry' or 'reads biology' has already been attacked. The scientist is, we saw, a man who investigates the nature of the world. His training, however, gives him a bias. For this reason, when a new area of study is being opened up, it is well to use an interdisciplinary team. The emergence of this sort of group in the early development of operational research has already been detected in the historical section. Now, in order to shake off the first attack of Tightness, the matter is considered in more detail.

In the first place, the brand of scientist who is already professionally concerned with the kind of problem that faces the management stands as little chance of escaping from the orthodox thinking of his own discipline as the manager stands of escaping from orthodox practice. The scientist, like those he seeks to advise, tends to be a prisoner within the accepted boundaries of the existing solution. In the case of the submarines that would not sink, there can be no doubt that plenty of scientific advice had been used before ever the OR team arrived on the scene. But that advice must have been stereotyped; it saw the problem as an abstraction on a blackboard, not as deriving from a real-life operation. The scientist too has been stereotyped, by the management and by himself. Often the research departments sponsored by industry and government house scientists of this kind. For example, if a firm makes a washing powder and its rivals claim to purvey a powder that washes whiter, the scientists in the first firm will be set to make a powder that washes whiter still. From a scientific point of view, this chase towards ultimate whiteness may be interesting (I do not know). It may involve good science: for instance, it may be possible to detect by spectroscopic analysis that each generation of powders does in fact wash very slightly whiter than the last. But exactly where does this get the management? Will the consumer take note of the powder that washes whiter than whiter than whiter than white, and prefer it? No; the management has become trapped in an orthodoxy and in a stereotyped notion of scientific advice.

Another example: the manager of a heavy steel mill may observe that when he rolls an ingot into a long product of small section, which has to be cut up into relatively short lengths, unsaleable pieces are left over and have to be scrapped. There is a tolerance on the lengths to be cut; if one knew the total length of product rolled from the ingot, and could do some calculations, it would be possible to make the cuts in places which would much reduce the amount of scrap. Unfortunately, the product must be cut very quickly, before it begins to cool; there is no time to measure the total length at all accurately (it varies considerably from ingot to ingot), still less to make the calculations. Now scientists can do something with this problem. They can install automatic measuring devices, coupled to an electronic computer, which will announce where to make the cuts. Here is the expert advising the management, and making a worthwhile advance. But the expert advice is of the same persuasion as the management itself—a persuasion that says this job is to do with engineering and nothing else. In fact, however, the steel is being sold against an order for steel, and the order is part of a lengthy order book. If the computer had access to that order book, it could compare various ways of cutting the steel with the requirements of various customers, then there need be no short pieces left over at all. This solution is several times more profitable than the first solution. But in practice the production manager regards the order book as the province of the sales manager; it is no concern of his. The scientific advice he wants is engineering advice, and the engineer in turn thinks of the salesman as a smart fellow whose fortunate job it is to take people out to lunch. The scientific adviser of the sales manager is an econometrician who does not concern himself with works' practice. The specialist advising the financial director is an accountant; he computes that a 1 per cent saving in the yield of steel is worth so many thousand pounds a year, and that the computer installation will pay for itself. Everyone is then satisfied with the wrong decision; an advance has been made, the orthodox divisions of management have all operated successfully, a number of experts have been used in a stereotyped way, the thinking has been shackled by the orthodoxy and the stereotypes, and a big opportunity has been lost.

The interdisciplinary OR team of scientists, properly led, should not make these mistakes. They do not play individually stereotyped roles; they do not owe special allegiance to one branch of the firm. This is why an operational research team is a different kind of entity from a committee, consisting of the same people, in which each man is there to represent the point of view of his boss's sectional interest.

There is a second reason for making an operational research team interdisciplinary, and for escaping from the stereotype of scientific advice. If operational research is to lead management to a completely novel solution, it cannot be predicted in advance which branch of science will be most useful in suggesting the breakthrough. In the case of the submarines, for example, ballistic experts and explosives experts were not the people to help. Think of the actual operation and what happened. Scientists used to the theory of probability, scientists used to measuring the speeds of human response, scientists used to evaluating fatigue and states of mind—these were the people actually required. Thus management replaces (for these policy-making investigations) its familiar ballistics-and-explosives team with an OR team of (perhaps) statisticians, physiologists and psychologists. It is easy, with hindsight, to recognize that these specialisms are relevant to the situation. It is not always so easy to see this before the problem is solved. So it is important for management to accept the advice of operational research people themselves, that OR teams should indeed be interdisciplinary in character.

This point is underlined because there is a strong tendency in industry today to accept for OR work only the kind of scientist that one would expect to meet within the industry anyway. In metallurgical industries, management is accustomed by now to meeting engineers, physicists, chemists and metallurgists. They are puzzled by the arrival in OR teams of biologists and sociologists, for example. But these are the very people who will be of most use in solving managerial problems of tactics and strategy. They are neither stereotyped nor committed in advance to a point of view.

2   The Second Tightness: Stereotyped Problems

The Wedged Bear has lost one degree of Tightness: its stereotype of the scientist. Now we turn to the question of the problem that has to be solved, for that has a stereotype too. This may be shortly described as the assumption that a problem really resides where its symptoms are first noticed. Thus a problem arising in the course of production is assumed to be a production problem; a problem arising in sales is assumed to be a commercial problem; and so on. A scientist set to work within the limitations of this stereotype of what the problem really is has little hope of success. The point to be made is this: operational research must encompass the *whole* of the problem situation, and management may not succeed in defining what this is.

Given that the solution to the problem lies outside the accepted boundaries of existing solutions, it is more than likely that the problem area itself extends beyond its traditionally recognized limits. Only the operational research team, then, can be held responsible for defining the scope of the problem. This is perhaps a revolutionary point of view; certainly it is one which management often resents as an abrogation of its prerogatives. But it is a rational attitude and one which management ought to embrace. It is worth recalling that many of the problems that most need to be solved, which are (as has been seen) those very problems in which the solution has not only eluded management but has not even been envisaged, arise precisely because of the way in which a company is organized. For practical managerial reasons, a company is divided into clear-cut areas of responsibility; and the manager, whose authority derives from his position in one of these areas, is conditioned by the whole of his experience to seek solutions in which he can feel confident from personal knowledge, and over which he can exert personal authority. But problems are not respecters of the company organization, nor of the talents of the company servant who first meets a symptom of the problem.

Of course it is the custom to argue that good management ensures adequate consultation across the departmental barriers, and that good organization will even create an inter-departmental committee structure whereby permanent liaison is secured. The first sounds very well when attested to in the happy afterglow of a company dinner; the second looks very well when inscribed on an organization chart. But as people interested in real operations, we simply have to face a few facts. Reflect how people actually discuss their colleagues in other divisions of the company; they are not seen as men who have something to contribute to the problem, but as men who just do not understand it. Therefore they are people who, despite many pious expressions of goodwill, have to be outsmarted. Reflect too how committees of liaison actually work. A busy executive, who has in all honesty been intending to study a set of papers since the last meeting, suddenly has them thrust into his hand by a secretary who announces that the car is waiting and he must hurry or he will be late. He thumbs through the papers during the ride, wonders what they are all about, wonders what some of his esteemed colleagues are up to, decides that at all costs certain ideas that have been mooted must be scotched, and works out conventional explanations for not having done the things he said at the last meeting he would do. In fact, he has no real need to worry; the chairman of the meeting to which he is speeding has already written the minutes in his mind. Yes; this account is an oversimplification. Even so, where is the senior executive of a typical modern company who can really claim to believe that the large problems of tactical and strategic management with which his company is concerned are really *studied* on an inter-departmental and inter-specialist basis so that the solution adopted is undeniably the best?

Operational research has this to offer instead. If a committee of responsible people is formed, they can commission an OR study of the problem before them. This will mean that a group of scientists, which is interdisciplinary, which has access to all the facts, which has permission to investigate difficulties wherever they may lie and to pursue ramifications of the problem wherever they may lead, is engaged full-time in objective scientific pursuit of the right answer. While this is going on, the members of the committee can happily go about their business. The OR report is then produced to the committee, and will have roughly the following form. The problem will be tentatively defined—possibly in terms rather different from those envisaged at the committee's first meeting—and an attempt will have been made to describe the whole of the newly-discovered problem area in a systematic way. The facts bearing on the problem will have been collected and collated, and fitted into this description. Various scientific activities (which will be discussed later in this book) will have been undertaken with a view to examining suitable courses of action. In the end, a number of possible answers will have been formulated which will be laid before the committee with an assessment of the probabilities, costs, risks and potential benefits of each. In short, the precise problem requiring managerial decision will have been pinpointed, and the area of uncertainty that surrounds it narrowed as far as possible. The committee may then have a meeting to discuss this report. Probably there will have been no time in which to read it, and therefore the meeting might well begin with an exposition of the OR findings by the man who led the OR team. He should then remain in attendance while the members of the committee discuss these findings, seeking further elucidation as they proceed. At the end of this meeting the committee will know exactly what has to be agreed at the third and last meeting. In the interval before this occurs, there is no real need to do further detailed work—for which the committee members certainly have no time. During this period, it seems reasonable to rely upon the capacity of the human brain to incubate decision. When the third meeting assembles, if there is any substance in the company's claim to managerial team-work at all, the proceedings should be plain sailing. For the results of incubation, coupled with some routine committee work, should produce an agreed decision. (The procedure outlined here is certainly effective, and suffers only from the demerit that it sounds trite. It is, then, particularly worth suggesting that anyone who supposes that the system is followed in the organization under his control should carefully examine what actually happens. Is it true, for example, that the operational research people are actually present at the meetings where their results are considered? If so, the acknowledgments due to any rarity are made here. It is far more usual to claim that an OR report must be freely discussed, that this cannot happen in the presence of its author, and that management is now on its own. No experienced OR man is subsequently surprised to hear that the particular policy that was explicitly condemned on the basis of detailed scientific research has been adopted.)

The importance of studying the problem *as a whole*, and not merely as a collection of local difficulties, emerges from the story of the submarines. As was said before, it is easy to view that problem as a matter of trajectories and explosives. It is only when a circle is drawn round the whole problem area (thereby capturing the weather, the pilot, attentiveness, bad luck, morale, and so on, as cogent factors in the problem) that successful science can begin. In this example there is no particular difficulty in detecting the boundaries of the whole problem; in other studies this detection can be extremely difficult. The reason is fundamental: a point from philosophy.

The philosopher Hegel noted that the relations by which terms are related are an integral part of the terms they relate. That is to say, the fact that a horse is bigger than a dog is part of dogginess and horsiness as well. If this dog were not smaller than a horse, it would not be the dog that it is; it would not, very probably, be a dog at all. This being so, everything in the universe is connected to everything else by a series of relations subsisting between everything in between; and if each relation helps to determine the nature of the thing that is related, then everything is what it is because everything else is what *it* is. This is perhaps rather confusing, and sounds metaphysical. But the resulting thought is important: the totality of what exists is an integrated system, and anything split off from the totality and considered separately is incomplete. In practice, we have to split things off and consider them separately, but we shall have to be extremely careful how we do it. An OR man who considers a suitable size for an interprocess stock would be mad if he failed to consider the cost of investing in it or if he insisted on considering the relevance of the position of Venus. Somewhere he has to stop; somehow he must 'determine the boundaries of the problem'. The point of this paragraph is to say that *this is the most difficult problem in operational research*. There is no standard technique for achieving the best answer. At least let us recognize that there is no such thing as a 'right' answer.

In practice, the scientist needs to enlarge the scope of his study in every dimension until the factors he is bringing in seem to make no tangible difference to the answers he is getting. Then he feels safe in stopping. At the very least, this process is going to take him outside the apparent problem area by one step in every direction. Most notably, if he is working for one of five managers all responsible to Jones, he will

have to consider the problem as Jones sees it. If this makes a vast difference to the way the tentative answer looks, he had better go on to the
organizational zone presided over by Jones' boss. This is a process
dictated to the scientist by the inter-related nature of the world. The
manager who commissioned the problem really must recognize this, and
not take umbrage. Other managers, who have nothing to do with the
remit and into whose preserves the OR man trespasses, really must
collaborate. More trouble is caused in the practice of OR by this business
than by any other aspect of the work. More potentiality for high profitability in the use of OR is thrown away through failure to see this than
through any other cause.

The management problem has no stereotype. It is unique. It is
malignant. It may involve all sorts of factors that no-one imagines to
be relevant. The job of the OR man is to handle it. Do not tell him what
the problem is, nor where his task may take him. Tell him what the
trouble is, and send him to find the problem. That is the first step. To
escape from the stereotyped problem is to lose another degree of Tightness for the Wedged Bear.

3   The Third Tightness: Stereotyped Science

The third of the important lessons about operational research that can
be drawn from the wartime example of the submarines has to do with
the question of chance. This is the God-given uncertainty of the future
for us humans; the likelihood that something unexpected will happen;
the risk of failure and unforeseen difficulty; the so-called 'human
element'; and so forth. People often assert that science cannot cope with
the questions of chance thus enumerated. Unless it can, indeed, operational research as a tool of management policy would be worthless. The
process of unwedging that Bear especially demands a right approach to
this matter.

It is as usual important that stereotyped opinions about modern
science are not accepted uncritically. After all, the idea of scientific
method that many senior people entertain is based (if they are honest) on
routine experiments through which they were conducted in the third form.
Moreover, their beliefs about the nature of science and its outlook on the
universe it studies may have been formulated somewhere between twenty
and fifty years ago. Just how carefully has anyone had time to review this
matter since? The new achievements of science are manifest to all, but this
question of the underlying nature of the work and of the sort of universe
in which modern science thinks we exist is rather more fundamental.

For example, nature (which is the subject matter of science) consists of a collection of various kinds of system. Early attempts to describe these systems were undoubtedly conditioned by the ways in which men had so far learned to manipulate nature. That is to say, the engineering competence of mankind determined for centuries the pattern of thought about the universe which naturally arose. At the time of hydraulic engineering, people seriously contended that the human brain squirted thoughts around the body in pipes which, anatomically speaking, they imagined the nerves to be. In the great age of mechanical engineering, the brain was envisaged as a system of pulleys, cogs and levers. And so, coming to our own era, the early discoveries of nuclear physics were pictured in highly concrete terms. Surely we have all met the 'billiard ball' version of the atom in which hard, spherical electrons circulated like planets in orbit around a larger sphere that was the nucleus of an atom. Perhaps our physics masters had all mis-spent their youth in acquiring proficiency at billiards; at any rate, the picture had this form. That picture is laughable and almost useless today.

In fact, the tremendous breakthrough of modern science in physics, in genetics, in biochemistry and many other subjects, is largely due to a realization that the universe is a collection of probabilities, and to the development of mathematical techniques capable of uttering descriptions of nature in these terms. The universe of hard solid separate things that collided with each other and bounced off, that rubbed against each other and lost energy, that became involved in sequences of events which could be neatly labelled 'causes' and 'effects', may still be the universe of engineering; but as the universe of science it has gone for ever. Each of the fundamental particles of matter is now pictured as being the size of the whole universe, and none has a definite location. Some locations are more probable than others, and matter is an agglomeration of these probabilities. But this is not in any sense at all an attempt to explain modern science. These points are made simply to emphasize that science is now supremely competent to handle probability, chance and mischance, risk and likelihood, and in general the vicissitudes of real life.

Secondly, it is undoubtedly a mistake to think about situations in terms of a clearly understood and absolutely determined set of developments, into which nature wickedly imports errors, and within which sportive deities play dice. Here is a thought on which to reflect: everything that happens is grossly improbable anyway. For example, a hand dealt at bridge which produced a complete suit for each player would cause consternation. Assuming that the dealer were a personal friend, the occasion would be worthy of a letter to *The Times*. People would compute the very long odds against this occurrence. What they might not realize is that every other hand played that night, and indeed any hand at all that can be dealt, is exactly as improbable as the one that divides the suits evenly. All these hands convey no sense of wonder, because they just are not interesting, but the play of probability is just the same.

Thus we argue that the behaviour of any natural system, which of course includes an industrial operation, is best described as a system of interacting *im*probabilities. A modern scientist has a considerable armoury of techniques with which to investigate that system and write it down. A real depth charge, one that is dropping from a real aeroplane in real weather and under real psychological conditions, will not arrive at a point in the sea with the precision that a dotted trajectory is drawn upon the blackboard. What is more, a real submarine that has already been submerged for one minute and has reached a depth of 100 feet will have begun to manœuvre. It will not be where the chalk cross is either. So, the intersection of the trajectory and the path of the submarine, as drawn in the classical exposition by the old-time tactician, actually depicts a gross improbability, multiplicatively compounded of two independent improbabilities. And the outcome is: no sinkings. But talk about the system in the way of modern science, define the areas of action in terms of probability theory, select the tactics which will bring (as it were) the 'shapes' of the two zones of probability into some kind of conjunction, and the chances of the bomb and the submarine colliding are brought to a maximum. This is the best that science can do. It offers no certainty in a universe which is now formally regarded as uncertain. It does offer an optimal strategy on the strength of such information as is available. But if it results in a 700 per cent increase in effectiveness, who shall complain?

The industrial parallels to this situation are legion. One cannot hold enough stock to *guarantee* that it will not run out. One cannot maintain plant so well that it is *certain* not to break down. One cannot *obviate* the risk of losing the most treasured customer. And if one adopts a crude, deterministic concept of profitability, and sets out to maximize it forthwith, the likely result would be to sell the company's assets and distribute the money to the shareholders. Life, as we know, is more complicated than this. We deal essentially in the judgment of probability. Thus the third key feature of OR work to which attention is here drawn, is a facility to discuss these probabilities in scientific terms, and to make the managerial leap in the dark a little more informed, a little less problematic.

Here we have considered one of the most disastrous aspects for management of the stereotype of science. Experience insists that this misunderstanding is widespread. It is one of the six powerful squeezes of Tightness that can assail any Wedged Bear. We shake it off in one sentence: Business operations are uncertain, and all future events are improbable; but these improbabilities can be measured and manipulated and from them a strategy can be scientifically contrived. Note that this is not the 'right' strategy; it cannot even be called the 'unqualified best' strategy. It is the strategy that best matches the managerial policy and intention.

4 The Fourth Tightness: Stereotyped Solutions

The fourth of the points that emerge from a consideration of the submarine story is in many ways the most important. The idea involved is simple but powerful, and something of a challenge. To introduce it, a thought will be taken from mathematics and another from psychiatry, and a joke that is both funny and deadly will appear in cold print.

The mathematical idea is that of a *phase space*. Now the tools developed by mathematics for handling quantities make it possible to enumerate an indefinitely large number of variables, to measure things that are indefinitely big, to ascribe numbers to processes that continue indefinitely, and to refine the scales of quantity indefinitely by slipping in a new number between any two existing numbers—however close together they may be. So there is for the mathematician a great cosmos of quantity, reaching out into eternity and infinity. In the more subtle regions of mathematics, it is capable of considering even infinities of infinities. When mathematics comes to be used, however, statements about a situation that has to be described are written down. These statements may be, for example, equations, and as everyone knows the main variables in these equations are designated by letters.

Now any particular set of equations limits the concept of quantity in general. It does not carve off a particular area of the universe of numbers as if one were to say 'between five and seventeen', because the numbers represented by the letters in the equation may be of any size at all. No, the universe of quantity is limited by these equations in that they select a particular *kind of space* and exclude other kinds. Plane Euclidean geometry chooses to talk about flat areas and forgets height and depth. A linear equation envisages the universe of quantity as a great mass of straight lines: one can imagine a prickly ball made up of an agglomeration of dressmaker's pins, inside which space is defined only by straight lines pointing in all directions. Just as the inhabitant of a Euclidean space knows no height, the inhabitant of this ball would know no curvature. When a mathematician sits down to describe a real-life situation in mathematical terms, then, the kind of mathematics he begins to write selects a kind of space.

As he continues to write equations down, he begins to define an area within that space. This is not because he is fixing actual numbers beyond which he is not prepared to go; it is because succeeding equations affect the earlier ones and limit their possible range. For example, my friend's house is roughly south of mine; it is not further west than south-west and not further east than south-east. So far no direct compass bearing has been put forward, no definite figures have been given. But the conditions laid down have successfully eliminated 270 of the 360 points of the compass from the search. The problem that is set—to find the house— now has a *phase space*: it is a particular, delimited chunk of plane space, with no numerical limit to the southward. This is a trivial use of the term concerned because we could quite easily describe all this in simpler ways. But recall that problem situations in real life have a large number of dimensions and not just two; and also that moving through the spaces generated by equations in many variables cannot be prescribed in terms of compass points. In these large circumstances, the concept of phase space becomes important because it picks out a useful and relevant frame-work of quantity from the vast cosmos of number. Within this frame-work, if it is properly selected, may be discovered the solution to the problem.

The second special concept needed here is that of *thought block*. Earlier on, the 'method of tenacity' was discussed as a mode of thinking and fixing belief. Remember the cars opening up a snowbound countryside, which by their passage facilitated particular pathways through it. This, it was said, is the mechanism by which the brain learns to find patterns in the world outside: the brain becomes conditioned. This process of conditioning, it was further said, is vital to survival, for in its absence the world would appear entirely incoherent and unpredictable.

Now a human being faced with a problem has an infinite number of possible reactions that he could make, and this universe of decision is like the universe of quantity discussed just now. There are no limits, other than those prescribed by the basic laws of nature, to what the human response to any stimulus *can* be. Someone offered a cigarette *could* respond by jumping off Beachy Head. Experience has, however, taught the brain to make coherent patterns of social behaviour as of everything else, and the range of *suitable* responses to this stimulus is fairly clear. In short, the problem presented by the cigarette offerer has an infinite set of possible solutions, within which a phase space has been marked out by the man at the receiving end as containing the solution he will actually give.

Most civilized men have marked out roughly the same phase space for a simple social situation of this kind. Even so, the phase spaces of the cigarette offerer and of his friend may not *quite* overlap, and if the friend chooses a response from the edge of his phase space which is not shared by the other man then he will be taken to have 'said something rude'. For instance, 'No thanks, I am trying to give them up' is likely to be acceptable, whereas the reply 'Not likely, I shall enjoy watching you die of lung cancer' is not. Note, moreover, that a savage who has never seen a cigarette may classify the act of being offered one in some completely alien phase space. For instance, he may classify it as belonging to the class of hostile actions and punch the man on the nose. (How will the pattern-making machinery in the offerer's head sort this one out?)

Collecting these ideas together, we now apply them to serious situations. The phase space for the solution of a managerial problem exists in the head of the man who contemplates it. It is therefore unique to that man. For a given problem, the phase spaces of the solutions envisaged by the production manager, the accountant, the engineer and the salesman are far less likely to coincide exactly than they are in the case of the simple social situation. The experiences, and therefore the learning and adaptation, of these men are different. So what is the best solution for the company? The solution normally adopted quite obviously lies in the common phase space—that is, in the area of overlap between the phase spaces of the individuals who comprise the management team—but there is no guarantee that this gives the most appropriate answer. The company itself has no brain. It has a phase space within which it always operates, but this can only be interpreted by human beings who inevitably get the company's phase space confused with their own. But suppose the company had its own brain and was aware of its own phase space. The answer to a particular problem might then lie on the fringes of this space, in an area not belonging to the phase space of any one manager in the organization. The best answer to the problem would therefore be missed, *because it would be strictly inaccessible to the management.* The thoughts of a man concerned with this particular problem cannot break through the barriers of his own facilitated pathways to reach the goal. This situation is called 'thought block'.

Here is the joke. A man went to see a psychiatrist who asked him what was the matter. The man said that nothing was the matter but his friends and relations kept telling him he ought to see a psychiatrist, so he had come. The psychiatrist asked whether they had given the patient any clues as to why they thought he should make the visit. The man replied: 'They seem to think it strange that I should be dead, but I cannot think why—death, after all, is natural enough.' The psychiatrist tried in vain to convince the man that he was not dead. The man would have none of it. And then came an idea. The psychiatrist secreted a pin in his hand. 'Tell me,' he asked, 'do dead men bleed?' The patient laughed im-moderately: 'Of course not.' With a sudden movement the psychiatrist scratched the patient's hand and blood flowed. 'How about that then?' The patient looked incredulously at his hand. 'Good heavens,' he replied, 'dead men *do* bleed.'

This story about thought block may be funny, but is it sufficiently deadly as promised? If not, consider the following actual experience. A famous company made slithy toves, and very little else (I cannot bring myself to reveal the product that actually masqueraded under this pseudonym). An operational research team working on a strategic development plan for the company had been evaluating the effects of a predicted collapse of the market for slithy toves, and a simultaneous increase in the national production capacity for them. The OR man was unfolding his prognostications about the future to a director who, not surprisingly, was looking rather grave. The director asked whether any ideas were emerging from the study as to what should be done. The OR man said yes, it certainly looked as though fairly large-scale investments planned for the improvement of slithy tove productivity should be switched to providing plant to manufacture alternative products. Gradu-ally the director's brow cleared, and a smile spread over his face. He put his arm around the shoulder of the OR man. 'You are a clever chap,' he said, 'but I do not believe you will ever understand the facts of this business. Please try to keep your feet on the ground, my boy, and realize that we don't make alternative products here—we make slithy toves.' And that happened.

Because the submarine story, on which this chapter is a commentary, was primarily concerned with just one measurement of the total system —namely the depth at which the explosive charge should detonate— it provides a simple one-dimensional example of this thesis. In this particular dimension, the phase space of the set of acceptable solutions was marked on the side of the depth charge, very likely engraved in brass. 50 to 100 feet was the phase space in the minds of those most concerned and, in taking the calibration of the gauge to a depth as shallow as 35 feet, the designers must have felt that they had allowed for all possible contingencies. In doing so, they at once reflected and reinforced a thought block. No-one working within this situation was at all likely to entertain the setting of 25 feet that actually worked.

This is the reason why it takes an objective, scientific, interdisciplinary investigation to arrive at a solution outside the phase space—a study undertaken by men who are by definition not prone to this particular thought block. A fairly detailed exposition of all this has been given, because it seems most important to accept that the manager who has failed to find this kind of answer is not culpable. He should not be labelled as incompetent, for if managers allow themselves too readily to wander imaginatively outside the phase space set up for them by their own knowledge and experience, they become rather dangerous. To go back to wartime prototypes: A Wingate or a Popsky has his impressive uses, but he is not likely to emerge as the Chief of the Imperial General Staff. A CIGS, however, who works within his acknowledged phase space and at the same time employs operational research teams to make scientific investigations outside it, is getting the best of both worlds, provided that he can sunder the thought block when it has been demonstrated that he should.

Fortunately, there have sat in Whitehall men who have done precisely this. Unfortunately, senior British industrialists have not taught themselves to use OR in this way; the few industrial parallels seem to have occurred in the United States. In general, the Bear seems firmly Wedged in the Tightness of stereotyped solutions, and every experienced OR scientist could give a dozen examples of particular problems mishandled as a result. The existing organization is likely to come very close to a good answer which does lie within its own phase space of solutions acceptable to all the managers, because there will be no thought block to prevent its so doing. Then the reason for employing operational research at all is to see whether there is a solution outside. If the report is then rejected on the ground that the proposed answer *is* outside the managerial phase space, while no-one makes any effort to break through the associated thought block, this fourth degree of Tightness will trap the Bear for ever.

5 The Fifth Tightness: Stereotyped Pay-off

Next, and fifthly, it is worth remarking that the kind of activity in the service of management here discussed is perhaps the only kind in which very large benefits are possibly obtainable with a very small outlay of effort. But to attain these benefits, another stereotype must be demolished.

It is often said that an operational research study may go on for a very long time, may consume the effort of a number of rather senior scientists, and may therefore be rather expensive. All this is true; scientists are not such fools as to pretend they can master the complexities of a really massive strategic exercise in a few minutes. The managers who are so quick to point out that this is the case, can hardly complain (although they often do) of the cost of the study that is made. The real point to seize on is the potential pay-off. This was, in the submarine example being examined, a 700 per cent increase in effectiveness.

But can operational research, in proposing to make a study at a given and fairly high cost, really guarantee a pay-off of this order? The answer is no. In the first place, there may not exist so lucrative a solution, and management must be prepared on occasion to pay the price of the investigation for the satisfaction of knowing that this is so. But, more usually, the reason why the scientist cannot guarantee such a high return is that he cannot tell in advance whether the manager will be able to cope with his solution—in terms of thought block. All too often, the reaction to the OR results will be 'we make slithy toves'. This risk arises in particular because of the watertightness of executive and administrative divisions in industry and government. Often the best solution will require an organizational uncoupling, a rearrangement of responsibilities. Consider the classic example of inventories of spare parts.

A company making elaborate machinery has to hold stocks of spares against the demands of its customers. As will be seen in a later chapter, operational research has developed many techniques for operating such a system of spares at a minimum cost. But if there is a very large number of parts involved, no amount of scientific effort can minimize the requisite amount of information about all these parts that has to circulate within the control system. Thus, typically, one can expect to find expensive computers handling all the data required. Yet how many of these spares are really necessary? Could the design of the machinery not be rationalized, so that there are more standard components? If so, the raw total of spare parts involved in this business could be cut down, and the inventory control problem is diminished in complexity by at least the square root of this reduction. So often, this fact is obvious to many within the organization. But 'design' is the responsibility of some person who flatly refuses to accept that financial and commercial pressures ought to be allowed to influence his work. His professional *amour-propre* is at stake, and he is able to defend it by specious talk of 'maintaining quality' and so forth. General management itself, if it is aware of this problem lower down, tends to regard it as a human problem, a matter to be settled in due course (that is, in a very long time ahead) by better selection of more amenable managers. They feel that the man concerned is so good at his job that this price will have to be paid in order to retain his services. But surely this is to misconceive the problem? If general management were to seize on the arguments advanced in the last section to justify their attitude, they would be misdirecting themselves. For the point is not that this design man has a thought block (although he has), but that the general management has its own thought block at a higher level of management.

The organizational phase space within which they are working is the *existing* structure of their company. Problems of this kind may have to be handled by altering the organization. The human organizational structure may need adjustment as a problem-solving phase space; so also may the physical organization. That is to say, a factory is a system for turning raw materials into finished goods, and this system has to be uncoupled at various places for many reasons. Among these are the production engineering methods employed, the need for inspection, the dispersal or conflux of flow lines at certain points and the sheer limitation of size of the facilities any one manager can control. But the particular uncouplings that exist in the factory are, after all, only one of an infinite set of possibilities. They exist only for historical reasons in the form they have now, and it could be that the newer technology, the improved methods, the change of personnel and the changing balance of products all demand a physical reorganization based on considerations supplied from a new organizational phase space. Very often in the metal industries, for example, material has to be cut up at a certain stage in order to ship it to customers who will use it as raw material for the next more finished product. This cutting up becomes standard practice. Subsequently the company itself lays down production facilities for doing the next more finished job itself. But the established practice for cutting up material is continued. The fact that the next process involves sticking the pieces together again goes unremarked. Thought blocks, aided very powerfully by special languages (that is, trade terms and works jargon), prevent our defining a process as anything other than it has always been.

Whatever is involved in implementing an operational research solution, a consideration to which we shall turn next, the present point is that the pay-off from an investment in an operational research investigation is more largely determined by the management than by the scientists involved. The management does not receive what it pays for, but what it demands and can assimilate. Consider the present reputation of operational research in some of the companies that have had internal departments specializing in this work for some time. Possibly the results are unrecognizable as outcomes of OR by the standards of this book. If so, who is to blame? Now managements are often loath to install new high-level activities in an established company because they create organizational difficulties and salary anomalies. Some monumental thought blocks are encountered here. Be that as it may, it is a fairly common practice to evade the difficulties by appointing some bright young mathematician, fresh out of the University, as an 'operational research officer'. He presents no organizational difficulties here, of course, because of his juniority. He lunches quietly in a junior mess, he does not confront senior managers, and he is paid about the same as a first-rate shorthand typist. The theory is that he will 'grow', that is, he will develop gradually within the organization in a natural and satisfactory way. If this young man keeps fairly quiet, he will gradually be assimilated into the organization and we shall hear no more of him. If he begins to be difficult, however, and to discover what operational research is really all about, and to advocate its proper use in the company, there is certain to be trouble. Probably the young man will leave. At this point, the more complacent kind of manager can be heard to say that he was not much use anyway, and had never once proposed a fundamentally new policy that could have been laid before the board. All this is sad.

What is, on the other hand, highly satisfactory is that operational research properly used can often increase effectiveness by an order of magnitude or more—at no other cost than the money paid for the study. This compares favourably with the years of expenditure which may well be involved in achieving effects of comparable value by research into the product and its mode of manufacture and subsequent development.

But it cannot be done while the Tightness of the pay-off stereotype holds management in its grip. This form of trouble is closely allied to that discussed in the previous section, for the unusual pay-off cannot be dissociated from the unusual solution. Nevertheless, there are separate issues here. While management does not know in advance what could possibly count as a particularly remarkable solution, it does know what would count as a really impressive increase in profitability. Therefore it can aid the whole exercise by setting the OR team a high aim in pay-off terms. This puts the scientists on their mettle, demonstrates to them that the management means business and will not be put off by the occasional thought block, and above all prepares the management itself for the answer to lie outside its own phase space.

6   The Sixth Tightness: Stereotyped Success

The last of these half dozen points of importance concerns the implementation of an operational research result. First of all, it will be as well to pick
up the moral that the submarine story directly points out.

Although, as has just been argued, years of research and development
are not necessarily required to obtain a lucrative solution to a managerial
problem, considerable development effort may need to follow in the
wake of an operational research solution. By selecting a new solution
outside the phase space of previously acceptable solutions, management
is almost certain to find that particular features of the existing situation
are no longer appropriate, or are inadequate, or are simply unworkable.
Just as the hydrostatic trigger for the depth charge failed to work reliably
at a depth of 25 feet until it was redesigned, so well-tried organizational
and control techniques in an industrial situation may have to undergo
change.

However, the economics of this development programme are likely
to be highly satisfactory. For by definition there will be a definite end in
sight, with a known reward with which to crown success. There are
likely to be fewer blind alleys to investigate than is normally the case.
Thirdly, the psychological tone of the development team ought to be
very high. But management should not fail to pursue these necessary
matters, which they sometimes do on the grounds that the answer can
be made to work without this additional expense. It must be remembered that an OR solution which postulates certain changes in the
existing situation, in order to facilitate a particular new policy, will have
built those changes into the validation of its solution. Thus the extent of
the dependence of success on the fulfilling of these conditions may be
harder to estimate than the management imagines.

This introduces the second facet of this topic of implementation, and
one which does not emerge from the submarine story because of its
unusual simplicity. To implement a portion of an OR solution may prove
disastrous. When the depth setting of 35 feet was installed to replace
existing practice of detonation at 100 feet, results substantially improved
—and at once. Certainly the full pay-off did not come until the development people had solved the problem of detonation at the recommended
25 feet. But no harm was done in the meantime. In more complex
problems, to adopt a '35 feet' interim solution may well position a complicated business operation in a context that simply is not viable. If a
submarine were a sort of vessel that could sink with extreme rapidity
through the 35-feet zone, then this interim solution could have resulted

in fewer, not more, sinkings. This state of affairs often exists in industry, and, one suspects, even more often in government problems; half measures may make the confusion even worse. At the best, if a given OR solution proposes a benefit of £50,000, to impose half that solution is most unlikely to result in a benefit of £25,000.

The three remarks made so far under this sixth heading may appear disenchanting, but the final point is much more hopeful. A typical breakthrough in the more familiar kinds of scientific research frequently raises more problems than it solves. A train of new difficulties will often arise. From what was said above, it might be imagined that the same is true of operational research, for have we not said that there will be consequential development matters to attend to when the typical OR solution has been applied? But the situation is in reality very different. It cannot be too strongly emphasized that an operational research project *must* take account of *all* the factors bearing on a situation. If it does not do this, then the work may solve some relevant problem, but not the actual management problem. For management, a solution only counts as a solution when it can be implemented without more ado. It is the function of an orthodox specialist adviser to say: 'From the point of view of my specialism, the best thing for you to do is so and so, but of course you will have difficulties with the unions, or you will have to face this or that consequential problem.' If the adviser is a chemist advising about chemistry, or an economist advising about economics, this is perfectly legitimate advice to give. But the operational research scientist specializes only in managerial tactics and strategy itself; therefore there can be no loose ends labelled 'your problem, chum'.

This point was made earlier, but it has to be mentioned again because of its bearing on the implementation of results. The stereotype of success in a piece of orthodox research stops short of managerial action. If the scientist can win a Ph.D. with his work, or even have it published in a learned journal, then the stereotype says he has succeeded. Where OR is concerned, managers and scientists alike may become Wedged Bears through this idea, and forget the whole point of the activity. An operational research solution should propose a complete answer, and in so far as this includes a demand that certain consequential matters be settled, it does at least specify what these matters are and how to settle them. It is perfectly all right for an accountant to put forward a new costing scheme, and to tell the management that the flow of data at some point is so great that a computer will be needed to handle it. But the management knows full well that completely fresh studies of computer feasibility and of detailed application will have to be made if the machine is to be installed successfully. In the case of operational research, on the contrary, the recommendation that a computer be bought will be rooted in the nature of the controls devised by the study. Thus, the OR solution that includes the installation of a computer is its *own* feasibility study.

Incidentally, the reason why an operational research team must have complete freedom to study whatever facets of a situation it regards as relevant again emerges from this sixth point, as it did explicitly or implicitly from the other five. If the managerial answer to an OR proposal can possibly be of the form: 'This is a good suggestion, but this is not the time to use it, or there is no money, or such and such a condition should be fulfilled first,' then something is missing from the operational research. At this the manager might well say that OR is trying to arrogate to itself a managerial function and prerogative. If there is no factor known to the manager that was unknown to the scientists, then (he may ask) what decision is there left for the manager to take?

The answer to this is really quite simple. Operational research exists to try and eliminate, or at least reduce, guess-work. Sometimes it succeeds; and when it does so entirely, there *is* no managerial decision left to take. No-one should be more pleased about this than the manager. Suppose that he began by recognizing courses A and B, and by having no idea as to which would prove the better. Suppose the following to be the OR advice. Course A is likely to pay a high return for the next three months, but then to lose money steadily for two years, at which time the company has a 90 per cent chance of going bankrupt. Course B on the other hand will be slow in starting but stands a good chance of doubling the profits in three years. How would the manager like the OR report to continue? By saying: however, this is no more than a scientific evaluation of the facts; it is now for you as manager to take a decision? That would be merely offensive. On the other hand, it is far more usual for an OR result to indicate that there is a number of possibilities which are equally valuable from the scientific point of view. Typically, for example, courses A and B may have an equal expectation of an equal financial return, but course A may reach this expectation more quickly than B, whereas B will involve less vigorous effort on the part of all concerned. Value judgments of this kind are the decisions that management really has to take. Once it has fully specified its set of values, a unique scientific solution should become possible. Sometimes the values can be quantified in advance and built into the study. In this case, the manager has exercised his prerogatives before the work begins, and can stand by to await a unique solution in the knowledge that he has already done his job. At other times, it takes an OR investigation to isolate clearly the value judgments that have to be made, and in this case the manager is left with a decision at the end.

So let there be no confusion about the nature of success, either for the manager or the scientist, or for the institution they both serve. The stereotypes of success for these two men may conflict, and each serves to nullify the other. The stereotype of success for the institution may itself be confused with theirs. There remains a good deal to be said about this point much later on. For the moment, it is enough to insist that as the novel solution is not an end in itself, so the novel pay-off is not achievable by itself: the novel concept of success is a necessary mediator. Above all, that concept involves a thorough-going technique of implementation.

And so, having eased off the Tightness of six stereotypes, the Wedged Bear becomes free. He may put down this Sustaining Book, and set off in search of more honey.

5

THE NEW LOOK

*ἐνταῦθα γὰρ τὸ μὲν ὅτι τῶν αἰσθητικῶν εἰδέναι, τὸ
δὲ διότι τῶν μαθηματικῶν· οὗτοι γὰρ ἔχουσι τῶν
αἰτίων τὰς ἀποδείξεις, καὶ πολλάκις οὐκ ἴσασι τὸ
ὅτι, καθάπερ οἱ τὸ καθόλου θεωροῦντες πολλάκις
ἔνια τῶν καθ᾽ ἕκαστον οὐκ ἴσασι δι᾽
ἀνεπισκεψίαν. . . .
τὰ γὰρ μαθήματα περὶ εἴδη ἐστίν· οὐ γὰρ καθ᾽
ὑποκειμένου τινός·*

Now it is for data-collectors to know all the details,
and for mathematicians to establish the reasons. For
they can demonstrate causes, often without knowing
all the details; just as people can entertain a
generalization without knowing each instance of it
singly—which they have not examined. . . .
Mathematical science is about pattern, not the
specific things that form its subject.

ARISTOTLE (384–322 B.C.) in *Posterior Analytics*

1 Whichsoever and Whysoever

Some authors suffer cruelly in the public esteem: for instance Aristotle,
and those who write government reports. People go around saying that
their writings are stuffy and irrelevant. Such people do not actually read
these authors (because they are stuffy and irrelevant).

Non-readers of Aristotle who are most familiar with his works may
find the passage selected to head this chapter irrelevant to the management topics of this book, but it repays a little thought. In the first place,
it is true that managements these days have acquired a respect for facts.
Accountancy deserves most of the credit for this: it has taught people
that they cannot make sound judgments, although they may make
inspired guesses, without a lot of detailed information. Admittedly, this

has led to some confusion, for a fact is 'that which is the case', whereas a good deal of information supplied to management is *not* the case, or is the case only in very special circumstances that have to be understood. Even the word 'fact' is monstrously abused; witness this sentence from a letter sent to a customer by a well-known British company: *We should not like you to believe the fact that we have disregarded your wishes*—rather not.

However, the difficulties surrounding the notion of 'fact' have been sufficiently well ventilated in a previous chapter. Presuming that there is plenty of information, and that it is factual, to know the details is still not enough. Facts propose necessary, but not sufficient, reasons for decision. The movement towards scientific management begins properly with a demand for facts, but it customarily stops short at this point. One has to know what the facts *mean* and *why* they fit together as they do. This entails uncovering the mechanism which underlies them. There is nothing in the routine of the accountant, the industrial engineer, the work study specialist or the O and M man which could possibly do this. Of course these people often do comprehend reasons in practice, as do managers themselves; that is because they are intelligent. But the words of the last sentence were chosen with care: 'There is nothing in the routine of . . .' As Aristotle said, the routine for uncovering reasons is a job for science.

In fact, Aristotle was very pithy on this point. In rendering the Greek into decent English, I have lost the economy of his opening thrust. His actual words run more like this: 'Now it is for data-collectors to know the whichsoever, and for mathematicians the whysoever.' Our modern collectors of data do know the whichsoever. It is stacked in the cellars on punched cards; it pours out of computers on magnetic tape; it is tabulated most beautifully on to clean white paper at a rate of 600 lines a minute; it appears on managers' desks in great wads that they are too busy to read; it is published by government departments in mammoth year books. For this is the age of 'automatic data processing'. Yet all this tells us nothing about the reasons why things are as they are. It takes some operational research to discover that.

But, answers the manager, the OR scientist works on a limited assignment. He cannot possibly assimilate all the knowledge the organization has accumulated about the whichsoever. Perhaps it is all locked away in people's heads; the data are just not there. Perhaps it is all locked away in the cellars on cards; the scientist will never get through it all. Aristotle had the answer to this one too. Consult the quotation. The scientist can assert that the three angles of a triangle add up to 180° because he knows

the whysoever. He has uncovered the fact from examining a few tri-
angles; he does not need to examine them all. This proposition, however, is deductive; most propositions about real-life situations depend
on inductive inference. But again the scientist can say: kettles of boiling
water have got like this through the application of heat. He establishes
this whysoever by a judicious sampling of experience; there is no need
to test every kettle. What is more, the modern scientist can go one better
than Aristotle on this matter. He understands the mathematical statistical
whysoever of the sampling process itself, and can achieve a higher degree
of reliability in his establishment of reasons, from less data, than the
Greeks knew how.

But this sort of work *is* a scientific job. It is worth remembering above
all that facts are no use without a specification of why they are needed.
It is obvious that they are not worth accumulating unless there is a
purpose behind their collection. That is a tautology; but its triteness
does not obscure the truth that a high proportion of facts actually
collected has indeed no purpose. Secondly, and this is a far more
sophisticated point, the purpose behind data collection *alters* the facts
that are collected. This particularly affects the standard of accuracy:
'The distance from *A* to *B* is ten miles' is a fact for a car driver who does
not care whether it is a mile or so more or less; it may not be a fact for
the man calculating how much white paint he needs to inscribe a line
down the middle of the road. Other aspects of decision making are also
affected, particularly where problems of classification are concerned.
'*Why do you ask* whether this expenditure is chargeable to capital or
revenue account?' is a relevant question; so is 'What is the profit?'

For reasons of this kind, the OR scientist seeking the whysoever of a
management's whichsoever must be responsible for the collection of his
own data. Of course, he may well use institutional information—once
he has fully investigated its nature. Again, he may not. But it is especially
noteworthy that the *absence* of information in a business is never a good
reason for not doing operational research. Many managers seem to think
that it is; that the scientist wants to be spoon-fed with predigested
victuals. He does not. Nor need the manager fear that the scientist's
hunger for facts which are not yet available will necessarily involve huge
delays and vast expenditure. Good OR scientists are proficient in specifying the purposes for which they need facts, therefore their precise nature
and also their minimum quantity. 'For they can demonstrate causes,
often without knowing all the details.' They should be told to get on
with it.

This admonition may result in the scientist's getting himself rather dirty. He has to involve himself in the operations that he is studying, otherwise he will never begin to understand what it is that he is really trying to measure. The point was obvious to all in wartime OR. Scientists with cameras hung out of aeroplanes; they sat up to their ears in mud. Today, perhaps, we take our fact-finding too easily, relying too heavily on others to tell us the whichsoever. The excitement and the difficulties and the dangers of war are missing. However, a scientist can get as bespattered and torn finding out what really happens on a night-shift in a steelworks (which turns out to be so different from what the log-book says), as he once did by falling off a motor-cycle into a paddy-field when trying to develop a way of measuring difficult terrain. Similarly, the risks run in interrogating the works' director about his reasons for backing the purchase of an electronic computer that neither sales nor accounts will be able to use, feel comparable to those run in seeking information in an Indian bazaar about the massing of hostile elements in outlying villages. The OR man who has done both experiences much the same emotion on seeing a hand glide unobtrusively into the folds of its owner's clothing, whether to produce a knife or a cigarette.

To be entirely serious: the facts that are collected within a business clearly do not tell *everything* about the business. It is very possible that they suppress precisely what it is most necessary to know in handling a particular problem. Especially, the official quantitative information never contains the facts about the value judgments and other so-called imponderables that are involved. The scientist has to find ways of measuring these factors—if they turn out to be relevant. For example, a system of priorities within a production control scheme based on a first-come–first-served rule is observed not to work. There are two reasons. The production people are grouping orders together, splitting them up, holding them back, accelerating them and regrouping them differently in order to get the most out of the plant. Everyone knows they do this and realizes that the habit saves money. But nobody, not even the foremen and chargehands concerned, knows *how* they do it. So the OR scientist has to analyse what they do, and find out. He may then be able to express the whysoever formally, and to embody the technique as a set of rules within the planning operation. If he does this effectively, it will save yet more money. The second reason is that the sales office awards special privileges to favoured customers, probably with good reason, and by importunity causes production to give these customers priority. This tendency can be measured by ranking the importance of customers (which of course introduces a set of numbers into a woolly situation) according to the judgments of the policy-makers, and then testing the ranking for consistency with its operation in practice. Much light may thereby be shed on the *real* importance of each customer. Moreover, it may again be possible to incorporate special rules in the planning scheme, this time awarding weights that reflect importance, thereby saving much trouble and temper all round.

In fact, while the manager is preoccupied with the *content* of his strategy, the scientist is studying its *form*. He is seeking the pattern behind the behaviour, trying to formalize it, testing its coherence and relevance. If he succeeds, he makes explicit what the strategy really is. Sometimes this is a blow to the manager. For example, if one asked the manager of an airline what price he put on each of his passenger's heads, he might be shocked. Yet, as Professor C. West Churchman has neatly shown, that manager's policy towards safety and the cost of buying it does indeed determine what a passenger's life is worth in the opinion of the management; the actual figure can be deduced. For the existing risk of killing a passenger could be reduced by spending more money, which the management does not in fact spend; or the risk could be increased by saving money, which the management does not in fact save. So Aristotle had this final point, too, in his last quoted sentence. Perhaps the most important aspect of this is that it tells us why OR experience is versatile in its future application. Managers are heard to complain that an OR consultant has no knowledge whatever of his particular industry, let alone of his particular company. But the scientist is concerned with the pattern of the strategy, not with its adventitious contents, and he *has* seen this before. Whysoever an investment in stock should and can be controlled, for example, does not depend on whichsoever items are held in stock.

These remarks apply to the whysoever of operational research itself. The lengthy Chapter 4 was concerned entirely with a discussion of the briefly told story in the previous chapter about sinking submarines. The OR men who undertook that job were concerned with finding a strategy for improving the rate of sinkings, not with investigating the nature of OR as we have been. With hindsight, more is perhaps clear now to the perceptive observer about their *own* strategy than was apparent to the scientists involved at the time. Any single OR job concerns the managerial whysoever, but deals in the whichsoever of OR itself. At the least, however, those men were aware of a scientific challenge, and were not obsessed with the techniques of their craft, for there were none. Today, with more than twenty years' experience of how to undertake managerial studies by scientific method behind them, typical OR approaches may be somewhat stereotyped: the freshness, the special virtues of a new look at any particular problem, are sometimes lost. The senior management scientist may become as stale in his own realm as the manager does in his; and the managers served by this newly emergent adviser may foster the stereotype of OR because it is easier to live with than the truth.

In the next section, a second case history of OR will be unfolded. Twenty years have passed. OR is now active in industry; it has acquired a corpus of knowledge and technique gained in the management service. The OR man sets to work on a problem to which the manager has no answer, and of which the scientist himself is totally ignorant; a new look must be taken. This time, however, the scientist begins by nearly falling victim to his own stereotype: his thinking is initially trapped in the methods of tenacity, authority and apriority that have grown into his own discipline and experience. But the method of science eventually wins through and the job reaches a successful conclusion. Thinking it over now as commentators on OR, we may observe the characteristic pattern that Aristotle would have the scientist seek. And we shall have occasion to remark on all six modes of tightness that can wedge the most well-intentioned bear.

2   A Modern Industrial OR Problem

In the generally rural area lay a large industrial town. This town was (and indeed is) dominated by a large and important industrial concern. A high proportion of the town's inhabitants worked for this company, and its own sense of involvement with the local community was highly developed.

The company was a heavy user of electricity. As is well known, there arises in the winter a particularly heavy demand for this source of energy, especially at peak periods of the day. In consequence, an industrial concern has to agree with the electricity undertaking on a maximum demand (MD). That is to say, the company undertakes not to exceed this agreed call for electric power during periods of peak demand, and in return a pricing system is agreed under which the electricity authority can be assured of a proper return on the proportion of its total load committed to this company. More significantly, the authority is assured that no load greater than that agreed as a maximum demand will be exerted on its supply system. But the company, which is fully connected to the grid, can fail to observe the agreed limit: what happens then?

Such a situation is fraught with great difficulty for the authority, and so a penal charge is imposed for all usage over the agreed figure. This forfeit will encourage the company to shed load as it reaches the level of maximum demand. But it can do this only if it is continuously aware of its demand from moment to moment, if it can forecast its fluctuating demand for the moments next ahead, and if a sudden decision to shed load would not entail disastrous consequences to production. It is by no means easy to satisfy this complicated set of conditions in a large works. At the end of one severe winter, the company discovered that it had exceeded its maximum demand level more than once. On each occasion, the period involved was roughly half an hour, after which time the situation had been appreciated, and load-shedding was efficiently organized to bring the consumption down below the MD figure. But under the agreement the damage had already been done: extra costs of the order of £20,000 were incurred for each mistake.

This situation was raised with operational research, although the difficulty appears at first sight to be open to solution by a combination of electrical engineering and accountancy. The managing director had, however, appreciated that a control strategy was required, and that this must involve many aspects of the business—for instance, its attitude to product quality and its production policies. He had also noted that routine methods had not in fact solved the problem, since the company had incurred undue expense, and he considered this was due to the probabilistic aspects of the case. The OR man was first confronted with this question at a management meeting, and had to make a quick appreciation. It is relevant to understand exactly what was going on in the mind of this scientist at the time (and this can be revealed—for sufficiently compelling reasons).

It was obvious, the investigator thought, that if all possible demands were assumed to occur together, and the total load aggregated, the maximum demand would be enormously and uneconomically high. The company had not done this, knowing from experience that only a proportion of the possible load would be likely to be in demand simultaneously. Nevertheless, the MD figure had evidently been fixed at too low a level. Clearly, then, this was a problem of probabilities. *Certainty* that any agreed maximum demand would not be exceeded by the actual demand at any given moment in the peak period, could not, of necessity, be reached. The following argument then emerged.

As the maximum demand ceiling is lowered from a level equivalent to the sum of all possible demands, the probability that it may be exceeded must steadily increase, though not as a linear function, because the expectations that each piece of electrically driven plant needs to

come into service at a given moment are not equal, nor are they independent of each other. Doubtless, however, these probabilities could be
computed: a curve could be established showing how the risk of needing
to exceed the maximum demand diminishes as the agreed level increases.
But, as the agreed level increases, the costs of the scheme (because of
the contract with the electricity authority) will go up—again, non-
linearly.

An optimal balance is required: a point at which there is so little gain
in the probability of not running into trouble for the added cost of
insuring this improvement that it is not worth paying the extra money.
Judging by last year's experience, for the maximum demand then operating, the curve must still be rising steeply; that is, it must surely pay to
increase the maximum demand substantially. But to what level? The
OR scientist hoped that when the curves of probability and cost had
been computed and plotted jointly against the level of MD, they would
turn out to have 'points of inflection'; he hoped, that is, that the curves
would suddenly and mutually flatten, thereby suggesting that the maximum demand should be fixed at the point where the curves changed
over from a steep to a gentle descent. He went so far as to draw a picture
of this possibility, as in Figure 1, which he showed to the managing
director.

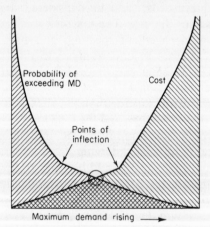

FIGURE 1. Preliminary econometric formulation of the Maximum
Demand problem.

Now the real work had to begin. The OR scientist, as manager of an
OR group, set up a small team to begin the study. As a first step, the
team was briefed to examine both the facilities for the works' control

of maximum demand and the legal contract with the electricity authority, and to produce a succinct statement on these matters as an internal document. After this, the OR manager met with the two senior OR scientists who would be concerned: one (a mathematician) as directing the project, and the other (a psychologist) as leading it on site. The three men formed an interdisciplinary team, and none of them knew more of the really technical aspects of the problem that lay before them than had by this time been compiled in their colleagues' notes. Discussion soon revealed some very interesting questions, to which no-one present knew the answers.

Following this meeting, then, the OR manager went back for a talk with the senior management about a number of matters. As far as the electricity demand problem was concerned, he was now intent on obtaining an answer to the following questions. When it looked as though the danger limit were being approached, the grid load would be shed. The first move in this direction was to switch on the company's private electrical generators. In order to use these generators, steam was required and this could be obtained by burning oil or by using one of two separate sources of gas supply—both of them originating in the works. The question therefore was: under what tactical control did these alternative fuels become used, what happened to the processes they were otherwise concerned in energizing, and who was responsible for the overall control of the many forms of energy that were apparently interacting in supplying the plant?

Answers to these questions were soon obtained. The accountants knew, as apparently 'absolute' facts, the order of cheapness of the whole range of fuels employed in the works—that is, they knew the cost of each as procuring a standard number of BTU's. It had therefore been ruled that any actions taken which would involve substituting one fuel for another should, as a matter of course, invoke the use of the 'absolutely' cheapest available alternative. As to the last part of the question, it was judged that, since this policy was so simple to comprehend, no one person need be charged with seeing that it was implemented. Everyone concerned knew the rules and obeyed them (an assertion subsequently verified as true in most cases).

The OR man was by this time becoming excited. How could anyone say what the relative costs of the fuels were for a given situation on the basis of some average costings? The costs actually incurred by a variety of alternative fuel policies at any one moment must surely depend on the opportunities available at that one moment to contrive some especially ingenious pattern of consumption to match some especially unusual set of demands. At this point the appropriate officials—the controllers of the electrical generating station, the gas controller, the man in charge of the steam boilers—were called into the meeting. These people contended vigorously that their preoccupations had nothing whatever to do with the problem of trying to fix the maximum demand from the grid. The OR man was impatient of these arguments, because he had been unable to complete his concept of the double probability curves without knowing what the peripheral conditions actually were. And it was in trying to convince these departmental managers of the motes in their eyes that he suddenly became aware of the beam in his own. The phase space of the problem as he had conceived it was entirely at fault; these 'peripheral' arrangements were not only relevant, they were an intrinsic part of the management's difficulty.

When the senior meeting resumed, the tack was entirely changed. Had the management in fact ever considered setting up a general control for energy consumption of every kind? The answer was that they had often thought about this, but they had discarded the idea, on the grounds that they knew of no similar works anywhere in the world in which a genuinely integrated energy control system operated. This bore out, they thought, their own intuition that the total problem was much too complex to be solved from moment to moment on such a broad front. As was remarked earlier, a manager is not culpable for fixing his phase spaces according to his own knowledge and experience; this is a necessary manœuvre, and is often correct. But no harm would be done in trying to devise such a control, since new scientific methods would be used in formulating the problem, and there would be a possibility of destroying many of the traditional difficulties within a completely new framework. This thought was based on the consideration that most of the problems arose from a failure to communicate between the different sorts of fuel controllers. Such information flow problems tend to disappear, however, if the centres between which the flow is supposed, and fails, to flow are in some way coalesced. So permission to alter the entire terms of reference of the investigation was sought. This was not a problem of determining the maximum demand for grid electricity, but a problem of discovering a company strategy for energy control.

The new proposal was strongly opposed—on the grounds that such ideas, even if successfully developed, simply could not be implemented in view of the company's organizational structure. The control principle adumbrated cut right across the established lines of managerial responsibility. Thought blocks began to rise like monuments all round the table, but the managing director was willing to give the idea a trial. The OR manager returned to base with what was, in company terms, a new commission—but which was, in his own mind, simply a new phase space.

The construction of a scientific account of the whole energy consumption of this company was a long and difficult task. It should be appreciated that to build into the scientific programme every source of fuel, together with the appropriate constraints and controls on its use, was an undertaking of a different order of magnitude from the original task. For although the electricity demand problem itself could only be solved by taking account of the alternatives which could be fed into the system, it had at first been understood that this would happen according to a set of simple and invariable rules. To allow for it in a situation where *every* fuel had a right to equal consideration as a poser of its own problems of profitability, made the problem perhaps ten times as great.

Gradually the scientific picture emerged. All the interactions of the fuels and the production situations that could occur were stated in terms of mathematical and logical equations. Few of the fuel relationships turned out to be symmetrical. That is, for example, the price paid for electricity imported from the national grid was different from the price received for works' electricity exported to the grid. There were many practical constraints on the apparent possibilities. Some of these constraints were not absolute, but themselves matters of probability. The most important of these, for instance, concerned a contract to supply the local township with gas. The company treated this commitment very seriously, with the result that gas-holding capacity which the OR scientists had originally regarded as a buffer in the system, turned out to have a restricted availability in that role. How far it was restricted would depend on the day of the week, because this determined both the probable level of the townspeople's demand, and separately the probable level of gas in the holder.

Figure 2 gives a general view of the total energy system which was now under study. Every entry in this diagram represents an activity that has some effect on every other entry. Moreover, no activity can be prescribed in exact terms; the whole system is a dynamic interaction of probabilities. Somehow a formal scientific account of this whole system had to be created, and this was done by a mixture of theoretical and practical work. The logic of the theory of sets was used to express the basic relationships; mathematical statistics expressed the probabilities; actual data were pumped into the formalizations to quantify the picture. In some cases, the data recorded were quite inadequate and more had to be collected. In some cases again, the data were insufficiently precise—and

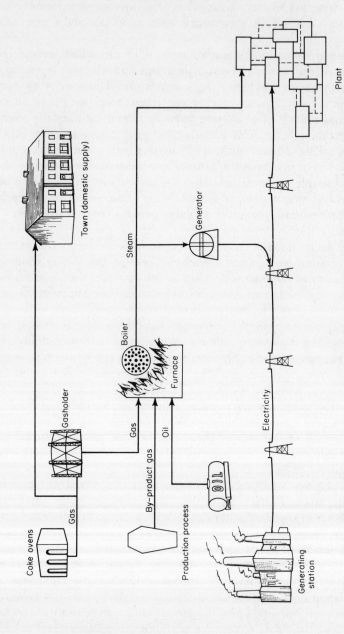

FIGURE 2. Diagram of the major interactions affecting the Maximum Demand problem.

could not be made more so; mathematical tricks were then used to estimate what more frequent readings would have recorded had the instrumentation been available. Many details of the system turned out to be unknown, and became the subject of special investigations.

For example, the optimal number of oil burners (as opposed to gas burners) inside the boiler had to be calculated. The generation rate of the private electrical sub-station had to be assessed in terms of the maximum output of five different turbo-alternator sets under different loads. This was done for available steam pressures representing residual energy available after intermittent and very heavy demands for steam had been met from the production plant. Lest the acquisition of these data makes the work sound like a straightforward engineering study, let it be noted that the object was not to find some theoretical best state for the system, but a control strategy that would actually work. Throughout, therefore, the interdisciplinary team was concerned not so much with the measurements quoted here, as with their *representation* in the system. The fact that counts is not that a meter registers somewhere, but that someone *knows* it has registered—after what delay, with what accuracy, with what reliability, and so on, and above all with what capacity to react to the information thereby conveyed.

In short, the scientific account of affairs involved the formalization of interactions between men, machines, materials and money, all spread over the complex system depicted in Figure 2. It took about nine months to complete the scientific appraisal, to evolve an optimal overall strategy for operating the total system, to test it adequately, and to present it in a form that would be usable in the works. For it is of course useless to present works' operatives with set-theoretic formulae; the rules for conducting the strategy must be translated into the practical language of simple charts and simple operations, such as pulling levers. In the end, however, the job was done.

The company was then informed of these developments, and told that the problems arising in creating a generalized control for energy had been overcome. Not surprisingly, the management immediately asked for an answer to the original problem: at what level should the maximum demand be fixed in future? The answer, assuming that the new controls were instituted, was that the figure could be *reduced to less than half* its previous level.

Inevitably, this conclusion caused consternation, and the arguments that followed showed clearly how important it is that management should really understand the nature of operational research. If the basic features of OR work which have been explained in these chapters had been comprehended, all might have been well. As it was, some of the people concerned had this familiar view of OR: that it is an impracticable attempt to beat a manager at his own game by theoretical mathematics. Apart from the total misconception of the subject thus indicated, this is a way of expressing things which, by its pejorative tone, is clearly intended to mean that such an approach cannot possibly succeed. It is high time to note, then, that a management group intending to obtain the advice of operational research should first provide it with a platform from which to explain its objects and methods to everybody who will be concerned. 'Everybody', moreover, means what it says: in particular, representatives of trade unions should be admitted to early confidence. A scientist has every prospect of obtaining first-rate collaboration from union men, provided he has an opportunity to explain his motives; for the scientist is interested in reality without a gloss, and the man on the shop floor is interested in this too. There must of course be every opportunity for those attending explanatory meetings, at any level, to argue; senior management should not seek to protect OR from open assault. Difficulties will be cleared up which otherwise would result in covert obstruction. Besides, these experiences are good for the OR man, who is thereby reminded that he intervenes in real life—a reality in which people stand to be hurt, or to be degraded, or to be exposed.

In the case of the MD job, permission to hold such meetings had been refused, but some time after the experiences here related the company made generous amends. It sponsored a whole-day conference on OR for all managers, and a half-day conference for union representatives. Thereafter, it is worth saying, the workpeople (who had hitherto barred quite rudimentary work study in certain locations) cheerfully permitted OR men to time their operations electronically to a fifth of a second accuracy in those same locations. This was because the OR men had by this time earned the right to be trusted to negotiate the arrangements and suitable safeguards by themselves—which they did.

Despite the difficulties caused by the failure in communications, however, the new control system was eventually installed. The operatives had to be taught the use of the practical tools which interpreted the scientific strategy—an operation in which the team leader, a professional psychologist, as well as an OR scientist, proved invaluable. Here was the new whichsoever of the job. The strategy itself, which had been prepared under the supervision of the project director (a mathematician of genius), was expressed in a symbolism that many who have studied mathematics at degree level would find hard to understand. It was therefore hidden away, labelled 'the whysoever'. And Aristotle was right to say that mathematical science is about pattern, rather than the specific things that form its subject matter, for three years later this strategy was taken out and used, to even more imposing effect, on another management problem of energy control. The situation was different; the very firm was different; but the whysoever of the whichsoever was the same.

3   Final Appearance of the Wedged Bear

There is no need to write a lengthy commentary on this case history, but the plan of these first five chapters calls for an explicit understanding of the managerial philosophy that is fundamental to the use of operational research. In particular, what was true of the nature, application and meaning of OR when it devised a method for sinking submarines during the war, remains true twenty years later in the creation of a strategy for controlling the use of energy in an industrial company. The last chapter tried to explain it, by considering six ways in which a manager can misunderstand. All these stereotypes were militating against success in this MD study, too, but we should be able to unwedge the bear with alacrity this time.

Firstly, the damaging notion of the stereotyped scientist was much in evidence. Here was a job apparently exposed to science already: an accepted set of experts had been handling it for years. What did these OR people know about it? Here are some of the disciplines represented, at various times, on the OR job: mathematics and psychology (already mentioned); philosophy; computer expertise; lubrication engineering; logic; economics. Before the follow-up work (to be mentioned later) had been completed, servomechanics and biology had been added to the list. This was indeed an interdisciplinary team, although it did make use of an electrical engineer who happened to be on the staff. These were the people who broke with tradition and found a new way into the situation.

Secondly, there was the stereotyped problem. And here the OR manager was himself a bear firmly wedged alongside the man he was trying to help. The problem, we have said, may not be as it appears: determine the *whole* of the situation, and forget the departmental barriers. But the OR manager went doggedly on, and got stuck. Fortunately, he fell out of the tree—because of a fluke, certainly, but also because in his ignorance of the proper way of handling a question of electricity supply, his tightness was not too severe. What really trapped him was in fact his too thorough knowledge of the company organization. Perhaps his less knowledgeable colleagues pushed. At any rate, the real need

was to consider the *whole* of the energy supply arrangements, and not
just those of an electrical nature. Again, with hindsight, this trick may
be regarded as frightfully obvious; one can only say that it had not often
been envisaged before and never attempted in a similar firm.

Thirdly, comes the role of chance in the situation: a formal treatment
of the subject, battling with the stereotype of science itself. Almost the
whole of the quantification of these strategies, policies and rules had to
be stated in terms of probabilities rather than clear-cut facts. This is a
matter not just of knowing some statistics, but also of understanding
science. Remember that people customarily use what the statistician
would call an estimate as if it were a cast-iron fact. There were those
absolute cost figures, alleged to measure the cheapness of fuels—regardless of the circumstances. There were maxima for wholes, computed as
the sums of the maxima of parts, which simply could not occur in any
universe governed by any degree of chance. And so on. It is the scientist
who can handle these probabilities and risks, not the accountant and the
engineer who tell him he cannot.

Next comes the question of phase spaces and thought blocks, which
insist on a stereotyped solution. It is so important to realize that the
treatment given to these matters in this book is not merely a gilding of
the lily that everyone has in a vase on his mantelpiece. It is easy enough
to say that people should be prepared to consider solutions that they
have not considered before, or that a good manager is imaginative. But
what do such exhortations really amount to in real life? In practice, they
are devoid of content. The exposition that was developed at considerable
length in Chapter 4 was intended to throw a genuinely helpful light on
the difficulty. Managers and scientists alike need to understand fully the
real mechanisms at work, and the limitations of the human mind as they
apply to this matter. It is not a question of the scientist being cleverer
than the manager, nor of the manager being obstinate and old-fashioned.
The two men have quite different roles to play in their quite different
jobs. The idea of culpability must be completely abandoned. In many
ways it is possible to argue that the old solution was the *right* one, for
without the change in conceptual framework the scientist could probably not have improved on it. It is not a manager's job to change his
own conceptual framework, but to get on with the responsibilities he
exercises within it. The onus on *general* management to consider such
changes is, however, much heavier. Perhaps this kind of decision is
their most important task.

Just how difficult it is to avoid the question of blame is well illustrated
in the present case. The OR team itself had, it can truthfully be said,

introduced no note of slander. They handled this question with tact. But the managerial hierarchy itself was not so understanding. Wedged firmly among his stereotypes, the top man (long since retired) hurled the OR report like a bomb at his subordinates. The shrapnel ricochetted. Various people were told by various others that they must have been losing the firm money for years. If a crew of egg-heads, including philosophers and biologists who did not know Ohm's law from an Act of Parliament, could do the job better than the array of responsible officials, the latter had better pack up. Two of them did; their resignations possibly had nothing to do with this rumpus, but it can be imagined what effect that outcome had on the reputation of OR in the company and its associate firms.

So much for the four points concerned with the tackling of an operational research study. The fifth point concerns pay-off. Again in this case history the rewards were really quite large; not only were there the decreased cost of the agreement with the electricity undertaking, the reduced cost of consumption itself and the elimination of the fines previously incurred, but there was an overall gain in the efficiency of energy usage throughout the works. If all these savings are brought into the computation (though the third can only be assessed problematically from a knowledge of the research work itself) the *annual* saving was certainly a six-figure one.

The stereotyped outcome of a small and respectable gain from operational research is in fact a comfortable notion for management. It carries with it the implication that everything was just about right. With the enlightened use of high-powered brains, suitably directed, a little more finesse can be achieved. But this is not the way to use OR. Where the work is used in that way, it deserves to be defined as the application of big minds to small problems. And who should bear the onus for that kind of prostitution? Truly the scientists concerned are to blame, for they ought not to acquiesce, but they may be defended on at least two counts. In the first place, many scientists are a great deal more diffident than managers imagine. The stereotype of scientific arrogance derives from a failure to understand science. A good scientist is never arrogant, although he may be conceited—as may be a good historian, or a good manager. Thus many OR men are actually doing work that is well beneath their powers, simply because they do not realize it. Secondly, however keen the OR man may be, and should be, about getting results that are managerially effective, the scientist in him has to be concerned about something else too. He wants to do good science and this is an end in itself. Hence the prostituted OR man, baulked in the search for thᵉ big company pay-off, will become more and more engrossed in the search for professional satisfaction. He may well achieve this in doing elegant and original science on assignments that are managerially fatuous.

No; the onus for this state of affairs rests largely with management itself. It can hardly be too much stressed that the sponsor of operational research is likely to get the pay-off he expects. But this is a topic locked up in the mode of fitting OR effort into the organization, which will be discussed at the end of the book.

The sixth of the stereotypes that wedged our bear was the stereotype of success. Agreement on what counts as success is sometimes hard to reach, and agreement on exactly what has to be done to achieve it harder still. The general discussion of this point in the last chapter concluded that the *whole* solution has to be implemented; parts of the total recommendation cannot be amputated because they are somewhat inconvenient. This, it was said, may entail consequential research and development.

As with the depth charge gauge, so with the MD control. The prospect of automating the whole of the energy control system had been investigated during the study. In principle, the idea was attractive: it is in most OR work. The reason for this is simple. Once a strategy has been examined scientifically, properly formalized, rigorously optimized, it is definite and precise. The rules for working it are, and must be, quite clear, even if the circumstances covered by the rules are not. This means that the strategy can not only be automated, but readily automated—because the basic work has been done. None the less, as in this case, full-scale automation is often just not economical. Some partial automation was, however, included in the energy control plan.

It had been realized that some links in the control sequence could not be reliably undertaken by human resources. The information that had to be passed would be too complicated to compute with sufficient speed, too long in transmission and too unreliably interpreted at the other end. In order to get the quick results that were so urgently needed, a plan was evolved to implement the strategy with human links. Inevitably this included simplifications to evade the troubles mentioned, thereby decreasing the effectiveness of the strategy and incurring a greater risk of error. The recommendations included the specification of certain automatic linkages to deal with these problems, and these called for the design of a small special-purpose computer.

It was tempting for the management to forget about this part of the solution. The simplified plan was adopted and worked successfully throughout its first winter. Why bother with these 'extras'? The fact, however, was that these were not extras, but an intrinsic part of the whole solution. To cut them out of the scheme would be uneconomical, or they would not have been in the scheme in the first place. This means that to save money on this development meant running a risk for which the long-run expectation of loss was greater than the cost of the proposed automation. Happily, the point was agreed. Designing the computer was a research and development task unsuited to an OR group, but the logical specification of the system derived from the original work. Thus a new, though smaller, OR project was mounted to complete the detailed logical design, and to collaborate with the electronic engineers elsewhere who carried out the circuit design and built the equipment.

Thus this commentary is completed. The bear, at his final appearance, has been unwedged again. This time the six stereotypes have been observed in action, as they actually impinged on a particular OR job. There is much to learn from the story, for both managers and scientists.

Here is a final lesson from this experience for them both. Although the stereotypes were gradually eliminated and the job was successfully commissioned, successfully undertaken, successfully completed and successfully implemented, the management did not know how to take the credit. They felt rather silly. Now this is absurd. A management which handles all this successful work should be very pleased with itself; it should declare that while others may fumble and misuse OR, it at least has discovered how to exploit the facility. Since it did not take this line and the credit it most certainly deserved, other managements within the group misread the situation. All who had been concerned were ill served by this development. It should not be thought that the OR people were gratified to gain a reputation for 'having put them right'. For one thing, this is not the OR task; for another, it makes other people very nervous.

Operational research is in this respect like musical chairs. If you're left holding the credit when the music stops, you're out.

4   Humpty Dumpty Rides Again

What then is operational research? There are roughly as many definitions of the subject as there are OR scientists. For these are thoughtful people, and if any one of them lacks the temerity to formulate a definition, his place is taken by bolder colleagues who have a range of definitions to spare.

The need for a definite set of words to express what the subject is must be real, because OR scientists are always being asked for one. On the other hand, it should be recognized that definitions refer strictly to the meaning of terms, not to the activities which the terms name. 'A straight line is the shortest distance between two points' says what the term 'straight line' should be taken to mean in a particular context. We could rewrite plane geometry using a different definition of 'straight line' altogether, something that we usually call a curve, for instance: tiresome, but perfectly correct. But if we adopt a new convention for a term that names an activity, the position is not so simple. 'In this article, the word *physics* means *the art of cookery*' is a convention easily, and again correctly, maintained within the boundaries of the article. Yet if the reader were to imagine that this gastronomic article told him anything about what physicists do, he would be misled. Humpty Dumpty paid words extra and made them mean what he chose; but he could not thereby change the behaviour of the things they named.

So it is with OR. 'OR is research into operations' is a definition of the term, and one which few people could possibly reject. But it says nothing about what OR men do; it defines a term, not an activity. Now of course activities themselves are not to be defined, as are the terms which name them. Activities are to be *described*. The first part of this book, which is now complete, has been devoted to description. Five chapters have been used up in saying what OR men do, why and in what context. If it is convenient to have a definite set of words to cover the meaning of OR, we must look for a compressed description, rather than for what could properly be called a definition.

The description had better start with the topic handled by OR. It is clear enough what this is: the complex problems faced by managers. Unless there were managers, and unless they had complex problems, operational research would not exist. Managers themselves, and most of their consultants, tackle these problems from knowledge and experience of the job. Specialist advisers, such as accountants, have a battery of highly developed techniques ready for use in this sphere. OR, however, as has been seen, investigates the situation without a preconceived idea of what it is like: its approach is that of research. That means taking a new look at the state of affairs. The method of investigation is the scientific method; an OR man attacks the problem as a scientist, using the ways of operating that he would use in any other investigation. These are, for instance, logical analysis, the identification and measurement of facts, the erection and testing of hypotheses, experiment, verification and so on: ultimately, the discovery of whysoever. But more than this, OR science imports into the investigation an interdisciplinary knowledge of the sciences themselves, of their formal languages and techniques, of their most advanced insights into the way the world works. All this must be compressed for the description. *Operational research is the attack of modern science on complex problems arising in the direction and management*—of what, exactly?

'Of enterprises', the answer would seem to be, for these are the things that managers manage and direct. And yet that term is rather vague, although everyone understands it. What really is an enterprise, as seen from the scientist's viewpoint? It is something that uses a collection of resources to meet a need. There is no point in being vague about the nature of the resources, either. To alliterate: men, machines, materials and money are the four specific lots of resources required to make an enterprise. And if four such radically different kinds of input are involved, they must be interlocked in the most intimate fashion. In fact they are; they interpenetrate to create a large, organic system. This is itself what makes the enterprise amenable to scientific examination. It is a system of which the internal mechanism can be discovered. Nor does OR care very much to what purposes this four-dimensional system is directed. Originally, as was shown, the systems studied were military; the defence enterprise remains a field of OR. Next came industry, the production-and-marketing system; and business, too, breeds enterprises that fit the pattern stated. Above all, government is an enterprise that calls for operational research. To compress all this is difficult enough. Not every enterprise can be identified by name. Schools, for example, and universities; hospitals, and doctors' waiting-rooms; all these and many other managed systems fit the bill. We shall have to hope that they occur to readers of the description as being covered by one of the terms used in this continuation: . . . *in the direction and management of large systems of men, machines, materials and money in industry, business, government and defence.*

So far the description briefly recounts the purposes, the topic and the fields of application covered by operational research. But 'the attack of modern science' says little about the methods it has developed since 1941. As will be seen in Part II, OR has in the meantime created its own armoury of special techniques. Although a short description cannot list these, some attempt should perhaps be made to crystallize the distinctive approach of the OR scientist. Now in trying to account for the behaviour of a complicated system, the scientist has first to represent it in the formal terms he knows how to manipulate. This stage of the work was clearly identified in each of the jobs so far discussed in detail. Looking over the scientist's shoulder at his working papers, one might see a whole series of boxes joined by arrows, and a whole lot of mathematics. Are these organization charts and formulae? Perhaps they are; but they are also more than this. They are attempts to get inside the system under study, to grapple with its intimate workings. The scientist is trying to re-create the system itself, not merely to describe some of its features: he intends to model it. The formal representation of the system that he builds is called a model. This model is something different from the diagrams that are drawn, different from the equations which inform their structure, different from the data which quantify the equations, and something more than the sum of all of these. The model is like looking at the real system through a filter; not a filter that polarizes light, not one that turns the picture red or blue, but one that turns it 'scientific'. All the major features of the system, suitably transformed, will be found in the model of the system. And these must include the so called imponderables. In particular, representation must be made within the model of such factors as chance and risk—we have already seen something of what this means. And so: *The distinctive approach is to develop a scientific model of the system, incorporating measurements of factors such as chance and risk.*

A deeper understanding of the nature of models must be sought later; meanwhile it is as well to make the reason for creating them fairly specific. The essence of a model is to be predictive. The scientist, it was said before, cannot foretell the future. But, if he is armed with an effective model of the system, he should be able to say a good deal about the way the system may be expected to operate in a variety of circumstances. By testing the model's reactions to different sets of possible eventualities, the scientist begins to evaluate the system's *vulnerability*. What can the manager do about the vulnerability of the system he manages? He uses his normal method, which might be divided into three categories. He can take a decision which could be defined as a switch that sets at least some part of the enterprise on a new course. He can adopt a strategy which could be defined as a coherent decision-making plan. He can install a control which in turn could be defined as a routine that implements a strategy and generates decisions. When the manager sets out to apply one of these remedies to a complex problem, he will certainly attempt to foresee the outcome. In fact, various alternative courses of action will be open to him. Before choosing one, he will want to predict and compare these outcomes—to know, in a word, which is the least vulnerable to a malignant future. This is what the OR model is for. So we may add to the sentence last formulated for the description of OR, an explanation of the model's purposes . . . *with which to predict and compare the outcomes of alternative decisions, strategies or controls.*

Finally, it should be made abundantly clear that the whole purpose of OR, of doing the things just described, is to aid the manager. People sometimes seem to fear that the aims of scientists in the managerial sphere are vainglorious. Some go so far as to imagine that the scientist wishes to establish dominance. Possibly a few scientists feel like this. If so, they are on the same footing as the historian or the classicist who feels the same way. Such men are either psychotics or potential managers and entrepreneurs. The scientist *qua* scientist seeks only to do science. But the OR scientist has a special motivation towards science in management, usually (one observes) because he cannot bear to look on quietly while decisions are taken, strategies adopted and controls instituted in important enterprises on the basis of guesswork. Though even this is not the worst, for guesswork can be inspired and the brain with flair is still the best computing machine we have. What really riles the scientist is that a course of action should be adopted for feeble reasons that masquerade as being scientific. For example, some cheap and nasty opinion poll is held in which too few people representing a biased section of the community are asked loaded questions which they do not understand, their answers being misinterpreted by unskilled interviewers for inadequate processing to demonstrate a pre-ordained answer. (This is not a general denunciation of opinion polls, many of which are excellently conducted. As with every activity, there are bad practitioners, however, and the question is whether their phoney results are uncritically used.) In fact, managers do often take advice which they honestly believe to have been established by proper study, but which will not stand up to five minutes of scientific scrutiny. They then assure their shareholders, customers, workpeople or constituents that the matter has been properly investigated—and these people have even less chance of knowing the truth.

OR sets out to give proper advice, after proper study, that management can trust. It asks managers to investigate its claim to be organized and competent to do this. Then management can get peacefully on with the job—using OR as an extra, scientific, lobe of its own brain. *The purpose is to help management determine its policy and actions scientifically.*

And so the description is complete; for those who really want a form of words, it will do. It is certainly not unique; but it is not entirely arbitrary, either. It was prepared for the Operational Research Society of Great Britain, after consultation with many leading British OR scientists, and the Council of the Society has underwritten it. The full statement is as follows:

Operational research is the attack of modern science on complex problems arising in the direction and management of large systems of men, machines, materials and money in industry, business, government and defence. Its distinctive approach is to develop a scientific model of the system, incorporating measurements of factors such as chance and risk, with which to predict and compare the outcomes of alternative decisions, strategies or controls. The purpose is to help management determine its policy and actions scientifically.

PART II

The Activity of Operational Research

Connective Summary

Having considered in Part I the origin and nature of operational research, how it came about and what it really tries to do, we pass to the exposition of how it really does what it tries to do.

Chapter 6 investigates the way in which managers solve problems, and contrasts this, in a rather formal analysis, with the way in which OR would tackle a similar situation. It shows how the predictive quality of the thinking is critical to a successful decision or policy, and expounds the concept of a 'model' as the basis of insight and prediction. The theoretical nature of models is examined, with the aid of really detailed explanation and practical illustrations. These examples are augmented in Chapter 7, and the methodology of OR is more fully brought out.

But scientific models have to be described in rigorous terms before they can be competently tested and used for predictive purposes. Chapter 8 explains how this is done: it specifies the role of mathematics as handling quantity, of mathematical statistics as handling probability, of symbolic logic as handling qualitative relationships. The basic vocabulary of these formal languages of science is explained in ordinary English, and case studies are quoted at length to illustrate their value.

Armed now with both a methodology and a set of languages for doing operational research, we begin to probe the real nature of the problem situation which it is the OR task to penetrate. In every case the manager is responsible for the control of some kind of system, and Chapter 9 considers how these systems may be described and analysed scientifically. Examples of almost every sort of management problem are discussed in this light.

Specifically, solving the problem of prediction within these systems is the nub of the management task. Chapter 10 goes into the nature of forecasting, and of the techniques used by operational research to help. Again, many problem situations are quoted, and it clearly emerges that OR can aid the manager through the identification and description of the mechanism which informs the system the manager controls. The model of this mechanism is the tool of OR which enables alternative decisions, policies and controls to be evaluated and compared in quantitative terms. And although the scientist cannot predict the future any more than the manager can, he is able to narrow the area of uncertainty and pinpoint the vital issues.

6

ABOUT MODELS

> Reason is the thing without which our state would be
> the state of wild beasts, of children and lunatics; it is
> the thing whereby we picture our intellectual acts
> before they become manifest to the senses, so that we
> see them exactly as though we had sensed them; then
> we represent these pictures in our sensual acts so that
> they correspond exactly with what we have
> represented and imagined.
>
> RHAZES (A.D. 864–925) in *Spiritual Physick*

1 'Too Many Variables'

A great deal has by now been said about the nature of operational research: its origins, its key features and its general relationship to the task of management. Hints have been thrown out about all sorts of applications, and two actual studies have been analysed in some detail. We have even essayed a definition. It is now time to discuss more systematically what operational research can do, and precisely how it does it.

Scientific method has already been talked about in a discursive kind of way, and most people can formulate some idea of how a scientist would go about investigating for example a plant or a mouse or a lump of lead. Physical objects such as these must be carefully examined; pieces are cut off them and scrutinized under microscopes; they are prodded, probed and in general analysed. One can see that, having obtained a great deal of information about a physical object, a scientist is in a position to begin to formulate his well-known hypotheses about structure and behaviour, to invent theories about how these objects would respond to certain treatments and perhaps to formulate possible laws which might inexorably govern these phenomena. All this could obviously be the subject of experiment and verification. As a matter of fact, however, modern philosophers of science are very critical of these traditional ways of describing scientific activity.

The simple-minded notion of 'objective measurement' collapses under close examination. It turns out that measurements are themselves based on theory, since there must be a purpose in mind when the measuring instruments are devised. It turns out that what is already regarded as natural law preconditions the design of experiments intended to verify hypotheses about natural law, because our idea of what constitutes proof is a late developer in our family of logical notions. And so on. In short, linguistic analysis shows that it is not possible to set the classical procedures of science in chronological order, so it is not particularly profitable to try and separate these procedures one from another at all. Moreover, the situation becomes still more confused when one stops thinking about physical objects and considers systems instead. The mouse and the plant may be physical objects, but they can be understood only as systems. Moreover, the boundaries of these systems are not the same as the boundaries of the physical objects themselves. If they could be entirely isolated from their environments they would no longer be the things that they are. To the atomic physicist, even the lump of lead is a system, and of course almost all the functions of management are concerned with systems rather than entities. At this point the scientist joins the philosopher in his assault on the classical notion of science: to measure aspects of a system—to observe it even—is to alter the system so measured and observed. This result is entailed by quantum theory.

For these and other reasons which there is no need to explore fully, we shall need a new kind of description of the scientific method in order to discover what is the fundamental approach of operational research. It has to be conceded that OR scientists themselves have not given much attention to this problem. Underlying most of their work is the classical philosophy of science, and they continue to get reasonable results in practice for the same reason that their scientific forebears were able to reach useful conclusions a century ago with the same philosophical equipment. The reason is that a cohesive collection of fundamental methods, which may be called a methodology, provides a framework for research which is neither right nor wrong, but only more or less useful. It is only at the limits of its usefulness, at the point where its concepts begin to disintegrate, that a methodology need be called in question. For example, the concept of the 'objective observer' worked well enough for Newtonian physics, but is useless when it comes to relativity. Likewise, a methodology based on the measurement of simultaneous events, which has been found perfectly sound and valuable in mechanics, in optics, in astronomy and in psychology, is totally useless to the modern physicist. For the term 'simultaneous' denotes nothing whatever in an Einsteinian universe. Similarly, it may be argued, the analytic scientific methodology most familiar to educated people today begins to disintegrate when it is applied to the consideration of large and complicated systems such as armies, businesses, industries and economies.

There are several very definite reasons for this accusation, which managers have been quicker than scientists to recognize. Traditionally, the scientist conducted an experiment by holding all the variables of the experimental situation constant—except two. He then manipulated one of these variables and observed the results on the other. This manœuvre is quite impossible outside the laboratory, because there is no means of holding all conditions but two constant in a real-life situation. The immediate answer was provided by developments in mathematical statistics, which enabled conclusions to be drawn validly when a considerable number of variables were all changing together. The tool of multivariate analysis was invented. From that epoch onwards, the scientist could in principle afford to laugh at the manager who cried in despair: *'There are too many variables.'* He knew that his statistical theory was competent to handle an indefinitely large number of them. But in practice his triumph was short-lived, because the theory demanded an ever-increasing amount of computation for every new variable that was added. Thus although it was now possible to carry out valid scientific experimentation outside the laboratory (for instance, in agricultural studies), it was still not feasible to keep scientific control of a real-life situation having the dimensions of, say, an industrial enterprise. But then electronic computers arrived on the scene. Today it is once again possible in principle to laugh at the manager who complains: *'There are too many variables.'* The theory of statistical computation has been matched by a practical computing facility; the only limit to the size of the problem that can be solved is set by the size of the computer's storage. Yet managers continue to say: *'There are too many variables,'* and scientists are prone to claim that managers are not up to date in their knowledge of scientific theory and practice.

I think these managers have been right all the time, although they might express themselves a little more precisely. The point really is much more fundamental than the arguments of the last paragraph supposed, for the prerequisite in handling a large number of variables is that they can be identified. Now the kinds of system under discussion exhibit

literally billions of variables. There is no *rigorous* means of knowing
which 'matter'. Indeed, the importance of a particular variable in such
a system is a question of degree, a question of judgment, a question of
convention. Moreover, the importance it has by any of these criteria
will change from moment to moment. This does not mean merely that
the numerical value assumed by the variable is changing—that is in the
nature of variables, and one of the things about the system that we know
how to handle. No, it means more: the *structural relevance* of the variable
inside the system is changing with time.

One class of variable in managerial systems is so notoriously difficult
to identify that it has drawn considerable attention from OR scientists.
This is the value judgment. In brief: the criteria of success adopted by
the management of an enterprise *must* be represented in the analytical
account of the system given by the scientist; this is absolutely unavoidable. Yet what manager can give a completely unambiguous account of
his criteria of success? He cannot say that he wishes to increase profit or
reduce cost—and leave it at that. For if he does, and that simple-minded
notion of success is built into the mathematics of an analytical treatment
of the problem, then the solution may well generate all sorts of unexpected side effects. One can imagine, for example, a situation in which
the manager who has asked for maximum profit is told that the solution
is (in a seller's market) to raise all his prices and to 'soak' his customers.
'But what about my goodwill?' he will say. 'And what about next year's
business, when all my customers have gone bankrupt?' But the analytical
scientist could reply that he should have mentioned these things earlier
on. The point of course is that however many desiderata the manager
may mention, there may be others which he takes for granted and will
not mention. Secondly, the longer the list becomes, the more likely it
is that the manager's objectives will not be consistent with each other.
Indeed, it is quite obvious that his objectives may actually be contradictory. He wants, for example, to maximize his profit, and *also* to be
a good employer. But if he spends a penny on amenities, his profits are
reduced by that penny. And by the same token every penny he retains
as profit he *might* have dispersed to his workpeople in some kind of
benefit scheme. The analytical scientist is potentially at a loss. For it is
in the nature of the optimizing techniques of mathematics, which the
OR scientist most familiarly employs, that *only one variable can be maximized or minimized at a time*. Should the scientist then complain that
the manager is muddle-headed? Not at all; it is this particular scientific
methodology that is limited. For as every biological scientist knows, the
primary characteristic of viable systems is that they try to optimize a

whole set of conflicting objective functions at once. They cannot do this —so far the mathematical analysis is correct—but they *try* to do it. The result is that their method of control is essentially one of contriving a stable *balance*, and not of seeking some unique maximum.

In practice, a great many operational research jobs escape this difficulty by limiting the scope of their enquiry. The study says, in effect: *assuming* that such and such conditions hold, and that the object is to maximize profit, then the correct strategy is given below. With this approach, operational research leaves it to the manager to interpret the results, and to strike his own balance with other factors which the study has not considered. But, as was forcibly argued in Part I of this book, this is not the kind of help which the management really seeks. It wants to know what is the best strategy having regard to *all* the circumstances. And so people concerned with OR, scientists and managers alike, need to think out the implications of these facts, and to contemplate a methodology which will satisfy all the circumstances. So far but one solution has been put forward.

This is, in brief, to say that in practice there is indeed only one scale on which value judgments, or managerial desiderata, or criteria of success, need be measured. This is the scale of *preference*. One can, the argument says, propose a finite number of distinguishable managerial policies and compute their complicated outcomes. One can then isolate a pair of such policies, show the respective outcomes to management, and ask which of the two outcomes is preferred. By repeating this exercise many times, one can eventually rank all the policies in order of preference. This position is vulnerable from many points of view. The scientific procedures which must be undertaken in order to arrive at a result are possibly defective. At the other end of the scale, it is fairly obvious that what is meant to be a scientific solution will in fact depend upon an arbitrarily subjective evaluation after all. Admittedly, this conclusion is obvious only because I have expressed the methodology in a way which makes it inevitable. Proponents of the methodology go to lengths which cannot be reproduced here to expound further scientific procedures intended to evade this difficulty. I do not think they succeed, and the point has been argued elsewhere.

At any rate, the arguments of this section have perhaps sufficiently shown that a new methodology of operational research ought to be propounded, and it is one of the purposes of this book to do just that.

2   Experiments with Experience

Let us begin by highlighting a particular aspect of man's reasoning faculty. It is the ability to make a forecast, and indeed it is precisely this capability in man which seems most clearly to distinguish him from other animals. There is no doubt that we all prognosticate; we can entertain possible consequences of the alternative policies which we might adopt. Unfortunately, there is also no doubt that these prognostications are often inaccurate, but the point remains that man has a facility to envisage the future. It is a fascinating and most difficult question to ask what is the mechanism whereby this act is accomplished, and whether it differs in kind or only in degree from the mechanisms available to other animals. But this need not concern us here. It is necessary to ask not how we *have* this faculty, but how we *use* it.

The quotation standing at the head of this chapter is an ancient statement of the process now under review. Rhazes was a Persian physician, who lived just over a thousand years ago and worked in Baghdad. His quoted account of reason concentrates on its faculty of adumbration. He says that before we do something, we contemplate doing it. Thus we visualize what actually happens when we do this thing, and then we try to copy what we have visualized in what we actually do. When the thing is now done in reality, our senses tell us what is actually happening, and we are able to compare this with our prior visualization. This mechanism will of course enable us to improve on the prognostications which we make in the future. In other words, rational conduct depends not only upon knowing what is really happening and being able to interpret it, but on having present in our minds a *representation* of what is going to happen next. This representation is not an account of what *is* the case, but a continuous prognosis of what is about to be reported to us as being the case. It is a prognosis continuously corrected by feedback.

Let us call this mental representation of the world that is not direct perception of the world a *model* of the world. The term is appropriate: models of things may be more or less accurate, and thereby better or worse able to predict the behaviour of what is modelled. Just because they are predictive, models are open to experimentation as a means of evaluating the likely performance of the thing modelled. In this mental representation too, experimentation goes briskly on, for, when we are about to do something, do we not rapidly explore various ways of doing it, selecting one of the ways for action? If we slow this process down, we can imagine ourselves contemplating a succession of representations, each depicting ourselves doing what is to be done in a different way, and systematically discarding the least convenient until only one is left.

Now science is a carefully thought out, professional, version of this rigorously rational behaviour. Compare the procedure just examined with the scientific methodology discussed in section one. Can the model be equated with a scientific hypothesis? Clearly not; the model does not postulate the causal mechanisms that underlie events, it simply represents the pattern of the events themselves in advance—by extrapolation. Is the model like a scientific theory then? Again, it is not; it has no explanatory content. A model is simply a reflection of whatever is the case, which is explicitly made available for experimentation. It is this which distinguishes it from perception. We can, in a very limited way, experiment with perception itself: for example, try to 'see' a cow in the room. If you have the faculty of visual imagery strongly developed, you may momentarily succeed in 'seeing' the cow. Typically, however, the mind which is accustomed to experiment with incoming perceptual patterns is diseased: 'hearing voices' is a classical symptom of schizophrenia, and the brain of the man who is aware of pungent smells which no-one else can smell is deteriorating. The normal, healthy person can however distinguish clearly between his sensations of reality, with which he must not tinker, and the 'spare copy' of this perceptual pattern which he takes off to use for experiment. There is no difficulty about envisaging the appearance of a cow in a recollection of the room that is clearly labelled imaginary. Moreover, he can classify his experimentation: most of it he uses for short-run decision-taking (as we saw above); some he may use for long-run decision-taking (as when he contemplates policies which will mature in ten years' time); and some he uses for other and stranger purposes to do with relieving tensions and resolving conflicts (the practice we usually call day-dreaming).

The scientist can certainly be described, as he was before, within this classification. He uses the short-run procedure continually in his work to guide his most mundane steps. The longer-run procedures underlie all his attempts at verification and all his assessments of outcomes. The day-dreaming procedures are in high demand by the scientist when he is in the process of inventing. The only difference between his handling of the model, and the use made of the model by the ordinary citizen (including the scientist in his private capacity), is that the scientist is *professional* about its use. He is self-conscious about the model he uses; he deliberates about it; he tries to make it richer—and therefore a better replica of reality; he examines how it hangs together—and may therefore try to express it in the rigorous language of science.

DC—H

This way of talking about the business of science is now quite common among scientists themselves, in that the use of the term 'model' is familiar. It seems doubtful, however, whether many scientists have thought very hard about the connotation of this term. Many of them are prepared to say that the word has itself been imported as a neologism which really does mean either 'theory' or 'hypothesis'. In fairness to them, it must be clearly stated here that this account of scientific methodology is my own, and must not be taken to be an agreed account of the matter. Mention of this fact makes this the right moment to dispose of a further point of usage. In scientific circles, the noun 'model' is very frequently qualified by the adjective 'mathematical'. According to the viewpoint offered here, a mathematical model is an algebraic statement of the representation already discussed. It is *not* simply an equation purporting to relate one set of variables existing in the world situation with another set—and this is the very much debased sense in which the term 'mathematical model' seems often to be used.

Returning now to the exposition of scientific methodology, the question that remains to be answered asks how scientists set about handling the model-that-everyone-has in a professional way. And, since we are talking about the uses of science within enterprises, we might well ask the parallel question as to how the manager handles the model in a way appropriate to *his* profession.

To answer the second question first, it seems that the manager contemplates his model, and compares it with models of other and similar situations that have been known to him. This is a way of saying formally that 'he brings his experience to bear'. Supposing, for argument's sake, that the manager has been in *precisely* the same situation before that he finds himself in now. If his memory is good, he can retrieve the model of the previous occasion; he will find that it corresponds point for point with the model at present in his mind. The process of prognostication is now trivial, because he also knows the outcome of the historical situation. In practice, of course, no situation is ever *exactly* repeated, so the status of the prognostications he makes now cannot possibly be dignified as certain. How probable, in fact, is it that his prognostications will be right? In the language of this methodology, this probability will reflect the extent to which the remembered models do correspond point for point with the existing model. This is the formal way of asking: 'How relevant is the manager's experience to this situation?' It may be noted that this account of the matter is consonant with our feelings about it. For the degree of confidence with which a manager will assert that a particular course of action is correct, correlates (he would surely agree) in some way with the extent to which he regards himself as being on familiar ground. If the situation in which he finds himself is utterly novel, he will assuredly feel rather unhappy about any decision that he may reach—because there is nothing to guide him. In formal terms: the translation of the model into reality requires that it undergo certain changes, and in the case considered the *rules* for making these changes are quite unknown. When, on the other hand, the situation is entirely familiar, we may say that the rules for making the changes are well specified. The prognosis from the model is therefore made with a high degree of confidence, and (supposing that the new situation really is almost identical with the historical ones) the transformed model will be a most accurate predictor of the eventual facts.

It now becomes very clear that the scientist who tackles a management problem is in a totally different situation, for he declares hopefully that he comes upon the situation 'with a fresh mind'. He believes this to be a good thing; but our explanation of his approach must begin with the alarming acknowledgment that he has by definition *no* historical models of the situation with which to set up correspondences to the present model, and that again by definition he cannot possibly know any of the rules for changing this model to make it fit tomorrow's reality. It is noted in passing, then, that in so far as the scientist can ever achieve success in solving a management problem, he is in no way imitating the manager. This decisively disposes of a view often expressed in management circles that an operational research team is best regarded as a group made up of men who have the time to undertake some detailed thinking about a problem which the manager would undertake himself if he were not too busy. This interpretation of OR is typical of the contemporary degradation of the word 'science' which was commented upon earlier.

Then how do we account within this methodology for the approach of operational research? The answer is that although the scientist has no historical models of the situation with which to compare his present model, he has other sorts of model which he can use. It must be remembered that the managerial task is concerned with the control of large and complicated systems. The scientist, quite apart from any relationship he may have had with enterprises, has inevitably been trained to understand the structure and control of *some* large and complicated systems. For example, he may be an expert in thermodynamics, in which case his memory will contain a richly endowed and profoundly understood model of the behaviour of systems whose activity is characterized by changes in entropy—and such systems range from heat engines, through communication systems, to the operation of the entire cosmos.

Then suppose the thermodynamicist seeks to make a detailed and formal comparison of the correspondences between this model and the model of the system which represents the enterprise. As was noted earlier, the model of any one system stands in *some* sort of correspondence with the model of any other system: the question is only whether the correspondence is great or small—and therefore more useful or less useful. If it is useful to a sufficient extent, and useful in the right way, the scientist will solve the manager's problem.

The reason is this. If it is possible, by effecting this correspondence, to discuss the enterprise as if it were a heat engine (under a methodology which declares precisely how valid such an exercise may be), many benefits at once accrue. For the whole of the insight which the scientist has into thermodynamic systems becomes, again within the limits specified by the methodology, an equivalent insight into the behaviour of the enterprise. Moreover, all the techniques of description, and experimentation, and in general of handling models, which the scientist has acquired in thermodynamics, will now be available to him for dealing with the manager's problem. The parenthetical reservations continually made in this passage about the validity of the correspondences, and the limitations of the methodology, will be examined properly in the next section. In the meantime, however, it will be well to complete the picture of an operational research team in action.

It was explained some time ago, and at some length, that it is of the essence of operational research to be an interdisciplinary undertaking. The team approach was found, for quite practical reasons, to be vital. It is now possible to comprehend the formal basis of this requirement. Although we have not yet specified the methodological justification for the procedure just outlined, we have already seen that this is not a matter of searching for a *perfect* correspondence between two models, and of discarding all those potential models which are at all imperfect. The matter is, we said, one of degree; confidence in prognosis derives from some measure of the extent to which the two representations can be matched point for point. So the thermodynamic insight which has been considered (just by way of example) is 'fairly useful'; that is to say, it is certainly not useless, and almost certainly not ideal.

But the next member of the OR group is a neurophysiologist. The model he really understands, is trained to manipulate, and so on, concerns the nervous system and particularly the brain. Now there are obvious resemblances between the controls used in an enterprise and those used in the human body. For example: both are hierarchical, both are redundant and both incorporate sub-systems of greater and lesser autonomy. Very well then; this scientist too can contribute to the matter in hand—under the same limitations and provisos as the thermodynamicist. And so the argument continues for any number of scientists and any kind of science. It is not perhaps difficult to see that a case of this kind can be made out to show how insight into *any* branch of science might be relevant to *any* kind of managerial situation. If there is any doubt about this contention, consider the limiting case. In the last resort, *any* physical system resembles any other to the extent that each endures. Admittedly, if this is the only point of correspondence which can be demonstrated, the attempt to enrich the managerial model by the scientific one will not be very efficacious. But it is really rather important to understand that the procedure is never totally irrelevant, never completely inapplicable.

Now comes the final point. If an OR team consists of a group of scientists, trained in different disciplines, and each capable of transferring his own scientific insights to the enterprise, the OR team as a whole is *focusing* spotlights from a number of different directions on the point at issue. The understanding of each, and the value of the contribution that can be made by any, may be defective and partial. But the insights supplement each other—supposing only that the scientists have learnt to communicate among themselves (and this is really the kernel of the problem of post-graduate training in operational research). The whole process may be compared, by a simile, with the process of triangulation in a survey of terrain. A point may be identified with great accuracy, given that approaches are made to it with fair accuracy from several directions at once.

3 Some Terms Explained

What has been said so far can hardly carry conviction, because of the vagueness of the sense in which the comparison between managerial and scientific models was drawn. As so far described, the methodology seems to depend on the examination of similes, which is well known to be dangerous and highly suspect. It is all very well to say that the control system of an industrial company is 'like' the central nervous system in the human body: but what does this mean? At the worst, this is a glib literary metaphor; at the best, perhaps, the analogy will hold a certain amount of water, but even then it may be of no real use. Everyone knows, in particular, that even when a comparison is basically sound, it is all too easy to employ it illegitimately: 'You are carrying the analogy too far' we customarily say. It is fully agreed that if nothing better than this can be done, the developing methodology is futile. If the grandiose claim to be expounding a new account of the scientific process is to be substantiated, a far more rigorous attempt must be made to specify what is going on.

In order to discuss this critical point with any precision, it will be necessary to use a few strange terms. The vocabulary of ordinary English is simply not adequate to the task with which we are now confronted, and a few new words will have to be introduced. Perhaps this calls for apology; on the other hand, the terms now to be explained are really extremely useful in discussing management systems. It is very possible to argue that one of the reasons why our thinking about the theory of management has been so thin and so ineffectual is because the only concepts available for which we have names are so trivial. In fact, the ideas to be discussed in this section are derived from three branches of modern mathematics, all of which use these words. They are: group theory, set theory and algebraic topology. Of course, no attempt can be made here to discuss the mathematical issues, but they are irrelevant to these purposes.

First, we shall often refer to a *set* of things. A set is no more than a properly specified collection of items, called *elements* of the set. Thus the whole of the plant in an industrial company may be thought of as a set, the elements of which are machines. Or the elements could be *components* of machines. A set is described, that is to say, by nominating its elements—and whoever is doing the talking is at liberty to choose what elements he intends to discuss. So there is a set of machines which exhausts the company's plant, a set of employees which exhausts the company's payroll, and so on. These are *finite* sets—they are exhaustible. There are also *infinite* sets, however, and these are the most important because they facilitate the discussion of collections of things which can be precisely nominated, but not exhaustively enumerated. The set of the natural numbers 1, 2, 3, 4 . . . belongs to this class. And of course it is also most convenient to use this terminology to refer to finite sets, the elements of which could be exhaustively enumerated, without bothering to enumerate them. This means being able to speak of the set of the company's present customers, for example, and knowing they are *all* included, without having to list them in an appendix.

Next comes the idea of the *partition* of sets. Obviously, sets can have sub-sets. The commonest form of partition in ordinary life, and particularly in the company organization, is to define a set of sub-sets which exhaust the set and do not overlap. An organization chart tries to do this. The set of commercial responsibilities is partitioned, for example, into home sales (heavy), home sales (light) and export sales. The idea is that any element of the set should also be an element of one, and only one, sub-set. Then the commercial manager can go home; this is the delegation of responsibility. In practice, of course, the rules which govern the partitioning are not always clear, the sub-sets may intersect, and there may be elements of the set which turn out not to belong to any sub-set after all. Because of the last point, it is often useful to nominate a *complementary set*, which is the totality minus all the sub-sets. This will account for anything left over from the major classification. If that classification is well made, however, nothing will be left over. This does not matter; it simply means that the complementary set has no elements —and this is called a *null set*. The utility of the complementary set may be noticed in many large business organizations in which a manager can often be identified whose responsibilities are those that arise from time to time and yet do not clearly belong to someone else.

Now it will be remembered that in speaking of models of managerial and scientific situations the idea of 'correspondences' between them was brought forward. To convey the idea of good correspondence, we spoke of models corresponding 'point for point'. See what this means formally. There is a finite set whose elements are the letters of the English alphabet. There is also a finite set of the natural numbers 1–26 inclusive. It is perfectly obvious that these two sets can be placed in correspondence with each other, and that if they are there is one number for each letter. This is called a *one–one correspondence*. And the process of making that correspondence is called a *mapping*. In this case, then, the set of twenty-six letters may be mapped on to the set of twenty-six numbers.

This operation could still be carried out if we used the infinite set of natural numbers. The twenty-six letters could be mapped, by one–one correspondence, on to *any* nominated sub-set of twenty-six numbers. This is the more general case of a mapping: we say that the alphabetic set is mapped *into* (rather than on to) the set of natural numbers. When a mapping is being made, an element in the 'target' set on to which an element of the original set maps is called the *image* of that element.

Suppose, then, that we wish to undertake a mapping. For example, a sentence could be encoded into a row of numbers by turning *A* into 1, *B* into 2, and so on. We establish our sets, we demonstrate the one–one correspondence. We now need the rules for changing the elements of one set into those of the other. Note that it is not enough to say 'change', for *A* could become 1, 3 or 25. It is necessary to specify a *transformation*. That is to say, one needs a code if something is to be encoded. So if, for example, the set 1, 2, 3, 4, 5 . . . is to be mapped into the set 2, 4, 6, 8, 10 . . ., the mapping is specified by the transformation $b = 2a$. This defines a one–one correspondence. The transformation $b = a + (5-a)$ defines a *many–one correspondence*. A mapping from the set 1, 2, 3, 4, 5 . . . now takes 5 as the image of every element.

So far nothing at all has been said about the internal relationship between the elements of a set. If the set is in fact identified with a system whose parts are the elements of the set, then each element is defined by its function. Consider an internal combustion engine, and break it down (in the engineering sense) to its ultimate parts. These are the elements of the set of components, and each can be defined by its function—which is to say its relationship to some sub-set of other elements. So there is also a set of the functions of components. Now take another engine off the same assembly line. Here are two sets of components, and they can be mapped on to each other. Not only is there a one–one correspondence between the elements of the sets of components, *but between the elements of the sets of functions*. In other words, if the first engine works, so will the second.

There is a special name for a mapping which not only involves a one–one correspondence of elements, but which also preserves operational characteristics in this way. It is called an *isomorphism*. The Greek derivation throws light on the denotation of this term: isomorph means 'having the same form'. Of course, all this ought really to be explained with mathematical notation, then the preservation of operational characteristics could be precisely observed, and the formal rules for establishing isomorphism could be explicitly stated. But here the concern is with borrowing the term, and therefore with its basic, not algebraic, description.

The final notion that we need is a little more difficult to grasp, but it is very important. Suppose the alphabetic set A–Z is taken, and divided into halves: the sub-sets A–M and N–Z. These are then mapped into the set of numbers 1 and 2. There is a one–one correspondence here, if the sub-sets are regarded as single-valued elements of the total set. Alternatively, the original elements may still be used: a mapping is defined whereby the transformation of *each* letter A–M is to the image 1, and of each letter N–Z is to the image 2. This mapping involves a many–one correspondence, and it is not isomorphic. Even so, the transformation can be arranged so that certain operational characteristics concerning the relationship of elements are preserved. When this is done, the result is a *homomorphism*. This is the end of the quest for useful new terms; and, since homomorphic transformations play a key part in what follows, some attempt must be made to illustrate the point about the preservation of certain operational characteristics—this being the aspect that is hard to understand.

As many people know nowadays, decimal arithmetic is a pure convention: computers use binary arithmetic (made up of the digits 0–1 exclusively), and the octal scale (in which the highest digit is 8) may be of more use to people in future than the decimal scale. Suppose we want to work in an arithmetic with a scale of, say, five—using only the numbers 0, 1, 2, 3, 4. Now it is possible to specify a transformation that will map the infinite set of natural numbers on to this other finite set. It could be written down as in Table 2. Clearly this transformation involves

TABLE 2. Specification of transformation.

$T \downarrow$

0	1	2	3	4	5	6	7	8	9	10	11	12	13	14	15	16	17
0	1	2	3	4	0	1	2	3	4	0	1	2	3	4	0	1	2

$T \downarrow$

18	19	20	21	22	23	24	25	26	27	28	29	30	31	32	33	34	35
3	4	0	1	2	3	4	0	1	2	3	4	0	1	2	3	4	0

a many–one correspondence. To illustrate this forcibly, the table might be rewritten as in Table 3.

TABLE 3. The many–one correspondence of Table 2.

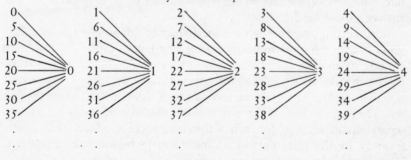

In the new arithmetic, there will have to be new rules of addition. For $4+3 = 7$ cannot be written this way—since 7 does not exist in the vocabulary. Accordingly, a rule for adding numbers must be provided (if this arithmetic were for normal use, that is, after reaching a count of 4 the calculator would go back to 0 and 'carry 1'). The rule is set out in Table 4. To find out what is the sum of two 'new' numbers, one

TABLE 4. Addition rule for five-valued arithmetic.

	0	1	2	3	4
0	0	1	2	3	4
1	1	2	3	4	0
2	2	3	4	0	1
3	3	4	0	1	2
4	4	0	1	2	3

of them is entered in a row, the other in a column: the intersection of row and column gives the sum. So $4+3 = 2$.

Is the transformation we have made homomorphic? Certainly it is many–one. To test for homomorphism, the mathematician would demand that certain operational characteristics of the arithmetic are preserved. It is now possible to exemplify this test, and thereby to give an indication of what is meant by the preservation of these operational characteristics. For this illustration, we shall add the numbers 11 and 19. As we know, the answer is 30. Here is the test. Consider these numbers as elements of the first set (the infinite set of all natural numbers), add them and transform the answer. Then transform these same numbers into elements of the second set (the finite set 0–4), and add *them*. The answer should be the same.

It is worth going through the mechanics of this simple test to understand exactly what is happening. In the first half of the test, the addition is done in ordinary arithmetic, thus: $11 + 19 = 30$. Transforming 30 by the given rule, which is read off either Table 2 or Table 3, the answer is 0. This is the image in the second set of the element '30' of the first set. The second half of the test requires that the mapping be effected separately, in advance, for each of the elements to be added. Thus: transform 11 by this rule—answer, 1; transform 19 by this rule—answer, 4. We now add these two answers, using the addition rule given by Table 3, and the answer is $1 + 4 = 0$. The two methods yield the same result, so we are dealing with a homomorphism. And we have seen how certain relationships are transferable between the two sets. We say in fact that in the new arithmetic the operations of the old arithmetic are preserved with respect to addition.

4   The Homomorphic Model

Returning now to the general argument about the nature of operational research, it should be possible to make clear what the formal scientific processes really are. The discussion so far is summed up in Figure 3. Here is the managerial situation, of which a conceptual model has been formulated: this means that we have 'taken a spare copy' of our direct perception of the facts. No doubt we have incorporated into this conceptual model all the insights that we have obtained into the way the

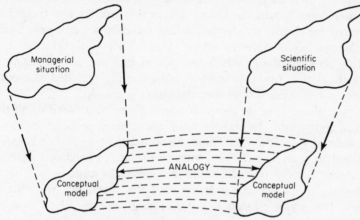

FIGURE 3. The process of 'scientific analogizing'.

system 'really works'. Similarly, the operational research team has selected from its scientific situation a conceptual model, incorporating its insights into how *that* situation 'really works', which it believes bears marked resemblances to the managerial situation. It then considers possible agreements between these two models. It tries to determine the extent to which the behaviour of the one system throws light on the behaviour of the other; in what ways the theories currently maintained by scientists in the one area might be transplanted into the other; whether the actual techniques of research and computation are appropriate; and above all, whether conclusions which hold for the one system hold (and if so, under what tests of verification) in the other. The question left over from the previous discussion, which has now been reformulated, was to know under what methodology the correspondence could be regarded as rigorously valid.

There are various levels of comparison at which the scientist might be trying to work. Firstly, there is the metaphor. But the metaphor is a

poetic device, and its validity is aesthetic; it can offer science no more
help than its verbal facility. Secondly, there is the level of analogy. The
validity of this comparison is a logical validity, and a lot has been written
by classical logicians to account for its usefulness and to circumscribe its
limitations. But the explanation is essentially philosophic rather than
scientific; the validity of a particular analogy must always be open to
disputation, and its relevance in a particular instance cannot be formally
demonstrated in a conclusive way. This leaves the third level of comparison: that of identity itself. If two things are literally identical with
each other, then conclusions that hold for the one will surely hold for
the other under similar conditions. But in this case the two things being
compared are clearly *not* identical in any ordinary sense, if only because
they are models of different things. The validity of the comparison of
identity between things which are not in fact one and the same is a
mystical validity. And mysticism is not generally regarded as useful to
science; it may offer insight, but the vision is cloudy.

In fact, there is in the research scientist's mind a blend of all these
levels of comparison. In his own head, the scientist probably is thinking
metaphorically; at the same time, he is aware of a need to couch his
metaphor in severely analogical form so that it can be closely examined
and tested; but the more he hopes to do this, the more he sees himself
as destroying the identity relation that the metaphor poetically en-
shrines. The whole process is self-defeating, and the description of it
is no more than an historical legacy. To use more modern terms, the
OR scientist is attempting to establish a mapping between the two conceptual models, under some transformation which he would like to be
isomorphic.

How can he proceed and set about this task? His two models are conceptual, literary things—they are not well formulated in scientific terms.
Therefore the first task must be to use the tools of rigorous science to
formulate them more precisely. The scientist must undertake this part
of the task in the only languages he knows how to use with precision:
the languages of mathematics, statistics and logic. All three are highly
developed scientific tools; basically, the first handles notions of quantity,
the second notions of probability and the third notions of quality. They
are languages whose grammar and syntax is developed to a remarkable
degree. The scientist therefore engages in a process of mapping each
conceptual model into a neutral scientific language. This is a process
in which some of the conceptual richness must inevitably be lost, for
some of that richness depends on nuance, and some on association, and
some on mood—none of which is transferable into rigorous terms. But

in return for this price, the scientist will obtain an account of the conceptual model that is precise and unambiguous. Returning once again to formal terms, the scientist now defines a set of transformations by which he can map contents of mind on to algebraic propositions. The correspondences are many–one. This is what a loss of richness means. And if the well-formulated result is to represent the antecedent set successfully, it should be homomorphic, too.

The conclusion of the argument should now be clear. Having refined the conceptual models, the contents of mind, according to this procedure, the scientist produces two deeper-level homomorphic models— *and these may well be isomorphic with each other.* So he has achieved an identity between the managerial and the scientific situations which is shorn of mysticism and of poetry, and which is completely free of the bedevilling disputation that attends analogy. This, it is suggested, is the character of the scientific model depicted in Figure 4.

A scientific model is a homomorphism on to which two different situations are mapped, and which actually defines the extent to which they are structurally identical. What is dissimilar about the original situations is not reflected in the mapping, because the transformation rules have not specified an image in the set the model constitutes for irrelevant elements in the conceptual sets. If the transformation has ignored as irrelevant elements which are in fact relevant, then the model will lose in utility, but it *cannot* lose in validity. This is its peculiar strength. Now the measure of utility is vitally important, but it may be accomplished by straightforward testing of the predictive value of the scientific model. If this predictive value is low, we had better start again. But if it is high, we can use it with confidence, and without further worry as to the appropriateness or otherwise of the analogy drawn at the conceptual level.

This exposition is meant to account for what the OR scientist does; it is not meant to state what he explicitly sees himself as doing. However, some operational research has been undertaken which quite specifically takes account of this process, and tries to use the explanation to validate itself by specifying the mappings involved, making rough measures of the information dissipated by the many–one correspondences of the homomorphism, and by testing the model within the terms of the description according to its reaction to partition. It is worth noting that university teaching in operational research is devoted mainly to the study of particular mathematical techniques, and that the thinking on which this instruction seems to be based is that the modelling process is one of the direct algebraic formulation of relationships believed to exist within the managerial situation. That is, the right-hand side of Figure 4 is altogether ignored, and the mapping processes of the left-hand side are not formally studied. Such activity should be referred to as applied mathematics, and not as operational research. In fact, the OR man,

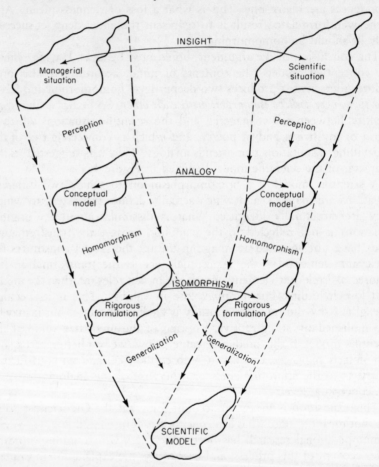

FIGURE 4. The nature of a scientific model.

whether he fully realizes this or not, is invoking analogical thinking derived from his scientific training in other fields, and it is surely best that this is recognized and the process examined. Where operational research has gone even further, by deliberately ignoring its roots in general science, and by trying to create mathematical models purely by abstraction from the system under study, the models have invariably been lacking in a reflection of the viability of the real-life system. The OR scientist should not only recognize his dependence on scientific insights from other fields, he should encourage it. For what is robust, dynamic and viable about the real-life situations which the manager handles is mirrored in the processes of nature which scientists study in all their forms.

In conclusion, and for the time being, consider just one exemplification of this methodology in action. It is designed to illustrate yet another feature of its special value to operational research, as distinguished from other modes of scientific activity.

An investigation is being carried out within industry, and a learning process is detected. For example, a big new plant has been laid down characterized by a number of novel features. When it begins to operate, its output is only a fraction of its intended capacity. But, as time goes by, the output rises: the plant is *learning its job*. Now this phrase may of course refer to many features of the total system. Doubtless the operatives are learning how to manipulate the plant; the engineers are learning how to sequence its output; the managers are learning how to control the whole project. Even the inanimate plant itself may be learning in some sense: all engines 'run themselves in'. But we are not concerned with these details and especially not with the precise sense in which any part of the total system may be said to learn. From a sufficient distance away, say the chair of the managing director, this plant is an indivisible whole; it has an output, and this output improves over time. The operational research people may be asked to estimate the level of output in a few years' time; they may be asked to estimate output of a *new* plant (one which has not yet been built) from its inauguration to the moment when the designed capacity is achieved as output.

Of course the very use of this word 'learning' implies a biological outlook; it is perhaps not the sort of term which it would occur to an engineer to employ. But if there is an animal psychologist in the OR group, he will quickly have observed that the task set by the management is indeed to describe a learning process of some kind, and he will contemplate his knowledge of animal learning processes, which have been rather extensively investigated. He may consider, for example, the case of a rat learning to run a maze. This situation has been carefully studied, because the task which has to be learnt can be unambiguously defined. The maze is an interlinked series of passages; there is only one entrance, but there are two exits. The rat is put in at the entrance; if he emerges from the 'right' exit, he will be rewarded with cheese; if he emerges from the 'wrong' exit, he will receive a punishment in the form of a mild electric shock. In running the maze, the rat has to take a number of binary decisions: it may turn left or right at each junction. Since there is no prior experience of this task, and if the maze is symmetric in relation to its exits, it may confidently be predicted that the rat has an equal chance of being right or wrong on its first run. Depending on the result of this run, the probabilities of the outcome will begin to change. After a sufficiently lengthy series of trials, the rat will learn the maze, and will almost invariably run correctly towards the cheese.

The animal psychologist in contemplating his knowledge of these facts is setting up a conceptual model of a rat in a maze. To inject any kind of scientific rigour into this picture, a new model must be created: one which can be formally expressed and tested. This process has already been carried out by the animal psychologists who did the work, and the OR man can look up the results. He finds a chart on which the horizontal axis is marked out in a series of trials, and the vertical axis expresses the probability of the rat's failure to run the maze correctly. It is easy to realize that the line found on this chart begins at the first run with a 50 per cent probability of failure, and that this probability declines over a series of runs until the line almost touches the horizontal axis itself— the probability of failure being very low indeed. The shape of the curve is concave, and the typical curve represents the typical behaviour of rats. Now this is, according to the terminology of this chapter, a homo-morphic model of this learning process. It is, after all, a many–one transformation of the conceptual model: a good deal of information has been thrown away. No data have survived concerning the colour of the rats, the noises they made, nor (if this chart shows only one line) the variation that is found between rats. But the particular relationship which is of key importance has been preserved. That is, we know on the average how long it takes to reach any given percentage of final success.

Let us now take this model as being isomorphic with another model of a machine which is capable of running a maze. That is to say, could we build an artificial rat whose behaviour in the maze would be in-distinguishable from that of a live rat? The answer is clearly yes, and indeed the job has been done. An artificial rat begins its learning task by making a random choice at each junction of the maze, and therefore has a 50 per cent probability of reaching either exit on its first run. It is then made to store in an electronic memory the successive experiences of its trials, and this stored information is used to bias the probabilities of a left- or right-hand turn at each junction of the maze. The logic of the control equipment can be designed so that the probabilities are actually used to procure a final learning curve indistinguishable from that of the original animal. So, following the methodology set out in Figure 4, a scientific model is now available, consisting of a mathematical expression which defines the learning curve, statistical information about individual variation from this curve and a logic which determines a behavioural link between stored probabilities, which change from trial to trial, and the rate at which total success is approximated. Let us note in passing that the methodology serves well in this respect, that we have an identity relationship between the live and the mechanical rat over a precisely defined area of activity—and not over others. It is no good, for example, feeding grain to the mechanical rat, or trying to disconnect the live one. These are judged irrelevant elements in the sets defining the two rats, and have not been mapped on to the scientific model.

The question now is whether this scientific model, already investigated in two dissimilar situations, will apply to the industrial plant. Again, the OR group would work backwards from the scientific model, which is of complete generality (it does not, for example, distinguish between live rats and artefacts), to formulate what is intended to be a homomorphic model of the learning plant. The conceptual model of the plant is already known, and it now remains to establish the homomorphic mapping between these two. It is probably found that some adjustment needs to be made, most usually by way of constraining the completely general model in some way. For example, the *a priori* probability of achieving the rated output on the first run may not be 50 per cent. Thus it is over this link that the more familiar experimental processes of science are carried out. But there is no need to be so vague as to say that the OR team is here engaged in trying to discover some mathematical formulation of the industrial problem which looks as if it might be appropriate, and then in proceeding to test it by any means in their power. We have instead, at this juncture, a rather precise problem of specifying a particular homomorphic transformation which will achieve a valid mapping between unambiguously specified sets.

The total picture is illustrated in Figure 5 in which the general methodology of Figure 4 is adapted to the present example. It will be seen that all three real-life situations, concerning the plant, the live rat and the mechanical rat, in some sense resemble each other. They all 'learn'—whatever that means. At the level of their conceptual models, an analogy exists between them which can be inspected by the methods of classical logic. Each is then mapped homomorphically on to a rigorous mathematical formulation, and these three homomorphs of reality stand in isomorphic relationship to each other. They are therefore embodied in a scientific model which equally represents all three situations over a well-defined range of activity.

Hence we have made use of a model from animal psychology: by pursuing it downwards to a scientific generality, pursuing it upwards to an experimental verification (the right-hand branch in Figure 5), and

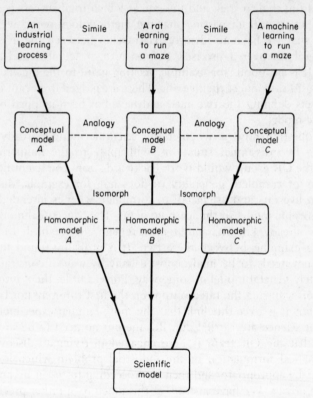

FIGURE 5. Application of the theory of models to a learning problem in industry.

then by pursuing it upwards once again to another problem-solving situation (on the left-hand branch). A predictive model such as this is eminently suitable for resolving the managerial problem originally posed. The peculiarly advantageous feature of this methodology for operational research is that a 'correct' answer is obtained (in so far as the OR predictions are fulfilled) by virtue of a behavioural definition of learning that identifies only what counts as being of interest to the management.

In other words, although this word 'learning' has been invoked, no-one in the OR team or in the management group has the least interest in isolating the nature of learning as such. He has no interest in arguing about the 'right' use of the word as a psychological term, but only in results. So the OR man is a special kind of scientist, for he does not have to bother with determining the·laws governing basic natural phenomena such as learning. This is a preoccupation for the academic animal psychologist who has a special responsibility to define the terms to be used in his science, and to denote the mechanisms for which the terms will stand. The OR man has, however, other concerns which do not preoccupy the academic scientist who normally regards himself as a specialist in a fairly narrow field. He must operate *across* the various scientific disciplines, being sufficiently knowledgeable and mentally agile to identify the model he needs. For, to take the quoted case, it is not every OR group that includes an animal psychologist. Or, if it happens to do so, it may not include the thermodynamicist whom we met before, nor the population geneticist whom we shall meet later. Secondly, the OR man seeks other kinds of natural law than those normally investigated academically, namely those which are themselves interdisciplinary. For there are laws that apply to systems in general, and to control in general—these are the laws that management would like to discover.

There are also laws, it may be thought, that have to do with logical induction and in particular with the conduct of operational research. Perhaps the methodology advanced in this chapter may diffidently be claimed as an example.

7

MODELS IN ASPIC

> The world is not made up of empirical facts with the
> addition of the laws of nature: what we call the laws
> of nature are conceptual devices by which we
> organize our empirical knowledge and predict the
> future.
>
> R. B. BRAITHWAITE in *Scientific Explanation* (1953)

1   Reflections on Models

The talk about models in the last chapter led to talk about laws: the laws
that govern systems and indeed the laws that govern nature itself—and
therefore scientific enquiry. It may seem that the concept of a model,
even when stiffened by the substance of homomorphism, offers but a
weak account of natural law. None the less, the laws of nature with
which we all grew up, are not the absolute truths most people think
them. They are essentially consequences of the conventions under
which we formulate our thoughts about the world; they are deducible
from the theorems which make formal languages consistent. This is a
complicated and philosophical point, and one which is therefore often
missed by scientists themselves.

For example, scientists have not been quick to follow up the last great
work of Eddington—his *Fundamental Theory*, a work which perhaps
gives scientific expression to that philosophic thought. For what
Eddington seems to be doing (although this is a personal opinion) is
to investigate the language in which science expresses itself, and to
generate from it facts about the world outside. Of itself, this appears to
be impossible, but if the idea is once grasped that a language that is
competent to describe the world must be a *mapping* of the world, the
process seems less silly. This may also be the answer to those who complain that modern philosophers, such as Wittgenstein, spent their lives
in 'sterile linguistic analysis'. If the language, whether mathematical or

120

metaphysical, is isomorphic with the world of fact, then its structure will reveal relationships which are true of the world itself. But how those relationships are expressed, where the emphasis lies, and hence in the long run whether those relationships are necessary or contingent, will depend on *which* language we use. For in practice, the mapping will be *homo*morphic—able to preserve some structure, but committed to losing some information. Thus our account of nature is 'true', but defective, and our account of such characteristics of nature as causation and law will change with the linguistic mapping we choose.

But if all this sounds obscure, the point is expressed with lucidity in the quotation given above. Science is certainly based upon fact and experiment; but the organization of its findings into coherent and useful generalizations is a subjective process. Perhaps the most pithy expression of this point was given two hundred years ago by the philosopher David Hume when he wrote: 'Necessity is something that exists in the mind, not in objects.'

It therefore comes about that the so-called laws of nature are contingent, and not absolute; they are contingent on the languages we use to express them, both as to the structure of those languages and their frame of reference. Thus as science collects more and more observations about the world, and undertakes more and more experimentation, discovery often awaits a *conceptual* breakthrough, a bursting of the thought blocks of the scientist himself. If the language is quite general and relatively unconstrained, we are not prompted to question the conventions it places on our thinking. And so a law of nature is derived from what is no more than a model of such general utility that it is never even recognized as such. Perhaps the ultimate model of the structure of the universe is indeed the structure of the human brain which contemplates it, for in so far as our brains can penetrate the mysteries of nature they are mappings of the universe. By the reverse argument, we can understand only those aspects of the universe into which our brains will map. This is such a serious and ineluctable limitation on human understanding that one never hears it expressed. Yet, by these same standards, the homomorphic models previously discussed entail consequences that are natural laws. That is to say, their logical status is the same as that of the more familiar general statements about the universe; only their applicability is more circumscribed. What we usually call a natural law is a statement about a particular model of the universe; what we here call a model of a problem situation entails its own localized natural laws.

All this is said to emphasize the validity of the processes under discussion, which must not be looked upon as tricks peculiar to operational research. Although the whole field of scientific induction is difficult to penetrate, the inductions made by operational research are no more and no less difficult to understand and justify than those of any other kind of scientific activity; they simply make a more agile use of models than is customarily necessary in science. If the theory put forward in the last chapter is an appropriate account of what goes on in operational research, it also explains to just the same degree the nature of every developed scientific activity. Indeed, any set of rules for the making of inductions is itself entailed by a particular descriptive language, and to quote Hume once more: 'They are very easy in their invention, but extremely difficult in application.'

Success in their application is a matter of practice, not on behalf of individuals but of a society. How the descriptive language is to be acceptably manipulated, how the set of rules is to be acceptably applied, and therefore what emerges that will count as a valid model: these things are social conventions. Any society of scientists develops these conventions although what is acceptable in one branch of science, or even in one school of that branch, will not necessarily be acceptable in another. Sooner or later, the model and all its trappings, so essential to actual progress, may begin to dominate truth. As new facts accrue, they are fitted into the language *in a way* that makes them consonant with the model, which expresses their consequences *in a way* that reinforces the rules of induction—and thence of behaviour itself. The italics draw attention to the fact that eventual outcomes are conditioned by this modelling apparatus. Facts, which are commonly supposed to be objective, turn out not to be unconditionally so: this was remarked elsewhere in this book. Now it is also seen that facts, which are popularly supposed to be neutral, turn out to be purposive, because of the way they are assimilated into a situation.

This state of affairs is dangerous to science, if it is not clearly recognized, for it can block new discoveries. Progress in science might well be defined as the overthrow of a model, and its appurtenances, that has exhausted its usefulness. The great scientist is one who sees the need and the moment to destroy a model—and who can also create its successor. Perhaps the same is true of the businessman and his business. But science itself is in the long run protected against the dangers of its own intellectual apparatus. In the first place, it is founded on observation and experiment. Eventually the model that is no longer useful (we say 'that is seen to be false'), and the model that can no longer encompass the scope of the scientist's insight (we say 'that is seen to be trivial') are overwhelmed. For if objectivity and neutrality in science are nowadays regarded with more suspicion than our fathers showed in them, *something* of the objective and the neutral breaks through into our work from outside ourselves. In the second place, and most significantly, the *intention* behind doing science is to expose a reality beyond our own imagination and desires. Even when the scientist is most horribly trapped within his own conventions, it is in his own acknowledged interests to escape. Thirdly, science (except in aberrant forms or moments) is *aware* that it deals in models and conventions; it is therefore well placed to keep a watch for insidious effects.

Science, in the form of operational research, serves managers—of business, industry and government. These operations too provide a social milieu for intellectual processes—of decision and control. All that has been said about languages and their conventions, models and their limitations, rules of induction and their consequences, applies as well to such occupations as to scientific pursuits. The dangers are the same; so are the opportunities. Only the protection allowed to science is notably missing. Management is *not* founded on observation and experiment, but on a drive towards a set of outcomes. These aims are not altogether explicit; at one extreme they may amount to no more than an intention to preserve the *status quo*, at the other extreme they may embody an obsessional demand for power, profit or prestige. But the scientist's quest for insight, for understanding, for wanting to know what makes the system tick, rarely figures in the manager's motivation. Secondly, and therefore, management is *not*, even in intention, separable from its own intentions and desires: its policies express them. Thirdly, management is *not* normally aware of the conventional nature of its intellectual processes and control procedures. It is accustomed to confuse its conventions for recording information with truths-about-the-business, its subjective institutional languages for discussing the business with an objective language of fact and its models of reality with reality itself.

Nothing emerges more clearly from this analysis than that management operates *through a model* of the business, a model in which the organizational structure, the structure of costs and prices, the structure of labour relationships, the structure of production itself, are all homomorphic mappings of the real thing. It is only in the works of Lewis Carroll (a mathematician, remember) that one finds a king who was really determined to have a truly *iso*morphic map of his country. He settled for the only one there is: the country itself. If a manager wants to do that, our theory can still handle the situation because there is an *identity* mapping in the language we are using which maps a group on to *itself*. The trouble is that no manager can really handle the full-scale isomorph of his enterprise unless he is the only employee. To delegate is to embark on a series of one–many transformations. The manager can at best settle for a homomorph consisting of all the ones.

Neither the earliest scientists, long since dead, nor the earliest managers, many still extant, were particularly concerned with problems that fitted this pattern of development. They had not got as far as seeking out systems and analysing their structures. For as men began to probe the nature of the universe, or as managers appointed men to probe the nature of their enterprises, careful and systematic observations were taken for the first time. And the things that were seen and measured themselves constituted important discoveries. As late as the seventeenth century, Leeuwenhoek was the first man to see bacteria; in doing so he discovered something new about nature. As early as the nineteenth century, F. W. Taylor was the first man to measure the work involved in a man's shovelling coal; in doing so he discovered something new about industry. Today the optical microscope does not 'make discoveries'; new insights into nature require that observations and experiments be compounded into hypotheses that explain natural systems. Equally, work study does not 'make discoveries' about industry; advances now depend on compounding facts obtained by such tools into models of business systems.

The lag between knowing the facts and knowing the system which generates the facts can be considerable. It is one thing, for instance, to cut up the bodies of animals and to discover that each contains a heart; this fact has been known for thousands of years. It is another thing to suggest that blood flows from the heart to the lungs and back again; the man who first did that was burnt alive. But it was not until much later still, in 1628, that *De Motu Cordis* was published, giving William Harvey's account of the circulation of the blood. This represented insight into the underlying mechanism: it really said something as to what the facts were all about.

Similarly there is a lag in passing from the stage in which sets of empirical observations constitute exciting discoveries, to the stage of insight into underlying mechanism, in every field of management today. In controlling the economy and diplomacy and society at large, in controlling business and industry and commerce, we have collected facts and perhaps identified systems. But we have barely begun to explain their underlying mechanism. *This is what operational research is for.*

It is in the natural course of the development of science to investigate such systems now. For they offer a new kind of challenge. In practice, they are not susceptible to total dissection, total analysis, total measurement; perhaps they are inherently insusceptible to such complete specification. But this does not necessarily mean that we cannot identify their underlying mechanisms. The process of homomorphic modelling is at the least a heuristic method for inferring the existence and structure of systems of which the complexity defeats isomorphic modelling.

It is now time to look more closely at a few operational models, to see how the process works in a little more detail. The examples which follow come up in no particular context; they are arbitrarily chosen to span the course of history, to span areas of application, and to span varieties of analogy. They are not connected with each other by anything more than their method, and they testify to nothing more than their own existence. They are models preserved in aspic: taste and see.

2   Applications: An Early Operational Model

If the early scientists did not use this method of consciously constructing a model, when did it first emerge? The technique of scientific analogizing in the more literary sense has a lengthy history; philosophers, for example, have always been prone to compare a metaphysical system with a scientific system in just this way. As we have seen, the comparison itself achieves a scientific status only when a rigorous attempt is made to construct a formal mapping. The earliest deliberate attempt to conduct an enquiry on this basis that I happen to have encountered was made by a scientist of no less eminence than the Hon. Henry Cavendish, F.R.S., who published his results in *Philosophical Transactions* in the year 1776—which, as it happens, was the year of the death of David Hume.

The problem facing Cavendish was this. There was a fish called a torpedo which delivered some kind of shock to anyone who touched it. A Mr Walsh had brought forward supposed proofs that the phenomena of the torpedo were produced by electricity, but there were features of the situation with which this finding appeared inconsistent. For one thing, shocks were felt when the fish was held under water, that is, when there was an easier route for the 'electric fluid' to take than through the human body. At the time of this work, 'some electricians' contended that electricity passes along the path of least resistance *alone*, and that there could therefore be no flow at all along a more resistant path in the same circuit. So the shock ought to pass through the water, but not through the more resistant human body—as it did. Moreover, when this fish produced its shock there was no spark, and no associated magnetism —two phenomena generally associated with electrical discharge in contemporary research. Cavendish wanted to verify or refute Walsh's assertions. Now it has to be remembered that when this work was done very little was known of the nature of electricity. Furthermore, the kind of apparatus available to scientists of the time for research into matters of this kind comprised batteries consisting of a series of discharging jars, 'Mr Lane's electrometer', and a pair of pith balls. In these circumstances, no very obvious way of deciding the matter unequivocally by investigating the fish itself was apparent. Cavendish therefore studied the problem *operationally*, and it might be fair to call what he did operational research.

In fact he constructed a model. It was indeed a physical representation of the fish, which is described in full detail in Cavendish's paper. The model was made of wood, the electrical organs on either side being represented by flat pieces of pewter fixed thereto. These were connected by wires, through long glass tubes acting as insulators, to the positive and negative terminals of the battery. The whole thing was covered with sheepskin leather and soaked or immersed in water. For the model to impart a shock, the circuit had to be completed either through the wood or around the surface of the leather—or alternatively the experimenter could touch both of the electric organs simultaneously. With this apparatus Cavendish made a long series of experiments, systematically varying all the factors involved. He was in fact trying to simulate the operational circumstances, and took great pains to do so.

In the course of the work he resolved all the difficulties that attended on Walsh's original explanation, and managed to get into mathematical form the relationships he discovered between various conductors in various kinds of media. He made tests in a tank, and also when the model was in air but still wet; he even simulated the effect of stepping on a torpedo buried in the sand while wearing shoes with wet soles. He attended also to the salinity of the water and recorded, for example, that sea water conducts 100 times better than rain water—a factor that goes up to 720 times in the case of what the paper most charmingly calls 'a faturated folution of fea falt'. So, by these operational means, Henry Cavendish resolved the problem. He did not *prove* the contention that the phenomena were electrical, but he did satisfy himself and others that this was a contention consistent with the facts. He also discovered the fundamental underlying relationships by experimenting with a model—which had predictive value in that it could successfully forecast what experiences one would have with the living fish in any circumstances one cared to envisage. All that was nearly 200 years ago; today the torpedo is more familiarly known to us as the electric ray.

Naturally, Cavendish would not himself have described what he was doing in the terms introduced in the preceding chapter: none of the branches of mathematics from which the terminology is taken were in existence at the time. It is none the less perfectly clear that in constructing his model Cavendish was undertaking a mapping. Momentarily at least, he set up a valid correspondence between the fish and the artefact. For example, his drawings clearly show that he copied exactly the outline of the fish in wood—hence its shape in plan is strictly isomorphic with that of the beast. In general, however, this was a homomorphic mapping. Cavendish was content with many–one correspondences (for example, the high variety anatomy of the living creature is mapped on to a set of two elements which are the sub-set 'electric organs' and its complementary sub-set). But at the same time he fully intended that the structural relationships with which he was concerned should be preserved in the model. As a result, his mathematical derivations measured the proportionality of electric charge flowing between various alternative sources and sinks.

The rigorous homomorphic model, then, obtained fundamental *structural* information about the *system* constituted by the electrical phenomena involved. This outcome was surely more important than the confirmation of Walsh's hypothesis about the fish: it had quite general relevance. It was a death-blow to the theories of 'some electricians' who held that electricity followed the path of least resistance and none other. And what had been their error? Precisely the familiar error of failing to observe a system as being such; they wanted a simple rule which would select the answer from a range of mutually exclusive possibilities. They had evidently set up a thought block against a complex solution, in which every part of the system would have some role to play, and in which the possibilities were not mutually exclusive but could be mixed in varying proportions.

This story is enchanting—rather fun. And admittedly the problem solved by this model was not a management problem. Oddly enough, however, it not only illustrates the key features of the OR approach, but points to the psychological difficulties which surround the use of that approach. Industrial managers faced with a problem in production control invariably expect a solution to be devised that is simple and uni-dimensional. They seek *the* variable in the situation whose control will achieve control of the whole system: tons of throughput, for example. Business managers seek to do the same thing in controlling a company; they hope they have found the measure of the entire system when they say 'everything can be reduced to monetary terms'. And the Chancellor of the Exchequer who tries to control the whole economic system by fiscal manipulations is in the same difficulty. None of these things is possible, and arguments can be developed in each case to show why. More important, however, is the reason which underlies the denial of all three cases—all four, if 'some electricians' are included.

It is that a ramified interacting system is strictly multidimensional and its structure cannot be preserved in a unidimensional mapping. In practical terms, this is because any conflict is apparently resolvable if it lies in a single dimension, whereas the homomorph required must reflect structures that support unresolvable conflicts. There is no unique path for the flow of electricity in a fully-connected network, nor for decision-taking in a fully-connected managerial situation. When Cavendish discovered this nearly 200 years ago he advanced electrical theory; if managers could discover it now they would encounter fewer strikes and fewer recessions.

3 Applications: A Recent Operational Model

Representations in physical terms of the homomorphic models underlying operational research work are however rare. They are instructive because they demonstrate, in a tangible way, the nature of scientific analogizing and of the underlying formalization, by rigorous statement of the identities that inform the analogy. Very often, physical manifestations of the analogy could be, yet are not, built. This may be illustrated by an immediate transition to modern times and to the *Proceedings of the Royal Society for 1955*. Here, 180 years later, we find Professor M. J. Lighthill, F.R.S., making use of the same technique. He takes a different scientific model for the purpose of his analogy; but he also gives a mathematical formalization of underlying identities. Of course, the terminology put forward here as a means of explaining the inductive process involved was by this time available. Lighthill did not use it; but then he was not intending to comment on the basic nature of his method, only to expound his results.

His problem was this. What approach can science make to the discussion and solution of the question: how should road traffic be organized so that the full benefits of our increased mobility can be enjoyed at the lowest cost in human life and capital?

Now there are two basically different answers to this problem. First, the topic proposed is *directly* susceptible to scientific attack, at least in part. Lighthill began by noting that there is already an experimental science dealing specifically with this matter: the quantitative study of traffic flow, together with the analysis of resulting data by sophisticated statistical techniques. Some might call this work operational research, but it is better called traffic engineering. This is because its object is to improve a process, not to evolve a management policy. There are several aspects to the question posed in the last paragraph which cannot be handled by purely empirical techniques. Moreover there is the problem of generalization, so familiar to science. To demonstrate that a particular street layout could be modified with advantage does not simultaneously educe a general principle about the management control problem posed. Even when many particular cases have been studied, so that (with luck) principles begin to emerge, the decision-taker's criteria may call for information that is not available from an analysis of the existing traffic flow by itself. Secondly, then, comes the characteristically OR approach: the construction of a model, based on some insight into an analogous system, and able to *generate* information not empirically available.

Lighthill's paper, then, introduces what he calls 'a quite different method' from that of the traffic engineer as such. His analogous thinking is derived from 'theories of the flow about supersonic projectiles and of flood movement in rivers'. He takes his model in fact from the science of fluid dynamics. According to the classification of scientific activity adopted here, he is now using the approach of operational research. Whatever it is called, it is quite clear that this *is* a different approach from that of traffic engineering itself—despite the highly scientific nature of the research sometimes undertaken nowadays under that heading.

The analogy used by Lighthill for his model begins from the insight of the fluid dynamicist that the flow of traffic along a road is analogous to any other kind of flow through any constrained channel. It is clear from the first that the analogy has limits of usefulness—its application will be focused on a restricted range of problems. The reason is that vehicles are not joined together in a continuous flow, and that therefore the pretence that moving traffic is a fluid introduces a simplification. However, and interestingly, this particular simplification is often made in science, and is not as serious as it might at first appear. It has been emphasized earlier that distinctions which appear to reside in the nature of the universe may in fact be introduced by the language in which we seek to discuss that universe. Whether a moving stream is composed of individual and separate lumps of stuff, or is literally an indivisible continuum, may in the first place be merely a matter of resolving power. Water is a fluid, but we may think of it differently if we can examine its molecular structure. More important, however, is the fact that the matter is one of convention.

130   *The Activity of Operational Research*

A man in a cinema can choose how to describe the film unfolding before him. He can examine his practical experience of the film show by introspection, and declare that quite certainly a film is a continuous process. Alternatively, he may examine the mechanics of projection and the piece of celluloid concerned. In this case he may declare that quite certainly a film is a collection of separate and distinct frames. In either case he is right; the assertions are not contradictory for their validity depends on the language being used, not on the facts described. Similarly, it is common in astrophysics to employ mathematical languages which assume that matter at intergalactic distances is continuous, but of very low density. That is instead of saying that it consists of lumps of solid material with a lot of nothing in between. This approach therefore treats solids *as if* they were gases—which at that distance seems quite acceptable; the comparison between thinking of the continuous and the discrete cases has the feel of a distinction without a difference. And so, in the present example about roads, we need not be concerned to ask whether the model from fluid dynamics is 'correct'; we should be concerned only to survey the limits of the appropriateness of the language we propose to use. Thus Lighthill points out that the analogy between his kinematic model and a real road system is likely to hold for large-scale problems only; but if one considers arterial roads, where the traffic is crowded and sustained, useful conclusions may well be drawn.

The model is then set up. According to fluid dynamics, the flow (in this case the number of vehicles per hour) is a function of the concentration (in this case the number of vehicles per mile). This structural relationship in the proposed mapping has first to be tested empirically. It holds. Mathematical curves connecting flow and concentration are investigated; their general shape is indicated in Figure 6. Naturally, the flow increases with the concentration until traffic becomes too heavy to be contained; the flow then diminishes until everything is at a standstill again. This is the point at which the underlying scientific model expressed in rigorous terms begins to emerge. Versions of the standard equations which describe this relationship in the case of fluid dynamics are developed in the language of traffic flow. If what the scientist is doing here be described in terms of a mapping, we can see that it is going to be homomorphic. For, if a continuum is to stand for a number of discrete objects, the translation from the one language to the other can be achieved conceptually by observing that the number of objects over any finite distance is infinite. Since one cannot compress an infinite number of *vehicles* into a finite stretch of road, the correspondence in this case is many–one. But that the system of relationships is none the less preserved is demonstrated by the research, which shows that the flow-concentration curve may yet be applied.

It now remains to investigate the implications of the model as rigorously formulated by Lighthill. According to the discoveries of fluid dynamics, slight changes in flow are propagated along trajectories known as 'kinematic waves', whose velocity is given by the slope of the graph connecting flow and concentration. The tangents *a* and *b* in Figure 6 indicate wave velocities for the two points indicated on the curve. When this fact is mapped into the traffic situation, it becomes clear that a driver will experience such a wave whenever he adjusts his speed to that of the cars in front of his: by reacting to the next man's brake-light, or by seizing an opportunity to overtake.

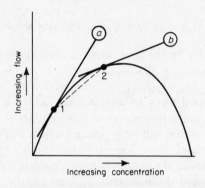

FIGURE 6. General shape of a flow-concentration curve.

Now if a stream of traffic is dense in front and less dense at the rear, the kinematic waves associated with (say) points 1 and 2 in Figure 6 have different velocities. Reflecting on this diagram, it can be seen that waves propagated from the rear are travelling faster than those propagated from the front; the former therefore overtake the latter. Given that a series of such kinematic waves can collide in this way, the model predicts the appearance along the wave collision route of 'kinematic shock waves'. In Figure 7 we see how such a shock wave (the thick line) is formed. Kinematic waves *ahead* of it have velocities given by tangent *b* in Figure 6, and are therefore drawn parallel to that. Kinematic waves *behind* the shock wave are parallel to the wave velocity represented by tangent *a*. The shock wave lies where these two sets of waves collide; it is in turn parallel to the dotted chord joining points 1 and 2 in Figure 6.

When traffic runs into a kinematic shock wave, vehicular speeds will be sizably reduced quite quickly. All this conforms to experience on

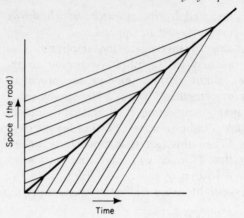

FIGURE 7. Appearance of a kinematic shock wave.

the road. The virtue of the scientific work lies in the predictive validity of the model describing this situation, for it is competent to forecast much more complicated effects in more elaborate situations. Suppose that a tributary road joins an arterial road, and that there is a period during which the traffic flowing in on this tributary is above the average. Clearly a knot of traffic will be generated which will continue to move down the arterial road. What happens when this intense local concentration of vehicles passes through a bottleneck—that is, a portion of road too narrow to accept the momentarily increased flow? What happens when the knot meets a junction? And how will the behaviour both of the traffic, and of the backward-propagating shock wave that it generates, vary for an uncontrolled junction and a junction that is controlled by traffic lights or a policeman?

It is to questions of this type that Lighthill's work offers a quantitative answer. People have sometimes commented that it seems absurd to set up a complicated scientific theory to handle such questions. The outcome (they say) is to declare (for example) that the driver at the rear of a column of traffic encounters shock waves, which force him to accelerate and decelerate in an uncomfortable fashion—his consequent irritation may be compared with the relaxed state of mind of the driver proceeding at a steady thirty miles an hour at the front of the column. One has only to take a car on to the road, it is objected, to discover the truth of this proposition, and no Einstein is required to detect the basic reason for it. Now this is a subjective impression of the fact that oscillations in speed are amplified towards the rear of a convoy. When all drivers concur in the same belief, the value of this judgment is improved to the point where the fact is socially accepted. Something may even be done about it. But it is evident that this belief has to be quantified before there can be any change in road design, since this demands decisions about quantities. Doubtless measurements *have* been taken to show the magnitude of these effects under different circumstances. But now a new question is reached.

When it comes to devising a whole new transport system, consisting of an interacting network of roads, many difficulties arise. The characteristics of every road have to be described in detail: the magnitudes of each, and the arrangements for feeding one into another; whether crossings should be controlled or not, whether such controls should be linked or not, and if so in what way; and so forth. Moreover, these exercises in optimal planning have always to be undertaken, not in the abstract as if they were pieces of geometry, but having regard to the practical limitations of geography and topography, custom and convenience, public service and finance. Those who object to the use of high science in solving problems of this extremely earthy kind, on the ground that they could more effectively be tackled by straightforward engineering techniques, are hoist with their own petard. For, to use their own criterion, they have only to take a car on to the road to observe that the results of precisely this practice are today an expensive failure. The reason is that the straightforward approach, even the straightforward *scientific* approach, has no real depth. It may succeed in quantifying the situation at a superficial level, and it does recognize some of the mechanisms involved; but somehow it does not manage to account for the underlying nature of the system at large.

Now the modelling process as outlined in the previous chapter, and exemplified in this, does provide that depth. Explicitly, the homomorph provides it—it reveals the deep identity between the problem situation and the model from science to which it is analogous. Given that demonstration of identity, profundity in the understanding of the scientific situation can be imported into the problem situation, where understanding would not otherwise be profound.

Moreover, the model is predictive: it can be used to generate information, to facilitate experimentation, and to check hypotheses and potential solutions. It is surely to a whole series of OR models that the national transport decision-takers need to turn, rather than to an even longer series of *ad hoc* studies leading to large numbers of local improvements. For the series of models may be combined into a complete homomorph of a large transportation system, and the characteristics of its optimal control strategy worked out. This global optimum cannot be expected to correspond with the aggregate of local optima: the whole is assuredly greater than the sum of its parts.

4   Applications: A Formal Homomorphic Model

Two examples have so far been quoted of the use of models for the solution of operational problems, ancient and modern. In each case it has been shown how the inductive theory based on the nature of homomorphism is useful in accounting for the processes undertaken by the two scientists concerned. It remains to illustrate the operation of this technique in a case where the method was used explicitly: that is to say, the mechanism depicted in Figure 4 was consciously in mind, and the homomorphism was formally constructed. This illustration is taken from my own work reported in *Transactions of the University of Illinois Symposium, 1960,* published by Pergamon Press (1962) under the title 'Principles of Self-Organization'.

The problem facing the scientists was this. The management of an industrial company involves its control as an organism within an environment which is sometimes propitious, sometimes hostile, but mostly unfeeling and arbitrary. Typically, a management seeking to exert this control organizes itself into a number of divisions—such as production management, financial management and so on—to which it allots different functions. Thus, to consider the cycle of company operations chronologically, some part of the organization must first of all be responsible for both stimulating and assimilating demand, and channelling it into the works. At this point, the production function assumes responsibility; it must find ways of converting this demand into goods, and of making these goods available for dispatch to the market. Another function is concerned with the purchase of raw materials, and another with all the transportation that is involved. Moreover, there has to be a financial function which supervises the economic activity throughout. This will seek to ensure that all aspects of these operations are financially viable, and will institute accounting procedures by which to verify this fact.

In the case under discussion, all these processes were unusually difficult to maintain. The production process was of a highly patterned kind: that is, its profitable operation depended on lengthy runs of production carefully planned into the future. But the demand pattern was totally adventitious; it proved impossible to forecast, even by the use of advanced statistical methods, and its day-to-day fluctuations had a highly damaging effect on the economics of producing the goods. Hence very large stocks of finished material were held, and even then market shocks penetrated through to the works and interrupted optimal activity. Moreover, raw materials were in very short supply, and were controlled by special and rather unfavourable agreements: the company was not buying in a free market. In almost every other department of its activity, this firm was in special difficulty. The labour position, for example, was by no means easy; the company had been held to ransom more than once by groups of skilled workpeople. In all these circumstances, which are not recounted here in great detail, orthodox methods of management were proving successful—but burdensome. The chief executive was by no means convinced that the best performance was being obtained. A new approach to control was being sought by the use of operational research.

The scientific analogy which appeared most apposite was, as already indicated, an ecological one. The company is an organism which must adapt to its environment; it must find ways of adjusting itself to changing conditions. Most living organisms manage to do this, because the environment is to some degree patterned, and the pattern is one which the organism can learn. Violent change is uncommon, and when it is encountered the organism may reel under the impact and become quite unstable and ineffectual for a period, after which it is likely to settle down to the new circumstances. This state of affairs, familiar to the organism, is also familiar to the typical industrial company. As has been explained, however, this particular company was atypical in precisely the ways which make ecological adaptation most difficult. A scientist therefore casts around within his ecological analogy for prototypes of control organizations which are competent to handle such extremely trying circumstances.

It seems clear that either of two possible creatures might expect to cope with an environment of this kind. One is an all-purpose, unspecialized creature: a blob of jelly, as it were, which can be tossed about unharmed by environmental storms. But this concept is a negation of an industrial undertaking, which must be in the very nature of things rather highly specialized: this is indeed what makes it so vulnerable. The second kind of creature, then, is one that protects itself by fast reaction, and moreover by perspicacious reaction. Now animal control systems of a purely biochemical kind do not have the required characteristics; one must pass to creatures having highly developed nervous systems. If the entire management process of the company under discussion is conceived of as a brain-like activity, the possibility of a successful outcome is assured. Accordingly, an attempt has to be made to expound the managerial activity in brain-like terms, to see whether this activity matches the activity already to be found in the company, and to try to develop better mechanisms on the strength of the comparison. And this is exactly what the study set out to do.

In this investigation, therefore, the scientific situation to be compared with the managerial situation is that of a brain-directed organism operating in an environment. The conceptual model of this situation is inevitably taken from the science of neurophysiology. Just how valid the use of such a model could possibly be is a question which is vigorously debated among scientists, and particularly by those scientists who though concerned with the brain (whether physiologically, anatomically or surgically) have no stomach for cybernetic formalizations of its nature, structure or dynamics. Too little, they argue, is known about the brain for such a process as is here envisaged to be remotely possible; and perhaps too much is known for anyone to suppose that an artificial structure such as an industrial company could parallel the wonder of the brain. Such objectors are trapped in an ambivalence which may derive, at the worst, from a fear that science is on the verge of penetrating the mysteries of their own natures; this they resent. Or the ambivalence may derive, at the best, from a profound unease—a sense of inadequacy in themselves and in their techniques to cope with the mysteries of this most complicated of control mechanisms. Let it be made abundantly clear that many of those, and certainly myself, who have ventured into this awesome undertaking share these feelings in large measure, and are certainly neither underrating the task, nor laying an overweening claim to a knowledge they do not possess. We are on the outermost fringe of both comprehension and our own ability to handle the situation as so far comprehended. But, armed with the methodology in which this book is now immersed, we may make a diffident start without falling straight into the traps of which we must all be well aware.

Anything that is said in attempting to explore the analogy now set up is, admittedly, a profound simplification. Opponents may suggest that a profound simplification is obviously dangerous, and possibly 'wicked'. Yet we are protected in the task by the highly developed methodology already explained. The object is to construct a homomorphic mapping of the brain which is by definition a simplification—and, by definition again, a simplification of which the limitations are understood. The really pejorative term here would be *over*-simplification; but that stage is not reached so long as a certain structure is preserved in the homomorph, and so long as we know exactly what that structure is.

In the case quoted, a homomorphic model of certain aspects of brain function was constructed and used to explore the mechanisms by which the company could possibly respond to environmental change. The formal language employed for this purpose was the mathematical language of set theory which, as explained earlier, is the very language in which the theory of homomorphism is itself expressed. Using this tool, it proved possible to state the required scientific model from neurophysiology—by following exactly, instead of inferentially, the refining processes depicted on the right-hand arm of Figure 4. Simultaneously, the attempt was made to parallel this analysis in the real-life procedures of industry. Experimental control systems were installed inside the company, with the collaboration of the management, to represent the left-hand arm of the methodology laid out in Figure 4.

Figure 8 is a schematic diagram of the neurophysiological model. It comprises four sub-models, marked *T*, *V*, *U* and *R*. These are respectively homomorphic models, worked out in set theory, of the sensory cortex, the motor cortex, the thalamic level and the reticular formation—each a major area of the brain. The diagram merely indicates how these areas are related to each other in the brain topographically, and shows a coronal section (the brain is cut through vertically, roughly from ear to ear). Obviously none of the detail can be discussed here: the mathematics is extremely involved. But, for the sake of interest, some comments are included about what was surely the first attempt to record the brain rhythms of an industrial company.

An electroencephalogram is a record of electrical activity in the brain: each line is inscribed by a pen activated from an electrode placed on a particular point on the skull. An electroencephalographer studies the rhythms produced from each of a number of different points simultaneously, and succeeds in detecting various forms of mental activity; he may also be able to diagnose an aberrant personality. It will be appreciated that the process of reading off electrical activity at a given point on the *skull* makes a many–one transformation from the electrical complexities going on beneath the skull in the brain itself. There, hundreds of individual neurons are firing, and thousands of nerve fibres are conveying impulses from one neuron to another. But only one stream of impulses is flowing down the wire to activate the pen recorder. Yet what is inscribed is a homomorphic record. There is certainly a structural difference between the rhythms generated by a sleeping brain and a brain engaged in conscious activity: the pens oscillate much more quickly in the latter case. Moreover, this structure of the rhythm preserves more important features of the very much more complicated structure of neural activity itself. For example, particular rhythm structures clearly indicate epileptic tendencies in the living brain. All this is possible, although the many–one transformation has thrown away all information concerning particular neurons, particular nerve fibres and particular neural impulses. The encephalographer has no idea what precisely is causing the rhythm to oscillate as it does, but he can interpret the oscillations none the less.

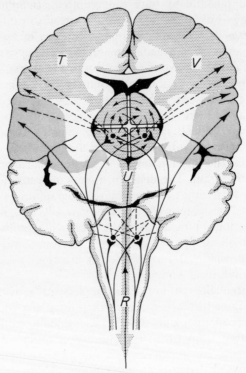

FIGURE 8. Diagram showing the connectivity of the four sub-models (*T, V, U, R*—details of which are not shown) comprising a neurophysiological model of the control of an industrial company. Successful management decisions were taken using this model of the company's 'brain'.

The parallel situation in an industrial company is clear. A financial expert diagnoses the state of the company from changes in rhythm read from balance sheets and profit-and-loss accounts. He also has no idea what particular occurrences in the works, what particular activities in the market and so on, have caused these changes. But, as will be argued later in this book, the rhythms he is studying are not generated by truly homomorphic mappings. The many–one transformation is there all right; but there are reasons why the all-important structure is not fully preserved. Some of it is preserved, of course; this is what makes his job possible. But the attempt to map every feature of the business on to a unidimensional monetary scale does not succeed, and this is why wrong decisions are sometimes taken.

Thus one of the objects of the OR study briefly described here was to construct a valid homomorphic mapping of the company on to a model of the brain. At the least, the order of complexity is right; there is therefore a possibility of preserving the important structure. In exploring the model, then, an 'electroencephalogram' was taken of ten areas of activity relevant to the company's management. This was not a genuine electroencephalogram, of course: it was an artefact generated by the company *through* the neurophysiological model. And it was all worked out by hand: we do not yet have machinery capable of doing the job. In short, it was an experiment. Part of the resulting chart is shown at Figure 9 which is laid out as a genuine encephalogram. The inset picture of the head would normally indicate where the electrodes were placed. Instead, this inset picture nominates the ten areas used to generate the rhythms. In reality, these activities have no definite sites inside the company that are topographically related in this way. The point is that *we do not know*, any more than the electroencephalographer knows, what particular events generate the rhythms. The model processes detailed facts available to the company, throwing away information steadily, and distilling structure. In the interpretation of such results one does not look for the usual information as to whether outputs or profits are up or down; one looks instead at the relationship between the ten lines. Some are correlated with each other, some are negatively correlated, some are correlated with a time lag. Above all, these rhythms are related to the major events of the world outside, and the research seeks to discover what bursts of rhythmic activity follow what major events, when, and how.

The results of this piece of operational research were, as were called for, the acquirement of insights into optimal ways of controlling the firm as a whole, and the establishment of formal decision-taking procedures for the control of its buying, stockholding, production and marketing policies. The rewards were sufficient for a piece of operational research. Of course, the study could also be conceived as an exercise in the science of cybernetics: an attempt to gain automatic control for the managerial, as well as the physical, activities undertaken by the company. Some advanced automation was indeed installed, and a development plan aimed at the more far-reaching targets of cybernetics

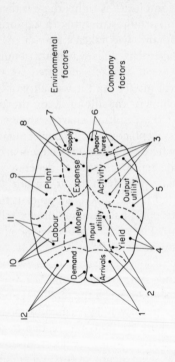

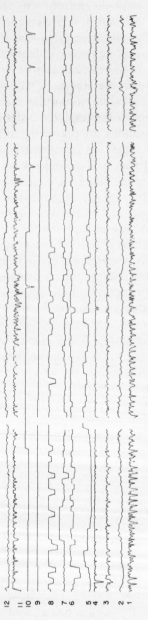

FIGURE 9. Encephalogram of the company's 'brain'. An actual trace made by an industrial company via the model shown in Figure 8.

certainly emerged. The advent of automatic decision-taking and policy-forming machinery for installation in companies must, however, await further investments. It will come. But these prospects are not of present concern to the argument here put forward, which is concerned with the operational research aspect alone. For this same reason, the model is not offered as a revolutionary technique for the presentation of company information. It was used as a tool for doing a particular job in a particular situation. Now it is a model preserved in aspic. We shall need it again.

8

THE FORMAL
LANGUAGES

Un enfant instruit en arithmétique, ayant fait une
addition suivant ses règles, se peut assurer d'avoir
trouvé, touchant la somme qu'il examinait, tout ce
que l'esprit humain saurait trouver.

A child instructed in arithmetic, who has made an
addition according to the rules, can feel quite sure
that—as far as that sum goes—he has found out everything that it lies within the human genius to
discover.

RÉNÉ DESCARTES in *Discours de la Méthode* (1637)

1   The Formal Language of Quantity

The importance of languages has been canvassed insistently in this book,
and a distinction has been drawn between social languages (those which
simply permit easy communication) and formal languages (those directed
towards maximum coherence and precision, regardless of the ease with
which they can be learned and 'spoken'). Having analysed the inductive
processes of operational research, and having discussed the nature of its
models at some length, we should now consider the formal languages in
which the scientific model is expressed. It is not one of our purposes to
investigate the technical details of scientific techniques, still less to
purvey a mastery over them. But it is a primary object to explain the
meaning of these techniques, and if possible to distil their essence.

As a means to this end, it should help to discuss how that which *is*
done can conceivably *be* done. For there is a no-man's-land between the
mere declaration that science is competent to express a conceptual model
in rigorous terms, and a full-scale exposition of what those terms actually
are. Each of these tasks has been adequately tackled elsewhere; it seems

142

clear that a managerial insight into the situation must lie somewhere between the two. Accordingly, we select the first of the formal languages used by scientists, namely mathematics, and try to answer the question why it is that this language is so important, and what special advantages it offers in the treatment of managerial problems which after all have nothing to do with algebra.

In the first place, someone who is not himself accustomed to use formal languages probably suffers from a thought block in their regard. Mathematics, for example, may be to him a grim and intractable subject —because he was not very happy with it at school. Moreover, it is clearly a dry way of discussing real-life affairs; so dry indeed that it cannot possibly cope with all the richness and colour of the world. Therefore mathematics is suitable for calculating numbers that managers want to know, and has no other relevance for them. Although this conclusion does not follow from the premise, there is of course a good point here. The mathematician trades in a good deal of the sensual delight of empirical scientific enquiry—and for what? Clearly the main answer is that his delight (and this necessary reward of labour *is* retained) resides in intellectual satisfactions. The mathematician is respected for this; people feel that he lives on 'a higher plane', but they do not really understand. Perhaps a clue can be obtained from Descartes, whose words head this chapter. The point is that a formal language is a *deductive machine*: it investigates itself, rather than the sensual world. Given a set of formal propositions, the mathematician investigates what they entail. He makes his work useful in society by matching his initial propositions to the world, so that what they entail is directly translatable into worldly consequences. What Descartes says is that the kernel of this process is a self-consistent, self-justifying business: it leaves no more to be said. The point to be taken for operational research is that formal manipulations inside the scientific model are assuredly the kernel of OR, but—for the very reason that they are self-justifying—this kernel must be properly embedded in its surrounding model. Hence models take pride of place over the formal languages used to make them rigorous. For a good homomorphic model that is less than rigorously expressed may be very useful; but a rigorous demonstration that derives from a poor model, improperly mapped from the problem situation, is highly dangerous and may be irrelevant.

Mathematics then is an *abstract* way of talking about quantities. This is not the naïve statement that it seems. There are mathematicians who would contend that it is naïve; that mathematics in fact deals with something more than quantities, namely logical relationships. But although that allegation is a more penetrating comment than the statement that mathematics is a kind of arithmetic in fancy dress, it is still not penetrating enough. If one goes into the philosophy of mathematics, it becomes clear that the relationships with which mathematics deals are basically quantitative: they derive from the nature of space and time. But the fact that the quantities involved are abstract is the really important point. Everyone who did school algebra knows that $a^2 - b^2 = (a+b)(a-b)$, and finds this interesting because it is a generalization. He does not demand to know what are the numbers of which this equation speaks, so that he may store them in his memory against the possibility of meeting them in practice. He prefers to store the basic pattern of the quantitative relationship, so that he may apply it to *any* set of numbers that he may encounter.

This argument may be extended to the handling of managerial problems. Mostly people behave as if each decision with which they are faced is unique. Strictly, it has to be conceded that, since we live in a world of flux, no decision is absolutely and entirely repeatable. But the pattern of decision-taking may well be repeatable. That is to say, it is possible to set down equations which adequately (by which is meant nothing more nor less than homomorphically) represent a wide variety of managerial situations. This being the case, it is possible to substitute actual numbers from a given unique decision-taking problem for the letters which stand in the equation, and to obtain a unique answer for a particular occasion. The advantages are twofold. In the first place, a decision which may appear to a manager to be qualitative, because he is hemmed in by the psychological exigencies of the moment, may now be instantly recognizable as belonging to a certain pattern of decision which can be quantified. In the second place, and reverting again to Figure 4, the same basic pattern may well underlie a host of apparently dissimilar managerial situations; therefore the amount of scientific effort which must be put into the task of modelling this pattern of decision is spread over many instances and becomes only trivially expensive. A point well worth adding on this score is that once a procedure has been discovered for solving a particular set of mathematical equations, a particular problem can not only be recognized and set up in rigorous terms quickly and cheaply, it can be solved quickly and cheaply too. Often, for example, the procedure may be embodied in a computer programme, so that the particular solution may be obtained for no more effort than that required to feed this programme from the library into the machine, together with the accompanying data that relate to this occasion.

It is worth trying to illustrate this point, if only briefly, and in one context. The example concerns a production shop containing a large number of machines, each of which can manufacture a range of items. Clearly, each machine can also operate at an intense or less intense level of activity. Into the department flow raw materials, which are converted by the machines into products, which then flow out of the department. Associated with all these activities are, naturally, costs. It is basically the problem of the production manager to decide how to fix all these variables to produce the highest profit within a given period. This statement of the situation does not of course reveal all the ins and outs of any particular example, but the general picture is surely sufficiently familiar. It is also too familiar to find that this problem is resolved on the basis of knowledge and experience alone. Probably no one man declares what the total answer is; rather, there is a group of men who plan the operation between them. They have a 'feel' for the situation, by which is meant that they tend to recognize combinations of activities which are advantageous and others which are disadvantageous, and they piece together a total plan of campaign which takes account of these intuitions. Normally, this group of people will not conceive that the answer to the problem is even in principle *computable*; on the contrary, experience tells them that it is a matter for negotiation between themselves— a negotiation in which each of the men concerned exercises his *judgment*. This belief comes about because no one man has a brain sufficiently large or sufficiently competent to undertake the computation that would be involved; therefore it is alleged that the answer is strictly noncomputable.

But suppose that by this point we are agreed that, given the facts, an answer *is* in principle computable. How should we then set out a statement of what has to be computed? Any attempt to do this in ordinary English will be most difficult; it will place a considerable strain on the comprehension and the concentration of anyone who tries to formulate it or to read it. Let us undertake a practical experiment on this point. What follows is a purely verbal statement.

Each machine has a definite average rate of production for each item at each level of activity. If we fix the item and the level of activity for each machine, we can see how many more or how many less units of production will come out of the shop as a whole in a given time, compared with some standard number (supposing for example that all machines produce a standard item at a standard level of activity). In order to procure such an adjustment to standard output, it would of course be necessary to add raw materials to, or subtract raw materials from, the standard set of raw materials going into the shop in the time period immediately preceding the one over which the output was measured. This consideration of a possible arrangement of work different from the standard arrangement of work might be more or less profitable than the standard profitability. In order to find out what is the *most* profitable arrangement, it will be necessary to consider in turn the manufacture of *every* item which that machine can make on *each* of the machines at the lowest level of activity; next we shall have to consider that whole permutation all over again at a slightly higher level of activity; and so on, until the maximum level of activity is reached. But then of course it would be possible to mix the effects, and to consider combining *this* item on *that* machine at a *certain* level of activity with some other item on some other machine at another level of activity—and so on, it might seem indefinitely. But take comfort: the number of possibilities is not actually indefinite, an end will be reached. Of course the number will be exceedingly large. Even so, all that is apparently necessary is to have the accountants cost each of this large number of possible arrangements, and then to choose the one that offers the highest profit. In practice, this cannot be done. An elementary mathematical argument is now used to quantify the basic problem—to show just what its magnitude is, and therefore why the accounting exercise cannot be done.

Consider the simplest aspect, and it is only an aspect, of this problem. There are N processes. Incoming material may be routed on to any number R of these N processes in any order, and the product may be sold at any stage. Admittedly, there will normally be side conditions to be met which make this problem as stated a little more fluid than one normally finds it—but think of a machine shop. In any case, this factor is compensated by making the shop in the example absurdly small. Suppose it has only ten machines in it. How many different routing possibilities are there: how many ways of allocating work to these ten machines? If anyone should wish to work this out, here is the way to do it:

$$\sum_{R=2}^{N} \frac{N!}{(N-R)!} \simeq eN!$$

And in case anyone does not follow this expression, or does not want to bother with it, the answer is over 10,000,000.

It is small wonder that most people have not yet realized that uniquely best arrangements can in fact be selected in circumstances of this kind, even for shops which are not ideal, which have a very much larger number than ten of non-interchangeable machines, and which in addition have to cope with thousands of different items and many different levels of activity. But surely the point has been demonstrated that the production planning man can hardly be expected to do the optimal job, and also that the mere task of stating what the problem is may produce a headache. Then let us just glance, without any detailed explanation, at a mathematical formulation of the original generalized problem. There is no algebra to be *understood* here; the object is to give a practical demonstration of the power of formal languages to be precise, and to condense long-winded verbal statements.

We are concerned with times, which are numbered consecutively 0, 1, 2, 3, 4 and so on. Typically, the time is t, and the time before it $t-1$; so the gap between them prescribes a basic interval, typically the tth interval. There is a range of activities which could occur in this interval, and a range of items which could be manufactured too. These could all be nominated by a string of consecutive numbers as well; but typically there is a jth activity and an ith item. Now if an increment a is defined as an addition to the cumulative flow function through the works, it must relate to a certain time interval, and it may pair off any item with any activity. The whole range of such possibilities is written $\alpha_{ij}^{(t)}$. Similarly, a decrement $\bar{a}$ is defined as subtracting from the cumulative flow; its particulars are specified in the same way. The first is an input coefficient, occurring at the end of the interval. The unknown, x (or series of x's), which must be calculated is in this case the number of units of each item that must be produced by each activity. The following expression accounts precisely for the equilibrial condition (that is, that the input to and the output from the system must match) of the dynamic system described above:

$$\sum_{j=0}^{n_t} \alpha_{ij}^{(t)} \, x_j^{(t)} = \sum_{j=0}^{n_{t-1}} \bar{\alpha}_{ij}^{(t-1)} \, x_j^{(t-1)}$$

Here the summation sign Σ shows how the system of equations entailed by this expression ranges over all possible activities in the shop. And 'system of equations' is the correct term, for it would take many pages to write out the entire piece of algebra prescribed by this one expression.

If we may revert briefly to the vocabulary introduced much earlier in this book for other purposes, this expression defines a particular mathematical space, namely a space which has the 'shape' of the situation under discussion. But it does not yet define the phase space of the problem. It is still of complete generality, and would permit answers to be given to the manager which (for instance) invited him to manufacture a negative number of items on certain machines. And so the phase space must be carved off this total space, not by the device which was un-covered in human psychology, that of erecting thought blocks, but by stating the limiting or boundary conditions which obtain. Thus the equations must hold for every item, and for every time; there must be a positive activity; there cannot be an implied decrement before the first moment of time considered; the search starts from that moment with the possibility that one item of something is produced, and a negative number of any item cannot be produced. So the equation has to be solved subject to these conditions, written respectively:

$$i = 1, 2, 3 \ldots m$$
$$t = 1, 2, 3 \ldots T$$
$$j \geqslant 1$$
$$\bar{a}_{ij}{}^{o} = 0$$
$$x_{o}{}^{(t)} = 1$$
$$x_{j}{}^{(t)} \geqslant 0$$

In practice, moreover, the range of possible solutions will be limited by more factors than these logical ones. For example, there will be items which cannot be made at all on certain machines, and items which can-not be effectively produced at certain levels of activity; there may be minimal quantities of certain items that have to be made to accord with outstanding commercial agreements, and there may be items which we do not intend to produce at all this month because no-one will buy them. In fact, all these limitations can be added to the list of logical constraints already given in similarly mathematical form. And here is an interesting comparison. When a human planner is given a long list of constraints of such a kind, he is prone to tear his hair—because his mind cannot assimilate all the ifs and buts. Scientifically, on the other hand, the more of these constraints that can be added the better, for they delimit and reduce the phase space which has to be searched in order to find the answer.

It is now clear that all possible answers to our question lie within the boundaries now fixed, and that one could prescribe the rules (presumably to a computer) which would enable all these answers to be generated and listed from the basic equation. But of course nobody wants all these answers, although they will all be feasible solutions to the management problem. Only one answer is required—that is, the most profitable arrangement of the lot. Therefore another equation is required, which will state quite precisely how to recognize this unique answer. To obtain this other equation, a measure of the profitability of every combination is required. If $\bar{\lambda}$ is the cost per unit produced of the jth activity, then its negative, λ, is a measure of the profit. Hence the profit, p, for the jth activity is $\lambda_j x_j$; and the total profit P for the totality of activities sums them all thus:

$$P = \sum_{j=1}^{n} \lambda_j x_j$$

Now time must be considered: another summing term has to be included to cover the range of times. And the resulting expression has to give the *maximum* profit. Hence:

$$P = \sum_{t=1}^{T} \sum_{j=1}^{n_t} \lambda_j{}^{(t)} x_j{}^{(t)} = max$$

The rule for finding the solution is now this: search the whole phase space for an answer which conforms to both equations (that on p. 147 and this last) at once. This is the best production programme.

These equations are typical of those devised to express this kind of problem rigorously. The credit for devising a rigorous set of rules for searching the phase space and recognizing the right answer belongs to an American, Dr George B. Dantzig. All this work was published as early as 1949. By now there is a large number of variants of this approach, collectively known as linear programming techniques. There are also variants of the original set of rules for finding the answer (to which the name algorithm is applied); Dantzig's own algorithm is called the Simplex Method.

It ought by this date to be possible to remark that every competent industrial management uses this method for analysing its production problems: but it is not. And please let no-one counter with the argument that his own production problem is *not* of this kind; for of course the illustration given is only an example of a whole family of patterns which could be used. Yet this presumably is just one of the thought blocks which have been erected to curtail the application of this immensely powerful approach. Because the plain fact is that most industrialists have never even tried it. Moreover, the results can be so startling that they fall foul of every one of the stereotypes of managerial thinking discussed in Chapter 4. On the first attempt of my own to use this approach a potential increase in the profitability of a small but very complicated works was disclosed of the order of 500 per cent. This at once set up in the management a whole row of wedged bears, transfixed in every possible attitude: it was an education.

We set out to exemplify the use of the rigorous language of mathematics in an operational research problem, in order to show how complicated verbal arguments can be succinctly expressed when an appropriate language is used, and to explain how decision problems which may appear to many to be qualitative can in fact be quantified. But there was a second point at issue. This was to demonstrate how a particular mathematical pattern informing a scientific model may underlie a variety of problems which appear dissimilar.

This mathematical model is in fact a formalization of a conceptual model drawn from an understanding of the nature of equilibrial systems. At the conceptual level, the model is not very rich: this is why many people concerned with linear programming regard it simply as a process of applied mathematics. Or they may call it applied economics, for it can be looked on as an extension of the famous input-output econometric models of Leontief. What then is the point of calling it operational research; or alternatively what is the point of insisting that the business of operational research begins in this case with a scientific analogy founded in a conceptual model? The answer is simple.

It is just because the conceptual model is not very rich that this technique is not as widely used as it should be. In our nomenclature, the mapping from real life is not strongly homomorphic. For there will be a variety of managerial considerations which were not included in the story as earlier set down. For example, the theory procures a statement of the 'optimal mix' of which the production programme should be compounded; but it tells nothing of what should be done if for some practical reason (a breakdown, perhaps) the manager is compelled to depart from the optimum. It simply is not true to say that his best course in these circumstances is to adhere as closely to the optimal mix as he can. Ideally, a new computation should be made—and if the situation is sufficiently fluid this may simply be impracticable. Again, even when the marketing constraints have been taken account of, and the phase space of the problem duly reduced, the very existence of a unique answer to the problem may itself offend against a hitherto unexpressed constraint.

To quote an actual case: the optimal mix, not of machine loads but of actual products, had been computed by linear programming in order to maximize machine utilization. The solution had the mark of a valuable OR result, namely the pay-off from the study showed an increase in profit of 700 per cent. And yet the solution could not be implemented, for the solution gave with *exactitude* the precise amounts of each product which would have to be made and sold. The commercial manager objected that, although the answer lay within the range of possibility which he himself had laid down, it would in terms of practical marketing prove impossible to sell *precisely* this balance of output. To come near to the result, it is emphasized again, is not necessarily the best policy if the target cannot be exactly hit. That is to say, then, that the solution in this example was not very robust. The reason for all this was that adequate account had not been taken of the environmental facts of the market (although the commercial manager had previously agreed that it had). Moreover, the prospect of uncoupling production from the market by the use of a properly organized and controlled stockholding system for finished goods, which would have resolved the difficulty, had not been investigated. The reason for this in turn was a serious commercial thought block: 'It is not our policy to manufacture for stock'. This fact was 'well-known' to everyone concerned, and in the event it proved impossible to question it—although it most certainly should have been questioned. Thus it comes about that a perfectly satisfactory piece of applied mathematics, entitled linear programming, was not on this occasion a satisfactory treatment of a managerial problem. In other words, it was defective operational research. And the trouble lay in the failure to formulate a good model.

When the matter is studied properly, and a genuine conceptual model of the real-life situation is formulated first, the actual technique of linear programming may prove invaluable in solving the computational problem which the model generates. There is a wealth of difference between trying to 'do a linear programme' on a situation such as this, and finding that in order to calculate a particular answer within the framework of (for example) the neurophysiological model mentioned in the last section, or of a 'systems' model that accounts for the company–market interaction, the technique of linear programming is indispensable. This story illustrates the difference in approach between the applied mathematician and the OR man, and it is not invented: rather too many instances have been observed in actual industrial work.

But, given a sound methodological framework as a setting, the technique of linear programming *is* invaluable. The technique was brought forward here in answer to a particular problem concerning the loading of a production shop. But it should by now be clear from the analysis of the problem that has been given, that the mathematical model *generalizes*. It can handle any equilibrial system of inputs and outputs, in which the allocation of resources to outcomes is permutable under certain constraints, and for which there is a unique criterion of success.

Hence the management of a warehouse can be controlled by the use of exactly this model. Such a warehouse maintains an equilibrium between the goods delivered to it and the goods issued from it; for each class of goods there is a rate of turnover which can be accelerated or decelerated within limits by various devices. The factor that might create the major managerial problem in this case is the price differential from season to season: what is the optimal mix of products, both the cost and the price of which vary from time to time—with a seasonal lag between the two? The model is the same and the technique is the same as the one already discussed. Again, if the problem is to transport goods from an alternative number of origins to an alternative number of destinations at differential rates of transportation charge, the underlying pattern of the decision to be taken is at once recognizable. Again, both the model and the technique are identical. In fact, this technique has been used widely and most lucratively in the coal industry, the electricity industry and the oil industry to solve this very problem. How, for instance, should crude oil from a number of oil fields be transported to a number of refineries to minimize the cost? One British oil company claims to have saved £1,000,000 a year by the use of this method.

And yet the success of such applications may confuse both the managerial and the operational research issues. They seem straightforward. The reason is that the model of such a transportation situation is indeed very straightforward: a simple network linking origins to destinations, plus information about the availability and cost of the requisite shipping. Thus the limelight does not fall on the model, but on the technique. When it comes to transposing the problem from a *given* set of ports and a *given* set of refineries to (say) a retail distribution network, the problem is more difficult. There are many destinations, and many routes to them; there is a variable number of possible warehouses, sited in an infinite number of possible situations—indeed the OR problem may be to find the optimal sites. The model is now all-important; the technique of linear programming is worthless until a homomorphic mapping of this retailing world is found.

2   The Formal Language of Probability

Mathematics, the rigorous language of quantity, provides the operational research scientist with a generalized way of talking about the measurement of his conceptual models in formal terms. In reaching the quantified answer to a particular problem, however, he has to substitute numbers for the letters that stand in the mathematical equations. What are these numbers, and where do they come from? Certainly, each of them is a measurement of some kind. People behave for the most part as if a number, having been measured, must certainly be 'right'. In fact, reflection will show that this claim cannot often be made, and that the circumstances in which it can be made are extremely difficult to define. We can exemplify the possibility: to say that there are three people in the room is to utter what is probably an incontrovertible statement. To enumerate the number of people milling about in a cocktail party, however, is not so easy; one would hardly take offence if told that one's count was in fact mistaken by one or two.

Many of the counts made in industry for managerial purposes, it must be conceded, are probably not exactly right. Moreover, the measurements used by managers for taking decisions are not often straightforward enumerations; they are more likely to measure some kind of average. Thirdly, they may not even pretend to be legitimate averages— only *estimates* of averages. So a particular measurement may turn out to be simply one of a number of estimates we might have obtained; a different answer would be 'right' had we taken a few more instances, or done the measuring on another day. In fact, the comforting solidity of the digits neatly listed in front of the manager collapses under scrutiny. There are many kinds of uncertainty attached to each number, and there is no need for present purposes to identify them all. It is sufficient to recognize that the real truth is something we never apprehend (which is why some people contend that 'real truth' is a chimerical concept altogether): it is always lurking elusively behind the measurements we are able to take. All this adds up to one simple assertion: the quantifiers of real-life situations are *variable*. Since the special circumstances which generate a number are never exactly repeated, never exhaustively enumerated, and never precisely measured, we are not entitled to regard that number as a sharp point on a scale.

It is unfortunately clear that some people do regard managerial data in this fallacious way. They were first educated in a universe of numbers with hard edges: things to be counted, concrete, discrete. It contained sixes that were by no means fives or sevens; those who said the sixes were fives or sevens were told that their answers were wrong. They grew up in this same universe of hard numbers; they knew that a balance had to be struck each night at the bank, and that everyone would be late home if a halfpenny were missing. All this promotes an outlook that is projected into management. A great industrial company will quote the capital tied up in stocks with the same precision: I have seen those big beautiful numbers myself, eight digits long, given to the nearest pound (a concession in itself). Yet the numbers of items in each stockpile have been estimated, multiplied by an estimated average weight per item, and multiplied again by the estimated average value per unit of weight. The company will be lucky if its stocks are evaluated correctly to the second of those eight digits. *Per contra*, managers do not call for the numerical penetration of quantity when they really do need it. For example, they may reject one process or product in favour of another when the difference between the two, though small, is clearly present 'on the average'.

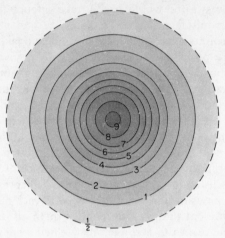

FIGURE 10. The contour map of probability. Associated with the measurement scale at the bottom of the illustration are the zones of likelihood surrounding an estimate of a particular measure. The true figure is most likely to be found in the centre; the chances of finding it further out drop steadily. The contours join points of equal likelihood, and the numbers ascribed to them indicate the relative frequency with which the true figure will lie as far out as the circle shown.

But if the variability of each set of data around its average number is relatively great compared with the small difference between the two average numbers, the decision may be invalid; the difference on which it is based is not statistically significant. Some managers reach this understanding by intuition, but even then they may fail to observe that the significance of this same difference, set within the same framework of variability, changes with the number of items considered. How often does one see tabulations of averages intended for comparison, which have been computed from sets of data containing wildly different numbers of instances, yet there is no mention on the tabulation of what these sample sizes are.

But this is not a dissertation on the proper use of figures; there is another point to be made. Thoughtful managers may well be aware of these difficulties, and resolve to be cautious in making decisions which depend on the precision of the data before them: that is one thing. But it is another thing altogether to use these insights to create a new approach to the problem of measurement, and to the use in decision-taking of the numbers that measurement generates. Figure 10 is a novel picture of a numerical scale, spread comfortably over two dimensions in order to make the point clear. This diagram looks like a contour map. The concentric rings represent zones of likelihood which display information as to where the number sought probably lies. The shading indicates that the *most* likely position is in the 'bull', and that the *least* likely place in which to find this number is on the periphery. This picture faithfully represents the account of measured quantity given above, and may be instantly recognizable as a fair description of the manager's own feeling about the matter. After all, if he were trying to shoot at this 'target' with a ·22 rifle he would mostly score bulls. There would be a rather high score of 'inners'. Very occasionally he might jerk instead of squeezing the trigger, so a few of his shots would fall on the periphery. And so he would say that any one shot would most *probably* hit the bull, or that the chance of scoring an 'outer' has a low *probability*. It is in just this way that concepts of probability derive from concepts of variability; the link is the notion of frequency.

But if this diagram looks like a contour map, we may proceed to treat it as one. A cross-sectional projection of a piece of terrain can be obtained by drawing a line, which positions the cross-section, across the contour map, and by scaling out the profile of the ground underneath. This is done for the contour map of variability in Figure 11. It can be seen that the most probable location of the required number on an ordinary scale of measurement is now represented as being at the 'top of the hill'. From there, the curve slopes away on either side. What does the vertical scale represent? Supposing that the number sought is an estimate of the average value of some variable, then the vertical scale represents the frequency with which the value indicated on the horizontal scale will appear. Obviously, in these circumstances (but not always), the average value is also the most typical value, which is to say the value most often encountered. Values close to this average on either side will appear with a lower, but still relatively high, frequency. As we move further and

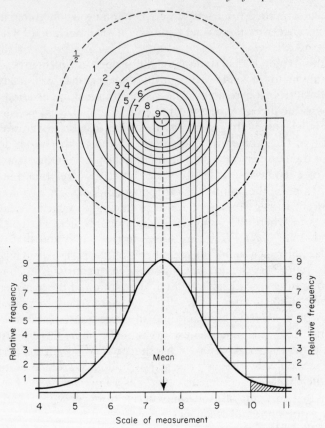

FIGURE 11. Projection of the contour map of probability on to
an appropriate scale of measurement. This 'hill' is a probability
distribution. NB. the proportion of the shaded area to the whole
area under the curve measures the chance of exceeding the
value 10.

further away from the mean, the values are less and less frequently
encountered.

   The picture obtained is, nowadays, familiar to many managers. It is in
fact a picture of a probability distribution. It is *certain* that the number
required lies somewhere under this curve; this is guaranteed by the fact
that the two tails never quite reach a zero frequency of occurrence—they
spread out infinitely on either side. This means to say there is always a
finite chance, however low, of encountering a ridiculously atypical value,
however freakish. (In practice, however, the chance of encountering an

extreme value at a really great distance from the mean is so remote that it can be virtually ignored. Indeed, there are often physical limits which cut off the long tails given in the theory.) Now if the number sought certainly lies under this curve, the probability that it does so is unity. Then it is possible to *measure* the probability that the number sought is actually greater than any given number. For example, it may be important to the decision-taker to know that 'on the average' the value with which he is dealing is $7 \cdot 5$; but it may be even more important to know in this case what the chances are that on any particular occasion the value will turn out to be 10 or greater. So we cut off the right-hand tail of this distribution at the value 10, and compare the area under the curve to the right of this division with the area of the whole. It is transparently clear that the ratio of these two areas measures the chance that any random occurrence of this event will have a value greater than 10.

If this curve is, as was alleged, so familiar nowadays, it may be thought impertinent to have engaged in this lengthy account of its nature. Forgiveness is sought as appropriate. In consulting with managers, however, it has been noticed that a use of distributions does not always guarantee an understanding of the nature of variability, nor of the way in which this in turn entails the concept of probability. The next object is to dispose of a clear-cut misunderstanding, which is this. Some people would say: on the one hand measurements may be taken to produce data which are correct; on the other hand some of the things we would like to measure keep recurring with slightly different values, so not one number but a spread of numbers must be considered. This is an incorrect, dislocated visualization of the matter. A better account would say that nature is mutable; every facet of the real world is quantified, but the attempt to label each variable with a unique number is incompetent and can only lead to misapprehensions. For one thing, what is measured may change; for another, our sample may be inadequate; for another, our measuring apparatus will not be 'perfect'. Most of the things we wish to measure may, for a large variety of different reasons, assume from time to time one of a range of possible values; in this case it is important to nominate that range, and to quantify each value within it by the probability of that value's occurrence.

Fortunately, it is not necessary to undertake fundamental research into the precise shape of this contour map and its associated topography in every instance of industrial measurement. Mathematical statistics has developed a codified way of describing the kinds of probability distributions which are most frequently encountered. The mathematical characteristics are known also; this means that we can readily write down probabilistic statements about chance and risk in a rigorous form. For example, it was said just now that the chance of a random value's exceeding 10 for the case depicted in Figure 7 would be given by calculating the proportion of the tail greater than 10 to the whole area under the curve. This can be done if a way can be found rigorously to compute the area enclosed in the tail. The expression to be evaluated is:

$$\phi(x) = \frac{1}{\sqrt{2\pi}\,\sigma} \int_{10}^{\infty} e^{-\frac{(x-\mu)^2}{2\sigma^2}}\, dx$$

When the number given by this equation has been calculated, the proportion it bears to unity is the probability of a randomly selected sample from this distribution having a value greater than 10.

This presentation illustrates incidentally how science should be put forward to the manager. The *principle* is easy to understand. The *theory* is necessarily complicated and difficult to understand—as that equation shows. Yet the *calculation* is easy again, because one can have a whole range of values tabulated for an expression of this kind. The manager, then, should be enabled to examine the bases and to obtain the outcomes of science with ease. And he should be given the hard science in between 'for the record', and perhaps for verification by other specialists. In a report such equations, and other formalizations such as are scattered through this chapter, would be found in technical appendices.

Now this particular curve, for which the integral has just been quoted, is the Gaussian or normal curve. It is encountered a great deal in nature, and in industrial and commercial activities too, for these after all are part of nature. But there are other varieties of curve, of equal importance to the Gaussian, with which any good introductory textbook on statistics will acquaint the reader. Suffice it to say, for present purposes, that many probability distributions are not symmetrical—and would not be expected to be so. For example, the distribution of the probability of making defective items in a plant will have its peak (the mode) well to the left of centre. The object is, after all, to make zero defectives; moreover, one cannot possibly make fewer defectives than that. Consequently, there is an expectation that the distribution will start on the left with a high probability of making zero defectives, a somewhat higher probability of making a few (and this produces the peak), followed by the usual tailing away to the right as the number of defectives increases and the probability of making that number decreases.

Mathematics is used in operational research because it knows how to handle the number of things; or it may suppress this raw number, and coalesce the things into groups (or somewhat differently into sets), going on to discuss *their* number. It knows how to relate these numbers and discuss their modes and rates of change. The subtlety of the subject does of course enable the scientist to undertake the investigation of such things without knowing what the numbers actually are. Algebras permit us to discuss them as generalities, and to solve a management problem subsequently by associating with those generalizations actual numbers, which are business and industrial data, at the moment when managers wish to know what the numerical answer really is. The building block of the mathematical language is really x, and the kind of problem discussed in the last section may be resolved because x is the number of machines (count them—there are seven), or x is the profit in March (ask the bank—it is £100,000), or x is the number of refineries to which oil must be shipped (add them up—there are eighteen).

But the building block of statistics is a *distributed x*. This is not just a number, but a range of numbers to which various levels of probability are ascribed. Armed with this concept, operational research is enabled to discuss those things that are clearly quantified, but to which no actual number can, equally clearly, be firmly attributed. For the manufacturer of a machine to quote a delivery promise, for instance, it will be necessary to know how long it will take to obtain all the components and to put them together. We want a collection of numbers, but what these numbers *are* will not be known until the machine has been dispatched. To do the planning, unfortunately, the numbers are required *now*. Eventually when it is much too late, we shall know that one of these numbers, for example, is (say) 17. At this moment, however, we may know that the most likely value of this number is 15. It would clearly be unwise to use this number and hope for the best—in the event the prediction will be falsified. But if we compute with probabilities, if the calculation ranges experimentally over all the values which this x could take, from the very lowest to the very highest value, computing in passing the probability of encountering each of the values between them, then obviously a better insight into the forecast will be obtainable. It will prove possible to obtain the limits within which the final answer is likely to range, and also to state the probabilities of missing the target date by any given time. This at once reveals the extent of the liability for missing the target date which the management can afford to accept (for example, in agreeing penalty clauses); it shows, when a number of forecasts for order deliveries are amalgamated into a production programme, how much slack ought to be allowed to encompass the risk that individual target dates will not be met; it shows, in a word, what the *vulnerability* of the production policy is.

The division of the quantitative aspects of a managerial decision or policy into determinate and probabilistic elements is important, but not often undertaken by managers. They seem to regard the situation with which they are dealing as predictable in principle, but likely to 'go wrong'. But if the whole situation is properly analysed, a clear picture is obtained of which elements are, or can be, determined, and which elements are susceptible to chance and in precisely what way; then the interaction between these two can be computed.

The theory of probability, which is central to this undertaking, is a full-scale subject in its own right. All competent OR men know something about it; all competent OR groups contain mathematical statisticians. But it is not an easy subject and there is no space here to go much further with the exposition. For, despite the existence of a vast range of mathematical statistical techniques, dilemmas still exist at the level of philosophy of science. No secret can be made of the fact that eminent statisticians disagree about the fundamental nature of probability and how to compute it. None the less, science has a great deal to offer the decision-taker in considering the impact of chance and risk. For the plain fact is that the man who has not studied these matters, but who works on an intuitive notion of what is likely, will often mislead himself quite wildly. There are, it may be suspected, biological reasons why this is so. The manager is not pure intellect; he is a living organism, and his basic impressions about chance and risk are derived inevitably from his need to survive as an animal. These impressions are not necessarily at all relevant to his profession as decision-taker.

For example, to take a straightforward situation, there are twenty-three people sitting in a room. What are the chances that two of them have the same birthday? (This is meant in the usual sense; it does not relate to the year of birth, but to the day and the month.) Most people 'feel' that this probability is exceedingly low. 'One in a million', people say; or 'there is not a cat in hell's chance'. In fact, the chances are better than evens. That is to say, if you made a bet that two people in the room had the same birthday whenever you saw twenty-three people gathered together, you would make a profit in the long run. If ninety people are present, the probability is not one-in-four, but virtual certainty. Even scientists familiar with probability calculations were surprised when Professor William Feller produced this example.

And so it behoves the manager to base his decisions on quantified assessments of outcomes, which are compounded of determinate and probabilistic estimates. Tools are available for handling each of these component factors. Mathematics is competent to build great edifices of quantities, showing the connectivity between aspects of the situation; statistics is competent to enrich this architecture with its calculations about chance and risk. Certainly the manager can employ a mathematician or a statistician (or both), and ask them to investigate a particular situation using these tools. But because of the arguments which have been advanced at considerable length in this book, these men may fail to understand the nature of the situation with which they are dealing —the fundamental character of the system which causes it to behave as it does. It is better to tackle the matter through operational research. The balanced, interdisciplinary OR team will examine that situation and that system, create a conceptual model of it by the use of scientific insights, and will *then* set about the task of constructing a rigorous model—by the use of those same tools which have been described in this and the foregoing section.

In short, what was said of the use of mathematics in OR applies also to the use of statistics in OR. This section is, after all, about a formal language which is, strictly speaking, a sub-language of mathematics itself—no wonder the same considerations apply. There are two reasons for discussing it separately, none the less. First, by no means all mathematicians are fully competent in statistics: a fact which should be known and borne in mind by both OR leaders and the managers they serve. Second, the topic with which mathematical statistics grapples is that of probability—a topic of peculiar importance to managers. This is because it underlies *every one* of his problems. If this were not so, the problem factors and their magnitudes would be known with certitude, the answer would be definite and incontrovertible, and there would not exist a problem any longer. Managers are needed because their zone of responsibility is subjected to chance and risk; in modelling such a situation the fact of variability must invoke the concept of probability. Statistics is the formal language for quantifying that concept with rigour.

3   The Formal Language of Quality

The appropriateness of discussing mathematics and statistics before turning to logic is dictated by a quirk in the syllabus under which scientists are trained. Few of them get round to a study of formal logic. From a more objective point of view, however, it would be proper to start with this subject. It offers a rigorous way of discussing the structural relationships of a language—and therefore of the realities which may be mapped on to that language. It seems reasonable to say that this qualitative application of rigour is methodologically prior to the rigorous treatment of quantity in the arithmetic sense. Logic indeed sets the stage for measurement, with its own special way of handling quantity through the distinction it draws between general and restricted cases: the 'all' and the 'some'—known as universal and particular quantifiers.

What counts as a coherent statement, what implies it and what it entails, whether an argument or demonstration compounded from such statements is valid and can support the conclusions it purports to maintain—these are all questions of logic. It is surely absurd to discuss the quantification by number of these statements and arguments unless they are themselves first recognized as competent. But, although the whole of life demands a minimal competence in the handling of such matters, few scientists go so far as to acquire a command of the formal techniques which sustain them. In fact, the subject of formal logic is an *arts* subject. Pedagogically, this strikes someone who is not a pedagogue as an aberration. From the point of view of operational research, there is a crying need to include a trained logician in the interdisciplinary team.

The role of formal logic in helping to supply the rigorous statement of a scientific model will be exemplified from two cases, one military and one industrial, previously unpublished. Again an opportunity will be made to show that there may well be an underlying formal identity between two utterly different problem situations.

The military situation is this. There is no war, but there does exist a complicated and dangerous political situation beset with the risk of uprisings on the part of various interested parties. A strange assortment of military and quasi-military detachments is responsible for law and order. They come under various different authorities. There is doubt about the loyalty of some of them (for example, one might suddenly decide to throw in its lot with an interested party). The efficiency and reliability of these forces covers the whole gamut from 'crack troops', to 'organized rabble'. Some of the detachments, although nominally accountable to the centre, are legally autonomous, and may do unexpected things. Communications are precarious: whole areas are sometimes cut off for days (in places the knowledge of radio arrangements is of the sketchiest kind). The situation deserves the adjective Gilbertian.

The orthodox military model used to study a situation such as this is, of course, a map—an ordinary, geographical, map. Locations are marked, and many conventions (flags, coloured pins, chalked lines) depict the state of affairs. Although one must confess that this is a homomorphic mapping of the terrain, the model is not homomorphic with the *operational facts*. The main reason is that the distances indicated are measured uniformly against a rigid grid. But what is interesting to a commander about such distances is not their absolute length. He wants to know how long it will take for a given detachment to move and to provide cover for a new area. This depends on a variety of probabilistic factors, as well as the determinate distance between the present and the intended sites and the determinate nature and size of the detachment. For example: its speed of advance has a range—which is weighted by a probability distribution. There is a finite probability that the detachment will simply not get there, and it matters very much what hostility, if any, is encountered on the way.

The orthodox model, which can itself be manipulated by mathematical techniques (the measurement of distances, the calculation of rates of change) had therefore to be redeveloped to meet operational needs. A probabilistic model was superimposed on the topographical model and its invariant quantities. This attributed statistical numbers to the terrain; it loaded all the determinate factors with measures of chance and risk. This effectively compressed and stretched the orthodox map, as if it had been printed on a sheet of elastic material. Using this more sophisticated model, it became possible to define a new sort of measure— that of 'coverage', a rather complicated statistic expressing the ability of a particular detachment in a particular place to give cover to some other nominated area. The use of this concept meant that a maximum time had to be fixed within which the forces of law and order had to arrive at a potential trouble spot (and the time allowed depended on the nature of the potential trouble). It also meant fixing an acceptable probability that the arrival occur within this time; for, once probabilities are invoked, there is always a finite chance that the detachment will *not* arrive in time, however long the delay that is allowed. The (elastic) distance reached for the probability fixed was called in this work the 'threshold of coverage'.

When any military activity of any sort occurred, it at once became impossible to know for certain what was actually happening—because of the feeble communications. (The OR scientist found himself contemplating conceptual models based on the Indeterminary Principle.) It was therefore necessary to amass such information as was available, to assess this within the framework of the 'coverage' model, and to infer such consequences as one could. Here is an example, based on an actual incident, to show what is meant.

There has been some kind of trouble, but no detachment, in Town *B8*. Five detachments were originally within threshold cover (as defined) of Town *B8*, which they encircled. According to the plan, one or more of these detachments should by now have entered the town. Communications with headquarters from this operational zone have broken down, but it is assumed that the five detachments can communicate with each other—if only by messenger. Their instructions are clear. A detachment asked to move on request from the authorities of such a town as *B8*, must do so if, and only if, its present location is within threshold cover of an adjacent detachment. (Initially, of course, the detachments were sited to guarantee this condition, but there may have been movements by now.) It follows that:

> *If all detachments that have gone to Town* B8 *have threshold cover from an adjacent detachment for the zone previously under surveillance, then some detachments have not gone to Town* B8.   (1)

Now if any one detachment has wrongly moved towards Town *B8 without* threshold cover for its zone (and this has happened before), the situation must have been remedied. For the rules provide for this situation by stating that *adjacent* detachments will continually check on their threshold coverage. It follows that the detachment adjacent to the defaulter will discover its default, and will then move in closer to the centre of the ring and close the gap, or it will call on the adjacent detachment in the network *behind* it to help provide new coverage facilities. Unfortunately, experience has already indicated a flaw in this plan. If the authorities in a town such as *B8* send out a general alarm, then *all* the detachments near to it on each side may begin to converge on the town. This produces chaos, because each detachment is relying on its adjacent detachment to cope with its absence, whereas no adjacent detachment is present either to do so *or* to provide the countercheck. Hence:

> *Either all detachments have gone to Town* B8 *or all detachments have threshold cover from an adjacent detachment for the zone previously under surveillance.*   (2)

In fact, if a general alarm went out, then all detachments which had threshold cover ought to have gone to Town *B8*. The suspicion is that some detachments without that cover may have gone too. So:

> *If all detachments that have threshold cover have gone to Town* B8, *then some detachments that have not got threshold cover have also gone to B8.*   (3)

The question is, does this follow? For if it does follow, there is by now something very wrong with the internal security of this neighbourhood. Now it seems that even when there are only three elements in the situation, as there are here, it is well-nigh impossible for the unaided mind to decide whether the conclusion (3) follows from the premises (1) and (2) or not. This, then, is the type of argument that can be examined by formal logic. There is still the same old x in the situation; this time it stands for a possible detachment. There are three 'schemata of x' (as there might be three functions of x in a piece of mathematics). These are: Fx (meaning that x is a detachment), Gx (meaning that x has gone to Town $B8$), and Hx (meaning that x has threshold cover from an adjacent detachment for the zone previously under surveillance). The algebra of the propositional calculus of logic is now used to link these schemata in order to restate the three propositions in a way which unambiguously expresses their meaning. As in the last two sections, they are written down here to show what this rigorous language looks like. (x) is the universal and $(\exists x)$ the particular quantifier; $\supset$ signifies implication; $\sim$ negates the following schema; $\vee$ signifies disjunction (either . . . or); the dot (.) betokens conjunction (. . . and . . .).

$$(x)(Fx . Gx : \supset Hx) \supset (\exists x)(Fx . \sim Gx) \tag{1}$$
$$(x)(Fx \supset Gx) \vee (x)(Fx \supset Hx) \tag{2}$$
$$(x)(Fx . Hx : \supset Gx) \supset (\exists x)(Fx . \sim Hx . Gx) \tag{3}$$

To find out whether the first two propositions jointly imply the third requires a formal test of the supposed implication. The analysis is not given here, but the point that must be taken is that no *thinking* process is now undertaken. Instead, algebraic rules are applied. The argument is first reduced to its simplest form, by appealing to logical theorems whose function is the same as those met with in Euclid. Then this formulation is subjected to a truth-value analysis which determines algebraically whether the implication holds. In this case it does. Something has been proved.

On a question of practicability, it should not be thought that the object here was to supply the military men with a 'logical slide-rule' by which, in the course of an engagement, to determine decisions. This point must be made clear, because any such notion must surely appear unreal. The objects were to investigate the plans that had been made, to test their good sense, to uncover weaknesses and to probe in retrospect actual incidents which in fact led to chaos. The example quoted is based on one such incident; even then it is not completely factual, for real problems are more complicated than this. And so the story has been condensed to fit a standard logical format—due to Professor Quine—

which well demonstrates that a problem in no more than three schemata of x is not easy to resolve without the proper tools.

The second problem to be discussed was tackled exactly five years after the military one just described. The same OR scientist was then to be found in an alloy steelworks in Britain, investigating the flow of steel ingots from three different melting-shops through varying selections of eleven different processes—the last being a rolling mill. Of the remaining processes, five were concerned with cooling (for highly alloyed steel must be cooled under controlled conditions to achieve a variety of metallurgical effects), and two with surface preparation prior to rolling; one was a stock-yard for cold material and two were concerned with heating prior to rolling.

A model was developed to account for this situation. Conceptually this too begins with a topographical layout, for the processes are related chronologically, and the flow of material covers actual terrain. But of course a mapping of geographical features is almost irrelevant. Once again we find that a perfectly good homomorph of the layout is not homomorphic with the operational facts. Instead, the important thing to realize is that we are confronted by an interactive system that is *zero-sum*.

This term means that if the system is disturbed, and in this case if products are routed to alternative pieces of plant, the sum total of all these changes is nothing at all. Take five ingots from A and put them in B; take seven ingots from C, putting two in A, one in B and four in D; put three ingots from B into C. Process A now has three less ingots than before and process B three more; process C has seven less and process D seven more. Everything is different: but $3 - 3 - 7 + 7 = 0$. Not all systems operate in this way (a warren of rabbits for instance), but systems that are zero-sum have interesting properties.

If more ingots arrive at one process than this process can accommodate, the extra ingots do not vanish. To preserve the zero-sum constant they have to appear somewhere else. In many circumstances, a machine shop or an office, for example, the extra work piles up in front of its next process, forming a stock or a queue. But when hot ingots of highly alloyed steel are involved this will not do. If they are allowed to cool in air they will pass too rapidly through a critical temperature range, and crack. So these ingots have to be put into another process. Even if the delay is too short or the steel is not highly alloyed (so that some delay in air can be tolerated), the situation is not a neutral one, for the ingots are losing heat, and the effect will be felt later—when they take longer to reheat to a uniform rolling temperature.

Now the steelmaking business would be uneconomical if a system of this kind had much 'slack' in it. This means that the process immediately in front of the rolling mill, through which all ingots must pass, is congested. It also means that when an ingot destined for this process has to wait, which happens often, it must go somewhere else—where it adds to the congestion. *And so on.* However, actual ingots are not allowed to trail around a works like so many frustrated passengers being shepherded round an air terminal. What moves around is *information*: statements about ingots and about processes, proposals and counter proposals, instructions and countermanded instructions. All this happens at a fairly low organizational level. If a serious alteration to plan is contemplated, it will be referred to the shift manager. The OR man, actually measuring the impact of one such change in the course of a night shift, recorded the manager as making twenty-eight telephone calls around the works in order to sort out the repercussions of that change; this gives an indication of the size of the repercussive effect. But no managerial intervention is called for in normal running—only the repercussive effect exists. How can this be investigated?

The conceptual model of this situation was taken from the science of acoustics. According to the analogy set up, a disturbance of the kind described sets up a 'noise' which reverberates round the eleven processes, and finally dies away. This reverberation may be measured according to the amount of re-routeing it causes at each point; the length of the reverberation will be affected by the occupancy of each process, for this determines its ability to absorb, or necessity to reflect, the noise. These two measures take the place of the sound intensities and absorption coefficients found in acoustical science, and facilitate the statement of a homomorphic model for this steelworks of an acoustic situation.

When this model is understood, the usual advantages accrue. It now makes sense to devise a reverberation constant, for example, and to work out the effects of changes in the control system which might reduce it. It is also clear that acoustical chaos supervenes when a succession of sounds fails to reach the acoustically steady state, for the reverberation of the first sound persists while the next sound occurs—they overlap. Equally, industrial chaos supervenes when the reverberating information from one process change is overtaken by the next. So a measurable criterion of stability begins to emerge. Moreover, we can as usual make use of the insights of the scientific model within the managerial situation by importing acoustical laws into the homomorphism. For example, we know that reverberation increases and decays logarithmically, with a steady state period in between during which the rate of emission and the rate of absorption are in balance. This produces the peculiar curve shown in Figure 12. Industrially, as acoustically, irregularities in the situation mean that this curve is not exactly followed; but we do know the basic pattern to seek.

This is not, however, the full story of an OR job; we must return to the use of logic as a formal language. When an ingot arrives at the penultimate process it may be accepted or diverted. Its arrival 'makes a noise'. If it is diverted, the noise reverberates. If it is accepted, the noise *may* be totally absorbed (for instance, if there is plenty of capacity available in the process), or it may yet reverberate—by interfering with the arrival of the next noise. This, then, is a *reverberating ingot*: one whose

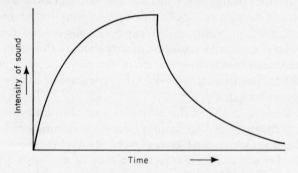

FIGURE 12. The pattern of reverberation.

arrival noise is not totally absorbed by the receiving process. No steelmaker would know this term, of course; it is special to this study.

The next special concept required is that of a *harmless ingot*, another term unknown to steelmakers. This is defined as follows. The penultimate process is a soaking pit: a special kind of furnace in which ingots, already hot, are 'soaked' in heat sufficiently long to give them a homogeneous temperature ready for rolling. The optimal soaking time had already been established by statistical studies of considerable elaborateness. An ingot which turns out to need no more than this time in the pits is designated harmless. An ingot which has to remain in the pits longer than this is harmful, because it causes a strange local effect different from reverberation. This is that ingots already withdrawn from the previous process are held up 'on the track' between the two processes—where, it is known, some of them crack as a result of being delayed too long at ambient temperatures.

What was actually happening on this track was not at all clear until the probability distribution of delay (the 'track time') had been evolved —a study that proved inordinately difficult. This most unusual probability distribution, unlike any other the scientist had ever encountered, was compressed, skewed and truncated, and had to be explained. Four factors accounted for it. First was the back-pressure from the pits just mentioned. Second was a special forward-pressure from the previous process deriving from surges in the flow of ingots caused ultimately by the 'bunching' of steel furnaces (that is, their propensity to tap co-incidentally). This was difficult to sort out, too, because there were three separate melting-shops using four different steelmaking processes. Third was a metallurgical instruction ruling that a given track time must not be exceeded because of the danger of cracking. Fourth came the effects on the records of clerical efforts to show that the ruling had been obeyed when it had not.

Now a harmful ingot in the pits would make this situation on the track worse, and could provoke a special delay causing a cracked ingot. Therefore measures had been taken to direct any apparently cool ingot into preheating furnaces *before* sending them to the soaking pits. But this had to be done at the cost of heat—which naturally set up ambivalent feelings in the management. Economic pressures suggested that everything should be direct charged to the pits; metallurgical pressures suggested that any ingot suspected of having been cooled somewhat should be routed via preheating. Everyone claimed that the metallurgical rules were obeyed; but cracking continued.

> *If all reverberating ingots that are direct charged to the pits are harmless, some reverberating ingots are not direct charged to the pits.* (1)

The truth of this proposition is clear, because reverberatory effects are being picked up—and a harmless ingot does not reverberate at all. If that condition of being harmless is not in fact being met, however, it is quite possible that all reverberation emanates from direct charged ingots. The economic pressure referred to means that the pre-heaters are not desperately congested: they may not reflect noise at all. Either this is true or all the harmful ingots are non-reverberating. For a control policy for reverberating ingots which makes free (that is, possibly uneconomic) decisions about their routeing will render them harmless. This is known, because in every trial of this freely mixed strategy no single ingot ever exceeded the optimal soaking time. Hence:

> *Either all reverberating ingots are direct charged to the pits, or all reverberating ingots are harmless.* (2)

What is the management trying to do? It is trying to save heat, and it would therefore wish to charge all harmless reverberating ingots directly to the pits, and route only potentially harmful ones through the pre-heaters thereby rendering them harmless too. But we begin to see that this is not possible within the existing situation:

> *Even if all reverberating ingots that are harmless have been direct charged to the pits, then some reverberating ingots that are not harmless have also been direct charged to the pits.*   (3)

This has been a difficult argument to present. It is hard to follow the establishment of premises (1) and (2), because the two concepts of reverberating and harmless ingots are elaborate ideas, and because the real-life situation is intensely complicated. So the possibility of feeling certain that (3), the conclusion, really follows is remote—without the use of formal logic.

The variable x this time stands for some ingot. Once again there are three schemata of x: Fx (meaning that x is a reverberating ingot), Gx (meaning that x is direct charged to the pits), and Hx (meaning that x is harmless). Again the propositional calculus will show that the conclusion is correct. For the record, this is what the three propositions look like in formal Quinean terms and employing those schemata:

$$(x)(Fx \cdot Gx : \supset Hx) \supset (\exists x)(Fx \cdot \sim Gx) \tag{1}$$

$$(x)(Fx \supset Gx) \vee (x)(Fx \supset Hx) \tag{2}$$

$$(x)(Fx \cdot Hx : \supset Gx) \supset (\exists x)(Fx \cdot \sim Hx \cdot Gx) \tag{3}$$

As before, the argument has been simplified and expressed in a slightly different way from that originally used. But this was indeed one of the logical investigations made of a quantified acoustical model in order to reach a managerial decision. (This was, incidentally, acted upon—with full success.)

It is worth comparing the two examples given, the military and the industrial, as the comparison throws a good deal of light on the nature of management science. In both examples there was a determinate and a probabilistic component of the situation. Neither model has been fully explained here, but the size of military detachment was analogous to the size of lots of ingots, and both examples were basically concerned with movements of these detachments or lots. In each case the speed with which anything arrived anywhere could be expressed only as a probability distribution. In each case, there was a finite probability of non-arrival (in the steelworks, the chance of making an unsaleable misfit cast or of rejecting a cracked ingot was measured). Above all, there is a resemblance in the fact that decisions have to be taken on incomplete information. This is the more important because it is not often realized and is often denied.

It simply is not true either that you can find out anything you want to know in industry, or that you absolutely cannot find out anything you want to know in war. As far as industry is concerned, situations change in the process of being measured (a model of which circumstance is readily available in quantum mechanics); information is slanted or frankly wrong; some things (like the reverberation effects) are hidden from observation and have to be inferred. Above all: gathering really deep, detailed and exhaustive information can be absurdly expensive. As far as warfare is concerned, any particular fact about a military enemy *can* usually be discovered if the price can be afforded—in money, trouble, time and men.

And so scientific enquiry, although it necessarily requires data, must make good use of what data it collects—inferential as well as direct use. The framework of the model helps vitally in this. In the military example, an initially orthodox topographical model (the map) had to be enriched by a special elastic geometry before any sort of homomorph could be understood. In the industrial example, an initially orthodox flow chart had to be enriched by a model from acoustics, for the same reason. In both cases, these conceptual models led to the identification of sophisti- cated and previously unrecognized concepts (thresholds of coverage and reverberating ingots), which could then be measured and manipulated. In each case, too, all three formal languages of science were used to express the scientific model in rigorous terms—although the logical language alone has been discussed here.

Finally, then, turning to the formal logic, one wonders whether the reader has noticed the trick played on him. In each case it was remarked that the presentation had been adjusted to fit a standard logical format. In fact, the logical structures of the military and civil arguments are identical with each other, as can be verified by examining the two sets of algebraic propositions. Needless to say this did not happen by co- incidence, nor would it have been important if it had. The trick was done to re-emphasize that situations are subject to laws which pertain as well to the field of decision-taking and control as to the physical universe, and that these laws 'are conceptual devices by which we organize our empiri- cal knowledge and predict the future'. That is what makes them useful.

9

A WALK IN THE RAMIFIED SYSTEM

Ita vita est hominum, quasi cum ludas tesseris;
Si illud quod maxime opus est jactu non cadit,
Illud, quod cecidit forte, id arte ut corrigas.

As when you play with dice, so is the life of men.
If that which you most need to throw does not fall,
then you should set right by skill the lot which has
    fallen by chance.

TERENCE (195–159 B.C.) in *Adelphi*

1   The Building-Block of Planned Chance

However vigorously the manager *qua* policy-maker sets about the task of determining events, the manager *qua* decision-taker is a professional manipulator of chance effects. Although he has determined the general pattern of his activity, the stimuli which assail him and call for response are randomly assorted. This is, in a lambent clause taken from a works' report of happy memory, 'owing to the day-to-day nature of actual events'. The manager sees what the fellow means.

In the quotation provided above, Terence forthrightly asserts a major aspect of the management task. A less literal interpretation was set upon the words by Raphe Robynson, when he quoted them in an introduction to the second edition of (Sir and Saint) Thomas More's *Utopia*, which Robynson had first translated from the Latin in 1551. This Tudor scholar lived in difficult and far from Utopian times—as do we; he favoured a more cynical account than the words of Terence strictly warrant—and so may we. His explanation runs: 'meanynge therein, if that chaunce rise not, whiche is most for the plaiers advauntage, that then the chaunce, which furtune hathe sent, ought so connyngly to be played, as may be to the plaier least dammage'.

Whether we seek to amend things when chance upsets the plan, or simply to 'get out from under' as Robynson would have it, we need a right approach. To the martinet, life 'must' abide by the plan. But the influence of the manager does not extend to the control of *force majeur* —it may not even cope with the foreman. A viable plan has to recognize the role of chance, and the manager who is not neurotic knows this. It is commonplace to say that therefore the plan must be flexible, and also to say that decisions should therefore be taken (or at least revised) sequentially. But it is not trivial to assert that chance is an intrinsic part of the plan, and necessary to it. In fact, entertaining genetic models (for genetics is about evolutionary plans) leads to a conviction that planning cannot be adaptive to changing conditions unless random mutations are included in the plan. According to this view, the manager is not the opponent of chance, but its collaborator. This is well understood by diplomats, politicians and perhaps big-businessmen; that is because they deal with men and events. The manager, whose decisions also largely involve things, does not think of himself as manipulating malice in the object—which is insensate, unresponsive—but he might well begin to do so: he needs to undertake engineering in probabilities.

To do this he may employ the conceptual system which will be outlined, with its applications, in this chapter. It begins by walking out on to the shop floor and confronting the first down-to-earth, hard fact that is encountered. Suppose that this is a production machine operating in a simple environment. This machine makes things, and takes on the average five hours to do so. Its total product is passed on to the next machine, which also takes on the average five hours to complete the next process. Machine *B* receives no other raw materials than the product of machine *A*, and since the two machines stand side by side no time at all is consumed in transportation. A naive account of this process declares: this is a perfectly balanced situation, there need be no idle time on these machines and there is no need for any inter-process stock. Now of course this 'on the average' talk will not do—as the man discovered who was drowned while crossing a stream of average depth 4 feet. Individual process times will be *distributed* around the mean of five hours. If the situation is as well-behaved as it appears, a scientific account of it will show that process times around the mean are those most frequently encountered; the risk of encountering a particularly bad time decreases the worse the time is, while the chance of encountering a particularly good time decreases the better the time is. Very occasionally, say, an especially favourable combination of circumstances arises, and the job is completed in three hours. Very occasionally also, a concatenation of unfortunate circumstances will conspire to make the job last as long as eight hours.

In short, for each of these machines, the time taken to do a job may be viewed as a spectrum of likelihood centred on the mean, and the attendant distribution of frequencies can be drawn (see Figure 11). In the present case, however, it will be noted that the distribution will not be symmetrical: the tail on the right will be longer than that on the left. Even so, an examination of past records will reveal what the distribution is in each case; it is no surprise to learn that statistical ingenuity can encompass this situation. In short, the probability of any particular occurrence can be measured. But to know what is really happening in this basic production situation, more than this is needed, for it is the *interaction* between the two processes that is managerially important. So time must come into the story. Suppose that a job is done on machine *A*; there is no means of knowing how long it will take (we are not fortunetellers), but we do know that this time will be a member of the population of times outlined by the distribution. The completed job is passed, at the end of this time, to machine *B*, which will now process it. The time *this* job takes is independent of the time taken on machine *A* (let us say—it need not be so). Again, there is no means of knowing what this time will be, other than to say that it is a member of the population of times depicted by the *B* distribution. This dynamic situation is illustrated in Figure 13. Here are the two distributions, dynamically connected by the transfer of two specimen jobs from *A* to *B*.

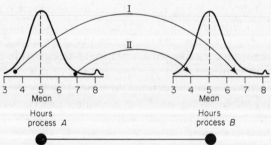

FIGURE 13. The building-block of planned chance. Here is shown the stochastic interaction between two processes having the same mean duration and the same pattern of probability. An infinitely long queue of work will be generated in front of the second process. The symbol underneath shows how this stochastic interaction is represented in subsequent diagrams.

Consider transfer I. The two machines start work together; *A* is lucky and takes three and a half hours to complete its job; *B* is unlucky and takes six and a half hours. Hence, when the operator of machine *A* hands his piece to the operator of machine *B*, he will not be ready for it. In fact, the piece will lie on the table between the two machines for three hours. This begins the formation of a queue. For, if by chance precisely the same thing happens next time, a second piece will join the queue at precisely the moment when the second operator picks up the first piece. If the same thing were to happen *again*, there would be two items in the queue three hours before *B* finished his second job.

Now consider the second sample transfer. *A* takes seven hours, by chance, to complete his first job. But *B* has been lucky and has taken only four hours to complete his. On this occasion, then, *B* will have nothing to do for three hours—until *A* completes his work. If this situation were to repeat itself several times in succession, *B* would enjoy three hours with nothing to do in every seven.

In practice, these runs of arbitrary couplings do not often occur. As a matter of fact, we can measure the probability that they might. If there is 1 chance in 100 that the extreme item we have considered should occur on machine *A*, and also that it should occur independently on machine *B*, then the probability that this *couple* will occur is the multiplicand of the two probabilities—namely, 1 chance in 10,000. To find the probability that this same couple would occur three times in succession, we should raise the probability of the couple to the power three. The answer is 10^{12}, or 1 chance in 1,000,000,000,000. It is clear that the manager need not worry very much about these particular risks. On the other hand, *something* must happen each time and there is no means of knowing what it will be. It might add to the queue of material between the machines; or it might suddenly cause idle time on machine *B*.

Now it should be fairly obvious that although no particular event can be forecast in this situation, it must be possible to say something about the dynamic interaction of the two machines. It is in fact possible to calculate, by the use of mathematical statistics, the extent to which this queue will grow, and at what rate. In the case quoted, it is clear that although idle time may be encountered on machine *B* for a certain period of continuous working, the chances that a queue will eventually begin to form are very real. Once the queue does begin to form, the likelihood that *B* will ever catch up becomes increasingly remote, because it would have to engage in a very long run of unlikely couples—the chances of which, as we have seen, get very rapidly more remote as time proceeds. This thoroughly basic situation is so important in operational research as applied to dynamic systems that a whole branch of mathematical statistics, known as *queue theory*, has been developed round it. One of the first results developed by this theory was to show that, in the conditions we have been examining, which is to say where the mean times are equal, the queue will eventually become *infinitely* long. This account has tried to reveal why this is so, but the result was, in its day, most unexpected. At the start of this story it was said that, naïvely, the production situation appeared 'in balance'. Surely this was intended to convey that a fairly satisfactory arrangement existed. Did we, in all honesty, at once suspect that the situation was foredoomed to run completely out of control? Most people do not; indeed our ways of accounting in terms of numerical averages precondition us to believe that this situation is all right.

Queue theory, it was said, accounts for the formation of queues in this way between a probabilistic supply and a probabilistic demand. On occasion, as has been shown, idle time is caused on machine *B*; one can see the sense in which this could be described as the formation of a *negative* queue. In the positive case, a collection of items forms on the table between *A* and *B*; in the negative case, a kind of vacuum is created on the table—a vacuum which seeks to suck material towards *B* and, failing to do so, results in idle time on that machine. These two terms will be useful. But the term 'queue' normally carries a pejorative sense; it seems to declare that it ought not to exist. In the situation recounted, however, the manager will probably wish to avoid idle time on machine *B*; he therefore *wants* a queue. In these circumstances he will surely call the queue a *stock*. Indeed, he will surely be asking *how much stock* is required between these two machines to avoid idle time on machine *B*.

It is not likely that refuge can be taken in the theorem from queue theory already quoted, because in real life these two distributions are unlikely to be identical, and their means though close to each other will not be identical either. Moreover, production will not be continuous for ever—it will be interrupted from various causes, and one machine may have the opportunity to catch up with the other. But these complications can of course be encompassed by the theory. Now although it was shown that the likelihood of long runs of unusual couples is remote, a finite probability still exists that any run we care to nominate, however bizarre, *might* occur. So there is no categorical answer to the manager's question. What can be calculated is the size of stock required *to meet a given level of risk that it will run out.* And so the key insight is reached. The manager should make no attempt to specify what the stock ought to be; his job is to specify the *acceptable risk.* Once he has said: supplies of these goods are so critical to our policy that I will not accept more than 1 chance in 1,000 that the plant concerned will ever be idle, the statistician can do the rest. He will be able to say, for this given probability, what stock should be held between the two processes.

The word 'statistician' was used advisedly, for this is a straightforward statistical job—as it stands. It seems very possible, however, that the manager will have no particular reason to nominate one probability rather than another. He will probably say: 'I do not really want to incur the risk that machine *B* will be idle, but on the other hand I am not prepared to see a huge stock investment laid down in order to meet this condition.' And so we reach the question: how much capital can we afford to tie up in stock? Obviously, this is a relative question; the answer to it depends on the state of other stocks in the production situation—and various other factors as well. It is for this reason that the wider view and interdisciplinary approach of operational research is necessary. But we shall return to this point later.

For the moment, it is salutary to contrast what has already been said with the ways in which stock levels are actually fixed in industry. For the example of machines *A* and *B* is no more than an archetype of any demand–supply interaction. Perhaps a little hyperbole will be forgiven in describing what happens: the language is not unrecognizably extravagant. Manager *A* declares that he will supply manager *B* with everything he wants; he prides himself on the service he gives; he declares that no intermediate stock is required at all. Manager *B* says that manager *A* is a very nice man and means well, but he would get no sleep at night if he had to rely on the absurd arrangements made by manager *A* to look after him. An argument develops. A financial man joins in, very properly doing his job of protecting the company's capital investment. Technical advisers join in: the stock will deteriorate, the stock will be unsafe, the stock is *strategically* vital because of scarce materials . . . and so on. Is it going too far to suggest that the stock level ultimately fixed will be proportionate to the resultant of all these forces—measured in decibels? Certainly, the senior manager called in to adjudicate has an unenviable task. It has been shown here, on the contrary, that this problem when shorn of factors which impinge on it from the side (which will be considered later) reduces to a scientific calculation.

This, then, is the building-block of planned chance: the notion that two interacting probabilistic situations are dynamically related in a way which can be measured by the use of probability theory. Throughout this chapter the notion will be used diagrammatically, and it will be depicted as two dots joined by a line (as shown at the foot of Figure 13). It is to be understood that each dot represents a measurable probability distribution, and that the line connecting them represents the statistical *convolution*, as it is called, of the two sets of probabilities. So the simple diagrammatic cypher which looks like a dumb-bell is not the over-simplification it appears: it stands for a very real and down-to-earth interaction of considerable complexity. Remember, too, that most dynamic situations can be thought of in this way. Some of the earliest queue-theoretic notions were developed around the problem of the doctor's waiting room—his appointment system, and the length of queue required to minimize his idle time. Queues form for buses too, and queues form in retail shops (especially in supermarkets). But one encounters precisely the same phenomenon in the queueing of capital development projects for available funds; in the stock of nuclear weapons which one country may be waiting to deliver to another. In all these cases, management seeks to cope with chance; but this is a chance whose pattern can be measured on the lines that have been indicated. Once this has been said, the notion of *planned* chance becomes tolerable. For although it is still impossible to predict any single event at all, the pattern of interaction is predictable.

This is to say, in turn, that any proposed alteration to one part of the system will have an effect on all the other parts—an effect which can be measured. Even the simple illustration given concerns a system; to improve the average time taken on machine *A* by five minutes will alter the idle time on machine *B* and have an influence on the stock held between the two machines. In the case of much larger systems, they may possibly be depicted by single interactions of this kind because the interaction of a large number of variables may none the less result in a *single* queue or stock. Finally, two special points must be made.

Firstly, the problem of transportation time between a demand and its supply has so far been ignored. In fact, however, it is not difficult to deal with. For the time taken to transfer material from one place to another has a mean value, and is itself distributed about that mean. So there is no difficulty in nominating 'transportation' as a process; in a scientific account of probabilistic interaction, this process will behave no differently from the production processes that are more familiarly called by this name. It also operates unpredictably within a predictable pattern. According to this view, machine *A* interacts with transportation which in turn interacts with machine *B*. Obviously this pair of interactions could create a need for *two* stocks—one awaiting transportation, and the other awaiting use at the other end. But, for the sake of the diagrammatic convention proposed above, the transportation distribution will be assumed to be accounted for on the line which joins the two dots. Thus the dumb-bell still stands for the interaction of two major activities, and their convolution is represented by the line which joins them. But this convolution may be mediated or not, as the case may be, by a probabilistic process of transportation appearing on the line.

Secondly, a point of technique deserves mention. It was said that the probabilities associated with this statistical model could be computed by the theory of queues. But this is true only in special cases which are as simple as that quoted. In other circumstances, although the theory is still perfectly correct, the mathematical apparatus for computing answers has yet to be discovered. For example, the pictures of the two distributions drawn in Figure 13 include one slight deviation from the account given of them in the text. A scrutiny of the figure will reveal a strange hump at the right-hand tail in each case. This hump stands for the occurrence of some kind of discontinuity—which is very common in real life. In this case, the idea is that these machines operate an eight-hour shift. Thus a job taking eight hours is bound to cross the shift boundary and have to be taken over by the next worker. This means that it will probably take still longer to complete. Hence the probability distribution may show an unnatural attenuation just before the hump (where completed jobs *ought* to appear, but do not because the operative is packing up), and an unnatural hump a little later (because the new operative is now completing the jobs his mate should have completed a half an hour earlier).

It cannot be over-emphasized that the existence of such peculiarities is the rule rather than the exception in actual industrial studies. Backroom-boy statistics is of little avail in these circumstances: it takes an operational research enquiry to elicit and to understand the full facts, and operational research expertise to discover ways of manipulating them. In this illustration, it is clear that the theory still applies; what is not clear is how the convolution should be computed, since there is no known way of solving the very peculiar mathematics which would result from an attempt to describe this particular curve.

The solution is the technique known as *simulation*. This is very easy to understand because a simulation was indeed begun earlier in this section. It will be recalled that a start was made in creating an artificial log of the behaviour of this system. A time was taken at random from the distribution of machine A times and compared with another time taken at random from the B distribution. The effects were evaluated. Another couple was then chosen, and so on. In this way, the behaviour of the situation is simulated, and it is clear that if this exercise is done sufficiently often and at sufficient speed we do not have to wait for a

work study measurement of what is happening in order to evaluate the
queues and stocks involved. In fact, in large studies of ramified queueing
systems such a simulation would be mounted inside an electronic computer, which could then generate the equivalent of (say) ten years'
production experience in (say) ten hours. By examining the artificial
log thus created, the scientist can estimate with great accuracy the
characteristics of the fluctuating queue or stock.

2   Controlled Dispersion

Having worked out with some care what is meant by this notion of a
building-block of planned chance, the conceptual modeller may now
build with it. It is clear that serial production could be envisaged as a

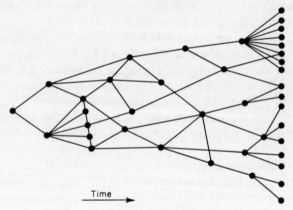

FIGURE 14. Dispersing stochastic network illustrating production
flow, retail distribution, transport system, etc.

long chain of dumb-bells: the output of each process is fed to the next
process, the output of which is fed to the next process, and so on. But
few activities in which the manager is interested are as simple as this.
The product of one process branches out to several more while the input
to any one process may derive from several sources. Hence the attempt
to picture any large-scale activity in terms of an assemblage of these
building-blocks will necessarily look like a *network*. One basic configuration of such a network is given at Figure 14. Time may be regarded as
unfolding from left to right, and very likely space does as well—although
the picture is not meant to be topographically correct. In this configuration, it will be seen, everything begins with one basic activity, the
outputs of which generate the activities of the entire network.

This network has a hard-and-fast look about it; it is necessary at first to remind oneself that each dot stands for some complicated probability function, and maybe the connecting lines do as well. What does it depict? Starting with production, it may be that the dot on the left is the output of a primary process, such as oil, or a plastic, or a flow of timber from a saw-mill, or a flow of metal ingots from a primary mill. In that case, the output is divided into two streams, which proceed to feed other processes, until a whole range of end points is served. The diagram does not of course neglect to indicate that in reality such flow lines are not normally isolated from each other: there will be a certain amount of interchange between them.

The problem of determining inter-process stocks, which has already been discussed for a pair of processes, can now be contemplated as a totality. In general, the inter-process stock gets more expensive as the diagram moves to the right; the penalties attaching to idle time will not be uniform throughout the system; a policy about the whole matter will be very much influenced by the possibility or otherwise of adopting alternative process routes. In short, the basic conceptual model, although quantified by the probability factors earlier mentioned, can now be weighted in various ways by other factors which may be obtained. As all the relevant information is made available and fitted into this picture, it becomes steadily clearer that we can talk of 'solving the network'. This is a strange phrase from a literary point of view; all it means is that the operational research man is now in a position to calculate whatever parameters of the system the management would like to know. The proper scientific model will not look like the diagram, needless to say. The pure connectivity of a network like this can be written down in terms of symbolic logic, thus doing away with the diagram. The functions by which the constraints affecting the network are related may be written down in terms of mathematics. And of course the general quantification of this essentially probabilistic system will be expressed in terms of mathematical statistics.

How to calculate the answers that are called for is a matter for the specialist; the object here remains to convey an insight into the nature of the problems involved, and if possible the conviction that the answers required are in principle calculable. The generic term for the behaviour of a system of this kind is *stochastic process*. Such a process is one in which chance governs the particular selection of events unfolding in time or affecting any particular item moving through the network, but where the probabilities which govern these chances are themselves patterned in the way earlier described. Thus although it is impossible to determine what the state of the network will be next Thursday at 10 a.m., or to say precisely when an item beginning today at the left-hand point will emerge at one of the right-hand points, it is possible to say everything about how the system should be managed. Particular stochastic processes are examined mathematically, or experimented with by simulation, or they may be subjected to control in practice by the feedback techniques which will be discussed in Part III.

It will not have been forgotten that in Part I one of the points stressed about the nature of operational research was that it must consider a situation in its totality, and refuse to be blinkered by the conventions of description which already exist. Note then how a network such as this can be fully specified without any mention of particular areas of management responsibility, geographical boundaries, technological phases or historical groupings. As a last remark on the stockholding issue, for example, it may be noted that solving the network could include the specification of its optimal uncoupling. That is to say, the location of present stocks is doubtless affected by the list of factors just enumerated. But stock ought not to be a device for uncoupling one manager from another, or one accounting schedule from the next. A stock is a machine for uncoupling demand and supply. It is a common outcome of operational research to demonstrate that the stock investment can be substantially lowered, not only by proper calculations as to optimal stock levels, but by a more ingenious distribution of the stock piles themselves. (Sometimes it is more profitable to *increase* the stock.)

Look for example at the top right-hand corner of Figure 14. Eight final processes are shown as deriving from a common source. A particular OR study showed that a large stock was held at each of these final points for immediate dispatch to the customer—and as in fact there were nearer eighty than eight the investment was large. No-one had thought of holding one stock at the *previous* process instead, a stock only fractionally as large as the total existing investment in finished goods. The reason for this failure to recognize an apparently obvious point was primarily that the production technology did not lend itself to the idea: set-up times on the final processes were long, and therefore lengthy production runs appeared to be economically vital. Secondly, the production control technique did not permit effective machine loading in the more flexible situation. Thirdly, the sales department was convinced that immediate delivery from finished stock was commercially vital.

Once the OR study had broken down the barriers that existed between the various functions, however, the whole matter was resolved with ridiculous ease. The engineers who had not been able to justify the expense of improvements in the machinery were assured of massive savings—and went ahead to change the plant. Once production control was assured that it had a new and different and readily resolvable machine loading problem, it speedily installed a paperwork system both cheaper and more rapid than the last. Once the sales department was assured that all these changes could be properly effected, it abandoned its diehard policy that finished stocks must be available on the shelves at all times (a ruling better described as a slogan than a policy), and closed down its section devoted to juggling with stock balances. The cost office noticed the difference; the customers got better service; the technical people gave up worrying about stock deterioration; and withal quite staggering savings were made (this was a good example of a non-zero-sum game).

Just how trivial is this example? Before anybody begins to complain about the use of steam hammers to crack nuts, let it be said that the annual savings in this case would have paid for the entire annual cost of the whole operational research department. Furthermore, the little example isolated here for discussion featured as little more than a footnote in the report which examined the network as a whole.

Just as the conceptual model nicely obscures the conventional descriptions of the system which are best avoided in any competent new study, so will its solution avoid stereotypes as well. It has just been shown in microcosm how an apparently stockholding study may have roots in both production and sales, and an outcome mediated by production control, costs and other departments. Again, this is not the truism it sounds. There are a great many firms, for instance, in which the finance people determine stock levels on the grounds that they are the controllers of capital investment. So they are; but finance is rightly regarded as a *constraint* on a stockholding policy. Finance has nothing whatever to contribute to the nature of the policy itself. This is an obviously correct assertion about the situation, when seen through the eyes of the conceptual modeller and his network. It ought to be obvious to management. That it is not so in the case of many famous companies may be brought home by observing their actions when the stock investment has risen to such proportions that some sanctions have to be applied.

It is common, for example, for an 'appropriate' stock level to be computed by such devices as comparison with other companies and indeed industries, or by extrapolating from earlier figures achieved when the company was quite different from the company that is now, or (and this is more reasonable) by making a financial judgment about the stock investment the company can possibly bear. In any case, having determined a suitable total level and having calculated the excess of stock now held over and above this level, it is common for an edict to go out that 'all stocks will be cut by 10 per cent'. This is totally inept management. The likelihood that such a policy will lead to an optimal distribution of the stock investment is virtually nil. Moreover, and ironically, the best managed sections of the business will already have the least margin of excess stock, and the blanket ruling may force these sections below the critical threshold of efficient operation. This is bad in itself, but it should be noted that the stock they *now* hold is bound to lose effectiveness in the return on capital it can provide. Now it is a common argument that when financial considerations make a stock reduction of paramount importance, there is no time to commission an operational research study which would master the entire production network and discover the best solution. If the firm has not had the prudence to compose the appropriate models before the crisis comes, this may well be true. But there is a matter of the degree of resolution to be considered here. A full-scale study of the detail might well take six months: this is admitted. But what does 'in detail' mean?

Remembering the inductive theory advanced in earlier chapters, we know that the most advanced study, even if it lasted six years, would still involve many–one transformations from real life. Thus, as usual, it is a *homomorphic* model that is being considered. A competent OR group should be able to carry the homomorphic reduction of the model down to a point where this problem could be solved in a day if necessary. To do so it would have to abandon a great deal of information and finesse, but it would produce an approximately correct answer. This very notion offends some pedantically minded people (scientists themselves more than the managers), but an approximately good answer simply must be better than a *bad* answer—such as we know the blanket reduction policy to be. The point has been made in a more scholarly way earlier, but it will bear a pungent repetition. The OR man is paid by the management to help it make decisions; he is not paid to write Ph.D. theses. If the management is compelled to take a decision tomorrow, it is incompetent in OR to reply that its scientific integrity demands a six-month study. If it literally can do nothing in the time available, of course it must say so, but normally OR can give some slight assistance, however short the time—particularly if it is an institutional OR group, which is already fairly familiar with the general picture.

Again emerges the justification for reminding young scientists entering the field of OR of the wartime origins of the subject, deeply as some of them resent this approach a generation later. For it should be so easy to see that if the enemy is standing over you with a drawn sword, there is no time to finish the calculation. Archimedes was killed in precisely this way, as is well known, thereby failing one of the important tests of an OR man. This is a pity, since in other ways he may be regarded as the founder of the subject. The manager he served was King Hieron II, for whom he brilliantly applied science to the strategic problems of defending the city of Syracuse against the Roman siege. (It was for Hieron too, by the way, that Archimedes solved the famous problem of the golden crown debased by silver; and OR men may be heard to cry *Heureka* to this very day.)

But to return briefly to the matter of controlled dispersion, it is worth a moment to reflect that the production system used here to typify the conceptual model could be replaced by many other managerial situations. For example, the left-hand point might represent a factory serving two huge depots (one for home and one for foreign sales), which in turn serve numerous warehouses distributing goods to retailers. This is the classic distribution problem: a commercial topic. And yet, when the underlying model has been located, the logical structure is seen to be no different from that of the production set-up. There are still the problems of stockholding, still the questions of location (how many warehouses, and where?), and there is the eternal dilemma of investment costs versus customer services. Again, just as we may wish to discover the best route for a product to take through the production system, so we may wish to find the best route for a travelling salesman to take from his factory through a complex of market possibilities. The product and the salesman are both taking a walk through a ramified system; they are both continually entering and leaving zones of probability. The same is precisely true of a message propagated from a source to a destination, through a series of junctions or exchanges or people; or of the progress of a virus from a single infected person through a population of potential invalids; or of the propagation of a brand image through a market of potential customers; or of a flow of spare parts to broken-down machines, such as cars or aeroplanes, that are in service.

In short, in a great many cases the dispersing network built of stochastic variables offers a basic insight into the system under discussion. We know how to describe it rigorously, how to quantify it both structurally and probabilistically, and how to calculate the decisions which the dynamic power of chance demands that management should take. Moreover, we can as it were float on this network a large variety of scientific models, competent analogies, whose ways of talking and laws and techniques can be imported to the problem in the standard way. One of them was slipped into the list given in the last paragraph: the propagation of infection. This is an epidemiological model which has been used as a basis for solving management problems in advertising. But particular models are matters for the OR group itself.

One of the benefits that managements should gain from these considerations is the notion of underlying identity between many of the systems they handle. Any two systems which can be visualized as dispersing networks can be mapped on to each other under *some* transformation. This is true of two managerial situations or of two scientific situations. It is also true of two situations one of which is managerial and the other scientific. There is the OR trick. There is also the reason why managers and ministers can often be moved successfully from one area of activity to another. It is one of our managerial beliefs these days that this should be done. The procedure is often justified by the broadening experience it bestows, and often accounted for by the tautology that 'management is management' (meaning, presumably, regardless of what is managed). It is suggested that this tautology expresses, on a single plane, the identity which is best understood by looking for the underlying and common conceptual model on that deeper plane on to which all managerial experience maps.

It has been shown how this works for a dispersing network, but obviously the networks describing systems that have to be managed do not all diverge. Then the question arises: does it make any difference if we consider converging networks?

3   Controlled Convergence

From the point of view of production, a converging network represents assembly operations. Just as the diverging network provides a picture of production in which raw materials are broken down into ever more highly finished products or into by-products, so the converging network is concerned with putting components together to form sub-assemblies, and sub-assemblies together to form complete assemblies. So the network pictured in Figure 15 might be the flow diagram for the production of a radio set, or an account of any other kind of construction— say of a cathedral, a power station or a submarine. Once again, however, this is not necessarily a picture of production at all. It might account for the supply picture of raw materials being brought into a factory; it might be a representation of demand; it might be the prognosis for a research and development programme.

It will be at once obvious that this new illustration has been obtained by rotating the last illustration through an angle of 180°. The two figures are manifestly isomorphic with each other. (Indeed, rotations are formally treated as a branch of mathematical group theory—from which our inductive theory was developed.) So there is a deep sense in which the answer to the question whether converging networks are different from diverging networks is that they are not. There is a different feel about them in management practice, and this is because each network unfolds *in time*.

That is to say, instead of rotating Figure 14, a similar result to that of Figure 15 (in fact its mirror image) could have been achieved by

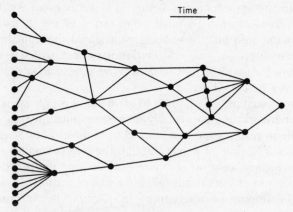

FIGURE 15. Converging stochastic network illustrating production assembly, construction of power station, capitalization of development, progress of research project, etc.

reversing the arrow depicting the flow of time. Since time is irreversible in real life, the diverging and converging situations do yield different features. For example, all inputs to the converging network must eventually reach one point, regardless of the route followed; whereas, in the other case, there is a wide range of terminal points, and an input will only reach one of these in particular as the result of a special switching procedure. On the other hand, the requisitions sent *back* through a converging network to obtain supplies have to be routed and timed to reach particular *initial* points.

Managerially speaking, each of these basic structures has its own peculiar difficulties. Nevertheless, the planning effort needed to guarantee results, and the amount of control effort needed to obtain them, are identical. Hence the structural isomorphism is very important; it uncovers the level at which the control problem in any ramified system of probabilistic components is invariant. The point may be considered again in another context.

One of the systems pictured as a divergent network was the distribution system of a company; remarks were made about the outward flow of material through depots and warehouses and retail shops to ultimate consumers. Instead of thinking of the flow of *goods* through this distribution system, imagine the flow of *information* which the movement of goods generates. That is, the changing balances at all the storage points are being monitored, and the flow of transport is being detected, so that information is seen to be diverging through the network. Now the target at which all this information is being (as it were) *aimed* is the ultimate level of demand at each terminal point. So if Figure 15 is now consulted, demand information is being propagated through the network in the reverse direction. This information may be regarded as representing a vacuum for goods: it results in negative queues and negative stocks in the manner described earlier.

Now the matching of supply and demand through isomorphically congruent networks is a particularly interesting phenomenon. For again it is possible to map a conceptual model from the physical sciences on to the situation. The flow of goods through the system implies a potential difference which is being offset: there is an evening-out process in train. Such a process in physics is measured in terms of entropy—a ratio which describes the amount of 'unevenness' in question. But information is a negative entropy. If a mathematical expression is developed for each of these notions independently, they are found to be identical—except for the minus sign in front of the second. Hence the energy transferred through the system is exactly balanced by the information flowing the opposite way; to speak of a change in entropy is *ipso facto* to speak of an equivalent change in negentropy. This equation at once provides a measure of the amount of control information that must be handled to contain the physical movements generated by the process of distribution. The model enables the OR scientist to determine the adequacy of the control system, the capacity of the computer required to automate it, and so on.

However, the most noticeable feature of any walk through a ramified system, whatever its basic configuration, remains the stochastic interplay that shimmers across the nodes and lines of the network. The word stochastic, incidentally, comes from the Greek στοχάζομαι, which means 'to aim at a mark'. (From this root, the word stochastic came into the English language, meaning roughly 'conjectural', and was current in the seventeenth and eighteenth centuries; today it is virtually obsolete in this sense, and has been taken over by scientists in the meaning already fairly closely defined.) Now the manager who is concerned with assembly or construction procedures, on the basis of a converging network, is indeed aiming at a mark. He has to bring together various items which converge on a single node; this itself represents not only their physical conflux, but their coincident arrival at a particular moment in time. It is not always easy to hit this mark in a well-laid-out shop using flow production; in a jobbing engineering shop, where large custom-built machines are made, it is yet more difficult; when it comes to building ships, motorways, power-stations and cathedrals, the task is more difficult still.

But the conceptual model that has been constructed still holds. The manager well knows that the mark at which he aims is not a unique point in space and time, but one of those target-like patterns representing zones of likelihood, which generate a probability distribution. The manager's plan takes aim at the centre of the target, and we can measure the chance that the arrow will miss by any given amount. And so the task of controlling the development of a massive construction project can be viewed as the generation of a stochastic process across a converging network, and as time unfolds and the target nodes are missed to a greater or lesser extent, the original network becomes distorted. A subsidiary job which is completed late will push the node representing its completion to the right on the diagram; there will then be consequences, in that the rest of the diagram must change.

In the simplest case, a tremendous new effort may shorten the time required to hit the next node, so that, by the time this point in the plan is reached, construction has caught up with events. If the plan were conceived merely as a long line of successive nodes, one might have a good deal of confidence that the errors in hitting the centre of the mark at each node would tend to cancel out, with the result that the final target date would be hit. Our problems in real life are exacerbated because this model does not hold: it is indeed a network with which we have to deal, and not a linear progression.

Thus, when a job is completed late, difficulties resulting at *one* of the succeeding nodes may be overcome. For example, a colossal effort may be made to restore the plan and to hit the original target date for this next operation. Or, quite possibly, we may be passing through a portion of the network which is not critical to the completion of the whole; in other words, there is some slack at this point which can be taken up without real damage. Unfortunately, while the staff is attending to this matter, a further chain or chains of events may have been started which it will prove impossible to control. For the node which represents the completed job that was late may feed *other* nodes as well as the one to which attention is most readily directed. These others may look less important, but in the long run they may themselves prove to have been critical points. Reflection on the diagram will suggest that secondary activities, which are begun late because of this primary delay, may feed other portions of the network, which might eventually deliver their effects in the main stream of construction with disastrous effect. Anyone who has ever been concerned with this kind of productive activity will understand the point. In the limit, a large and expensive machine which is virtually complete may be held up for a long time awaiting the completion of some relatively minor aspect—which suddenly achieves monumental importance, for the simple reason that the completion of the contract, as a whole, now depends upon it.

If this is not to happen, it is vital that the plan should recognize which of the various links between nodes that are under stochastic implementation at any one time really *is* critical to the success of the ultimate aim. Nor can the most critical of the momentary links be recognized unless the antecedents and consequents of *all* the links are examined. This is, after all, a ramified system; the object must be to consider its ramifications. It thus comes about that a necessary stage in planning of this kind is an examination of the entire converging network, and the isolation of that route through it which is composed of all the critical links. This is in fact the longest route through the network, for time once used cannot be reclaimed. In rugby football, the ball may be thrown in one direction alone; in a converging net, to commit a foul against this rule is equivalent to a demand that time run backwards. The longest route is uniquely the route which guarantees that all the subsidiary loops of the network can be accommodated within the time allowed. This route is called the critical path.

A whole collection of operational research techniques has evolved from this concept. These techniques all depend upon the recognition of the critical path, but they differ in their recognition of the criteria by which the longest route should be ascertained. For example, if the major object is to finish the entire job in the shortest possible time (as happens in the case of a defence programme), the critical path may be different from that which would emerge if the criterion of success were that the job should be completed at the minimum possible cost. The basic reason for this difference is that, if cost is not of overriding importance, a stochastic delay can be made good to the extent that the probability distribution at the succeeding node may be assumed to operate at a low level of probability in favour of rectifying the plan. In real life, this desirable consequence may be achieved (if there is sufficient warning) by taking special, if costly, precautions—such as increasing the labour force.

Naturally, the critical path through a converging network can be discovered under any criterion or balance of criteria. The corpus of techniques which flow from this particular aspect of the conceptual model is known as *Critical Path Analysis*. In some quarters, highly specialized versions of the approach have been developed with particular criteria in mind, and the resulting technique has been given (as it were) a brand name. Thus managements are sometimes offered these techniques under their brand names as ready-made means of optimizing performance on a construction job—provided that the criterion of success can be stated in advance. But it is not really in the spirit of operational research that techniques should be sold in this way as pre-packaged commodities. Their application, sight unseen, is risky. It is, on the contrary, most important that proper research into the managerial desiderata in a particular case be undertaken before the programme that will isolate the critical path is settled. When it is settled, however, the critical path is of paramount importance to the management of this kind of production.

In the first place, it will be clear that to know what is the critical path enables a manager to concentrate his managerial resources on the task of meeting the delivery dates represented by the nodes that lie on this path. Provided that this particular collection of nodes can be adhered to as a series of target dates, it is guaranteed that the total job will be finished on time. Managements have been aware of this fact for many years, and have often tried to isolate the critical path as a guide to their control of the situation. But it is only since the advent of electronic computers that the full possibilities of this idea have been developed as a practical proposition. For the fact is that quite early in the production process difficulties are likely to be encountered which will involve a late completion at some node on the critical path. Hitherto, it has been a practical necessity to adhere to the pre-arranged path, and to use one's resources to try and catch up on the pre-arranged plan. But, given that a delay does occur, it is probable that the critical path from that point onwards is not the same as the critical path originally foreseen.

The balance of interacting probabilities in the stochastic progression through the network causes a shift of emphasis—which dictates a new critical path from the point at which things began to go wrong. In practice, this means that the critical path should be re-evaluated more or less continuously in the course of construction. This is a very difficult task when there are (to quote the particularly famous case of the Polaris missile) no less than 30,000 nodes in the network and 11,000 different contractors responsible for achieving the target dates they represent. In such circumstances a computer programme alone is competent to re-evaluate the critical path more or less continuously, and thereby to guide management in its control of the situation.

It is worth considering just one example of a situation that can readily arise, in which the value of this technique becomes fully apparent. Let us suppose that a stage of a construction job is most seriously delayed early on in the proceedings. The completion of this phase is two weeks later than envisaged in the plan. Now it is simply not true to say that everything can be delayed by two weeks, and that the completion of the entire contract will also be two weeks late. The network, if it has been properly constructed as a model of events, will undoubtedly wander outside the sphere of influence of the management itself. For example, if there are indeed 11,000 contractors, then the entire job is heavily dependent upon their co-operation. The fact that the programme is now two weeks late may prevent one of these contractors from undertaking his part in the programme at the expected time. If this happens, there is no guarantee that his services will be available precisely two weeks later. The economics of his own business may compel him to embark on other work, and to get out of phase with the programme in which we are interested.

It could thus happen, by a concatenation of such circumstances, that a two-week delay encountered within the construction programme itself might result in (let us say) a six-month postponement of the final com-pletion. This outcome would be thanks to the ramifications of the system concerned: it begins to act as an amplifier of delays. Now the managerial consequence to be drawn from such a situation is of the keenest interest. Instead of embarking on the new critical path, which has been com-puted to result in a six-month delay in completion, it is open to the management to determine that they will after all adhere to the *original* critical path. This is usually a physical possibility: by taking quite extra-ordinary measures it may be possible to achieve very high speeds on the next phases of the programme. Normally, if these exceptional measures are extremely costly or otherwise causes for alarm, no-one would seri-ously consider them. The stereotyped answer is that since a delay of two weeks is in question, only two-weeks-worth of expenditure—at the most—is justifiable in order to catch up. So the phase space of acceptable solutions is narrowly determined. Once it has been calculated, however, that a *six-month* delay is now inevitable, the losses that would accrue from *this* delay (in extra costs and perhaps in penalties) are the measure of the opportunity loss incurred in accepting the situation.

This is a scientific measure of something that would normally be regarded as imponderable. It may suddenly become clear that the cost of taking utterly extraordinary measures (such as, for example, flying in craftsmen from the other side of the country) is much less than the loss which would be involved in accepting defeat and adopting the new critical path. Without the benefit of this operational research result, many mistakes are made by acquiescing in alternative routes to the conclusion which are simply not economic. It has to be noted that orthodox accounting procedures will not be able to measure the amplified loss generated by the ramified system following an initial delay—for the simple reason that orthodox costing procedures have no means of including this factor in their measurement task. Hence in practice, in a case such as that quoted, the cost to the programme of the initial two weeks delay will be costed as an *ultimate* loss of two weeks. And this is quite wrong.

These then are some of the insights into managerial situations that are obtainable using the converging network configuration. It has been shown how a situation of this kind can be controlled, despite the risks and chances that are built into it. The key thought remains that the probabilities built into the system can be measured and accounted for by various means: the manager is not at the mercy of fate. Of course, he already knows this, and he seeks by determination and skill to amend the hand that is dealt to him by chance. But if he should decide to call in science to aid him in this task, he will find that much more about the system can be measured and predicted and controlled than he hitherto believed. It is vital to make use of the understood patterns of stochastic processes. With a knowledge of these patterns and how they can be manipulated, the concept of control returns to a situation which might otherwise be no more than a sustained fight between inflexible intentions and bad luck. Control, seen in these contexts as the confident manipulation of apparently random events through an understanding of probability, remains possible. To achieve it, the manager must engineer with probabilities; he must build an edifice with the building-blocks of planned chance.

4   Controlled Hierarchy

By rotating the now familiar network through another 90°, a new diagram is obtained (Figure 16). This at once creates the impression of an hierarchical structure, but one which differs in a number of important ways from the familiar 'family tree' type of organization chart. In the first place, the nodes in the network which now represent individuals are not very tidily placed in ranks of equivalent importance. This is realistic; whenever one lives close to a group of managers alleged to be of equivalent rank or status in the organization, one rapidly discovers that this is not strictly true. Because of a differential importance in the

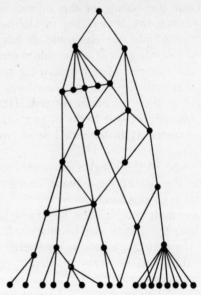

FIGURE 16. Hierarchical stochastic network illustrating company organization structure, the devolution of government, military command in the field, etc.

activity each commands, or because of historical associations, or in the limit because of the personalities of the men concerned, it is possible to produce a rank within the rank—to decide of any two of the men which is the more 'senior'. Secondly, there is diffuse responsibility and authority indicated by this diagram; in places we may detect the normal rule that each man has only one immediate superior, but in other places he appears to have two or more. Again, this is no more than realistic; this diagram has not been handed out by the firm as an account of the way it is managed, it has been created by an operational research investigation which has sought to depict the relationships which actually exist. Very often a man will accept instructions from someone who is not his nominal superior, and equally he may be able to influence people of

senior rank to whom he does not nominally report. Thirdly, it is important to remember the convention of the 'dumb-bell': this diagram does
not represent merely a chain of command, but a flow of information and
decision. Consequently this is (as in the previous two diagrams) a
dynamic picture of stochastic interaction.

This network, with its three distinctive features, forms a good basis
for discussing models of organization. One of the first questions which
ought to be put to any alleged representation of a management structure
is: what happens when someone fails in his job? Supposing that a
manager, having received various information through the network,
gives a wrong decision (and it must surely be conceded that this often
happens), what capability has the network for rectifying the error? An
excellent model through which to discuss this problem, and indeed to
quantify it and to reach conclusions, may be taken from neurocytology.

Parts of the brain contain networks very like the one shown. Each
node or decision-taker is a nerve cell, called a neuron. The neurons are
connected together by nerve fibres, of which there is a very large number.
The diagram poorly represents a neural network, because the nodes are
firmly connected by single lines. In brain tissue, a neuron is approached
by a large collection of transmission lines which are themselves net-like:
they are the dendrites which impinge on the neuron and cause it to
change its state. Nerve impulses arriving at a particular neuron, therefore,
do not come thumping in as might be imagined from Figure 16; they
dribble in with more or less reliability. And yet, the convention underlying the networks printed here is that the lines drawn on them represent
stochastic interactions; so information flowing through this particular
network must be regarded as arriving at any one node *with a certain
probability*. Whether the neuron 'fires' or not, thereby transmitting information down its axon, is also a probabilistic matter: the brain is a
computer having 10,000,000,000 unreliable computing elements. So
the analogy again holds; few managers would claim that the stream of
decision which emanates from them all day long is uniformly of very
high reliability. Remember that people often speak of decision as if the
word related only to that vital moment when a verdict must be reached
that changes the future course of the company. We are here considering
instead the total communication of a manager within the network, a man
whose judgments are flowing upwards, downwards, and (significantly)
sideways through the organization whenever he writes, speaks, uses the
telephone or has lunch. So this is a viable conceptual model; now it
must be followed down to the rigorous level.

Figure 17 shows a formal neuron. It has two imputs, *A* and *B*, and a single output *C*. Its job is to compute $A + B = C$: that is to say, the neuron should take a decision when it receives information from both *A* and *B*, and then pass on a message. Thanks to the general unreliability of the network of which this node is a part, it may well be that the information coming in down both channel *A* and channel *B* is (let us say) only 70 per cent accurate, while the neuron itself fails to draw the right deduction 1 in 200 times. These figures may well be realistic ones to use where the brain is concerned; perhaps they are also reasonably good estimates of the kind of situation in which a manager finds himself.

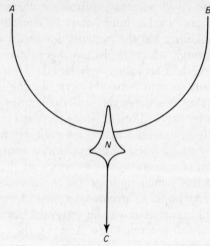

FIGURE 17. Decision-taking node of hierarchical network. With error-rates *A* and *B* 30 per cent, *N* 0·5 per cent, *C* gives wrong answer most of the time.

A manager whose two sources of information are on the average 70 per cent correct, is, perhaps, fairly lucky. After all, the men who advise him may have misunderstood the situation, misinterpreted the facts, incorrectly conveyed their own understanding, or they may have changed the emphasis either by accident or design. As to the manager himself, even in this elemental, archetypal situation he may very occasionally produce the wrong answer. The first question is: what are the chances that the neuron or the manager will give the wrong decision?

This probability is very readily computed. The probability that *A* is correct is 0·7; the probability that *B* is correct is also 0·7; the probability that the decision-taker is correct is 0·995. Since the chance of making a mistake at any one of these three points is independent of the other two, the total probability of obtaining a right answer is 0.7×0.7

$\times 0.995 = 0.48755$. The chance of getting the answer wrong is then the complement of this, namely 0.51245. That is to say, the neuron will be wrong *most* of the time—and so will the manager.

In this situation, it looks as though some very extraordinary advice ought to be given to the manager. His chance of being right is less than evens. In fact, out of 100,000 trials he can expect to be wrong 51,245 times. Had he given the opposite answer every time, then, by saying *yes* instead of *no* and *no* instead of *yes*, he would have been wrong only 48,755 times. The advice appears to be that he should most carefully consider the evidence, take a cool and deliberate decision, *and then reverse it.*

A manager who felt constrained to spend his life in issuing the opposite of his most carefully considered decisions might well regard it as a mockery. And if this is the best that the computing elements of the brain can do, then equally it is a wonder that we humans are as well served by our brains as we evidently are. There must be an answer to this extraordinary paradox—and there is.

Historically, light was first shed on this problem when that great mathematician, the late John von Neumann, asked the following question about the taking of alcohol. It seems that a modest amount of alcohol in the blood stream will cause a neuron to change the threshold at which it fires. That is, the amount of stimulus received from A and B before C will be triggered off alters. Now if the brain consists of an intimately interconnected network of 10,000,000,000 neurons, and if the taking of alcohol causes all of these to change threshold, how can the brain possibly function when people are drunk? Of course, drunkenness causes people to behave in strange ways—this is known. But considering the radical change made in the whole computing circuitry, it is surely extremely remarkable that people manage to behave in a manner in the least approximating to that of a normal human being when alcohol has been taken. Von Neumann soon showed that the basic trick used by the brain as a means of making reliable computations with unreliable components is the *principle of redundancy*.

If one suspects that a vital telephone line may be cut by the enemy, the obvious precaution is to lay a number of lines in the hope that at least one of them will survive. This is known as multiplexing the channels of communication. Equally, if it is suspected that the telephone instruments themselves may not work, it becomes possible to consider the connection of these multiplexed lines to a collection of instruments. One could then take, as it were, a vote on the outcome. This design is called a majority organ. Computations of the probability that a message will be correctly received show that the chances increase very rapidly as the level of redundancy in this circuitry rises. From these early calculations, several scientists have developed an advanced theory of redundancy in neural nets—notably McCulloch and his collaborators.

It is now clear that the brain manages to achieve its high level of reliability by multiplexing its nodes and its channels according to a very complicated logic. By doing so, it overcomes not only the influences of such threshold-changing stimuli as alcohol, but also the inherent unreliability of the components themselves. Living components have an inevitable tendency to atrophy and fail, and it seems likely that the neurons in our brains are cutting out at the rate of *100,000 a day*. For example, McCulloch has estimated that at the age of sixty a man will have lost between 10 and 20 per cent of the Purkinje cells in his cerebellum. Yet the machinery still works. The cerebellum continues to control his posture, and he does not fall flat on his face. The brain is in fact imperfect, from the very beginning of life to the very end, and its machinery is moreover constantly falling into disrepair; so the trick by which it produces a reliable output is important.

Using the model to comment on the managerial situation, it is clear that human societies have adopted the same device. Not only is there a tendency to form boards, committees, conferences and meetings of a formal kind; there is also the tendency to undertake a great deal of unofficial consultation within any managerial group. Hence people are accustomed to monitor each other, in both formal and informal ways, and sometimes the informality can extend to complicated networks which extend out of the organization and return to it—having passed through quasi-members of the organization on the way. This band of quasi-decision-takers may include people from supplying or consuming companies, from university research departments, or from comparable companies in the industry; and they may include such people as bankers, stockbrokers, city editors and even wives who have been talking to other wives. That all this kind of consultation goes on is well known, but its importance has not perhaps been fully understood. Had it been understood, it seems impossible that the kinds of organization chart with which we are most familiar could ever have been drawn, or that responsible teaching establishments could continue to instruct senior managers on the importance of defining unique responsibility within an organization. The trick of redundancy is the means of reliability, and it has to be represented within management theory in a measurable way. In that case it will be well to examine a redundant network, which might either be a neural net from the brain or a management consultative situation.

Figure 18 shows a redundant network in which the same two inputs *A* and *B* are multiplexed into five-line inputs. The error rate on *each* line remains 30 per cent as before. These inputs now stimulate four unreliable neurons, *each* of which gives the wrong answer 1 in 200 times. It will be noted that all the lines are connected to all the neurons, and that the assembly of neurons then commonly supplies the output *C*. The diagram is drawn to suggest a section of the cerebral cortex, but it shows the formal connectivity just explained.

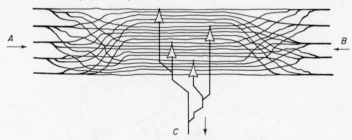

FIGURE 18. Decision-taking cortical-looking system with un-reliable components and five-line inputs. Gives the wrong answer once in 100,000,000 trials.

The computation of the probabilities is now more difficult. Here, at any rate, is the expression that has to be evaluated to find out how often this network will give the wrong answer:

$$P \simeq \{1-[(1-0\cdot3^5)\times(1-0\cdot3^5)\times0\cdot995]\}^4$$

The result of this calculation is:

$$P \simeq 9\cdot37\times10^{-9}$$

This is to say that there is only 1 chance in 100,000,000 of obtaining a wrong answer. Using the same input information as before, and using decision-taking elements of the same order of reliability as before, a fantastic increase in reliability has been obtained.

This cortical-looking network is further formalized in Figure 19. Here, for the sake of variation, ten-line multiplexed inputs are used; these are enclosed in cables the more clearly to indicate the connections. This is still a brain-like system which may be copied electronically. Alternatively, the diagram shows a group of four managers, well supplied with unreliable information, reaching a corporate decision. With this system, the probability of obtaining a wrong answer is $0\cdot63\times10^{-8}$. That is to say that there is only a 63 per cent chance of obtaining *one* wrong answer out of 1,000,000,000 trials. This network (Figure 19) is in fact over 800,000,000 times more reliable than the original (Figure 17).

It has to be reiterated that Figure 19 is very much simplified; for example, it makes assumptions about the nature of the error in the system and about what counts as a correct output at *C*. On the other hand, it uses only the crudest of the logical devices made available by this research. In fact, we learn from the brain how to use inhibitory impulses as well as excitatory ones; and in practice the whole treatment is vastly more complicated than this simple example suggests.

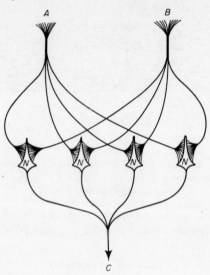

FIGURE 19. Decision-taking system with unreliable components, and ten-line cables. With the same error-rates as before (Figure 17), this network is 800,000,000 times more reliable.

Even so, on seeing this demonstration, some people may think that there must be a fault in the argument somewhere, for it appears that something has been created out of nothing. It is well known that one cannot have a perpetual motion machine, and that something is always lost (for instance in friction) when any kind of activity is undertaken. But here something seems to have been gained—a great deal in fact. The reason for this mistaken notion is that a wrong model is being used. It is a model taken from heat engines or from mechanics. Now it is certainly true that redundant networks are inefficient in terms of the energy they consume, or of their cost. But this is not the parameter of the system in which we are interested. The concern here is with *information*, and the information in this example has been *amplified*. So the right model to have in mind is perhaps a radio set. The sounds emitted by radio transmitters fill the air around us, but (fortunately) we cannot hear them. A radio receiver amplifies them to the point where we can listen without difficulty: it is a device that consumes a great deal of *energy* in the process of providing amplified information. So the trick is possible.

Now von Neumann propounded a mathematical theorem which showed that if one is prepared to go on increasing the redundancy of a network without limit, it is possible to obtain an output of arbitrarily high accuracy from a network whose components are of arbitrarily low reliability. This is an extraordinary guarantee. Neither brains nor company organization would work if it were not so. It is one of the uses of operational research to deploy this neurophysiological model in the analysis of organizational structure and in the design of more effective organizations. For it should be noted quite clearly that for a *given* level of redundancy it is possible to construct a network whose reliability is either almost the same as the equivalent non-redundant network, or one which is enormously better. The difference lies in the skill with which the logic of neural nets is deployed.

This has been an example, no more, of the thinking which operational research can bring to bear on organizational problems. The principle of redundancy is relevant to any sort of control system, whether this is an industrial management, a government policy, an army command in the field, or (for that matter) a signalling system on a railway. The neurophysiological model (or more generally models from every sphere of biological control) has much to offer the designer of managerial control systems—as will be investigated further in later chapters. This discovery is very recent. In fact, before it can be exploited in even a small degree, people at the top of major organizations will need to assent to the propositions that management structures need to be, can be, and should be designed at all, and that they are stochastic, not formal, networks. Experience suggests that they prefer to rely on the self-generative properties of social groups, on over-simplified pictures of the stochastic interactions of their nodes, and on the guidance of this growth on the organization chart according to the principles of aesthetics. Whoever saw an organization chart that was indefinite, redundant, or even asymmetrical?

The lack of cogent thought about these problems, let alone of a competent scientific formulation of the principles involved, explains much that is inefficient and even futile about the direction of contemporary affairs. Above all, it explains the unhappiness and frustration of many junior people: in the lower and often middle levels of management, among professional men such as accountants and Civil Servants, in the research laboratories and other fields of scientific endeavour. The more lowly placed individual sees himself at the bottom of a massive organizational structure, the weight of which bears down upon him, and the limits of which fade out of sight and comprehension. He does not see the 'top of the pyramid' in all its simplicity. He sees the man above him and *his* colleagues, and the rank above them; he knows that at this point other sister organizations merge with his own, multiplying the list of high officials; he hears tell of associated enterprises oversea, and visualizes how they add to the score. Certainly he may know the name of the

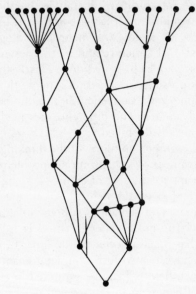

FIGURE 20. Hierarchical stochastic network illustrating the limit of upward vision of a lowly-placed person in a large organization.

chairman, but the limit of his practical understanding is a pantheon, not a father-figure. He simply does not understand; nor, in the context of an irrelevant organizational model, is he understood. This lengthy chapter ends with the fourth and final rotation of the stochastic network: it gives some idea of how this person feels.

The difference in viewpoint for the lowly individual is now obvious, yet its importance might still be underestimated. Professor R. W. Revans has made a study of what he has labelled the 'opaqueness of organizations'. How many people believe that they understand the problems of those who work beneath them, or that those for whom they work understand theirs? Revans found that 28 per cent of shop-floor operatives believe their own foremen understand the operatives' problems; of these same foremen 88 per cent believe that they understand the operatives' problems. Of these foremen 43 per cent believe their own works' managers understand the foremen's problems; of these works' managers 94 per cent believe that they understand the foremen's problems. Of these works' managers 59 per cent believe their own general managers understand the problems of works' managers; and (it can be assumed, says Revans) all general managers believe they understand the works' managers' problems.

Looking down from above, we can roughly quantify what Revans happily calls the 'downward transparency' of the enterprise by multiplying out the levels of belief which people hold about their own understanding of the next junior rank: 100 per cent × 94 per cent × 88 per cent, which is roughly 83 per cent. This is the degree to which management corporately believes it understands operational problems. The man shown at the bottom of Figure 20 might measure management sympathy for his problems as: 28 per cent × 43 per cent × 59 per cent, which is roughly 7 per cent. This is the 'upward opaqueness' of the enterprise.

However critical one may be of the crudity of these two assessments, they are supposed to measure the same thing. The disparity between 7 per cent and 83 per cent is sufficiently large to indicate that the observer's vantage point conditions his results (an outcome familiar enough to scientists), and to imply criticism of communications within the enterprise.

10

APOLLO'S GIFT

Quicquid dicam aut erit, aut non:
Divinare etenim magnus mihi donat Apollo.

Whatever I say will either happen, or not:
truly the great Apollo grants me the gift of forecasting.

HORACE in *Satires* (30 B.C.)

1   The Archetectonics of Planned Chance

A particular configuration of a network was used in the preceding
chapter, and all four of its right-angled rotations were mentioned in
turn. This was convenient for expository purposes, but the whole idea
can be generalized in the picture of an unspecified, undifferentiated
network, having no origin and no terminal points, no apices and no
directionality. It is stochastic, in the sense already described. It is probabilistic, moreover, in a further sense. That is to say that no route or
trajectory through it is fully determined. So far a pathway through a
network has been treated as definite; each node presents a set of alternative possibilities, it is true, but one of these is chosen at each successive
node—whereupon the route is prescribed. But now the picture is further
generalized so that each node presents a number of alternatives *each* of
which has a finite probability of being chosen, the sum of their probabilities being unity.

No diagram is given of this picture, for any one exemplification would
betray the qualities of abstraction and generality which inform it. The
object now is to give *texture* to the talk of management topics. Just as a
picture may be painted on canvas, or a decoration may be printed on
paper or cloth, this discussion is mounted on a stochastic network. Just
as the picture will be affected by the texture of the canvas, or the fibrous
structure of the paper, or the woof and warp of the cloth, so the dis-

204

cussion in this chapter is affected by the substratum laid down for it in Chapter 9. For the flow of decisions and events through time and space is spread inevitably across a stochastic network of probabilistically interconnected nodes, and the pattern shows through in the picture of management activity. The chances with which management copes are always there, and they are planned chances in the sense already given. Their reticulated structure has an architecture devised by nature; and systematic knowledge about the principles which guide that architecture is called 'architectonic'.

Although the use of the term 'model' in this connection has been avoided, the network notion may have been thought of as being one. Indeed, some writers refer to it in this way. A fresh reading of the preceding paragraph may make my own attitude clear. The network notion is part of the structure of the *language* we use to talk about these matters. A real-life managerial situation which (inevitably, it was said) conforms to such a network, is best discussed in a language which implicitly expresses network-like notions well. This is the language developed in the preceding chapter. The same is true of any network-like conceptual model which operational research draws from science to map on to the situation. The generalization propounded in the first paragraph informs our discussion of both situation and conceptual model. When the real science begins, and the scientific model which underlies them both is sought out, a rigorous language of networks will be needed in which to express that model. This is given by the branch of modern mathematics called the theory of graphs, of which more will be said later.

The aspect of models to which attention now turns is their predictive value. The adjective 'predictive' has been used to qualify the noun 'model' many times in this book. Models are devised to describe what the situation is, but if they can do no more than this, any decision based on a model will be competent to determine the existing situation alone. Since the existing situation already exists, there can be no point in seeking decisions which would bring it about. Not so. The model may be required to indicate decisions which, when applied to the existing situation, will change it in some desired way; or it may be required to say what decisions will offset an anticipated or possible change in some desired way. So the use of the model is predicated of the future. The attributes that are desired are called *criteria of success*. The formulation of a set of states for a model which meets the criteria of success is called its *objective function*.

Now the sense in which a model can be called predictive must be considered with care. Neither managers nor OR men are fortune-tellers; on the other hand they cannot afford to be as blithely helpless as the satirical Horace suggests at the head of this chapter. Apollo does not hand us a crystal ball, and the man who declares that he can foretell the future is no scientist. Yet in some way or other and to some extent or other we 'know what will happen'—otherwise all management is meaningless. Apollo's gift is best described as an architectonic of planned chance.

There are three main points to make about the kinds of prediction that can justly be called scientific. The first is that the uncertainty of the future may relate only to the details of a pattern which is itself highly likely and therefore predictable. For example, the manager of a retail shop selling clothes cannot tell whether the next customer will be tall or short. But he can say that, over a period, the proportion of customers of each height of individuals is randomly spread over a scale where the frequencies follow a Gaussian distribution. So the scientist can help the manager to calculate the probabilities of his 'having a run on' the less common sizes of garment, and can help him also to fix the required stock levels for any given interval between deliveries of stock—at a quoted risk of not being able to serve the randomly arriving customer. He can in fact specify the *reorder rules* (which, incidentally, can be operated entirely automatically by a computer in a large establishment). These rules say when and how much material to reorder. Similar problems occur in production processes too, and although such statistical techniques are patently relevant and useful, it is amazing how infrequently they are applied. When the situation does not declare itself as patterned in this stochastic way, the techniques are not used at all. This is where the question of prediction is so important. If the manager believes that the future is veiled in mystery, he may have a thought block about the very possibility of perceiving a stochastic pattern in events.

The second point to make about scientific prediction has to do with induction. In arguing from an enumeration of particular instances to a general proposition, a precarious conclusion is reached. 'The seven Danes I have met have blonde hair, therefore all Danes are blondes' is such an induction. The conclusion is in fact false, and the reason for the mistake is that the sample size is too small. But, given a properly designed sampling scheme based on statistical theory, an inductive conclusion can be raised to an arbitrarily high degree of probability (and therefore credibility) although it remains precarious. Now some people confuse this logical process, which is enumerative, with another which is quite different.

Consider the general proposition: 'Any kettle placed on a fire will boil.' Is this an induction by simple enumeration? There have been a great many kettles placed on a great many fires; as far as anyone seems to know they all boiled; no-one ever seems to have recorded that a kettle left on a fire indefinitely failed to boil. This argument appears to be all right; the sample size is enormous, so the conclusion becomes highly likely. In fact, however, science provides an entirely different argument from this. It explains what happens when water is heated; it knows the chemical change that occurs, and why it occurs. In short, science has discovered the mechanism involved, and has no need to rely on the argument from multiple coincidence. That is the third point.

In a great many management situations the possibility of prediction is denied because the manager's attempts to learn inductively fail. He is searching for the reiterated coincidence which will link two sorts of event, and he does not find it because it is masked by the complexity of the ramified system. Science can come to his aid. It may be able to identify the elusive correlation by multivariate analysis—which sorts out the interactions of more variables than the unaided brain can simultaneously contemplate. Then prediction, based on what J. S. Mill called 'concomitant variation', becomes possible again. This process is scientific, because there is statistical evidence that the two variables are correlated. Therefore an hypothesis can reasonably be formulated that they are linked by some common causal nexus, although what this may be is unknown. (By the way, the procedure remains scientific only so long as we remember to call this an hypothesis. If we lapse into calling it a *law*, a belief has been fixed by the method of tenacity—recall the arguments of Chapter 2.) Alternatively, and preferably, science may discover the linking mechanism itself.

If this happens, it seems unlikely that the scientist will refer any longer to 'prediction'. One does not *predict* that a kettle will boil. Very often in operational research, however, the scientist penetrates what has hitherto been regarded as a mystery in a circuitous way. He may identify only part of the mechanism, or the whole of the mechanism imperfectly; real life is after all extremely complicated, and its ramifications may defeat perfect understanding. In this case the scientist may buttress his insights with inductive arguments of the other two kinds. He looks for some statistical inference, either in the form of a stochastic pattern in events or in the shape of high-probability generalizations based on samples, which will enable him to interpolate numerical relationships in models at points where the deductive mechanics are unknown. When he has to try and assert what will happen in the future against this background, he is not fully confident. So he may call his effort a prediction after all; the manager certainly will.

Expressing this account of prediction in terms of the network language is straightforward. As time unfolds, history 'fixes' the uncertainties; the probabilities and the stochastic elements vanish in ascertainable facts. But although *all* the facts are in principle ascertainable, only a few will be ascertained. So the record of the changing network of the past is a many–one reduction of what actually happened. If its key characteristics are to be understood well enough to make a reliable prediction about its future states, that many–one reduction ought to be a homomorphism. That is, we must get its structure right, and we must decide on the selection of facts to illuminate that structure.

It is, however, logically impossible to use the language of the network's description to comment on its own structure. There are profound reasons for this which belong to metamathematics. The commentary has to be made in what is called a metalanguage, which is to say a language of higher order than that of the system itself. There is no need to go into the technical details; the point may be exemplified through any of the well-known logical paradoxes. 'The barber shaves all those, and only those, who do not shave themselves.' It is impossible within the linguistic framework of that sentence to discuss the problem of who shaves the barber. If he does not shave himself, he shaves himself; but if he shaves himself, he does not. Logicians call a proposition of chis kind an *undecidable sentence*. But we can and do discuss this problem; we observe that the language in which it is couched is self-defeating. A language competent to express this discussion is a metalanguage. Now the network language which spans the gap between a problem situation and its conceptual model also contains undecidable sentences. This matters little in the course of managing, perhaps; but it can matter a great deal in operational research and the practice of management as applied to its own procedures (note the reflexive statement). For it is then necessary to analyse the structure of the language spoken within both the problem situation and its conceptual model if the deeper-lying scientific model is to be made rigorous. This analysis of the network cannot be undertaken in 'networkese'.

This problem is of course resolved by the creation of the scientific model, the language of which is a metalanguage with respect to the network language of the practical situation. From within the model, that is, one can discuss the situation which the model analogizes and ultimately maps, without being trapped into undecidable statements. All this is said at the level of philosophy, but its practical relevance is great, particularly in the context of forecasting. Here is an example.

In a labour dispute a bargaining network is set up between employers and employed. Each of the contestants is himself a member of a wider network, and may see himself as spokesman for and responsible to his brethren—be they other trade unions or other employers. Sometimes, particularly when points of national interest appear to be involved, the stands taken within the bargaining network become reinforced by positive feedback from within the supporting networks on either side. For instance, some tough demand that was initially advanced with due caution across the negotiating table is reported through the press; the supporting network hums with activity; the negotiators are pushed forward when perhaps they would rather withdraw. (If we wished to study this process scientifically, a model from servomechanics would be useful.) At any rate, deadlocks develop across the total system of networks because the 'equations' that the network is trying to solve are insoluble. One sees the same thing in international diplomacy.

In the limit, the labour representatives may refuse to settle for less than would literally bankrupt the firm, while the employers refuse to give more than will hold the employees to the firm. It is rare to see the undecidability of the conclusion quite starkly, because other forces tend to intervene—which they do in a metalanguage. But the *structure* of the network language itself is undecidable in the limit, because if the employers 'win' they cannot continue operations, and if the workpeople 'win' they have no jobs. In short: whoever wins, loses. Again compare international affairs, particularly unworkable peace treaties, which reveal that intelligent people, trapped in undecidable situations, cannot always find a way out.

The disruption of undecidability may come with official arbitration, speaking a metalanguage. But it could also be achieved through the metalinguistic OR model. This would probably be taken from the *Theory of Games*. The situation is studied as if it were a game, with two sides and certain rules—this is the conceptual model. The rigorous model requires the mathematical analysis of the game's structure and constraints, followed by an evaluation of all possible strategies for each player. Since the likelihood is that an implacable opponent will select his own optimal strategy for each move in the game, the other player selects *his* strategy on that assumption. The OR scientist would seek to compute the best strategies by interpreting the players' criterion of success in mathematical terms, and using it as the objective function for his matrix. For instance it may be decided to select the *minimax strategy*. This is a prudential course to follow, because it computes the maximum risk and then selects the strategy which minimizes this. Notice how the architectonics of planned chance permit the discussion of future situations according to a mixture of the three predictive methods: the game is the mechanism; the matrix is quantified by enumeration; the strategies are stochastic patterns.

However, if the players have committed themselves to impossible positions, the game-theoretic enquiry will quickly show this. Then what happens depends upon whether the game is zero-sum or not. It may be recalled that a zero-sum game was explained earlier. It is a game in which the *total* pay-off is fixed, and the bargaining decides how this total is to be divided. Perhaps the contestants in most important games nowadays (from labour disputes through national economics to international diplomacy) too readily regard their games as zero-sum; it is a possible opinion. If the game is non-zero-sum in principle, and those mentioned surely are, it certainly should not be constrained to a constant pay-off. For a game that is freed from this constraint can generate a new and higher pay-off to share, with the result that each contestant now receives a much better reward than he conceivably could have done under the old conditions. To do so, the players must form a coalition with respect to this particular game; the extra reward is generated by their refusal to lose pay-off 'in friction', and is called *collaborators' surplus*.

A metalanguage in which it is possible to talk like this is clearly competent to resolve the undecidability described earlier. Moreover, the scientific objectivity of the model, and of the scientists who compute within it, might help to reduce psychological tension between the contestants. It seems possible that something of this kind has already been successfully operated in international affairs, and within the affairs of an industrial company. But there is no sign whatsoever that the available OR approach has been used at national level to resolve the problems of social and economic affairs that are normally labelled 'political'.

Meanwhile, and instead, policy-makers in both government and industry play strategies that are not so much good or bad as meaningless—because no metalanguage has been created in which to discuss them. They are caught up in undecidable sentences, which is the reason why no-one ever wins the argument, and no decision ever turns out to be wrong. The nation suffers for this.

For example, the industrialist who adopts a bad development plan and begins to make a product of national importance uneconomically is supposed, by classical economics, to go bankrupt. In fact, when he raises his prices, his 'competitors' (who have actually but unknowingly formed a game-theoretic coalition with him) smile and raise their prices too. Legislation exists, of course, to stop this happening—and can do so when formal coalitions (which we call monopolies) are formed. But the unexpressed, even unconscious, search for what is actually collaborators' surplus goes on. The theory on which we work supposes that this cannot be done without chicanery—deliberate abuse of the competitive code of Western society. But this presupposes that everyone in the game really knows what his costs and profits are, in detail and absolutely. He does not: large ramified systems obscure these issues, and accounting systems are not clever enough to penetrate their complexities. Hence the smiling competitor who raises his prices too is probably saying in all honesty: 'I *thought* we were not charging enough for this product, now I am sure.'

The worst feature of all this is that it destroys the learning mechanism by which decision-takers ought to learn through their mistakes. For an undecidable language has been revealed here in which no mistake can possibly *count* as a mistake. The (genuinely) bad development policy is shown by subsequent events to have been an (ostensibly) good one all the time. The industrialist, or the minister, who is trapped in this undecidability is all too happy. '*Quicquid dicam aut erit, aut non*: whatever I say will either happen, or not. In either case I am going to be right: good old Apollo.'

2   Decision Theory

The foregoing discussion of the nature of prediction is set within the general theory of model-building. The sense in which a model may be called predictive has now been explained. A methodological amalgam is required, having three separable aspects: a correct (that is homomorphic) identification of underlying structure and mechanism, a stochastic scheme of quantification and a knowledge of statistical interaction. Decision, then, is an event detectable, describable and indeed determinable, by the parameters and states of a model—whether this be formulated rigorously by the scientist, or unconsciously by the manager. Decision is effective to the extent that it is competent to modify future states of the system in a way which meets the pre-established criteria of success. Given this framework, the process of reaching the best decision is known as *optimization*, and the corpus of theoretical knowledge which bears on this process is called *decision theory*.

Decision theory comprises a large number of mathematical techniques, details of which need sponsor no delay. For, using the network language, it is very easy to understand what kinds of problem will yield to these techniques, what is their fundamental nature (for in this respect they are all the same), and through what kind of rigour they may be approached. They are divided arbitrarily here into three groups.

(a) Geometric approach

The rigour of the first group is geometrical. Clearly the network is a geometric construction, and this may be valuable in tackling certain kinds of problem in which physical space is actually involved. Most notable among the applications of this idea (and incidentally one of the earliest techniques of OR to be developed) is *search theory*. This is of predominantly military relevance: it has to do with the optimization of tactics for finding an elusive target. If allied and enemy forces are each regarded as following a line depicted on the network, then they may encounter each other at a probabilistic node. Targets for each force are randomly distributed as the potential intersections of lines advance—according to certain probabilities of which the density can be measured.

The search procedure to be followed will depend on the information available about the enemy: whether his probability densities are uniformly distributed or are concentrated in particular areas, for example; and whether the likelihood of one tactically significant event is contingent on another or independent of it. Criteria of success in such problems are formulated as (for instance) the requirement that the probability of a target entering the range of the allied strike force as it moves down its path should be maximized; or that the number of randomly assorted targets which could enter this range should be maximized; or that the proportion of potential targets which can escape detection is minimized. The scientific elucidation of these strategies is of course important in the field of operations itself. But perhaps the most valuable management aid which the technique provides lies in the comparison which can be made of the effectiveness of alternative weapons systems and detection equipments. For it is possible to assess which is more effective when using its optimal search technique, and which is more vulnerable to failure if strategic exigencies compel the forces to depart from optimal tactics.

All operational research techniques, once they are properly described in an appropriate language and are correctly referred to their underlying models, turn out to be relevant to a variety of problems—some of them not envisaged from the start. Search theory is potentially applicable to *any* sort of searching process, for searches are conducted outside the sphere of military operations, for example in the quasi-military searches undertaken by police forces. But we also speak of search in connection with patents, legal precedents, library references, genealogies and so on. These searches are not conducted in physical space as were those studied by military OR men. Nevertheless, this is not to say that search theory is altogether inapplicable, for perhaps a given programme of logical search could be *mapped on to* a geometric programme of search through physical space.

The barrier to such a development is conceptual rather than scientific, for in the geometric group of applications decision theory is concerned with an ordered series of decisions which trace out a course or pathway of action. It is of no theoretical importance whether this pathway exists in physical or logical space. For example, the search by a commercial company for customers requires a serial decision procedure on the part of the management which optimizes the use of its selling resources. Whether each sequential decision refers to the selling technique to be tried next (logical space) or to the direction a travelling salesman will next take (physical space) is scientifically immaterial in terms of the geometric rigour of a network—on to which both sequential decision problems can be mapped.

(b) Statistical approach

The rigour of the second group of decision-theoretic techniques is statistical. This group has to do with decisions that are in fact determined by the probabilities generated at each node of a network by the statistical convolution of the probabilities which flow into that node. Sequential decisions are not now concerned with tracing a pathway *through* the network, but with an instantaneous change in the state of the entire network as between one moment and the next. Mathematically speaking, if we write down the probability that the system is in one particular state at a given moment, and add to this the probability that it is in another particular state at the same moment, and so on until the probabilities are exhausted, we have a way of describing the stochastic nature of the system in its entirety. For the expression just calculated for a given moment in time is complete—it has unit probability. And it has all the resolving power needed by a network description, because it enumerates in mathematical shorthand all possible states of the system. (Technically, this is called a probability vector in Hilbert space.) Now it is fundamental to this thinking that the probability that a system will be found in a given state at a given time is conditioned by the state it was in at the previous instant. The passage of a system from one state to the next has, then, a *transition probability* which can be measured in terms of the likelihood of the immediately preceding state. This is called a *Markov process*, and a sequence of such transitions is called a *Markov chain*.

When decision-taking is based on a theoretical foundation of this kind

DC—P

we are (despite the abstruseness of the last paragraph) in precisely that area of forecasting most familiar to the practical man. He is often heard to say that the most reliable method of prediction is to assume that what has just happened will happen again—rather than to work out a theory which will attempt to compute from scratch what the next state of the system will be. In fact, however, the scientist also knows full well that real life is a self-perpetuating business; the system with which the manager is concerned is (the manager will say) a *dynamic* system, and not merely a random succession of states of affairs. This is precisely why the scientist who studies the stochastic processes implicit in a given network regards it as Markovian, and seeks out what he will call the *dynamical equation* which links the probabilities that one state will transform to the next. Moreover, the practical man knows that if a system is left alone it will run to some kind of equilibrium; a great deal of management technique is indeed based on this expectation. The question the manager wants to answer is: given that the profitability of the system is so-much when the system is in a given state at a given time (in other words as I now find it), to what level will the profit rise in how long before it levels off at equilibrium? Alternatively, if a profit is generated in the act of the system's changing state (for example, when a sale is made), what can I expect this profit to be in the equilibrium condition? The scientist computes this answer with ease, once he has established the transition probabilities of the Markov process, and found the dynamical equation of the system.

It is with this statistical rigour that operational research tackles a large variety of problems which depend on stochastic interactions in the network. Queues and stocks and inventories are all residues of statistical interactions—as was described in some detail earlier. According to *queue theory*, it is possible to determine how long a queue should be to ensure that the process for which queueing is going on will undergo no delay—for any given probability. In hospitals, this conclusion is important to consultant physicians who do not want to waste their time, but who do not wish to keep patients waiting unnecessarily. It is important to production economics if a machine is not to experience idle time. It is, conversely, important to a supermarket to ensure that—even at the risk of some idle time on the part of the cashier—a queue of customers does not get too long.

The same arguments apply to stocks of raw materials, finished goods, warehouse stores, bins of spare parts, and so forth. They are all affected by exactly the same statistical considerations, and *inventory theory* seeks to determine how big these stocks should be and what are the appropriate policies for managing them—for a given probability. With techniques of these kinds, decision theory can take its stand on prescribing a queue discipline or a reorder rule after the manager has prescribed acceptable probabilities of failure to meet the criteria of success. Once he says what these probabilities are, all the parameters of the network fall into place, and the system can be optimized to procure a minimal capital investment, for example, or a maximal profitability. But it is most important to take note of the case where, instead of prescribing these probabilities, the management decides to allow the stock levels to fluctuate of their own accord. Normally, this happens *faute de mieux*, in which case the fluctuations may be embarrassingly large and the investment involved may become uneconomic. All this can, however, be avoided if the control system underlying the entire operation is properly designed. This probably means floating a scientific model on to the network language in which the system is described.

For example, a model may be taken from servomechanics, and the system designed to become self-regulating. For the point about any servomechanical system is that, when it is distributed, it goes into an oscillation of which the behaviour can be measured. Basically, one of three things may happen. Either the oscillation will be amplified by the servomechanism, so that stock fluctuations grow ever more wild; or the oscillation may simply be perpetuated, so that no-one is ever quite sure what is happening; or the oscillation may be damped—finally to disappear. This admirable outcome does not happen by chance: it is fully determined by the design of the servomechanical control. If, then, the OR model succeeds in identifying a set of communications and decision rules across the stochastic network which conform to the laws of servomechanics, the queues and stocks and inventories can be guaranteed to be self-regulating. In this case the whole of the mathematical theory recently described can be brought into play. The system is running to an equilibrium whenever it is disturbed: very well, we may calculate the economics of its steady-state behaviour. Operational research has made good use of this model from time to time in the context of particular problems. More recently, however, the model has been extended to cover the entire operation of a business. The topic of *industrial dynamics* deals with this class of model.

These are powerful tools indeed for any management. And the list of specialized OR techniques which belong to this genre may be expanded still further. For example, mention was made earlier of the technique of *critical path analysis*—which is of course just such an application of stochastic theory across a network, considered with statistical rigour.

Renewal theory concerns itself with strategies for replacing worn out parts, machines, aircraft or anything else that has to be renewed. This work depends on the notion of life-cycles, and its terminology is roughly actuarial. Here are the *birth–death processes* which have been studied extensively mathematically, and which lead to policies for making replacements, and for undertaking preventive maintenance. These ideas naturally lead to the whole question of breakdowns and the way in which they influence the smooth running of any whole system. And breakdowns need not refer to mechanical failures on the part of production plant: they may refer to any kind of stoppage. For example, in the process of weaving, an automatic loom may be stopped by the breakage of a thread. Thus the amount of time lost in such a situation will depend on the availability of the relatively few operatives available in a large weaving shed, and a variety of decisions about the labour force and the production system itself will be determined by stochastic interactions. This leads to the *theory of machine interference.*

Finally, at any given node in a network where there is an interplay of probabilities, a random fluctuation will be acceptable. But if something goes wrong, that is to say if the system goes out of control, these fluctuations may become dangerous and they will have to be detected. Decisions are required as to the correct moment for intervention and the correct action to take. All such cases are governed by the need to recognize when some fluctuation is no longer due to chance. In the simplest case the techniques of *statistical quality control* are fairly familiar from applied statistics. At a more advanced level, there are the *sequential decision techniques* which consider not only individual instances of fluctuation, but accrue whole runs—so that the moment of decision is recognized far more quickly than the unaided brain can possibly detect a significant change.

There are indeed many highly developed ways of looking at this group of decision-theoretic problems, and there is a risk that their very multiplicity will persuade the sceptic that somewhat trivial notions are being proliferated here for the sake of effect. On the contrary, an entire literature exists for each of the theories italicized above, and there are many first-rate scientists working in industry (one hesitates to call them operational research men in the round) who specialize in the application of these particular techniques to the exclusion of everything else. Their activities are confined and their lives may be boring; but it has to be faced that there is enough waste, enough lost production and lost profit, enough futile occupation, enough sterilized capital and labour, to keep an army of such scientists indefinitely and most profitably busy.

(c) Algebraic approach

The third and last group of techniques of decision theory relies not on a geometric nor a statistical rigour but on an algebraic treatment of the network language. These techniques are the optimization methods *par excellence*: they may be summed up under the name *mathematical programming*. The original, and still the most potent of these methods in practice, is *linear programming*—which was discussed in Chapter 8. According to this, all possible permutations of the resources available to the management in a complex situation are connected to all possible outcomes; this can be viewed as a complicated and tangled network existing in as many dimensions as there are resource–outcome connections. Such a network of possibilities carves out a phase space within which the solution of the problem, good or bad, must inevitably lie. The problem is handled by the algebra of convex sets and, as was shown in the earlier example, an optimal solution to this allocation can be discovered—given that the criteria of success can be properly formulated to create an objective function for solving the mathematics. But phase spaces are not always built up of a tangle of straight lines, and a network of curved lines can easily be envisaged. Such curves would represent the fact, for instance, that the relationship between the amount produced of some product and its profit-earning capacity is rarely linear. For the handling of such problems, more involved techniques of *non-linear programming* have been devised.

Now all these approaches are directed towards a static situation. Given that there exists a range of possible resources and a range of possible outcomes, the best connectivity between them can be found. It is not usual, therefore, to regard these approaches as offering a forecasting technique. On the other hand, the solutions they propose are offered to management as policies which they may adopt; if the management responds by altering its existing arrangements to conform to the optimal solution, then it is indeed expected that the profitability which has been computed will accrue. And this is what happens in practice. So the procedure does amount to a forecasting technique, and the solution is a prediction in the sense discussed in the last section. The sense in which 'we know what will happen' has been pinpointed. The interpretation most definitely requires that the situation be static, or at least that any drift in conditions is slow and sure, so that its effects can be taken out of the calculation. The case may well arise, however, where the static assumption is obviously a wild oversimplification. Perhaps the situation is changing markedly and in a not very straightforward manner. In this case the technique of *dynamic programming* is used, for this is a form of the general technique especially adapted to the description of changing situations.

These then are the main techniques of decision theory, arranged arbitrarily here in three groups for ease of understanding. Decision theory provides the engineering lore for building management policies within the architectonics of planned chance. It was said in the first section of this chapter that the most useful scientific language for discussing the networks that underlie all this is really the *theory of graphs*. Yet the mathematics of decision theory is not historically of this kind; as has been seen it is basically geometric, statistical and algebraic. The answer to the implied question is that graph-theoretic approaches to OR network description and manipulation have only recently started to acquire a coherent form. Clearly a network is a graph, and clearly a graph is a geometric entity. Also, a graph whose transitions are probabilistic is clearly a statistical entity. Thirdly, a graph which is unoriented (where the lines indicate the edges of spaces rather than vectors) is an algebraic entity. These viewpoints have been considered; and a fourth might well have been added: the graph as a logical entity, consisting of an arborescence of binary relations to be treated by Boolean functions. Now the modern mathematical statement of graphs is achieved with the help of the theory of sets, and it looks like subsuming all the other descriptions in one. (The vertices of a graph are regarded as elements of a set which is mapped into itself, of which set the whole graph is then a multi-valued function.) All the techniques of decision theory can, it seems likely, be expressed in these common terms—once the theory of graphs is more widely taught and understood.

But these technical diversions, although important, should not hinder understanding of the general argument. The techniques of decision theory exist, and although OR scientists will eventually discover more economical and elegant ways of expressing them in a consolidated form, they exist to be used now. As a battery of weapons they have already proved themselves immensely useful, and indeed most of the literature of operational research is concerned with them alone.

In fact, some authorities declare that operational research itself is simply a part of decision theory, since all OR is aimed at helping the decision-taker to optimize, and since decision-taking situations exist in which OR cannot help at all. Yet in this book the matter has been dealt with in this one section of this one chapter. So definite a rejection of the popular view, and so cavalier a treatment of so wide a subject, merits some explanation.

3   Against Scientific Impetuosity

Despite the technical brilliance of many of the decision-theoretic techniques, and despite the very large savings which they have brought about in practical industrial and governmental situations, classical decision theory suffers from three major limitations: one mathematical, one methodological and the third pragmatic. From these small points consequences of some moment flow. It was said at the very beginning of this Part II (Chapter 6, Section 1) that the kind of science which is preoccupied with analytic method is not altogether adequate to the task of dealing with large and exceedingly complex systems and situations. It was indeed for this very reason that the whole theory of modelling and mapping was embarked upon. It is therefore rash in the extreme to charge at a real-life managerial problem, with an impetus derived from pure mathematical thinking which claims to have penetrated the nature of this problem in its generic form. Operational research is an empirical science; it is concerned with actual situations and not with idealizations of them—and what is important to the manager may not have been present in the minds of those who developed the technique. Put dramatically: there is no point in making a coruscating scientific presentation of the reasons why a factory should be built at site *A*, if the manager has his eye on the trout stream at site *B* and his wife prefers the shops there. This is not at all to say that decision theory is of no use. But, as with every other kind of tool, one must know and understand its limitations.

(a) The mathematical difficulty—and value theory

As was explained in Chapter 6, it is mathematically impossible to optimize more than one variable of a situation at a time. That is to say, when a mathematical model has been set to maximize profit, or to minimize cost, that is *all* that it can do. If the management has other objectives than this, they have to be handled by other means. In the limit, the really impetuous decision-theorist will ignore these other criteria of success altogether, acknowledging to the management that he has done so. His recommendation is of the form: this is the programme that makes the largest possible profit; I cannot guarantee that your employees will not immediately come out on strike, nor that your customers' goodwill will be retained, nor that the plant will withstand the battering I propose to give it, but you are the manager and had better take care of these matters. This is incompetent operational research, because OR is supposed to be giving the manager scientific advice on a policy which he can actually follow. It is fostered partly by academic research, which sometimes forgets that OR is an empirical science, and partly by managers who feel that their prerogatives are usurped if the scientist is allowed to try and cope with all the facts. But it will not do; and we have to seek out ways in which the unidimensionality of the decision-theoretic approach can be handled.

The method usually adopted in practice, usually by people who have not thought much about it and who do not recognize precisely why they are doing this, is to prescribe constraints to delimit the phase space of a feasible solution—so that the answer looks sensible. If an optimal solution to a production-planning problem acknowledges a sufficient number of constraints about the way the labour force is used, then it is most unlikely that there will be a strike. If the optimal solution to a stockholding problem acknowledges the constraint that only 1 chance in 1,000 will be accepted of failing to meet an order (whereas a chance of 1 in 100 or 1 in 1,000,000 might equally well have been chosen), then the customers' goodwill is likely to be retained. If the optimization of a scheduling problem accepts the constraints put on plant performance by the most lugubrious of the maintenance engineers, then it is unlikely to fall apart at the end of the year. In this way, a large number of other desiderata appears to be met, although the optimization is quite strictly concerned with one variable alone—such as cost or profit.

Considered as a solution of the problem as it was originally raised, however, this answer is trivial, bad science and actively misleading to the management. For of course it ignores the nature of the ramified system; it pretends to know the absolute boundary conditions of the system which are not in fact known, and not in fact absolute. The whole point about prediction within a ramified system is to be able to see how existing restraints will be moved in or moved out or utterly changed by an alteration in policy or environmental circumstances. So the approach freezes all the degrees of freedom which the system naturally has—except one. And there is usually no justification for doing this. Sometimes, however, there is; it is at these moments that decision theory comes into its own.

Now it will have been noticed that of the restraints which surround a problem situation, some are of fact and some are of value. That is to say, that whereas the maximum speed at which an engine will turn before it blows up is accepted as a fact, the proportion of late deliveries which a customer will accept before he seeks a new supplier is accepted as a value judgment. For example, it is typical of a manager's life that he should have to take a decision between two clamant customers, each of whom is demanding a service which only one of them can have. And yet this dichotomy between fact and value, when projected into an actual decision-taking situation which refers to the future, turns out to be invalid. In the manager's mind, the judgments he makes about value are as clearly facts of the problem as are physical limitations. The real nature of the manager's dilemma is not that he has to arrange a marriage of fact and value, as so many analysts presume, but that his decision is taken with incomplete information.

What normally pass as facts and values are both ascertainable (albeit by different methods) in a completely specified situation alone. Important decisions, which concern a fairly distant future, relate to conditions which are not completely specified—which is why there is a decision to take at all. The future circumstances which can so easily affect and change a value judgment can just as easily affect and change the facts of the case, because of the ramified system. Hence the criteria of success which are applied to a given problem are in very large measure arbitrary choices made by the management in the face of a large measure of ignorance about what the circumstances will really be like at the time. They are statements about how the decision-takers envisage that they will be conducting themselves at the time when the decision becomes operable. For this reason, when a management group takes a corporate decision, it is probably solving a problem in social dynamics. The decision taken will be the one that minimizes the expected level of conflict.

We are now in the field of value theory, the subject which attempts to bring managerial value judgments within the compass of decision theory. But it has already been argued that the distinction between fact and value is unreal in a particular practical context, and this makes the attempts to escape from unidimensionality somewhat unreal as well. For according to value theory, one should try to ascribe numbers to value judgments in order that they may be built into the decision-theoretic model. There are various technical problems lying in wait, which there is no room to go into here. (They include the issue of subjective and objective probability, the problem of additive capability in the value numbers, and the likelihood that a numerical scale of values is based on a notion of absolute preference which may well be chimerical.) But overriding all problems of theory, comes the point that the whole approach assumes rationality in decision.

Now the allegation is not that decision-takers are irrational (although examples of this could be found). It is to say that most important decisions are non-rational in so far as they contend with incomplete information. The people who have gone furthest with a decision theory incorporating a value theory as a means of meeting the difficulties discussed above, seem to gloss over the arbitrariness of temperament. If decision can be lifted out of the emotive plane altogether, as some of them would claim, then there must be a way of measuring an appropriate risk which is independent of the attitudes of the managers who will be taking that risk. If not, then the managerial temperament has to be built into the model. This is sometimes done unwittingly by theorists who are not immersed in empirical OR science.

Econometricians and game-theorists who are not also operational research men, are inclined to classify managerial strategies according to value-theoretic criteria which they have *themselves* devised. When the *minimax criterion* (which minimizes the maximum risk) was mentioned in the earlier discussion of game theory, it may well have been thought that this is quite typically the prudential policy which managers follow. But suppose it is not? An extremely conservative management probably follows the *maximin criterion*, which maximizes the minimum pay-off. Even so, a really impetuous manager might look at the possible outcomes of each of his possible strategies and consider only the most favourable outcome in each case (which he feels sure he can achieve); he may then select the strategy whose best outcome is highest—the *maximax criterion*. Or again, a management which is not only prudential but rather pessimistic by nature, may look at the problem less in terms of the pay-off available and more in terms of the cost of making a mistake—which is called 'the regret'. Hence a manager may seek to minimize the maximum risk of opportunity loss, which is called the *minimax regret criterion*. When all these criteria refer to 'risk' they are actually seeking to measure the advantage available to the other player (which may be nature). This is because in a zero-sum game you lose what he gains. But when the game is being played against nature, it becomes rather absurd to think of an opponent actively attempting to 'do you down'. Hence, although it is possible to work out the consequences which flow from considering nature as an opponent who is trying to win, it might be best to embody one's ignorance of the future and of 'nature's policy' by assuming that nature will play every one of the strategies open to it with equal probability. This is known as the *Bayes criterion*.

There is no point in going on with this list, to which various ingenious modifications have been proposed from time to time. In any case, instead of resolving to adopt the one strategy which uniquely meets one of these criteria, many possible situations arise in which it can be shown that the most sensible policy is to mix various strategies in certain calculated proportions at random. The great advantage of a *mixed strategy* is that when playing a real opponent, he is unable to deduce under which criterion one is playing. This makes the problem less predictable for him. There is a second advantage to be gained in terms of stability. A game is said to be *equilibrial* if the minimax pay-off for one player is the same as the maximin pay-off for the other. Not all games with a finite number of pure strategies have this equilibrial property, but if the players are allowed to use mixed strategies, the game is always equilibrial.

There is a number of whole books written on the topic of game theory, but this is not one of them. The present object is to show that the values adopted by the management in formulating policies under the uncertainty of the future, are in practice affected by temperament. For these strategies, which depend on degrees of prudence, determination, pessimism, and such like, refer not only to situations which can be formulated as formal games, but to the whole range of decision-theoretic situations. With all of the techniques discussed in the last section, there are choices to be made which depend on an attitude towards the future; so to talk of scientific forecasting without taking these attitudes into account is delusory.

The preferences of management can be handled, it is sometimes argued, by setting them in order and assigning numbers to the outcomes which are so ranked. This view seems to be defective, both for the reason that nobody knows whether it is true that a manager's judgment of such matters is unambiguous and consistent, and also because an adequate account of the matter would have to include, at least implicitly, a model of the manager's brain—which is the computer that does the ranking. Here is another way of showing that this whole problem is metalinguistic, compelling the inference that analytical decision-theoretic techniques are not as straightforward as they appear once an uncertain future is drawn into the problem.

To sum up this argument: decision theory is mathematically limited to optimizing in one dimension. Constraints operating in other dimensions than this one are really fluid, and a ramified system under uncertainty which is generating a future we wish to predict will cause them to change. To overcome this difficulty, it is alleged that the constraints are not genuinely fluid: they are determined (regardless of the ramified system) by managerial value judgments. By quantifying these values on a numerical scale (using techniques not examined closely here), the optimization can still be effected in respect of the future. To this we have replied that, although the distinction between fact and value is illusory, the whole system of constraints (of whatever kind) is fluxing in the course of adaptation to unpredicted change. The conclusion is that the value-theoretic approach enables decision theory to escape the mathematical limitation of unidimensionality in a static situation, where a result can be implemented now, if the managerial temperament can be correctly assessed or indeed deduced from current practice. But it is of little help in a problem involving long-term forecasting.

(b) The methodological difficulty—homomorphs again

The methodological difficulty encountered in applying the orthodox OR techniques, which is also ignored by the more impetuous OR scientist, is that decision theory leaves out the formulation of an explicit scientific model from the operational research process. It tries to jump directly from the real-life situation to a mathematical model, without investigating the nature of the mechanism of which the mathematical model is supposed to be a rigorous statement. Now to be quite strict, this is impossible; what is really happening is that the mathematical model is a rigorous account of a very loosely formulated and altogether untested theory about the natural mechanism involved.

In inventory theory, for example, a great many assumptions are usually made about the statistical form of the probability distributions that will be encountered. These rest on *a priori* notions which are often falsified in practice—because of the ramified system. There are so many interactions and feedbacks in the network that the distributions which are supposed to appear are very often radically distorted. Again, mathematical programming techniques also tend to ignore this stochastic and interactive feature of real life. They may in a particular application be very sensitive to both errors and probabilistic fluctuations in the coefficients entered into the input–output matrix. The list could be prolonged indefinitely. It is all a matter of identifying structure in the real world—which is an empirical, heuristic, undertaking. Too often the proponents of decision theory assume that they know what this structure is.

If lengthy experience of doing operational research shows up such weaknesses so clearly, why are the techniques acclaimed, and, more particularly, why do they so often succeed? If we can answer these questions, we shall be able to join in the acclamation and the success without falling into the traps being discussed here. There are two answers to the question.

Firstly, situations are quite frequently encountered in which the simple-minded and latent scientific models on which decision-theoretic techniques are based are roughly homomorphic with the facts. With luck, the *a priori* distributions of probability will not be distorted; and with skill, a practised OR man will recognize the fact. He can then use the classical theory. Or take the case of the most successful application of linear programming: the transportation problem, in which the technique is used to decide what is the optimal (that is, the cheapest) way to transport materials or goods from a number of sources to a number of destinations. There is no deep underlying mechanism to these situations, and the linear programming network itself is certainly homomorphic with the facts. This is why the techniques work. There are moments when impetuosity pays off.

But because the inversion of a linear programming matrix can generate the total number of ways in which oil can be moved from a number of oil fields to a number of refineries under certain transportation constraints, and because we have an algorithm for discerning which of these ways is optimal, it simply does not follow that the same device can be used to describe and optimize the national economy (for instance). An economy is *par excellence* an exceedingly complex ramified system, too unspecified, too deeply interactive, and for that matter too undecidable to be mapped on to the orthodox linear programming matrix. It is ironic that champions of technical rigour should be so methodologically slapdash as to make the attempt. They need to erect a theory about the way the economy works, expressed as a scientific model which can be tested as a homomorphic mapping, before even contemplating a technique which would identify optimal economic policies within such a model.

Secondly, decision theory is immensely useful in providing a language in which to discuss managerial problems. Even in the case where a technique cannot be pressed home to the point where a computed numerical answer is available and correct, it can certainly be used to explore the situation—if only to find out in which ways real life is more rich and interpenetrative than the mathematical model allows. It would be interesting to know in how many cases where decision-theoretic techniques have been used, and published as having been used, an exact numerical solution was both obtained and also precisely applied to real life. Let us be bold and say: this very rarely happens.

If this sounds like heresy in some OR circles, it is because some professionals imagine that their only claim to scientific respectability resides in making the opposite claim. The doctoral student on his first assignment may be forgiven for thinking so, because it is right for him to submit to academic discipline. But from a professional OR standpoint, it must be confessed that the manager is not particularly interested in providing the scientist with Nobel prize fodder; he wants answers that work. Well, the manager is himself a professional, and it is not to his credit that he has no vocabulary capable of discussing his own problems properly. Ordinary English simply will not do, as anyone can hear who attends a managerial convention. The penetration of the vernacular into the deep nature of a managerial dilemma is slight indeed; hence the discussion of this dilemma is more a matter of exchanging slogans than of conducting an enquiry. Decision theory can certainly claim to have devised ways of talking about these problems which are penetrating and quantitative by nature. Therefore they are extremely useful—whether numbers trickle out at the end of the enquiry or not. It should always be remembered that in many managerial problems science has done all that is necessary in the way of quantification if it can get the sign right. That is to say that a policy should make a profit rather than a loss, or that course B will make more rather than less of a profit than course A.

The moral is perfectly clear. One dare not slap a decision-theoretic technique on to a problem like a poultice. The relevance of the mathematical model has to be examined with the greatest care, and this is in itself a full-scale scientific investigation, involving the collection of facts, the formulation of hypotheses and the undertaking of experiments. In fact, the mathematical model does not exist *sui generis*; it ought to be a rigorous formulation of a scientific model that is itself a homomorphism of the problem situation. This is the reason why the job of selecting a technique and certifying its relevance must be left to the scientist, and should not normally be undertaken by the manager himself. A manager is ill advised to say: 'Do a linear programme on this', or 'Use inventory theory on that.' The scientist is not a tradesman to be summoned with his No. 5 kit of tools to mend a leak in the management regimen. The manager should say instead: 'Kindly examine this dilemma by the methods of science.'

The analogy with a doctor can hardly be overlooked. It is too easy for a man with a stiff arm to say to his physician: 'Prescribe a liniment for me to rub into my stiff arm.' It is only when the patient tells the doctor what his symptoms are and asks for help that the doctor has the opportunity to discover that the stiffness in the arm is caused by a weakness in the heart. Correct diagnosis depends on the physician's having a strongly homomorphic model of the patient's whole anatomy, and the freedom to investigate its mapping on to the patient.

The lengthy consideration given in preceding chapters to the methodology of operational research should help to display the nature of this extremely important matter. There is always a conceptual model in OR and, since it is a trained scientist who has the concept, a scientific model underlies it. It is vital for the scientist to acknowledge the exist-

ence and to investigate the nature of this model before proceeding to give
a rigorous account of the matter in mathematical terms.

(c) The pragmatic difficulty—better versus best

The third of the limitations inherent in decision theory is specified as a
pragmatic difficulty because one of the startling features of real life is
that things are indeed as they are. What is the case is true. It is perhaps
the most important ability of the OR man *qua* professional, as contra-
distinguished from the OR man *qua* scientist, that he should be able to
recognize the truth in the guise of what is already the case. If the truth
is not discernible in this, of course, he must say so—and seek to alter
things. But it is a limitation of the decision-theoretic approach that it
impetuously declares what the structure of decision *ought* to be, without
first investigating what it is. So again we find the competent OR man
setting his knowledge of technique within the framework of scientific
methodology.

Observation of the managerial process certainly suggests that its aim
is to improve matters steadily, rather than to seek a rigorous optimum.
The reason why this should be so is also clear. The manager is not at all
sure that he can find in his own understanding a conceptual model which
really represents the situation he is trying to control, nor that he can
specify the relationships within it, nor that he knows all the criteria of
success. And so he changes things cautiously, altering the parameters of
the situation in ways which his experience suggests may be valuable,
noting the outcome, and reinforcing success when it occurs. Now the
scientist ought to be able to recognize in this approach a perfectly valid
mechanism of control. It may be learnt of nature in the processes of
genetic mutation and natural selection. And indeed the OR scientist has
many ways of handling models to emulate this approach. The most
familiar of them is most appropriately named *evolutionary operation*.
This is quite straightforwardly a rigorous version of the managerial
practice just described. It uses mathematically planned experimentation
to direct a sequential decision-taking process; this is aimed at a steady
increase in the kind of satisfaction which is only recognized after it has
occurred, and cannot be uniquely specified in advance. Other ways of
looking at this problem will be discussed in Part III.

But, for the moment, it is enough to say that forecasting itself is best
treated as an adaptive process, and that this conclusion also militates
against the impetuous use of decision theory in situations which relate
to the future. The reason for the allegation can be formalized: it is not
simply a matter of emulating what managers do. For if we look at a

distant outcome as the end-point of a converging stochastic network, it becomes very clear that it will be possible to improve the precision with which the characteristics of this point are adumbrated as the moment 'now' moves from left to right across the diagram. The number of outcomes lying on the critical path towards the final outcome steadily diminishes; the extensity of ramification around the critical path also attenuates. And, if we consider the situation from the standpoint of information theory, it is sure that as we move from left to right our forecasts of the final outcome reach out towards it and, as it were, bounce back. Today, on the fourth of the month, I see myself in Birmingham on the fifteenth; because I reach out in my mind to this future event, I seek to make arrangements with a man whom I wish to meet in that town; unknown to me he will not be there. But in two days' time his letter bounces back from that notional future date to tell me, on the sixth, that my forecast of what it will be like on the fifteenth is defective in this respect at least. Adaptive forecasting is like radar locating events in time instead of space.

As an example, we may consider a production programme manufacturing for stock. The balance of this programme requires that future demand be forecast. Now consider a person who, though ignorant of many things, knows all about optimal scheduling techniques. His impetuous nature demands that he should at once compute the production programme that gives least idle time on the plant, or meets most orders, or minimizes stock or whatever (let us hope that he remembers to find out which of these desiderata—if any—the management is prepared to have optimized). The schedule he is about to prepare relates to the future, and must therefore include estimates of future demand. He declares that no-one knows what the future will be like, and that the best that science can do is to extrapolate present trends. He does extrapolate them; and he takes the figures and puts them into his computer.

Now to extrapolate means to draw a line (either by eye or some more sophisticated statistical means) through all the points that have been recorded in the past, and then to extend that line on into the future— taking a reading at the date in which one is interested. This procedure gives equal weight to *all* the points that have been recorded in the past. As was said when the question of forecasting demand was last discussed, however, there is in fact no guarantee whatsoever that circumstances are generating change with a guaranteed underlying pattern, whether we are looking at an increase which appears to be linear, or exponential, or for that matter follows a sine wave. The very identification of such patterns can often be misleading, because they powerfully suggest that there is some secret mechanism generating the change. Indeed there may be. Yet, as we all know, some really important event may suddenly occur which radically alters the whole thing. And so, as was said before, the practical man is likely to assert that the best forecast he can make does not delve far back into the past (when circumstances were very likely quite different) but assumes that the most recent experience will be repeated. In other words, his forecasting procedure is a Markov chain.

Pausing for a moment to consider these extreme viewpoints, we might well come to the conclusion that each is a little too extreme. Surely experience suggests that although the second argument makes pretty good sense, the very last point may itself be something of an aberration, and perhaps one ought to go back a bit further. The question then is how far. It would be nice to evade that very difficult query, and in fact we can. For if we argue that the most recent event may well be repeated, we can also argue that the one just before it may also influence the event about to come—though perhaps rather less. And the event before the one before the last may also have a bearing—but rather less still. In fact, the influence of history *is* felt from way back, but its impact is decaying as it retreats into the past and may be losing its relevance to the future. Let us then take all the events we have on record into account; but let us weight each one by its distance (and therefore irrelevance) from the present.

Of course we have no way of knowing at what rate relevance is being lost. On the other hand, we are very familiar with this process of decay in nature, and we know that it tends to follow an exponential curve. That is to say, the decay begins rather rapidly and gradually flattens out: an example of this was given earlier. So if exponential weights are allocated to historical data, the most recent event will have the biggest impact on the forecast, and its predecessors less and less impact—according to this mathematical function of decay. Because the exponential curve is asymptotic (that is to say, it is always approaching the base line but never hits it), every event of recorded history could be accorded some weight in making the forecast, but as time recedes the weights will become indefinitely small. This is what was meant by saying that we do not need to declare how far back we are prepared to go. On the other hand, scientific decisions must be taken about the rate at which the exponential curve is to take effect, and this is admittedly a tricky matter. But it can be resolved by competent analysis of the records.

This way of handling demand statistics is known as *exponential smoothing*. It turns out to be a reliable method of predicting demand, and it allows for the 'feedback from the future' effect. For as time passes each new event improves the estimate of the final outcome, which it does by being awarded the largest rate—while everything else is pushed back one step. So instead of deciding on the optimal production schedule for one point in future time, it becomes possible to conceive of the programme as being something which already exists, and something which is continuously modified towards a future that is never reached. Adaptive forecasting is effected by feeding the model which computes it a continuous input consisting of an exponentially smoothed demand.

And so we pragmatically acknowledge that whatever is, is true; that whatever was, is less relevantly true; and we say that we shall get an ever improving estimate of what will be true next, because it is formulating itself to be so, regardless of the computed optimum.

Having said all this, it remains the case that if a proper investigation should reveal that the structure of production is homomorphically represented by a mathematical programme, and that demand is either stable or can otherwise be forecast realistically (for instance because it is already agreed), then the best thing to do is to optimize the production schedule for that future date. And, having reached this conclusion, it will pay the company for the OR man to make the lives of managers a misery, until they have specified what criteria of success should be applied to create an objective function. The outcome of this procedure will be to overturn the methods used by management in the past to feel its way towards a better state of affairs, and to replace them with a scientific high-precision tool. The result, as was seen in an earlier chapter, could be a 500 per cent increase in profit.

4   Heuristic Forecasting

Having seen the way in which decision theory handles the future, and having examined some of the difficulties inherent in this approach, we should give further consideration to what is altogether another line of attack. This is to use the technique of simulation, which was expounded earlier, as a tool of heuristic forecasting.

Briefly to recapitulate: when a situation has been described in terms of a stochastic network, which has in turn been quantified by expressing its probabilism in terms of statistical expressions having parameters that are expressed numerically, a language competent to discuss that situation has been created. Valid talk about the situation consists in speaking this language. We may say: from this node the flow passes down one of three lines in the proportions 20 per cent, 50 per cent and 30 per cent, but which of the three routes will be followed by the *next* item is not known. The time the next item will take to travel down this line is not known either, but in the long run the distribution of times taken will conform to a known stochastic pattern—describable by a statistical function which has been measured. The next item will then undergo the process represented by the node it has now reached; again the time it will take is unknown, but again the pattern of times traced out over a period is known, and so on. By speaking the language in this way we begin to delineate a model of the dynamic situation concerned, for our talk about the way the system operates, and the way it actually operates, are both unfolding in time, and each leaves behind it a trace consisting of an intricate web of events which have been related to each other in certain ways. One of these traces is a statement about real life, the other is a *simulation model* of real life.

The extent of the isomorphism between the two may of course be examined. To specify the simulation model, it is necessary to arrange parlance in the network language: that is, a quasi-history must be written. Hence, a moment of time is selected, and a particular state of affairs which is plausible in real terms is expressed in the network language. A process then begins of unfolding time artificially to see what will happen next. This involves random sampling procedures which select routes, transportation times and nodal process times, from the stock of information held about these matters. The *random* sampling guarantees that the patterns which will be established in the long run are known. All this is a way of generating artificial but representative information about the system. It is an experimental method singularly appropriate to operational research, which is an empirical science. The advantages of doing this, it is also recollected, are threefold.

First of all, simulation provides artificial experience of the real system very much more quickly than it could otherwise be obtained. Simulated time can be made to run, say, ten times faster than clock time—or if a large computer is available perhaps a hundred times as fast (and it really is ludicrous to note that some simulations are undertaken in which the time ratio is the other way round). Secondly, the experience is gained without running any risks. If we want to know what the system does under a particular set of circumstances, this can readily be discovered without putting the real-life system to the trouble and expense of running a trial which may in any case prove disastrous. Thirdly, it is even possible to alter the system as it now is, to see what would be likely to happen to it under a new kind of régime; and this may also be done without jeopardizing the success of an existing profitable situation.

It may be gathered from these comments that simulation is really a forecasting technique. Simulations are not run to see what is actually happening now under existing conditions—for this may more readily be discovered by going to see. The clue is that simulations tell us what *would* happen, if . . . . I have called this kind of forecasting heuristic, because it is not an attempt to deduce what must necessarily happen, but an attempt to induce what is likely to happen—by feeling out a plausible route from the here and the now through space-time, considered as structured by a stochastic network. If the reply is made: yes, but this will only give a *plausible* interpretation of the future, and not a particularly likely one, the answer is that science is accustomed to making inferences of this kind and knows how to handle them. For the whole procedure is, in scientific terms, an experiment, and it is of the essence of experimentation that a particular outcome should be reproducible. So the facility of a simulation to act as a time machine can be used to replicate the experiment perhaps a hundred times in the span which would be taken to try it once in real life. Naturally these replications will not produce precisely similar outcomes—nor would the replication of the situation in real life. What is important is the recognition of common features in the set of outcomes; these are the inductive inferences which may be classed as forecasts. We say that the system is *robust* in respect to a particular set of outcomes.

Great use has been made of simulation by operational research, often with an air of apology which is altogether misplaced. Some people say that what is really happening is this. A mathematical model of a situation has been constructed, and quantified statistically. If mathematics were yet sufficiently powerful (which it is not) to work out the convolutions of probabilities across all the ramifications of the system, then a rigorous statement about what the system does would be available. Simulation, say these people, is a rough and ready means of approximating the answer—which is really rather disgraceful, and should be supplanted at the earliest opportunity by some respectable mathematics. From the standpoint now reached in this book, it is possible to repudiate this view altogether.

A description of a dynamic, probabilistic, real-life situation in terms of graph theory and stochastic processes is not a model at all. It has here been called a language—which can be spoken to generate a model. This is an important distinction; because if the mathematical statement itself were a model it would be incapable of the homomorphic preservation of situation structure, which is time-based. The mathematical statement collapses the temporal dimension into an instantaneous statistic. Now this is itself capable of temporal expansion (it involves for instance the use of things actually called probability generating functions), but in its mathematical form it has not in fact generated anything at all. Mathematicians may reply that this does not matter, that, for example, one need not write out the full expansion of a polynomial in order to specify it completely. The answer to this is that the analogy is incorrect, and for two reasons.

It has to be shown that the instantaneous statement in mathematical terms of a stochastic network does not usefully specify its spatio-temporal expansion (except in a trivial way). Firstly, then, it should be noted that real life is far too rich to be encapsulated in the so-called model: a great many variables will actually be missing. Secondly, unless one is going to assert quite dogmatically that the universe runs on deterministic lines, even to include a complete statement of all the variables and their relationships would not finally determine the future. The physicist may account for this fact by speaking of Brownian motion, the geneticist may invoke random mutation, and the theologian may assert free will, but the philosopher of science may content himself with the remark that conclusions, however likely, that are based on inductive arguments, remain precarious. In any case, and whatever may be said theoretically about the matter, the state of affairs is adequately indicated in practical operational terms by referring to the influence of noise in the system.

The second reason is more recondite. It is at least possible that the structure of a network configuration is governed by some uncertainty principle analogous to that associated with the name of Heisenberg in quantum physics. The work referred to in Section 4 of Chapter 7 produced a theorem indicating a law called the *Indeterminacy of Configuration Structure*. This says, in rough terms, that if a network (which can by definition take up a very large number of possible configurations) retains an identity of configuration through a period of time, then it cannot be denoted by a general algebraic function—which is to say that the transfer functions at the nodes cannot be completely specified. On the other hand, if such a general algebraic function can be stated, it is impossible to guarantee that the configuration will retain its identity through time. This argument does not apply to all networks of course; it applies to those whose own behaviour is determining the configuration which the network adopts.

For these two reasons, so briefly nominated here, it is argued that it will never be possible to forecast the future state of one of these systems with mathematical rigour to produce an answer which is either certain or complete. But these complicated arguments have not been developed in full, and may be unconvincing. If so, it will be quite sufficient for present purposes to agree that these outcomes, if not actually impossible, are at the least impracticable.

For these reasons it is not appropriate to speak of simulation as an improper or makeshift way of reaching conclusions which ought (in some sense) to be reached by pure mathematical reasoning. But there must be some reason why certain scientists hold the contrary view, and it seems that some confusion may have arisen. Perhaps to bring out what I think the confusion is will help to clarify the whole matter. Many people have in fact confused the OR method of simulation with the mathematical technique known as the *Monte Carlo method*. Faced with a mathematical expression of such hideous complexity that he is unable to evaluate it, the mathematician sometimes devises an algorithm (that is to say a set of procedures) which, when applied numerically to the expression, will lead to an approximate answer. For example, there is an experimental method of determining the constant π which is very well known (as indeed it should be since its originator, Buffon, expounded the matter 200 years ago). If a regular rectilinear grid is marked out, and a needle having precisely the length of the grid interval is thrown at random on to the grid, the probability that it will intersect a grid line is $2/\pi$. Thus, if the experiment is repeated a great many times, a steadily improving estimate of the value of π may be obtained. It is obvious why the Monte Carlo method is so called; obvious too what this method has in common with simulation. It is an experimental, heuristic, non-rigorous technique. But the vital difference is that the Monte Carlo method is not trying to handle a ramified and exceedingly complex real-life system, but a fully determined geometric constant. The value of π is completely specified by the radius and circumference of a circle; no amount of noise, uncertainty or ramification can possibly influence this relationship.

Now the whole virtue of simulation is that it explores the influence of these difficult features of real life. Having run a simulation and procured a set of results, it is possible to postulate influences which were not originally taken into account—and to run the simulation again. This is a full-scale experimental method. We are used to this approach in ordinary life. Suppose, for example, we approach a baby. It is true that we identify some of the variables in the stimulus–response system consisting of ourselves as observers and the baby as observed. But we do not in fact seek to make to ourselves a model of the way the baby works in detail; we treat it as an organic system and enter into an experimental situation with it. The major parameters of the system may be considered as fixed within certain limits, and if we are wise we will keep an eye open for the operation of certain major variables. Having thus defined a phase space, and identified some of the more obvious features of the situation, we teach ourselves (and the baby) about the way this situation works— heuristically. This is the sort of situation with which simulation deals, and it is quite different from the misapprehended notion of simulation (based possibly on confusion with the Monte Carlo method) which purports to be a numerical method for estimating something too difficult to calculate.

Consider, for example, the psychiatric treatment of disorders of the brain. Only five major physical techniques of therapy are known: leucotomy, continuous narcosis, shock therapy (electrical or insulin), psychotherapy (hypnotism, for example) and drugs. All five methods acknowledge our inability to produce a detailed model of the operation of the brain; they rely instead upon large-scale effects which will absorb a great deal of intricate and idiosyncratic neural behaviour generated by the disorder. In the economy, which is another large and complex system, the bank rate is used for the same purpose. The same thing happens in industrial simulation. We cannot get a complete and systematic analytical account of what is only a relatively isolated system, and we try to absorb the very high yet indefinable variety of the system we observe by a homomorphic representation in the model. This does not require recognition of all the variables and their relationships, but provides instead a series of transformations for the information which the system is generating. Note the form of the verb 'is generating'; it reiterates the time-dependence of the model.

Now although the rigour of all this is a methodological rigour, rather than a mathematical one, it is none the less real. When a manager says to a statistician that he cannot hope to handle a given problem scientifically, because no-one knows what is going to happen and the plans are always falsified by events, the statistician has an answer. He laughs at such naïvety, and declares that he has a technique for handling the uncertainty which so worries the manager; although he cannot predict individual events, he can produce a stochastic account of them. Yet the same statistician may say to the OR man that he cannot treat an exceedingly complex system scientifically, because his analytic tools are inadequate and it is impossible to identify all the variables and their relationships. The OR man may return a similar answer. There is a methodological rigour which will handle this kind of system despite its indefinability, just as there is a statistical rigour which will handle a defined situation despite its uncertainty. The statistically-susceptible approach deals in stochastic methods which can specify probabilities without specifying events; the OR-susceptible approach deals in group-theoretic homomorphic models which can specify systems without specifying their contents.

The OR scientist has to recognize that the span of behaviour in the kind of system with which he deals is so great that 'typical' behaviour is impossible to recognize objectively. Behaviour that is alleged to be typical usually turns out to have been manufactured in some way by the observer—usually through the language he has used in order to describe the system. This remark epitomizes the criticisms made in the last section about the general utility of decision theory, just as it vindicates the general utility of simulation.

Finally, there is something to be said about a rather special kind of simulation known as *management gaming.* This is generally regarded as a training device, whereby managers may be given an insight into other fields of management than their own—fields spread about them either horizontally or vertically. A simulation is run of a fictitious business situation which has been described to a computer in the language of stochastic networks; the student managers supply the necessary decisions. The simulation computes the effect of these decisions according to the language of the game, thereby generating a model of a real business situation—underlying which is a mathematical model of this heuristic decision-taking process. Experience of this training technique suggests that it is difficult to find a compromise between two dangerous extremes.

On the one hand, the game may be constructed to resemble so closely the operations of the company whose managers are playing it that they become conditioned by their gaming experience. That is, they may become profoundly convinced that a certain policy is correct, and transfer this afterwards into real life. This is by no means the object of a business game. The mathematical model has been thought up by an OR scientist as an intellectual exercise; it is not even intended as a mapping of the business concerned. Its resemblance to the business derives not from a non-existent homomorphic mapping, but from a comparable vernacular language which beguiles the student. On the other hand, in an attempt to avoid this trap, the OR scientist may construct a game so different from the situation which the manager normally confronts as to be virtually useless to him. The experience of watching the manager of a steel rolling mill trying to take decisions in a simulated situation dealing with the retail of toffee apples is bizarre. But management games are the concern of industrial pedagogues who employ OR men as engineers in fabricating the required procedures. They are mentioned here only because there is a point of contact between this training outlook and operational research itself.

Consider an OR simulation of a decision-taking situation, the object of which is to make heuristic forecasts about the future behaviour of the plant under certain alternative régimes of control. Typically, the operational research scientists run this simulation under the different régimes consecutively, *sampling* typical management decisions at the nodes of the network. Experience with management games suggested that instead of developing the experiments with a statistical artefact of management decision, the managers who actually conduct the operations being simulated should insert their own decisions in the model being generated. This slows down the simulation because the computer has to stop whenever it reaches a management decision, declare what the situation now is, and wait for a manager to supply the next move before it can continue with its next section of programme.

However, the advantages are manifold. Most of them are obvious, and the one selected for special mention is that the participation of managers in the operational research work at this point breeds a confidence in what OR is doing which it would be difficult to achieve in any other way. The manager finds himself increasingly involved in and committed to the developing simulation. His initial opinion that a mass of advanced mathematics and electronics, presided over by a collection of long-haired scientists, can have no possible relevance to the job he actually does is rapidly dissipated as he gets the feel of the game. A group of highly sceptical managers who embark on this simulation-game at 9 a.m. because they have been told they must, may by lunchtime have undergone a week's artificial experience. Their conversation over the meal is then quite alarming: they give the impression that they may seek to raise money for capital development on the market at any moment, for which purpose they would doubtless issue a fraudulent prospectus. By the same token, a general involved in a war game situation has been known to suffer something suspiciously like battle fatigue. Such is the power of a competent simulation. It follows that forecasts made about the future, and the way in which that future should be handled in terms of policy, acquire such verisimilitude in the minds of the managers concerned that the normally serious problem of 'selling' the results of the OR study vanishes altogether.

Simulation, then, is an important, valid and perfectly respectable method of forecasting in wide use in the empirical science of operational research. As usual, the technical details have been ignored here; we have concentrated instead on the meaning of the work.

It was argued at the start of this long chapter that the difficult task of using science in the business of forecasting could be tackled (by sufficiently experienced men) using a blend of three methods. These were the search for stochastic pattern, the enumeration of connected events, and the uncovering of mechanism. But in what does pattern inhere, do events cohere, and does mechanism reside? The answer is always: in a system. It is to the identification of the system and its nature that OR is directed, and the ability to forecast any feature of its behaviour must depend in the end on our ability to reproduce that system in a form susceptible to experiment. This is what matters. Whether the experiments are conducted on the actual system (if that be conducive to such work itself), on a model (by decision-theoretic analysis), or heuristically (by evolutionary techniques or by simulation), is a matter for well-instructed and scientific choice.

PART III

The Relevance of Cybernetics

Connective Summary

Operational research, as has been seen, means doing science in the management sphere: the subject is not itself *a* science, it is a scientific profession. In turning now to the relevance of cybernetics, we encounter a science in its own right. For the new science of cybernetics is the science of control and communication—wherever these occur in whatever kinds of system. The core of cybernetic research is the discovery that there is a unity of natural law in the way control must operate, whether the system controlled is animate or inanimate, physical or biological, social or economic. Now if cybernetics is the science of control, management is the profession of control—in a certain type of system. Hence we may recognize the subject of management cybernetics—which is seen as a rich provider of models for doing OR.

In Chapter 11, then, a start is made in exploring the real nature of the large, complex and probabilistic systems that management must control. Ways of describing and measuring such systems are discussed, and the origins of cybernetics are explained in this context. The argument is continued in Chapter 12, with a more complete account of the cybernetic discoveries and ways of talking that are useful in operational research.

Against this background, Chapter 13 deals with the control of operations. A cybernetic critique is offered of orthodox practice, using production control as an example. A new treatment of industrial control, of considerable generality, is then put forward based on a cybernetic model. But operational control is not the whole of the management function: senior management is in command of an organic whole—the enterprise itself. Accordingly, the treatment must be extended to deal with the control of enterprises to make the story complete.

Before this can be done, further cybernetic thinking has to be outlined in Chapter 14, which is about self-organizing systems. The manager, who does not always recognize this fact explicitly, relies largely on the capability of a large, viable system to control and even to structure itself. The properties of such systems have to be understood before they can be invoked, in Chapter 15, to improve the design of the company or governmental organization. This part is more difficult than its predecessors, but the concepts and terminology required are steadily developed from the groundwork laid down in Parts I and II.

11

ABOUT SYSTEMS

. . . we have for the most part, if not always, as clear
a notion of the relation as we have of those simple
ideas wherein it is founded. . . . If I know what it is
for one man to be born of a woman, viz. Sempronia,
I know what it is for another man to be born of the
same woman Sempronia; and so have as clear a
notion of brothers as of births, and perhaps clearer.
For if I believed that Sempronia dug Titus out of the
parsley-bed (as they used to tell children) and thereby
became his mother; and that afterwards, in the same
manner, she dug Caius out of the parsley-bed; I had
as clear a notion of the relation of brothers between
them, as if I had all the skill of a midwife. . . .

JOHN LOCKE in *An Essay Concerning
Human Understanding* (1689)

1 The Rudiments of System

The idea of *system* has emerged as all-important, and indeed the situation
confronting the manager at any moment represents one state of a
system undergoing dynamic change. This system is characterized by
various features which are fundamental to the management problem.
It is exceedingly complex. It is highly probabilistic. It is, at least in
certain ways, self-regulating (otherwise it would be chaotic). These three
characteristic features of the system controlled by management will have
to be discussed more fully later, in Sections 3 and 4. First of all, however, it is important to grasp the nature and the magnitude of the
problem faced by the manager of a system. These are the topics of this
section and the next respectively, numbers 1 and 2.

To speak of a system is to speak of the coherence of a number of
entities called parts of that system. What constitutes a system; what

241

identifies the collection of entities as being coherent? Surely this is an act of mental recognition. A system is not something given in nature, but something defined by intelligence. An internal combustion engine is 'clearly' a system; we subscribe to this opinion because we know that the engine was designed precisely *to be* a system. It is, however, possible to envisage that someone (a Martian perhaps) totally devoid of engineering knowledge might at first regard the engine as a random collection of objects. If this someone is to draw the conclusion that the collection is coherent, forming a system, it will be necessary to begin by inspecting the relationships of the entities comprising the collection to each other. In declaring that a collection ought to be called a system, that is to say, we acknowledge relatedness.

But everything is related to everything else. The philosopher Hegel enunciated a proposition called the Axiom of Internal Relations. This states that the relations by which terms are related are an integral part of the terms they relate. So the notion we have of any thing is enriched by the general connotation of the term which names it; and this connotation describes the relationship of the thing to other things. In fact, Hegel's Axiom entails that things would not be the things that they are if they were not related to everything else in the way that they are. We do not know what all these relationships are; certainly we do not bother to enumerate them. In considering a matter to do with mice, we do not have to remember that a mouse is smaller than an elephant. On the other hand, this fact *is* part of the mousehood of a mouse. If someone said: 'Consider a mouse larger than an elephant', we should at once be in difficulty. It is all this relatedness, whether expressed or not, in our view of nature, which gives coherence to our thinking and assures us that nature itself is coherent.

In practice, however, we acknowledge relatedness only when we are ready to declare its relevance. The engine is coherent to us, rather than seeming a collection of bits and pieces, because the relationship between the pinion and the gear (for instance) is obtrusively relevant. When a general pattern of relatedness is detected, we call the set of relationships systematic. Even then, the collection is not dignified by the unitary notion of *a* system until some unifying purpose is devised for it. Thus there seem be three stages in recognizing a system as such. We acknowledge particular relationships which are obtrusive: this turns a mere collection into something that may be called an assemblage. Secondly, we detect a pattern in the set of relationships concerned: this turns an assemblage into a systematically arranged assemblage. Thirdly, we perceive a purpose served by this arrangement: and there is *a* system.

Does this mean to say the engine would not be a system if no-one were there to observe it? The question is meaningless—because the engine was designed by a mind to be what it is. It was observed, so to speak, in advance of its manifestation. But coherence and pattern and purpose are, all three, acts of mental recognition rather than characteristics of physical things. These acts, in increasing sophistication of insight, derive from a primary recognition of the importance of particular relationships. We select, from an infinite number of relations between things, a set which, because of coherence and pattern and purpose, permits an interpretation of what might otherwise be a meaningless cavalcade of arbitrary events. It follows that the detection of system in the world outside ourselves is a subjective matter. Two people will not necessarily agree on the existence, or nature, or boundaries of any system so detected. Nor is it possible to *prove* that a system exists, or is thus and thus; it is possible to say only that the treatment of a certain collection of things as a system is helpful.

Now this account of systems is highly reminiscent of the account given earlier of models. It may well be that systems detected in the world outside ourselves *are* models—mappings of our own brains on to the world. It does at least seem certain that one person will nominate a system that others cannot detect, and also that the one may communicate his recognition to the others. This he does by pointing out the relevance of relationships which the others had not noticed, commenting on their coherence, pattern and purpose. The whole point may be tested, as the value of a model is tested, by checking on the predictive capability of the insight.

Mankind was slow to appreciate these matters. For most of the time, what seemed relevant to man about relatedness was physical contiguity, temporal continuity and strong causal connectivity. A dog has always been a system. Because, although a dog has parts, the parts are actually jointed together; because the collection of parts retains its identity through time; and because dogs growl if their tails are pulled. The parts of a dog always and everywhere come in a recognizable parcel labelled 'dog'. But even today, because the relevant relationships are not obtrusive, we often fail to treat *situations* as the systems they are. 'The economic system' is a term which declares that the economic situation is indeed to be identified as a system. But the relevant relationships within the economy are mostly not obtrusive, and so no-one is sure about its coherence, pattern and purpose. These remain matters for debate. Meanwhile, we are inevitably rather unsuccessful in manipulating a system we have not managed to specify properly.

Looking back over history once more, it is very difficult to find any significant awareness of system in the thought of even the greatest minds of the Western world until the seventeenth century. This deficiency clearly had to do with the failure to recognize the importance of relations. Admittedly certain relationships were identified, but these were so obtrusive that their recognition led to the identification of systems that are themselves directly experienced as entities. The relations of contiguity, continuity and strong causal connectivity specify systems which come, like the dog, in discrete parcels. They retain their identity and their unity through time; therefore for most purposes they can be treated not as systems but as things. Thus it was that existential propositions, rather than relational propositions, became central to Aristotelian logic—which dominated man's attempt to think rigorously for the next 2,000 years. In this logic one asserts that things are or are not; and it is very difficult indeed even to express the notion that A is bigger than B.

It was the philosopher Locke who broke right through this barrier for the first time. He saw quite clearly the importance of relation, even contending that knowing the relation rightly is more valuable than knowing rightly which things are related. One of his more lighthearted statements of this view heads this chapter. It is significant that Locke's greatest contribution to human thought was his analysis of causality, for here was a relation very much more subtle than had been realized before. The 'strong causal connectivity' mentioned above was a trivial notion of cause, a notion derived from the clashing together of things. Causation is something far more difficult to understand than this.

But mankind's thought moves slowly, and Locke was alive a mere 300 years ago. Thus today, when two different market research organizations produce statistical estimates of some firm's market share which differ, the managers they advise are still likely to become incensed. The reason why they differ is not because one or both is 'wrong', as these managers suppose. It is because the two organizations have not identified identical systems. Each is making a perfectly competent measurement of *some* system it has itself nominated to be *the* system. And the system being considered in each case is so complex and so ramified (remember Hegel's Axiom) that the simple descriptions of them which are put forward conceal, or at least fail to specify, the differences that are causing the confusion. No: what matters is what Locke knew, and what many managers have still to be taught. This is that the important issue is whether this month's market share *as estimated by the same methods for the same system* is bigger or smaller than last month's market share. Note that this comparison can be made even when no really adequate account of the system being measured is available. The relation is more important than the things related.

Locke has been called the initiator of the philosophy of the environment: he must surely be regarded as one of the founders of modern science. For science itself has worked on the notion of relation ever since. But, as was seen in Chapter 6, science had other troubles of its own. It could not cope with big systems, because it did not know how to handle many variables at once. It dealt with this problem by making big systems little. Consider, for example, the weather. Weather is the result of a big-system operation. But meteorology to this day, judging by the predictive quality of its models, cannot cope with as large a system as the term 'weather' encompasses. The trick which guaranteed the advance of knowledge was the selection of one pair of variables at a time from the mass of variables, and the examination of the relation between them when other variables were held constant. Having identified this relation, other variables could cautiously be moved in turn, and the results for the relation be discovered. If the results were nil, that is to say if the relationship were constant, the big-system complication disappeared. And so the laws connecting mass and distance in a gravitational constant, volume and pressure in Boyle's law, current and resistance in Ohm's law, and so on, were discovered. These laws express relationships between two variables which are reckoned to be invariant with respect to the behaviour of all other variables. So far, so good.

But later on it became clear that these kinds of conclusion were only approximately correct. For instance, and most notably, objective science had always been proud to say that one of the ubiquitous variables of which its laws were independent was the observer himself. The discoveries of Einstein ruined that claim. Science, in this century, has come to understand the importance of multiple relations, and the relevance of relations that are not obtrusive. Hegel, with his Axiom of Internal Relations mentioned earlier, was not a good scientist, and scientists have had some fun at his expense. But the last laugh may be his. Today, science is at last aware that everything is related to everything else—and that this may turn out to be important. The OR scientist brings this knowledge with him to management science.

Thus it is that when an OR man seeks to identify a management system, he is wary of over-simplification. He will want to trace relationships a long way back—and forward, and sideways. This may exasperate managers, who suspect that if they ask an OR scientist to advise on the capital development of a company, he may vanish down the nearest gold mine with a view to tracing out the relevant system. But the

DC—R

principle is correct; and it is in the management interest that the scientist should question the institutional identification of the system. Certainly he should not gaily accept the system delineated by the conventions of management structure.

(Lecturing once on stock control, the OR scientist was arguing that science could contain the problems involved, whereas managers often relied on emotional argumentation. Science, he said, can identify the appropriate system—which has nothing to do with Mr *X*'s anxieties, nor Mr *Y*'s table-thumping, nor yet the phases of the moon. A manager stood up and said that *his* stock control system was in fact heavily dependent on the phases of the moon; the goods came in on a tidal river in boats of critical draft. The OR man, like anyone else, can be hoist with his own petard.)

The system in the situation, at any rate, is the topic with which management is primarily concerned. The situation is more or less coherent, patterned and purposive. To recognize these characteristics and how they inform the system is half the battle. This act of recognition is precisely the formulation of a conceptual model of system. When the OR scientist sets about the task of making this particular model rigorous, he is using the tool called *General Systems Theory*.

Clearly to identify, to quantify and to make inferences about a ramified system in this way is more difficult than to diminish the system to pairs of variables, between which the relations can be more readily contemplated. Just how difficult the task really is will be assessed in the next section. But there is not really any alternative. The practical reasons why were unfolded in Chapter 9. The theoretical reasons have now been disclosed as well. Put it this way: if we ask what is the nature of a man, chemical analysis can be used to give an answer. It is perfectly good science to separate the elements of the system and to measure their amount. The result would be a short list of chemical elements, together with the percentages of each discovered in the human body. *This*, then, is a man. That answer is a perfectly scientific one too; but it says nothing of any use to the observer concerned with man-the-system, its coherence, pattern and purpose. Equally one might ask how much a balance sheet, which is correct and factual, tells about the *system* that is a firm.

2   The Proliferation of Variety

It is necessary, then, to study the relations which exist between things in the management situation, if systems are to be identified and modelled.

Expressed thus baldly, the point sounds trivially obvious. But we under-rate the magnitude of the task.

If this magnitude is to be discussed sensibly, it will have to be measured. A clearly-formulated concept of complexity is needed, and its scientific name is variety. The *variety* of anything is its number of distinguishable elements. This seems sufficiently clear. Here is the thing to be considered: separate it into distinguishable elements, and count them. This provides a measure of the thing's complexity. And, as with any good measure, it is unambiguous: the answer will be the same who-ever does the measuring. But it seems that the lessons of the last section are already being forgotten. For if the intention is to measure the com-plexity of a system, to state its variety, everything will depend on how the system is defined—in short, on who defines it. In particular, it will be vital to know how deeply the observer's insight has penetrated into the nature of the system.

Little has been written about the measure called variety, although it is a term quite widely used. Most authors have been content to say what has been said before, and no more. A certain amount of confusion has resulted—due, not indeed to the ambiguity of the term, but to the ambiguity of the situations to which it is applied. The use of the measure will now be illustrated using the classification loosely developed in the last section. In every case there will be just seven *things* involved. One might think this means that the variety must in every case be: 7. But it will be seen that *the number of distinguishable elements* (variety) in-volved in the seven-ness depends entirely on what the elements are thought to be elements *of*. The classification itself, being arbitrary, is of little importance. It is very important, however, that having defined the members of the catalogue there should be no doubt at all about the measurement of the variety of each.

(a) A collection of dissimilars

The set of seven things in Figure 21, known to be dissimilar, forms a collection because (in the act of nominating their number as seven) the things have been separated from the rest of the world (hence the circle). Nothing more is known. The variety of this collection is 7. Note the sense in which this answer gives a measure of the *information* supplied by the dia-gram. Note also the sense in which the answer says how much uncertainty exists inside the

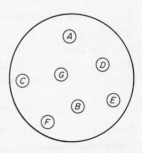

FIGURE 21. A collection of dissimilars.

circle: if these seven things are dissimilar, the identity (or which-is-whichness) of them is uncertain to a sevenfold extent.

(b) A collection of partial-similars

The set of seven things in Figure 22 is very like that in Figure 21. But in fact four of the things are quite literally identical with each other; and the remaining three are identical with each other as well. Remember: *nothing more is known*, although this (or any) diagram of the situation gives the impression that something more is known. The variety of this collection is 2. This is because the universe represented by the circle contains only

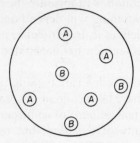

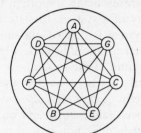

FIGURE 22. A collection
of partial-similars.

FIGURE 23.
An assemblage
of dissimilars.

two distinguishable elements. The seven-ness is illusory. For, since we are told that four (and then three) of the things are 'literally identical' with each other, there can be no way of distinguishing between them. The diagram does distinguish, because the representation of this collection (if it is to be drawn at all) has to be spread out in space. On the information given, four (and then three) of these things are actually coincident. Imagine the diagram of this state of affairs that cannot be drawn. The information it yields is binary; the uncertainty it offers is twofold. Perhaps the best way of understanding this rather difficult case is to say that if the four A's were interchanged with each other, and the three B's were interchanged with each other, no-one could tell the difference. The *variety* is 2.

(c) An assemblage of dissimilars

In Section 1 it was suggested that a collection could be called an assemblage when the relatedness of the things it comprised was acknowledged. In Figure 23 the seven things *are* recognized as related. At this point a mere collection *begins* to be recognized as some kind of system.

It has now acquired the quality of coherence. Since it is the coherence that interests us, we join Locke at this point—losing interest in the *things*, and taking note of the *relations*. All seven things are related to each other, and the number of distinguishable elements is the number of lines on the diagram. That is to say, having counted them, the variety of this assemblage is 21.

The points now being made are central, and although the mathematics is elementary it is worth thinking this out. Each point is connected to six other points. There are seven points, so there must be forty-two connections. But when a connection between (say) B and F has been specified, the uncertainty as to the existence of some relation between these two things has been removed. Therefore when it comes to drawing the connection between F and B it is already there. Half of the forty-two expected lines will not have to be drawn. In short, the number of ways in which n things can be related is:

$$\frac{n(n-1)}{2}$$

For $n = 7$, the variety of an assemblage (as defined) is, as was counted, 21.

(d) A systematic assemblage of dissimilars

Having discussed the introduction of coherence into a collection, and called it an assemblage, Section 1 went on to introduce pattern as well. Hence the title of 'systematic assemblage' came about. The idea here is that, beyond coherence, a special kind of relationship is detected between the entities. This is depicted in Figure 24 by orienting the relations between the things. It is perfectly clear that this case is the same as case (c)—except that the halving of the number of connections has not been carried out. This is because a connection between B and F is no longer the same as a connection between F and B. Observe: $B \rightarrow F$ is different from $B \leftarrow F$.

The fact is that once *more information* is added, the variety goes up (recall the notion of variety as a measure of information). In case (c) coherence was asserted: each point stands in some relation to every other point. Nothing was known about the relationship concerned, except that it had become obtrusive. Now, it is alleged, the relationship is known. For example, F is the son of D, the brother of B. Then the relation depicted by the arrow in $B \rightarrow F$ is 'uncle', while that depicted by the arrow in $B \leftarrow F$ is 'nephew'. These two relations are cognate, it is true; but an uncle simply is not a nephew, nor a nephew an uncle. B–F would express the relation in general, true; but it kills half the information now available, because there would then be no means of knowing what the *pattern* of the relationship may be. *B–F* is still uncertain; to remove the uncertainty the connection must be nominated twice.

In reality the relations given in the network do not have to be merely directional. They may take on many values, rather than two. *B* is *F*'s uncle; he may also be taller than his nephew (in which case the nephew is shorter than his uncle); and he may be balder, richer, older, and so on indefinitely. Hence the relationship between two things may have many modalities. In management science, we may be interested in a considerable number of them. In this way, then, variety proliferates.

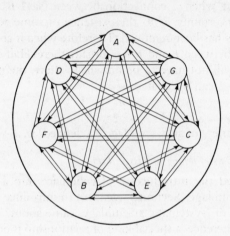

FIGURE 24. A systematic assemblage of dissimilars.

For every new class of information added, the number of possible connections increases alarmingly. And to specify what is actually happening a greater amount of uncertainty must be removed.

But, for the present, it is enough to record the simplest case of a systematically arranged assemblage—one with an oriented relationship. The formula is obviously $n(n-1)$; the reason for dividing by two has vanished. The variety in case (*d*) is therefore 42.

(*e*) A dynamic system

Finally, we identify a system. This means to say that not only are the seven things coherent, and not only is their relationship patterned; they are unified in a purposive whole. Hitherto the variety calculations have been made about a static set of things. But now the collection-turned-assemblage springs to life. It is seen to be a system because it *works*; it operates; it does things.

Interestingly, it is a condition of actual operation that the relations which subsist between the parts should be capable of change. The electrical connections in an internal combustion engine (which trace relations between parts) must go on and off; the petrol vapour flowing into the cylinder must be controlled by a valve going on and off; and so on. If a particular relation inside a system cannot assume more than one *state*, that is to say, the system itself and as a whole cannot change its state. It cannot therefore *do* anything—let alone be purposive. In Figure 25, a system of the simplest form is drawn; each relation has two states: on and off. To measure the variety of this dynamic system, it is, as always,

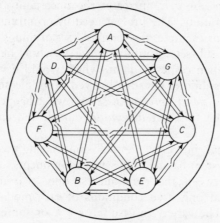

FIGURE 25. A dynamic system.

necessary to count the number of distinguishable elements. If the dynamic quality of the system is now relevant, the elements will be *states* of the system. Consider that the first state of the system has the switch on line $A \rightarrow G$ open, while all other switches are closed; the second state closes this first switch. The third state opens the line $A \leftarrow G$, and the fourth closes that. The first four states of the system derive from the connection between two things. There are two lines, and two positions of the switch on each: $2 \times 2 = 4$. If another line is now brought into the picture, say $G \rightarrow C$, it will contribute two more states—and the original four states may be associated with either of them, yielding two lots of four, or eight, states in all. $2 \times 2 \times 2 = 8$. And so on. Because there are forty-two lines, the number of distinguishable states consists of forty-two 2s, all multiplied together, written as 2^{42}.

This is the variety of the dynamic system depicted in Figure 25. Only those who commonly use numbers of this sort are likely to have any idea of the actual size of this number. In fact, it is well over 1,000,000,000,000. This is the variety of the sevenfold set—once it is nominated to be a dynamic system. And of course this colossal proliferation of variety is based on a two-position switch in each line. Each line in a real-life situation might easily have ten positions (say ten different levels of probability that it is 'on'). In that case the variety would be 10^{42}. So one could go on.

Variety is a concept of profound interest, and its magnitude is important for reasons that will be laid bare in the next chapter. Every conceptual step which enriches the nature of a system under study increases the information about it, increases the uncertainty informing it, and proliferates its variety. The process need by no means stop at the point reached here. For example, the sevenfold set of things could be regarded as operating in sub-sets of arbitrary size; a whole new arrangement of configurations then comes to light, which would have to be permuted with the 2^{42} possibilities already observed. And, please note, all this can happen within a *closed universe* of seven; what happens when the relationship between this and the world outside the circle is taken into account has yet to be seen.

For the present, however, we shall stop; having measured the variety of a dynamic system having only seven components, only one obtrusive relationship between the components, only two modalities of that relationship, and only two conditions of each modality that alternate through time. The variety in case (*e*) is 2^{42}, or something greater than 1,000,000,000,000.

(*f*) The logarithmic measure

It will have been realized that, because the relatedness of entities within a system is of prime importance to its understanding, the process of measuring its variety will inevitably feature the number 2^n. Also, when two separate 'lots' of variety begin to interact, the total variety is not additive, but multiplicative.

For these reasons it is highly convenient to use logarithms in computing with measures of variety. If two systems of variety 2^n and 2^m are compounded into a single larger system, the variety will become 2^{n+m}— since the addition of the exponents (or logarithms) is equivalent to the multiplication of the n and the m writ large. Moreover, it is not surprising that logarithms to the base 2 should be used, instead of the more familiar logarithms to the base 10, since the numbers we expect to handle have the form 2^n rather than 10^n. Hence variety is a measure often quoted in the logarithmic form. If the variety of a system is x, where

x is a very large number of the size we have learned to expect, it will be convenient to quote $\log_2 x$ instead.

The added advantage is that it may never be necessary to *calculate* x at all. In the last set of paragraphs, (*e*), we considered an x larger than 1,000,000,000,000: it was the expansion of 2^{42}. In fact, $\log_2 x$ in this case is indeed: 42. A precise measurement has been made; and yet the precise value of x itself has still not been calculated.

The additive property is illustrated as follows. If five things may each take on one of two states, the variety $\log_2 x = 5$. If there are six things, the variety $\log_2 x = 6$. In the first case $x = 2^5 = 32$; in the second case $x = 2^6 = 64$. If the two sets of things are considered as a totality, the variety must be $32 \times 64 = 2048 = 2^{11}$. That is, $\log_2 x = 11$; and this could have been discovered simply by *adding* the original logarithms: $5 + 6 = 11$. There was no need to compute the expansions.

3   Introducing Cybernetics

In earlier chapters of this book the difficulties of making a scientific analysis of a managerial situation by classical methods have been ventilated. The manager has to handle a system of great complexity, it was said; just how great is the variety that must be handled is now beginning to emerge as a measured quantity. The erroneous idea that the problem could in principle be contained by nominating the most important variables in the system, and writing down some kind of equation to show how they are connected, has surely been demolished by now. But even with the whole methodological apparatus of homomorphic modelling, many problems yet remain. As has been shown, a homomorphic mapping makes a many–one reduction in variety; and it does so legitimately, because it preserves relevant structure. But it is important to consider just how big a reduction in variety may be involved in propounding the solution to a management problem. By the means so far described under the heading of operational research, good decisions can be taken and cogent policies formulated. But the third major element in the managerial task, that of control, is not fully illuminated by these means. The reason is that what makes control difficult is precisely the proliferation of variety. To pinpoint decisions and to clarify policies will provide a proper basis of control; but the *business* of controlling demands ways of containing a variety so large that it may defeat the controller.

The operational research scientist seeking a solution to this problem may turn to the science of cybernetics. The name cybernetics was defined by the mathematician Norbert Wiener, who named the science in 1947. It is the science of communication and control in the animal and the machine. That is to say that cybernetics studies the flow of information round a system, and the way in which that information is used by the system as a means of controlling itself; it does this for animate and inanimate systems indifferently. For cybernetics is an inter-disciplinary science, owing as much to biology as to physics, as much to the study of the brain as to the study of computers, and owing also a great deal to the formal languages of science for providing tools with which the behaviour of all these systems can be objectively described.

In a sense, the science of cybernetics, new though it may be, offers the OR scientist who understands it a source of models. If a model is re-quired of a control process in conditions of high complexity and high probabilism, it is natural enough to look for one in the discoveries of a science which studies these very matters. And yet this science stands in a special if not unique relation to the management task. For cybernetics is the science of control; and management is the profession of control. It follows that models drawn by the OR scientist from cybernetics have a direct bearing, an immediacy, which models drawn from other sciences lack. Their relevance to management problems is found at one remove; they describe situations which may be analogized to manage-ment situations. But the relevance of cybernetics is more straight-forward; the processes that it studies are to be found among brains, colonies of animals, and economic, social and managerial systems too.

For this reason, the relevance of cybernetics has one part of this book to itself, and some attempt will here be made to elaborate the point. On the other hand, this is not the place to enter into a detailed account of the nature of the science: this was done in an earlier book, *Cybernetics and Management* (English Universities Press, 1959). That book pro-pounded the basic orientation of the subject, dealt with its main divi-sions, explained its first major discoveries and examined its promise in the managerial field. There is no space here to make another attempt to meet these terms of reference. A brief introduction to the subject is included in this chapter at this point, but the four which follow will be concerned to develop in some detail a general theory of management control which can be used in practice.

Cybernetics, then, derives from the way in which various scientists were individually beginning to think during the late 1930's, and the way in which their thought developed jointly when some of them came together in America during the Second World War. Each was a scientist specializing in the theory of control in his own field: in engineering perhaps, or in neurophysiology, or in mathematics; and it was the stimulus of special wartime assignments which caused most of them to enlarge their thinking in unexpected directions. From their conversations the science of cybernetics was born and eventually named. By this time, scientists elsewhere, whose thinking had led them in strikingly similar paths, heard of the work of these pioneers, and recognized a kinship with them. In particular, several British workers were quickly to become identified with the new science—which was itself soon to be internationally acknowledged. Since those times the work has expanded rapidly, and mention of the subject is nowadays made in university syllabuses—even in Great Britain.

It was soon discovered that there were certain principles or natural laws governing the behaviour of systems under control, which, regardless of the particular form or context of the system, were quite general, and to which scientific expression could be given. Very soon it was realized that control is not a mandatory exercise, in which people are bullied or things are coerced to operate in a desired way. Rather is it a question of coaxing a system towards optimal performance; or, even better, of arranging for the system to regulate *itself*. In this way, the vital importance of the principle of feedback was soon realized and formalized. The job of control was seen to be less a job for the autocrat as for the steersman; or, in engineering terms, the job of control is typified less by the perforated programme of a Jacquard loom and more by the kind of equipment invented by James Watt as a means of governing a steam engine. The Greek word κυβερνήτης was adopted to name cybernetics. It means *steersman* in Greek, and from its Latin form *gubernator* is derived the English word *governor*.

Before cybernetics, most of the scientific work done on the subject of control had concerned relatively simple systems in isolated circumstances. Or, if the systems being considered were not really characterized by either of these properties, they were treated as if they were. For example, the engine governor is a genuinely simply and genuinely isolated stimulus–response system, in which control is exerted by negative feedback. As the engine revolves, the governor revolves with it; centrifugal force causes the arms of the governor to fly outwards, and this mechanical movement is used to regulate the input of energy to the system. Hence, the system is brought under control *in the very act* of going out of control.

A Pavlov dog, however, is neither a simple system nor an isolated one; it can be described so that it is artificially both these things. In his stimulus–response experiments, Pavlov treated the animal as if it were

no more than a 'machine-for-eating'; moreover, he placed it in an artificial environment consisting of nothing beyond pleasure-inducing food
and pain-inducing electric shock, monitored respectively by positive and
negative feedback arrangements. The discoveries of Pavlov in regard to
conditioned behaviour were genuinely prototype discoveries in cybernetics. But it is important to realize that these discoveries about the
nature of control in animals were made by classical methods of science.
That is to say, the variables were separated out; the complexity of the
system was suppressed from view; and the results were of the kind that
links the behaviour of two variables by some law that is invariant with
respect to other characteristics of the situation.

Thus the basically simple system of the engine governor, and the artificially simplified system of the dog, both obey valid control principles,
but represent rather trivial cases to the new science. For what cybernetics
specifically sets out to recognize, to describe and to handle, is the complexity of the real world. The reason is that viable systems are always
complex in their own structure, never entirely isolated from the world
outside themselves, and they always act as a whole.

The structure of living organisms invariably turns out to be highly
complex: even that so-called simplest of living things, the amœba, is
amazingly complex at the biochemical level. It is now suspected that any
other system, whether social, economic, industrial or purely managerial,
must reach a similarly high level of complexity if it is to attain viable
characteristics. What are the essential characteristics of a viable system?
No rigorous classification has yet been developed, and certainly we are
not here concerned with problems of taxonomy. But the sort of capability
involved may certainly be indicated, as for instance in the following list.
Viable systems have the ability to make a response to a stimulus which
was not included in the list of anticipated stimuli when the system was
designed. They can learn from repeated experience what is the optimal
response to that stimulus. Viable systems grow. They renew themselves
—by, for example, self-reproduction. They are robust against internal
breakdown and error. Above all, they continuously adapt to a changing
environment, and by this means survive—quite possibly in conditions
which had not been entirely foreseen by their designer.

Now the systems that must be handled in the economic, social and
industrial worlds are indeed systems of such viable characteristics, which
tend to have (when they are successful) the properties just listed. Cybernetics has demonstrated that they have these properties *only if* they have
high complexity; they must exist beyond a certain 'complexity barrier'
to be viable. Therefore to insist on treating them through concepts,

models and controls that are deliberately of *low* complexity is to rob
these systems of their viability. Hence it at once follows that caution
must be used in applying the OR methodology to a management system
of very large size. If the viability of that system is due to high variety,
and since the object of a homomorphic mapping is to make a many–one
reduction of variety, the resulting model (although it may appear in other
ways legitimate) may have been robbed of that very feature which
matters most.

Secondly, viable systems maintain equilibrial behaviour only by
multiple contact with whatever lies outside themselves, much as a tall
mast can maintain equilibrium only if provided with numerous guy
ropes. For if an organism is to adapt to unforeseen circumstances, it
cannot rely on the information built into it by the designer. There is a
rigorous proof (in the mathematical theory of communication) of the
fact that enough channel capacity must be provided in the feedback
loops of any system under control to match the capacity of the system
to make an erroneous response. Other proofs show that unless this
capacity is used to feed in fresh information about the changing world
outside, the organism's ability to formulate adaptive strategies must
steadily decline. Hence to isolate the system artificially from its environment, as is often done in industrial control situations as a convention for
ease of management, is also to rob the organism or system of its viability.

Thirdly, if one starts cutting pieces out of a viable system in order to
study them, or if one insists on considering the behaviour of bits of the
system as if the rest of it did not exist, they cease to function—or at least
begin to behave atypically. The organism itself is likely to die. It is characteristic of a viable system that all its parts may interact; not indeed to
the extent that all possible permutations of all possible parts with all
other possible parts must manifest themselves, but to the extent that
subtle kinds of interaction drawn from all these permutations can and do
take place. Yet how often in industry is a manager responsible for getting his own bit of the company organism right, regardless of the rest;
and how often is it said that if all managers succeed in this the sum of
their success represents success for the whole. It clearly is not so. The
theory does not even hold inside a football team.

These three attributes of a viable system (its innate complexity, its
complexity of interaction with the environment, and its complexity of
internal connectivity) turn out to be so important that to override them
and to treat the system through a simplified, isolated or incomplete
model, places a definite and measurable limit on the knowledge of that
system that can be obtained. This limit is very quickly reached. Most

control activities in artificial systems, from a laudable desire that they should be cheap and direct, offend against these principles. Fortunately, the formal control is usually backed up by an informal one. It is important to recognize two things about this. First, this is not necessarily inefficient and intolerable; nor is it simply a demonstration of team spirit —a good thing in itself; it is a necessary method for maintaining viability. Second, without it (and orthodox thinking about automatic control techniques for complex systems *is* without it) the organism will die.

So the problem of extreme complexity has had to be faced by cybernetics, and facing it has led to unexpected advances. For it appears that the twentieth-century understanding of control has been an anachronism in comparison with the twentieth-century understanding of most other aspects of nature. The 'complexity barrier' stopped science, and incidentally society, from imitating the advanced control systems of nature. Moreover, it generated an ill-considered outlook in which living systems were thought to have special facilities not allowed to inanimate systems. Thus learning, for instance, came to be regarded as a prerogative of brain, so that a machine that could learn from its own experience was by common consent a concept of science fiction. The invention of learning machines, one product of the last ten years or so of cybernetics, is based essentially on a recognition of extreme complexity in the system that learns, and on control techniques which are competent to deal with complexity of that order.

Similar remarks apply to the problem of uncertainty as have already been applied to the problem of complexity. For, as was seen in the last section, the measurement of complexity in terms of variety specifies also a measurement of complexity in terms of uncertainty. Just as in the search for comprehension of complex systems the tendency has been to conceive of them too simply, so there has been a tendency to conceive of them too deterministically. The account of unconditioned reflexes in physiology could not satisfactorily be extended to conditioned reflexes in terms of the mechanism called 'reflex arc', because of the essentially probabilistic character of the processes involved. Similarly in economics, and for the same reason, the mechanism of manipulating the bank rate is not an accurate and fully predictable means of control. In commerce the price system, and in industry the incentive bonus scheme, are again instruments of control whose concepts belonged to a deterministic universe, but whose practice belongs to a probabilistic one. In the outcome, the control instruments themselves inevitably become regarded as probabilistic, although they are not. They are likely to be more or less efficacious to an unpredictable degree because they are fixed and certain mechanisms operating in an unfixed and uncertain world. It is possible to visualize at least three different levels of uncertainty in systems, each of which demands somewhat dissimilar treatment from the others. In the first place, there is pure mishap. This is almost a trivial level of uncertainty, and yet so oversimplified is the orthodox model of a real-life system, and so deterministic, that a mishap has come to be regarded as the breakdown of the system. The control is not even expected to deal with it. In man-designed systems, an emergency service is usually switched on at this point to take *ad hoc* crisis measures.

But surely a mishap is simply one mode of expression for the uncertainty inherent in real-life situations, and a control adequate to the task of dealing with those situations will encompass the mishaps too. Nature heals its own wounds, and all viable systems find ways of reorganizing themselves in case of mishap. In some cases, as with tissue and certain nerves, the affected parts regenerate themselves. In natural control systems, such as the brain, the technique is to circumvent the trouble by using highly developed processes employing redundant circuitry— as was shown in an earlier chapter. The statement made about the matter then, about the structure of these systems and the logic of these processes, was in fact a cybernetic statement. And the application of such work to industrial control as a means of dealing with mishaps is indeed an example of management cybernetics.

The second level of uncertainty is the level of inherently probabilistic behaviour—not that deriving explicitly from mishap, but that deriving from the unpredictability of the behaviour of other systems which impinge on the one to be controlled, and the natural variability of its own parameters. It has already been noted that a chunk of the world cannot be isolated completely from the rest and considered as a self-contained whole. However large the stocks which protect a department from the failure of its sources of supply, sooner or later the outside world will reach through and administer a shock to the system. Probabilism infiltrates into any real-life situation: supplies of raw material are never certain; the regularity of demand is never certain; the working order of all the plant is not perpetually guaranteed, nor is it certain that replacements will be there; tolerances wander away from their limits; men are off sick; the quality of product suddenly degenerates without obvious cause; and so on.

Management is a battle to cope with probabilism in the system and to reduce it. But this cannot best be done by starting with a pretence that the situation is not really probabilistic at all. This would make sense only if management were empowered to extend the limits of the

situation under its control and to analyse the causal relationships beyond. But there would always be new boundaries, at which events
would again appear to be arbitrary. Hegel's Axiom of Internal Relations
would defeat us. The probabilism in a situation, then, is not necessarily
due to the fickleness of nature, but is an effect of limited knowledge and
experience.

Again, however, the living organism provides a prototype system to
map on to such a situation. It too suffers from probabilism imported into
its life and language by these same limitations. It too seeks to extend its
own boundaries: first, by equipping itself with a massive sensory input;
and second by its search for pattern in that input which will make prediction possible. Here is the lesson to be learnt. Industrial control
systems are insufficiently aware of what is happening: they are normally
designed with minimum input facilities, so that incoming information
is so sparse that its patterns are undetectable. And the system has no
facility for recognizing the patterns anyway. Thus, for example, the
complex and probabilistic network of events that produces the total
demand for a product is completely suppressed in the chart which
shows the general manager what the level of demand has been for the
last twenty years. What pattern is he supposed to detect in this wandering, attenuated line? He can do no more than try to extrapolate the curve.
The answer is usually quite wrong because all the really vital pattern-
generating information is missing. It cannot even be provided, because
the organism that is the company is sensorily deprived. Again, the conclusion must be to begin by accepting the effective probabilism of the
universe, and to organize means of handling it as the organism does.
The pretence of determinism is the real danger.

The third level of uncertainty encountered in cybernetics is very
much more difficult to understand, and is possibly analogous to the
principle of indeterminacy of physics. As is known from quantum
mechanics, the very measurement of the value of one variable of a
microphysical entity produces changes in the value of another of its
variables. Thus, for example, regardless of the accuracy of the measuring
instruments which might be developed, it is impossible to know *both*
the position and the momentum of an electron exactly, because whatever
means are taken to get close to the first value will drive accuracy out of
the other value according to a known relation. It may be that the uncertainty resides solely in the process of observation; it may be that there
is a deeper significance in nature. At the least, here is an uncertainty of
a third kind.

Now a control system of the complexity discussed by cybernetics consists of a structure, that is some kind of network through which information is passed, and a set of parameters that characterize this network—each of which determines (for instance) the transfer function governing the transmission of information at each node. The indeterminacy theorem for cybernetics, to which allusion was made earlier (Chapter 10, Section 4), has to do with the structure of these configurations. It says (roughly) that the exact specification of the microstructure of the network at one point precludes the exact specification of the transfer function at that point—and vice versa. The relevance, then, of this third level of uncertainty to the theory of control is that really advanced control systems for real-life situations of high complexity and high probabilism can never be fully designed in the sense in which an electronic computer is designed. There is a third kind of uncertainty here too, quite different from the uncertainty of either mishap or probabilism. For the difficulties that derive from mishap can be reduced to an arbitrarily low level, and probabilism can be driven out of the system by enlarging one's knowledge of the system's environment; thus inductive conclusions about the system can be raised to as high a level of likelihood as is desired—or can be afforded. Theoretically, the probabilism goes altogether, and the induction becomes certain, when the whole universe is included, and every example considered. But indeterminacy of the third kind may in practice prove to be ineradicable in all circumstances susceptible to observation.

If this conclusion is correct, then clearly completely new approaches are required to the problem of designing advanced control systems, and much research is currently going on into this problem—in theory, experimental practice and in applied research.

And so the heading 'uncertainty barrier' has also been explained. For three reasons, it has been said, real-life situations cannot be treated as if they were deterministic. Orthodox ideas about control erect a barrier against the admission of uncertainty to the model and hence to the control of the system; viable systems such as living organisms, on the other hand, have to break through this barrier in order to survive. Uncertainty must be accepted; it is there; it is ineluctable.

4   The Paramouncy of Self-Regulation

Complexity and uncertainty are invariable characteristics of cybernetic systems. They have to be measured, and new ways must be found of handling them. For, as has been seen, the massive variety reduction involved in the classical methods of science is likely to destroy in the model those viable features of the real-life system which most interest management. Before making a full-scale effort to give a cybernetic answer to these problems, we should give some preliminary consideration to the third of the really basic characteristics displayed by all those large assemblages in which we recognize system. This, as was said at the outset, is some facility for self-regulation. The idea behind this is familiar enough to all engineers, and something has already been said here about the role of feedback and governor-like processes. But the readiness with which people have acknowledged the cybernetic discovery that these engineering principles reside in biological systems has often blinded them to the real nature of that discovery. Something must be added to the general arguments for self-regulation, something which follows from what has recently been said.

An organic system is extremely complex, probably too complex to make its definition in detail a practicable proposition. Moreover, if the arguments advanced about the third kind of indeterminacy are correct, then it is in principle impossible to define the organic system in full detail. When the whole picture is completely assimilated, it becomes evident that attempts to regulate this system fully by intervention from outside are by definition doomed to failure. Too little is known about the system, its environment, and the interactions between them (in both the dimensions of complexity and uncertainty) than is needed to make a volitional act of interference from outside certain to produce the required effect. In fact, the truth of this proposition may be proved by recourse to technically very difficult logical methods taken from the subject of metamathematics: a verbal explanation is available in *Cybernetics and Management*.

To be more practical: many examples could be educed of the relative failure of control measures imposed on viable systems from outside. Shock therapy on the brain, sudden curtailment of credit facilities in the economy, generalized instructions of management about the control of capital expenditure, and so on, all offer massive interference with the natural workings of the system and are in principle not subtle enough to achieve their objects without damaging the delicate mechanisms that conduce to survival. They are all inadequate control procedures, because they seek to cope with the infinite variety of fluctuations in a complex system without detailed insight, without understanding the patterns of events, and without sufficient channel capacity. All of them sometimes work; but that outcome is not good enough.

From the logical theorems of network theory, from the mathematical theorems of information theory, from the strategic analysis of the theory of games, and from other scientific sources, it can be shown over and over again that viable systems cannot be entirely regulated from outside. Therefore, if they are to be regulated at all, they must be regulated from within. This is the real force of the concept of self-regulation. A useful contrast may be drawn between the engine governor described in the last section and the prison governor—whose duties are much the same.

The duty of both governors is to hold certain variables within given constraints. In the case of the engine governor, the object is to prevent the engine turning at a faster rate than its limiting speed. The prison governor has to constrain certain runaway variables, too, called convicts. The prison governor therefore installs in his prison a variety of ingenious alarm arrangements, which will inform him of the escape of a variable from its constraint. Suddenly the warning is given and a whole train of regulative procedures is set in motion. But what does the alarm really mean? It may well mean, for example, that a prisoner has been gone from the prison for several hours, and is already at some distant and unknown place. The convict has in fact outwitted the alarm system, setting it off only after a considerable time lag—for example, when the roll is next called. But the engine governor automatically operates the regulatory device *in the act of going out of control.* Here then is the notion of intrinsic control, of self-regulation as distinguished from mere regulation.

In other words, the principle of error-controlled negative feedback is important not only because it is a clever piece of engineering, but because it immediately demonstrates that systems can be designed that are inherently capable of responses not envisaged in detail by the designer. It is one thing to list all the things one imagines might go wrong and to legislate for them; it is quite another to provide a system with a criterion that something must be wrong (whether we have thought of the possible cause or not) and a routine for taking corrective action. It seems unlikely that James Watt himself, in inventing the steam engine governor, really understood that he had discovered a principle of life. It is a case of scientific serendipity. Now of course it will be argued that the provision of such control devices is not *really* of such fundamental importance, because they could still go wrong. But this is not true, except in the very special case that the system is either annihilated altogether or so radically damaged that it ceases to be the system that it is. We should agree that the human body is capable of adaptive response to many forms of stimuli, and that belief is not vitiated in any way by saying that the body cannot adapt to being hit by a high explosive shell and blown to smithereens. Within a reasonable range of normal operating conditions, a self-regulating system will regulate itself.

If it fails to do so, this is evidence of fundamental damage. If, on the other hand, an ordinary regulating system fails to work, it is probably because some environmental change has occurred which the designer of the control did not envisage.

It may help at this stage to discuss the meaning of intrinsic control through self-regulation by quoting elementary industrial cases. Firstly, some of what has been said can be 'brought down to earth' by considering the control problem of a rolling mill manufacturing steel rods through more than twenty mill-stands at a finishing speed approaching 70 miles an hour. Techniques are now available to make the whole physical operation virtually automatic, and yet this concept of automation does not normally include any organic, intrinsic, self-regulatory device for handling the lowest level of uncertainty: mishap.

In this context, mishap characteristically occurs when the steel misses its guides, and collides with a mill-stand itself—instead of passing through the rolls of this next stand as intended. Within seconds, long lengths of red-hot steel are thrashing around the shop and tangling with the equipment. The accepted action is to detect this situation by eye, and to press an emergency button that switches off the mill. The scene of wreckage is then surveyed; not many years ago (before even limited automative devices were installed) the scene of wreckage was a scene of carnage too: the steel would loop itself round human limbs. Even today a most primitive form of emergency control within this general zone of automation is deployed: a squad of men armed with hand shears. They have to cut away the product from the plant before the mill can start to roll again.

This illustrates a failure, not so much in production engineering, as in conceptual outlook. A rolling mill is visualized as a magnified version of an automatic wringer, and the whole plant is a collection of such machines: a simple and deterministic model. Consequently, if something goes wrong the model has no means of accounting for the mishap. Therefore there is no alternative but to cry a halt, cancel the model for the time being, suspend all the routine regulative mechanisms and bring the situation 'back to normal'. Replace this concept by the model of an organism, of a viable system, and it is at once seen to be short of any adaptive mechanism for dealing with the problem—even though the problem is in this case well known in advance. This is because the plant itself is not sentient; it has no 'nervous system' capable of reacting at electronic speeds to disasters of this kind, and above all no intrinsic controller which could obey the signals. Therefore the cybernetician seeks to install such arrangements.

The difficulty about this idea is that while everyone knows how to recognize automatically that a product has arrived where it ought to be—using say photo-electric devices—it is not immediately obvious how to recognize that it has arrived where it ought *not* to be, since the number of possible wrong destinations is infinite. Here is the proliferation of variety again. The engineers faced with this problem did, as a matter of fact, try to instrument the environment so that wherever the 70-mile-an-hour product turned up it would be recognized. But as was said, and as has been seen by anyone who has ever entered such a mill, the product goes up to the ceiling in some arbitrary trajectory, and therefore this solution to the problem of handling high variety is quite intolerably expensive. The cybernetic solution is, as so often happens with hindsight, absurdly simple. We have noted before in this book that a vital capability of a viable system is (in some sense hard to define) the ability to forecast. Living systems become aware of crises less because they can detect, in a field of colossal variety, the appearance of something which ought not to be there, as because they can forecast where that something ought to be—and recognize that it is not there. Given the capacity to forecast, a high-variety decision is replaced by a decision of variety two.

This is in itself an important point. In a situation of (roughly) constant high variety, a high variety problem may be solved by solving the complementary problem that has low variety. In this case, all that is required is that the plant should be sentient to the extent that it can recognize two distinguishable states. When the product leaves one mill-stand it should forecast the time of arrival (in milliseconds) at the next stand, which is only a foot or so away. The next stand, armed with this knowledge, will 'know' that if the product does not arrive as forecast it must have gone somewhere else where it is not supposed to be. The plant will stop. This is indeed a very simple example; the fact is that it took a cybernetician to discover the answer, and the first impact of the answer on the orthodox production engineer was one of intense surprise. Perhaps the sense in which this passive plant has become an active organism (within the very simple definitions that are appropriate) is sufficiently clear. The plant now has a kind of *tonus*; it is 'on its toes'; it anticipates.

Secondly, what about this control machine itself? It too could go wrong and make mistakes. This risk appears to haunt many managers: they fear that once control is handed over to machinery, no-one will be left competent and accustomed to take action if it fails. In fact, we need a control machine that is itself sentient and adaptive to its own failures.

Otherwise the problem of mishap is not really solved, but merely pushed one stage further back. Fortunately, the cybernetic theorems relating to reliability through redundancy (which were referred to at the end of Chapter 9) are applicable here. There ought to be at least a chance that throwing a brick into an industrial control machine would result in no adverse effect on the operations being controlled. For real life is uncertain and perhaps nature (or a Luddite) will throw that brick. But of course this is an exaggerated form of the real need. Patients will inevitably suffer impairment if vital centres are damaged in the brain, even though they may survive wounds or necessary surgery in other parts without any apparent loss of function. The more important proposition is that failures in components should not cause the machine to give up altogether, and without saying so. In the case now being quoted, the ultimate defeat of the redundant control machine was not signalized by a loss of control. The machine itself was capable of registering: 'I perceive that I am no longer competent to carry on, please take over.' This is the cybernetic version of a fail-safe device.

But cybernetic hardware is not yet the most important product of industrial cybernetics; its application to decision-taking systems is of the first importance. Consider any modern plant, largely automatic, requiring lengthy runs at one setting for its economic operation. Almost every industry contains such factories nowadays. Now the market, not caring very much about the economics of this plant, persists in throwing up an odd assortment of orders. Some of them are themselves sizable, yielding long runs; others of them can be amalgamated to produce artificially long runs; others again cannot. This situation leads to long cycles of production, in which the first class of order can be happily contained, and the second is handled by hard work and skill; the third class is accumulated to form a rather uneconomic period within the cycle of odd job lots.

Some strongly production-oriented companies deal with this situation by ignoring the environmental uncertainty, manufacturing to fixed cycles of long runs only, and meeting the probabilism of the market from its warehouses. This method inevitably involves high stocks, which may of course pay for themselves. A strongly sales-oriented company, on the other hand, may well insist on intervening continually in the massive production machinery to demand the immediate manufacture of some trifling order. This process is often justified by claiming the trade concerned is essentially a jobbing trade, depending on this policy for its goodwill. Again, the process might pay for itself (although this is sometimes an illusory piece of economics based on a costing system which is incapable of measuring adequately the cost of lost opportunities incurred in meeting these special demands). Thirdly, a near-monopolistic company may be specially privileged in being able to adopt the first policy, by insisting on longer runs, without incurring the loss of large stocks. This can be done by the simple expedient of holding the customers to ransom and making them accommodate the necessary stocks. It is fortunate for the national economy that few companies are in a position to get away with this, for it ties up unnecessary amounts of capital.

In these circumstances the operational research scientist is inclined to say that although there is an inherent probabilism in the market situation, scientific techniques can be used to predict its likely movements. This is often the case, and predictions can usually be made which have at least the effect of reducing the buffer of stocks required to uncouple the production unit from its market demand—as was also seen in Chapter 9. In the particular case study here described, however, the most intense statistical investigation and the most imaginative use of OR itself failed completely to master the environmental probabilism. This can happen particularly in those cases where the company has not an over-large share of the market. Consequently, the sample of demand that it draws every month can change very markedly from month to month. The point is that forecasting itself is not a question of divining the future, as we have insisted before, but of trying to recognize a pattern inherent in nature.

The cybernetician is now coping with the second level of uncertainty: not mishap this time, but probabilism in the environment of the system. The solution must be to embark on a sequential decision procedure, based on the continuous assessment of all the data coming in as they arrive. Again this thought derives from the analogy of the living organism, and reflects that a control system in these circumstances must be abundantly and continuously supplied with information. This remark sounds altogether truistic, but everyone having practical experience of industry knows that the information coming into the company day by day in the way of orders, modifications to orders, complaints and telephone calls of diverse purposes, is not in fact immediately fed into the production control system and evaluated. Indeed, anyone can produce examples where the absence of this information meant that production plans were altered on the grounds that certain conditions were not fulfilled which were in fact fulfilled; or that false information (oddly enough, unduly lugubrious as often as unduly sanguinary) was fed to the customer because the real situation was not known. It is not enough to say that these shortcomings reflect crass stupidity on the part of some individual, bad management or bad documentation. The fact is that the control system has been designed on the wrong model: information does not circulate in intrinsically self-regulating paths. This is not merely because the system is sluggish, but because there is an insufficiency of feedback, of interconnection between the parts of the system and of local centres of command, and because the circuitry is not sufficiently redundant.

In the case being discussed, anyway, there could be no proper forecast, and certainly no final solution to the problem of the optimal cycle of production, because demand really was unpredictable. But by installing a sequential decision procedure based on the capability to respond with speed and sensitivity to *every incoming order*, a cybernetic solution was obtained. As usual, the adaptive solution is a function of a viable system. Looking at the office procedures installed to handle the problem, at the charts and the calculating machines, the whole business appears to be very simple. A decision to change the length of production cycle, which is no longer made at some monthly meeting as before but at the instant when it first becomes clear to the control procedure that such a change is necessary, is indicated by the line on a chart crossing from one zone (representing a production cycle of given length) into another zone (representing a production cycle of another length).

But, as before, it is all too facile to say with hindsight that 'it should not have taken cybernetics to deal with this matter'. This problem had resisted the efforts of some experienced and senior workers in production management, production engineering and operational research for some years before this solution was discovered. It is also worth nothing that the immediate result of this new control method saved enough time in resetting the plant and in working optimal cycles, to produce an overall increase of 8 per cent in throughput. To learn from these examples, one has to realize that it is not the solution itself which merits close attention, but the formulation of the appropriate model within which alone it is possible to arrive at the solution. Until the institutional method of handling information had been changed, until the language in which production cycles were discussed had been radically altered, and until the whole method of cost accounting had been exposed as inadequate and replaced, it was not only impossible to use this solution, *it was impossible to say what it was*. We are back to the question of undecidable sentences.

But this chapter is purely introductory to the use of management cybernetics, and we shall soon pass to more elaborate examples. For the moment it is enough to have established the meaning of a viable system, to have introduced the notion of variety and its measurement, and to have pointed out the fundamental problems posed in terms of the philosophy of science by its extreme complexity, its various kinds of probabilism, and its latent capacity for intrinsic control by self-regulatory means. All these points, and particularly the last, will receive more attention later on. In the meantime, here is a peroration.

The reference of cybernetics is always to viable systems. That means, in the first place, to genuinely living organisms: to amœbæ, to animal populations, to the brain. No cybernetician has yet had the effrontery to attempt the construction of either an amœba or of a cerebrum; thus his science is, in this connection, descriptive and elucidatory. Next, a collection of viable systems may interact with another collection to form a new and larger viable system. For example, there is the prey–predator system, and in general the system of organism-within-environment; there is also the genetic system whereby life forms are perpetuated and evolved. In these systems the cybernetician again detects natural principles, laws and mechanisms of control. Now he begins to say, if one is confronted by a system such as an industrial company or an economy, and if this system has many of the formal properties of a living organism as well as its critical aims and objects (such as surviving in reasonable comfort), then these entities belong to the class of cybernetic systems. They ought to respond to the same control mechanisms.

So he looks at the internal control arrangements (physiology), at the interaction-with-outside arrangements (ecology), at the surviving and evolving arrangements (genetics), and at what happens when things go wrong (pathology, psychiatry). Then he creates cybernetic controls: these may be actual machines—hardware attached to the plant—or new modes of organization, information handling and decision-taking among people. Ultimately, he predicts, there will be machines with enough brain-like attributes to be capable of doing management jobs, as well as of advising managers as at present.

But whether cybernetics is looking at brains, constructing mathematical models of learning processes, installing a new decision procedure in a works, helping a company to be more adaptive, reorganizing the structure of a group of companies to be more responsive to change, or constructing ironmongery that will teach children the multiplication table, it is still the same interdisciplinary science of control.

12

COPING WITH COMPLEXITY

ὃ δὲ σαφὲς καὶ φανερόν, καταφρονεῖσθαι εἰκός,
ὥσπερ τοὺς ἀποδεδυμένους. Διὸ καὶ τὰ μυστήρια ἐν
ἀλληγορίαις λέγεται πρὸς ἔκπληξιν καὶ φρίκην,
ὥσπερ ἐν σκότῳ καὶ νυκτί. ἔοικε δὲ καὶ ἡ ἀλληγορία
τῷ σκότῳ καὶ τῇ νυκτί.

What is clear and evident is likely to be scorned, just
like men stripped naked. Mystery is spoken in
allegory to excite such fear and awe as exist in
darkness and night. In fact, it is the allegory that
compares with the darkness and the night.

DEMETRIUS *On Style* (A.D. ? 50–100)

1   The Relatively Isolated System

It has been shown that the science of cybernetics sets out, as does
management itself, to deal with proliferating variety. Both the science
and the profession, moreover, are concerned with the study of viable
systems, and especially with the identification of those characteristic
features of animate things which conduce to survival. In addressing our
thinking to such matters, it is important to beware of especially strong
psychological barriers to understanding. For what we are really doing
is setting out to investigate *ourselves*. We are the viable systems *par
excellence*, and are aware of the characteristics of animate things largely
because we experience them as our own. There is therefore a risk that
they will seem to be our own prerogatives; there is a resistance to
explaining them, because we might seem to be explaining them—and
therefore ourselves—away.

Many years ago a cybernetic machine was built which was capable of
learning from its own experience. When this machine was demonstrated,

people could see that it did this: it was given a simple task to fulfil, and as it obtained practice in the task it took a shorter and shorter time to succeed. Behaviourally speaking, at the least, the thing was learning; and so the audience would agree. When, however, the lid was taken off the box, and the mechanism explained, people were prone to say: 'Oh is *that* all.' In other words, when we receive an explanation for something that has hitherto been mysterious, it ceases to be mysterious; we then have the choice of declaring either that the mystery has been explained or of saying that the explanation is improper, because we *know* that there is a mystery after all. What we call the mind is not extended in space; it is not a thing. Whatever it is, it is surely a function of the brain—which is extended in space and is a thing. As the mysteries of the way in which the brain works are uncovered, science moves towards a day (yet far distant) when it will say: this explains how the brain works, and that accounts in turn for how the mind works. Everyone will then be able to say: 'Oh is *that* all you have done.' And probably none of us will believe it.

Where the behaviour of very large systems, with their proliferating variety, is concerned, management faces the mystery of how it all works. As cybernetics begins to demolish what is mysterious, we must be on the look-out for the Oh-is-that-all rejoinder, which is too glib. There is no doubt that we enjoy the mystery; it is veiled in allegorical language by businessmen themselves, by city correspondents, by the way everyone talks. If science can strip away the allegory and expose the naked mechanisms of viable systems, we are likely to complain that the exercise is spurious. But science could well retort that the systems are not inexplicable: it is the way they are discussed which plunges us into darkness. The warning then is clear; it is given above by Demetrius who, like most of the ancient authors quoted at the headings of these chapters, well understood the point a long time ago. Scientists are not however daunted from their attempt to make things both clear and evident, always recognizing that they can hope to do so only within the limitations of present knowledge.

It has already been argued that no system can in fact be isolated from the rest of the universe, to which any set of entities with a circle drawn round them remains related in innumerable ways. It has also been shown that many advances in the earlier days of science were due to the scientists' insistence on treating a small set of entities *as if* they were susceptible to being isolated in just this way. Subsequent advances were made when the 'as if' clause was dropped; the laws of gravitation had to be modified, it had to be admitted that Ohm's law does not hold in

all circumstances, and so on. Yet the unsatisfactory concept of an absolutely isolated system had proved its worth; indeed it is evident that if
scientists had refused to use it they might have been forced to concentrate
on the indivisibility of nature, and they might have discovered nothing
at all. But there has been occasion to comment on false dichotomies
before. The fact is that systems consisting of something less than the
whole of nature can be recognized, manipulated and managed. It is
therefore essential that we discover how to retain the concept of system,
which implies distinctness from the rest of the world before it can be
recognized, without at the same time formulating the concept in a way
which would entail absolute isolation. The concept required is that of
the *relatively* isolated system. Quite obviously the difficulty about making
such a concept clear and therefore useful is that 'relatively' is a term
which in normal usage is itself imprecise. We have to say quite definitely
what 'relatively' is supposed to mean.

Consider then a system enclosed within boundaries, but which is still
interacting with the world outside. In terms of Hegel's Axiom of
Internal Relations, the system is interacting with *everything* outside. But
we would certainly agree to be practical about this, and only to count
relationships which cross the system's boundary if they appear to matter.
That is to say, if we can explain what is happening within the system
without drawing attention to some entity outside we shall do so. For
example, an industrial company stands in a certain relationship to the
sun, a relationship defined by a set of relations: the company is roughly
93,000,000 miles away from the sun, much smaller, less bright, less
hot, and so on. But this relationship is to all intents and purposes
unchanging, nor can the directors of the firm attempt to change it;
therefore it will be disregarded. But there are other relationships which,
if ignored, will make the behaviour of the system inexplicable. These
relationships, and the specific set of relations which determine them,
have to be identified.

In practice, the most noticeable feature of the interaction between the
system itself and things outside it, is that the relationships are directional.
Either the thing outside is affecting the system, or the system is affecting
the thing outside—or both. There are of course many relations which
are not oriented in this way, but they could hardly be called interactions,
nor could their omission from a description render the behaviour of the
system inexplicable. This firm may be smaller than that firm, in which
case that firm is larger than this firm; but what of it? The relation
becomes relevant to the behaviour of this firm only if that firm *uses* its
larger size to take action (such as selling for a period below cost) which

influences this firm. So in fact it becomes possible to divide the relationships which represent important interactions into two classes: those which affect the system, and those affected by the system. These are respectively called the *inputs* to the system, and the *outputs* from it.

Thus a relatively isolated system is a set of entities, having properties discussed earlier, that is separable from the rest of the world except for two specially chosen sets of relationships with things outside, called its inputs and outputs. The man who first put forward the phrase 'relatively isolated system' as a technical term and who has since made a formal development of the logic of such systems, is the Polish cybernetician Henryk Greniewski. He has developed an elegant formal account of various processes common to viable systems, using the notion of the relatively isolated system as a building-block.

But it could well be objected by anyone who has followed the arguments of this book with any care, that this division of all relationships with the external world (of which the system is alleged to take cognizance) into inputs and outputs is arbitrary. Surely this is just another of those dichotomies on which the author is fond of pouring scorn. And this is true. There will be difficulties to meet, the first and most obvious of which is this. The notion of a feedback coupling has already been displayed, and its importance in the characteristic behaviour of viable systems has been emphasized. In fact, this notion can be expressed in the present terminology only by saying that an input is an output, and an output is an input. Greniewski noticed this, and dealt with it formally by the use of matrices in which coefficients on the diagonal (which would normally be empty, because they show the relation of a thing to itself) have meaning. A positive value on the diagonal means that an output from A *is* an input to A. The British cybernetician, Ross Ashby, had noticed the point too. His rigorous treatment is based on the theory of sets, and therefore he can surmount this technical difficulty in terms of an identical transformation: one in which an element is mapped on to itself.

But there is more to this problem of dichotomizing interactions than the technical problems of description which these cyberneticians have encountered and conquered. It is well to be aware of the relativity of oriented interactions, for their direction is not invariant under all transformations of the system. For example, consider an educative system consisting of a teacher and a class. The ignorance of the schoolchildren, as represented by their questions, is an input to this system; the response of the teacher to these stimuli is an output. Or, alternatively, what the teacher says to the class is an input to the system; the acquisition of knowledge, as represented by the passing of examinations, is an output. Everything depends on how the system is defined, and this in turn depends on who is the observer: the dilemma of modern physics appears once again.

In fact, the question of who is doing what to whom can be answered no more than arbitrarily when any two parts of a system are adapting to each other. The reason is that, as a formal analysis of the process of adaptation reveals, one sub-system adapts to the stimulus represented by another sub-system by seeking to imitate it. A teacher tries to construct a model of his pupil's state of mind, and the information fed to the pupil is an output of this model. The pupil in his turn is seeking the model in the teacher's mind, and his outputs offer approximations to the teacher's outputs as inputs. The process is very clear in any formal analysis of a particular teaching (or adaptive) task. When a human pupil is learning from an electronic teaching machine, for instance, it is impossible to tell from the electrical monitors of the interactive system which sub-system is the human pupil and which the cybernetic teacher. The inputs and the outputs of a relatively isolated system, then, may not be easy to nominate; moreover, which is which depends upon the observer's point of view and the conventions he unconsciously adopts. It is most important to bear this in mind. When it comes to the consideration of a system as complicated as the national economy, it may well be misconceptions and prejudices about which are the inputs and which are the outputs of the multifarious sub-systems involved that lead to managerial chaos.

The same may well be true of industrial unrest. The management probably regards the effort put in by workpeople as an input to the system, and the wages paid to them as an output from the system. The two are coupled in the eyes of management, but by a transfer function having to do with costs and profits—the wages (outputs) are then a direct function of the effort made (inputs). The labour force, on the other hand, probably regards the wages paid to them as an input operating through a transfer function which conditions their effort as output. Perhaps this kind of argument should be classed as semantic legerdemain; alternatively it may offer a perfectly sound explanation of certain examples of industrial unrest. For if 'the two sides' are using different models of the system—different to the extent that the one is oriented in the opposite direction from the other—then bizarre consequences must follow. For example, the management may seek to reward the system by supplying positive feedback in the form of some kind of incentive. To do so, it will need to change an output of the system into one of its inputs, and it has only its own model on which to operate. It therefore intervenes in the wage structure, using a measurement of productivity to adjust the wages in a way which will cause them to modify the original effort. The labour force, *with its model*, must see this manœuvre as adding a new input—which (evidently) is not a reward for effort but an attempt to impose sanctions on inadequate results. The *systems* are formally the same, the one being a mirror image of the other, but the standpoint of each observer causes him to see the system in a totally different light. The existence of a feedback driven by a comparator (measuring the difference between a norm and an actual) means that the system responds in an invariant way—regardless of who observes it. But the management sees the norm as something to be exceeded, and an incentive for higher rewards, whereas the labour force sees it as a threat to its standard of living. It cannot be long before each side accuses the other of bad faith.

These then are some of the difficulties and peculiarities which arise in the attempt to designate a relatively isolated system. The initial concept is simple and perhaps even elegant, but a great deal of care is needed in its application to management cybernetics. It is indeed often best to assume that a two-way interaction is going on between any two subsystems of a large and complex system. This is not, as it might at first appear, a betrayal of the notion that relationships are in fact oriented— which they are. Rather is it a recognition that systems rely quite fundamentally for their viability on ecological interactions between themselves and the environment, and also on physiological interactions between their own sub-systems, of a richer and more elaborate kind than the analyst customarily assumes. The phenomenon is one of the marks of proliferating variety.

2   The Laws of Variety

The system in which both the manager and the management scientist are interested may well be described as a relatively isolated system. It will be called a *situation*—namely, the one with which the manager has to deal. A situation corresponds to the definition of system given in the last chapter, plus the concept of its *relative* isolation. But of course it has to be recognized that in appearance it is quite unlike the kind of system normally denoted by that term. It is exceedingly complex (to the point where full definition becomes impossible); it is extremely probabilistic (to the point where causal relationships are discernible as no more than tendencies); and it is internally self-regulating to some extent.

The manager responsible for this situation knows full well that it interacts with the world outside itself; he can, to a degree, isolate his responsibility for the situation, but he cannot isolate the situation itself. This state of affairs is pictured in Figure 26. The physical appurtenances of the system may well lie within a geographic area in which the manager has supreme authority, and his post may endow him with authority over the purely internal relationships to be found there—in so far as he can exert it. But the world influences this situation, in a way the manager cannot control or even foresee, and the situation itself influences the world, initiating a chain reaction which the manager cannot follow through. The box containing the situation is irregularly drawn,

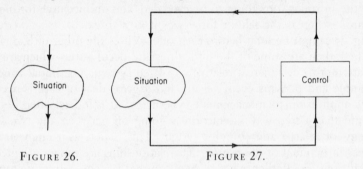

FIGURE 26.   FIGURE 27.

as before in this book, as a constant reminder that the boundaries of real-life problems are not rectilinear, but amorphous.

For the moment, all the influences on the system will be channelled through a single input, and all the effects it exerts will be channelled into a single output. In order to simplify the thinking which follows, it will be assumed that the set of inputs to the situation derives from another system into which the outputs from the situation are fed. A closed loop is thereby artificially created. It will be seen that in the eyes of the manager next senior to the one who is trying to manage the situation from within, a new system of higher order is now created. This is (again for the moment) an artificially isolated system; moreover, it is one in which the senior manager uses the second system to *control* the first. Thus information about the situation passes into the control, while instructions pass from the control to the situation. From the point of view of the manager inside the situation, these two channels carry the output and the input information respectively from and to his system. Such a state of affairs is depicted in Figure 27.

As we know, variety proliferates within the box labelled 'situation'. A measure of this proliferation was developed in the last chapter and it is very large indeed. Given that sufficient information about this pro-liferation of variety can flow along the output channel, and that it reaches control, what is control to do about it? There are broadly two schools of thought. The first, corresponding to orthodox management practice, declares that a study of this information will reveal patterns and trends in the data, which will enable experienced managers to feed instructions back to the situation through its input loop—and thus to modify its behaviour. The second school of thought, corresponding roughly to the position of operational research, is more realistically aware of the magni-tude of the problem. It says that the human brain cannot cope with all this information, and that the thing to do is to create an analytic model of what is going on. The two policies are in principle identical, but the second insists that the processes entertained by the first can be made far more efficient if modern scientific techniques are used.

These two standpoints may be examined in the light of an analogy from rugby football. The football pitch represents the artificially isolated system depicted in Figure 27. Fifteen men in red jerseys are installed at one end of this pitch: they constitute the first sub-system—the situation. Now the purpose of this sub-system can be readily identified in this case because the rules of the game are known. The object is that they should convey a ball to the opposite end of the pitch and touch it to the ground. Since each of the fifteen men is free to follow any kind of trajectory up the pitch, and since the ball (subject to certain constraints) may be passed freely among them, the variety of this sub-system proliferates to an enormous extent. Now control in this context means containing the sub-system: that is to say, these fifteen men in red jerseys have to be stopped from achieving their purpose. The question remains, how should this be done?

The manager belonging to the first school of thought is inclined to say that he would like to watch the fifteen men in action for a bit. He notes that they adopt a rather characteristic formation which in practice reduces the available variety. He notices that a few of the men (those known to their colleagues as good handlers of the ball) tend to dominate the handling. The pattern of running and passing so develops that it is most usual for one or two men, called wing three-quarters, to make the final run: one or the other comes sweeping in from one or other touch-line and grounds the ball between the goal posts. The conclusion is fairly obvious. If a man is placed between the posts, he will be able to stop the would-be try-getter. The objection may be raised that sometimes another of the players is seen to cross the line. Never mind; they all seem to make for the same spot, so it doesn't matter. So an attempt is

DC—T

made to control the situation in this way. Unhappily, the attacking system outwits the defence—it is content to cross the line a little outside the goal posts if necessary. In recognition of this, other defenders have to be added, and by a process of pattern-seeking and variety-trapping an extensive group of defenders is eventually built up.

The man with the second approach laughs at this ineptitude. He sees at once that a large number of games will be lost before the really operational patterns are identified, and the trial and error process succeeds in determining a control system which will thwart the attackers for roughly half the time. Clearly, we need a modern, analytic and scientific approach. Nobody knows what the attacking system will in practice do—so we must find out. Inspection of the nature of the system, rather than experience of it in operation, reveals that each of the fifteen components of the system is itself governed by a control mechanism called a brain. Obviously a way must be found by which the brain processes can be continuously monitored when the system becomes operational. Accordingly, our man wires up each of the fifteen players with an electroencephalograph and, if possible, a system of electrodes implanted in the internal regions of the brain as well. The multitude of wires leading from each man's head must needs be fed into light, flexible, multicore cables, which have to be specially developed in view of the practical difficulties of recording in these circumstances. A computer is then installed on the touchline, and the cables run to it. At this point there will be a pause of several years while transduction equipment is invented and manufactured to amplify the cerebral micro-voltages, to digitize them and to programme them as input to the computer. As the team begins to run down the field, the computer (which works at the speed of light) analyses what is going on, constructs a model of the strategy being employed, and makes predictions (of ever increasing reliability) about the point where the line will be crossed. The computer is then able (by radio) to direct an automaton to this point in time to block the try-getter. In the context of the example, this is a caricature; in the context of real management it is not. A great many schemes for automation actually realized in industry are quite as stupid.

The cybernetician, for his part, regards these massive arrangements with amusement. Certainly they are scientific: they recognize the proliferation of variety of which the attacking system is capable and take measures to deal with it. But of course the cybernetician knows that the best way in which to control the system of fifteen men in red jerseys, is to put fifteen men in white jerseys on to the field. This solution, the cybernetician contends, will be at least as effective as the last one. Moreover, if the white system can be trained to proliferate its variety a little more quickly, or to pattern it within the system a little less uncertainly, the control is likely to succeed for most of the time. The plain man with commonsense who is watching all this agrees with the cybernetic solution. He says, rather drily, that although he never even went to a university, he himself could have proposed this solution without a moment's thought. But this is where the analogy breaks down. *This observer knew how to play rugby all the time.*

The manager in real life, who seeks to control an industrial, military, social, political or economic system, does not have this advantage. He is playing a game of incomplete information, in which only a few of the rules are known, and he has to cope with far more proliferating variety than the men in our example. He is therefore debarred from adopting the commonsense solution of the observer who knew how to play all the time. Basically, he adopts the first of the three courses of action. If he is a modern, well-informed and aggressive manager, he will use operational research to help him—avoiding the excesses of the second example above. That is to say, he will not embark on a fully analytic, fully automated control system unless the situation for which he is responsible is remarkably straightforward. He will use his operational research teams to help him quantify decisions and to choose between alternative policies. Should he not, however, make some use of cybernetics—the science of control? In short, how did the cybernetician reach the commonsense answer in the example? If this can be explained, the information may well be useful in those cases where a commonsense answer is no longer available.

The answer to this question may be found in one of the really fundamental laws of cybernetics, adumbrated by various people, but disclosed in its most general form by Ross Ashby. It is called the *law of requisite variety*. There are various rigorous formulations of the law, but it may be expressed (in Ashby's own words) 'picturesquely: *only variety can destroy variety*'. There seems no point in going into a great deal of detail and close exposition about this law. In terms of the example just considered, it simply says that if each red-jerseyed player is *marked* by a white-jerseyed player (who is after all safely assumed to have roughly equivalent physiological resources) then, on the average, whatever the actual play undertaken by the red team, sufficient variety can proliferate in the white team to match it. The two levels of variety must be equivalent. If, for instance, the referee sends one of the white men off the field, there is certainly a statistical expectation that the red side will win the game. There is really no more to be said by way of explaining this law.

It has to be confessed, however, that the exposition is abandoned with a sense of great unease; such brevity shows scant respect for what is a major discovery of cybernetic science.

But there must be readers clamouring at this point to know what on earth the fuss is all about. For, they will say, all this is entirely obvious. Of course it is obvious—with hindsight. It seems safe to say that all the great natural laws that operate on the same scale of resolution as we humans do ourselves, and which can therefore be directly experienced, are obvious too. But this by no means diminishes their importance. Besides, if the law of requisite variety is a truism, how is it that we try to disobey it all the time? And how is it that, although this disobedience causes us to fail in our task of control, we *still* do not recognize what has gone wrong? It will be necessary to justify the assertions implicit in these two rhetorical questions. So a comparison will now be drawn between the operation of controls in natural, animate systems and in fabricated, artificial systems.

Firstly, consider any natural control system: a coupling of the general kind depicted in Figure 27. Ask whether there is not *prima facie* evidence that the law of requisite variety holds. Suppose that what interests us about the natural system is that it consists of a population of animals of some species. This population forms a social system, with intricate relations and a proliferating variety. Schoolboy mathematics applied to the basic laws of procreation in this system quickly reveals that it embodies a latent power to overrun the entire locality in a very short time. But the proliferating variety is controlled by another population of animals which prey on the first. If every individual predator eats one individual prey, then the population of the first species can only be held constant if there are as many predators as preys. Perhaps, however, the population representing the control system is notoriously small. There may, for example, be only 1 per cent as many individual hawks as there are individual quadrupedal land-based animals on which the hawk preys. If so (and assuming this system to be isolated) it is entirely obvious that if the population preyed upon is to remain constant, the predators must catch and kill a hundred of the preys each. Requisite variety must be there; it does not have to exist on the basis of a raw count of items, but the purposive and systematic assemblage that is identified as a system must be capable of proliferating requisite variety. Otherwise the system goes out of control. Admittedly, this example is not very impressive biology at all: it is well known that ecological food webs are exceedingly complex and resist isolation in this way. But however many interacting sub-systems of preys and predators, big fleas and little fleas, are invoked, it is none the less evident that the balance of animal populations would be grossly upset very rapidly unless the law of requisite variety held in general throughout nature.

Consider next any artificial system which could be modelled by Figure 27 and enquire what is going on. Contemplate the solitary policeman trying unsuccessfully to sort out a ramified traffic jam through a network of roads. He fails, because he does not have requisite variety. When the jam eventually clears, by the way, it is because the residual variety required has been supplied by the motorists themselves—in their efforts to escape. Or consider the factory manager whom we met in Part II. He may well know, from econometric studies, that twice as much capital as is really necessary is tied up in stocks. With due caution, he issues an edict that *every* stockpile must be cut by 10 per cent. That should be all right. But it is *not* all right, because the system proliferates so much variety. Not *every* stockpile is twice as large as it should be: the figure is an average. Some stockpiles are only *just* large enough, so when they are cut by 10 per cent they cease to be adequate at all. This manager has the right information and has taken what is in principle the right decision. But he does not have requisite variety and therefore makes a nonsense of the control function. Again nature exerts its laws—even on artificial systems. The human beings in this factory will in practice proliferate sufficient variety to circumvent the manager's disastrous ruling, as anyone who has ever worked in industry would agree. So the system will remain viable; the only trouble is that the manager will not achieve his object of running the place more efficiently. The examples could be multiplied indefinitely. No-one could possibly claim that any government department has requisite variety to exercise the control function which a modern economy demands that it should. But this is not to say that it is impossible to devise controls of requisite variety for all these cases— as will be shown in the next section and exemplified in the next chapter.

There are other laws of variety which can be discussed even in terms of the radically simplified diagram of Figure 27. Most of them derive from the work of Claude Shannon and his mathematical theory of communication. In 1948 Shannon published twenty theorems on this topic, all of them dealing with the passage of information through electrical systems. If the particular system of which some theorem is true can be isomorphically mapped on to some other system, then the theorem (under some suitable transformation) will hold in the second system as well.

The example most relevant to general cybernetic theory is found in the case of Shannon's Tenth Theorem. Reverting to Figure 27, we have so far discussed the relationship between the two boxes, situation and control, in terms of requisite variety. But what of the input/output channels by which they are linked? It is certainly obvious that each of the two channels marked on the diagram must have sufficient capacity to transmit the variety proliferated in each box to the other. This in itself looks a formidable task, until it is recalled that the diagram is a simplification in which a multitude of connections between the two boxes is compressed into one line. For example, if a management were compelled to rely on the information reaching it through 'orthodox' channels of communication, it would certainly never have anything like requisite variety for controlling the company—for the simple reason that the orthodox channels could not transmit it. No, the management has many other ways of obtaining information, as has been remarked before, and the permutation of variety between them brings the quantity of control variety up to something like the desired level. In fact, however, the channel capacity required in the control loop is considerably *greater* than the amount of variety proliferating in the situation. This is because of uncertainty in the system at large. In any real-life system, the signals emanating from the situation will be 'noisy': that is, they can never be quite precise and unequivocal. Shannon's Tenth Theorem is not adequately explained here, because it involves the concept of entropy which it would be a digression to discuss, but it may be described in the present context as saying that the channel capacity must be sufficiently great as to resolve the ambiguity in the signals transmitted.

As Ashby himself has pointed out, this theorem bears a close resemblance to his own law of requisite variety. For in so far as noise (or uncertainty) creeps into any real-life system, this is one of the bases on which variety proliferates. From the standpoint of the control box, the variety to be absorbed is not just that generated by the situation itself at a distance. What matters is the variety observed at control—and this includes any extra variety multiplied in by transmission errors. Ashby has gone so far as to wonder whether his own law and Shannon's Tenth Theorem are not different ways of saying the same thing. But it seems that in suggesting this he is too modest. For, if any distinction is to be retained between the boxes and the lines in Figure 27, then the considerations that apply to them are very different. The transmission of information along the lines is spread out in time; 'obviously' the control must wait to get sufficient information before it can act effectively to modify the situation. But it is a deeper insight to contend that, communications apart, the capacity to proliferate variety within the control box must be as great or greater than the capacity of the situation box to proliferate variety.

3   Environmental Disturbance

These then are some of the basic considerations about variety and its relevance to processes of control. So far, the whole discussion has been derived from Figure 27—which is an absolutely minimal representation of the problem. It is necessary to extend this, if only by a small amount, to show how the management cybernetician can begin in practice to account for the more involved situations of real life. The next element to introduce into this isolated system, and one which will again make it only relatively isolated, is an environmental disturbance. As can be seen from Figure 28, the sub-system called the situation is likely to have another class of input than that which emanates from its control. The figure does not show how this originates, only that it represents the extramural interactions which make the situation relatively (and not absolutely) isolated from the environment at large.

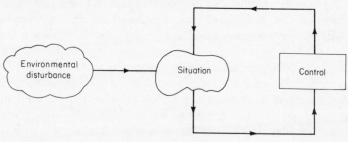

FIGURE 28.

This modification to the diagram produces an effect on the emerging theory of control which is both evident and innocuous. Manifestly, the variety of the situation will now proliferate even further; therefore by the law of requisite variety the available variety in the control must rise by a similar amount; and the channel capacities of the communications loop must rise—both by this amount and by the increment of uncertainty which an inexplicable environmental disturbance inherently injects. There is thus no particular problem in understanding what has happened, although the practical effects may well be serious—since greater variety-handling capacities must be supplied all round. However, there is an important moral to be drawn.

Suppose, to revert to earlier arguments, the manager of this system were relying on either the first or the second strategies discussed earlier. It will be remembered that the first strategy was based on the idea that a recurrent pattern could be detected in a situation, while the second proposed to use science to discover analytically how the situation really behaves. Now it is clear that if a large injection of variety from the environment enters the system, neither of these strategies has any real hope of providing adequate control. There were always difficulties, but at this point in the story it becomes virtually impossible that either of these strategies should retain the least verisimilitude. By definition, that is to say, the environmental disturbance now introduced is quite arbitrary, unpatterned; from the standpoint of the observer managing this system it is inexplicable. The management cybernetician is, on the contrary, unmoved by this development, for he has not claimed that he will recognize pattern, nor that he will explain away the behaviour of the situation. He has said only that by designing the control loop to obey the law of requisite variety and to meet the provisions of Shannon's Tenth Theorem, control is implicitly possible. It has yet to be explained how all this works in practice; but at least the necessary provision is there.

To be explicit, what has emerged by this point is a new notion of what constitutes control. Because of the dichotomy between animate and artificial systems, we are accustomed to take the controls implicit in the first for granted, and to make the wrong specification for the second. The orthodox notion of control is frankly fascist; it is mandatory; it is a bully. Orders are issued and it is expected that they will be carried out. But by now we have put on nature's spectacles. We see that the fundamental nature of the self-regulatory control implicit in a viable system is that it can *absorb* proliferating variety like a sponge. But, it may with reason be objected now: since the relatively isolated system is *not* absolutely isolated, and since it has now been conceded that environmental disturbance will be injected into a real-life situation, this concept of the absorption of the variety which results begins to look an impossible task. It was shown in the last chapter that even a tiny system, with a minimal set of relationships and states, proliferates a thoroughly alarming level of variety. If we take a real-life situation, and moreover allow that unknown, and doubtless very large, quantities of environmental disturbance are to be pumped into it, the final tally of variety that has to be absorbed—and therefore equated in the control system—is astronomical (no, it seems impossible to find a suitable adjective). Perhaps this fact will render the whole approach impracticable.

It does not; the cybernetician can learn a trick from nature here, and endow the control with requisite variety despite all. But before going on to the next section in which this trick is explained, we must for once acknowledge that there is something about the way nature works which operates in the manager's favour.

Thanks to the fact that nature is indivisible, an organic whole, arbitrary disturbances from outside the system as depicted in Figure 28 are not really as disconnected from it as they seem. This admission does not mitigate the difficulties just touched upon, for it is still impossible to carry the analytical process of investigation and explanation far beyond the boundaries of the system for which the manager is responsible. But we can usefully draw on the notion of the ramified system, and the Hegelean Axiom of Internal Relations. From these considerations the following argument may be evolved. The disturbance under discussion was called an environmental disturbance. This means to say that the disturbance is at once something separate from and inexplicable to the system, *and* something that is in some other way intimately bound up with the system. For, after all, the environment of a system not only affects it; the system *belongs to* its environment. It may be separate from it, but it is not utterly foreign to it. Thus whatever it is that remotely causes the environmental disturbance *impinges indirectly on the system too.*

Gert Sommerhoff was the man who made this insight explicit, and provided a rigorous framework within which to discuss it. He created the concept of a 'coenetic variable'. The word he coined comes from the Greek word meaning 'common', and the coenetic variable is the common causal determinant of the state of both the environmental disturbance and the situation at the same time. Now it is important to see that the belief in such a variable is not a gratuitous assumption. In respect to certain results which accrue from the interaction of the situation with its environment, the former is said to be adapted to the latter. We cannot conceive of a viable system as being totally enclosed, and totally foreign to the environment with which it interacts. What 'adaptation' means will be discussed much later. But certainly, in the pragmatic terms of the results of the interaction, adaptation implies some kind of mapping between the situation and its environment. Sommerhoff's contention was that adaptation implies not only the actual existence of a particular mapping which can be inspected, but also the potential existence of a whole variety of other specific mappings which *would have* existed if the environmental disturbance and the system had been different from what they are. Hence Sommerhoff is led to contend that some prior and causal state of affairs exists which is common to both the situation and its environment, and which influences the adaptation of the one to the other. The correspondence inherent in the mapping is in fact observable as a correlation of behavioural states; the argument says that the two are *directively* correlated by a coenetic variable.

More sense can be made of Figure 28, then, by invoking the concepts of a coenetic variable and of directive correlation. In Figure 29, the previous figure is redrawn making use of these concepts. The lower half of this figure is a natural control loop which helps to constrain the proliferation of variety in the situation which we have learned to expect. (Neither Ashby nor Sommerhoff can of course be blamed for any infelicities in this account of a type of management system which neither of them explicitly considered.) As can be seen, the coenetic variable contributes to the state of the situation and to the nature of the environmental disturbance that impinges on the situation. Similarly, when the situation adapts to this stimulus, the results that accrue are also affected directly by the environmental disturbance—since this has modified the environment in which the results occur.

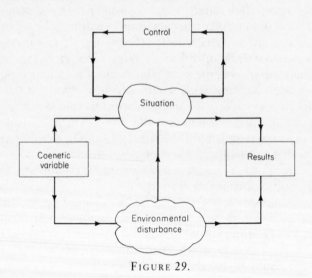

FIGURE 29.

It must have been noted that, in each step forward that has been taken, it has turned out to be valuable to close artificially a system which began by being open. Figure 26 had inputs and outputs trailing out into the unknown. These could not therefore be accounted for until, in Figure 27, the relatively isolated system was turned into an artificially isolated system. Managerially speaking, this meant stepping one rank higher up in the hierarchy, to view the problem of the manager of the original situation through the eyes of his immediate superior. When Figure 28 introduced an input from outside *this* system, the second loop was closed in Figure 29. The managerial implication of this manœuvre is that a step should be taken sideways, rather than upward, in the hierarchy. For the manager who can understand the nature of the lower control loop in Figure 29 probably has a task that is functionally different from that of the manager working in the area represented by the upper control loop.

To exemplify: if the situation is a production situation, it has a production manager. He is inside the situation, battling with its proliferating variety, and using the system's own self-regulative properties to help. This was the position in Figure 26. The manager does not·'speak the language' in which the larger system, of which these inputs and outputs are part, makes sense. But a more senior manager, his superior, does speak this language. He completes the larger system, which includes a control element designed to constrain the behaviour of the situation. But along comes an environmental disturbance, say from the market. The whole pattern of ordering suddenly and inexplicably changes. Now not even the second manager can understand what is happening, because he does not speak the language of the market. The man who does, and who can cope with the closure of the lower control loop in Figure 29, is the sales director. This time it is he who completes the system from outside. Meanwhile, the production manager has to obtain results: that is, he must ensure that the situation adapts to the environmental disturbance, by dispatching to the customer a new balance of new kinds of product; but his problem is not as difficult as it might at first appear. The changed order book, which is the environmental disturbance, does not somehow present the production manager with an overwhelming challenge. It might seem a little weird, but he is half prepared for it. The reason is, of course, that the production manager and his unknown customers (unknown because their existence, their nursing, their entertainment and their status is the responsibility of the sales director) belong to the same industrial milieu. The pattern of technological change which has influenced the market to demand a new pattern of products, has also influenced the production manager directly. Even though he may not make prognostications about what the market will do, because this is not his job, he knows what it is like to be living in this branch of industry. The pattern of technological change will have caused him to make various adaptations to the prevailing climate himself. Thus the state of technology, as it applies to this milieu, is the coenetic variable in Figure 29.

Now it is clear that new external influences could be brought to bear on this double-looped closed system from any direction, to impinge on any component. That means by definition that there is no-one in the system as depicted who can speak the language appropriate to the explanation of this new input. So the management tends to close the system again. The process can go on almost indefinitely. This is why commercial companies pay the heavy expenses required to send some top executive to the opposite ends of the earth to find out what conditions are really like there. This is why an industrial company will invest money in research so fundamental that it seems to have no relevance to the business at all. (Industry may often be surprised carrying out research of a kind that the local university would regard as overly 'pure'.) But this is not altruism, as it is often represented. The series of loops generated by the opening and closing of the system has simply taken the search for languages in which to comprehend environmental disturbances further and further away from the commercial operation.

There are various cybernetically technical aspects to all this which are of absorbing interest. What is happening here is in fact an exemplification of a basic law in advanced logic known as the Incompleteness Theorem. These studies are apparently so remote from real life that it is often said that this theorem, though intellectually interesting, has no relevance to anything practical whatsoever. In *Cybernetics and Management*, I tried to show that this theorem underlies the whole problem of organizing control in a large system such as an industrial company. The fact is that if a system is only relatively isolated (that is to say, *open*), it has to be absolutely isolated (that is to say, *closed*) by an artificial convention before its mode of control by the natural laws of cybernetics can be discussed. I have called this *the principle of completion from without*. But it must be remembered that the closure of the system is *artificial*, for the reason that (as was agreed earlier) all systems are in reality relatively isolated and not absolutely so.

This turns out to be extremely fortunate. Briefly: it is possible to prove in cybernetics that if a system such as those described here is to maintain stability under disturbances not foreseen by the designer, it must behave 'equifinally'. This means that there must be various different ways in which it can reach a specified goal, or final state, from different working conditions. Now Ludwig von Bertalanffy has proved by the use of general systems theory that closed systems cannot behave equifinally. Therefore viable systems are not closed. (This result conforms with commonsense, for if it were possible to isolate an animate system absolutely, it would quite obviously not be alive for long.) So a number of conceptual models of the way in which the management of a complicated enterprise has to be structured for purposes of control, map on to each other at this point.

The general systems model, as indefinitely extended from Figure 29, can accommodate all the conceptual models so far brought to bear on the problem. Philosophically, Hegel's Axiom of Internal Relations shows that the boundaries drawn to contain a system are purely conventional—and the indefinite extensibility of the model exemplifies the point. Ecologically, the viability of a system as guaranteed by its interaction with the environment is exemplified in the model by the metamorphosis of inputs into outputs and vice versa. Servomechanically, the model obeys the laws which govern communication channels transmitting error-controlled negative feedback. Logically, the Incompleteness Theorem of Gödel is acknowledged in the application of the principle of completion from without. And so on.

4 The Variety Sponge

The kind of control mechanism with which we have been dealing is known as a homeostat. According to many cyberneticians, this is the basic control mechanism used by nature. It is certainly the type of system which promotes biological homeostasis. Homeostasis is that feature of an organism which holds some critical variable steady within physiological limits. The most usually quoted example is blood temperature. Whether we work in the refrigerators of a meat packing station, or on the melting-shop stage in a steelworks, our body temperature remains 98·4° Fahrenheit. There is, of course, a statistical variation about this mean figure. What is important to the organism is not that the figure be maintained precisely as a constant, but that its value should not wander so far away from the mean value that physiological damage ensues. One of the key features of any viable system, and a sure index of its submission to control, is that it can maintain a homeostatic equilibrium. Not only the blood temperature, but the entire biochemical system of the body has to remain in balance—within physiological limits. And this is surely true also of the industrial, social and economic systems with which managers have to deal.

It should be noted at once that neither biological nor artificial systems employ homeostasis as a control device for the reason that they wish to be static. All the systems in which we are interested intend to learn, to evolve, to become more effective and in general to 'improve themselves'. They do this by making excursions from a state of balance with a given pay-off, and an internal régime for the system which yields a better pay-off than heretofore will be adopted only if it is still capable of achieving a homeostatic steady state. For example, if a man finds it profitable (for some reason) to run very fast, he may do so for some time. But he cannot adopt running-very-fast as a permanent characteristic of his existence, because he will quite soon run into an oxygen debt. The body can in fact sustain unphysiological behaviour for a period by such a trick, but sooner or later the debt has to be repaid by rest. So the running becomes a profitable short-term behaviour pattern of the system which is *part of* a more general bodily homeostasis. The same phenomenon occurs in artificial systems too.

This is not to say that an organism cannot find a more profitable state than it now has—which is itself homeostatically tenable. An industrial company typically exemplifies both points. Every businessman knows how to make a very large increase in the profits of his company for a month or two—after which the homeostat underlying the system must take effect (because a physiological limit has been reached) and the debt is then repaid by an unprofitable period. But a genuine advance, one involving a new mode of operation which has been learnt from experience, or one worked out (say) by operational research as offering a better allocation of resources to outcomes, may be sustained indefinitely within the natural homeostasis of the business. The intuitive recognition of the difference between these two ways of improving the state of affairs is, in many circumstances, what makes a good businessman.

The basic homeostatic control loop will now be looked at in a little more detail to see how it operates. We know that, given requisite variety, the sub-system called control is competent to absorb the variety proliferating in the sub-system called the situation. We also know something about the transmission of information between the two sub-systems. But what goes on inside them? The formal account of this matter is due to Ross Ashby, who discovered the principles underlying homeostasis by building a strange machine which he called The Homeostat. This machine had only one object: to settle down as quickly as possible to a stable condition after it had been disturbed. The homeostat is therefore a mechanism for achieving stability—the constancy of some critical variable (its output). But of course many kinds of system can do this much: even an ordinary balance will resume a horizontal steady state after it has been disturbed. Ashby was in fact chasing a more elusive concept, which he called *ultrastability*. In ordinary language, an ultrastable system is capable of resuming a steady state after it has been disturbed *in a way not envisaged by its designer*. This is the really powerful feature of a homeostatic control mechanism. It is all very well for a system to be, as it were, programmed to respond to disturbances in a sensible way. The difficulties into which viable systems, whether natural or artificial, characteristically run are due to environmental disturbances of an unexpected kind. A homeostat can deal with these, as was explained in the last section, and in the simplest possible terms this is how.

In Figure 30 is shown a homeostatic control loop of the kind already discussed. The space inside each of the boxes denoting a sub-system should now be taken as including a large number of points, each of which represents a possible state of the system. That is, if the system were actually two-dimensional as is the diagram, its state at any particular moment would be represented by a pin-point somewhere inside the box. At the next moment, its state might have changed to another such point. The boundaries of the box delimit the possible states of the system. In real life, of course, systems are not two-dimensional, but multi-dimensional, and it is necessary to envisage the point representing the

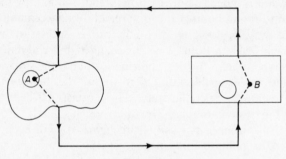

FIGURE 30.

state of the system as fixed in a phase space of many dimensions. Now if the host of possible points within the situation represents all possible states, it is only to be expected that the manager of the situation will find some of these points more satisfactory than others. Indeed, in so far as the manager can either allow the state of affairs to continue, or intervene to alter it, the host of points in the box might be classified as being either acceptable or unacceptable in every case. Characteristically, the number of acceptable states will be much fewer than the number of unacceptable states. In Figure 30 the acceptable states are collected together into a circular blob. What is true of the manager of the situation, is also true of the senior manager who has responsibility for the whole of this system. He is not concerned to manage the situation as such, but he is concerned with the homeostasis of the whole system, and also with recognizing within the control box what appears to him to be a satisfactory state of affairs. So the acceptable states of the control are also gathered together into a small circular blob.

It is clear that the influences on the situation, here again represented through a single input channel, help to identify the present state of the system; and also that it is precisely information about the present state of the system which passes out through the output channel towards control. So the dotted lines in Figure 30 close the entire loop for a particular moment in time. At this moment, the situation is in state A and the control is in state B.

Now it will be seen that, from the point of view of the situation manager, the state of his system is satisfactory. Any information sent to the control will indicate this. As far as the control is concerned, however, the state of affairs is not satisfactory. Control wishes to define a *trajectory* (the cybernetic term) that will guide point B into the sub-set of acceptable states. Its decision about this is transmitted as an input to the situation, and is indeed an instruction intended to modify the state of affairs, without driving point A into the region of unacceptable states. If the analytical way of looking at things proves successful when this happens, all will be well. Point A will be changed, but will remain in the region of desirable states; the new information about the situation transmitted to control will enable point B to follow the planned trajectory into its own region of desirable states. Homeostasis has been achieved. But because the system is relatively (and not absolutely) isolated, an environmental disturbance not shown in Figure 30 will eventually jog either point A or point B into an unacceptable state—whereupon the homeostat must operate again.

But the more interesting condition is the one in which the analytical treatment of proliferating variety fails to work successfully. The trajectory planned for point B by control gives rise to a message which in fact drives point A into an unacceptable state; the message transmitted from situation to control is now one that asks for help. Point B may be able to follow its planned trajectory at this moment; or it may not, because of the new information arriving from the situation. In either case, control will certainly know that some new message must be passed to the situation. However, given sufficient time, it is evident that this system will eventually reach stability. For each sub-system vetoes any state adopted by the other sub-system (whether that state be satisfactory internally or not) which does not favour itself.

This then is the *self-vetoing homeostat*. It has a plan for stability, even in the absence of adequate analytical knowledge, for in the last resort the proposals made by each sub-system to the other can be random trial-and-error mutations. It also has a plan for ultrastability. Imagine that some stream of disturbances which no-one has hitherto contemplated impinges on the situation from outside. Variety then proliferates within the situation, and it is a species of variety that no-one (not the situation manager, nor the controller, nor the senior manager) understands. Even so, because control has requisite variety, it has the capacity to go on vetoing every *B* that is unacceptable, and therefore to force *A* to continue changing state (even within its own region of acceptability) until *B* is itself acceptable. Requisite (control) variety absorbs proliferating (world) variety like a sponge. The only difficulty about all this is that the length of time taken to reach homeostatic equilibrium may be far too long. In general, if the average time taken for the control mechanism to operate is longer than the average gap between environmental disturbances, then the system will oscillate interminably. This problem will be discussed in Chapter 14.

Meanwhile, the question for us here is the following. Given that variety proliferates naturally in the situation sub-system, how is requisite variety expected to proliferate in the control sub-system? After all, the control sub-system is artificial, and we are simply not accustomed to the idea of a machine or an office which is meant to be a variety proliferator. The answer to this problem lies in the notion of the black box.

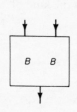

FIGURE 31.

The term *black box* has been used in a great many contexts in recent years. The meaning of the term in cybernetics is that of a box to which inputs are observed to lead and from which outputs are observed to emerge. Nothing at all is known about the way in which the inputs and the outputs are connected inside the box—which is why it is called black. The reason why we contemplate a box having such odd properties, is that the more familiar box in which something *is* known about the internal connectivity has its variety constrained. The variety of a transparent box may be measured by enumerating the switches inside, and calculating the number of possible states which the box can take up. Even if an arrangement having fairly high variety were chosen, the potential variety of all the other arrangements which could have been built in is suppressed. But a black box is assumed to be able to take on any internal arrangement of input–output connectivity at all; it can therefore proliferate maximal variety. The next question is how this is to be measured.

Figure 31 shows a black box with two inputs and one output. As usual, the simplest version of the mechanism will be considered. That is to say, each of the transmission lines may take on one of two alternative states—nought or one. Given that the box is black, and that any mode of connectivity may exist within, let us measure the variety of the system. The input variety is $2^2 = 4$. This may be checked by enumerating the number of distinguishable input states as follows: 00, 01, 10, 11. If there were three inputs, the answer would be $2^3 = 8$; and in general the input variety is 2^n. But the box has an output line as well, which may take up a 0 or 1 response to any input pattern. People often think that the variety of the whole box is therefore twice the input variety. This is incorrect, and the point is of such importance that the correct answer is argued here in detail.

Consider a specific black box, of the Figure 31 type, which responds to the setting 00 for its inputs with the output 0. This fact by no means determines the behaviour of the box. For instance, when the input pattern is changed to 01, the output changes to 1. This says a little more about this specific box. Consider a second specific box which *also* responds to the 00 input setting with a 0 output. When the input pattern of this box is changed to 01, the output remains at 0. The second box is different from the first because its response *pattern* is different. Since variety is a measure of the number of distinguishable things, the variety of a Figure 31 box can be determined only by considering the set of permutations of input against output. This set of permutations defines a *machine*. Here is an exhaustive account of a specific black box which defines the kind of machine that it is.

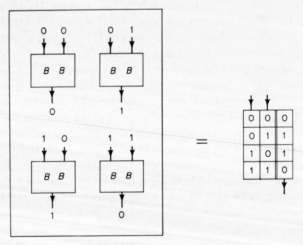

F<small>IGURE</small> 32.

The drawing on the left shows the response it actually gives to each possible input pattern. The schema on the right shows a convention for writing the drawing down in simpler form. The question now is: how many distinguishable *machines* are specified by the black box in

Figure 31? A tableau, using the new convention, is provided in Figure 33 which gives the complete answer.

The variety (count it) is 16. This is because each distinguishable machine specifies each of the four responses that it makes to each of the

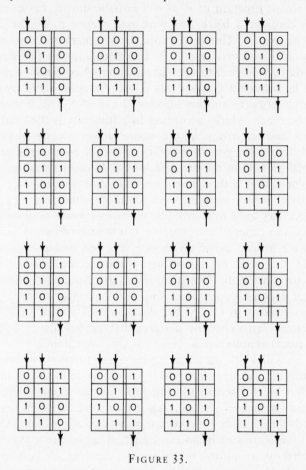

FIGURE 33.

four possible input patterns. The response in each case can take one of two forms: the outputs 0 or 1. So the variety of the machines is the output variety (2) raised to the power of the input variety (4)—that is, $2^4 = 16$. But there are four responses simply because the input variety is $2^2 = 4$. The breakdown, then, is really $2^{2^2} = 16$. The first 2 is the output variety, which is raised to the power of (the second) 2, which is the input variety on one line, which is itself raised to the power of (the third) 2, which is the number of input lines. In general (as was shown) a box with n inputs has an input variety of 2^n. So the machine in general has a variety of 2^{2^n}, where n is the number of inputs.

This measure is the characteristic variety generator of a black box. It is a very potent function of n, as will now be shown. Let us arbitrarily choose to consider a black box with one output and eight inputs, as shown in Figure 34. This box is capable of generating a variety of 2^{2^8}. Since $2^8 = 256$, the variety is 2^{256}. The calculation of this number by hand is tedious; suffice it to say that the answer has seventy-eight figures in it. Just how large a number this is may be appreciated by contemplating its closeness to another number: $\frac{3}{2} \cdot 136 \cdot 2^{256}$. This is the so-called Cosmical Number, which, according to Eddington, is the total number of protons and electrons in the entire universe. The black box in Figure 34, therefore, generates sufficient variety to name almost every fundamental particle in the universe with a different name.

The point is that, although it is necessary to acknowledge the way variety proliferates in a real-life situation, it is not necessary to be over-awed by the task of trying to supply requisite variety for its control. But to understand how to make proper use of this device, it is first vital to understand the need to reverse our orthodox mental approach to complexity. The plain man, and especially the classical scientist, copes with complexity by suppressing the proliferation of variety, by killing off variety until almost none is left. Then he declares that he has discovered a fundamental relation between (say) two things;

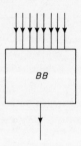

FIGURE 34.

after this he will work outwards again, trying to take account of a few more factors in the situation which appear to influence it most profoundly. But by this technique, and however far we go in specifying a complicated interaction within a transparent box, we shall never begin to approach the capability to generate variety of a box that is altogether black and therefore totally unconstrained. This immense variety is the raw material of a control mechanism competent to handle real-life situations. We have to learn how to fabricate systems from this raw material without de-naturing it.

When talking about natural situations, we have said that variety proliferates. This conveys the idea that the system just naturally breeds variety. When talking about the control element in the homeostat governing an artificial system, however, we have spoken of the need to generate variety. This is intended to convey the idea that deliberate 'black box engineering' can be undertaken in the design of managerial systems. This chapter closes with a simple two-dimensional model intended to illustrate the nature of a *variety generator*. This is a device, not necessarily a machine made of ironmongery as will be seen, which is not only capable of proliferating variety, but is deliberately organized to generate it for a purpose. And the precise purpose is not known in advance, although of course the *kind* of purpose is known.

Consider the situation in which you wish to meet a friend at a beauty spot for a picnic. Each of you has heard of this place, but neither knows exactly where it is. You consult about the matter on the telephone, each armed with a similar map. You find the place on the map, and you wish to indicate to your friend over the telephone where to find it on his map. This is a high variety two-dimensional situation. The first question is: how great is the variety? The map is about a yard square and is covered with a quarter-inch grid. Obviously, the primary scientific problem of placing a suitable scale on a continuum has been solved; once the right square has been isolated, your friend will be able to identify the place within it. So it is correct to consider the variety of the grid as a suitable measure of the variety of the situation. The number of distinguishable squares, then, is upwards of 20,000. To reach an answer it is necessary to match this situation with a control mechanism of requisite variety. The most obvious way of supplying this is to identify each square with a number. Consequently, you suggest to your friend that each of you should sequentially number all the squares in turn. It seems possible that this will take about seventeen hours, working very hard. At the end of this time, however, success is at hand. You can say to your friend: the place where we are to meet is in square 13,472. The law of requisite variety has triumphed. But none of us would do this. Instead, we draw attention to the grid numbers which quantify the two co-ordinates of the map. You will say to your friend: we meet inside the square *selected* by the co-ordinates 48/79.

The variety of this more effective control device is (say) $2 \times 144 = 288$ —the total number of distinguishable elements along the two co-ordinates. But considered as an unconstrained system it can generate a variety of $144^2 = 20,736$. So, for the expense of recording and handling a variety equal to twice the square root of the requisite variety, the law has been met. Moreover, in a system such as a real-life situation that has (say) 100 dimensions, requisite variety will be obtained for the price of handling the hundredth root of the proliferated variety of the system. This all looks very simple because the example chosen is familiar. But, if we consider a phase space in which we have preconceived notions about the relationships between variables, it is all too easy to specify a control system which constrains the variety of the black box to such a degree that requisite variety is no longer obtainable. Think of any recording system with which you are familiar. Is this not arranged according to a classification which reduces variety by a vast factor? To illustrate: we divide some people into Scotsmen and Englishmen; we divide the Scotsmen into those wearing kilts and those not wearing kilts; we divide the Englishmen into those wearing bowler hats and those not wearing bowler hats. The next thing that happens is that we meet an Englishman, wearing a kilt and a trilby. The classification cannot cope. Our man becomes 'miscellaneous'. Before we know what has happened, 95 per cent of our records are in the miscellaneous file. The arrangements lack requisite variety.

These ostensibly irrelevant and irreverent examples will repay careful thought. In the next chapter, the application of these cybernetic principles to certain industrial problems will be considered. Free use will be made of the notions of homeostasis, requisite variety, channel capacity, black boxes, variety generators, and all the cybernetic trappings of the relatively isolated system.

13

CONTROLLING OPERATIONS

वास्तवमें सम्पूर्ण कर्म सब प्रकारसे प्रकृतिके
गुणोंट्टारा किये जाते हैं तो भी जिसका
अन्तःकरण अहङ्कारसे मोहित हो रहा है, ऐसा
अज्ञानी ' मैं कर्ता हूँ ' ऐसा मानता है ।

> In reality, action is entirely the outcome of all the
> modes of nature's attributes; moreover only he whose
> intellect is deluded by egotism is so ignorant that he
> presumes 'I am doing this'.

THE LORD KRISHNA
in the *Bhagavad–Gita* (*circa* 3000 B.C.)

1   Implicit Control

Here is the oldest cybernetic quotation of them all. Some effort has
been made in the selection of remarks made by various Western authors
to show that our understanding of system has been slow to emerge,
although our understanding of some other scientific subtleties has been
acute. Eastern philosophy has, notoriously, followed a very different
course. In this quotation from ancient Hindu scripture is revealed an
insight into the nature of system, secondly into the proliferation of
variety, and thirdly into the generation of spontaneous control activity.
The first clause, translated directly into cybernetic jargon instead of
English, might read: 'Output is a self-regulating black box function of
input variety.' But the sting is in the second clause. It speaks of the
self-determination of the system from its own nature, of the *implicit*
control which cybernetics purports to discover in nature 5,000 years too
late to count as original.

The intention now is to make a rather detailed study of the problem of
management control at the down-to-earth level of industrial operations.

299

What follows immediately is in part a recapitulation, but it is important to transplant the ideas developed in the last two chapters into the working environment. The scene of the analysis must be set.

Control mechanisms are designed to make situations behave according to certain desired performance criteria. Control engineering in the context of an automatic production line, for example, designs control mechanisms for *artificial* situations, for the situation is itself created by the engineer and is his creature. A situation in the sense so far meant, one that is simply a chunk of real life, will be distinguished in future from such an artificial situation by calling it a *world situation*. For instance: an area of a factory, a battlefield, a zone of a market, and the traffic in a city, are all world situations. In industry, a world situation is usually some thriving, complex, uncertain, interacting collection of men and machines, materials and money; one may stumble across it as a going concern.

What are the performance criteria by which world situations are judged and for which their control systems exist? The point was made long ago that these criteria are not very clear. A company seeks to make a profit, but not ruthlessly, to its long-term disadvantage. It seeks to offer a service to the community, but not without regard to the interest of its shareholders. And so on, almost indefinitely, runs the list: for every desideratum there is a counter-desideratum that is incompatible with the first, and perhaps even contradictory to it. In a traffic situation, for example, one object is to minimize the maximum time through the system, and another is to see that no-one gets killed. These criteria are fundamentally incompatible—as are the main criteria in a maintenance situation. In the limit, an aircraft operator can reach maximum safety by maintaining his aircraft on the ground all the time; or he can achieve maximum sales of seats by doing no maintenance whatsoever. In either case his system will soon be dead. Viable systems have to do better than this; they have to survive. And so usually no particular object, however desirable, can be pursued to its maximum or minimum value, any more than it can in the personal life of a man.

Now the general theory of self-regulation in control engineering demands that performance criteria be explicit and consistent, and that the quantities to be controlled should tend to limiting values. Similarly, orthodox control procedures for world situations try to accept these principles. Thus aspects of organization within world situations which are recognizably contributing to control are frequently called by names like 'rules and regulations', 'the book', 'the Bible', or just 'the system'. These names, which are often used pejoratively (or at the least in a despairing tone of voice) seem to imply that world situations are really controlled by such mechanisms as divine right, Mosaic Law or a systematic appeal to precedent. But what, on cybernetic analysis, appears really to control such situations is a facility for implicit control.

According to this insight, world situations themselves, as contra-distinguished from the people and things of which they are comprised, behave organically. Like living organisms their parts interact so that local objectives are thwarted by incompatible objectives elsewhere. The formal device, explained in the last chapter, to account for this facility is the self-vetoing homeostat. Also like living systems, world situations have the power to learn from their own experience, to recognize patterns in their own circumstances, and thence to prepare directively for their own future behaviour. That they do this unself-consciously does not alter the behavioural facts. We do not have the right words to talk about such behaviour, because the language we use about living things is teleological, and it is the only language available. In fact, it makes as much sense to say that a world situation has what looks like an evolving purposive pattern as to say this about the slime mould Dictyostelium. Neither, as far as we know, has any conative faculty, no volition; yet both look as if they have to the observer. Both, in short, adapt to their environments.

Something has already been said about the formal mechanisms involved in this process too; recall the importance of the variety-reducing coenetic variable and the concept of ultrastability. It must have been noted that none of this is achieved by the application of any unique and unequivocal performance criterion for the system at large. Self-regulation is here more subtle and more profound: it affects not the parameters of the whole system, but those of interacting sub-systems—and through them the organizational structure of the system at large.

The cybernetic commentary on world situations is that controls for them cannot be designed in the sense in which most people would understand that term, because there is nowhere near sufficient understanding about the detailed structure of the organism itself, nor of the environment to which it has to adapt, nor of the interaction between these two. But this is not to say that controls for viable systems cannot be designed at all. Certainly, we can design those error-regulating negative feedbacks that directly reduce the powers allowed to a wandering variable, and indirectly force it back to its acknowledged best level. But it has also been shown that feedback must operate on the entire structure of whatever proliferates variety, on its organization, on the built-in sub-systems that produce aberrant behaviour. It is this deeper-level control that can be designed: a 'meta-control' mechanism capable of amplifying such control power as is built into it by its designer to cope with the unexpected.

This is what is meant by implicit control. Arrangements are not made to record every possible state of the system and every best answer to every state. Arrangements are instead made to ensure that the system will be able to find, or to learn to find, the answers to problems it is set. In the case of the man with the map mentioned in the last chapter, he did not know in advance which square he would be required to select, nor had that square been given a name in advance. None the less, the system was organized so that he could find it. No-one is born with the facility to solve diophantine equations, but people are born with the facility to acquire the facility to solve them. The organic archetype of a system with implicit control is the embryo.

In industry, the world situation is controlled by such methods as production planning, cost accounting, sales forecasting and budgeting. The basic problem that confronts any would-be controller of the world situation by these methods is to delineate the boundaries of the situation with which he hopes to deal. We have already provided an analysis of the nature of relatively isolated systems and we know the difficulties. Any viable system, whether it be a plant, an animal or the company itself, must interact richly and continuously with its environment. Otherwise it loses its bearings, loses its facility to adapt and, in brief, 'goes mad'. Thus, even if a particular situation appears to have very definite boundaries, it can be most dangerous to seal off the area and consider it *in vacuo*.

Whether doing this matters or not depends, not on the system as such, but on who the observer is and what he is trying to do. It is a matter of relativity. A man is encased in an envelope of skin; he appears to begin and end at well-defined points. But this account of a man might be worthless to an atomic physicist, who would see the fundamental particles of matter entering and leaving the envelope continuously; it would be worthless too to the psychologist (for whom a man's personality is nothing when divorced from personal relationships), worthless to the chemist, to the economist or to the biologist, each of whom understands a man in a particular context alone. Above all, the envelope account is worthless to the man himself. For if a man is experimentally deprived of all sensory input, so that he can neither see, hear, smell, touch, taste, nor sense his muscles and joints, he begins to hallucinate in a very short time—and after a little longer ceases to be, in a verifiable sense, the man that he was before.

The cybernetician seeking to account for the behaviour of a company and its controls does well to redefine the boundaries of world situations, and ought not to accept uncritically the conventional boundaries he finds. The operational research man decided this quite firmly in the first half of this book, but by now he has been offered a cybernetic model of the underlying reasons why his experience leads him to this conclusion. The point to remember is that even when the people running the company realize that the divisions they have created are artificial, they do not regard them as particularly dangerous. Whether the division should be accounted dangerous or not depends on who wants to know. Even when the boundaries have been drawn, it will be necessary to remember that they are quite arbitrary, and care must be taken to check that conclusions reached within the area selected will not be completely invalidated if the boundaries of the area are somewhat changed. For all anyone knows, nature may have a different idea of where these boundaries lie.

Time t_1

W1

FIGURE 35.

Figure 35 is a picture of a world situation, showing its arbitrary and untidy boundaries. Inside it there is a large selection of events: machines operating, standing idle, breaking down; men working, resting, waiting, men being happy and miserable and absent from their work; power being consumed, dials going round, instructions being given; pieces of material, products, spares and defectives moving and being moved; money being committed and being saved, successes and failure, opportunities being seized and lost; satisfactions being offered and withheld for men, managers, shareholders and customers alike. Each event is related to many of the other events, and the whole pattern changes continuously as time goes by. So the state of the world situation cannot be discussed timelessly; its states are associated with particular times. Hence *this* state is called $W1$ and it is associated with time t_1. Within this picture there is no homogeneity. Some hint of this is given by the 'drifts' of events as depicted; but remember that this is a two-dimensional picture of an n-dimensional situation. In reality, these 'drifts' are sets of highly complex interactions.

Now comes the problem of choosing the sorts of event in which to be interested, for it seems clear that an infinite number can be discerned —depending upon who the observer is and what his interests are. There is no objective, no absolute truth to be stated here. Take the matter of a stock of interprocess material. The accountant sees the events making up the story of this stock, its additions and subtractions and the kind of stock that it is, as a process of continuous investment of capital against a fluctuating risk. The foreman who runs the next process may be completely unaware of the existence of these financial events; he is interested in production events. And so on.

Now although the manager of the world situation has so to conduct himself that the entire system with its proliferating variety behaves itself properly, he will certainly be interested in particular events. In particular he will wish to discriminate some one event from the great confusion of events, and to make predictive judgments about it. In management accounting, for example, a costing system of some kind will be required to supply information. Modern costing systems recognize the inadequacy of a historical basis, and they seek to account to a predetermined standard which is prospective rather than retrospective. Thus the manager should be able to make use of his management accounting facility to discuss expectations about the future: the effects of doing one thing rather than another, the profitability of accepting certain orders, and so forth.

Similarly, if work study is used to analyse the work content of whatever tasks are undertaken in the world situation, standards of another kind will be set which also have a prospective character. The manager will be able to make use of this tool also in evaluating expectations. The same point applies to the complex of activities which embrace order control, production planning, production scheduling, production programming, machine loading, and the arrangements for dispatch against delivery promises. In sponsoring all these activities, the manager is asking that those to whom every kind of control function is delegated should be able to discriminate some one event from the general confusion of events, and to make predictive judgments about it. For this reason, it will be convenient to nominate six sample events, which it will be assumed are of special interest, within the world situation. These are ringed in Figure 35, and in subsequent figures they appear as standing for any sample of six events chosen from the proliferating variety. In the course of examining the creation of a managerial control system, we shall study these six events to see whether they can be projected into the future with predictive value.

The plan is to discuss how management controls are normally contrived, and to develop a critique of orthodox practice in the light of cybernetic theory. This will be done in the next section. After this, we shall look in detail at the novel kind of control structure which cybernetics itself has successfully put forward. There is just one word of warning: although we shall continue throughout this chapter to treat of concrete industrial cases, some little effort of imagination will yet be required of the reader. If he will cast his mind back over the arguments of this book, he will recall many objections to the compartmentalization of management functions. Therefore he should not expect to find that the explanations which follow deal either with a costing system, or a production control system, or a sales control system, or any other departmental activity. The topic to be discussed is the control of a world situation, for which a manager is uniquely responsible.

Just how many control systems does this manager want? How many different standards can he accommodate in evaluating his expectations from how many different advisers? These matters, it is submitted, are getting out of hand in modern businesses. The control function becomes sub-divided geographically, functionally and professionally; a selection of empires is sustained: the whole arrangement is both confusing and costly. This attack on orthodoxy has to be made, or else the provision of a cybernetic control notion is certain to be regarded as adding yet another speciality control, yet another empire, yet another set of standards, yet another expense. But the real purpose is totally different from this. It acknowledges the control function as an indivisible whole and seeks to devise arrangements for exercising it. If costs are required, and machine hour rates, delivery promises, quality controls, and so on, then they should be *aspects* of a general technique of control. It is with this general technique that we are concerned; but that fact will not be used to avoid the practical implications for any one specialized function.

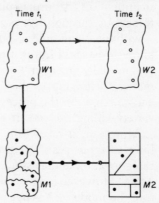

2 A Cybernetic Critique of Orthodox Practice

The world situation just defined appears again in Figure 36. The time is t_1 and the state of the world situation is $W1$. Its outline can be recognized, and the six sample events already mentioned alone are marked.

The first act of the would-be controller of a high variety system is to find means to

FIGURE 36.

reduce the variety in a way which would make it possible to deal with the situation at all. He has no choice in this, by definition. And so in this system the designer makes a model $M1$ of the world situation. In the orthodox practice now under discussion, it is the accountant or the work study man or the O and M officer who does this. The first move is to divide the area into what appear to be convenient sub-divisions. In industry, this is commonly done (depending on the purpose of the system) by demarcating product groups, machine groups, delivery zones or something of this sort. Something must now be written down and recorded for the use of everyone concerned. $M1$ is a conceptual model and looks very like the world situation it is meant to describe. The sub-divisions introduced are themselves complicated and hard to specify. They reflect the comprehension of real-life complexity by the experienced man who is doing the work. However, in so far as he must now begin to write, or to create a filing system, or to design a punched card record, he is compelled to introduce simplification.

To trace the boundaries of the situation and its sub-divisions in a truly organic way, that is by studying the living and interacting behaviour of the system, will involve a treatment of a large proportion of the whole system's variety: the description would be intolerably voluminous and it would take an immensely long time to complete. Thus the model that is committed to paper has to be a simplified version of the conceptual model so far in mind, and this new model is designated $M2$.

It will be noticed that the detail of the boundary lines has had to be sacrificed. They have all been straightened out. This exemplifies the process whereby one says: 'All steels of *this* analysis will undergo heat treatment' or 'All orders placed by *this* firm have top priority' or 'Everything put through *this* process must undergo 100 per cent inspection' —without being able to put in all the detailed exceptions that everyone knows exist. Still less is it possible to include all the exceptions that will undoubtedly arise in the future, when experience will be gained of matters belonging to these classifications which have never before been encountered. So the process of constructing the working model $M2$ is a variety-killing exercise. It has to be.

Moreover, it takes time to complete. In practice, it can easily take as long as three years to invent a recording system, make a reasonable categorization and classification and arrange for the collection of data to begin. However long it takes, it is not an instantaneous process; therefore the model $M2$ is not ready until time t_2 (whenever that happens to be). The line on the diagram bearing dots is intended to indicate that variety is lost in this transformation: information has had to be sacrificed. During this lapse of time, the world situation (shown on the upper line) has been unfolding, without any particular increase or decrease in variety. It will be noted that in the lapse of time t_1 to t_2 the world situation has changed somewhat—this is inevitable. So $M2$ is not a model of $W2$, as we would like it to be, but a model of $W1$—that is, it is already out of date. In the example given in the diagram, this does not seem to matter very much. Each of the six sample points is to be found in one of the six zones demarcated, roughly in its original position. So the man who has been doing the work has done it satisfactorily.

It has to be noted at this point, however, that in real life the exercise that has just been described is *not* done satisfactorily, mainly for the reason that it takes too long. A case is recalled where three accountants spent three years in reaching the stage $M2$ for one third of the events in the world situation. The manager, who was a nice man, was at a loss as to how he should tell them that he was about to reorganize the entire third of the works which they had studied. In another actual case, the very possibility of writing down an $M2$ control system, which was required for purposes of standard costing, had appeared so remote that no-one had ever tried to do it. Consequently, while the top management believed that the figures placed before them were standard costs computed in the ways laid down, they were in fact fabricated by the old fashioned method of adding a uniform oncost to the labour costs involved. The memory of that extraordinary oncost figure is imperishable: 1,029 per cent. As a third example, there was the case of a schedule of piecework prices *for a single machine*, in which the tabulation covered more than seventy foolscap sheets.

It is obvious that all three examples (and many more could be given) were grossly impractical attempts to handle high variety. The point is that they do occur. Moreover, we can isolate the precise difficulty. These people were all trying to cope with complexity by exhausting the real-life proliferation of variety in the model $M2$. It is to be hoped that anyone who thought the example of the map reader (where all the grid squares on the map were exhaustively numbered) to be fatuous will now quietly apologize. In fact, it would be safe to accept a challenge that a misguided attempt to cope with proliferating variety by exhaustive enumeration could be unearthed in any actual managerial situation.

The analysis must now continue. A long interval in time is assumed to intervene before the vital moment arrives when predictive control is expected to operate. That is to say, we will look at this system a year or two after it has been put in. Forecasts about the six particular events are required for time t_n, and the system is preparing to make them. So the time now is t_{n-1}. It must be borne in mind that the control system that now has to generate these forecasts still has the basic structure of the system defined by $M2$. What has happened in the meantime, is that

*M*2 has been filled out with all the extra data that have accrued since time t_2. But in practice the variety of *M*2 is still less than its designers intended, because when one creates a recording system, one visualizes it as eventually filled with data. However it never does fill with data; whole categories remain uncharted. Thus when the control office, marked *C* in Figure 37, draws on *M*2 for information, the model that emerges (*M*3) is of still lower variety.

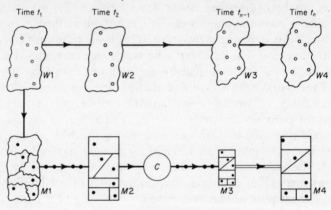

F<small>IGURE</small> 37.

What is happening is this. The control office receives (as the uninterrupted straight line shows) the full variety available in *M*2. The function of the control office at this moment is to operate on this model and to predict something about the six sample events selected for this exercise. When it comes to examine the data which are supposed to have filled out *M*2, it finds that the *M*2 variety potentially present, which would contain all the quantitative information needed to describe the events, is largely missing. What it actually can describe is no more than it can glean from the experience it has accumulated since it began life—which is only a fraction of the potential variety of model *M*2. Furthermore, the process presupposes that whatever information has been available to the control office in the past can be retrieved: in real life, retrieval is not a very efficient process. For these two reasons, the predictive model *M*3 produced by the control office to include forecasts about the six sample points has very low variety compared with its ancestors as models, and still less compared with the *W*1 world situation from which the whole process began.

However, we must do the best we can. In order to make use of the information available, it must be amplified (or, as the office possibly says, extrapolated) to have at least the appearance of matching the variety of the world situation itself. Otherwise there will be no possibility of mapping a predictive model on to the world situation at all. Now, as has been remarked before, the amplification process in communication theory is well understood. Suffice it to say, that to amplify a signal is also to amplify the noise surrounding it. In the absence of any new information to interject into the system at this time, the final predictive model *M*4, although amplified, contains exactly as much variety as *M*3. So although the transformation from *M*3 to *M*4 in Figure 37 shows a double line indicating an amplification, the notion that variety has been increased is not genuine. It is in fact impossible to retrieve the information thrown away during the process $M1 \rightarrow M2 \rightarrow C \rightarrow M3 \rightarrow M4$. It follows that in using the sample events shown in *M*4 as predictors of the world situation, there is no hope of attaining to requisite variety.

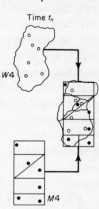

FIGURE 38.

In Figure 38 can be seen what happens when the attempt is made to map the model (now *M*4) on to the real-life world situation. What this means in practice is that work tickets go out on to the shop floor bearing alleged production rates; or that the standard cost for some process has to be compared with the cost actually incurred on this particular shift, on this machine, for this particular product; or that the customer takes delivery now and compares this fact with the promise made to him. Time t_n has arrived and the chips are down.

What has happened? The boundaries of the world situation, which is now *W*4, have changed; the arbitrary sub-divisions originally made have wandered off their courses. This means to say that people have slightly changed their responsibilities, the technical rules of the game have altered somewhat, the contracts made with the customer are not quite the same as they were before, some people are working harder and others less hard than before, and so on. The position of the sample events has consequently been altered by the distortion of the whole reference frame. In fact, in the diagram, all but one of the sample events have been predicted in the wrong sub-division, and two of them are now outside the world situation altogether (that is, they now fall in some other manager's area of responsibility). All this is only too likely to happen in real life.

Now of course this mis-forecasting will not be allowed to go on indefinitely. The whole technique of orthodox control has not yet been

uncovered. If this were indeed all there was to it, the control arrangements would rapidly deteriorate and the entire function would become
meaningless. But before going on to see how good control systems
accommodate the difficulty, it is only fair to remark that the description
as so far given can be verified. Anyone having industrial experience will
have met control arrangements in every speciality which have indeed
broken down at this point and never been put right. In every large company there is an expensive planning board tucked away behind the filing
cabinets. We can uncover examples of elaborate costing systems which
happily perpetuate themselves at great expense—while the managers
they are supposed to serve make rule of thumb judgments about the
expected costs of a job, because everyone knows that these are more
realistic than those produced from a cost office which has broken all ties
with the real world. On the shop floor, one can always find an example
of a machine-loading arrangement which 'controls the flow and allocation of material around the shop'. What it actually does is to make desperate attempts to keep the job cards posted as they are returned—to
provide something like an accurate reflection of what is going on. To
the objective cybernetician, then, the shop floor is a control system
generating variety for the purpose of controlling the planning office, and
not vice versa. The reasons for these unhappy examples have been
formally uncovered. They are: lack of requisite variety, disobedience
of the theorems of communication about channel capacity and so on,
and above all, a static, inadequate, unadaptive model of what the world
situation *used* to be like several years ago.

But fortunately these examples, which justify the analysis to this point,
are not found universally. There is a characteristic way in which control
procedures keep themselves viable and rectify their mistakes. This is
indicated in Figure 39, which completes the diagram that has been
evolved. It will be seen that the mapping of the predictive model $M4$
on to the real world situation $W4$ is now marked AHC, which stands for
ad hoc control. For the action the control system can now take is to
compare each real event with each of its predictors, and to feed back the
discrepancy for future reference. Thus there are six feedback paths
marked by dotted lines on Figure 39, one for each of the events under discussion, and these pass back information to the control office. This is now
enabled to modify its records in $M2$ and to improve the predictive quality
of the *next* real world situation—as indicated by the amplifying forecast
marked at the bottom of the diagram. In short, the control sub-system is
struggling to acquire requisite variety, and has constructed willy-nilly a
(horribly inefficient) variety generator. Consider how it works.

The control office takes the original low variety available at C from $M2$ and augments it by the feedback from AHC. If C is well designed in the O and M sense, so that the feedback information is well codified and readily accessible, then future forecasts (exemplified by the lower double arrow on the diagram) will indeed have much higher variety than the original model at $M2$. This amplification, in terms of information theory, offers a valid increase in $M2$ variety. Now of course the process as described for a particular time t_n is in reality a continuing one; that is, these things happen at *every* time t_n. So the control system does acquire a certain adaptability; it learns to become a better predictor.

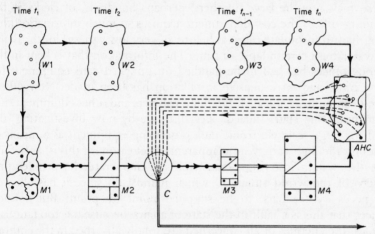

FIGURE 39.

Given that the proportion of completely new events (which this kind of control is very bad at handling) is quite low, and given that C really can organize the feedback information, there is no reason why everything should not run fairly smoothly. It usually does.

Although everything is now working fairly well, which happens because the system is operating the laws of cybernetics in an unconscious fashion, the major weakness of this orthodox approach has now been revealed. For there is no doubt that the intentions of the constructors of this control arrangement were to 'keep it simple'. Indeed they are most likely to have received a very definite briefing on this point from the management. Nothing elaborate was required; nothing costly; 'we want something so simple that it cannot go wrong'.

The whole trouble is that these arrangements are typically so simple that they cannot go *right*. In the description just given, the management has got what it asked for: a very simple arrangement indeed—the simplicity being directly measurable by the amount of variety un-accounted for in model $M3$. But in the course of time, and because of the vital necessity for creating a spate of continuous and detailed feed-back, the management policy has had to be abandoned. Everyone is rather unhappy about this and does not know quite how it happened; they do realize (and rightly) that unless this control organization had been allowed to grow, the control arrangements would have lapsed as being irrelevant. But think of the following consequences, which are by no means uncommon.

The control office, C, has grown to large, even outlandish, proportions. There may now be large numbers, perhaps hundreds, of clerks in the planning office; the cost department acquires so much information that it has had to formulate rules (as before, of very low variety) for throwing it away after a certain lapse of time. The information that is kept in the various offices has had to be handled on punched card equipment for some time, and an expensive installation has been made. New offices have been built to house all the filing cabinets and other equipment, not to mention the staff. Indeed, specialists are by now investigating the need for large-scale electronic data processing equipment as a means of handling the high variety now apparent. The reason for this is, as before, that the system is trying exhaustively to enumerate the proliferating variety of the world situation, which it must do since it has allowed the necessary feedback to be supplied point by point. But nobody notices that this is a fault in the state of affairs, because it is too familiar; besides, the energies of all concerned are totally absorbed in the enthral-ling business of arguing the merits of alternative computers. The picture is fairly gloomy and not much exaggerated in this sketch. Typically, the absurdities inherent in the situation are obscured by the *appearance* of modernity and technical competence which all this activity betokens.

Turning from offices to production departments themselves, a very similar situation results as the emphasis switches from machinery that makes goods to machinery that controls plant—automation. In earlier times, the combination of a low variety model in the charge-hand's 'little black book' amplified by the high variety brain of the charge-hand himself, used to produce quite good results; but all this was long ago replaced by 'the simple system'. This was probably so rapidly over-whelmed by its own feedback that sophisticated work study techniques may have been invoked as a means of bringing back a great deal of the variety thrown away. What more natural today than that plans be in train to spend £250,000 on a digital computer to handle all this variety? The system for controlling spare parts in the engineers' department, the system for buying stationery, the system for controlling purchases and the system for organizing despatches have all very likely followed the same path, by precisely the same mechanism. It would seem that it is the same mechanism, although evolving far more slowly, which underlies the techniques of control used by senior management for evaluating capital development schemes for the company—and indeed policies of every kind.

The lesson is simply this: world variety is controlled by equivalent control variety, and cannot be competently controlled by less. We mislead ourselves into thinking that we can outwit the natural law of requisite variety, just as many imagine that they can beat other natural laws on the race-track or at the casino. People who believe in the natural laws that affect *things* will not believe in the natural laws that affect the way things interact, and surely the difficulty derives from the historically meagre comprehension of system in Western thought. Even when people come to accept that the laws exist, they will not face up to their consequences. To this day, learned institutes continue to receive 'solutions' to Fermat's last theorem, to the problem of squaring the circle, to the challenge of the perpetual motion machine. And society, whether social, industrial or economic, still reckons it can solve the problem of providing cheap, low-variety control of expensive, high-variety systems.

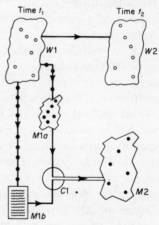

FIGURE 40.

3   Creating a Cybernetic Model

The cybernetic approach to this problem must also begin by constructing a model which greatly reduces the variety of the world situation—because there is no alternative. But it rejects the use of conventional sub-divisions as its method of categorization, because these have only a certain verbal convenience to offer. Its task is to accomplish the variety reduction in a way which will allow at least some of the lost variety to be regenerated later on. The first step in this new process is shown in Figure 40.

It will be seen that the initial model of $W1$ is in two parts—$M1a$ and $M1b$. Neither of these components of model $M1$ attempts to make a classification of experience within which all occurrences can be exhaustively enumerated. $M1a$ is a *structural* model of the world situation.

Just because a full-scale analytical model of so complex a system eludes the OR man, there is no reason to ignore altogether the more evident constraints of the system. In the same way that we should describe the brain in terms of its gross physiology, without claiming to know either its microstructure or biochemistry, so we try to set down the gross physiology of the situation for which the manager is responsible. For example, it is possible to make a list of plant or other capital assets, to make variety measures of the market (the number of customers and their relative size, for instance), to look at the geography of a distribution system, to investigate the capital structure of a business.

An attempt is made here to understand the underlying mechanism of the processes concerned, and to produce a rigorous account of their basic relationships. This means finding out the pattern of such connectivity as really does exist, as distinguished from amorphous and problematic connectivity, but not measuring the quantities that impart size to those relationships. For example, the time taken for a piece of material to pass through a machine is a definite and known function of the speed of the machine and the length of the material, which is in turn a definite and known function of its cross-sectional area and weight. This little formula is deterministic, for no power on earth can alter the implicit relationships. But the 'trimmings' that have to be added, provision for the variable gap between successive pieces of material for instance, feeds and speeds, and so on, will certainly have to be expressed as probabilities. Even so, to provide this *structural* model of every class of event mathematically is not too onerous a task—even when the realities of works' practice are taken into account. We know that it is idle to pretend that when material has to be moved from one place to another by a locomotive, for example, the time taken is constant. It will vary over a wide range of times. But the statistical pattern of this distribution is knowable, even though one does not attempt to make lists of the particular transportation times associated with every sort of circumstance. We have already seen how patterns of statistical variability can be modelled by generating functions which, when expanded, produce the probability of a journey's taking any particular time one cares to name. And we know how to link these structural statements about real life in chains called stochastic processes.

Fitting little structural models of this kind together gradually creates a large structural model of the world situation. This is a low variety model, because it includes no actual quantities, but it already has the latent capacity to generate variety: for the letter a in the model may stand for a whole range of values, as does the letter b. The product ab

in the model stands for the multiplicand of *any pair* of values selected from the two separate ranges; a probability generating function will produce all the coefficients of a power series. This kind of structural modelling of events and their basic relationships has already been dealt with in Part II: it is the standard modelling process of operational research. As usual, most of the model $M1a$ can be written down in terms of mathematics or statistics. But other aspects of the structure of the world situation are more difficult to handle, and call for the more sophisticated language which is specially adaptable to the statement of relationships—logic.

For example, the events involved stand in complicated relationships to each other, in that alternative process routes may be discovered for the same product—depending on the state of the material, the plant or the order book. These relationships constitute a body of constraints on the behaviour of the system, and may be expressed as networks of conditional decision. 'If this product has a good surface condition, every effort is made to put it on the first machine; if not, it must go forward to the second machine if at all possible. In the first case, if it proves impracticable to use the first machine, it passes to the third machine; in the second case, if using the second machine is impracticable, it is put to stock.' The structure of conditional decision networks of this kind can be written down in the language of symbolic logic. To show the neatness of such a set of logical constraints, the statement just made could be written:

$$x \supset :. \, y \supset . \, \alpha a \lor \tilde{\alpha} c : \tilde{y} \supset . \, \beta b \lor \tilde{\beta} s$$

Demonstrations of this kind of statement were made earlier, and do not need to be repeated here. The above example is quoted as a reminder that the structural model $M1a$ of the world situation is not to contain numerical data; it therefore reduces the variety very greatly. But even the structural variety may become too great to handle, and the ordinary operational research technique of homomorphic transformation must be used to keep it down. It will be remembered that this technique coalesces several points in the original structural scheme into just one point, thereby reducing variety as such, but arranges for this to be done in such a way that the formal relationships between the points are preserved— thereby maintaining its latent complexity. Using it can ensure, for example, that important rhythms or periodicities in production are reflected in the model, while the need to store all the data disappears.

$M1a$ is thus an accurate structural model of the world situation, although of much diminished variety. The suppressed variety is of four forms: (i) numerical data which do not appear at all, including actual measures of probabilities; (ii) relationships which differ in quantity, such as those defining blocks of material which are in fact all different, but which can be represented by the same three variables—width, thickness and length; (iii) relationships which differ in topography, such as process routes, but which can be represented by the same decision network; and (iv) the homomorphic reduction of certain structural complexities. This last group may be pictured as reducing an account of the relationship in which every note on a piano stands to every other note, by an account of the relationships obtaining for a single octave.

To give some idea of the variety reduction achieved by this kind of modelling, an actual case is recalled in which the world situation of three separate steel melting shops, all their associated equipment such as casting bays, stripping bays, soaking pits, annealing furnaces, tempering furnaces and so on, down to and including the primary rolling mill with its pre-heaters, and incorporating also an account of the flow of material between them all *and* the probabilities of material rejection, was written down on one (very large) sheet of paper. This model was no use as either predictor or control instrument on its own: it was a model of the class $M1a$.

Next it is necessary to deal with the problem of quantifying the structural model. To do this, numerical data will be required: actual quantities that are descriptive of the world situation. This is attempted in the parametric model $M1b$. Here again, however, a large-scale reduction in variety is necessary; for it would be an absurd and wasteful operation to attempt a complete record of the numerical history of the structural model. Even though the problem of structure has now been uncoupled from the problem of quantity, it would still be possible to make an error of the kind exemplified in the last section. No-one can possibly assimilate information contained in records of this type, which have not in fact much predictive value. It is not helpful to retain in one's memory a perfect quantified record of the thirty-ninth move of a famous game of chess, on the grounds that should this precise position recur in one's own play one would be able to make the brilliant fortieth move which was played by the world champion. It is better to have mastered the principles on which such moves can be constructed, and to generate them in one's own play as required. Still less is it profitable to remember all the moves in one's own games of chess, and to repeat (after huge feats of memory) all the mistakes that were made before. In short, a cautious approach is made to the problem of quantification, realizing that it is possible to distil numerical information from volumes of figures, but realizing too that some methods of making the distillation (such as numerical averaging) kill variety so finally that it can never be regenerated.

A better choice for the kind of data to record in model $M1b$ is performance optima. In the first place, optima can be investigated with considerable objectivity, and without making value judgments about current works' practice and current works' difficulties. Optimal weights, optimal sizes, optimal tolerances, optimal speeds and feeds, and so on, can be tabulated with precision and neatness—if they can once be established. In fact, the practical problem posed is not very difficult to resolve. For example, the optimal weight of a certain class of consignment may be well known to all: variety is proliferated in real life because there are variations about the optimum. But it is necessary to record only the optimum value itself in model $M1b$, because the pattern of variation that is appropriate can be selected from the structural model $M1a$. We shall see how this happens later on. To take another example: if a machine (including its modifications) has been designed to run at a certain speed, this may be written into $M1b$ as its optimum speed. The fact that this speed is never quite achieved in practice is of no relevance at this moment, because the pattern of relationships which determine the speeds actually achieved by comparison with the optimum is already written into $M1a$.

To be even more specific: formal analysis of a structural network may well reveal (as shown in Part II) that only 67 per cent of the sub-assemblies destined for a point Q can possibly reach there by the promised time. This is a quantified statement of a sort, but it yields no numerical data about a particular situation—for it is couched in terms of proportionality. This is the limitation of $M1a$. Equally, if nothing more realistic is to be recorded in the numerical model $M1b$ than some idealized figure, it is a limitation of this sub-model that to say '200 sub-assemblies *ought* to arrive at point Q' is to say nothing of practical relevance either. And yet, if *both* these statements can be derived from the model $M1$, they enable us to say that in reality the number of sub-assemblies reaching point Q is 134.

In other words, although these data in $M1b$ are no use as predictors of actual works' performance, this is not the immediate object of the modelling process. What is vital at this stage is to create a numerical model which properly reflects the fundamental quantitative relationships in which classes of events stand to each other. If the situation is well managed, then as time unfolds actual values will tend to move towards optimal values rather than away from them. They are the relationships

318 *The Relevance of Cybernetics*

that the world situation, governed by its good manager, is 'trying' to make manifest. Therefore they are recognized in $M1b$, just as structural relationships unencumbered by numerical ifs and buts were recognized in $M1a$. Now it is clear that the object is to construct a variety generator. As was shown above, statements selected from $M1a$ may be married to statements selected from $M1b$ to produce other statements which are valid comments on what really happens. But it may not yet be clear how this process improves on the orthodox practice of listing experience according to conventional classifications. In that case, it is well to recall the co-ordinates of the map again. $M1a$ and $M1b$ are co-ordinates of the world situation. The variety generator is much more than two-dimensional in practice, because each of the sub-models has itself a number of dimensions. But this fact obscures the main point. We can select any sub-set of numerical information from $M1b$ and apply it to any sub-set of structural information from $M1a$.

As with the structural model, it will again be found that the record of the numerical model can be contained in a small space. For example, such a model covering a shop with over 100 different machines and 120,000 different machine-jobs, was recorded in a loose-leaf book of some twenty pages. This is a tremendous variety reduction, and it is obtainable for the following reason. Theoretically, ten machines of the same type behave in the same way: their optimal performance, then, generates one set of responses to the same stimulus. In real life, they do not behave identically; as time passes they may become effectively ten different machines. Thus actual shop-floor measures, such as the figures of average performance, generate ten different sets of responses to the same stimulus. Furthermore, at optimal performance, a set of different stimuli (such as working different qualities of material) may produce the same response. At actual average performance, the same machine may be responding differently to the various qualities. By the time the whole range of possible stimuli has been run through the whole range of machines, variety has proliferated seriously. Hence the method of recording numerical data based on optimal performance may lead to a variety of just *one*—for ten qualities on ten machines. Whereas the method of recording average performance, on the other hand, could lead to a variety of 100. And this last example includes only one sort of stimulus (quality) of the many stimuli (size, weight, design . . .) that the product characteristically offers to the machine.

The model $M1$ is now complete in its two parts, structural and parametric. Let no-one be concerned about the lack of realism of this model for predictive purposes on the shop floor. This question has yet to be dealt with in the design of the system; for indeed the aim must be to attain requisite variety. If, in the case just quoted, the real-life variety is 100, whereas the variety recorded in $M1b$ is 1, then variety generators will have to be found to make a hundredfold amplification. But for the moment the concern is to express in the lowest possible variety an account of the fundamental qualitative and quantitative relationships of world situation events. The overriding merit of this model is that, although constructed at time t_1, it is valid for the future. For no ordinary fluctuations in practice or efficiency affect either the structural relationships of $M1a$ or the numerical optima of $M1b$. The first is constructed to encompass all possible kinds of behaviour; the second is based not on what currently happens, but on what could ultimately happen. Of course, if new sorts of plant are introduced, or old plant is scrapped, the model must be altered; but given the same sort of plant and the same sort of product, there is no need to change the model so far constructed.

The process of using this model to obtain predictions, comparisons and decisions must now begin, and the first stage is to produce an amplified model $M2$ through control operation $C1$. The unreal quality of model $M1$, in which relations exist that have no quantity, and numbers exist that stand in no relation to each other, is immediately left behind. The concern now is not for a description that could generate all possible modes of the world situation, in its proliferated variety, but for a model of that situation as it is right now—the time being t_2. So the task is not really one of finding more variety to cope with the real situation, but one of reducing the potential variety that could be generated from the marriage of $M1a$ and $M1b$ in an appropriate way. Thus this variety amplifier (note the double line in Figure 40) is not simply a magnifying glass to enlarge the image of an oversimplified model to a size that will fit the world situation—as it was in the earlier example. The control operation $C1$ is the use of a valid generator of variety to some definite end. And, in the case of the example we have been following, this end is the prediction of six world events.

On this occasion, then, it is not necessary to look up the six events in a vast dictionary of alleged standards, only to find that five of them are not available or are out of date. By consulting the co-ordinates of $M1a$, the position of each event in its structural phase space is isolated; by consulting the co-ordinates of $M1b$, the relevant optima are selected. The two answers are applied through each other as being the two major co-ordinates of the system. This process produces the model $M2$, which contains statements about the events going on in $W2$—and no others.

The rest of the modelled variety, together with its capacity to generate much more, is left behind in $M1$ for future use. It is now time t_2, and as shown on the diagram there is little resemblance between the picture now obtained and the world situation at time t_2. The reason is of course that the model so far obtained is still an idealization of real life. The fundamental relationships and the fundamental quantities built into the model are valid as an account of how the works ought to operate, and not of how the works will actually operate at time t_n.

Now at this stage there is an actual world situation, and there is a model of it, having requisite variety, which is supposed to be competent to be used as a control. But these two systems, which are shown as separate from each other in Figure 40, are precisely the components of the self-regulating system discussed in the last chapter as a self-vetoing homeostat. If the homeostat is to operate at all, connectivity must now be introduced between the two sub-systems. This is done by mapping them on to each other inside a black box. A further injection of cybernetic theory is to be made to the design; let us review the present position which makes this necessary.

Although the design of the mechanism to date has been based on cybernetic considerations, and in particular the need to generate requisite variety from low variety components, the operational research so far done to establish the actual models has used analytical methods. So far, so good: we have always recognized the possibility of producing analytical models of gross physiology (as in $M1a$) and of quantified patterns (as in $M1b$). But as cyberneticians, we have also found it necessary to say that an entirely analytical account of this kind, however exhaustively conducted, will not give the complete description of the world situation that its controller would like to have. This is not to say merely that the task is too great; it is to say that the task is theoretically impossible, and that means must be found for proceeding rather differently from this point. It is worth recapitulating briefly here three of the many reasons already produced for this state of affairs, in order of increasing profundity and difficulty.

Firstly, it is assumed in an analytical model of the system that it can be subjected to consistent performance criteria. Within such a model, only one criterion can be maximized at once, and it is meaningless to speak of incompatible (still less contradictory) criteria. But in world situations these limitations cannot be accepted. When the manager indulges in a conversation with the OR scientist about maximizing profit, he does not mean to say that nothing else matters; nor does he mean that there will never be occasions when the highest profit is deliberately rejected in favour of some other desideratum. But the accounting system, for instance, has to be based on this unique kind of outcome so long as it is analytic; within the accounting framework itself alternative *a* must be preferable to alternative *b* if it is cheaper. It is left to the manager to override this conclusion for other reasons—if he can think of them, and is prepared to accept the responsibility. But in the system developed here, management must be offered facilities to handle all its desiderata simultaneously.

Secondly, analytic models lead to closed systems—otherwise they cannot be made internally consistent. But it has been established that what is really necessary is a series of ever larger open systems, each of which is closed by 'completion from without'—within the framework of a larger system which is also open, but is closed in its turn. The position now reached, and drawn in Figure 40, is precisely such an open system which has to be closed.

Thirdly, the analytic model attempts to discuss a control system for the world situation in the language of the world situation. But, if the principle of completion from without is to be used to close a succession of open systems, we know that the language of each higher order control system must be a language of higher order than that of the world situation. Otherwise, the language will be 'incomplete'; that is to say it is possible for things to happen of which one cannot adequately speak, and about which one certainly cannot decide. The model at $M2$ is expressed in the language of the world situation, albeit that use has been made of a good deal of formal science. But this language, like the control loop, is incomplete; and the language used at the closure must be one in which it is possible to assert that the descriptive language of $M2$ simply will not do.

In Figure 41, then, homeostatic connections are introduced between $M2$ and $W2$. But it is not enough to say, as before, that if these two subsystems are left to interact they will eventually reach a stable situation that is mutually acceptable. For time is pressing, and in any case no machinery by which the one could modify the behaviour of the other has been prescribed. What is proposed instead is that a *black box* should be introduced at this point to monitor the instantaneous interaction of $M2$ and $W2$, and to supply its output information to the system. The use of a black box of inherently high variety permits the entrance to the modelling line of unanalysable high-variety components from the behaviour of the world situation line. In doing so, it proposes the closure of the meta-system, and offers a new mode of description in a metalanguage. In short, this piece of designing fulfils all the requirements that have just been enumerated, and follows the principles that have been learned. It remains to explain exactly what this involves in practical terms.

The particular manifestation of the black box depends on the actual situation to be controlled. Basically, the technique is this. By taking a statistically adequate sample of actual events in the situation as they occur, and comparing each with a prediction derived from the variety generator $C1$ in the model $M2$, a self-vetoing homeostat is set up between $M2$ and $W2$. The interaction is shown in Figure 41. Express each

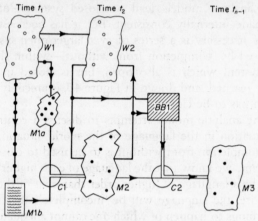

FIGURE 41.

of these comparisons not as an error of prediction (which it is not), but as a ratio. Thus if the time taken for a certain machine-job in $M2$ is twenty-seven minutes, and the sample from $W2$ turns out to be thirty-six minutes, the black box will produce an output reading of $\cdot 75$. This means that the analytic model, $M2$, has accounted for three-quarters of the influence of the factors that the world situation brings to bear on this event, and that a quarter is injected by an unknown mechanism inside the black box. Now of course it would be possible in a given case to analyse further this 25 per cent of mystery, and to account for it analytically in its entirety. For with hindsight the facts of the matter may well be uncovered. But what purpose would this serve?

In a given case, a manager might wish to know the complete list of components of a machine-job time: this is by way of a post-mortem on some job done on his plant, and is a perfectly reasonable undertaking. But the control system itself is interested in producing valid predictions, not in the pathological information provided by a post-mortem. Besides, for other events belonging to the same class as this event, these residual details will be different—although their net effect will be the same. We rely on the statistical laws of large numbers. Even if the analytical model could be extended to account for somewhere near 100 per cent of the facts, the efficiency of the recording system for this increasing variety in the model diminishes logarithmically. Moreover, assuming all this were done, the resulting model would still be open to all the theoretical objections advanced earlier.

So $M1$ is left alone. The task now is to consider the output of $BB1$ which (by analogy) may be thought of as a procession of creatures of unknown parentage. We want to produce a behavioural account of their responses to the actual stimuli provided by $M2$ and $W2$ at time t_2. And this is not difficult. For if a large sample of the ratios mentioned earlier is considered, it will be found that the ratios fall into patterns. This is by no means surprising; the world is a place for pattern, a pattern in which nature follows its own simple laws—while concealing them from observers under a misleading cloud of mutation and apparently random appearances. Thus the genetic structure of identical twins is identical: but they do not lead the same lives. Similarly, different jobs which share the same structure in $M1a$, but have different lives in the numerical sense of $M1b$, may belong to the same race of creatures emerging from the black box; and their behavioural ratios, although not identical, may belong to the same statistical population.

It is in any case a matter of fact that if some extensive sample of behavioural ratios of $BB1$ is taken over a considerable period and analysed statistically for pattern, patterns are found. Events concerned may then be grouped according to their behaviours in this sense, and the black box becomes a measure for each population of the interaction between the analytic model and the world situation. No-one can account for the discrepancy of which this is a measure, nor does he need to do so. For this is not a matter of despair, as would be a simple error-correcting feedback; it is an attempt to complete the incomplete language of the analytical model through the real world—a process which itself cannot be undertaken analytically. The method relies on the theoretical principles mentioned earlier: it is essentially a process of completion from without.

This system has now revealed the basis it implicitly offers for providing classification rules. The scientist has so far entered (into the model $M1a$) the crude structure of the world situation as discovered by operational research. But proliferating variety in the world situation causes the system itself to distinguish between different classes of events which the highly simplified analytical model tacitly recognizes as the same. For if we treat the output of ratios from the black box as a statistical population, it will turn out to be heterogeneous. By advanced but none the less orthodox statistical analysis, it is possible to break up this population into a number of statistically homogeneous groups. By determining which features the members of each group have in common, a classification system for events determines itself. Experience of the application of these methods shows that this classification system is quite unlike any conventional breakdown of the total system which people happen to think of.

Is $BB1$ a meter for measuring discrepancies between the analytical and empirical predictions of an event; or is it a logical strategy for providing the system with a metalanguage in which paradoxes can be restated and resolved; or is it a practical device for maintaining touch between the control system and the world situation? It is all these things simultaneously. Why then was $BB1$ called a species, having races of creatures?

The reason is that any particular ratio measured on the meter is but a sample of a whole class of ratios belonging to the same homogeneous population. What defines the unity of this population or race? Nothing more than that each of its members *is a relationship* between a statement in $M2$ and a statement in $W2$. Biologically, the creature typifies an interaction between the world and a neutral control picture of the world, and creatures are classified into races on the basis of that interaction. Sparrows and eagles are quite different in their natures, and one might be an event in London and the other an event in America; but they are both birds, and they both fly. So *this* production event and *that* production event are different in their natures, and one occurs in *this* place and one in *that* place. But they are both 'ratio sixty-niners', because this is how they relate themselves to real life. $M2 : W2$ as $1{\cdot}0 : 0{\cdot}69$.

Understanding this is of the first importance, for it reveals a completely new method of categorizing industrial experience. It ignores the attributes which make either events or their control models look alike and look different, and concentrates on ecological factors—those that relate the organism to its environment. Such a classification is supremely valuable, because it works in operational terms. The metaphor of creatures and their races emphasizes this ecological outlook, and it also gives these $BB1$ ratios *substance*. This is right, because they are recognizable entities—not just the pure numbers which are their names. That is what makes it possible to take this vital, variety-generating, next step: it does not matter if an event whose characteristics are to be predicted has never happened before, if it can be recognized as belonging to the right race of $BB1$ creatures. This is quite different from saying, as one normally would: this product is 'rather like' that product, and will there-fore take the same time to make. Perhaps it will—but perhaps it will not. Its modest differences may easily be causes of completely different be-haviour on the shop floor. There lies the key advantage of an ecological classification.

Incidentally, the cybernetic theory underlying the design of *BB*1 makes it impossible to describe what is happening at this point purely in terms of statistics. Some people who have examined the technique in operation have declared with surprise that the whole thing can be described as a form of statistical control. (The oh-is-that-all fallacy.) A little later they begin to express doubt as to whether this 'piece of applied statistics' is quite valid. All this confuses what is done with the way it is done. What is done is fundamental cybernetics: statistical control is used to express and to monitor its operation.

The barrier confronting full comprehension at this stage of the argu-ment is of the kind discussed in the methodological part of the book. It is no good judging the system by its external appearance alone; one has to look for the underlying system which makes it work. A Martian statistician confronted with a clock face at noon might observe by 1 p.m. that the big hand had moved twelve times as far as the little hand. But he would be angry with the clock designer who contended that after another revolution of the big hand the little hand would point to the figure two. That is not a valid statistical prediction, the Martian would say, and of course he would be right. It is necessary to explain to him how the clock works.

The underlying cybernetic mechanism here is not deterministic like the gearing of the clock. It does, however, justify the technique at a level of logic which the statistical description does not itself reach. But because what has been said about the black box is conceptually difficult to understand, it does not follow that it is difficult to operate in prac-tice. Actually, it is quite easy. But because its operation is quite easy, it does not follow that the underlying mechanism is trivial, or not worth investigation.

The black box *BB*1 thus re-establishes numerical, metamathematical, logical, statistical and ecological connection with the world situation. Its immediate outputs are the pure numbers which express a numerical comparison between the quantity ascribed to a particular event in the analytical model *M*2, and the actual event when it occurs in *W*2. But, having understood the nature of the pattern-producing mechanism going on inside the box, it becomes possible to produce its outputs through a filter which duly registers each comparison not as a number,

but as a designation of membership of its appropriate statistical population—which defines an ecological race. Thus the output channel from
$BB1$ is again reduced variety: it carries a non-analytic model of the black
box's behaviour.

We now return to the design of the system as a whole. A considerable
step forward in time is now taken, as happened with the last system, and
the moment t_n is approached at which it has been assumed reliable
predictions of the six sample events will be required. First of all, then,
the situation just before this will be described: the time is t_{n-1}. The start
of the next phase is also pictured in Figure 41. Control $C2$ has as input
the output of model $M2$, from which the variety generated by $C1$ is
maintained, plus the output of $BB1$ which has just been described.
Control $C2$ proceeds to generate a new model $M3$, which is done by a
further process of variety amplification. The analytic value for each of
the six sample points becomes associated with, and weighted by, the
$BB1$ measure for the statistical population defining the ecological family
to which each event is recognized to belong.

It will be noted that once again no attempt is made to associate each
model event, as it were personally, with its own ratio of inadequacy in
the real world of $W3$. For this is not the best estimator of future outcomes: there is no special predictive value in this sample of one, and
what happens to occur at time t_{n-1} for this sort of event could easily be
an historical fluke. Predictive value lies in identifying the class of black
box output (the race, as it was called) to which events of this sort tend
in general to correspond. This is not difficult, since the black box has
been allowed to generate its own system of classification. As was said
before, the system may have to handle events which have never occurred
before, and will not occur at all until the critical time t_n. In practice, this
method of control has been found precisely as accurate in its predictions
about entirely new events as about familiar ones.

How efficient is this first predictive model $M3$? Now as was said in
Chapter 10, the scientist does not subscribe to a theory of forecasting
which bases itself on mere extrapolations from the past. Scientific
analysis confirms what common sense comprehends, namely that information cannot be had for nothing, and a predictive model is only as
good as the information fed to it. So far, no account of information arising
in the world situation has been taken beyond time t_2. Thus it is not
surprising that the new model $M3$ fairly well reproduces the world
situation of $W2$; within this situation the six sample points will be predicted with an accuracy that depends only on the statistical error implicit
in the pattern-forming operations of $BB1$. But meanwhile the world

situation itself has moved to *W*3, for the time is now t_{n-1}. Thus a drift has doubtless occurred, which it is now necessary to correct. This is the object of *BB*2, which is added to the evolving diagram in Figure 42.

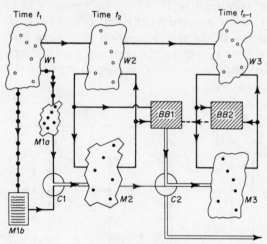

FIGURE 42.

Once again, no explanation of the drift in the world situation is required. All that is needed is an output from the black box which will bring the control language into line with the world language, and the model estimates of quantity into line with the numbers now characterizing real life. Thus *BB*2 is effectively a statistical control procedure modifying the operations of *BB*1; this is shown by the feedback line (dotted) in Figure 42. (At this point a convention of the diagrams must be explained. Obviously a feedback cannot operate backwards *through time*—as it appears to do. In fact, the control *C*2 has been moving forward in time, ready to receive the *BB*2 output just after time t_{n-1}. This is justified by the fact that *C*2 is persistent; the new *C*2, the whole of which apparatus could be re-drawn between *M*3 and *M*4, is the same *C*2 as before.)

This persisting *C*2, considered as at time t_{n-1}, now has three inputs: one from the model *M*2, one from *BB*1, and the new feedback from *BB*2. This feedback is used to modify the output of *BB*1, and impinges on *C*2 by that route. Hence in making predictions for model *M*4, which is the final model required to predict the world situation *W*4 at time t_n, the control is still using a model (*M*3) with slightly less than the information required to generate a perfectly accurate final model. This time, however, it is taking account of world information *up to* *W*3. Thus it is now only one time interval out of date, regardless of how far away in the past t_1 and t_2 may have been.

The final outcome is shown in Figure 43. The predictive model of the six events actually used is $M4$. This, by a process of modification by the system's variety generators $BB1$ and $BB2$, brings the initial model $M2$ up-to-date with the world situation $W3$. Since the prediction has to be made at time t_{n-1}, this is the very best source of information about the world that there is. By time t_n the world situation $W4$ will not have

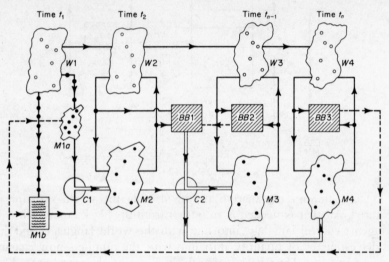

Time t_1 Time t_2 Time t_{n-1} Time t_n

FIGURE 43.

altered radically, and an $M4$ that takes account of $W3$ makes a good predictor. The six sample events inevitably match closely their realizations in the world situation. Predictive control has been achieved.

One further requirement of this theory needs explanation. As was said earlier, there is no need to alter the basic model $M1$ for as long as the plant and the class of product it produces remain substantially the same. However, these characteristics of the works do ultimately change as time passes; amendments to $M1a$ will be required to account for substantial alterations to the plant and to $M1b$, to deal with fundamental changes in practice which alter such numerical parameters of the world situation as the optimal speeds of machines. For these purposes, a final feedback loop is required to $M1$ which is taken from $BB3$: this is the black box comparing the world situation with its model at the moment of effective action—in the case of this example, at time t_n itself.

But this feedback concerns the evolution of the *race* of black box outputs; it does not concern all the individual predictions—which are no more than sampled. So this all-embracing feedback is fired by a variety generator, and is therefore highly economical to work. It will be two or three orders of magnitude less costly than the massive feedback channel of the orthodox system.

In fact, *BB2* and *BB3* are one and the same black box, just as control *C1* and *C2* are one and the same control. Their functions are distinguished by the fact that the information used at one moment of time to modify the forecasting machinery is used at the next moment of time to confirm or deny the structural information contained in *M1*.

Thus the account of this generalized theory of control is complete. Once it has been designed and installed, there should be no need to take any further action. For the system (like that which controls a living organism) regenerates itself continuously. It bestows the formal characteristics of learning and adaptation, characteristic of an organism, on the system it controls; it is indeed consciously based on what cybernetics has to say about the formal mechanism responsible for these brain-like aptitudes. So the control system can be expected to grow with the world situation, and to match it event for event as required. But, like an animal brain, it would be upset by violent interventions which ruptured its communication paths; and, also like an animal brain, it needs nourishment—in this case the energy and attention of those who operate and use it.

But it does have one more organic characteristic of high importance when it comes to worrying about the capacity of human beings to tend the system. If they make a mistake, this system is competent to rectify it—and will do so automatically. Consider the operation of this facility at the weakest link in the whole chain of operations described here. This is undoubtedly the formulation of the model *M1*, where the scientist has to take arbitrary decisions about how much structure to enter into the model, and about what data constitute optima. Supposing he judges all this badly, and that in fact this leads *C1* to generate a good deal of rubbish at *M2*. Now the rubbishiness of predictions made at *M2* is instantly detected by *BB1*—because it has requisite variety. And, because its inputs consist of information about the operations of the self-vetoing homeostat $W2 \longleftrightarrow M2$, *BB1* 'has the intelligence' to set the matter right. Consult Figure 42 and consider the following very simple example of this capability.

Suppose that *M1* produces through *C1* a prediction in *M2* that the duration of an event will be ninety minutes. In fact, this event in *W2* takes one hundred minutes. Then the output of *BB1* will be $\frac{90}{100} = 0.9$.

If this same event could be repeated at time t_{n-1} the prediction through C2 at M3 would also be ninety minutes, obtained from the input from M2, *modified by the input from* BB1. This would mean that the ninety minutes is multiplied by the reciprocal of 0·9. Thus $\frac{90}{0·9} = 100$: the prediction is now exactly correct. If we take the case where rubbishy information is delivered by model M1 through C1 to M2, so that the prediction is only (say) ten minutes as against a hundred minutes in real life, then the output of BB1 will read 0·1. When the M3 prediction is reached, C2 receives an input of ten minutes from M2 and an output from BB1 of 0·1. Multiplying by the reciprocal, we get on this occasion $\frac{10}{0·1}$—which again equals 100. This is the self-correcting facility at work. It is effective in dealing both with gross errors in the initial analysis, and with noise in the system.

Again, however, the example short-circuits the actual mechanism for purposes of illustration. Because, of course, the comparison between particular descriptions and particular events is not used to modify the *same* particular predictions in relation to the *same* particular events. The procedure works, as it were, genetically—through the races of BB1 creatures.

4   Some Practical Points

The account just given of a general theory for management control of physical processes is a distillation of advanced research in theoretical cybernetics and its practical industrial application already spread over about fifteen years. In this final section, the practicality of these ideas is emphasized. Firstly, there will be an account of precisely how a black box can be designed—since it seems that the very blackness of the box is liable to promote confusion about its actual nature. After this will follow comments on the results that can be expected from this work.

(a) Creating a black box control unit

In order to discuss the really practical detail of this process, a new kind of diagram has been drawn at Figure 44. This does not depict a control system any longer, but rather a process of applying the black box within that control system. The letters used, however, are the same as before. The diagram is divided into six zones, each of which will be discussed in turn.

In zone 1 the first world situation (W1) and its first model (M1) are shown. For the purposes of this example, it will be assumed that the world situation is reduced to the behaviour of a single machine. The machine has an infinitely varied output, because products of all kinds of dimensions may be made on it. The process of devising model $M1$ (with its two parts a and b) has already been discussed. The most general mathematical formula possible would be written to account for the time taken to do a job on this machine. Using an algebraic notation, rather than any actual figures, it will doubtless prove possible to write $M1a$ on a single line—for the entire operation of $W1$. Typically, the equation will relate widths, thicknesses and lengths, weights and numbers-off, machine feeds and speeds, and so on. In model $M1b$, the data that appertain to this situation will be classified; lists will be made of possible ranges of quantification for all the variables that occur in $M1a$. Typically,

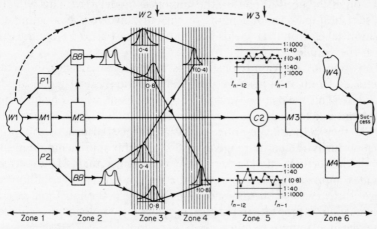

FIGURE 44.

there will be lists of the scalar intervals over which each variable may range, together with the maximum and minimum in each case. It will be noted that (in this simplest possible case) the output of the machine operating in $W1$ is divided into two major components, $P1$ and $P2$. This is the customary works' classification, which everybody uses. Let us call $P1$ 'white pieces' and $P2$ 'red pieces'.

Now the task of setting up the black box begins, and we are in zone 2. First of all, an historical sample of events taking place on this machine is selected. Normal statistical criteria are used to create this sample which must be suitably stratified with respect to the white and the red pieces, with respect to different operators and different shifts, and with respect to the range of shapes and sizes produced. Again, normal techniques will be used to decide on the sample size. Having obtained these data, we shall make a spurious forecast of the machine-job-time for each job in the sample. The forecast is spurious, of course, because the job has already been completed and the actual time taken is known—but we shall not consult this yet. To make the spurious forecast, the basic data about the actual job are applied to the equation in $M1a$, and missing numbers are supplied from the tables in $M1b$. For example, if a machined bar to given dimensions is to be produced in one-foot lengths, several of the values by which to quantify variables in $M1a$ are given in the specification. But what length of bar will be supplied as raw material? This is important, because it will determine how much handling time is required for each item actually produced. There is nothing in the *order* to specify from what size of raw material the product must be made; now comes the need to consult the numerical model $M1b$. This will give the statistical pattern of lengths or weights involved. Evaluating the equation taken from $M1$ yields a spurious forecast at $M2$—one for each job in the sample.

The spurious forecast (from $M2$) is now compared with the actual time taken (from $W1$) in every case, and the ratio is calculated inside the black box. This yields two statistical populations of ratios, one for white pieces and one for red. These are the creatures of the black box: to what race do they belong? We notice that each of the statistical distributions covers virtually the entire range from 0–1. A ratio approaching 0 means that the job actually took a very great deal longer than $M2$ expected; an index approaching 1 means that the job was carried out with maximum efficiency; and an index of 0·5 means that the job took exactly twice as long as forecast. In practice, virtually the whole range is covered —but inevitably there is much clustering—and this is what creates the familiar statistical pattern. Incidentally, if the model building has been well done, it is virtually impossible for an index to exceed 1·0, for this would mean that the job was done in real life more effectively than the model would predict using optimal performance as its criterion. There are two black boxes shown in zone 2, simply because the whole recording system is built on a difference between the white and the red pieces: the data are in different log books, for example. But we observe that the statistical pattern emerging from each black box appears to be roughly the same. Moreover, it is bimodal.

Now if a statistical distribution is genuinely bimodal (and this can be tested) it means that the population from which the sample is drawn is not homogeneous. The likelihood is that two distinct populations are involved in each case, and the next task is to separate them. Remember that the box being used to generate these outputs is black: we have no idea *why* any of these indices should have turned out to be less than one, but we know that they have. By the same token, when we come to separate the two statistical populations involved, the question of *why* there are two is not to be asked. The object of the enquiry is to *define* the two distinct populations from which the sample of black box output has been drawn. Again, orthodox statistical techniques enable this to be done. The characteristics of each job are known, and so is its ratio. Correlation techniques will discover a classification by which to separate the overlapping distributions.

In zone 3 the two distributions in each case are separated from each other. In the case of the white pieces, a roughly homogeneous sub-group has been identified, having a ratio of 0·4 at the mode. Attached to this group is a definition, perhaps rather involved (and certainly quite unconventional), which says what kinds of white pieces belong to it. Similarly, a second sub-group is defined, having a value of 0·8 at the mode. In the case of the red pieces it turns out that there are also two groups, having the same values of 0·4 and 0·8 at the mode. This at once suggests that although the company and its clients clearly distinguish between white and red pieces, and see them as different, the machine doing the production cannot recognize the difference at all. On the contrary, it recognizes a difference between a 0·4 and a 0·8 order. There is now a logical problem: are the two 0·4 sub-groups and the two 0·8 sub-groups drawn from the same two statistical populations? In statistical terms, they are indistinguishable; the problem is a logical one because it is necessary to see whether the elaborate empirical definitions coincide or not. Assuming that they do, the sub-groups which match can be coalesced—and this is what has happened in zone 4 of the diagram.

A good deal of rather elementary statistical expertise is required to fulfil the operations disclosed in zones 3 and 4. Moreover, various extra duties are required of the statistician at these stages. Firstly, a check sample ought to be taken to ensure that the classification system which emerges (as was promised in the last section) is robust. There is a risk that the primary analysis has stumbled on some arbitrary grouping, and we want to ensure that the grouping is real—reflecting some genuine difference. Since there is no rational explanation that would satisfy us (the box is still black), we have to seek the same assurance by inferential methods. But statistics is perfectly competent to continue with check samples until the measured risk that the differences are unreal has been lowered to virtually nothing. Secondly, the statistician has some rather more difficult work to do.

The distributions as drawn in zone 4 are regular—and in fact Gaussian. This is very convenient, because Gaussian distributions are themselves robust: they are symmetrical, and very easy to keep under surveillance because their characteristics are so well understood. But the original distributions from which they are composed, those appearing in zone 3, do not look Gaussian at all—they are mis-shapen. In practice, it is found that they are almost certainly skewed (that is, asymmetrical), and the reason for this is fairly obvious. They are distributions of ratios, having an upper bound of 1. So the distribution is, as it were, piling up at the right-hand side against a limit which it cannot exceed. Distributions with modal values approaching 1 will inevitably have a precipice on the right-hand side; and even those with low modal values turn out to be affected by the existence of an eventual limit. This skewness can be eliminated by transforming all the ratios mathematically. (It is a technical problem for the statistician to decide how to do this; in the work here described, the inverse sine transformation was used.) Moreover, the distributions may be either leptokurtic or platykurtic—that is, either too peaked or too flattened to be Gaussian. Again, the statistician can make suitable adjustments.

Some emphasis is placed on this zone 4 operation of turning the distributions into a standard form. This is by no means necessary for purely scientific reasons, because the actual distributions could themselves be handled. But it has to be remembered that this discussion concerns a simple case involving one machine. In real life, the controller may end up with thousands of these distributions to keep under surveillance. So there is no doubt that the standard form is valuable, because it is convenient. There may be some doubt whether the transformations referred to are legitimately made. Is one entitled to doctor the data in this way? The answer is yes: because the use to be made of the *transformed* statistics occurs only in zone 5. A special language is being invented for this purpose. When it comes to making real-life use of the data contained in the distributions, they will be transformed back to their original form.

The problem in zone 5 is to keep the distributions, which are at once a classification of the black box creatures and a measure of the size of each race, under surveillance as time goes by. For the world situation is constantly changing, and the values associated with the distributions of black box output may then change. Now when Gaussian distributions are involved, only three possible changes can occur. Firstly, the modal value (which is also the mean value in a Gaussian distribution) may drift. Secondly, the *variance* of the distribution may change—this is a measure of the spread across the distribution. In this case, the variance statistic measure changes in the variability of the machine's performance. Thirdly, the underlying classification system may break down. For

example, the machine may suddenly decide that it can distinguish between two classes of work which it has hitherto treated in the same way.
If this happens, one of these apparently stable distributions will bifurcate
and itself become bimodal.

If any of these things happen, it will be necessary to find out and to
take remedial action. Accordingly, zone 5 depicts a battery of statistical
control charts which observe the behaviour of the mean and variance of
each distribution. To work the control chart (which is established under
the ordinary techniques of statistical quality control) routine but small
samples of production must be taken. As a matter of interest, schemes
have been run in which this sampling was done monthly, and others in
which it was done weekly; probably the best arrangement, however,
was to have a running sample going on continuously, using sequential
statistical control. At any rate, the behaviour of the charts controlling
mean and variance will signify not only incipient changes in these two
statistics, but also give warning of a tendency for the population from
which the sample is being drawn incipiently to break up.

The story is now almost complete. When in real life it is necessary
to produce a forecast, this is done by the original operation of using $M1$
(which is virtually fixed) as a variety generator for $M2$. $M2$ is extrapolated to $M3$; but on the way the $M2$ forecast is modified by the
appropriate black box output—as processed through the statistical
arrangements just described—at $C2$. Because of the continuous monitoring of the statistical groups, the weighting applied to the raw forecast
from $M2$ at $M3$ will be entirely up to date. Consequently, when $M3$
generates forecasts to be applied to $W4$, it will be found that they match
the actual situations that have developed in $W4$ very closely indeed. This
is because $M3$ has taken $W3$ into account, and $W3$ is as closely related
to $W4$ as is possible. A successful mapping has been produced, then, in
zone 6. The rest of the control system operates in the way described in
the last section.

There are various comments to make on all this. Firstly, it should by
now be quite clear that actual events are not being used to forecast
themselves. This is a meaningless proposition, but people do fall into the
trap of thinking this is what the system does. In fact, actual events are
being used to create a structure for the situation, a structure designated
by a set of statistical control groups. This structure is inexplicable
(because the box is black); but it provides, and must provide, an effective
and realistic way of describing the world situation, because it obeys all
the cybernetic principles of control. It will adapt, and must adapt, to a
changing situation, because it is self-regulative. It provides *intrinsic*

control of the situation. This structure is then used to classify the jobs that are coming along: and because the structure is realistic rather than conventional, and because it has been quantified by a black box having requisite variety, and because it is characterized by an elaborate definition, it is almost infallible in recognizing the job to be done *by the time it will take*. In other words, it is an excellent predictor.

In particular, this means that a control system based on these principles is capable of dealing with jobbing production, in which a large proportion of the work has never been attempted before. It 'knows' how to recognize the job for what it is. It might well be thought that an inanimate system of this kind, however well designed, simply could not do this particular job as well as a man who has worked all his life in the business. This challenge was so interesting that it was put to the test.

A group of experienced foremen was selected, each man having an average relevant experience of about thirty years, and asked to estimate all the machine-job-times for new work received over a certain period. Of course, we have been talking here about one machine-job; a customer's order might involve (say) twenty machine-jobs from start to finish. The foremen's forecasts were then compared with the times actually taken in production. They varied between 20 per cent and 250 per cent of the actual times, and the distribution of these percentages was almost flat. That is to say, the chance of saying the job would take 25 per cent of its actual time was about the same as saying that it would take about 30 per cent of its actual time—or 40 per cent, 80 per cent, 100 per cent (in this case being correct), 150 per cent or 250 per cent. This means that within a uselessly wide range of error, as good an answer could be produced as the foremen produced using a set of dice. The cybernetic control system, however, used on this same sample at the same time, produced a mean error of only 2 per cent, and was in no case more than 6 per cent out.

Finally, a refinement to the system as described should be noted. The statistical surveillance of zone 5 may indicate a time trend. That is, the mean value of the black box output for one group may rise or fall steadily. In this case, the control chart will eventually register a need to charge the mean value ascribed to the group. But in the meantime, the rate of change can itself be picked up and measured by the statistician in charge of zone 5. He would therefore be able to provide an *extrapolated* value for the black box output as used in $C2$, instead of the actual present value. This enables the control system as a whole slightly to anticipate changes, as well as to react with maximum speed and confidence when changes have already occurred.

(b) The effort involved

The example just worked through is clearly minimal in size and complexity. How massive is the task of designing a cybernetic control system for an entire works? This question is a very fair one, and no-one could pretend that a job of this size could be completed without a lot of work. However, the effort involved must be contrasted with the effort put into the construction of orthodox control systems.

The first point to note is one made earlier: this system is designed to provide control—full stop. Once it is installed, it can generate all kinds of managerial information, for use in production control, accounting, and so on. By orthodox management means, the control system has normally to be instituted for every purpose separately. Secondly, and this point has been made before as well, the cybernetician does not embark on a process of enumeration. The virtue originally claimed for this was that the cybernetic variety-generating processes were more sound scientifically. In practice, though, and despite all the analytical work that has to be done, the speed with which the control can be instituted is a very potent advantage too. Experience shows that this kind of system can be installed in a small works (which might be defined, say, as containing 100 pieces of plant, all at least slightly different) in roughly six months. If this is a high-variety works, then any system based on the exhaustive enumeration of all possible products must take several years to introduce —if only because the bulk of the possibilities simply do not occur in a lesser time span.

Next, there is the question of the commitment involved in personnel. Now the implementation of a scheme of this kind involves an operational research study based on a cybernetic model. A team of (say) three to five OR scientists may be required in a large works or, more particularly, in a whole factory. They will need some computing assistance, access to punched equipment, and so on. If an electronic computer is available the task will be very much easier. But the once-for-all cost of instituting a control is a minor one, since it is a valuable investment against the future. It is more interesting to ask what commitment is involved in keeping the thing running.

The answer to this is rather impressive. At first sight, to undertake continuous sampling of production and the statistical surveillance of (say) a thousand of the groups referred to, sounds formidable. In practice, a staff of about ten should suffice. These people must be of high quality, though not necessarily highly qualified. A residential graduate statistician is probably necessary, but his subordinates—he only needs about four—can be trained from high grade clerical staff. The remaining five or six of the staff will be girls working desk computing machines. (Again, the availability of an electronic computer alters all this.) Now this staff replaces all the people throughout the company who would be working on jobs which this system makes unnecessary. There may be several hundred of these. It is not easy to say, because the people hitherto concerned will be doing other work as well. All these figures are provided from a desire to answer obvious questions, and they are based on experience. On the other hand, every company is different, and they should be construed as no more than a guide to the magnitude of the question.

(c) Production control

Although the general theory just expounded was designed to provide an integral means of providing an indivisible managerial control, it can be applied (as was said earlier) to each of the traditional *aspects* of the management of processes which demand predictive estimates. As a matter of historical fact, the stimulus for the creation of the prototype system of this kind was found in production control. The methods described were devised in 1949 and 1950 for the solution of a practical problem; the full and more generalized account of the underlying theory in the terms set out here was not achieved until later.

The first challenge came in this way. Here was a works containing over 100 different machines, and as many as 2,000 works orders in progress (from the progressing of raw materials to final dispatch) at any one time. The order book, extending nearly a year ahead, contained a sizable proportion of orders which had never been attempted before. And this proportion could be substantially increased by adding on those orders which, although undertaken in the past, had not been produced sufficiently recently to enable the records of the performance at that time to relate at all reliably to performance now. The major problem as posed was to quote delivery promises that could be met.

It hardly needs emphasizing that this world situation was controlled by a first-rate management: after all, it commissioned an advanced scientific attack on this problem at a time when the words 'operational research' were almost unheard of in industry. Even so, the complexity of the situation was such that only 27 per cent of the orders delivered were delivered within the promised period of four weeks. If this sounds incredible, it should be explained that the jobbing work, the technical difficulty and the chance of mishap which characterized this trade were notorious; even this performance was perfectly comparable with the best attainable elsewhere.

The installation of the cybernetic control arrangement, under tenacious management invigilation, somewhat shortened the delivery promises quoted, but had within six months increased the percentage of orders delivered on time to 90 per cent. The remaining 10 per cent were up to about six weeks late, compared with delays for this 'lost' minority of over a year under the previous method of control. Because the planning was now clear-cut and realistic, a reduction of stock levels at the input side of the production system was effected, and the capital committed here fell by a third. A reduction of work in progress on the shop floor inevitably followed better forecasting, planning and progressing methods. This meant a further reduction in capital commitment, as did a two-thirds cut in finished material stocks.

It would hardly be possible to achieve results on the scale just mentioned without so smoothing the flow of material through the works, and increasing the utilization of machinery, that the net productivity failed to rise. In fact, in the case quoted, the productivity had been carefully measured for a year before the cybernetic system was installed, and was found to be constant. This assertion is based on an aggregate of job-by-job comparisons between ultimate capacity and actual performance. As soon as the new control, so rich in feedback, was operative, the productivity began to rise: after six months it had risen by 15·2 per cent. About a third of this rise was due to the introduction of incentive schemes, made in parallel, which were based on work study investigations of particular bottlenecks pin-pointed by the overall control. The total savings were therefore very considerable.

The general theory has also been applied in production control situations of other kinds, using other criteria of success. For example, there was a time when there were such acute shortages of a certain major product that it was dispatched according to an allocation system. Owing to the overriding necessity to attain full production, and to surges in the system caused by orthodox planning techniques, only about 35 per cent of the customers received their allocation in a given period—although the total deliveries were equal to the total allocations. It was quite obvious to all that this lucky minority was receiving very much more than a fair share. But all attempts to rectify the position failed, because inquests always revealed excellent reasons why unduly favoured customers had received so much more than the published allocation. The application of the theory given here showed that its more sensitive controls would be able to suppress the surges. Even so, the organizational structure of the control function in this very large works was misconceived, and was acting as an amplifier for any deviant inputs.

A highly diversified organization was uncovered, in which fourteen different clerical sections (responsible to eight different senior managers) were involved in controlling the production of the plant. A study of the information flow, the feedbacks and the time lags was fascinating. Roughly speaking, each of the sections was trying to instruct the other thirteen, while the impact of the entire control effort on what actually was going on was negligible. Thus, in addition to installing the control principles already discussed, cybernetics provided the model by which operational research reconstructed the organizational structure. All fourteen sections were abolished, and re-created as part of a new organic system. Despite the extra difficulty created by the need to get the new organization working in human terms, and arranging whole sets of new procedures not directly connected with the control problem as described, the percentage of customers in receipt of their full allocation had more than doubled after six months; after a few more months the proportion was brought up to 96 per cent and maintained there.

Actual experience reveals a further cybernetic mechanism in operation. The existence of this mechanism might well have been predicted in advance; in fact it was not, and it makes a good example of the self-regulating properties of viable systems. Once there has been a break-through in control, so that the more notorious problems of the world situation have been resolved, various positive feedbacks operate to improve the position still further. For example, if better control results in a reduction of work in progress stocks, there will be less material cluttering the works basis of the shop floor. This was mentioned before as an economic advantage, but it also means that the flow of material is further facilitated.

To sum up under this heading: the general theory put forward has always proved competent to handle a high-variety, probabilistic world situation. It does seem to have general applicability. There is, of course, simply no need to invoke a cybernetic model for operational research work on a control system if that system can be adequately accounted for by a more tractable and rigorous model—for instance, one taken from servomechanics. But when such models lack requisite variety, as do the unexpressed models underlying most production control procedures found in orthodox practice, a radically new concept is needed to establish control.

(d) Costing

As was mentioned before, it is an impossible job in practice to investigate, record and keep up to date a complete library of machine-job performance standards for a large and complicated shop. Although attempts to do this are constantly made, and are often believed by senior management to have been successful, they do not bear close examination—for good and sufficient cybernetic reasons. However, the costs involved in a production system of the kind described inexorably attach to machine-job-times, delays and mishaps, stockpiles and process routes. That is to say, in our terms, that production control and cost control are isomorphic systems. It is surprising that this fact is not more often recognized by management. This seems partly due to the fact that different specialists responsible to different functional chiefs may be involved, and partly to the fact that there exists no underlying general control theory on to which each of the functional specialisms may itself be mapped.

Drawing again on the first case quoted, 120,000 basic machine-job cost standards were required. At the highest possible rate of empirical investigation and clerical recording, a library of standards of this magnitude would take years to compile—and of course by the time the jobs were completed most of the first part of the library would be out of date.

The control system based on the cybernetic model used its black boxes to generate all this variety sequentially, as required, and all costing information was kept up to date automatically by the feedbacks given in the general theory. It was found that standards provided in this way, with almost no clerical commitment, could predict the actual production cost with an error of less than 1 per cent. In fact, in the very first month to which this arrangement was applied, and on a monetary turnover in six figures, there was a discrepancy between the predicted standards and the calculated cost of £46. (Although scientists take a sternly professional attitude to matters of chance, it seems that nature does not therefore withhold their fair share of luck.)

To sum up the key point under this heading: cost control is the function of cost accountants, and these people are specialists. This means that their activities tend to be regarded as entirely separate from those of everyone else. Yet if the control model which underlies the costing system is different from that used for other purposes, the manager is in a real sense being misinformed. If, on the other hand, the unexpressed costing model is the same as that used by everyone else, an extraordinary waste of money is implied by the establishment of a completely separate costing scheme. Again, the notion that every specialist control function should be an isomorphic mapping of every other, and a homomorphic mapping of a basic control theory which expresses no particular specialist function but is modelled on the manager's own role, is seen as a valid and economical concept.

(e) Management control

Turning now from the two specialist control functions that have been considered as examples, we reach the function of management itself which makes use of them both. The essential importance to the manager himself of a cybernetic control system is that it automatically filters the vast amount of proliferating information about the world situation that is accessible, and can present him with that very small proportion which is of real importance. For a system that is self-regulating must be capable of the automatic correction of small and large errors alike; and in the course of correcting them it must of course detect them, and can therefore report them according to whatever criteria are laid down. These criteria should certainly be based on probability theory, so that a manager is not troubled with discrepancies, however large in absolute terms, that are explicable by chance variations.

This is of course an example of the long-standing technique of management by exception. But it does add something to that technique, for the cybernetic system is able to define, operationally, what counts as an exception. It is surely possible that an excess of £5 on one job may be more important than an excess of £500 on another—for the reason that the larger belongs to a population which is statistically variable in high degree, whereas the smaller error belongs to a population that is very closely controlled statistically. It follows that a time-consuming inquest about the loss incurred on the larger amount will reveal explanations that are perfectly acceptable and call for no action; but there will be no inquest on the apparently small loss. In fact, this small loss is a warning signal that something is going seriously out of control: next time the losses in this area may be vast.

Since, according to the general theory, all information is passing through black boxes competent to classify its relevance to the self-regulating property of the system, and to measure its probabilism, an 'importance filter' can be installed with little trouble and no expense. All that is required is that the information channels marked in zone 5 of Figure 44 as modifying the transformation from $M2$ to $M3$ should be *tapped*. Using statistical improbability as a criterion of managerial importance, a few items out of very many thousand can be siphoned off for the manager to investigate. This has been done in the practical applications quoted here, with the result that a monthly cost report some seven inches thick (in which the manager had to browse in order to *select* possible exceptions) was replaced by one sheet of paper quoting those matters which the self-regulating viable system 'became aware of' as being exceptional. This device leaves the manager almost entirely free of routine monitoring activities, which are so time-consuming.

Moreover, the predictive capability of the model (originally created for purposes of forecasting a multitude of interacting events for routine, planning) is powerful as a warning system to management. In detecting inefficiency and the drift towards unprofitable operation, it may also detect abuses of production facilities. Remember that the model $M1$ which underlies the control is based on performance optima. In general, then, the appearance of black box outputs greater than $1·0$ indicates that too great a stress is being placed on the relevant plant. This can easily happen in a ramified production system. One machine, for example, may be an almost unrecognized bottleneck; it is operated under pressure from both its supply and demand functions; it receives (perhaps) un-authorized help—safety devices may be removed, minimal time allow-ances may be cut, and so on. At any rate, when the control ratios consistently exceed unity, one of two things is very likely to happen. Either the plant breaks down, or the product quality collapses. The case studies quoted in this chapter have given rise to several examples of both outcomes.

The explanations of this general theory have all been taken from the production situation: its planning, programming and progressing to delivery; its stocks, productivity and costs. But exactly the same theory applies in other fields of management where processes are being con-trolled. For instance, it has been applied to market situations, where it can make adaptive forecasts in the same sense as already defined in the production situation.

In this case, for example, the rate of ordering and the bunching of orders offer a measure of demand which can be forecast with ever-increasing accuracy. But a system based on these measures alone will not provide an adequate criterion of a *healthy* demand. Again manage-ment is faced with a system of many dimensions and many performance criteria. Thus the models implicit in this kind of control must take into account not only the rate, size and stochastic flow of orders, but their profitability—having regard to the state of the factory. We are in an area of opportunity costing, in which OR models of complex systems and cybernetic models of exceedingly complex systems can profitably be geared together.

Similar remarks could be made about the outside world of suppliers, as well as of customers. Indeed, the general theory is not impotent when it comes to such rarified questions as those involving major capital development. The fact is that the problems of management are created by the proliferation of variety. The thinking advanced here offers means of governing this variety scientifically, in an economic and predictable way.

14

SELF-ORGANIZING·
SYSTEMS

Regem locusta non habet et egreditur universa per
turmas suas.

The locust has no king, but he marches out at one
with his troops.

Book of Proverbs (?600–250 B.C.) **30**, 27 in *Vulgate*

1 Structure and Maturity: The Ecosystem

Having elucidated in some detail a cybernetic approach to the management problem of controlling operations, we wish to advance to the consideration of even larger managerial issues. In order to do so, it will be
necessary to add further insight into the nature of systems. Hence, just as
the last chapter was preceded by an account of the cybernetic theory
needed to talk about operational control in management, the next
chapter on these wider problems of the manager is preceded by this
explanation of *self-organizing* systems.

Up to this point, the emphasis has been on systems capable of controlling themselves implicitly. They have to do with self-regulation: a
complex system generating high variety must be controlled by requisite
variety; requisite variety is not readily to hand in the orthodox mandatory notion of control; it is best obtained by installing as controller
a variety generator capable of absorbing proliferating variety like a
sponge. This was demonstrated in Chapter 12 and exemplified in the
management context in Chapter 13. All this, however, presupposes a
structure of the situation within which to operate: the manager was
dealing with a given world situation which it was his responsibility to
manage. In the higher functions of management, whether in industry,

business, defence or government, it is precisely the structure of the world situation that has to be managed.

For management, the problem of structuring the world situation emerges from policy formulation. We know what we want to do; how do we *organize* the system to do it? Once the system is organized or structured, we know how to endow it with the facility for implicit self-control. The basic answer of cybernetics to the question of how the system should be organized is that it ought to organize itself. For reasons entirely analogous to those deployed in connection with control, we are not likely to be very successful in imposing rigid organizational structure on a complex system. Not only is the task too difficult in handling the system as it now is, but we cannot easily foresee the organizational needs of the system as it will become quite soon. In current management practice, this is allowed for by legislating for a certain flexibility. '*This* is the organization, we think, but we reserve the right to modify it—particularly if good old Bill should be run over by a bus, for we shall not see *his* particular combination of talents again.' But in nature, the structure of control—its effective organization —is not monitored by a pantheon of directors which decides to change the structure. The structure . . . just changes. This is why the cybernetician speaks of self-organizing systems, and also why we need to investigate their nature before we can contemplate the applications of the natural model to the managerial situation.

A prevalent concept in science is the process of evening out. That is to say, if a system is divided into a pair of freely interacting sub-systems, and one of these has more of a certain commodity than the other, then an equilibrial state of the whole will eventually be reached in which the dispersion of the commodity over both sub-systems is equivalent. Water, we say, 'finds its own level'. But this is because the force of gravity operates equally on any two hydraulic sub-systems. More typically, and more 'self-organizingly', we say that *energy* evens out. The archetypal example of this process concerns energy in the form of heat, and is expressed in the second law of thermodynamics. Very simply: if a hotter body and a cooler body are interacting, heat will be transferred *from* the hotter *to* the cooler until they share the available heat equally; then the transference stops.

Now the system consisting of these two bodies was active. Energy, in the form of heat, was available for transference from the first sub-system to the second, and could do useful work on the way. The measure of *how much* useful work it could do is called *entropy*. Entropy is a measure of the disbalance of energy in a system. In a thermodynamic system, it is the ratio of the amount of heat available for work to the absolute temperature of the system. By the time all the heat has been evened out, this ratio has risen to unity. The system is then *dead*, in the sense that activity within it necessarily stops. The rise of entropy happens automatically; it is a law of nature that, other things being equal, entropy tends to its maximum.

The concept of entropy is difficult to understand, especially because it turns up in several branches of science in a slightly different form. In cybernetics, in particular, we meet its negative version called negentropy. Surprisingly perhaps, negentropy is a measure of information. That is, a system gaining in entropy is also losing information. By the time entropy has risen to unity, the energy has all been evened out and there is nothing to say about the *system* as such—which is dead. It has no information to yield.

These concepts, and this basic law of nature, bear very relevantly on matters of self-organization. Consider again the system divided into two freely interacting sub-systems. Suppose that one of these is more *organized* than the other. Does it follow that it must share its degree of organization with the less organized system? Is the 'commodity of structuredness' analogous to heat, and will it even out? The answer is no; in fact, the reverse is true: a system that is organizationally dis-balanced will tend to become more so. The reason is that organization is more akin to available information than available energy; its elaboration is therefore measured by a growth in negentropy rather than in entropy.

Suppose that the two sub-systems both begin with the same amount of energy. Sub-system *A* uses up a lot of this energy in the process of organizing itself internally. Sub-system *B* uses up less of its energy in the process of organizing itself to a lesser extent. So *A* is more organized, and more depleted of energy, than *B*. Accordingly, since interaction occurs, energy must, by the rules of entropy, flow from *B* to *A*. It is now, as it were, too late for *B* to catch up in degree of organization with *A*. It has a decreasing supply of energy available to use for organizing itself, while *A* has an increasing supply. So the more organized *A* feeds on the less organized *B*. Eventually *A* will destroy *B* altogether (in an isolated system). Note that the boundary of *A*, which is its interface with *B*, has to be visualized as advancing into *B*'s territory. That is, the degree of organization moves against the direction of the flow of energy.

The phrase 'feeds on' was used with deliberation, for when an elabor-ate organism, such as an animal, lives in an environment of less elabor-ately organized living things (including lesser animals and plants) it

literally eats them. The immature animal is highly structured organizationally, according to its genetic nature, but it is very short of energy. It
takes energy from its environment, by feeding itself, and converts this
energy (using its genetic codes) into more and more organization of its
own fabric. Consider an immature animal (sub-system A), placed in an
environment of foodstuff (sub-system B), and suppose that the entire
system is then isolated. This is exactly what happens in a zoo; an animal
is isolated in a cage or a tank, and supplied with food from outside. But
make the food supply finite. The animal will now assimilate all the
energy available, converting this to organization in the sense of its own
growth (a highly structured fabric); then it will die, for there can be no
more energy transference.

The processes now under discussion are ecological: they relate to the
interaction of an organism and its environment. Hence the sort of system
referred to is called (for short) an *ecosystem*. In talking about the aspects
of general systems theory which are important to viability, we have
already encountered feedback. Hitherto, we have concentrated on the use of
feedback as an error-correcting mechanism; this is essentially *negative* feedback. Negative feedback is important to the ecosystem, too; it cuts back
excessive animal populations, for example, through ecological homeostasis as already described. But in the ecosystem, rather specially, we also
encounter *positive* feedback: the tendency of some change to be automatically reinforced. The expansion of the more highly organized at the expense
of the less highly organized is a typical example of positive feedback.

Both types of feedback are demonstrated at work in the simplest
organism we can investigate: the living cell. Nicolas Rashevsky, another
of the men who have devoted themselves to the scientific investigation
and rigorous formulation of biological mechanisms, expounds the theory
(though not under this heading) in his *Mathematical Principles of Biology*.
A cell exists in homeostatic equilibrium with its environment by exchanging substances both ways through its membrane. If a certain metabolite
is produced inside the cell so that there is a higher concentration of the
substance inside than outside, then this substance will tend to diffuse
through the membrane—to leak away into the environment at a measurable rate. But if the metabolite be used up inside the cell, so that the
concentration of the substance is higher outside than inside, then diffusion will occur *inwards*. This is an entropy-like process, but it does not
reach finality because it is not isolated; the cell, for example, may continue to produce the metabolite indefinitely. But the tendency is there;
the perpetual seeking of balance is there. Rashevsky expresses this
homeostatic mechanism in a system of equations.

The rate of diffusion through the membrane depends on the permeability of the membrane, and it is this which governs the nature—in particular the size—of the cell. If the rate of production of the metabolite were spontaneously to increase beyond the possible rate of outflow, then the concentration inside the cell would increase to infinity. Now the production process requires energy, in the form of oxygen. Since this is being used up inside the cell, and assuming there is an infinite supply of oxygen outside, then the evening-out tendency requires oxygen to flow in. But Rashevsky's system of equations shows that the rate of oxygen consumption tends to a limiting value. This fact must inhibit production inside the cell. In particular, it limits the rate of production to something less than the rate of diffusion outwards—otherwise the cell would explode. The cell in fact has a critical radius, above which no stable state for the diffusion interaction exists. Perhaps the mechanism (as distinct from the chemistry) by which all this self-organizing capability is achieved is not properly understood. Yet the behavioural facts are clear. The need to adjust the production rate to the outflow rate is met by a governor of the oxygen intake. This checks the rise in concentration of the metabolite in the very act of its going out of control. That description maps isomorphically on to the description of the Watt steam engine governor. In the cell there is no pair of weighted arms driving a valve by centrifugal force; but there is quite evidently a cognate negative feedback phenomenon.

Conversely, we may detect in the same cell a positive feedback phenomenon. Although this has little to do (directly) with ecological homeostasis, it has a great deal to do with self-organization. Suppose that the production of the substance already discussed is internally monitored by a catalyst, the function of which is to inhibit that production. The catalyst is particulate. Since the produced substance is flowing outward, it must propel the particles of catalyst outwards. Therefore the production of the substance is inhibited round the periphery of the cell. Next, as familiarly happens in nature, casual variations procure a cluster of these catalytic particles at one point on the cell periphery. At this point, then, production of the substance will be differentially inhibited: it will arise in higher concentration everywhere else. That means a diffusion flow *towards* the point where the catalytic particles are clustered —a flow which will carry more particles with it. Here then is the positive feedback. The accidental cluster of particles is not dispersed by entropy, but reinforced by the influx of more particles. And these in turn will accelerate the trend. In this way the cell acquires more structure, more organization. For the catalyst is not uniformly distributed throughout the cell, but concentrated in one section. The cell has now a self-organized and self-regulating polarity.

This cybernetic account of the mechanisms of self-organization would not necessarily commend themselves to Rashevsky, whose examples have been quoted. But other workers have also noted the biological activities on which this commentary is based. In particular, the laws stating that the flow of energy is from the less to the more organized sub-system, and that the latter tends to grow in a direction opposite to the energy flow, have been promulgated on experimental evidence by the Spanish ecologist Ramon Margalef. He refers to the gain in structured-ness that accompanies the entropy change in a biological system as a gain in the *maturity* of that system. The word is obviously well suited to describe structural elaboration, and it will be adopted here for artificial as well as natural systems—if only because the word 'structured-ness' is an unpleasing invention.

2   The Nature of Self-Organization

The criteria by which to recognize a complex system that will organize itself are, it must be frankly stated, in dispute among cyberneticians. Some contend that many and complicated conditions must be fulfilled; others that almost any complex and richly interacting system will undertake a measure of self-organization if left to itself. The latter viewpoint will be argued here, but for a rather special (perhaps idiosyncratic) reason. This is that organization is an attribute of the observer of a system rather than of the system itself; it represents an extension of the arguments advanced earlier about the recognition of a system as being a system at all.

It is assumed that the subject of this enquiry is a high-variety, complex, interacting system. Such a system has innumerable modes of behaviour; and according to the sense this behaviour makes in the eyes of an observer he is likely to describe it as either inchoate or organized. But even if he cannot account for the behaviour, and calls it chaotic, the observer may well concede that 'there must be a reason' for this behaviour. What he is saying, then, is that the apparent chaos is a measure of his own ignorance. In view of the connectedness and coherence of natural phenomena, it is wise to assert *on principle* that a system is organized.

A telling example of the arbitrariness of these descriptive words may be taken from thermodynamics itself. In a system made up of gas molecules, there may exist a radical disbalance at a given moment: a concentration of molecules in one part of the system. By the process of entropy, the disbalance evens out, until there exists a completely homogeneous gas within the confines of the system. It is an experimental fact that this happens, and the reason why it happens is thoroughly understood. No-one disputes that entropy has run to a maximum. The interesting thing is that, conventionally, the thermodynamicist calls the disbalanced system *ordered* (because the disbalance has a kind of order—the more and the less concentration of molecules), and he calls the ultimately balanced system *disordered* (because it is homogeneous, and the gas molecules may be found rushing about anywhere at all). The process described is called the order–disorder transition. According to him, then, the system gains in entropy and loses in organization. But what could be more ordered, or better organized, than a completely uniform molecular distribution? In this, the probability that any one space is filled by any one molecule is exactly the same for all spaces and all molecules. This is (if we choose to say so) perfection in organization, absolute orderliness. It is only when the probabilities are different, and the molecules are concentrated in particular zones of the whole region, that disorder has set in. Thus, on the same facts and the same mathematics, it might be preferred to call the transition disorder–order—instead of the other way round.

It does not matter at all what we *say* about this system. What matters is what we understand by what we say. We may even convert the one answer to the other, if battle is joined by the protagonists of the two points of view, by redefining the terms (which are arbitrary) so that the sign of the answer is changed. What matters is that the two ways of talking are not 'in disagreement': they are diametrically opposed as contradictories. To the layman, this may sound like the ultimate sort of disagreement; to the logician, however, it is a guarantee that the two sides are actually saying the same *structural* thing. And they are.

The purpose of these explorations is to make clear why the following proposition is tenable. There is a natural law—refer to it as entropy—which causes isolated systems to change their internal structure if they are left alone. The tendency is irresistible, and is found everywhere in nature. The process of change thus determined will be named *maturing* (following Margalef); and every state of the system during maturation will be designated more organized than any preceding state, and less organized than any subsequent state. The argument is thereby settled *per definiendum*. Organization is a monotonic-increasing function of maturation.

But, it will be protested, by the standards of ordinary conversation, the connotation of 'organization' must include remarks about complexity.

One cannot say that a system is maturing to a more organized state if in fact the process of entropy is causing it to disintegrate—to lose its complexity. Suppose that a perfectly moulded ice-cream pudding is removed from a refrigerator and left in a warm room. According to this definition, the system will *mature* to the point where the dish is full of a runny liquid—which must then be declared more *organized* than it was before. If this outcome offends ordinary usage, which of course it does, the reason is not because a reference to complexity has been omitted. The ice-cream pudding has indeed progressed to a more probable condition than it had before, and is therefore more and not less organized in respect to its environment. No; what has been omitted is a reference to the *purposes* of the pudding.

It is in fact the teleological context of the system which determines whether a system is to be called perfectly organized or totally disorganized. The scale of organization connecting these extreme states is calibrated by the *fitness of the system to achieve a purpose*. The whole point of the specification of an ice-cream pudding is that it should be (relatively) cold, and retain its moulded shape. The acknowledgement of its purpose thus determines the physical state that will count as perfectly organized on the scale. On this understanding, the pudding that disintegrates in a warm place is after all losing its organization: so usage is satisfied. But the entropy of the system is increasing—and we said that this meant the organization must be increasing too. What is the solution to this paradox?

The answer is that the pudding should never have been taken out of the refrigerator. In taking it out, the teleological context was changed. The pudding was set the task of 'adapting' to a warm room, which it proceeded to do—thereby maturing. If the pudding is *meant* to stay cold, to retain its shape, then the relevant environment to which it must adapt is the refrigerator. All this means to say is that if maximal entropy defines maturation and therefore maximal organization, then the contextual system (S), consisting of the original system (s) interacting with an immediate environment (e), must be specified in relation to the purpose of the original system (s). If and only if it is so specified, then particular values are (tautologously) specified for the entropy equation so that entropic processes carry the system (s) to a maximally organized state and to nowhere else. This in turn means that system (s) and environment (e) are considered as a relatively isolated system (S) within the larger environment (E).

Analysing the original paradox, it becomes clear that the system (s) gaining entropy in relation to environment (E), is the pudding melting away in the warm room and becoming more organized in respect to it. When we say that this concept of organization is unhelpful, we mean that the purpose of the pudding is to be cold and shaped; it is therefore isolated from the room, with a refrigerator around it. The entropic drift *within* this system is determined by the relation $(s-e)$. Since e is even colder than s, the pudding becomes more organized in an acceptable sense (that is, in relation to its purpose). What then is the role of the larger environment (E), the room outside the refrigerator?

From the standpoint of the system $(s-e)$, which is also the standpoint of the pudding-fancying observer, the room is a source of environmental disturbance which has to be catered for as a challenge: it is a destroyer of puddings. Now of course a refrigerator is specifically a machine for achieving homeostasis in the loop $(s \leftrightarrows e)$ despite environmental disturbance from outside. The system $(s \leftrightarrows e)$ is ultrastable. All manner of un-programmed disturbances can be undertaken in the room outside by ice-cream pudding abolitionists. They may light fires on the floor (which the refrigerator designer did not expect); they may freeze the room in the hope of lulling the refrigerator into a false sense of security, and then rapidly heat it up again. It is all without avail. We who know how refrigerators work perceive that the machine has intrinsic control: equilibrium is restored *in the act of* being lost.

The meaning of self-organization is now emerging and will be brought home fully after a distinction has been drawn. Consider the usual complex, high-variety, richly-interacting, probabilistic system that has to be controlled. The first and inevitable question is: why? If this question has no answer, there would be no meaning in asserting that it has to be controlled, for it would be impossible to state what counts as being either in or out of control. In saying why the system has to be controlled, we implicitly provide a criterion of success—and that means that the purpose of the system is specified. The form of the specification will surely be the statement of a set of goals. The promised distinction arises because there are two quite fundamentally different ways of approaching this task.

First: one may design, that is to say organize, the system to be of such a kind that its set of goals will be achieved. This process consists in determining the inputs to the system and their characteristics, and then undertaking some engineering on the system so that control can be exercised and the goals attained. Think of a computer laboratory, for example, with a large computer chassis, a whole heap of components and wires, related systematically in an experimental mock-up. We may set out to *organize* this system, so that the system will do what the sales literature says it ought to do. When it comes to managing a business, or an economy, we may use this approach to organization as a model, and try to design the system to meet a set of goals. This turns out to be very difficult, for reasons mentioned *passim* in this book.

Secondly, however, we may begin from the knowledge that the system already *is*: it does not have to be designed or organized to be a system—it is there already. To exercise control, however, and to meet the appropriate set of goals, something must be done. The answer is not to design the control, but to constrain the system. *Let us so uncouple a sub-system that the natural movement of increasing entropy within it will tend towards one of the goals.* If we can do this throughout, we have created a system that is self-organizing. The design or management task is to set the structure of the system to determine sub-systems in which the process of entropy is so defined that it will find a way (which we may neither detect nor understand) to cope with disturbances from outside.

There is conceptual difficulty to cope with in all this. We simply are not educated to understand that order is more natural than chaos. People expect nature to be chaotic, and think of order as something imposed upon nature by clever human beings. As with the order–disorder transformation in physics, however, which we have declared it is preferable to call the disorder–order transformation, so with the realm of living things. Already in this book there has been much talk of ecological balance; yet the fact that every ecosystem that surrounds us has its own orderliness as dictated by the entropy of maturation is not generally noted. This story may help to bring home the point. It is a particular example of ecosystemic control, to the existence of which attention has been drawn several times already.

The cabbage aphis is a plant-louse. It weighs about a milligram, and sits on cabbage leaves, feeding. Suppose that just one aphis is taken at the beginning of the summer season. Breeding occurs (by parthenogenesis). Aphides breed quickly and with great fecundity. If nothing were to interfere with the process, that is to say if all the lice lived and bred in turn, given enough cabbage, it is obvious that by the end of the season there would be a great many aphides about. People are well aware that this exponential breeding process is impressive—but just how impressive? Just what weight of aphides would result in the example quoted? We do not know the answer, but are prepared to be impressed by a total which clearly might run into several tons. But according to a report by the New York Academy of Sciences, the answer is actually *822,000,000* tons—which is roughly five times the weight of the entire human population.

This fantastic propagation of aphides does not happen; the variety generation that is the procreative power of the aphis is absorbed within the ecosystem by homeostasis. There is no Comptroller of Aphides, no licensing procedure, no rules whether legal or moral by which the world's engulfment by aphides (or indeed any other beast) is prevented. Nor does the process of massive retrenchment of an animal population misfire to the extent of annihilating the entire species. This is not chaos, but the most remarkable order. And it is into this orderliness that the horticulturist advances with his pesticide—not to make order out of chaos, as he may think, but to introduce a local variation into the homeostatic equilibria of one of the set of sub-systems involved. This is done by changing the local framework of the sub-system so that the entropic drift is towards the destruction of aphides. As with the aphis, so with other beasts; with the locust, for instance, whose self-organizing ability was remarked upon at the head of this chapter in the words of the school of Solomon.

The management of high-variety systems is always concerned with a definition of entropy which serves particular goals, and with defining success as the maturation of a system in its maximal entropy.

3 Learning to be what One is

The notion that a self-organizing system becomes what it is by virtue of a tendency akin to entropy is vital, and its implications must be understood. In this section, a closer look will be taken at what is involved. The question has to be answered: what makes nature so clever?

Once the property of self-organization has been defined as a structural adjustment to a set of disturbances within the context of a set of over-riding goals, it *ceases* to be anything 'clever'. The 'cleverness' of a self-organizing system resides in the minds of observers who try to imagine themselves specifying the rules: they boggle at the difficulty of the task. How would one set about programming a bee, for example, to construct a honeycomb as an hexagonal lattice? Or how—and indeed what—would one programme to ensure that a cloud of hot gas in space should maintain an equilibrial temperature in excess of 6,000° Centigrade? Provided that we adhere to our knowledge of natural law and refuse to place ourselves in so false a position as to envisage programming nature, we can understand how such tricks are brought off. It is then no more than a step to see how self-organizing systems can be created in the managerial fields too. Thus, now that the concept of entropy has been introduced in various ways, it will be useful to obtain a rather more precise notion of what it is.

In classical thermodynamics, the notion of entropy is explained quite simply like this. There is a system made up of parts, some of which are hotter than others. In every small amount of time, a tiny quantity of heat changes place within that system (until finally it is all evened out). The significance of the quantity of heat that is transposed is clearly relative to the overall temperature of the system at that time. So the change that is being measured, which is the entropy, is measured by the rate at which the ratio alters. It is this consideration which yields the classical mathematical formulation for entropy:

$$S = \int_0^T \frac{dQ}{T}$$

which shows the 'little bit of heat' (dQ) as a ratio with the 'temperature at the time' (T), the sum of all these tiny changes being computed from the original absolute temperature, 'zero'. The expression holds subject to various overriding conditions which are not enumerated here.

Now when heat is being exchanged on the basis of entropic drift, each of the states on the way from a disbalanced system to an evened-out system may be realized in innumerable ways. That is, so long as the heat evens out by stages, no-one needs to know where any particular molecule is at any particular stage. If the innumerable ways, of which there are (say) g, are all equally likely to occur, then the entropy moves as the logarithm of g. This is the formulation of entropy as it is found in statistical mechanics, and it is written even more simply than before as

$$S = k \log g$$

(where k is a constant—Boltzmann's constant to be precise).

Obviously any system at all has a large number of possible states, which is to say g of them, and for the moment we are regarding them all as equally probable. So the entropy of the system is the logarithm of the probability that the system is as it is. When the system is fully mature (as described earlier) it is in its *most* probable state. So entropy is the natural 'force' which carries a system from an improbable to a probable condition.

To get the full benefit of this discovery, we need to appreciate it in a form which recognizes that all states of the system are in most cases *not* equally probable. Consider state i. The probability P_i that the system is in state i, is less than 1, since it could be in some other state. So the expression for S given above must be rewritten to accommodate the sum of all possible states, measuring the probability of each. Hence:

$$S = -k \sum_i P_i \log P_i$$

As a check, suppose that there are just four possible states of the system and that each is in fact equally likely. Then the new expression would read:

$$S = -k \, 4 \, \tfrac{1}{4} \log \tfrac{1}{4}$$
$$= k \log 4$$

which would have been given by the original expression.

These classic expressions are given as an aid to understanding alone; we shall not start computing with them here. The point is that a system tends to move from a less to a more probable state, and that the rate of its change is proportional to the logarithm of the disbalance of probability existing at any one time.

Now it was explained that entropic movement carries the structure of the ecosystem towards a pattern which guarantees an equilibrium between the system and its environment. When the observer has defined a set of goals as appropriate to his purposes, and has spotlighted an entropic drift which conforms to these needs, he will dub the system self-organizing. He then refers to the changes taking place as evidence of *control*, which from his standpoint they certainly are. Surely, if a system is moving towards what he regards as desirable ends, it is 'under control'. Moreover, the control which is exerted in the process of self-organization is proportional to the system's 'self-awareness' of its own improbability—as measured relatively to the most probable end-state of maturity. That term 'self-awareness' can surely be used too; for the system is in process of organizing itself, and to the observer the movement must look evolutionary and purposive. What the observer does is to project his own notion of purpose on to the system. Thus the system appears to the observer to be under control in proportion to the amount of self-awareness—that is, information about itself—that it exhibits. Or to be precise: the degree of control exerted is proportional to the logarithm of the amount of effective information available to the system.

These conclusions may be tested in the cases of the bees that have to be programmed to build a hexagonal honeycomb, and the cloud of hot gas that has to be programmed to maintain a high temperature. Each of these systems is in fact self-organizing, its 'control' being founded in an entropic drift. They do not have to be programmed, in fact; only recognized for what they really are.

Consider the bee. He secretes wax, and he builds his own cell by spinning around within an exudation of wax. Thus the bee may be thought of as surrounded by a cocoon in the form of a wax cylinder. The question then is, given a host of similarly cocooned bees, how should they be programmed to construct a hexagonal honeycomb? To insist on asking the question in this form leaves the observer gasping at his own ignorance and the bee's 'cleverness'. For the bees evidently have to be taught mathematics; they must communicate with each other in mathematical terms; and so on. The bee, then, is exceedingly 'clever'; we wish we could construct computers of equal ingenuity; and so on. But the problem is quite illusory. The cylinders, while being formed, are jostling together under a gravitational pull. Each one will therefore progress downward as far as it can go. Given a floor to the hive, then, there must develop a closely packed bottom layer of cylinders, lying side by side. If there were any gaps, gyrating bees would fall into them. Consider the first bee to descend on to this bottom layer: it might land right on top of another bee. But this is an abstraction; in fact a host of bees is simultaneously jostling at every level, so the bee concerned can hardly balance his cylinder in unstable equilibrium on the one below —he will be knocked off his perch. Obviously the second layer of bees will inevitably lie in the troughs between the bottom-layer bees. And so on.

Next consider a bee somewhere in the middle of all this activity. He lies in a trough formed by two lower-level bees; he has a bee touching him on either side (making three in a row at his level); and so two more bees at an upper level lie in the troughs thereby created. Hence his cylinder is touched tangentially by six other cylinders equally spaced around him. The wax is still malleable and capillary forces cause the arcs of the circles to close together. The honeycomb, which looks so ingenious, is simply an ecosystem being what it is.

The self-organizing system in this case is called organized because it appeals to the observer's criteria of design: it has aesthetic appeal, regularity; it has superb economy (maximum bees in minimum space), and therefore looks purposive to the waste-conscious, cost-conscious citizen. It manages to organize itself by an entropy-like process, however, and not by a conscious or even instinctive planning function. For the organization is affected by the evening out of a system subjected to three generalized forces: gravity, capillary attraction and a random movement. Notice how the requisite variety in the 'hexagon-constructing-control-unit', which is non-existent, is supplied by having as many bees as there are bees—not a difficult condition to fulfil. Notice how the control regulations necessary for hexagon-constructing are supplied by specifying a uniform transformation for each bee: 'fall, jostle, cohere'.

In thinking about control, it seems, people have been too mechanistic and too introspective. Ideas have been mechanistic, because in engineering we do not achieve results unless the parts of a system operate in an entirely preordained way: the infrastructure of a workable machine must be fully specified. Ideas of control have been introspective, because the most impressive natural system in a man's eyes is himself, and he is controlled by a brain. Hence if a system is under control, being organized, we tend to look for the box that contains 'the works', 'the programme', 'the computer'. But the big lesson of cybernetics is that most commonly in nature there is no such thing. Natural systems organize themselves over a period of time to be what they immanently are. To the observer, who determines the criteria by which the end result is called organized, this process looks like learning or, in general, adaptation. In fact, it is a process of entropy.

But there is still more to say. Some natural systems appear to be not only organized, but *responsive*. Here again is one of those words which seem to imply that an intelligence is at work inside the system. Consider, for example, the cloud of hot gas mentioned at the start of this section. If the temperature of this cloud is greater than 6,000° Centigrade, it is likely to 'blow up'—for a very definite reason. An ordinary gas is composed of molecules which simply wander about. They do not exert powerful attraction or repulsion among themselves. But in a gas as hot as this, particles carrying electrical charges are released. The temperature is a function of the speed of these ions. If an increase in temperature is postulated, there will be an associated increase in ionization, and it looks as though the whole system must be unstable and disintegrate. Indeed, these strange features of a very hot gas make it a special phenomenon: this has been called the fourth state of matter and given its own name of *plasma*—something different from a solid or a liquid or a gas. How then can a cloud of plasma remain stable in these circumstances?—for it does. No outside agency impinges upon it in a way which could be regarded as a plasma-controller (think of the sun, for instance). So even the cybernetic expectation that there might be an environment-system homeostatic stabilization is not the answer. The answer must lie in the system itself. If we call a cloud of plasma self-disciplined, able to keep itself under control despite the powerful forces locked within, just what is implied? If a human being can do this trick, we say he is ethical; Freud said he had an endopsychic censor. If a company can do this, we know it has an authoritative management. There are so many misleading models. For once again this is a self-organizing phenomenon; as is now shown.

Oppositely charged ions are so strongly attracted to each other that they tend to cohere and form atoms. The hotter the plasma, the more and the faster the ions that are rushing about. This increases the probability that atoms will be created, and decreases the supply of ions. Thus the rate of atomic recombination balances the rate of ionization, and the stability of the plasma is given by the equivalence of these rates. Hence in so far as a plasma, despite all its terrible power and internal stress, maintains a peaceable equilibrium, it does so because it is what it is. It self-organizes its stability because its nature is to be stable. If that is remarkable, *who says* it is remarkable? We do; because we wish we could organize ourselves, our economies, our societies to be nothing other than equilibrial, and we fail.

But there is nothing particularly remarkable in a system's seeking a more probable state than the improbable state it has at any given moment. And from a statistical point of view, the state of any system is usually highly improbable. Of course we do not recognize this either. In ordinary parlance, things that *are* tend to be seen as highly probable because they *are* as they are. We may recall an argument from Chapter 4. If four people sit down to play bridge, and each player happens to be dealt a full suit of cards, what happens? Assuming the players trust each other and do not conclude that some chicanery is afoot, they will become very excited; they may write to the newspapers to discuss the astronomically long odds against this happening. In doing so, however, they may not stop to think that this particular distribution of the cards is no more improbable than the particular distribution obtained from every single deal they ever witnessed. Any particular distribution is highly improbable; yet some particular distribution may be obtained quite readily by merely dealing the cards. The excitement is generated by the recognition of the pattern produced when a full suit falls to each player.

Now the business of self-organization becomes finally clear when it is realized that a system has to be recognized as being organized when in its most probable state. A prime example of this occurs in the process of growth. A seed has to be considered as a variety-amplifier, for it carries the specification of something larger than itself. But it also carries a temporally-based plan for growing to maturity: a self-organizing capability. Not only does this plan specify a set of architectural relationships, it specifies a criterion of maturity. That is, any organic seminal programme that inaugurates and controls growth 'knows when to stop'. This capability applies not only to the macrostructure, so that you and I are roughly the right size to be recognizably human; it also applies to the infrastructure of the organism: every limb, every organ, every parcel of tissue however delineated, from cranium to toe-nail, grows to a limit.

During growth, further growth is by definition due to follow; development (except by massive intervention from outside) cannot be arrested until the plan is complete. To this extent, a partly-grown organism is in an improbable state, and is driving towards its most probable state—adult completion. Growth can be regarded, that is to say, as an entropic process. The growth process stops when the genetic information is used up, actuality having been finally and in sum exchanged for potentiality. Any form of the entropy equation will serve to formalize this process.

Growth, then, is a self-organizing activity of a system in which that system 'learns to be what it is'. The seed 'struggles purposively' to free the adult imprisoned within it. For the seed has requisite variety as a genotype, which it continuously amplifies by generating more variety from its environmental input to form a phenotype. Yet the genotypical variety is preceded by requisite variety in its turn; the amount of information and its orderliness are specified by the parental genetic template. Thus the processes of procreation and growth betoken the advance of a certain orderly structure, which we have called organization, through nature and through time, across the span of the life-cycle for any individual. Energy exchanges explain this possibility in terms of sustaining an organism, but only entropic exchanges can account for the maintenance of organization without rapid degradation across the generations. Organization is in fact maintained from parent to progeny by supplies of negentropy in the environment, which the variety generator in the organism can utilize. This is how evolution becomes possible, in so far as the degree of organization moves against the flow of energy, and increases with the entropy. So evolution, just like growth itself, is a self-organizing characteristic.

4 Adaptation and Evolution: The Teleology of Development

It becomes more and more apparent as the argument proceeds that the features of living organisms which we most admire and seek to understand are properties of self-organizing systems. Learning and adaptation, growth and evolution, occur through entropic processes which do not demand 'control centres' but utilize pervasive natural laws. Some insight at the verbal level has been derived in this chapter into them all. All are founded in the capabilities of the evening-out machine, the homeostat, of which a slightly more formal account was given earlier.

Then the claim has been made that the purposive nature of these viable characteristics is projected on to the system by the observer, who interprets entropy in teleological terms. The essence of the idea is that, since systems run by nature towards an evening out of energy, and since organization is preserved in this process by means already discussed, then those systems are robust against disturbance. The observer, interpreting this, declares that a homeostatic system has adaptive capabilities: because although the environment alters all the time, the organism perpetuates its own structural identity, its organization. Equally, when the observer notices the preservation of identity across the generations, accompanied by a long-term increase in organization, he declares that a homeostatic system has evolutionary capabilities. For the species survives, and improves its survival-worthiness in the process. These capabilities are purposive, in the observer's opinion, just because he can see that they conduce to survival. In view of the influences which apparently assault the adapting organism and the evolving species, the observer thinks of success in both cases as highly improbable: hence his teleological explanations. As has been shown, however, success is not improbable (on the average), but certain; because the improbabilities are no more improbable than any alternative improbabilities, and are in any case moving continuously to more probable states all the time.

Let it be noted please that these explanations of teleological mechanisms do not explain 'purpose' away. They do not assure us that self-organizing systems are not purposive, only that there is a natural mechanism to which the name of purpose is given. How anyone should interpret this is a subjective matter and must depend on the connotation he accords to the word 'purpose'. So, for example, it does not seem possible to draw atheistic conclusions from this work of science nor to endorse theistic conclusions. But it may be necessary to say that what remains to be explained, whether theistically or atheistically, is not the cleverness or the tenacity of an organism in seeking survival (for these qualities appear to be artefacts of self-organizing systems), but the existence, universality and simplicity of the law of entropy.

Yet scientifically there is more to say; and the clue to this may well be found in a subjective reaction. If teleological aspects of systems are to be accounted for in this way, how did we ever come to regard them as so 'clever' and 'competent'? Why, if they refer thereby to the processes of a blind entropy, were they not more readily recognizable as posing no special problems? In short, is anyone really satisfied that the kind of explanation given fully accounts for the observed facts? The motivation of these questions, it is suggested, resides in an intuition (which has yet to be dealt with) that a system engaged in a purely blind entropic development would (*a*) blunder about, and therefore take a long time to reach stability, and (*b*) never achieve anything really new, exciting or creative. The theory of natural selection, for example, as put forward by Darwin, belongs precisely to the class of teleological mechanisms here defined; and because the world has existed for an unthinkably long time people are disposed to believe that animal life could have reached its present state of organization by the blind entropic process (in this case, random mutation followed by survival of the fittest). Yet in the shorter term, where the growth of an individual to maturity is concerned, or a learning process is studied, or the adaptation of a particular moth to the changing colour of its surroundings is contemplated, the blind process of entropy is more clearly unconvincing.

The last of the major problems to be discussed here arises from these thoughts. Even the evolutionary explanation is suspect, as it happens, because the time that was actually available to evolve man from the amœba or the first protein molecule, though unthinkably long in everyday terms, is just not long enough. This will be explained in a minute. To be general: the process of adaptation by which any very large system adjusts itself to an environment, cannot be restricted to a so-called 'random' process of trial and error. That process provides an ecosystemic feedback in itself, true. But there is another mechanism to uncover.

Consider then, side by side, two of these vital processes—two which appear to be very different. These are: the problem of adaptation for the brain of a single human being (this is a process we call learning), and the problem of evolutionary adaptation for a whole species (the process we call survival). These turn out to be closely analogous processes after all. That is to say, a high-variety generator is set to work; it produces all sorts of possible behaviour patterns. The task of the learning human or the adapting species is to discover a strategy for selecting particular patterns of output that are survival-worthy. The generator available to the individual human is his own brain; for the species it is the DNA (deoxyribo nucleic acid) molecule that carries the genetic code.

The magnitude of the two problems can be crudely measured. However inexact the following figures may be, they do at least convey an idea of the difficulties so readily glossed over in ordinary talk about these matters. The brain contains roughly 10,000,000,000 (10^{10}) nerve cells—the neurons—each of which, though apparently an analogue system internally, can be regarded as a binary system in so far as it produces a binary output (a pulse, or no pulse, in the axon). So the variety of the brain, which is its possible number of states under this description, is $2^{10^{10}}$. This variety may be compared with the total genotypical information in the mammalian egg cell—which is that information carried by the DNA molecule. According to Perutz, the number of nucleotide bases in the total length of DNA in a mammalian cell is about 3,000,000,000 (3×10^9). Now these bases are the genetic information carriers, and each may take on one of four chemical forms. As has so often been said, the genetic code is written in a four-letter alphabet. The variety, then, of DNA might be written as $4^{3 \times 10^9}$. This is equivalent to 6×10^9 bits. These estimates have been verified by Raven, in his work on oogenesis, by other modes of quantification. He agrees that this figure is roughly correct. Now the variety of 6×10^9 bits is close to $2^{10^{10}}$.

It seems then that the problem of learning for a single human brain, and the problem of evolutionary adaptation for a whole species, are roughly equivalent—not only in quality, as argued before, but in magnitude. Each system demands that a competent selection of survival-worthy states be made from a total range of states of the order $2^{10^{10}}$. Here, one might think, the resemblance ends; but the comparison is not over yet.

The basic rhythm of the human brain, its alpha rhythm, averages some ten cycles per second. Thus it might be taken that a change of state occurs in the brain every tenth of a second. (A faster rate of change in brain-state might contribute to this periodicity, but it has little meaning to assert this as important: we have to bear in mind the delay times imposed on input and output data by the speed of nerve conduction.) Given then a change in brain-state every tenth of a second throughout life (for the rhythm continues during sleep), the time required to explore all the possible $2^{10^{10}}$ brain states is that number of tenth-seconds. In the case of evolutionary adaptation, the calculation is different. If a mammal reproduces, it cannot create progeny at the rate of ten a second. Wasted ova and spermatozoa do not of course count; there is no way of testing survival-worthiness in mammalian progeny except by observing whether the offspring does survive. And the only way of incorporating a success, even then, in the genetic constitution of the species is by waiting for this individual to breed. Thus the basis cycle time for running through the possible states of DNA is not a tenth of a second, but about twenty-five years (in the case of man). This makes genetic learning (that is, adaptation) 7,884,000,000 times slower than individual human learning —because there is that number of tenth-seconds in twenty-five years. But the individual human is on his own, by definition; the species at any given time contains millions of individuals, all of whom contribute to this experiment. There are 3,000,000,000 human beings alive today; by the time they have all reproduced 2·6 times, the genetic learning rate has caught up with the rate required for individual learning.

It is not clear whether these very rough calculations about learning

rates, which indicate a problem of similar magnitude for both individual
and evolutionary adaptation, point to a conclusion of any importance.
Certainly the cybernetician, in his dealings with viable systems, begins
to suspect for many reasons that life and the capabilities of living things
may have to do with measurable thresholds of variety. But it is too soon
to make predictions based on casual computations of the kind made
here: there are too many complications. For instance, had our calculations been done when only a few men existed at all, the figures would
not have worked out; but the state of evolution at *that* time might have
demanded that other mammals than men be included as affecting the
evolution of man. So it is no part of this thesis to claim that numerical
constants, magic numbers, characterize all modes of survival behaviour
in viable systems, for the evidence is neither satisfactory nor sufficient.
The numerical result computed here may be a risible coincidence.

Even so, the point that has to be made survives, and it is this. If
learning for the individual is no more than a process of trial and error
in arranging the states of the brain, and if adaptation in a species is no
more than a process of random genetic mutation, we know something
about the time factors required to achieve both. *There is nothing like
enough time.* As will be seen, there is little need for accuracy or refinement in the calculation—because that assertion is not marginal. The rate
at which either system can explore its possible states equates (we said)
to $2^{10^{10}}$ tenth-seconds for a complete exploration. Expressed in years, this
yields a figure ending in 3,000,000,000 noughts. Thus, if each page of
this book were crammed with noughts, the book would have to contain
1,000,000 pages to quote the figure in full. Compared with this fantastic
lapse of time, the individual human has merely a hundred years at most
to make his exploration; as to the human race as a whole, a mere
1,000,000,000 years have elapsed since life of any kind emerged on this
planet—which was itself in a gaseous state only 4,500,000,000 years
ago (see how short the length of that number as printed actually is).

Random mutations are a necessary prerequisite for any kind of learning—whether this is adaptation in the individual or in the species. The
psychologist and the geneticist knew this already; cybernetic research
has demonstrated the point formally. But we cannot stop there, as some
psychologists and geneticists would wish to do. Although there may be
no need to explore *all* possible states of a brain or a DNA molecule in
order to adapt, it is obvious that competent adaptation must entail a
degree of organization in the available material—and by the definitions
used here this would require a process of *self*-organization. That would
impart a directional mechanism to the adaptation, deriving from the

structural constraints by which the organization was defined. Only thus can the necessary success in learning be achieved in the time available. It is precisely this mechanism which we describe as teleological; and rightly so, because it conduces to survival. It is precisely this mechanism which we have sought to account for as an entropic shift. What is defective about the account up to this point has been the blindness of the machinery, for the stumbling about takes too long.

Earlier in the book the mechanism underlying learning was identified on a conditional probability model. In Chapter 12, the homeostat was explained, and discussion of the time it takes to settle down to stability was reserved until now. The new contention, then, is that the mechanism of adaptation is in principle similar, and that it can be accounted for on the *same* model. There is a process of random mutation in genetic change, true; but this process is carried by another goal-seeking process which steadily improves the chances of success. The more survival-worthy characteristic is more likely to be reinforced than a less survival-worthy characteristic is likely to be selected only to fail. The dice are still thrown, but they are weighted dice. If we can reward the dice for turning up as a double-six, and reward them a little less for turning up the six–five combination, and so on, they will learn how to behave. They will increasingly tend to produce increasingly good scores. Because of the underlying randomness of the throw as such, however, there is always a finite chance of doing badly (genetically, we get a 'sport'). All the arguments show that it is essential to preserve this possibility, as a loophole of escape from the trapped double-six stability which suddenly turns out to be undesirable.

This happens when there is an environmental change. That is, if the rules of the game alter, so that (say) double-two becomes the best result, the dice will adapt to this outcome. It is not necessary to recognize with analytic insight what has happened. The reward system begins to indicate pain instead of erstwhile pleasure on the high numbers, and the dice reduce the weights attached to their falling accordingly. At the same time, pleasure instead of erstwhile pain begins to be indicated for the double-two, and the weights accordingly increase. Had the double-two been *eliminated* from the game during the earlier phase, as being worthless, the power of adaptation would have been lost. Hence, in biology, we find that when a highly specialized (double-six, say) organism becomes *over* specialized (eliminating the double-two mutation), a radical change in environment (alteration of the rules of the game) leads rapidly to extinction—if it should happen to call for a double-two organization in response.

Unless the cybernetic arguments advanced by the geneticist C. H. Waddington have been misunderstood, he identifies just this sort of mechanism as underlying evolution. The genetic process, with its random mutations, is none the less conditioned by the prior history of the species. Where we have spoken of loaded dice, whose weights adjust themselves in a self-organizing way, Waddington speaks of an *epigenetic landscape*—a most graphic term. Under this image, a ball (representing a genetic determinant) is thrown on to a landscape of hills and valleys, the contours of which are as they are because they have been formed by the prior experience of the species. The randomly-running ball *can* finish up anywhere: if its energy runs out at exactly the right moment, the ball *could* come to rest on a ridge. But obviously it is far more likely to run down one (we do not know which) of the valleys. If the progeny is (statistically) successful, it will transmit its inherited genetic data to *its* progeny. And these data will specify not only the physical characteristics of the parents, but the underlying epigenetic landscape (or conditional probability model) of the species—suitably modified by one more generation's-worth of successful survival.

Much the same device could be nominated as preconditioning the brain, to explain the time factor in adaptation for the human individual. The overall measure of $2^{10^{10}}$ makes no assumptions about constraints which may be exerted on the free proliferation of variety. There surely are some of these in the actual topography of the cerebrum. The brain has an inherited macrostructure: its pons, its diencephalon, its cerebellum, its cerebral cortex; and we know that some functions are at least partly localized. Therefore *every* state of the neuronal population does not have to be examined, because many states would be absurd. Activity in one part of the system presupposes activity somewhere else. Similarly, the finer details of brain macrostructure (for instance, the convolution of the cortical surfaces) develop in infancy and childhood. Can it be doubted that the growing physical configuration places further restraint on the capacity to proliferate variety? Finally, if the conditional probability model of learning has a neurophysiological basis of any kind, this too must add restraints. The evidence that this happens lies with memory. We speak of associative recall, meaning that one set of ideas is more likely to follow this set than other arbitrary sets; so the neuronal states representing the less likely sets of ideas are having their variety generating potential diminished.

In general: it seems that we must add to the theory of the homeostat, and its blind entropic process, a self-organizing capability which tends to reinforce survival-worthy patterns within the variety generator. This is done by the pain–pleasure (algedonic) loop, the reward function, teaching, bribing, the epigenetic landscape—what the mechanism is most aptly called depends on the kind of organism being considered. But it is unequivocally clear, despite the confused terminology, what this feedback loop does. It interferes with the alleged randomness with which the variety generator poses solutions, as well as vetoing further attempts to pose the same unsatisfactory solution as before. It biases the throw of the dice. Unlike some workers, I believe that no precise statistical formulation of the effect on conditional probabilities is necessary. Nature does not need an exact or even closely predictable process here; nor does the cybernetician. It is enough that the mutations of an adapting system should not be entirely hazardous, but should be biased, for positive feedback can be relied upon to steer the progressive bias towards viable behaviour—once the bias exists. This is what the self-organizing capability means. It is extremely interesting that no-one seems ever to have observed a viable system (organic or not) in which mutation is 'strictly random'. In fact, it is notorious that science cannot quite satisfactorily define what 'genuine' randomness is. This may well be because the concept is a mathematical artefact, which does not match any observable process in the systemic world. That world is self-organizing, and it must have 'biased randomness' as a raw material.

So the teleology of development can be described by the type of machinery discussed in these chapters: it is mapped on to the general concept of a self-organizing system. Moreover, it becomes more and more clear that the laws which govern such systems are relatively few. If we envisage any self-organizing system as modelled by a high-variety homeostat, having requisite variety, obeying the information-theoretic rules regarding connectivity and channel capacity, and now as having its internal variety generators continuously modified by conditional probabilities which are reading off success and failure from the environment, we shall observe a viable system.

The entropic process which drives self-organization is still homeostasis, but we have learned here not to think of it as blind. Viable governors are still entropy-driven, but the variety generation yielding proliferated states from which successful patterns must be selected is conditioned from outside. Some of this influence doubtless antedates the system's own behaviour by means of coenetic variables, as discussed before. A coenetic variable diminishes proliferating variety by preempting certain sets of the possible range of sets of states. Secondly, variety is diminished by feedback of an annihilating kind—based on environmentally tested mutations found wanting, as in Darwinism.

Thirdly, variety is cut back by a learning mechanism which biases the alleged randomness of mutations—thereby creating an epigenetic landscape, as in Waddington's theory.

This is what the ecosystem is all about: *responsive* mutation. It gives the homeostat a task which at last can be done in the time available. The species can evolve, the individual can learn. The viable system, of whatever kind, can adapt. This is a control device which takes the fortuitousness out of randomness. Instead of meaning 'totally unpredictable in form and content', random means 'largely predictable in form, though not in content'. This was the very definition advanced, in quite another context, for a stochastic process. And learning, adaptation and evolution are indeed stochastic processes, monitored and conditioned in special ways by feedback through the algedonic loop. This chapter began by asserting that ecosystems are the archetypes of self-organization. But a more complete understanding, as taught by nature, of what self-organization involves reveals why (to the observer imbued with teleological insights) these systems appear to be purposive. The self-organizing system with the threefold responsive mutation device discussed here may be called a *sentient ecosystem*.

15

CONTROLLING
ENTERPRISES

Si loin que la Science pousse sa découverte du Feu
Essentiel, si capable devienne-t-elle un jour de
remodeler et de parfaire l'élément humain, elle se
retrouvera toujours, au bout du compte, face au même
problème posé: comment donner à tous et à chacun
de ces éléments leur valeur finale en les groupant dans
l'unité d'un Tout Organizé?

However far Science pushes its discovery of the
Essential Fire, however capable it may one day
become of reshaping and perfecting the human
element, it will still find itself in the end confronting
the same problem: how to give their final value to all
and to each of these elements in grouping them within
the unity of an Organized Whole.

PIERRE TEILHARD DE CHARDIN in *Le Phénomène Humain* (1955)

1   *Laissez-faire* and Direction

In the last chapter but one a cybernetic model was devised through
which operational research is enabled to provide the manager with an
integral scheme for the control of operations under his command. But
the enterprise as such is something more than the totality of operations:
it is a whole organism. The term enterprise, by the way, is used here to
denote the firm, and indeed any kind of massive undertaking such as a
quasi-monopolistic industry, a public service corporation, or a national
transport, education or health service.

Any such enterprise should certainly be regarded as an ecosystem. It
is by its very nature a complex organic entity, interacting with an en-

vironment. Moreover, because of its immensely high variety, it has to be a self-organizing system to a large degree. To handle it at all, as manager or minister, we have to understand it as indivisible. The purpose of this chapter is to determine, with the guidance of the general considerations advanced in the last chapter, which principles of cybernetics can be invoked to institute and maintain the control of the enterprise.

The task is almost terrifying, and one which has very largely been given up by practising managers. They rely mostly on the self-organizing properties of sub-systems, which they seek to link together by a macro-structure of relative simplicity which they can understand. And indeed it has to be admitted that the human head cannot contain all the variety of which the enterprise is such a potent generator. But courage may be drawn from the fact that to find a means of contemplating the enterprise as an organic whole is much less a problem, after all, than finding a way of treating life itself as meaningful—and this is a problem faced by every human being. It is for this reason that the words of Père Teilhard have been chosen to state the major thesis above. Here was a French Jesuit who was also a palaeontologist; his was a book which attempted to give a conspectus of the entire history of the world, in an evolutionary sweep passing from inorganic to organic, from inanition to sentience, from awareness to self-consciousness, from mental to spiritual. This is the ultimate among organic wholes: the ecosystem of man. Undaunted by the magnitude of the task, Père Teilhard put forward an integral treatment of the entire range of human knowledge and belief. Always, as in the passage quoted, he adhered with the utmost tenacity to the notion of the organic integration of things, of the organized whole. His book is a contemporary re-statement, in terms of modern science, of the Axiom of Internal Relations of which we have already spoken. It is a triumph; it both heartens and guides the man whose target is to understand nothing more than a vast enterprise in its integral state.

The enterprise, then, is an organic whole. It is a homeostat built of homeostats. It is an ultrastable machine. It is, very largely, a self-organizing system. We know a lot about its control in detail, ranging from the highly developed business methods, which are now widely taught, to the cybernetic treatment of its operations. But we have yet to discuss its macrostructure. How in fact does one do cybernetic engineering on the architecture of an enterprise, and how in practice does one seek to influence a system composed of such directed energies? For it is not enough to say of a self-organizing system that it is ultrastable. That characteristic entails robustness and a capability to survive, it is true. But it tells us nothing of any criterion of success which is external to these aims. The interesting thing about an enterprise, on the other hand, is that once these homeostatic conditions have been fulfilled, the 'owners' of the system seek to discuss its future in a metalanguage. The operational managers speak the language of the system: they are content that it should survive in a stable condition, that it should make a profit which is a guarantee of its future, that it should learn from its own experience, evolve and adapt. But at a higher echelon there are the policy-makers: those for whom this state of affairs is necessary but not sufficient; those who would re-direct the *motives* of the enterprise as distinct from its *aims*.

These are the gods of the system. To the operational managers of the firm, they are the directors who represent the shareholders; to the civil service, they are (or ought to be) the political masters who represent the electorate. Thus it is perfectly possible for a self-regulating engineering company, for example, to evolve satisfactorily as a supplier of markets—even to diversify its products, to re-design them and to change the entire technology of production and distribution. But it is as inconceivable that such an engineering company should suddenly become a publishing house or a shipyard as it is to suppose that a dog should suddenly evolve into a rabbit. With a sufficiently strong notion of the organic wholeness of nature and its history, it is not impossible to envisage such a change as occurring *eventually*—because one can contemplate the infinitely large number of tiny yet directed mutations which might carry the former state to the latter. But the heads of enterprises are distinguished by their ability to take decisions of this kind overnight. Their problem of control is to know what to do to the ultrastable self-organizing enterprise which will give effect to the new policies which reflect a change of motivation. This need is nowhere more apparent than in the government sphere, since a change of party in power presupposes a change of fundamental political motivation.

Moreover, and although we have accustomed ourselves in this book to thinking of the dynamic forces generated inside an enterprise as susceptible to intrinsic control, the self-organizing posture taken up may be unsatisfactory. It is clear that in the language of the system itself it cannot be unsatisfactory, because it is directed towards viability and survival. But in a metalanguage, in terms of which the gods of the system seek to implement their own changes of heart, it is possible that this posture will be regarded as self-defeating.

It is the pathology of self-organizing systems to take a self-defeating turn. Some evolutionary adaptations, such as the increasing size and weight of prehistoric animals, which were viable learning systems in one language, turned out to be metalinguistically defeating. That is to say, some of these animals paid so much attention to relatively short-term ecological adaptations (such as the securing of food and other necessities) that they failed to notice as it were the unendurable strain the adaptations placed on their own internal economy. Many of them became far too large in size to support themselves mechanically. The only animal fitting this description which has survived to this day is the whale, which took the weight off its legs and the strain off its heart by entering the water and acquiring new mechanical support from there. But companies and economies can overload their internal structure in the search for ecological viability: the firm may over-sell and over-commit; the economy may encounter a balance of payments crisis with the countries with whom it too anxiously trades. Especially, the size of the enterprise as measured by the variety it generates may result in a kind of organizational elephantiasis. This pathological condition, already visible in some large firms, some quasi-monopolistic industries and some massive governmental schemes, is due to a self-defeating quality in adaptation.

A self-defeating system, in short, is one which succeeds in its self-appraising language and fails in the metalanguage of its top direction. Since this explanation is becoming turgid, the point may be illustrated anecdotally. Two very sick patients lie in adjacent hospital beds separated by a screen. The one who is less ill rouses himself to enquire of his neighbour: 'How are you this morning?' The man in the next bed, anxious to reciprocate, rouses himself to a supreme effort. 'Fine', he shouts back; and the effort kills him. Or again, consider the interesting logic of the following epigram written by the sixteenth-century English poet and mystic John Donne:

> *Thy Father all from thee, by his last Will,*
> *Gave to the poore; Thou hast good title still.*

It is the function of executive management to make the effort to respond when interrogated by the market, and to cut subsidiary companies out of its will if this seems sensible. It is the function of the board to observe, metalinguistically, when these executive adaptations will prove self-defeating in larger terms. We shall now see how this pathological insight reflects on the most basic of all disagreements about the organization of enterprises.

Comment has been made more than once already about the way in which the human mind seems impelled to declare false or at least artificial dichotomies about the world. In the matter of controlling enterprises, there is in the minds of many a dichotomy between the *laissez-faire* and mandatory approaches. As is well known, the *laissez-faire* economy was originally conceived as one in which all producers were allowed to make what they liked; the term has been extended and is now generally used to refer to any theory of control which relies upon a natural system of checks and balances between the sub-systems of the whole. What could be more closely analogous to the self-organizing system as defined by cybernetics than that? The mandatory approach to control, on the other hand, declares that the *laissez-faire* mechanism is too slow, too arbitrary, and likely to involve local and short term disbalances. These may be acceptable in some inanimate system or even in a population of cabbage aphides; but they are not acceptable in a human society where they may involve pockets of high unemployment, severe poverty and social injustice of other kinds. So the mandatory controller declares that human reason should be able to triumph over these environmental difficulties, and do better than the (apparently more natural) system which relies on intrinsic control. Thus is justified an economy based on forward planning, on regulations of various kinds such as licensing, and on the political mandate of the governor to govern. And what could be more closely analogous to a hierarchical neural network as defined by cybernetics than that?

In other words, there is *some* cybernetic justification for using either of these approaches; but there are two points to note. Firstly, whereas either of these systems may work in practice for a given epoch of time, each may easily turn into a self-defeating system. The *laissez-faire* economy may become so preoccupied with its own stability as to run down and die of high entropy; or it may become an ecological centrifuge which is so outward-looking in the search for nourishment (in foreign markets for instance) as to wreck its own interior, delicately balanced, economy. The mandatory system, on the contrary, may become so powerful that it overrules the self-organizing homeostats of the sub-systems altogether, so that they become de-natured. If this happens, the control will fail: because it cannot supply requisite variety without this aid. The second point is this. Although both these approaches masquerade as theoretical solutions to the problems they seek to handle, they are not intellectually neutral approaches to the facts. The head of a firm will choose one or other of these alternatives as a matter of temperament, just because he is like that, while convincing himself that this is the logical way to behave. The political party will choose one or the other, as determined by its own social history, while attempting to show the electorate that this is the logical way to behave. In fact, and in both cases, the proponents of either course have selected *one* of a variety of available models, and have declared that real life works like this. Roughly speaking, the doctrinaire *laissez-faire* man is backing a model of the ecological system, and the doctrinaire controller is adopting a model from the neurological system.

Now we know from the general philosophy of science as applied to operational research that every system maps on to every other system, that any model 'will do'. We spoke of a 'triangulation process', whereby a variety of models would be mapped on to the problem situation and conclusions drawn from an insight which would be an amalgam of them all. If this is not done, after all, the particular scientific model adopted will provide the scientist with a structured phase space, surrounded by thought blocks, every bit as arbitrary and every bit as dangerous as the one that the manager has become conditioned to accept by virtue of his experience. In the present case, we want neither of these models; because they are manifestly partial. If we are to adopt a useful model of an organic system, we must use a model taken from an organic system. Only a complex creature, such as a man himself, provides an adequate model, for he has problems of *both* internal and external adjustment to contend with.

Given such a model, which will be developed in more detail in succeeding sections of this chapter, it is interesting to observe at once that a great deal of the talk which is customarily applied to the enterprise can be seen to be incompetent. Why do people talk (another dichotomy this) about the relative merits of centralization and decentralization? Because this seems to be a clear-cut issue on which a decision is required. But it is so only within the context of an inadequate and partial model. To take instead the model of a man, and then to ask such a question, quickly shows the dichotomy to be absurd. If the reader were centralized, in the sense in which some would advocate that enterprises should be centralized, so that all decisions of any weight whatsoever must be consciously monitored at the top, we should find the autonomous nervous system abolished. Thus, for example, the reader would have to remember to keep his heart beating—however interested he became in these paragraphs. If he became too interested, he would drop dead over the book; and although this would constitute an impressive effect from the author's point of view it would do little good to anyone. On the other hand, if the reader were quite decentralized, in the way advocated by some theorists about the enterprise, his autonomous nervous system would *really* be autonomous; in this case, and again however interested he became in these words, a mild feeling of thirst overtaking him would cause him to rush from the room in search of water. No: the dichotomy is ridiculous. One could claim, perhaps, that the economy of a man is some judicious blend of the centralized and decentralized control arrangements; but how judicious is 'judicious'? To define what one means by this blend is as difficult a problem as the one with which we began—so the dichotomy of control procedures helps not at all to resolve it.

Many other arguments that are classically put forward in economic, social and political theory can be demolished by cognate arguments. Questions of monopoly, including in these days questions of nationalization, quite certainly belong to this class. Political tempers become roused about such issues, precisely because neither side can possibly be right or possibly wrong. The question is formulated within an incompetent model. If Society has to decide how to control primary industry which is, of its very nature, monopolistic in character, then it should do so by seeking a cybernetic model which provides the kind of control that will give the effects which are desired—and these *effects* are not too difficult to define. What is difficult, and what makes the whole question so fraught with electoral danger, is the attempt to specify a mode of control in a language which makes sociological sense to the electorate and operational sense to the managers in charge of the industry simultaneously. This seems to be formally impossible because, although we are talking about the same *thing*, we are talking about two different ecosystems mapped on to two different models. In short: we try to deduce the control system from a preconceived model in which there is a *belief*, instead of doing the operational research work required to specify a model in which the language of the control system is meaningful to both the electorate and the operational people at the same time.

There is much the same dilemma about so large a national issue as the foreign market orientation of a country. Great disquiet has existed in Britain as to whether the country should join the European Economic Community (the so-called Common Market), or whether it should seek to create an equivalently coherent marketing system inside the British Commonwealth. Interestingly, the protagonists of both points of view each selected a model, declaring this in advance to be 'right', the language of which was competent to express only the one conclusion or the other. Thus, for instance, one group (led by the then Prime Minister) declared that common marketing is possible only among nations of equivalent technological advancement. The attempt to resolve this problem in terms of that model, not surprisingly, points to an inevitable conclusion: Europe. There is in fact no other choice. And of course, once this model has been adopted, one cannot even express the argument that perhaps countries of inequivalent technological advancement could very well collaborate, using the entropy of the system as measured by technological imbalance precisely as the driving force of marketing. Conversely, the other group adopted a model based on an historical conception of Britain's role in the world. Once this model is adopted, Commonwealth marketing is the only answer. It becomes impossible now even to express the counter argument that a new economic bloc is emerging in a Western Europe which by definition includes Britain, for the model states as part of its own structure that Britain is *not* included in Western Europe. So how can anybody be so absurd as to think it should join the European community at all?

We could say in the terms of straightforward logic that the parties were incurring the fallacy of *petitio principii*, in which the conclusions are assumed in the premises; but that kind of analysis impresses no-one. The reason is that the conceptual models we adopt are far more potent than the propositional assumptions we put forward in the course of debate. The latter can be challenged and perhaps falsified; the former structure the universe for the speaker and make it impossible for him to know what the opposition is saying. This mechanism seems to be characteristic of all political argument in particular, and also of the kind of argument which arises in a firm of a heavily institutional kind. The 'old family business', for example, knows what it is, why it is there and how it works. Any suggestions about the modifications of these tenets, which ought to be entertained in a changing world, will be met with heated rebuffs—on the basis that the adviser has not properly understood what this firm is all about.

To summarize, then, the contention is that many of the great arguments, the unresolved dilemmas, about the ways in which enterprises should be controlled are chimerical. The possibilities are herded together into two massive camps which are in contradiction, and each of these camps propounds a model of the problem in which its own thesis alone can be expressed. Hence no cognizance can be taken of the opposed viewpoint; hence no compromise solution can in principle be evolved. In practice we encounter compromise solutions, for the simple reason that neither side proves capable of effecting an isomorphic mapping of its own defective model on to the real world. Policies for adaptation, then, as expressed in terms of the language appropriate in any one model, turn out to be self-defeating in terms of the metalanguage of any higher-order model which could subsume the two. It has been shown that both the *laissez-faire* and the mandatory schemes of control rely upon partial models, mapping respectively on to different bits of the structure of organic control as found in nature. It remains to specify a model of higher order, based on an integral notion of what constitutes a self-organizing system.

2 The Cybernetic Solution

It is against this background and armed with the insights of cybernetics in the previous chapter, that we come to consider the control of the enterprise. To be crisp: there is no doubt whatever that the enterprise has to be very largely a self-organizing system; nor is there any doubt that the *laissez-faire* approach to it reveals gross inadequacies, which nevertheless are not to be remedied by the installation of mandatory controls. A paradox is revealed; this is immensely important, because it does appear to be precisely the paradox with which the enterprise (whether in industry, business or government) is faced in a free, democratic and mature country such as Britain in the second half of the twentieth century. Most of our affairs are in precisely this state, and it will not do.

The resolution of the paradox is not at all difficult to find, once a grasp of managerial cybernetics has been obtained. We can adhere to the largely black-box homeostat-of-homeostats system approach; but in order to make it work we have to enrich the structure of the system that constitutes the enterprise under study. Homeostats consisting of a large number of interrelated sub-systems will not work unless they are very richly interconnected. This was entirely clear from Ashby's original work; it becomes an unassailable conclusion in practical affairs, once they are studied cybernetically. Secondly, it is perfectly possible to super-impose a hierarchical organizational structure upon the self-organizing system, provided the reason for doing this is borne continuously in mind. We must neither regard it as a fiction, powerless in the face of the colossal inertia of the homeostat itself, nor must we regard it as the 'real' control which is hidden from all except the *cognoscenti*. For here is a false dichotomy once more.

Many thinkers have adopted the first view, including representatives of widely divergent psychologies; and their philosophies affect our thinking, for they are part of the cultural inheritance of man. In Zen Buddhism, for example, as in the meditations of some Western Christian mystics, we find the notion that the world outside ourselves is not for structuring. The world happens to us, and its own structure is meaningless or irrelevant. Even when the structure outside is recognized, and acknowledged as critically relevant to ourselves, the role of the individual lies in a passive submission to that structure. The idea is found in

Leninism, for all its revolutionary appeal; the idea is found in Karma-Yoga, within the Hindu ethic. The former accords to the dictator special rights, which accounts for successful purges within the hierarchic structure—and for the fact that the dictator's activity is doomed to become a self-defeating system. The latter accounts for a caste system which makes social evolution virtually impossible. Strangely, the Karma teaching turns up in the peace and quiet of Victorian England: 'God bless the squire and his relations, and keep us in our proper stations.' One finds traces of all this in modern Existentialism too. So many outlooks, so many divergent views, and yet there is a common notion of control for the individual *vis-à-vis* society. The part is less than nothing in relation to the whole, and either cannot or should not seek to influence it.

The other half of the dichotomy comes sometimes from thinkers, more usually from men of action. It asserts the right of the individual, and his capability, to structure the world outside. This is the philosophy of fight, of non-acceptance. It leads to individual heroism and to piracy; to empire building and to the welfare state. From it comes Fascism and aristocracy; it accounts for the concealed (and therefore potentially irresponsible) authoritarianism of the 'inner wheel' in an apparently democratic constitution—whether in politics or in business. Its temperament is different from the former class; but with the temperament comes theory—to justify, to rationalize.

If we adhere to the organic model, as advocated in the last section, we can see the cybernetic validity of a control system based on objective assessment of effective results. It requires that we escape both from temperamental notions of what is best, and from theories that are conceived *in vacuo*. The thought block that obstructs the view is immense, for we have been brought up and educated in a world which accepts some implicit belief as to the nature of control on this scale. We have also learned, if our wits have been sharp, that the system (whichever it is) to which we are thereby conditioned does not actually work. Therefore the skilled manager tends to experiment with the *opposite* view. This is why management consultants, or new company chairmen, quite typically attempt to destroy a centralized management structure in favour of a branch-autonomous one—and vice versa. What is the objective, scientific approach?

Firstly, the richly interconnected homeostat that constitutes the self-organizing system must take priority as the only means of obtaining coherence in a situation of such high variety that no other technique of control can be sustained for long. Secondly, the hierarchic system which is superimposed upon it, or rather by which it is implicitly informed, can be seen as that arrangement which speeds up the operation of homeostasis, and which can evoke quick responses when danger is threatened. Above all, that structure is needed which can choose between a mode of survival which is viable yet unprogressive in terms of some intellectually selected criterion (for homeostats operating in a given language do not generate ideals expressed in a metalanguage), and a mode of survival which is viable yet progressive in these terms. There is a simple but quite fundamental distinction here. Any viable system is evolutionary, a learning and (in part) optimizing creature. But its teleology is an artefact: it is something understood *post hoc*. It is, as was seen in Chapter 14, driven by a 'purpose' which is defined by the 'goals' it did in fact hit. It is only the forecasting, forward planning, *intending* human mind which chooses goals on the basis of deliberately formulated ideals. These *ante-hoc* goals constitute the metalinguistic policies of enterprises.

Now it is obvious that if we seek to have an enterprise which can attain a goal formulated in advance, but whose structure and mechanism is that appropriate to an organism whose goals are formulated only with hindsight, then our managerial task is one of *organizational design*. The job is to modify the structure, without destroying the self-organizing properties of the system, so that the goals it 'just happens' to achieve (the ones recognizable only after the event) turn out to be the goals which the human managers wished to attain all the time. In the arena of policy-making, the brilliant manager (be he government minister or company director) knows intuitively that this is what he has to do. And because the whole of the mechanism by which he operates is verbal, inter-personal and political, he is able to achieve his ends. Politics is the art of building organic structure into a universe of discourse, of debate, of climate of opinion. An analysis of any major policy-making manœuvre reveals this elaborate structuring of ideas: how certain opinions are used to neutralize each other so that a third opinion (apparently less cogent than the other two) becomes acceptable by default; how individual personalities behave homeostatically and produce the kind of expectant deadlock in which some one personality becomes uniquely acceptable as being the only common member of the sub-sets of preferred states. Then the way in which hierarchical structure in argument and the command of opinion is floated within this self-organizing is also clear: we talk about it in terms of loyalties, of personal ascendancies and of character. But when the same task is faced in the control of the enterprise (which included the political level of control), there arises a much wider realm of things, relationships and even people which are quite outside the policy-making group.

It is this part of the system which people, for all their intuition, do not seem to understand how to engineer. They lose the subtlety they show in political matters, and begin to plump for one half of the false dichotomy. Lower down in the enterprise, moreover, as the lower echelons are reached, it is not even so simple a matter as a dichotomy with which we have to deal. Rather do we discover a universe broken up into a great many mutually exclusive categories. Thus in government, each ministry is set up to deal with an aspect of affairs, as if it could cope with that aspect *in vacuo*, whereas in truth no one aspect can be supervised without the intimate collaboration of all the others. So in industry, there are directors of production, sales, finance, engineering and research for whom the same is true. We try to put these pieces together again by an overriding amalgam of their interests, calling the result a cabinet in the field of government and a directorate in the field of business. But the most elementary analysis of self-organizing systems shows that the interactions obtainable at this level, if they are not mirrored all the way down, are impotent to produce the cohesion of the entire enterprise which is essential. To use the model of the living organism, it is as if we created a frontal lobe of a brain and a group of autonomous control systems throughout the body, and omitted altogether to furnish the system with the older parts of the brain which do in fact mediate all sensation and all motor activity, co-ordinating the autonomous functions of local control centres on the one hand, and infusing the whole with conation and volition on the other.

Cybernetic insights show, in particular, that the totality of the organization ought to be made up of building-blocks that will be called *quasi-independent domains*. This is the compromise notion lying between actually independent domains (decentralization) and no domains at all (centralization). These domains have a certain local autonomy and may (in their own language) claim to be altogether autonomous. But they are not autonomous in the metalanguage of the whole system, which monitors their activity according to the laws of cybernetics. Managers will recognize that this is what enterprises are really like; only the languages are not properly distinguished and may prove incompetent to express the facts properly. The extent to which the domains are (metalinguistically) independent derives from the need for local fluctuation without which local homeostasis, still more local learning, is impossible. Without this local facility, the organism certainly explodes—from a lack of requisite variety. All nature is replete with examples. Without local facilities for biochemical interchange inside the brain, the overall cerebral balance of oxygen and carbon dioxide (for instance) would be strictly impossible: any attempt to achieve this control in a centralized way would turn the interaction of localities into a self-defeating system. This is observed in pathological states when the mechanism goes wrong. Similarly, in the sphere of electrical activity, it seems likely that a lack of local independence in solving problems of electrical balance is the defect responsible for epilepsy. On the other hand, it is vital that all these local controls be *mediated* centrally; otherwise they will sub-optimize and destroy the total system by (as it were) internecine strife.

Thus the design of the control that is needed for enterprises lacks (what can be thought of as) a central nervous system. What we see of control in industry is a collection of separate and specialist functions: order processing, sales allocation, demand forecasting, forward planning, plant programming, machine loading, stock controlling, order pro-gressing, production controlling, dispatch sequencing, invoice process-ing, cost accounting, budgetary controlling, and perhaps some other monitory activities. Ludicrously, each of these activities may be caught laying claim to being the key mechanism of managerial control. In fact, as the senior management knows and the careful observer can detect, the success of the enterprise depends upon the ability of the senior managers to coalesce these many activities into some central theme. But the theme remains notional; there is no physical, tangible, substantial thread—such as the central nervous system itself provides in the body. Hence all the modes of control that are visible, are no more than out-ward signs of control-like activities which have no ultimate connection. They are epiphenomena of a central control which does not actually exist.

The same is precisely true of government enterprises, except that financial control is more utterly dominant than it is in industry—where technological and entrepreneurial enthusiasms reduce its force. Yet from a cybernetic point of view, the appearance of a central thread of control contributed by the Treasury is even more misleading than the appearance in industry of no central thread at all. For all one can actually get hold of in the exercise of financial controls at the government level are indeed epiphenomena themselves. The point is that they speak powerfully of a central *thing*, driven by an overriding fiscal policy. Yet there is in truth no such thing, and the fiscal policy belongs to the class of goals that are recognized with hindsight. For national budgets are not goals that are met. Either they are exceeded, because the self-organizing system that is the economy causes them to be exceeded in the struggle for viability; or else they are adhered to by force—it is always possible to refuse to pay out more money than one had allowed for. But in the latter case, an

economic oscillation is at once set up by the refusal to allow this particular parameter of the system to take up its natural (that is, homeostatically determined) value. Thus politicians habitually claim that constraints
which have artificially been clamped on to a homeostat, with sadly unphysiological results, were in fact goals which the system has met. It is
the same trouble: the organizational structure of the economy is not
sufficiently rich or well designed to procure outputs which satisfy predetermined goals *of its own natural operation*. And once that prerequisite
of a self-organizing system is falsified, overall success can be attained
only if conscious and directed intervention in the system can itself be
sustained throughout. But of course this is impossible—by the law of
requisite variety.

Some attempt will now be made to expound what the structure of a
control system for the enterprise should be like: an essentially self-
organizing system, with hierarchical overtones. It is a control system
which operates itself, but which can be monitored from on high, and
given new directions towards predetermined goals which it does not
itself recognize and of which it cannot indeed be made aware.

3   The Structure of Institutional Information

A practical system for achieving these ends in an enterprise must face up
squarely to the following problem. A situation to be controlled is of
immensely high variety, and if all this variety is allowed to impinge
directly on to a control centre (whether a management group or a
computer) two quite disastrous results will follow.

The first is that, in order to sort out such vast input, the controlling
centre must itself be enormously large. No management group, indeed,
can be conceived which would be sufficiently large for the purpose—
this is why the trick of averaging has been so extensively developed in
the provision of institutional information. Unfortunately, really senior
management receives data which are actually averages of averages of
averages, and this means that only biased estimates of global means are
available, while the most vital movements in the outside world are all
too readily obscured. When it comes to the possibility of using a computer, people imagine that this problem can be dismissed. All the raw
data can be ingested. But that is not the case; calculations have been
made to show that a computer competent to accept *directly* an undifferentiated input of such high variety would have to be so big that its
area would cover approximately 100 square miles. But of course technological progress continues, and we pass from the miniaturization of

electronic components through micro-miniaturization to molecular engineering; so it is just possible that this difficulty might one day be overcome.

Even so, the second problem, which is more basic, would remain. If we imagine an on-going control of the kind envisaged, its central operation is quite clearly one of homeostasis. Now, if a homeostat in an equilibrial state be bombarded without respite by wave after wave of input data, it will go into an oscillation from which it can never recover. That is to say, and here we encounter the practical version of the theoretical argument advanced in a previous chapter, if the periodicity of the input is very much faster than the cycle time of the homeostat itself, then clearly it has no opportunity to settle. This means in practice that the policy of the enterprise as manifested in an actual plan of campaign would become chaotic. Every order sent from control to the enterprise would be rescinded and countermanded before the physical mechanisms of the business could possibly carry it out.

The problem is exactly of the form to which the discussion of the last chapter led us. The high variety of the external world has to undergo a many–one transformation before it is allowed to impinge on the central control. And we have discovered something of the way in which this ought to happen.

In the first place, it is necessary to transduce information about the enterprise into the control system. This transduction is an isomorphic mapping: we require a one–one correspondence between what is actually going on and what the control system 'knows' is going on. Such a transduction can be envisaged as any kind of recording system, whether manual or automatic. But it will certainly be convenient and in keeping with the state of technological progress if the latter case is more seriously contemplated. Mechanical, electrical, photo-electric and electronic means can be used to detect the information sought. A range of so-called data-capture devices is already available for the purpose, though not widely used. Doubtless the range ought to be extended and codified. However, this phase presents no real problem.

The next phase consists in a many–one variety reduction of these data. The machinery for this should be thought of as an echelon of small, rather simple black boxes, each receiving a sub-set of the inputs, and emitting a single output. The operation here is closely analogous to that described in Chapter 13 for the control of operations. It will be recalled that (for instance) we have a measure of industrial output if we take the weight of the product. But variations in this weight may well be meaningless, in so far as a collection of the variables influences it. Certainly we must avoid hitting the delicate equilibrium of the central homeostat with an input which declares that the weight of output is halved (thereby throwing the control into violent activity), if the reason why it is halved is known to be that the cross-sectional area of the product has been reduced to the point where it is twice as long for unit weight. Equivalently, there is no point in causing terrible trouble within the homeostatic control centre by saying that demand today has suddenly halved, if the reason turns out to be that (over a large area of the market) yesterday was a public holiday, with the result that demand tomorrow is doubled. That is to say, the black box dealing with these inputs will need to operate such devices as exponential smoothing techniques in order to make legitimate variety reductions for onward transmission of the data.

Similar types of argument can be put forward for every area of activity within the enterprise, although there is a problem which must be noted at once. Some mixtures of input are fixed by physical constants and determined relationships and this makes it possible to specify them with complete confidence in advance. In these cases the box, far from being black, may be almost transparent. But in the case of genuinely black boxes, we shall have to posit a learning system within the black box, which is also evolutionary, adaptive and teleological in the sense recently described. But the genuinely black boxes of Chapter 13 were competent to handle this difficulty where *operations* were concerned; there is in fact no difficulty in designing a precisely similar system to handle other kinds of input such as market states, and the financial and personnel situations. Furthermore, the statistical transformations, extensively studied in Chapter 13, by which the output of these many–one black boxes ought to be transformed to eliminate the noise of statistically insignificant variation, will also be fully applicable.

It is at this point that the arguments contrasting the apparently mutually exclusive alternatives of a *laissez-faire* and a planned strategy become relevant. It was suggested that, on the model of the living organism, the strategies are *not* mutually exclusive, but that a mixed strategy can be played. In fact, in the account of controlling operations, such a mixed strategy was seen at work. In Figure 45, the conclusions of Chapter 13 are redrawn, in order to reveal the extent to which what we have hitherto called a black box is actually transparent. This is purely a recapitulation; but the new terminology of transparency and opaqueness, as applied to black boxes and the new type of diagram, will be needed for what follows.

In Figure 45, then, the familiar amœboid shape at the top represents a world situation. The box marked *T* is a fully-thought-out transformer of the inputs regarded as relevant: six are drawn here. The output of this transformer is, as before, a pure number which blends the inputs: it is the mean of a statistical distribution of recent events. The many–one variety transformer that is actually part of the control system is represented by the large gridded square. The large dots in the compartments of the first row are transduced inputs in their raw state. These are combined together, according to a pre-set formula, which reproduces the

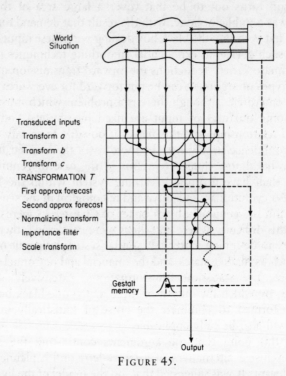

World
Situation

T

Transduced inputs
Transform *a*
Transform *b*
Transform *c*
TRANSFORMATION *T*
First approx forecast
Second approx forecast
Normalizing transform
Importance filter
Scale transform

Gestalt
memory

Output

FIGURE 45.

transformation *T*. Hence the transforms marked *a*, *b* and *c* are pre-ordained blending operations and routeing instructions. They lead to the heavily marked compartment depicting the result which is obtained *now*, if the processes which set up the generalized transformation *T* are gone through for the present state of the situation. To this point, then, the box is transparent. No self-organizing characteristic has yet entered the system. In the next row, however, the weight of previous experience is applied to the answer. The arrow entering the situation from the right represents the output of an entire system, centred on box *T*, such as that depicted in Figure 44.

This is to say that the output from transformation T as measured *now*, is read off (as if it were the final output of the box) and compared with the generalized experience stored in box T. Thus the result of coalescing the crude inputs is treated as the output of a theoretical model, and it is now referred to codified experience to produce a first approximate forecast. At this point in the design we have the best kind of estimate which can be made using analysis—both of the structure of the situation, and of the totality of experience in stock when the system was set up. But, as happened before in Chapter 13, this estimate can now be taken off to a dynamic control centre in which *current* experience is constantly being sampled and recorded. This experience is being continuously codified by its statistical pattern, and provides the sampling framework against which the immediate forecasting problem will be solved. It is labelled 'gestalt memory' in Figure 45. When a further adjustment has been made from this source, the trajectory of the coalesced input is moved into the next row, called 'second approximate forecast'. This operation is entirely opaque, because no-one can say why current experience weights the conclusion in the way it does. Yet the second approximation itself is viewed through a transparent window—it can now be inspected, at the least.

So far the situation has been treated as static; and indeed the location of this point on the trajectory will not change unless the feedback from the comparator changes. This can only happen infrequently, because the statistical criteria applied to the building up of the store of generalized experience in the gestalt memory recognize significant changes alone. But once the behaviour of this system is viewed dynamically, once *time* is as it were switched on, the real-life raw inputs to the box will begin to vary. Therefore the first approximation will vary, and so will the second (even though the relationship between the two remains the same —namely that read off from the box T feedback). If this happens, the output of the box will continuously vary—this is depicted by the wavy line of small dots emerging from the diagram from the second approximation row—and it is precisely this chance variation which must not be allowed to impinge unnecessarily on the central control later on.

Hence further transformations are required before the output can be allowed to escape. Three of these are readily identifiable and are shown in Figure 45. The first one is a normalizing transform. The 'quality' of the number representing the second approximation is only to be understood in terms of the mathematical set of which it is a member. For this is no longer a straightforward measurement of the world, but a ratio computed from a comparison of the perceived state of affairs and recollections of past experience. The set of such numbers will constitute a statistical distribution that is markedly skewed—because the representation of experience is a ratio having a finite upper bound of unity. Thus, since it will be valuable for control purposes later on to treat outputs from this box as belonging to a Gaussian distribution, it is necessary to modify the second approximation. This can be done by applying a statistical transformation (such as the inverse sine)—which was precisely the device used in the operational control of Chapter 13. The second operation, called here an importance filter, is also familiar. This exists to eliminate variety, where variety constitutes noise as measured by a statistical test. And again this is an operation depicted in Figure 44. The third of the transformations has not been encountered before. This is simply a scale modifier. For this is one black box of many that will be needed in the total system, and it will be advantageous to have the outputs of them all varying over the same range. So the final operation is not one that affects the structure of the system: it simply alters one of its conventions.

It is to be hoped that this exposition, up to this point, can readily be seen to recapitulate the operational control theory of Chapter 13. The all-important feature is preserved: namely, that which comes out of boxes of this kind should not without good reason propose problems to the homeostatic controller. But instead of the elaborate structure of the original theory, in which various absolutely opaque black boxes operated alongside various transparent boxes, the whole thing has been enclosed in a quasi-black box. This has only two genuinely opaque operations: those resulting in the first and second approximate forecasts. Operations prior to these are transparent; and the final three transformations might be labelled 'cloudy'. The reason for this is that we know precisely what the transformations are doing in principle, but are certainly not going to inspect these compartments of the system to discover why.

Only now do we reach the nub of the present argument. In a cybernetic system for the control of the enterprise, we require a large number of features (those discussed in Chapter 14) which were not present in the operational control system. The reason is that the enterprise as a whole talks a metalanguage in which the language of operations can be disputed. Hence, although we were right to make the upper half of this box transparent for the former purpose, its structural rigidity is inimical to the organic wholeness of the enterprise as such. As was seen in the previous section, we require some self-organizing freedom in place of the structural rigidity—for the precise algorithm which determines transformation T must be open to modification by an adapting, evolutionary organism. On the other hand, as we said when discussing biological evolution, it would not be feasible to allow the transduced inputs to this box to combine themselves in arbitrary ways, mutating their connections for ever, for a viable result simply would not emerge in a reasonable time. Freedom there must be, but a freedom constrained by experience.

Therefore the pattern of squiggly lines representing transforms *a*, *b* and *c* is to be treated as the epigenetic landscape of this transformer. Moreover, the cloudy part of this system as so far described is also open to change. In particular, the importance filter can operate only with a rule about the levels of statistical significance which will be allowed to count. In the orthodox practice of applied statistics, various levels of significance are traditionally chosen and adopted as conventions by the profession. But this viable controller must have the capability to experiment with the levels of significance it is using. At any rate, to complete the theory of the black box transformer, it will be necessary to make the whole of this box genuinely opaque. We shall be able to guess only the *sorts* of things that are going on inside it, because we are going to endow it with a certain structural *propensity*; but no completely fixed rules will be retained. In order to show how this can be achieved, it will be necessary to add a third dimension to the diagram. In Figure 46, which is a cubic lattice, Figure 45 figures as one slice.

In Figure 46, then, the previous figure is repeated in a perspective consisting of a cube. Obviously this cubic lattice would be made up of a number of such slices, and it is most important to understand that these slices do not represent the handling of an equivalent number of sets of inputs. So far we are talking of only one set of inputs; the slices then are *alternative* configurations for handling these inputs. If each of the input lines be traced down the slice (Figure 45), it will be seen that their paths coalesce and emerge as a single output—which is the trick which achieves the variety reduction. As before, this configuration is called the *trajectory* of the input set to an output. The facility offered by the cubic lattice, then, is that the trajectory through the cube is a three-dimensional one. Such a three-dimensional trajectory is illustrated in Figure 47.

The point about this added dimension is precisely this. Each slice through the cube (Figure 46) provides a sequence of *known* transformations (each separate row) which, with one exception, are not strictly opaque. It was said that the top half of the slice is actually transparent, while the lower three rows are cloudy. This is because the transformations represented in transmitting the trajectory from one row to the next below it are fully specified. But supposing, to take an example, that on this particular slice the importance filter is set to operate at the orthodox

5 per cent fiduciary level. This means that on the average only one impulse in twenty will be regarded as deviating beyond the limits of chance variation. Thus, from this cause, nineteen out of twenty of the occasions when this set of inputs is fired will result in the absorption of the trajectory by the cube: there will be no output at all. But this ortho-

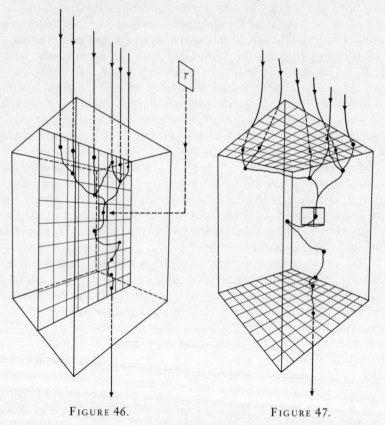

FIGURE 46.   FIGURE 47.

dox five percentile may not, in the particular circumstances, have the right survival value. Only the gradual maturing of the ecosystem of which this black box is part can ultimately select a proper level. Thus the alternative next slice may have the level fixed at 4 per cent instead of 5 per cent, while the slice of the other side has the level fixed at 6 per cent. Alternatives of this kind are available across the set of slices.

Thus the three-dimensional trajectory that will be followed by a particular combination of inputs will gradually be determined by usage. In fact, an epigenetic landscape will gradually be established, computed in terms of this machinery as a conditional probability model, which will steadily reinforce an output reading for this set of inputs which is meaningful, and has survival value to the system. But, as explained earlier, there will always be an opportunity for a mutation to occur— although the probability that it will do so decreases with maturity.

The box as now understood (Figure 47) is certainly opaque, and deserves its description of a black box. But it does constitute the kind of learning, adapting, evolving, teleological mechanism, the need for which was established in the last chapter. Moreover, the opaqueness referred to is not a warranty of chaos within the box. We have achieved here just the sort of 'free yet structured' machinery that the arguments from biology have prescribed. Indeed, this whole account is based on the set-theoretic model of some parts of the brain referred to as far back as Chapter 7.

4 The Structure of Institutional Organization

A vantage point has now been attained from which it is possible to discuss a general theory about the control of enterprises. In this section, it will be necessary to draw deeply on the material of Part III—of which this story is the climax. Inevitably, an account of how enterprises are to be controlled is an extraordinarily complex business. This is the reason why Figure 48, which reduces the matter to its absolute essentials, is none the less complicated and difficult to study. However, if all that has gone before has been well comprehended, the task is not insupportable.

As usual, the study begins with a (or in this case, rather, *the*) world situation. For the enterprise, this world situation may be understood in the form of two fairly well contra-distinguished aspects. The first is the internal world situation, which is the one that the enterprise *is*; the second is the external world of the enterprise environment: that part of nature which has a direct bearing on the internal state. As has been recognized before, these two systems are not absolutely separable; they do not have absolutely clear-cut boundaries. One of the reasons for the problem of separability is that each is influenced by a set of coenetic variables to be found in the world at large. All this is illustrated at the top of the diagram, where it will be seen that a set of preferred states is marked off (as a circle) from the totality of states represented by the phase space. In these two small pictures, as in those others which follow, the present state is shown within a preferred set of states. To go back to the drawing: the input from the set of coenetic variables is shown helping to determine this happy state of affairs.

Each of these world situations may be observed to be amplifying variety. This plethora of information is seen cascading from the side of each picture. As we know, the first problem of control is to become

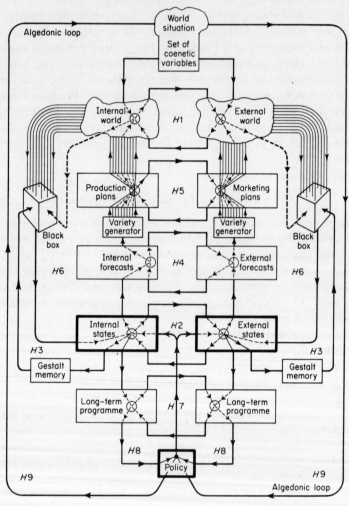

FIGURE 48.

aware of this variety, and in each case data is shown cascading on to the lid of a black box. But before attending to its subsequent use, it will be noted that the internal and the external world situations are depicted as interacting through a self-vetoing homeostat (*H*1). This is no more than

a formalization of the actual state of affairs, for whatever the management does or fails to do about controlling the situation, it will in some
sense control itself through the interactions which its two halves necessarily have. Management, however, will wish to influence this interim
interaction for motives of its own, and the model now continues by
saying what is to happen.

Consider the two black boxes on to whose lids information about the
internal and external world situations is constantly falling. By some
means or other, whether by human speech or by letter, whether by
manual or mechanical recording, whether by mechanization or full automation, the system must become aware of these data. Thus we posit a
collection of data-captured devices, capable of transducing this input
into the black box. Thereafter, the mechanism described in the previous
section operates; a much lower variety output emerges. This output is
the vital information on which the enterprise must be managed. As has
been seen, it is processed in a sophisticated way within the black boxes,
and is led to the second homeostat, $H2$, which is the basic control centre
of the enterprise. $H2$ is a homomorphic, homeostatic model of the
moment-to-moment state of affairs. Quickly to connect this picture with
the previous three figures (45, 46, 47), we can see that there is an input
to the box from the world situation which is separate from the general
cascade of information about the variables concerned. This is a direct
statement of the representative point which defines the immediate state
of affairs, and it will be recalled that this is fed into the black box as a
first stage modifier of transformation T. It will also be noted that the two
boxes of homeostat $H2$ are constantly recording their states in the box
labelled 'gestalt memory', and that this historical experience is fed back
to the black boxes, where it is used to modify the first approximation and
to create the second.

Hence the homeostat $H2$ is supported by the two 'historical' homeostats labelled $H3$. It is mainly for this reason that the model $H2$ can be
regarded as a representation of a mature ecosystem. It is not simply a
reflection of the momentary state of affairs $H1$. On the contrary, it is a
highly structured and very stable homeostat. This (by its structure)
reflects the history of the system, and in particular the epigenetic landscape created in the two black boxes; and (by its stability) announces
the fact that the world situation does not directly impinge upon it. So
the homeostat $H2$ is the 'still centre' at the heart of the control system
for the enterprise; it does not change its state without good reason.

When it does change its state, finding a new stable condition, it is in
response to inputs from the two black boxes which declare a definite,

significant and structurally assimilated change in the outside world. It must then proceed to act. This it does, by transmitting such changes in the representative point as are necessary to the homeostat $H4$. This system ($H4$) is the control system which prepares for immediate action in the real world. In the original model from the brain, $H2$ and $H4$ corresponded respectively to the sensory and the motor cortex. That is to say, $H2$ is primarily concerned with receiving information and evaluating it in terms of the mature ecosystem of which it is the core. $H4$ is a parallel activity which prepares to transmit instructions on the basis of its knowledge. Because these instructions will have to lead to specific actions in the real world of equivalent variety to that world, a variety generator is now needed to regain requisite variety for the intentions of the control system. Thus the output from $H4$, in passing into $H5$, undertakes a variety proliferation of the kind discussed earlier. $H5$, then, far from being a homomorphic model of the world situation required for purposes of overall equilibrial control, becomes a planning system couched in the terms of day-to-day decision. In operational research language, $H5$ is an optimizing device. This is the place to remark that all these diagrams pretend that the world situation and its representations exist in a two-dimensional space, whereas of course they are multidimensional. This is the reason why, in $H5$, the huge variety of the input and the output is shown as diminishing to a point. There is in fact no reduction of variety intended by this pictogram; the point itself is multidimensional, that is to say it defines a whole profile of variables, but it is shown as a point because it is unique. The output of homeostat $H5$ is then a detailed programme of activity which is passed back to the world situation itself.

In following through the course of these controls, we have in fact defined the new operational homeostat $H6$. Again this appears in the drawing as two $H6$'s, one for each of the halves of the homeostat. $H6$ is the homeostat which interlocks $H1$ and $H2$. A constant comparison and adjustment is going on between the world situation and its homomorphic model in $H2$, the flow of information undergoing first a variety reduction (in the black boxes) and then a variety amplification (between $H4$ and $H5$).

It should by now be clear how all this operates as a controller of immediate events. The picture does of course differ markedly from that normally advanced in either industry or government. The whole system is immensely stable, because the six interlocking homeostats sequentially uncouple the deep considerations of balance in the enterprise from the day-to-day hurly-burly of decision and action, through four modifying stages. Moreover, they uncouple the variety levels involved in a way which conforms to the laws of cybernetics hitherto educed. Finally, they uncouple the past and the present in an acceptable way, through the concept of epigenetic landscape and an entire learning theory. The criteria of success which are introduced are complex and ill-defined— just as they are in any real-life situation—for the major object of the system as so far described is simply to maintain equilibrium. This might possibly be described as 'making a profit' in a short-term and narrow sense. The wider sense in which this enterprise can be led to succeed is examined next.

If we return to the central core of the control, the homeostat $H2$, we may see that it sponsors a further activity at the bottom half of the diagram. Just as $H2$ can be used to generate immediate forecasts of events, so it can be used to examine long-range prognostications. The homeostat $H7$ is a continued management exercise, not operated in real time, in which the internal and external situations are balanced for many years to come. The representative points are determined, at least in part, by extrapolated outputs from $H2$. The adjustment of these points is determined by the operation of the homeostat $H7$ itself. It is the output of this homeostat which largely determines the policy of the enterprise —as can be seen in the drawing. Now this policy is at once fed back to the homeostat $H2$, for it is the long-range intention of the management which conditions the way in which the present state of affairs ($H6$) is to be conducted. The ability of the system to cope with this fact is recognized in the two-part homeostat $H8$ which produces an interaction between what is now going on and the policy for the future.

Now this whole system 'ought' to work, just as a biological system (whether a brain or an ecological interaction) 'ought' to work, on the strength of a structure aimed primarily at systematic adaptation. However, the lesson that can be drawn from the biological model is that such processes tend to be sluggish and (as it were) self-satisfied. They appear to require a more immediate challenge; a kind of crisis impact. After all, if a crisis should occur in a system of this kind, it will be monitored by so many centres and mediated by so many sophisticated techniques (the whole object of which is to be 'unflappable'), that there is a clear risk of the system's ultimate response being very ingenious and appropriate— but far too late. The mechanism by which nature deals with this risk, without at the same time making the system neurotic or over-responsive, is the reward mechanism of the algedonic loop.

To recapitulate in context the argument of Chapter 14: a child undergoing a learning process is producing an adaptation; but he may never become adapted, through sluggishness or a lack of *conation*. Accordingly, he is stimulated into speedy activity by a system of rewards and punishments. Similarly, at a non-intellectualized level, the older parts of the brain receive collateral inputs direct from the sense organs. That is to say, although these inputs are processed through the cortex by an elaborate pattern-making machine (which may well be closely analogous to that described here), danger is monitored by the reticular formation of the brain stem. In this way, we may find ourselves running away from some serious threat long before we have worked out intellectually that a threat is indeed being offered. This algedonic mechanism, which resolves the dilemma between the twin yet contradictory needs to be stable yet responsive simultaneously, is just one example of a more general natural phenomenon. For example, a comparison between the flight of man-made gliders and of birds has been made by R. H. J. Brown of Cambridge. A glider without a tail fin will lose its stability, and crash. Anatomically, then, a bird is aerodynamically unstable; it uses its highly developed neuromuscular control of the shape and position of wing and tail to maintain flight. In fact, all animal mechanisms are in this sense unstable—which is why they can be brought under control by small forces, if the sensory information and speed of response is sufficiently good. If animal mechanisms were highly stable, their response to gross perturbation would be too sluggish and would call for huge control energies.

In the same way, then, the model under development has to resolve this fundamental dilemma. The system so far is robust and not easily upset. Yet if there is real trouble, its very robustness will make it a poor adaptation machine. So the whole system is enclosed by an algedonic loop, which can effectively short-circuit the total machinery. This will guarantee speedy reaction to pleasure and pain (cashing-in on the market and crisis respectively), without damaging the routine, self-organizing, self-regulating control procedures. This loop is the channel defining the final homeostat, $H9$, by which the policy being promulgated through the system is allowed to impinge directly on the world situation through other channels (such as an announcement to the Press about the intentions of the enterprise), and the reaction of the world situation is directed straight back to the policy. Here is the reward and punishment system for the enterprise, a mechanism by which the management may decide to alter its policy (see the input in the bottom right-hand corner of the diagram), regardless of the elaborate control activities which are governing day-to-day affairs.

Moreover, this final arrangement is the one that makes sense of the more subtle managerial intentions that lie behind the enterprise. No system of day-to-day control can do more than work smoothly towards a criterion of success which is defined in its own language as 'profitable'. But it is clear that the senior management may have, and very possibly should have, aims and objects which can only be expressed in a metalanguage. This metalanguage may be spoken around the algedonic loop. It is perfectly possible to conceive of a company chairman or a government minister formulating, modifying and *measuring* his policy and its effectiveness in consultation with parts of the world that do not directly impinge as environmental circumstances on his enterprise. Those employees whose lives are dedicated to the operation of the company as they know it will never understand these overriding intentions and success criteria, because they do not speak the metalanguage. This is an important point: it is one of those aspects of the enterprise which lead to misunderstanding between governor and governed, to industrial strikes and to electoral disasters.

The model of the control of the enterprise is completed. The explanation given has been minimal; otherwise it would fill the entire book. But it is not difficult to see how this control is used to handle particular problems of kinds not explicitly mentioned here. For instance, it is possible to contemplate any operational research problem of the enterprise as a facet of this cybernetic model. Although we may use standard OR techniques in solving such a problem, using the approaches set out in Part II, this wider concept of organic control enriches the insight and safeguards the application.

Before leaving this chapter, however, a special declaration needs to be made. This is the only case, of the very large number of studies and models and approaches put forward in this book, in which what is no more and no less than a theory has been advanced. There is, at the time of writing, no enterprise which would confess that its method of overall control had been built on this advice. Even so, the theory is more than an untried operational research model. In the first place, it is a descriptive account of how enterprises actually work; in this capacity, perhaps, it throws light on that problem—and at the least it forestalls the kinds of description as given in balance sheets and organization charts (which, as so often argued here) over-simplify to the point where they are a positive danger. But secondly, it can be claimed that a fair number of partial applications of this model have actually been made in real-life situations.

Finally, it is suggested that the use of this model would radically change the *appearance* of an enterprise-controlling system. For although it was just said that controls are actually exercised rather like this, no-one acknowledges the fact; nor is the machinery explicitly designed—and therefore it must be inefficient. For this model is about control, it deals with the core of the problem. Most descriptions and most manifestations of an enterprise-controlling system are about the epiphenomena of control. What is really the core and central nervous system is locked within the communicating minds of a managerial *élite*. One of the reasons why the replacement of the existing state of affairs by something more formal and better understood is so vital, is because of the movement towards automation. In so far as we increasingly remove the human element, we must increasingly replace *all* its functions. The acknowledged functions to do with giving decisions, signing papers, endorsing plans and so on, are well understood and have often been imitated by computers. But without a theory of the kind discussed here, there is no basis for the automation of what is central to the control of the enterprise. Beware the risk that automation will march on without this being noticed. The point will be presented again, in a more directly relevant context, in Part IV.

So ends the discussion of the relevance of cybernetics to the great control problems of management. The arrangements made have to do with the ecosystem; they should attend to its sentience; they should attend to hierarchic structure as informing the homeostatic balance by which systems are in fact self-organized. Finally let it be said again that we have been concerned with what only looks like a grandiose general theory of management control. The first half of the book, in a way, gives the lie to any belief that such a theory can be clamped on to a real-life situation. For operational research is empirical science. What this part has really been about is a novel and demonstrably rewarding approach: a newly oriented insight, an enriched vocabulary, a way of thinking that rises above the platitudes of orthodox management training. Cybernetics is about control, which is the profession of management.

PART IV

Outcomes

Connective Summary

The whole of Part I was spent in considering the nature of management decision, policy and control in the light of science. We saw how operational research meant doing science in the management sphere. In Part II all this was amplified by a discussion of the way in which OR actually operates: its methods and techniques were introduced; we saw it in action on behalf of management. Science, it was seen, could arrange to model and to quantify the large systems with which managers must deal, and from these quantified models conclusions about managerial policies could be drawn.

But these large systems turn out to be no more than parts of exceedingly large systems, and the classical techniques of OR do not deal with these very successfully. A special class of models was therefore introduced in Part III, drawn from the science of cybernetics. This science has been developed with exceedingly large systems, and particularly viable ones, especially in mind. By using this class of models as a basis for doing operational research, the topic of management cybernetics is born. We saw how this works too.

The time has now come to consider the outcome of all this in the world of affairs. Although the first three parts have been full of examples, case material and the discussion of explicit management problems, these have not yet been drawn together to form cohesive lines of attack. A vantage point has now been reached, however, from which to attempt a conspectus of applications—to include not only what has already been done, but what ought to be done next.

We begin with industry. In Chapter 16 is considered the use of OR in the firm, and the management science approach to modelling its entire activity. This leads into an extended discussion of the special issues which arise for industry, and indeed for every kind of enterprise, because of the changing scientific attitude towards information and communication. Especially in this Chapter 17, the consequences of the new computer technology are worked out and discussed. These arguments lead in turn to the outcome for government, which is conceived as essentially an informational process. Chapter 18, then, discusses the use of management science in dealing with national and international problems.

It is impossible to ignore the bearing of the approach of this book on the profession of management science itself, and this topic is considered in Chapter 19. How both OR men and scientifically oriented managers ought to be trained, and how the use of both ought to be organized, is discussed at length. The book ends with concluding thoughts (Chapter 20) on what counts as practical management and practical science in this era of difficulty and change.

16

THE OUTCOME
FOR INDUSTRY

... ἡ εὐβουλία, δῆλον ὅτι ἐπιστήμη τίς ἐστιν· οὐ
γάρ που ἀμαθία γε ἀλλ᾽ ἐπιστήμη εὖ βουλεύονται.

... ἔστι τις ἐπιστήμη ... ἡ οὐχ ὑπὲρ τῶν ἐν τῇ
πόλει τινὸς βουλεύται, ἀλλ᾽ ὑπὲρ ἑαυτῆς ὅλης,
ὄντιν᾽ ἂν τρόπον αὐτή τε πρὸς αὐτὴν καὶ πρὸς τὰς
ἄλλας πόλεις ἄριστον ὁμιλοῖ;

Good counsel is clearly a science in some sense;
nowhere do men give good counsel through
ignorance, at any rate, but through knowledge.

Is there any science ... which does not deliberate
about some one particular thing in the city, but
about the entire city itself, and in what way it may
best orient itself towards itself and towards other
cities?

PLATO (429–347 B.C.) in *The Republic* (Book IV)

1 OR and the Firm

Rather than to solve problems, it is clever to dissolve them; there is then
no residual task of implementation.

This is certainly one message of this book; for what has been written
in the first three parts includes throughout an appeal to think again about
the nature of the management role. As far as good practice is concerned,
management improves steadily. It makes increasing use, as it should, of
work study, of O and M (which turns out really to be the work study of
office work), of ergonomics, of production engineering, of management
accounting, of product planning and of marketing techniques, as tools
in the fight for better results. All this implies a scientific approach to the

401

402

day-to-day task of decision and control, because all these management aids are based on the collection of facts, on measurement and on a statistically competent appraisal of the resulting data.

But beneath the level of practice lies the level of problems. Managers work under great pressure very often, and have little time to think freshly about the nature of the problems which their good practice handles. That is to say, managerial practice assumes the real nature of the problems to be known. Yet it is far from true. Quicker and more organized ways may be found, for example, for producing cost comparisons between different products or process routes, but the basis on which those costs are calculated may possibly never be questioned. There are many impressively elaborate systems of costing which hide the same old assumptions about the distribution of overheads—assumptions which vitiate the meaning of the whole exercise.

It is at this level that the *fruits* of a quarter century of operational research experience can rapidly be garnered. Many of these problems are classics of OR, and they can often be reduced to a characteristic shape. Because so much work has been done on questions of stockholding, queueing, the allocation of resources, and so forth, the problems which underlie management practice in such areas can be examined through mathematical models which do not require further justification at the systemic level of model-building. In such cases good answers, which provide more enlightened bases for management practice, can be obtained virtually by calculating a formula. And because of the interdisciplinary nature of OR, we are entitled to subsume under this heading those econometric techniques of which the same is true. The economic model of the firm that enables us to examine the relationship between marginal cost and marginal revenue is a vitally useful management aid; and no manager with any pretention to professional skill would fail to calculate the break-even point of his business. It is for these reasons that two professors of operational research have classified management problems into 'eight basic forms, which singly or in combination account for most of the problems that confront executives'. Their conveniently small book (*A Manager's Guide to Operational Research*, Rivett and Ackoff, Wiley 1963) is a vade-mecum for managers who wish to make rapid and inexpensive use of the OR approach to the clear definition and quick solution of a large range of familiar problems.

But it is just because these answers *are* known that they were called the *fruits* of OR, rather than OR itself. There is no need to undertake Research into Operations, if it can be taken as given that no real research is needed—but only hard work in applying a known result. Thus the position taken here is that such fruits of past OR ought to be assimilated into management practice as a matter of course. Those responsible for stockholding systems ought to include people specially trained in the techniques which OR has developed for controlling stocks. Those responsible for running allocation systems ought to include people trained in mathematical programming. And so on. But none of these people needs to be an OR scientist, for his function is to do the research that will establish answers to problems *to which no answer at present exists.* This is not a captious distinction. If either management or the OR profession pretends to itself that applying established results constitutes doing operational research, then it will be living in a fool's paradise in which no breakthrough is ever possible. Naturally, the known work must be exploited; and because we know what it is, there is little difficulty in organizing the exploitation. But for operational research itself is reserved the novel problem with no apparent solution; the determination by scientific method of an outcome which would otherwise have to be guessed. (There is evidence from their other writings that both Professor Ackoff and Professor Rivett would agree with the substance of this paragraph, despite the foregoing quotation from their joint book.)

This brings the argument to a deeper level still. Below the problems which underlie the practice, are found the policies which determine how those problems appear and ought to be approached. This is the major arena for operational research: the sphere of policy. There exists no formula to help the scientist to assist the manager in formulating his criteria of success; and this is the problem with which OR always begins. Nor is there a formula for redesigning policy to meet those criteria, once it is admitted that the whole issue is open to reappraisal. To be graphic: the manager who thinks he is sponsoring OR because he has a mathematician studying the behaviour of a queue, ought to pause to ask why the queue is there in the first place. Genuine OR might so recast the policy, with managerial connivance, that the queue was abolished. In this way some applications of inventory theory to decide which items should be held in stock turn out to be pointless, if original OR should happen to show that either all items or no items should be so held. In this way, too, applications of linear programming to decide the minimum cost allocation of a set of resources to a set of outcomes turn out to be pointless, if original OR should demonstrate that either the resources or the outcomes can and should be radically altered. Nor is it right that management should be advised by the use of game theory that a certain policy is the best of those available to meet a competitive situation, on an unexpressed assumption that the manager really wants to minimize the maximum risk, if this wish is either temperamentally anathema to him or can be shown to be silly in a particular case. And so on, indefinitely.

Thus *within a given and accepted framework* it may well be true that problems of management can be matched to one of eight templates, for quick handling by someone trained in the appropriate mathematical technique. But the whole purpose of OR as described here is to join with the manager in questioning that very framework. It is for this reason that the chapter opened with the remark that problems are better dissolved than solved. In the early part of the book a picture was created of a known and all-too-familiar company situation, in which the nature of things is structured by the people who are involved in them, people for whom real life is a specialized phase space surrounded by thought blocks. The manager who appreciates the sense of this description, and the limitation of his whole organization as a machine devoted to handling an arbitrary account of the way things are, will use OR in a correct way. He will deliberately send his OR team into orbit around the phase space, using the power of objective science, coupled with the sheer ignorance of his particular business enjoyed by the scientists, as the energy which achieves escape velocity. He will enjoin the team to explore the outer space to find out what is going on beyond the confines of his own managerial universe; to think afresh about the nature of his problems in the context of the whole. For it is in doing this, in thinking systemically, that OR scientists have their expertise.

In short; what is the entire enterprise all about? In what way may it best orient itself towards itself and towards other enterprises? This is the proper question for OR; or, at the least, it is the proper *context* in which a more particular and perhaps pressing policy question should be set to OR. It is the very question that Plato thought good management should set out to answer, as quoted above in the second passage from *The Republic*. And, as quoted in the first passage, Plato thought that counsel in this matter ought to derive from knowledge rather than ignorance—that it should approach what we now call a science. He was, even then, perceiving the need for the OR facility that we now have. And if it seems almost trite to say that advice should derive from knowledge rather than ignorance, it behoves us to reflect on the difference between assumed and genuine knowledge. To listen at the board-room keyhole will naturally not reveal that ignorant decisions are *thought* to be other than knowledgeable by the directors inside. But the experience of applying objective tests for the degree of genuine knowledge in use within can be shattering. We reach 'good' decisions, which are soundly argued conclusions from totally false premises; and we believe the false premises to be true because we could not bear it if they were not.

In the rest of this chapter we shall discuss how OR for the firm works out in practice, if it is approached on this scale and with this breadth. Certainly the most alarming issue which this approach immediately raises is the question of time and money. The untutored manager can be forgiven for feeling that any such research is bound to last for years and years, and to cost him a small fortune. But it can be hoped that, after reading this book, another manager will be more sanguine. For he will realize that the OR team does not start work with a blank cheque. It knows that it is dealing with an organism operating in an environment; it knows that every science can propose ways of looking at such a situation; it has (if it is experienced and properly led) long practice in devising appropriate models. Once the model is created, it has access to all the techniques developed by science for handling models of that special kind. And the whole process of doing OR, it ought to be remembered, is self-organizing on a sequential basis.

The particular relevance of this last point arises in the matter of obtaining information. Managers themselves are often quite overwhelmed by the difficulties which they assume OR will encounter in the attempt to quantify any scientific model of their firms. There are two reasons. First, they expect that the model must reflect in every detail every facet of the operation; and they well know that the data for this assumed purpose are by no means available. Second, they perceive that some of the critical information is not only missing in terms of an available record, but is not a conventionally measurable entity at all; value judgments belong to this category. The answer to this twofold difficulty is really quite simple. If a systemic model is constructed, it may well elicit the major features of the situation quite quickly based on quite crude data. For example, each of us as a private individual can know whether he is solvent if he has a statement of his total assets to compare with a statement of his total liabilities. His solvency in no way depends on the answer to the question whether his wife has paid the butcher's bill.

The next step is to decide from the systemic model which sub-system of the total system needs further resolution in detail, and precisely what quantities need to be measured to provide it. *Which* sub-system is determined by the model, and not by the manager—who (with respect) usually cannot judge; mainly because he is looking at the conventional breakdown into sub-systems whereas the scientist is not. *What* quantities to measure are decided by the needs of the model, and not by the needs of the manager whose daily task is quite different from that of this study.

DC—DD

The criterion to be used by the scientist in reaching these decisions is the criterion of requisite variety. So whether 'exhaustive records' of what everybody thinks is happening are readily available or not may well be completely irrelevant. It has been argued repeatedly here that OR is empirical science; its prime responsibility is to discover what and how to measure, and to undertake (or at least to supervise) the measuring. So there is the answer to the second difficulty too. The scientist will seek to construct the sort of model that he *can* quantify, not one that he cannot. This does not necessarily mean that he must omit some of what the manager considers as critical variables; it means that he will try to express the system in another way. The whole history of science is studded with examples of discoveries made in the absence of critical information, or of the facilities to obtain it. The history of science is also studded with examples of people who were martyred for declaring that aspects of life could be measured, which their persecutors 'knew' could not be measured—or thought it would be blasphemous, dangerous or immoral to try to measure. We none the less progress. Let the scientist try; let the manager not try to tell the scientist what he can and cannot do; the scientist will report back soon enough.

OR *explores.* It feels its way along. It ought not to set itself impossible methodological targets, and then complain that there is no way of hitting them. Its models are models of structure, and not of the history of particular events. It has to feel out the structure, to express it scientifically and to quantify it in its own way. It is the manager who tries to be his own OR man who, by specifying the required technique and the 'actual' problem and so forth in advance, makes solutions impossible. It is the OR man who prejudices all these questions by picking on one of eight templates of technique before he has constructed a systemic model, who comes whining to management that there are not enough data. They make a perfect pair, and will get nowhere. Let us get on with some real OR.

2   Modelling the Total System

There is, we have often insisted, no 'right' or 'correct' model of anything at all; there are only more or less appropriate models for particular purposes. If, however, we are to approach Plato's desideratum of discussing not some one particular aspect of an organized whole, but the whole of it at once, we need a model able to encompass not only the firm but all its interactions. The methodology to be followed has been expounded, and its critical point ought to be reiterated. It is this. Since we cannot account for the entire detail of a system as big as a firm, the model must be a many–one homomorphic reduction. Requisite variety can be obtained in such a model, by including in it data generators. But any conclusions drawn for managerial purposes from this model must be supported by a level of variety commensurate with their own variety. This in general can be done, *either* by resolving in more detail those parts of the system which relate to the decision, *or* by generating variety stochastically in a simulation.

There are probably many models in science to choose from that would offer a mapping of the whole firm and its interactions. Anyone who has read through the first three parts of this book, however, will understand

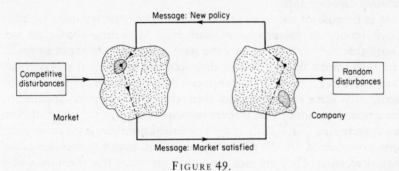

FIGURE 49.

the author's own predilection to work from a biological basis. For the problem as defined, namely that the firm is an organism interacting with an environment, is instantly recognizable as an ecological problem. Thus there is one OR scientist at least who embarks on the operational research task of modelling a global industrial situation by turning to cybernetics for a model of the sentient ecosystem.

Figures 26–30 inclusive are increasingly complicated pictures of the key interactions governing ecosystems, drawn to illustrate a text dealing with the problem in a cybernetically general fashion. When we come to considering industry, we need to elaborate a more specific version. Figure 49 quite clearly belongs to the same generic set of illustrations as 26–30. It shows a self-vetoing homeostat, in which the company and its market are constantly interacting. (The market is for this purpose defined as the environment in which the company operates.) The state of the system as depicted in Figure 49 shows that the market is satisfied by the present balance of the homeostat, but that the company's representative point is not in its preferred set. Therefore the company's policy must change in an effort to move its own point into its own preferred set of states, without driving the representative point of the market outside its own preferred set of states—thus upsetting market satisfaction.

The company box in the diagram receives information from the market environment box, and reacts by passing information back to influence the market. This is the basic feedback loop of the total ecosystem. It is at once obvious that the company must be in possession of enough information about its market if the system is to attain to a homeostatic balance. Since the variety generated by the market is very large, the lines of communication back to the company must have large channel capacity. Equally, the information travelling in the other direction must be large enough to influence the market, and the same measures of channel capacity apply.

It is because of the high variety in this loop that we must spend so much money in the process of marketing. Marketing people are well aware that they are trying to cope with a high variety input by means of a high variety output. Indeed they seem more aware of this necessity than any other branch of management. Some members of top management, even some marketing men themselves, are somewhat appalled by the amount of money that is spent in the process. One notices at marketing conferences, particularly those concerned primarily with advertising, how preoccupied are the executives concerned to justify themselves and their profession. They are nice men; they are aware that the money they disperse would look after a significant portion of the starving and needy families of the world; they are not quite sure if there is an ethical basis for their lives and their means of livelihood. But it is not really an ethic of which they stand in need: they are short of some raw cybernetic theory by which a scientific demonstration that a marketing campaign demands this kind of expenditure can be made. This does not excuse them from responsibility for its proper use. But the law of requisite variety does demonstrate in this context how very great is the information that must be generated and paid for in a competitive society.

Without benefit of the cybernetic model, management tends to behave towards this situation of Figure 49 in its orthodox way. The world outside the company is seen as somewhat chaotic, indisciplined and anarchic. It is a hostile muddle; something into which order and discipline must be imported. Thus in the orthodox picture money, the working capital allocated to marketing, is pumped outwards towards the public who purchase the goods. But the working capital is (let us admit it) a rather arbitrary sum. This has to be divided (again by somewhat arbitrary means) between the various functions of marketing: advertising, distribution, packaging, market research, product research, and so on. Each of these functions may well have its own management and organization, and is indeed a distinct activity in its own right. Nor does the process of cutting up the marketing function stop there.

In advertising, for example, further breakdowns of the appropriation have to be made as between the press, television, hoarding displays, and so forth: this is the problem of the media mix. At this stage, operational research scientists may be brought in to use such techniques as linear programming as a means of determining the best (minimum cost) way of obtaining coverage for a particular audience. Even this is not the final division. Decisions have to be taken not only between newspapers and journals, but between full, half and quarter pages, thirty-second and one-minute television spots, and so on—until the money is spent. And what applies to the advertising branch applies to all the others.

This picture is of the kind that has been painted before in this book, because it is common to the whole of business and industrial management: a division of functions, a division of staff, a division of money. And the process of division is one that continues down from the single point of the total marketing appropriation, through a very large number of stages, down to the great variety of separate bills that are eventually paid. The whole of this money and effort is directed to the public who are potential purchasers of the company's products. The model which underlies this orthodox outlook, although it may be unexpressed, concerns a teeming population of irrational, unpredictable individuals due to be 'controlled' by the marketing pressures directed at them, and demonstrating the degree of their being controlled by the making of their purchases. The pattern of purchasing is then studied, analysed and used for predicting the effect of the next round of expenditure in every division and sub-division. More and more sophisticated methods are employed to make these analyses and predictions; but somehow marketing men do not work themselves out of a job. Most of them believe that the major decisions are matters of judgment and flair.

With the ecosystemic model of marketing, however, a completely different picture is obtained; one which may well demand an entire re-orientation of outlook. The question is: can Figure 49 be turned into a usable account of the firm's interaction with its market? In Figure 50, a more elaborate version of Figure 49 is put forward. Note that its structure is identical with the earlier simplified picture. Although an attempt has been made to give more resolution of the detail, this system is clearly a self-vetoing homeostat.

Examining the diagram for significant detail, the very high variety

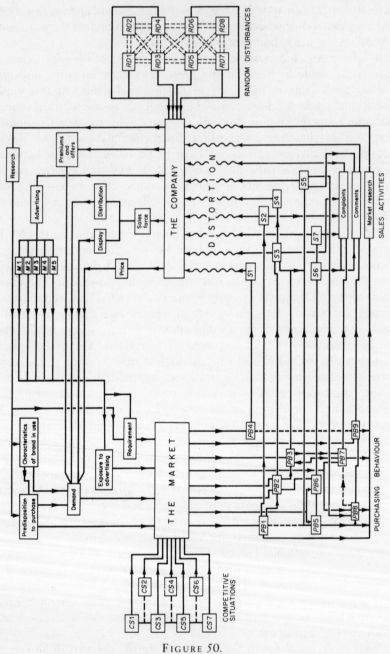

FIGURE 50.

which the market is capable of generating emerges in the bottom left-hand corner as a mass of sub-systems representing kinds of purchasing behaviour. These sub-systems all interact, and indeed the collection of boxes marked '*PB*' is itself a homeostatic assemblage. Secondly, the torrent of high variety information which eventually reaches the company through its sales returns (bottom right-hand corner) is rather seriously distorted. Everyone knows that it is extremely hard to collect sales data which are directly attributable to a particular campaign, or a particular state of mind of the public, because of time lags, interference of every kind, stockholding complications, and so on. But fortunately this model does not call for any causal analysis of the sort normally undertaken. In practice, the study will be interested in the characteristics of the mechanism marked 'Distortion'; but the ultrastability of the system does not depend on an ability to unravel that mechanism.

In the top right-hand corner of the diagram is the organization of the company's affairs over which the management has direct control. It too is pumping high variety onwards: promotion, towards the market. And as was pointed out earlier on, this is very essential. Indeed, the variety can be measured scientifically and its obedience to the laws of information theory can be studied. In the top left-hand corner of the diagram appears an attempt to unravel the mechanism by which the market is influenced. This abbreviated diagram contends that only one product is involved, whereas the product *range* is itself a source of variety that has to be multiplied into the measurement of total variety as depicted.

Finally, the external influences shown on the extreme left and right are not explained at all, although they could well be to some extent. It is possible to make secondary homeostatic models of the competition which is affecting one's market, and also of the disturbances which may affect the company itself. Interestingly, and despite the geometry of the diagram, it often happens that apparently unassociated disturbances on the extreme left and right have a common cause in the outside world. This *tertium quid* is precisely the coenetic variable discussed in Chapter 12 and illustrated in Figure 29.

Figure 50, then, is a diagram of a generalized model from cybernetics of the company considered as a sentient ecosystem. Attention is drawn to the fact that the market itself and the company itself are both depicted as black boxes: all the detail is to do with their interactions. And this is in the best tradition of operational cybernetics, since we know that it is the interactions which embody homeostatic equilibrium. But of course, in any given study, it may be very necessary to resolve the structure of these two black boxes, either more or less, according to further models as required. Before passing to a discussion of this matter in the next section, however, we should consider the managerial value of the global model itself.

Suppose that a model of the kind illustrated in Figure 50 had been made of the firm. This is not nearly as difficult an undertaking as it might appear, and might be expected to take no more than a month of work by a small OR team. It is also a fairly easy job to set up the logic of this system inside an electronic computer. The model must then be quantified, using real data about the real situation. Let there be no mistake about this: real data do usually exist. A great deal of money is spent in determining the parameters of a system of this kind; but because analytic methods do not enable statisticians to make thoroughly reliable predictions, we tend to assume that we need more data. This belief is chimerical. The reason why the data do not yield fully accurate predictions is not that there are insufficient of them, but rather that life is uncertain and the system extremely complicated. The reason why actual marketing decisions seem to depend so fundamentally on flair and judgment is because marketing activities are broken up into a rigorous organizational structure (as mentioned earlier), and the bits are then treated as if they had nothing to do with each other. On the contrary, experimentation with the model will quickly confirm the cybernetic expectation that the mode of interaction between the boxes is the most important element in determining the behaviour and stability of the whole. Thus the object is to quantify the model with data that do exist, rather than with information which everyone would like to have but which turns out to be missing—such as a reliable measure of advertising effectiveness. The effectiveness of advertising is a behavioural phenomenon of the ecosystem; that is to say, it is a measure of the metabolism of the system's dynamics. This is why people often (but not always) fail to measure it when they try to identify a *result*. It is rather like asking the question: whereabouts in the engine of a car can one find the speed?

So the point about the computer simulation on which OR would now embark is that it arranges well-known data in probability patterns, which then become the raw material for simulating a stochastic network. This experimental approach to the dynamics of the ecosystem yields an account of the stability, rate of adjustment and learning, and so forth, of which the situation is capable. Experimentation in which one alters the arbitrary variables, notably the various arbitrary appropriations, over a considerable range will reveal just how sensitive the stability of the system is to parameters within managerial control.

Everyone has fixed ideas about the way in which a system of which he has vast experience actually works; but these ideas are really beliefs and not tested truths—they are not even, scientifically speaking, hypotheses. Thus, as we have come to expect, scientific work can bring under the spotlight all manner of prejudices, superstitions and convictions. Ultimately, the following question should be answered: what is the optimal state of the company's total marketing policy? But long before then it should be possible to discover the answers to some formal basic questions of the kind: to what particular facets of the system, both qualitative and quantitative, is profitability most vulnerable? To what remedial actions are particular dangerous states of the system most susceptible? What features of the system are more or less invariant whatever we do? The answers to all these questions are missing from any analytic research results, however sophisticated. They are locked up in the intimate, dynamic interactions of the homeostatic ecosystem.

A tabulation of the actual output of a computer simulating a purchase–repurchase feedback loop within the overall model depicted, is given at Figure 51. This is a simulation of a two-brand marketing situation, in which a group of 1,000 customers is assumed to be influenced by a wide range of marketing pressures. It illustrates how a particular facet of a global model can be investigated. The particular computer programme, devised by Dr B. T. Warner, enabled the behaviour of a sub-group of 100 consumers over a period of two years to be simulated in less than two minutes; still higher speeds could be attained on a larger machine than the one actually used. The investigation concerns two brands competing for an economic share of a total market that is quite inelastic. Decisions by either manufacturer on the amount and type of advertising, sales effort, premiums, offers, price changes, and so on, can be injected at periodic intervals and the effect on sales observed. As long as the simulation is continued, the customers preserve their memories of their attitudes to, and use of, the two products—although these memories are arranged to decay, and do so unless reinforced.

This kind of investigation, and this kind of model, may well be the start of a scientific attack on a firm's existing situation. Although it is global, it can tell us, really rather quickly, what are the major features of that situation, and how different sorts of behaviour could be elicited from the ecosystem. This means that plenty of major policy problems can be solved without ever penetrating the darkness of the black boxes which generate ecosystemic behaviour. For example, many problems to do with the siting of factories, depots, warehouses, retail outlets, and so forth, can be dealt with, starting from this point, in terms of interactions alone. Considered in orthodox terminology, these are problems

Week number	Brand	Promotion[a] Advertising TV	Promotion[a] Advertising Press	Promotion[a] Sales force (%)	Promotion[a] Offers	Promotion cost per 100 homes (£)	Wholesale price in pence/unit	Description of situation	Resultant sales per 100 homes	Sales income per 100 homes (£)	Profit per 100 homes (£)
1–20	A	5	1	100	none	8·5	20	Brand *A* starts with a heavy TV advertising campaign. *B* relies mainly on the press and is more cautious.	1135	94·6	29·4
	B	1	3	100	none	8·5	20		848	70·7	19·8
21–40	A	*7*	1	100	*yes*[b]	12·5	20	*A* seeing the advantage of TV promotion steps this up to seven per week and introduces an offer to win over loyal *B* purchasers.	1287	107·3	30·2
	B	1	3	100	none	8·5	20		676	56·3	14·0
41–60	A	7	1	100	**none**	9·8	20	*A* withdraws his offer as the resultant sales did not appear to justify the expense; *B* increases his sales force and switches part of his advertising budget to TV.	1459	121·6	38·8
	B	*3*	2	*150*	none	10·6	20		439	36·6	4·0
61–80	A	7	1	100	none	9·8	20	*A* maintains his obviously successful policies. *B* abandons the additional sales effort and following *A*'s lead steps up his expenditure on advertising.	1484	123·7	39·7
	B	3	*4*	**100**	none	11·0	20		507	42·3	5·9
81–100	A	7	1	100	none	9·8	20	*B*, forced to the wall, increases the price of his product to finance a massive advertising campaign. *B* has now more than recovered his share of the market.	821	68·4	17·6
	B	*6*	*6*	100	none	15·4	*21*		1177	102·9	28·6

[a] Italic type shows an increase in marketing effort; bold type shows return to previous state.
[b] Italic type indicates that the offer applies to 50% of retailers' sales with an apparent price reduction to the consumer of 2*d*. although the actual cost to the manufacturer is 1*d*./unit.

FIGURE 51. Results of simulated marketing situation.

of plant balance, marketing and distribution. The particular purpose of the global model from ecosystems is to put together again the Humpty Dumpty of marketing, which has been shattered in pieces by over-elaborate organizational structure and over-refined specialization in the various aspects of the problem. In less orthodox terminology, however, we are really talking about the survival-worthiness of the firm, its viability. Thus another set of problems which can be approached from this standpoint would generally be called by the title: problems of capital investment.

3   Resolving the Sub-system

It has been repeatedly emphasized that any piece of operational research can be undertaken within the context of a global model. And indeed if it is not, then there is a risk of misunderstanding the interactions which surround the sub-optimization contemplated. To see how the resolution of sub-systems works out, using the full OR concept of the homomorphic mappings of interlocked models as discussed in Part II, two examples are now given. In these, the black boxes that were respectively the company and the market in two different ecosystemic models have to be further resolved.

The first example quoted is taken from an actual study, and the diagrams which follow are actual diagrams taken from the case papers (which is why the names have been removed). The problems being considered concerned the acquisition and use of raw material, and the consequent capital investment in the plant which would be involved in any changes in purchasing policy and production practice that could be made. The work began with the creation of an ecosystemic model very like that already discussed in the last section. But it had these complications. Since raw materials were very much an issue, the environment of the firm had to distinguish between input and output. The 'supply environment' considered the outside world in so far as it offered raw material, and the 'demand environment' stood for what has hitherto been called the market. Because the possible change of works' practice might involve labour complications, a 'working environment' was distinguished; and because of capital requirements, a 'financial environment' also. So the first resolution of the company–environment ecosystemic homeostat looked like Figure 52 which shows a quadripartite resolution of the environmental situation. It is a family of homeostats, constituting one large homeostat. Now preliminary investigation based on the conceptual model at this stage revealed that the financial environment could be expressed as an integral part of the company's *internal* activity, for the reason that there was no question of raising money from outside. Any financial operations, such as the capital investment which was contemplated, would have to be paid for in a very short run out of the revenue accruing over that period. Secondly, the working environment should be similarly treated; the factors affecting labour could almost entirely be accounted for within the firm itself. This would not happen, for example, in the case of a dockyard, or in any other situation where there is a highly mobile in-and-out-flow of seasonal labour. Thus the

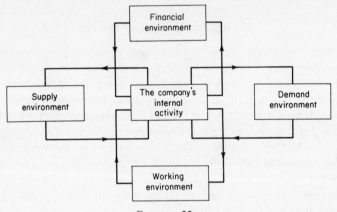

FIGURE 52.

next model, it could now be decided, in order to make the earlier ones simultaneously more specific and more elaborate, ought to depict the relationships of men and money integrally with those of materials and machines, as one interacting system. But both the supply and the demand environments, which turned out to be highly critical to the whole policy of the firm, would have to be set up as distinct from the firm itself.

At this point, a considerable degree of resolution was attempted and a second model was evolved. This model derived from general systems theory, and a diagram showing the relationships that emerged is given at Figure 53. Here, the supply environment is the smaller horseshoe on the left, embracing three main material sources and their alternatives. The demand environment, the larger horseshoe on the right, is made up of ten separate markets. It will be clear that the sources and sinks within this general systems theory model are still treated as black boxes. The object is to make some more resolution of the company activity which links the two environments together. Now given that the relationships in this picture, denoted by the lines and arrows, could all be statistically quantified in terms of magnitudes and probabilities and time cycles, quite a lot could already be said about the stability of the system, and about the vulnerability of the organism. Note that anything inferred at this point is in fact inferred from the ecological relationships, and not from information about the content of all the little boxes. Although many more of them are shown, so that more structure is resolved, the individual boxes are still black.

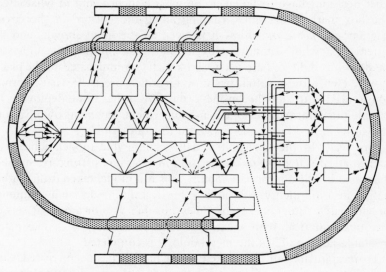

FIGURE 53.

Having learnt, from the analysis of this model, a great deal about the behaviour of the total system, it became possible to specify what a yet more rigorous scientific model should be like. An interlocked model of greater precision, expressed in still more formal terms, was needed. The model used was chosen from the science of servomechanics, and is exemplified in Figure 54. The required description has now been reduced to completely rigorous terms, using the language of electrical engineering (a system designed by Mr R. H. Anderton). This design depicts an analogue computer which would behave exactly like the organic system in the previous figure. From this could be computed how one locality of the system would stabilize itself when perturbed by inputs from another locality. In fact, any large-scale mixed system that is a going concern has features, call them intrinsic governors, which tend to make the total system self-regulating. If managerial systems were not basically self-regulating, it would never be possible to manage them. They would generate too much variety for us to cope with. So, as usual, we start from the premise that we are confronted with a system which works, and is working. The task of management is to do things to the system which will achieve particular results, such as making a higher profit.

In this servomechanical model there is a special facility for identifying precisely what is self-regulating about the system. This in turn reveals, by default, what is not self-regulating about the system: that is to say, what decisions have to be taken, on what evidence, and to what effect. The box marked 'decisions' running along the bottom of the circuit diagram *will not work* unless it is given all the input shown; and the system as a whole cannot realize its maximum profitability, unless all the decisions indicated are taken and are all communicated to the places shown. Hence the research has now identified precisely what information is needed to run the business, and how it has to be deployed. To provide this information alone is an achievement, having its own pay-off. Few firms indeed know the answer to this question.

This leads to the final and actually computable model, which is a mathematical statement of the decision-making box's structure, suitably quantified by the appropriate inputs. This is a model taken from mathematical decision theory. By running this decision model on a computer, for alternative situations, it becomes possible to indicate what sets of decisions will deal with what sets of circumstances in a maximally profitable fashion. Thus the methodology is completed.

To recapitulate: an interlocked set of models has been created, each mapping on to its successor, each seeking to perform a different function in the chain. Using the nomenclature put forward in Chapter 6, there were two conceptual models from ecology; three scientific models, one from general systems theory, one from servomechanics and the last from decision theory; and there was a mathematical and computational activity resulting—as would be expected.

It is surely sufficiently evident that this account of the firm as an eco-system, with its resolution in given detail of the plant, can be used as the basis for answering almost any question of policy relating to the physical part of the firm. Perhaps, in a conceivable case, there is insufficient resolution to obtain that answer even now. If so, further resolution of the relevant locality can readily be written into the chain of models to obtain the required answers. In fact, this study was used to determine optimal investment decisions. Every local request for capital within such a system, as every accountant knows, is accompanied by a water-tight 'story' explaining why the investment will yield precisely that return on

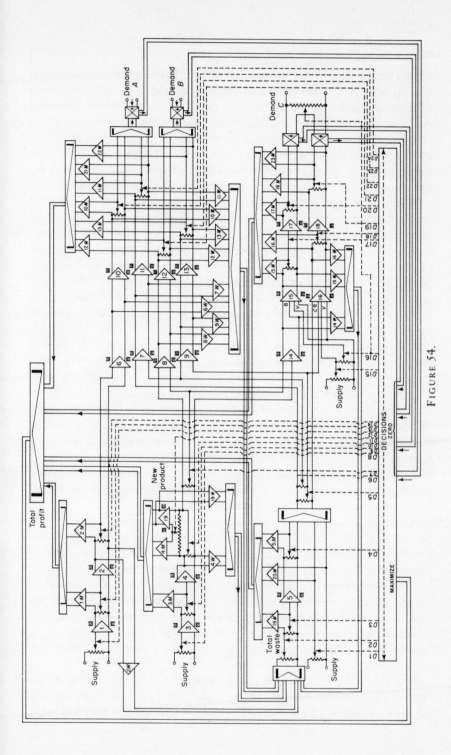

FIGURE 54.

capital demanded by the company's board. It is a strange coincidence. But, as was said at the outset, to reach a rational decision among these competing claims, it is vital to re-evaluate the behaviour of the entire ecological system assuming that the change has been made. Quite obviously the answers obtained will be different from those worked out in the immediate locality of the new piece of plant. Reverberations throughout the whole ecosystem will occur, and these will determine the influence of this decision on the total profitability of the company.

It has been argued before, but here we see the point in context, that the best investment decision is the key that will 'unlock' the entire system. Cases have occurred where new strategies have been prepared to increase overall profitability by several hundred per cent per annum of the *local* investment required. This is not an orthodox way of computing return on capital, quite obviously, since the use of other assets is involved. But if a small local investment can so facilitate the overall behaviour of the system, then it is worth selecting—and the new level of profit is absolutely attributable to this change.

The second of the promised examples, this time dealing with a resolution of the marketing black box, is also a real-life case study. The company concerned makes a product consumed by the general public through a very large number of retail outlets. These outlets are served from depots, which are in turn served either from warehouses or direct from factories. In addition, both the factories and the warehouses may deliver directly to the outlets. The initial question posed was: where should the major factory be re-sited, since it has to be rebuilt? Here is a typical management problem which appears to be susceptible to standard econometric techniques—if not indeed to a standard costing exercise. But the operational research approach is quite different.

An ecosystemic model of this situation still looks like Figure 50. But the market box is really very black: rather little is known about the details of its operation, still less about its trends. And these are of great importance if a major capital investment is in question. Now any black box is defined by its inputs and outputs, and these are shown in Figure 50. The resolution of the market black box depends, in this case, on the input line marked 'Distribution', and the set of outputs indicating purchasing behaviour. A model was indeed constructed to account for the latter aspect, but it is with the former aspect that this discussion is concerned.

It could, and normally would, be said that the blackness of the distribution aspect of the market can be resolved by setting out the existing network of connections between factories, warehouses, depots and retail outlets. But once this apparently definite and unassailable apparatus is contemplated within the context of the global model, an interesting thought quickly occurs. Since the major factory is to be rebuilt, and could be re-sited, it might pay to re-design the entire marketing network. Of course, this would be costly. On the other hand, a network of this type usually is (and in this case certainly was) the result of many years of historical accretion: viewed in the context of the total, present-day homeostat it could conceivably pay handsomely to change it. Thus, with the agreement of management, the original problem was re-stated as follows. What is the optimum investment policy, given certain constraints about the money available and the rate of return required? This problem is really immensely difficult, because the marketing box is now genuinely black. No transparency can be obtained by studying what is there on the ground, since it *could* all be changed. Not only are the factories, warehouses and depots all wandering about inside the black box, it is no longer certain how many of each of them there are. How many there should be, and where geographically located, can be settled only by fitting the ecosystemic inputs and outputs to the black box, and resolving the detail within in an optimal fashion.

The first step was to construct a logical model of the possible modes of connection of an unknown number of factories to an unknown number of warehouses and depots, showing all possible interactions between these three types of plant and the known number of retail outlets. It is necessary to establish this kind of model as specifying the underlying structure of the system, to ensure that any future computations are properly directed to available alternatives. Again, this model must ensure that the computations will not commit such solecisms as attempting to send goods from the outlets to the factories, instead of vice versa. Now this network logic has to be superimposed on the topography of the geographic system, according to the economics of the operational system. Since goods can be transmitted by a limited number of routes, defined by roads and railways, it is not very difficult to make an appropriate many–one mapping of the country's geography. Normal map-reference devices were used to give a computable account of the terrain, adding logical constraints to avoid such solecisms as attempting to drive a lorry through an estuary. Making the econometric model of distribution was more straightforward and familiar. It involved a mathematical generalization of the cost of making a journey from any point A to any point B, taking into account handling factors and such restraints as the number of hours a man is committed to drive a lorry at a stretch. The model has also to deal with the costs of investing in various types of transportation, and this was handled on the basis of discounted cash values.

Thus an interlocking set of models was established, consisting of one drawn from logic, one from topography and one from econometrics. These did not form a sequential chain (as in the last example); they had to map on to each other simultaneously. It is as if a three-dimensional model had been created, and the whole of it was translated into computer language and set up inside a machine. Some effort must be made to visualize what this elaborate scientific model really means, and the following picture (which is quite unreal) may help. Imagine the country in question as a map. The contour lines on this map are not those connecting points of equal height above sea level, but those connecting sites for plant of equal annual cost. Thus at the top of a 'hill', the cost of a plant would be the highest in the locality of the hill, while at the bottom of a trough would be found the cheapest point.

A procedure must be found for hunting over this economic terrain for the best arrangement of plants; that is to say a *search algorithm* is needed. The discovery of this algorithm, or systematic procedure, was a difficult research task; but again it is possible to illustrate what it involved through the image of an economic terrain as just explained. Suppose that one man is asked to walk over this terrain looking for the site of a factory. Unfortunately, there is a thick fog; he cannot see anything at all. This constraint comes about because our searcher is not alone. Other people have been appointed to look for other factory sites; still others are looking for sites for warehouses and depots. All these people are setting out simultaneously, because the required solution must satisfy them all at once. But as they move about, each changes the terrain continuously for all the others—since the movement of a factory (for instance) continuously changes the cost of having the depot it serves at a given point. Thus all the searchers, of whom the number is not yet known, have to move about a shifting terrain in a fog seeking low points; and they have to arrive at the best combined solution.

There is only one rule that any searcher can be given. He is standing at a point, and cannot see. Then he must seek around with one foot for a foothold lower than the one already held, and move to it. If he continues to do this until any step he attempts to take is *up*hill, he has arrived at the lowest place. Provided that there is no sealed-off hollow on the map, that is, provided there is always a descending route to the lowest place of all, the searcher will find the best site. It is difficult to visualize how this provision can be met in real space, but it can be achieved in the phase space of the model by technical devices from logic.

The searcher cannot think of himself alone, however. There must be wireless communication between all the searchers. Otherwise one of them, in a fanatical attempt to reach his own lowest point, may ruin the attempts of the others to find theirs. This man may raise the ground level for everyone else, so that the *total* cost is exorbitant. This need for communication, so apparent in this parable, exemplifies the systemic nature of the problem.

This rather crude attempt to explain what is going on, in the use of a tremendously complex model inside a computer, is helpful for several reasons. Firstly, it does indicate how big is the task which the management has to face. It is surely a task of such immensity that there would be no hope at all of examining by orthodox methods every possible answer in looking for the best. There is an infinity of possible answers. The best that can be done without operational research is to list what experience suggests are the most likely solutions, and to evaluate these by accounting exercises. Even if this can be successfully done on a static basis, the dynamic interactions of the system cannot possibly be taken into account. Moreover, the management will simply never know if there is a better answer that they just do not happen to have proposed for evaluation. The search algorithm, however, does in a sense examine an infinitely large number of solutions, because it must end by selecting the best—even if no-one has thought of it. When that best answer is reached, the fog clears: the new network becomes visible, and the box is no longer black.

It has to be emphasized that all this takes into account the cost of any changes implied by the solution. That is to say, if some *existing* pieces of plant have moved when the fog clears, then it is already established as right that they should move. This is not a separate issue, because capital has been taken into account in constructing the global model. In the case quoted, a fairly new plant of considerable capital value was shown to move in the optimal solution. The management, not unnaturally, found it very difficult to believe that it could possibly be an economical proposition to pull down the splendid new plant that had recently been opened. Yet it was eventually agreed that this was so.

Finally to emphasize the immensity of the task, it is interesting to record the amount of computer work actually involved. Because a search algorithm is an heuristic process, no-one could say in advance what course the experiments with the model would take, nor in consequence how many there would be. In the event, some seventy experiments were required to complete the search. Each of these involved the evaluation of the entire set of interlocking models a huge number of times. Twenty of the experiments each needed no less than 250,000 such evaluations of the total system. Even so, thanks to the speed of modern computers, the answer was found in a day.

It had taken about six months to do the whole job. At the beginning, the position was that a new major factory would produce (thanks to technological advance) a very handsome saving in production cost. Unfortunately, however, the managers tried to fit this factory's output into the existing marketing scheme and, wherever they thought of siting it, the whole of this saving and more besides was lost in increased distribution costs. The completely new plan produced by the study preserved the production saving, and procured a new saving of equivalent amount through more effective supply to the market.

So much, then, for the resolution of sub-systems within the initially black boxes of global ecosystemic models. The great virtue of both these case studies lies, it is suggested, in the fact that they answered managerial problems of policy within the context of the total system, taking into account the fact that black boxes really are black. Had the OR scientists *not* considered these problems in the global setting, it is quite clear that although the questions posed by management would have been answered, the optimal company policy would not have been discovered. Secondly, had the scientists *not* recognized the boxes as black (that is to say, had they assumed that the existing networks were necessarily unalterable), neither of the solutions could possibly have been found—since both of them involved radical changes in the structures that already existed. It is time to say more about structure.

4   The Question of Structure

The scientific attack on the managerial problems of an industrial firm should, it is contended, be seen as beginning in a global model, the details of which can be resolved in greater detail as required. The by now classical techniques of operational research, drawn from its mathematics, its statistics, its econometrics and its computer technology, may be most successfully and safely operated within that context. And it seems that there are few problems which cannot be tackled by these means. This is not to say that *all* management problems must be tackled in this way, nor that the manager may now lay down his burden and hand over to the scientist. The point is that managers should begin to look at the situations for which they are responsible through descriptions which acknowledge the natural law. They need scientists to help them to do this. They need competent models, and the aid of a comprehension illuminated by the best thinking-tools that man has yet discovered for the purpose of dealing with nature; they should quantify those situations if at all possible. It is not the substitution of science for management that is advocated; it is the appeal for a professional rather than an amateur approach to the managerial task.

Now if this appeal is justified, then the very first thing to do is to think in a scientific way about the constitution of the management itself—since this *is* the control structure of the enterprise. This task is more fundamental than any other; more fundamental even than the construction of a global model of the firm. For once OR begins to model the totality spread before it, it makes the fundamental acceptance of the structure which controls it. This is because that structure can be discussed only in a metalanguage. The language in which one describes the firm itself is simply not competent as a vehicle for discussing objectively why the firm is as it is. And since the normal occupation of management is to be expert in using the practical language of the firm's operations, there is a particular risk that the management will never learn to speak the metalanguage in which its own structure can be discussed. The phase space of management is defined by what everyone knows management to be; the thought blocks which threaten managers when it comes to discussing management are often well nigh impenetrable.

In Section 4 of Chapter 9 some preliminary remarks were made about the problems of industrial organization. Those remarks derived from the discussion of operational research, and were made before we embarked on the chapters dealing with cybernetics. People often think that the relevance of cybernetics to organization has to do solely with automation. But this is not so; and what has to be said about automation is in any case reserved for the next chapter. This is the place for the elucidation of various organizational matters in the light of cybernetic thinking, regardless of the degree to which advanced machines are in use. It is a common error to suppose that the relevance of cybernetic science to the organization of a firm depends upon its mastery of computer systems and the like. But in truth cybernetics, which is defined as the science of control in the animal and the machine, is precisely *about organization*—for this is the medium through which control is exercised. Therefore cybernetics may also be defined, as it has been by certain Russian writers, as the science of effective organization.

We have to face the facts of our present situation. Here we are, in an atomic age, running companies which themselves employ a highly sophisticated technology in all departments, and basing our mode of control on folklore. It is perhaps good folklore; much thought has been devoted to what management schools call the Principles of Organization. But these principles are the outcome of experience: they are rules of thumb. Just as we prefer to replace rules of thumb in (say) production by more scientific analyses, so must the time come when the chairman and the managing director will demand a more scientific attack on the question of how the business is organized.

The drawing of the traditional 'family tree' has already been criticized, because it fails to depict real relationships but only formal (and thus possibly unreal) ones. Never mind, say its adherents; it does not pretend to do other than state the 'chain of command'—it attributes responsibility. But that it does so despite the real relationships, and in ignorance of them, is precisely the criticism. For responsibilities in a complex viable organism *cannot* in general be handed out like rations. Certainly the managing director, in discussion with his senior managers, can say: 'I hold *you*, Bill, responsible for *this*.' It is likely to be clear from the context exactly what that means. It has to do with getting some particular agreed action done, some specific project implemented, some definite decision enforced. Everyone, including Bill, knows what he has to do, and he does it. The responsibility is eventually discharged. But the responsibilities allocated by an organization chart are not at all of this kind, unless they are to do with very special skills. The company medical officer, like the financial accountant, has a responsibility for a particular activity whenever and wherever it arises; that too is clear to all and can be discharged in each instance. But the divisional responsibilities of general management to which we are accustomed are not susceptible to being *discharged* in these senses.

The sales manager is 'responsible' for selling, and the works manager is 'responsible' for production. One can see the sense in which these two men can be differently oriented, the one facing outwards to markets, the other facing inwards to the plant. So the notion of 'areas of general responsibility' is born. But meanwhile the notion of some definite task that can be discharged is dying. In the limit, a kind of organizational decadence may set in within the firm, in which the sales manager sits in an office 'owning' the commercial policy, while the works manager sits in another office 'owning' the production policy. What are these policies? They are, in this limiting case, incompatible ways of envisaging the same thing—namely the company's survival.

But, it will be objected, each of these men is taking the important decisions that arise within his general area of responsibility. What sort of decisions are these? A sales decision concerning the selection of one retailer in a town rather than another as the unique outlet is clearly a *sales* responsibility—but it is not 'important' at the general management level. A production decision as to the process route to be followed by a special one-off job is equally clearly a *works* responsibility, and it is also 'unimportant'. Then enlarge the importance (presumably, then, the *value*) of the sample decisions. The sales manager 'decides' on a sales campaign; the works manager 'decides' on the purchase of a costly piece of plant. But just a moment. Each of these possibilities has inevitably been the subject of months of study by junior specialists and under-managers. They recommend a course of action which the senior man is asked to approve. On what basis can he refuse approval? He does not know anything like as much about this project as the staff on whom he has laid the genuine responsibility for discovering the right answer. They know it; he knows it; he knows they know he knows it. If he refuses approval, he is reprimanding his staff for incompetence. Anyway, why should he regard himself as more competent than they?

There is only one basis on which any senior manager can take a genuine *decision*: the basis that he knows something his staff does not know. Well, he ought to have told them what he knows; and he will in fact have told them what he knows about the topic they are studying. So what he uniquely knows, or subsequently discovers, is not to do with the topic of their study. It is something to do with another facet of the company's survival; a facet, it is now clear, that is not within his own 'responsibility' but somebody else's. The strength of the senior manager is in fact nothing to do with the divisional policy he is alleged to own; it is to do with his integration into the general management team.

Now this is good cybernetics. In all natural control systems and in all mechanical artefacts, we find components and assemblies, sub-systems, that discharge particular responsibilities. Let us adhere to the idea that a responsibility is something which is definite and *can* be discharged; at which point the responsibility is over and done with until a new respon- sibility is allocated to this sub-system. Computing the flight of a ball in order that a man may catch it, or computing the flight of a missile in order that another may intercept it, are both examples of control acti- vities. Each involves a series of interlocking activities which must be accomplished. Each of these activities is awarded as a distinct respon- sibility that can be discharged to some sub-assembly of the control system. Each has specialized optical circuits, for instance. The brain has the eye lens, the retina, the optic nerves and the occipital lobe of the cortex as a specialized, analysing sub-system. The tracking device has radar antennae, oscilloscopes, tape storage and differential analysers. The sub-systems all parallel each other; both major systems rely on homeostasis as between the sub-systems, monitored by extensive feed-back. All this makes sense in terms of responsibility and its discharge. And arrangements of this kind are paralleled in the firm by functional specialism and the humbler levels of line management.

But how is the decision to catch the ball, or to intercept the missile, to be taken? In the ball-catching case, the brain, which includes apparatus for this purpose, no longer operates (as far as we can tell) with localized cerebral sub-systems: its top level decisions are functions of its total behaviour. The reticular formation of the brain stem is a *generalized* monitor of input information; the prefrontal lobe of the cortex, which inductive research suggests is connected with processing moral decisions, has no specific sub-systemic control responsibilities. But we do not know how to work the orthodox computer as an integrated, undifferentiated control device in this sense. It ought to follow then, if this argument is correct, that there is no procedure by which the tracking system can of itself decide to intercept the missile. That checks. In the case of the firm, by parallel arguments, we look to the top management *as a whole* to take policy decisions which have to do with the company's survival.

In a lively, well-led firm this is exactly what happens. It amounts to well-led cabinet government. But in the decadent case the sales manager and the works manager (to continue with these two as exemplifying the argument) may openly opt out of the generalized computation proceed-ings. They may spend their talking time on the board or the management committee, trying to demonstrate their independence within a situation of which all aspects are clearly interdependent. The discussion is about a new product: then the sales manager finds that this is *his* province, and only he is competent to take decisions about something which (after all) has to be sold. But no-one, least of all the sales manager, is going to be allowed to tell the works manager how to make this product. It turns out that every feature required by sales makes the product impossible or uneconomic to manufacture, while every feature required by the works to facilitate production turns out to make the product unsaleable. How is the managing director to cope with this? His organization chart does not help him, and he has to rely on human attributes: his own powers of per-suasion or force of character, the weaknesses and vanities of the two men. If he is any good, he will overcome the difficulty. But this probably means that he has to do the actual decision-taking alone. Now although this *is* the limiting case, it indicates a pathological syndrome that is terribly common in senior management groups. Indeed, if the decadence has gone thus far, it may be an advantage, for surely both these men will soon be removed altogether. The real trouble arises because they usually have the good sense, in practice, to restrain themselves sufficiently to obscure what is happening, and thereby to avoid the ultimate showdown. But the firm is deprived.

In particular, the company loses the redundancy factor previously remarked (Chapter 9 again), which is its only reliable protection against major errors of policy. In some actual cases noted, even this appallingly dangerous situation is offset by the good sense of people lower down, who begin to enlarge their communications beyond their official limits and to arrogate to themselves the integrating functions of their seniors. This is good cybernetics again: the redundancy factor elsewhere permits lower hierarchic levels to change their actual function—just as seems to happen in a brain affected by gross lesions (through war wounds, for example). It happens, too, in battles. Nowadays, communications are supposed to be too good for this trick to be necessary. But certainly in (for instance) Nelson's day, a sub-system of a few ships could be isolated by bad visibility from the flagship, and would then have to undertake its own integrating functions based on a prior knowledge of the grand strategy. Yet again it must be observed that the organization chart says nothing of all this: it specifically denies any such possibility by omitting to show any kind of horizontal interaction at the lower levels. Thus once pathological symptoms appear in the higher management control system, the organization chart (which ought to come to the rescue) becomes a blueprint for the disintegration of the firm.

There are problems in all this that must be tackled, and it is going to pay the firm to embark on a scientific study of its organizational structure. No ready-made theory of organization is available, but various models have been tried out in particular situations. The solutions to organizational problems are without doubt the most difficult sorts of operational research to implement. So it is not a question of finding radically new answers to ancient problems, which must then be put into effect by commands ordering the whole senior management to start being different people. This cannot be done; and if it could be done it would induce a traumatic shock to the organism so great that the firm would probably die. But this does not mean to say that *nothing* can be done. The object should be gradually to improve what happens by modifying structural relationships according to valid cybernetics. This ought to be an improvement on common sense. After all, the organizational confusions which can be uncovered in almost any large firm are precisely the fruit of common sense. The inoperable structure which pundits have installed actually works, but only because the natural laws affecting the behaviour of viable systems have operated since then. If

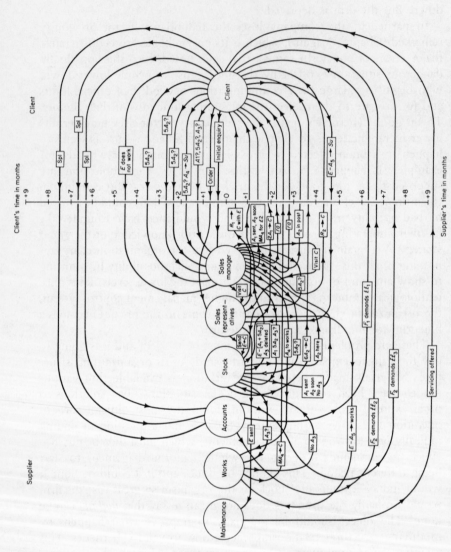

FIGURE 55. Case study: Activities involved in failing to sell a single item worth less than £100.

we work with a knowledge of those laws, and use them deliberately, we must surely reach a better answer.

Consider Figure 55, for example. This diagram (devised by Mrs. G. E. Gillott) shows the progress of *one order*, placed by a single customer, for a single item worth less than £100, produced by a large firm. This is an actual case history. The customer placed the order and tried to have it filled. The start of the process is at the centre of the vertical line. Time works outward in *both* directions, up and down, to enable us to distinguish between the company's (left-hand) and the customer's (right-hand) activities. A closed-loop system is clearly in operation, which becomes depicted as a spiral—since the time scale spreads out the looping information. As can be seen, it took more than nine months to complete the transaction—with no sale recorded at the finish. The process ended for the customer after four and a half months when he finally sent back the product in disgust, and refused to pay the bill. The process ended for the company five months *after* that, when the service department offered the customer a maintenance agreement for the product he did not have.

Obviously the organizational structure of this company is total nonsense. Somehow it got like this, somehow it cannot be put right. If we apply OR, using cybernetic models, to the situation, then the design of the structure can certainly be improved. Moreover, it is possible for OR to validate the changes made—by scientific experiment. This kind of experiment does not have to be based on simulation. It is possible in cases of this kind to test the ecosystem at work by actually buying products, and charting the customer's progress on diagrams of the sort shown in Figure 55. It is obvious that quantitative comparisons, using various criteria, such as the number of operations and the time elapsed, can be made between earlier and later charts. The machinery for a scientifically directed evolution of the management structure is all available. But the results in this case cannot be demonstrated. The example has deliberately been chosen in an attempt to bring home the reality of those thought blocks. For the distinguished businessman who is managing director of the famous company concerned, having studied with astonishment the facts recorded in Figure 55, declared that nothing could be done. 'X, who is responsible,' he said, 'is a very good man. Any other organizational structure than his would probably make things worse.'

Is it a good joke, or bad management, or incompetence, or indifference, that stops managers from managing themselves? Perhaps they are simply not trained to speak the metalanguage. It is in the language of the firm that problems are posed, and are solved or not solved. It is in a metalanguage alone that it is clever to dissolve them.

17

INFORMATION AND
AUTOMATION

A rose by any other name would still smell like
phenylethyl methyl enthyl carbinol.

The Sciences, Vol. 3, No. 20 (1964)

1 Reorienting Towards Management

In the last chapter, a discussion of organization from the cybernetic
viewpoint was begun. The idea that it is possible to use cybernetics to
help resolve management structures was offered as being independent of
automation. But the availability of advanced machinery certainly makes
it urgent to think afresh about the modes of organizing that have been
inherited. In short: whether the firm is run entirely by men, or entirely
by machines, or by some mixture of both, is irrelevant to the question
whether the structure of the control function is properly designed. Given
a properly designed structure, on the other hand, its appearance in the
flesh or in the metal is a matter of convenience; 'that which we call a
rose, by any other name would smell as sweet'—for the reason given at
the chapter heading.

It is not good operational research to attempt to formulate general
principles *a priori*. Yet cybernetic considerations, reinforced by much
observation, begin to suggest that other ways than those that are familiar
could be found for distributing duties at the very top and, as a consequence, for specifying modes of interaction lower down. At both these
levels, the topic is now horizontal integration: a task at present attempted
by two major techniques, the one formal, the other informal. Formally,
the answer is to hold meetings, from the board downwards, which are
generally called (at the lower levels) committees. Informally, social
interaction is sought. The board itself, because of its very seniority and
its consciousness of the power to go wrong, tends to behave very much

432

as a social group. This is its cybernetic salvation. The amount of interaction is immense; and it does not much matter what is the content of
communication, be it official or unofficial, if it produces the sense of
unity and the climate of opinion which betokens a high-redundancy
decision-taking control system. But, lower down, the orthodox committee system, which at first sight procures both the inter-communica-
tion and the high redundancy demanded by the cybernetician, by no
means meets the need.

Each committee member represents some special function or department to which he owes a loyalty. In practice, he is usually present not to
procure an agreed policy which integrates the views of all members as
alleged, but to procure his sub-system's policy as the agreed policy if
possible or, failing that, to stop any other sub-system's policy from
being foisted on to his own. Second, he does not arrive fully briefed with
an objective knowledge of all the facts. He knows what his chief expects
him to achieve; for the rest, he has thumbed through 'the papers' in the
car *en route*. Third, the conduct of the meeting is not a homeostatic
interaction of like minds seeking a company optimum, but a political
foray in which it may be that no genuine communication takes place
at all—only the striking of attitudes already well known. Fourth, the
account of the meeting afterwards that is given by each member to his
own sub-system, is a dramatized and distorted account of what happened
which supplies positive instead of negative feedback. That is to say,
instead of the delegate's bringing home error-correcting information, he
returns with an emotive judgment about the foolhardiness of everyone
else's views which reinforces error. Fifth, the official account of the
meeting, given in its minutes, which are the means of informing everyone
(and especially higher management) who is not directly concerned, contains almost no information. They are short, terse statements about long,
involved negotiations, totally lacking in requisite variety, even when
objectively drawn. But the need to be sure that no-one is 'given away'
(otherwise he will object to the minutes), coupled with the machinations
of the meeting's convenor who instructs the secretary, reduces their
value further.

If anyone objects to this account as being exaggerated and ridiculous,
it is possible again to fall back on the argument used before. Namely:
even if committees are not really like this, they run these risks; even if
the more egregious absurdities can in practice be avoided, it is still
wrong that the whole arrangement could in theory conduce to them.
(But secretly we may prefer to agree that committees really are shock-
ingly like this in most cases; especially if we, as judges, have ever

actually sat on them ourselves.) At any rate, thoughtful firms, which have no professional cybernetic advice, do in most cases acknowledge the defects of such formal horizontal communication, not by admitting to faults but by supplementing the arrangements. Social interaction is encouraged. For rather misty reasons, which may be formulated in surprisingly altruistic terms, many firms find themselves subsidizing this social interaction at considerable cost in actual cash. If challenged, those responsible tend to embark on set speeches about *esprit de corps* and 'happy ships'. If they but knew it, they have clear, precise and scientific cybernetic justification.

The net result of all this seems to be the following. We have a two-dimensional control system for the firm. One dimension is formal and has the advantage of being highly structured. Thus when people are operating in this dimension they know how to behave. The rules of the game are clear: everyone knows whom to call 'Sir', whom to address as 'Mister', whom to speak to by surname and whom by Christian name. Everyone knows, moreover, who is responsible for what, and by what means he may set about achieving the outcome his side has selected. But control in this dimension is unstable for the reasons discussed (and many others). So a second, intersecting, control dimension exists: the informal dimension. This is the plane of social interaction, which maximizes genuine communication regardless of the rules, or of the relevance of the information passed. This second system refuses to obey the so-called Principles of Management. It is no longer clear who is senior to whom. It no longer matters who is 'responsible' for what. No-one any longer pretends to believe that each man answers to one and only one superior, or that no more than five juniors can report to any one senior. (Where did that magic number come from?—the fingers and toes, some say. Historically, it was apparently the dictum of a forgotten French writer.) Again all this is cybernetically sound. Most viable systems depend upon this particular form of redundancy as well as other forms: a two-dimensional, structurally inconsistent, control system. Consider, as an example, the central nervous system and the endocrine system in the vertebrate body.

This is the basis on which industrial organizations actually manage to work. People seem to see it as a one-dimensional system (the formal, of course) which is imperfect, and which has to be buttressed by informality. The cybernetician is likely to go much further and to say that the system is intrinsically dual in its fundamental character, and that this duality is the structural mode of protective redundancy. There is a particularly interesting outcome of this disagreement, which helps to resolve it, and which is worth further exploration. According to the formal organization chart, decisions are taken by the 'responsible' people —who are just those whose labels authorize them to decide. According to cybernetics, this is impossible in a system which is to survive. Decisions are always taken by the node, or the plexus of nodes, in a network which has the most information. In a brain-like system, that is to say, as investigated by cybernetics, the first element or sub-system of the system to attain requisite variety to match an input situation acts. It is knowledge, not the laying on of hands, which bestows the power to decide. And it is a corollary of this theorem that it will not always be the same element that acts on a given class of input.

The exploration of this contradiction between formal industrial organization and the conclusions of cybernetic inference, highlights the equivalent status claimed for the informal organization. For, according to arguments advanced earlier, the way in which informal controls (the social ones) counteract the formal controls might well be defined by their requisite variety in relation to a given decision. The board decision is not put together like a jig-saw puzzle composed of logical pieces—the sales element, the production element, the financial element—whatever the organization chart may seem to imply. It is created through like-mindedness: the responsive awareness on the part of each director of the direction of thinking taken up by all the other directors as a whole. One director can influence that direction of thinking; if he is vehement, his own vector may dominate all the other vectors, so that the board's direction is his direction. But the vehemence, if the board is competent, is not defined in decibels: it is a measure of knowledge. This director is communicating insight into the whole problem; he is not contributing the facts that concern 'his areas of responsibility', and sitting back until the chairman has put the jig-saw puzzle together. The jig-saw theory of board decision is a *post hoc* rationalization, and the organization chart is its blueprint.

What applies to the board applies to the shop floor, and the issue under discussion is indeed more readily understood at that level. Department B requisitions its raw material from department A, in order to deliver raw material to department C. The formal organization provides elaborate procedures to make sure this is done properly—and they largely work. The stock-control files operate, the multicoloured forms flow, the planning boards are set up. Yet none of this apparatus has requisite variety to provide control of an imperfect and uncertain world. It works in theory, but would not work in practice because real life injects too much variety—especially in the form of noise. But we said: it *does* work.

The reason is that extra control variety is pumped into the formal control system by the informal control system. The shop floor in big industry is notoriously interactive; everyone is someone else's cousin; everyone meets his opposite number in the charge-hands' mess, the local public house, the pigeon-fanciers' society or the gardening club. The directors of the firm should give thanks that this is so—and without cost at that. For here is decision-taking in action, based on the cybernetic principle that requisite variety acts. 'By the way,' says Joe, 'you won't be getting that lot of crimple-bars until Thursday: we had a breakdown.' The work is replanned two days before the official notification comes through (if it ever does; the departmental manager may have a sensitive spot about crimple-bars). By then it would have been too late.

There are surely reasons in contemporary industrial society why boards and shop-floor foremen, charge-hands and planners, form intimate social groups at their two disparate levels. There are also reasons, in Britain at least, why middle management does not. Wherever the state of the management profession is discussed in Britain, whether among directors or on foremen's courses, whether in universities or in management schools, the same concern is expressed. The effectiveness of middle management is everyone's worry. Yet pick on a middle manager in the flesh and interrogate him: one finds an upright and intelligent citizen, competent in his job, anxious to work and to collaborate. The cybernetician answers this dilemma. The middle manager, alone of the management hierarchy, is operating (almost) one-dimensionally as a control element. There is no pressure on him, as there is on higher management, to interact vigorously with his colleagues; he may meet them at lunch, but this is not enough. The others still wonder what sort of woman could possibly have married him, and cannot understand why he likes or dislikes a particular television programme. He is an enigma, and (again in Britain) he commonly lives in a suburban society of peers far away from any of his colleagues. So there is no village-life species of interaction among middle managers, as there is in very junior management—where each knows the other's business because their families are intermarried and because they are neighbours in a community of gossip. The (virtually) missing informal control dimension among middle management is modern industry's greatest weakness.

This is the kind of thinking which cybernetics can apply to the way existing organizations work, and the minimal claim is that if we can once sink our scientific teeth into organizational problems we shall begin to understand them more clearly. But obviously a rather more ambitious claim than this ought to be possible. If we once have access through science to the very nature of viable organization, then we begin to formulate OR models which can be used to achieve improvements. Something can usually be achieved *within* the existing management structure to increase efficiency: to make clearer what has to be done in the way of redefining responsibilities, reorganizing information flow, reconstituting the committee system, restating policies for management succession, and so on. But there is more than this.

In the last chapter it was said that the problems which underlie practice should be restudied, and that below the level of problems, again, should be uncovered the level of policies. But, it is now argued, there is a yet deeper level: that of structures. If a firm is ready to reconsider the very structures of organization, then the outcome for its policies may be a considerable change. In that case the nature of its problems may appear radically different. And in that case, in turn, what now counts as either good *or* bad practice may cease to be at all relevant. It is here that the initial remark about dissolving rather than solving problems is finally justified. For although new structures, which bring new policies in their train, will doubtless not eliminate problems but simply create a new set of unfamiliar ones, something important has been gained. This is the capability to tackle the new problems by an exceptionally well endowed management; a management, that is, which really understands how these problems arise, because it understands the structures which provoke them. 'Understand', in turn, in a truly scientific sense, because the structures are scientifically designed—and that means that their limitations are precisely known. A managerial situation of this kind is thoroughly amenable to OR attack.

As was said some pages back, it is not good science to assert that we now know what the answers would be in general. We do know, from particular studies, what particular answers can sometimes be given; but far more work on special cases is required before there is much hope of enunciating general principles. Yet a conclusion to this essay may be reached in terms of one (cautiously drawn) conclusion. It is this. It is knowledge, momentary knowledge, in an element (or sub-system) of a system that really confers authority to act, not the arbitrary allocation of responsibilities. This has been argued as an information-theoretic principle, as a practical induction from a study of controls in nature, and as an analysis of what really happens in industry anyway. If this is so, then it could well be more satisfactory to determine organizational structure around the ebb and flow of requisite variety (for meeting disturbances) in a firm, rather than around seniorities and boxes drawn on organization charts.

DC—FF

This would mean that the two dimensions of management control would cease to be the formal and informal dimensions. They could instead become the functional and the problem-orientated dimensions. This is to say that responsibilities-that-can-be-discharged would indeed be allocated to individuals. But since, as has been seen, these usually involve 'unimportant' (tactical, rather than strategic) decisions, the managers involved in the process would either be junior managers or functional specialists—such as accountants or production engineers. The more senior part of the firm would be organized around particular problems, which of course would change from time to time. The board (or top management committee) is already organized like this, according to earlier arguments, although it pretends it is not. At this highest level, the team is trying to solve problems of survival, and there is a good case for suggesting that its members should not waste time by pretending to be the ultimate decision-takers within 'areas of responsibility' which are in fact covered by redundant control systems of lower rank in the hierarchy. At the middle management level, however, the change (in outward appearance at least) would be traumatic; instead of being busy managers who rush off to committee meetings, the men concerned would really become full-time members of problem-solving teams who occasionally accept particular and dischargeable local responsibilities.

The mechanism suggested can be most clearly envisaged in the context of a problem which arises because of a change in technology or circumstances (such as the new product mentioned before), although it could equally apply to more familiar problem-generating situations. If a group of the best (most experienced, well qualified, etc.) managers are banded together as a project team to handle the new product, then they can be given—as a group—a dischargeable responsibility. Occasionally in modern industry this is done, though because of inhibitions about organizational structure, the people selected have to be seconded from the formal 'I-own-a-policy' organization, and senior management is never quite sure whether to relieve them of departmental duties altogether or not. Of course, if the firm were differently organized, then this difficulty would not arise. Specifically: if the best men do not *have* departmental pseudo-responsibilities, then no-one would have to decide whether they should be relieved, who should stand in for them, or how to convince those concerned that they were not being effectively sacked. It is better to dissolve problems than to solve them.

A management which took it for granted that the *status quo* could be maintained by junior managers, functional specialists and a certain amount of automation, would feel free to use its best managerial talent in the way suggested. It would mean that new situations would be conquered more quickly, that changes in technology would be encompassed and assimilated more readily, and that the old familiar problems would actually receive competent attention, instead of being for ever relegated to low priority. There was once a scientist who wrote on a memorandum from the chairman: 'I regret I cannot deal with this, owing to the pressure of less important work', and got away with it. There have been many strikes (could it be *most* strikes?) which have occurred because the problems which generated them have been too trivial for a manager, busy with papers and his policy-owning industrial democracy, to consider urgently. Whatever is management doing while its work force is building up a ferment of unrest so serious that it eventually shuts down production? The answer is nothing; nothing, that is, about the problem. It is too busy taking pseudo-decisions, and 'being responsible' for areas—which are not things-that-can-be-discharged.

The new kind of middle management teams would attract more adventurous and genuinely decisive men. They would lead a more exciting and valuable life. Their *modus vivendi* would utterly change, from a nine-to-five attendance at work to a series of thought-intensive projects, each of which would gradually build up to fever pitch and immense personal commitment. In return, these people would be beneficiaries of fresh thinking by top management about how to employ managers. As a result, there would be sabbatical leave schemes involving visits abroad and attendance at (the newer and more aware) universities. It goes without saying that these people would know how to make operational research work for them in a truly problem-oriented way. Not only would they have time to read OR reports, they would be major sponsors, critics and users of policy-investigating science.

2 Reorienting Towards the Computer

It is against this background of what management really is like, and what it could more effectively be organized to become, that the real problem of managerial information is correctly seen. If management groups ought to be problem-oriented and to use problem-oriented science, then the measures of the world that they will require will be special to the problem as well. The managers will call for measurements of parameters of systems, and not for 'the facts'. They will demand that systemic qualities be measured which no-one as yet knows how to measure—hence their need for operational research. By then, there will be no longer any need to pretend that all major decisions are purely economic in character. As we have seen, there is normally a set of conflicting criteria by which a decision or a policy must be judged, a set which includes the criterion of economic viability but is not subsumed within it. Therefore there must be a change in the kind of information which is at present circulated for the running of a firm.

At present, all choices are presented as economic choices. The main reason why this has happened is that the language of choice and its conventions are provided by accountancy. The models that underlie the structure of management information are, as was seen in earlier chapters, the balance sheet and the profit and loss account. The rule of induction is: *that the alternative action* (expressed in terms of these conventions) *which costs* (using these conventions) *least* (using these conventions) *by comparison* (using these conventions) *with the standard or predetermined* (using these conventions) *action for given circumstances* (using these conventions) *is correct.*

The force of these ubiquitous conventions is little understood. They may result in an institutional way of talking, or (as we have learnt to refer to it) a special language, which does not even permit the expression of vital facts. Here is an actual example. A production manager refused to acknowledge that his works ever produced defective items. An item that failed to pass inspection was simply given a code number. The effect of this code was to send the item for corrective treatment. The corrective process was not referred to as such, for there is no need for salvage operations in a works producing no defectives. Therefore this process came to be regarded as a production process undertaken by certain products at technical discretion. Acknowledging all this in the costing system meant building the process concerned into the accounting model of *standard* processing, with a certain level of occupancy—one in fact reflecting the level of defectives. In weeks during which this process was not used at the expected rate, it threw up an 'idle time charge' against the product. Hence to reduce the actual rate of defectives appeared to increase costs. The only way apparently to reduce costs was to make enough defectives to keep the corrective process fully occupied. In this language there is no way of saying: 'To make a better product is a good thing to do.' The accounting model is not homomorphic with reality and it therefore generates nonsense. Let it be noted that in this story the ludicrous outcome was by no means the fault of the company's accountants. They were doing as they were told, and believed in the existence of this spurious production process. The conceptual model of the enterprise in use is created by management as a whole: it is a social phenomenon.

The balance sheet too is a social entity because it is *purposive*: it intends quite openly to express the company's financial stability for the benefit of creditors who do business with it, of shareholders who invest in it and, more generally, of the financial world which underwrites the business confidence which surrounds it. It is a teleological model. But, if it is to be of any use at all, it should be a homomorphic model too. Obviously the transformations which operate on the company's affairs to produce this piece of paper are many–one. The structure they preserve is the measure of stability that is expressly given by the equation 'total assets = total liabilities'. Prior to the Companies Act of 1929, the information available from the balance sheet of a British company may have been virtually nothing more than this. The effect of that Act, and also of its successor in 1948, was to provide a richer mapping, to reduce the many–oneness of the homomorphic transformation. More information thus appears on balance sheets nowadays. Now those who are highly skilled in the reading of a balance sheet, are precisely engaged in seeking out the structure preserved by the homomorphism. When they explore, for example, the flow of circulating capital, they may compute the ratio of annual turnover to current assets, which gives the speed of that flow in revolutions per year. How this speed varies from one year to another expresses a relationship that has preserved its structure under the homomorphic guarantee.

To fit the modelling account of what is going on to the businessman's financial technique may reveal, in a given case, a great deal about the validity of the management's criteria for decision. But it also shows clearly that the balance sheet is a model that exists in one dimension. If the balance sheets of the nation answer to the tests prescribed by the financial world, 'all is well'. Hence if the return earned on capital employed in a particular company is both stable and comparable with the average for the industry, the shareholders (or more realistically the financial commentators) will conclude that the company is well managed. But there is no knowing whether this return could not have been very much higher if other policies had been pursued. Moreover, there is no knowing if the position will hold in changing circumstances.

It is precisely the fact that circumstances change which restricts the value of the whole existing approach. There is a well-known story about the attempt of a large departmental store to discover which department had the highest turnover and return per square foot of floor space, and to see whether any conclusions could be drawn from the answer. The cost exercise revealed that the most profitable department was the ladies' room. There is a kind of managerial mind which, supplied with this information, would conclude: we must turn the entire departmental store into a public convenience. Observe that there is a spurious 'now' in which this conclusion is correct: that is, if everyone now in the store could instantaneously be enabled to use this facility now, the profits would exceed any ever made. But quite obviously this is impossible, and quite obviously the system that constitutes the departmental store will not permit the successful implementation of this policy in the future, for the new system created to maximize profit will not in fact have any customers.

The conclusion drawn is not wrong just because it is ridiculous; there is a very definite reason for the mistake. It is this. *In changing the character of a system which has generated a profit in one part, we alter the expectation of profit in that part.* Therefore a policy for change which is based on analysis of the present situation, and the extrapolation of the results into a future which will have been made different by that very change, is probably wrong. We might well find that the new system does not generate any profit at all in the part that was so profitable before. This is surely the reason why so many grandiose development plans undertaken by industry do not make the return on capital which was forecast. The error is frequently met.

It seems very possible that the succession of crises that have characterized the British economy since 1945 derive from these two limitations of the balance sheet model of the enterprises which compose that economy. Apparent booms have been illusory, because the return on capital (and hence the dividend) has measured up to accepted but arbitrary levels that have themselves not been effective measures of the need. During these periods, proper advances (those which would measure up to the *unexpressed* need) have not been made. This is not surprising psychologically, for people are in general unwilling to interfere in a situation they regard as satisfactory already, partly from laziness and partly from fear that the disturbance they create will damage whatever unknown mechanism it is that apparently serves them well. Studies of actual firms and also experiments with simulation games support this conclusion. The second point is that the static accounting model is a bad predictor of stability in the face of change. The effect of this is to amplify recessions. The mechanism here is that policy-forming and decision-taking undertaken against a background of the balance sheet during an easy period, fail to recognize the relevance of the boom. That is, the policies are all right if the boom continues. The moment it is noticed that the boom is illusory, selling becomes difficult and the expansionist policies cannot be supported. Their collapse makes the recession worse.

These arguments reinforce the need for models that are both systemic and dynamic. Policies have to be tested in context and against alternatives —not in isolation and against the preconceived notional policy that offers 'a reasonable return'. Their vulnerability to the unknown future has to be assessed on a variety of assumptions about the state of the market. Naturally enough, managements typically declare that these things are done, and they may genuinely believe that they are. Even so, what is important is that there is literally no language in which to express such arguments competently in an orthodox business, and there is certainly no model from which to generate meaningful answers. The economic model has a unidimensional objective function, namely profit. It is a myth to say that all the other criteria of management can be translated into this language of profit; even if this were possible in principle, the mapping transformations are simply unknown. It is moreover this unidimensional language which promotes the rules of induction referred to earlier, which assume that any activity can be costed independently of any other. For although this assumption holds for the particular model in use, it is unfortunately falsified for the real-life multidimensional dynamic system with which management has in fact to be concerned.

Now the new kinds of measurements which managers require will differ from all this in two major respects. Firstly, they are likely to be pure numbers rather than raw data measuring world events. This point was explored rather fully in Chapter 13. There is no point in presenting the unaided human brain with multidimensional information which it cannot appreciate. We saw how an exceptional cost has to be contemplated in terms of exceptional technical considerations, for example, or perhaps in terms of the weather or of something (such as labour goodwill) that is strictly incommensurable. So the measures that managers want are measures of a system's overall behaviour—in which the collection of variables involved has already been suitably entangled. The importance of a measurement which is a pure number compounded of raw data cannot possibly be its momentary value, for this has no meaning. The importance of such measurements lies in the rate and periodicity of change in the pure number. Secondly, then, the information that managers require is information *about* these sophisticated measurements— they do not require the measurements themselves. The cybernetic arguments of Part III must again be invoked: the situation which the manager handles is a black box. No amount of accounting will make it much more transparent, although that is the specific aim of accountancy. It is better to set up an aim of examining the system's behaviour through the changes of its output, in order to modify its input. Management is the sentient filter of the feedback loop.

It is in the context of this information need that we encounter the electronic computer. Computers have been mentioned before in this book, but their facilities have not been dwelt upon. The reason is that it is possible to be side-tracked very quickly by the capacities of these machines, and to forget to think out what are the real objects of the firm. The existence of computers has been taken for granted, in so far as many of the scientific calculations required by the techniques that have been discussed can be undertaken in no other way. But at last the role of the computer becomes a central issue in its own right. The point is this.

A computer is not a very fast, very accurate calculating machine—or it is so only incidentally. A computer is a logical engine, an essentially deductive apparatus. Computers can do arithmetic because the procedural rules of any arithmetic are tautologous deductions from the logical axioms of that arithmetic. Hence number systems are floated along on the fundamental binary logic of the machine, which is itself indifferent to what that number system is. Now ordinary decimal arithmetic (the kind in which raw data normally accrue, are averaged, and are in general handled) is a trivial instrument in comparison with the task already enunciated. The object of management is *not* to obtain quick delivery of parcels of data—those data which it has always received in the past— in ever greater volume and at ever greater speeds. The management requirement is quite other: it is to obtain very few and highly digested data at those moments alone when the system calls for a decision. Since the system is fundamentally self-organizing, this should happen rather infrequently. In fact, and this is entailed by the cybernetic arguments of Part III, genuine policies and genuine decisions are formulated meta-linguistically. There is no point in interfering with the natural homeo-stasis of the firm as it is running unless the manager is operating in a higher order language than is the system he manages. But the present-day languages of the manager are the languages of the system itself.

So it is a logical problem of some complexity to devise languages fit for the manager to use, although it is a task which can be accomplished (as was seen several chapters ago). The equipment needed to speak the manager's metalanguage is precisely a logical engine—the electronic computer. Without it, the task of discussing the information in the feed-back loops metalinguistically is too great for the human brain to encom-pass *in numerical terms*. This, and not either genius or cussedness, is the origin of management intuition. Intuition is the name given to the operation of the cybernetic computer in the cranium. Intuition does not give precise numerical answers, not because the brain is computing in 'qualities' or 'ideas', but because its computations are too complicated for its output transducer to express arithmetically. The task of replacing intuition by scientific method is therefore not a task of abrogating human qualities in favour of the robot; it is a task of modelling a biological mechanism which is of its own nature quantified by a homomorphic mapping on to a cybernetic black box. The difference between quality and quantity becomes this: qualities emerge from quantitative procedures to which we have no access; quantities have hitherto been treated as raw data too crudely handled to give rise to qualities.

The computer, then, is a machine to be used as an absorber of raw data and a distributor of judgment. In this it resembles a manager. It is meaningless to ask the question that is perennially asked: will the computer replace the manager? The answer is self-evident. The computer will replace the manager only in those functions which the manager (aided by science) is able to elucidate. The class of judgments which the manager is able to elucidate continuously grows. There is always something left over. Moreover, there will be something left over as long as the human brain with its 10^{10} neurons remains so much bigger than a computer, and so much more sophisticated in its built-in logical programmes—most notably, the one referred to as the epigenetic landscape. But that machines should one day, in the long run, outclass the intelligence of their designers is not only possible but virtually guaranteed.

To return to the practical affairs of our lifetime, however, the initial task of installing machines to undertake even the simplest of human functions has hardly begun. It cannot be too vehemently emphasized that this is neither because the machines are inadequate, nor because the scientist's use of them is inexpert, but quite simply because management has not yet understood what the machines are *for*.

3   Reorienting Towards Automation

Putting together what has been said in Section 1 about organization and in Section 2 about the computer, it becomes possible to see in what direction the automated future lies.

If management ought no longer to be carved up into arbitrary empires so that functions and responsibilities which in reality interact are artificially divided, then it is a mistake to install computers special to those empires. Because firms are organized as they are, this is exactly what is happening today. Each manager, and each functional specialist, very reasonably believes that it is his duty to examine the impact of technological change on his area of responsibility. The computer is available to him, and he naturally sets out to make use of it. Accordingly, the vast power of automation is harnessed to the service of the part and not the whole. Hence offices, which consider themselves as production departments with paperwork as the output, have installed data processing machinery, so that the productivity with which more and more paper is produced rises. They have not asked themselves the question: what is to happen to the output? There is no particular reason why they should. Sales offices have automated their order books, enabling themselves to keep a close watch on customer behaviour and on the way in which the customer is treated by the works. They do not (they dare not) ask themselves the question: what is the good of acting as a speedy reference library of information, if neither the market nor production can be influenced by the knowledge acquired? Just as change cannot be produced without information, so information that does not result in change is unreal—it does not truly exist. Factories have installed on-line control computers so that the plant may be more efficiently controlled, but production managers have not asked themselves the question: to what end is this greater control of the process? It is so easy to become obsessed in an engineering sense with better practice within a given framework, without understanding that elasticity in the framework itself could lead to a different definition of practice altogether.

This trend leads to an extraordinary conclusion. We are using the very discovery, namely automation, which in principle frees the firm from its historical divisional preoccupations, to reinforce them in practice. We automate what is there. Now what is there exists because the human hand is limited in its capacity to manipulate, the human eye is limited in its capacity to channel input, the human brain is limited in its ability to process information and to trigger output. These limitations have led to an organizational structure and an approach to problems which the integral social effort of human beings can resolve. Thus when automation is brought in to make all these same activities automatic, most observers see only that what has hitherto been done slowly is done quickly, what has been unreliable is more reliable, what had to be estimated can now be calculated properly. And they are impressed and pleased. What they are really observing, however, is the automation of human limitation; we are enshrining in steel, glass and semi-conductors the very limitations of hand, eye and brain which the computer was invented precisely to transcend.

No, the task is different from this. An elaborate attempt was made in Part III to expound a theory of control for the enterprise, and in the present chapter it has already been argued that management—the society of men—ought to be built around problems. To serve these ends of effective control and management service, automation must set out to provide a generalized information network. That is to say, far from automating what is there already, we should automate what is not there at all—namely, a new control system for the firm at large. The control systems that can be studied today inside firms are not control systems in the sense that they provide a coherent means of ensuring viability at all. They are regulators which operate on stereotyped aspects of the firm's existence. Imagine for a moment a control system which would govern an integral organism in its battle for survival. Then the control systems we know about are no more than epiphenomena of this control.

The obvious analogy to use is that of the control system of a known viable organism such as the human body. Here, unlike the firm, the information system is more than the sum of the local sub-systems which relate to special functions. Autonomy of the production or sales side of the business, as of the spinal reflex or the liver, is all very well, but if it is not to be inimical to the health of the whole organism it must be monitored and mediated by a central system. This is not dedicated to any particular mode of control. It exists to ensure viability and survival, and it serves the autonomous functions. Equivalently, it is perfectly possible to envisage an indivisible automated information system to run a modern firm, which would be installed for the enterprise as a whole, and which would none the less meet the needs of divisional, departmental and functional activities as a by-product.

This system, designed on cybernetic principles, is one that calls for information to effect action and not to invite perusal. Since the main institutional controls depend on people at every decision node, everyone is trained to the notion that information is a commodity presented to men for them to read. But in a natural control system, most of the quantities computed are used directly to procure results: they are simply transformation rules for mapping one black box on to another. In the firm, it should be a rare thing to make an automatic computation available to conscious inspection. Under automation, digital access is not required to most of the numbers. To use the terminology that is used of human beings, the behaviour of computers should *look* intuitive. This is perfectly clear within the framework of the cybernetic models presented here, but it is a complete denial of the outlook sponsored in practice by most data processors.

If the entire management of the firm is to depend on an automated central nervous system, as it were, the question of its reliability can no longer be evaded. One of the apparent advantages of the piecemeal approach to automation within orthodox divisions, and assuming good management, is that each unit tends to support the others. If something goes wrong, then it may be possible to check and to remedy the fault by cross-checking with an independent system. This is perfectly good cybernetics; it invokes the principle of redundancy. And of course this is the clue to the answer, even when an integral control system is envisaged. It was explained at the end of Chapter 9 that the brain (itself integral) uses a very high order of redundancy to obtain reliable results from unreliable elements. Von Neumann's theorem was referred to: outputs of arbitrarily high reliability can be obtained from computing elements of arbitrarily low reliability if the redundancy factor is large enough. This theorem simply must govern the development of automation in industry. It costs more to build a redundant system than a system that is not redundant—of course. But it will pay to introduce redundancy, bearing in mind that the level of reliability then rises very rapidly for a modest increase in the system's elements. Certainly there is no need to approach the redundancy factor that is found in the brain itself, which may well be of the order of 20,000 to 1. That machinery has to be reliable in a highly diverse environment and a vast number of possible circumstances. The control system of the firm is not placed under anything like the same potential stress, but redundancy there must be: in the transducers of output, in the channels, in the computing elements and in the outputs which activate response.

This understanding of automation entails a consequence of high importance, which seems by no means to have been noted—either by managers or by scientists themselves. It is this. A control system of adequate redundancy is protected not only against the inherent unreliability of its elements, but against their eventual failure. In the brain, for example, it seems probable that some 100,000 neurons fail every day throughout life. This is a very serious failure rate: a man ends his life with perhaps only two-thirds of the elements with which he began. But his brain does not have to be 'maintained'. No-one replaces the failed elements, nor do they regenerate themselves as do some other kinds of tissue. The failed components, like the unreliable components (for failure is simply 100 per cent unreliability), do not result in the collapse of the control system, because they have been allowed for in its design.

Now it is perfectly possible to envisage an automated industrial future in which most of the labour force consists of white-coated technicians, armed with soldering irons and technical diplomas, whose job it is to replace the electronic packages which comprise computer circuits when one of their elements fails, or when a preventive maintenance scheme requires the replacement as insurance against failure. This is the picture often quoted, and many social consequences derive from it—the alleged need, for instance, to train huge numbers of technologists and technicians. But it is equally possible to provide for industrial plant with a built-in control system that is guaranteed to last the lifetime of the plant. It is made of unreliable components; many of its components will fail. But because it is a redundant control system, it will continue to function satisfactorily. It is quite clear that this could be done—now. The costs of such meta-reliability would naturally be high, but the saving in highly paid technological service would be enormous. And what can be done for an individual piece of plant can, and *a fortiori* should, be done for the proposed central control system of the firm.

In fact, the scientist has a great deal of freedom in deciding on the best way of achieving the desideratum of reliability. He can obtain it through the design of the electronic hardware, by having more components and more connections. He can also obtain it by taking a larger computer than he would otherwise need, and *programming* redundancy into it. That is to say, there can be redundantly organized software as well as hardware, and there can be any mixture of the two. What will happen depends very much on the extent to which intrinsically reliable components can be developed by the electronics industry. But for any given state of the electronic art, it is a relatively straightforward operational research exercise to decide on the amount and mode of redundancy that is required to achieve any given level of functional reliability. The challenge to managers consists in the implicit demand that they abandon the thought block whereby systems are seen as reliable or not. This false dichotomy describes a completely unreal world. There is no such thing as a completely reliable system, whether in nature or in man's handiwork. There are only more or less reliable systems, and it is for the manager to work with the scientist in specifying an agreed level of reliability which can justify its cost. At any rate, the cost criterion is likely to be fixed in terms of replacing a system more than of repairing it.

Finally, it is important to say that these matters are very specifically matters for general managers to consider. The tendency, noted all around, is for the general manager to abdicate genuine responsibility for the problem: how do we use computers? But this is just one of those issues for which he should hold himself personally accountable. Consider: this is a problem of vital importance which affects the firm at large, and responsibility for it can be discharged. The general manager alone (although advised as necessary) should say what he demands of automation. If the issue is left to under-managers who run parts of the firm, they will inevitably proceed to reinforce the barriers between their divisions—by divisional automation; and they will inevitably entrench their old, discardable, methods—by the automation of hallowed techniques. Thus, if there were a genuine need for automation specifically in the office or specifically in the works, the company secretary and the production director are the very last people who should be charged to decide about it. Yet, under the present structure of management, the onus is likely to fall entirely on them. If it does not, it may fall on an automatic data processing specialist within the firm, or seconded from the firm whose equipment is to be bought. This is also quite wrong, for these people must inevitably seek to adjust the world situation to the equipment—instead of the other way round. When general managers, commissioning the appropriate research as their own thinking develops, begin to demand that automation be used thus and thus, and that equipment be devised to operate thus and thus, the advance of automation can begin. It is held up at present by the equipment manufacturers, who must perforce sell the machinery they make, simply claiming or assuming that this is the right *sort* of equipment. Of course, they are not to be blamed; it is the general manager who is culpable. At this stage of the game, there can hardly be a more important matter to compel his own attention.

4   The Art of the Possible

This challenge leads straight to the question: how much can the general manager demand? What really is possible, and when, are critical issues, and unequivocal answers must be attempted here.

It is a maturely considered and not reckless statement that any automation that is required can in principle be done. That is to say, it would be wise not to reserve any activity or capability as a solely human prerogative. Hence thinking about these matters should begin in an open state of mind that considers what would be desirable rather than what appears to be attainable now. For there are certainly two views about this attainability. Some experts, gloomy in their awareness of the development difficulties faced by any new project, understate what it is already known how to do. They confuse the design attainability with the hardware availability. Other experts, excited by their knowledge that something *can* be done, forget that we do not yet know quite *how* to do it. There are, then, three distinguishable levels of attainment. Firstly, there is the mathematical demonstration that a particular facility can be automated; secondly, there is the design specification as to how to do it; thirdly, there is the availability of reliable ironmongery.

It was argued earlier that the immediately available equipment may be wrong for the job, because it has been designed in acceptance of a structural framework we may wish to destroy. So although some automation has been done, and some novel applications not yet seen could none the less be done forthwith, most of the automation advocated here would require a development phase. This means working in the gap between the second and third levels of attainability. However, the gap between the first and second levels is not nearly as populous as most managers believe. Practically all decision processes belong in the second–third gap. The capabilities that do belong in the first–second gap (of 'can' but not 'how') are the strictly biological rather than psychological processes. For instance, we can show that it is possible for a machine to reproduce itself, but we are unable to demonstrate other than trivially how it works. This is mainly because we are short of suitable fabrics rather than suitable concepts. In short: there is no synthetic protein.

Now if even the most advanced notions of control of the firm by automation belong in the second–third gap, the outlook is bright. A personal judgment is that the lead time required is of the order of ten years. Many management people, and even electronic experts, would put the ideas described here in the wrong gap, because they have not paid any serious attention to developments in cybernetics. The result is that they would suspect a need for huge investments which would not pay off until all of us were dead. No wonder there is not much incentive to press forward, and practical automation advances at a snail's pace. But of course these results will not in fact be attained in ten years if managers leave developments to the existing inoperable system. It is only the artefact of biological *processes* which perforce waits on new ideas of fabric, that may take fifty years to mature—whatever managers do. The artefact of biological *system*, with its capacity for decision and control, can be mounted today as a viable project for operation in about ten years.

Suppose that a general manager did mount such a project, what would it involve? In the first place, as argued, it needs his personal direction. Second, it calls for a first-rate OR team to work for him directly, and this team must include a cybernetician as well as computer experts and automation specialists. Naturally, under the interdisciplinary dispensation of OR, the team would include scientists from other fields too. It would be wise to second an imaginative senior manager full-time to the group—this being a second-best arrangement from that proposed above for later use, in which the entire senior management might itself become a problem-oriented group. This idea cannot yet be considered, for the firm would grind to a halt.

Next, the terms of reference must be imprecise: the general manager is directing the work personally and he is thinking aloud through his OR team as he goes along. But the object of the project is clear: to design an automatic nervous system which will as far as possible automatically control the company according to the policies from time to time laid down by its human management. Now two points about this are very important. The ultimate goal must be established. This is said contrarily to the possibility that some piecemeal alterations be made 'to see how we go'. Second, the route to the goal must be established. There are both practical and theoretical reasons for these demands. In practical terms, one would no sooner think of destroying and rebuilding the management structure overnight, than of pulling down the entire plant and rebuilding that at one blow. But this does not prohibit the rebuilding of plants. The old must be dismantled in planned steps and replaced by the new.

The theoretical point is this. There is cybernetic knowledge about the seeking of known and unknown goals. It is certainly possible not to fix the goal, but to evolve towards an unknown solution which would not be recognized until it were reached. Let us suppose that the goal lies in a phase space having 1,000,000 possible states: this is the measure of the problem's variety. The phase space can be imagined for convenience as a square array of side 1,000. If we hunt over this phase space for the goal, the search will take on the average 500,000 steps. If however the goal is known, the task of reaching it becomes the task of inspecting the two co-ordinates of the array: a search having a mean expected number of 500 steps in each case. Thus the reduction of effort in the known-goal case is from 500,000 to 1,000 steps. Hence if it is possible to know the goal (as in the circumstances here discussed), and the manager none the less prefers to adopt an experimental and evolutionary approach (which British managers often do prefer), the inefficiency of the attack is measured as $0 \cdot 2$ per cent. Of course, the selection of a two-dimensional space is arbitrary, as is the size of this particular problem: the case is merely illustrative. In general, the known-goal-seeker is operating on the nth root of phase space variety in any n-dimensional space. The more structured the problem, the higher the n, and the much more efficient is the search. (All this is formally equivalent to the variety generator expounded and deployed in Part III.)

Returning now to the question of imprecise terms of reference, which are not to be confused with the precise goal for the project that is to be

developed by the research, the arguments of Part I of this book are recalled. Here is an outstanding case for applying those arguments. It will
be necessary to ask whatever the firm is all about, what it is trying to do;
it will be necessary to avoid any preconception about structure at all.
Therefore the real phase space of the problem is very wide indeed, and
the thought blocks enclosing the accepted and much smaller phase spaces
must be battered aside. To exemplify the dangers now in mind, it is
worth considering a business, rather than industrial, situation for a
change. Some operational research work has been done in the business
(as distinct from industrial) arena, but not a great deal. Yet in considering
the information and automation aspects of science in management, the
business world is a major potential client. Banking, insurance, stockbroking, finance—these are all great undertakings whose stock-in-trade
is information itself. So the relevance of scientific thinking about information is not confined to the management of affairs, but applies to the
affairs themselves. Consider, then, the example of banking in its day-
to-day activity of handling current accounts.

The British bank, to the depositor, is a particular building. This building is open for business from 10 a.m. to 3 p.m. on all five working days
of the week, and also (at present) for two hours on a Saturday morning.
The depositor arranges for his personal salary to be paid to the credit of
his current account at this bank, which money the bank holds—paying
no interest. The depositor has a book of cheques with which he may pay
his creditors, who pay his cheques into their own banks. The banks all
clear the cheques, reconcile the accounts, and charge the depositor for
this service. Alternatively, under the relatively new credit transfer system,
the depositor may arrange for his bills to be paid directly by the bank,
using a single piece of paper to authorize the payment of them all; the
bank then sees that the accounts of the creditors are duly credited. If the
depositor requires cash, he goes into the bank, writes out a cheque, and
receives money in exchange. All this activity requires much paperwork.
The depositor writes out many cheques in long-hand; these have to be
read by cashiers, read again by ledger clerks, posted, and so on.

Here then is an immense flow of information, and the question of
automation arises. Can machines be made to do any of the work? In the
first place, a machine cannot read what is written on the cheque. It
would be possible to make one that could, true; but it would be very
difficult because people write so badly. However, a machine can read
print of known fount, and a machine can read stylized symbols—easily,
too, if they are printed in magnetic ink. Obviously, then, the first thing
to do is to transcribe the depositor's long-hand statement on the cheque

DC—GG

into such symbols, so that it can be read by a machine which can then post the ledgers automatically. Of course, someone must read the cheque in order to print the symbols so that no-one will need to read the cheque; and of course the cashier must still read the cheque himself. Never mind: a common language for banking is in process of elaboration, and this is a valuable outcome. It is not denied. Nor is the painstaking committee work of the banks and their technical advisers open to challenge. But it is surely permissible to ask whether automatic cheque processing is what ought to be done for banking by automation.

From the standpoint of the management scientist, armed with the discoveries of cybernetics, the methodology and techniques of operational research, and the ironmongery of modern electronics, the whole idea is absurd. Here is a devastatingly obvious case of the automation of human limitation. Moreover, it is a case in which the phase space of the banking operation considered (current accounts) has been rigorously set by history. No-one has thought of reconsidering, or alternatively dared to reconsider, the entire situation, although this is manifestly and not covertly required. The depositor does not enjoy writing out cheques; he could not care less about the cheque except as a means to a distant end—the payment and perhaps receipting of bills. Yet the cheque is the centrepiece of automatic cheque processing and the cause of all the trouble. Then there is the depositor's need for cash. Is this sensibly met by operating hours fixed for just those times when most clients (especially, note, potential clients) can least easily use the facility? Clearly not. In fact, the facility available, as described in the penultimate paragraph, is almost certainly not what the depositor would like in any particular. But to alter all this, it is protested, would involve radical change: not in processes alone, but in the formulation of the problem, in the policies underlying the present answer to the problem, and even in the organizational structure of the bank itself. Which is just what these chapters are all about.

One vast and general thought block appears to be holding up any prospect of major reform. It is the belief that customers demand a personal service. In the first place this might turn out to be wrong. Some people, it may well be, would rather be serviced by quick, accurate, machinery, yielding comprehensive clear-cut statements, than be bumbled over by people who may appear to know less about the matter in hand than they do themselves. In the second place, what customers demand is subject to change by various pressures and incentives. Thirdly, the reputation for personal service can, if deemed really necessary, be retained as a gloss on efficient automation rather than as the substance of administration. One startling feature of the automatic cheque processing system, in some banks, is that the periodic bank statement remitted to the depositor has lost the name of the payee of each cheque. Instead, the cheque number alone is quoted. This loss is a highly significant sacrifice, for the naming feature was one of the very few aspects of the old system which most depositors appear to have approved. But the banks concerned did not flinch from inflicting this trauma on their clients, once it became an indicated outcome of the data processing investigation. Thought blocks, it seems, are unselective and arbitrary.

Now it may be disappointing to learn that no pat statement about what ought to be done will be offered here. The competent research has never been commissioned; therefore the answers are unknown. The competent research has been offered; but the banks' reply was to say that the matter was well in hand. In order to prove what long-range, careful thinking was being put in, one bank advised that a young accountant had been charged with the task of exhaustively examining the bank's procedures. He would report on their possible automation in due course. Moreover, said the bank proudly, they realized that this was not a simple matter; they would not expect to hear from the young man for fifteen years. The reader is left to work out just how many of the conclusions drawn in this book about modern management methods have been violated by this policy.

It seems quite clear that the banks should seek to meet the needs of the depositor, and should first find out (from depositors) what these needs are. This is a job for OR with a strong human sciences orientation. The next job is to work out how these needs should be met, under the major constraint of security. That is the situation. Without knowing what the outcome would be, it is certainly plausible to suggest that cheques as we know them might vanish, and that bank cashiers as we know them might go too. As to computers capable of reading symbols written in magnetic ink . . . the likelihood is that they would never have been heard about. But, to exemplify an argument set out earlier, the plausibility of removing these cheque-reading machines *now* (that is, once installed) is weak. The old irrelevant system is becoming expensively and concretely entrenched.

Hence, for example, the chance that a depositor's 'own' bank will ever be more than the building down the road is minimal. If the depositor needs money in a strange town, he has to make arrangements for facilities there; if he is caught unexpectedly, he has to pay for the branch where he finds himself to establish those facilities with his own branch. But given automation it ought to be possible to interrogate a current account,

wherever it is, from wherever the depositor may happen to be, as easily
as if the depositor had walked into his own branch. Now the banks are
attempting to move in this direction by relating branch accounts to a
zonal computer. It seems very doubtful to the cybernetician, however,
whether that intention can be pressed very far. The reasons for this
allegation are to be found in Section 4 of Chapter 15. The idea of
'communicating computers' is unsound, because the amount of requisite
variety available in existing social systems cannot be duplicated by the
channels that link the computers. So if there is to be 'one bank', and not
just a collection of virtually self-contained branches, the whole system
must be rethought as an entity. The policy of gradual automation,
whereby branches in the same vicinity are zoned, and then the zones are
linked, and so on hierarchically, is bound to fail. It is the old story of
interconnected autonomous organs in a body that lacks a central nervous
system.

What has been said of banking applies, *mutatis mutandis*, to other
industries that deal in information. The archaic worlds of insurance and
stockbroking have a desperate need of automation, applied on valid
cybernetic principles. So has the whole majesty and profundity and
chaos of the law. So has government administration, both local and
national. As the standard of living rises in any country, a higher level of
social sophistication demands more and more of all these information
industries. They are less and less able to provide the service needed. The
attitude they adopt to the facilities of automation is unscientific and
trivial. What is possible for them all, however, is nothing less than a
new, cheaper, more effective activity which could revitalize those aspects
of society with which they have to do.

But no amount of serial *replacement* of man by machine, or of machine
by better machine, will make good this promise. The automation of
limitation will prove disastrous. We must return yet again to the question
of structure and to the definition of cybernetics as the science of effective
organization. When this point was discussed at the end of the last
chapter, the requirement of organizational redundancy was stressed.
In the information industries, above all, redundancy of information
in the system is vital if errors are to be avoided. There are three quite
different aspects to this redundancy, two of them obvious, the third
less so.

An information system is a network of channels and nodes. The
channels are subject to two defects: they may be disrupted, and they
may be noisy. If a channel is disrupted, then it ceases to transmit information; there must therefore be a procedure that ensures that alter-

native channels are invoked. If the channel is noisy, then a sufficient proliferation of alternative channels will ensure that the message is passed correctly. Here is the redundancy of which examples have already been given. In information-theoretic terms, it may come down to the question of adequate band-widths. In the terms of computer technology, it may come down to the question of using error-correcting codes. At any rate, the user can be sure that reliable operation is always possible, if science is charged with ensuring it, to a given and arbitrary degree. This, it will be noted, says more than that commercially available machinery should be 'installed', because every piece of machinery has its built-in capacity to fail, and the vulnerability of each part of the system interacts with that of the rest. This involves the question of the defectiveness of the nodes that link the channels. And again, explanations have already been given of the need for nodal redundancy. The network of channels and nodes has to be designed as a whole, with redundancy in both of those elements, to achieve effective and reliable results.

If there are two sorts of element in the system, and both are organized redundantly, where is the scope for yet a third measure of redundancy to be introduced? The answer is: in the way the system is arranged to work. It was argued in the last chapter that it is the possession of information, rather than bestowed authority, that confers the right to act. So in any network of channels and nodes, some sub-system of the total system acquires a commanding state of knowledge at a given epoch of time. A particular ganglion of nerve cells, or a local plexus of the network, achieves command—because it holds, and is processing, critical information. In a completely established hierarchy, it is known in advance what sub-systems work as entities, and which of them command what aspects of control. But in a self-organizing system, or in a system designed for learning, adaptation and evolution, it is necessary for alternative groupings to be possible. So the third form of redundancy lies in the potential for command: it is a behavioural, not a structural, component of the system. The trick was learnt from the brain, once again, and may readily be observed in operation in any social group. This subtle feature of effective organization was named 'the redundancy of potential command' by the distinguished American cybernetician Warren McCulloch. He has also been responsible for much of the pioneering work in the investigation, analysis and rigorous description of neural nets.

These characteristics of the systems to be automated for use by the information industries are brought out here in an effort to persuade those responsible that the design of structure is all-important. They

should wonder no longer at the inadequacy of their own efforts to understand and to employ automation, since the man–machine replacement
policy they pursue will obviously not deal with these issues. And it is
this very same point that must be made to those who are concerned at
large with the social consequences of automation too. It ends this
discussion of automation considered as the art of the possible.

The advance of automation within a country is at once a determinant
of economic progress and a threat to the stability of society. This is well
known and well realized, but it is not well understood. People insist on
regarding automation as the replacement of men by machines, and they
do not penetrate to the structural implications for society. We have seen
how industries make this mistake, and how they then fail to progress.
Society itself faces the same lack of progress because of the same misunderstandings.

In Britain, as in other advanced countries, the labour force demands
less work for higher pay. If automation is to come, less work (in the
manual labour sense) will be necessary, and higher pay will be available.
So that is all right. Meanwhile, however, government and management
on the one hand oppose the reduction of the working week and the
award of pay increases, and on the other hand worry ceaselessly about
the proper use of increasing leisure. In this they are misguided. If people
are compelled to discuss these matters in a language which equates hard
manual work with income, then the increased use of automation will
compel them to talk about unemployment, not leisure. The insistence
that this is the right language to talk compels people to resist automation. Then the authorities who have determined all this complain about
restrictive practices and increased costs.

The fact is that the labour force is paid too little to ensure that management finds automation worth while. The way to decrease costs is not to
minimize the wage bill, but to rethink the structure of the work and to
use the facilities made available by science. Thereafter, the wage bill
will figure as an overhead, and not as the critical component of product
cost—as it generally does today. Meanwhile, the citizen can begin to
reorganize his attitude to work as something which fulfils his needs,
rather than something which conditions his income. The time must come
when the opportunity to work is regarded as a privilege and not as an
unpleasant necessity. Today, those who are driven to work hard from a
sense of duty, or because they are temperamentally inclined that way,
maintain (almost uniformly) an attitude of ineffable condescension towards those who acknowledge or betray that they would not work at
all unless they had to. Social commentators have spoken of the Puritan

ethic which sponsors this attitude. The pragmatic approach to the problem is quite other. Society can afford to accept the demands of labour in exchange for a peaceful revolution in *modus operandi*, and it can afford to foster a constructive attitude towards leisure. Before it can do so, its own leaders have to think out what revolution is in the making, and to commission research into the consequential social changes that ought to be brought about.

There is, after all, plenty of leisure-work required. Most of our industrial towns are not fit places for habitation by human beings. They lack every kind of cultural and recreational amenity, unless we are to judge them by last century's standards. Judged by the needs of an increasingly educated population, a social life largely restricted to television at home and various forms of gambling outside is a disgrace. Britain has an enormous heritage of artistic treasures, which no-one attempts to make available to the public (the public can gain access to them, but this is not the same thing). Britain has fine orchestras which can be heard only in a few suitable halls; the public therefore has a thought block about serious music. And while the citizen is invited to pack himself into various sports stadia in the spectator role, there are intolerable difficulties facing him if he wants to take his family for a swim. Amenity centres are required in every town and township; education needs to be geared to a society in which the intentions of education have some outlet. Hitherto, this ideal has seemed Utopian because there has been no money or time available for such 'unproductive' activities. But the availability of labour, under automation, means money.

Hence a properly phased plan for the introduction of automation in the firms of a township, needs to be geared to a properly phased plan for the improvement of the township itself. Collaboration between the firms and the local authority could effect this. As automated firms became richer, the industrial rate would rise; the local authority could afford to pay for massive developments, the very existence of which would dissolve the man–management problems of automation for the firms. As usual, we are faced with a series of false dichotomies in which everyone seems to believe. There are the dichotomies between unpleasant and pleasant work; between leisure and unemployment; between industrial and social enterprise; between 'useful' and 'useless' activity. The most usually quoted social problems of automation are compounded of these dichotomies; they are not real. But they may easily become real, if people insist on talking in these terms. As usual, it seems that an integral solution is available if people will stop trying to sub-optimize those parts of the socio-economic system which they personally decide are important. Apart from the failure to exploit the benefits of science which this entails, the most absurd and unprofitable conflict is arising within each sub-system. The industrialist, for example, with his limited aims, is caught in an ambivalent position. He wants his labour force to work harder (more output, less cost, equals more profit), and he wants new methods involving less hard work at the same time.

Does the art of the possible condemn society to an extension of the miseries of the first industrial revolution, while the benefits of the second are held back? The social engineering for which we must appeal is often held to be an unavoidably slow process. One recalls slogans about the inevitability of gradualness, from Aristotle to the present day. But, historically speaking, there have been plenty of societies which became too hidebound to be tolerable, and which were therefore overthrown by political revolution overnight. Sudden change is certainly possible, then. Brought about by revolutionary methods, it is also horribly wasteful and sadly inefficient. But socio-economic cybernetics should be able to do better, if anyone determines to try for rapid change. It is, after all, a question of management; the reactions of the mass of the people are remarkably predictable, once they are provided with the language in which they should talk.

If that sounds sinister, it is because it is a principle which has been abused from time to time. Whether we like it or not, the future of automation depends upon the cybernetic good sense of the plans made to introduce it—and this includes the cybernetic good sense of the language in which those plans are couched. We can speak, if we wish, of the Age of Machines, of human degradation in the face of cybernetic advance, of labour redundancy and unemployment. This way, which dominates today's top-level conversation, will lead to social trouble. Alternatively, we can base our policies on the correct notion that a man who does work that a machine could do is thereby degraded. We can speak of the Age of Freedom, of man the master of his environment, of labour as a personal fulfilment and a social boon, of responsible and constructive leisure.

The Luddites of the eighteenth century were ignorant workers who retarded progress by smashing machines. The Luddites of today are ignorant managers and ministers who talk of the dangers of automation instead of its reliefs. It is their duty to circumvent the dangers, not to frighten the populace.

18

THE OUTCOME FOR GOVERNMENT

διὸ μίαν μὲν εὐνομίαν ὑποληπτέον εἶναι τὸ
πείθεσθαι τοῖς κειμένοις νόμοις, ἑτέραν δὲ τὸ
καλῶς κεῖσθαι τοὺς νόμους οἷς ἐμμένουσιν. . . .

Therefore one mode of good government is taken as
being to obey the laws as laid down, but an
alternative is to lay down well those laws that the
people abide by. . . .

ARISTOTLE (384–322 B.C.) in *Politics*

1 The Law and the Profits

Government is a stabilizing informational process of complex systems.
For most of his history, civilized man has regarded government as
juridical: a matter of giving instructions, exercising controls and, above
all, enacting and administering laws. But we have come nearly to the
end of a lengthy book about the nature of control as modern science is
able to discuss it. From this vantage point it seems clear that orders,
government controls and laws are best regarded as regulators of a self-
organizing system. Orders and controls are the kinds of input which
enter into the equations of motion which govern the behaviour of the
interacting homeostats which compose the State; laws themselves, on
the other hand, fix the parameters (in the short run at least) of this
macrosystem. Society is, however, a sentient ecosystem and, being self-
aware, it is quite capable of rebelling against its systemic parameters.
This is an unusual condition for any system, and is the basic cause of
political disturbance and difficulty.

Aristotle appeared to understand this point in what may well be the
most cybernetically perceptive remark he ever committed to posterity.
It is quoted above. For rebellion and the overthrow of governments

461

derive from frustration in the citizens' attempts to make private and corporate profits (by some definition) within the existing parametric framework. If only, say the citizens, this framework could be changed we should all be very much happier. People who, historically, do not rebel, are those who regard themselves as living in a free society; that is to say, they do not regard themselves and their institutions as confined or frustrated by systemic parameters. Since, on any objective analysis, a social or economico-political system *must* be so constrained, it can only be concluded that acceptable parameters are those which people accept regardless of any attempt to impose them. It would be too facile to represent the acceptable and the potentially unacceptable parametric frameworks as characteristic of particular political creeds. Rather, the former is characteristic of a self-organizing state, and the latter characteristic of a state which is in the grip of some kind of tyranny. It is important to realize that what counts as a tyranny is not the state objectively assessed as tyrannical by the historian, but one understood to be so by the majority of subjects under the given system at a particular time. The cleverest kind of tyranny is one in which the populace is hoodwinked into believing that it operates as a free society; this can happen both under some form of apparently self-organizing democracy and under some kind of autocratic dictatorship. Machiavelli did not live in vain. If people on the whole wish to live in a certain fashion, then those laws which make this verdict precise will seem to the citizen to maximize his profit.

Thus it is that government depends upon informational processes rather than upon mandatory powers. It was observed in Chapter 15 that many of the notions most commonly entertained about social and economic control are based on false dichotomies. For example, centralization and de-centralization, monopoly and free competition, nationalization and private enterprise, were all regarded as dimensions of argument which had no basis in systemic law. Equally, then, the regulators which deal in these terms are not the vital instruments of government that they appear to be. On the contrary, wise and clever government does not begin with many precise notions about what people and institutions ought to do; nor does the basic information circuit begin with government as transmitting instructions to the populace. Rather does it begin with the receipt of information about how the populace, both privately and institutionally, is behaving. If government, with its mandate to govern and its special prerogatives, then wishes to change that behaviour, its task is to *change the structure* of the system that produces it.

After all, the mass of the people is not competently organized to generate anti-government behaviour patterns (unless an actual rebellion has been mounted). All its objectionable activity can amount to is a self-organizing behavioural characteristic of the system as it is now structured. That is to say, reverting to the arguments of Chapter 14, that the system-as-structured is moving to a more probable state by its own entropic drift. To procure another set of outputs, government must so change the structure that the direction of these entropies changes in its favour. This is done only incidentally by issuing instructions or exhortations; it is done fundamentally by changing the role of institutions.

As has been concluded in so many instances quoted in this book, people misread these structural changes as economic changes—because they always discuss them in economic terms. For instance, the importance of nationalization is not that it puts 'the means of production, distribution and exchange' into public ownership. 'The people' are no more competent or indeed able to alter the course of an industry than were the erstwhile shareholders of the companies of which it was composed. What matters about a political change of this kind is that the structure of the industry is fundamentally changed, both internally and in relation to suppliers and customers. In Britain, the various nationalization moves that have been made, under various auspices, in this century, have failed for the most part to make explicit what the structural changes *vis-à-vis* the *external* environment were supposed to mean. The meaning of *internal* structural changes becomes quite clear once modes of organization have been settled. But the external relationships depend upon such factors as whether the transmogrified industry is supposed to be making a profit out of its customers or not. This has been left notoriously inexplicit. Thus the law falls foul of the profits, for the intentions of law cannot go beyond the notion of service to the nation, whereas no-one knows how to measure service except in terms of its profitability. The operational research has not been done.

Inside the country it governs, then, the task of a government is to define structures so that their entropies move towards a more probable state desired—*and also made explicit*—by the government. One might think that, in invoking the principles of self-organizing systems, it would be unnecessary to make explicit what the aim of the system was supposed to be. But this reckons without the psychological factor which is in fact the *major* variable with which the government must deal. What is the law and what counts as the good citizen's reaction to the law are both major determinants of what people and institutions will actually do. Some groups regard themselves as bound by the law but not by the intention of the law; some regard themselves as bound by both; certainly a relatively small but virulent minority wishes to circumvent both if it can. Thus a government's engineering with complex probabilistic systems within the state is quite largely a problem of arranging to do things in a way which produces a predictable (in the mass) pattern of psychological reaction. Behaviour will remain the criterion of success and failure, but this behaviour is conditioned by psychological predispositions—and those in turn are part of the informational circuitry. It is the predisposition of the governed which closes the loop of government.

To recapitulate: this loop begins with the government's receipt of information from the populace, but the foundations of this information are based on predisposition which is in turn created by the government's activities. This ecosystemic loop is closely analogous to that expounded in Chapter 16 to account for marketing problems. Indeed, the government which does not wish to provoke a rebellion does well to regard itself as marketing its policies.

At this point it should be noted that once the dependence of a control system on an information circuit (if indeed these are not best regarded as equivalent) has been recognized, the inevitable failure of a complex system to provide *perfect* information has to be faced. Requisite variety can be obtained, as has been seen, and the channel capacity for it can be provided too—once the idea is secure that two halves (or n $n$ths) of a vast system interact through a rich elemental connectivity rather than by means of an exiguous thin stream of information passing from one bloc to another. In the case where either an hierarchic structure or the appearance of human beings as nodal points arises, however, special problems of informational corruption also arise.

Those at the head of hierarchical organizations 'invite' biased advice and information. They are as it were lethally cocooned by their staffs; their greatest problem is to ensure that the state of the real world, and particularly the error-controlled feedback messages which it generates, are reaching them. The informational model that uses entropy is valuable here. Since the entropy of the system is, by the natural law, increasing, a complex system self-organizes itself to denature its leading spirits. They, for their part, are seeking to attract and to store *neg*entropy— which is another word for information. Hence a familiar battle automatically occurs in the very task of keeping a complicated hierarchical structure in being at all. Such a system that is growing needs an immense input of education and training, of selecting and conditioning, merely to retain its existing level of sophistication. This applies as well to a civilized nation considered as a whole, as to any particular enterprise.

The conclusion is contrary to the law which says that structure spreads through a self-organizing system as it matures, because of the 'polarity' introduced by insisting on a particular hierarchical pattern. That demand has to be supported by organizational energy.

In the case of interactions between two human beings who are peers (the non-hierarchical case), the corruption of information arises mainly because each has an inadequate model of the other. John understands the behaviour of Cyril only through his model of what Cyril is really like; therefore messages transmitted by Cyril will be degraded to the extent that any mapping from Cyril on to John's model of Cyril involves variety reduction (and it always does). The behaviour that is transmitted will in any case depend upon the adequacy of the other model—that which the transmitter entertains himself. For example, John comes to dinner with Cyril and is given a finger bowl. John, while reflecting that Cyril uses oddly shaped glasses, drinks the water; Cyril registers John as the sort of man who drinks the water out of finger bowls—clearly an iconoclast. Each of these men is using quite valid information which is passing between them, processing it through a false model, and drawing incorrect inferences which may well affect his future actions.

Nowhere is this kind of failure in communication and therefore control more apparent than in international affairs. If two diplomatic terms take the place of John and Cyril, it is evident that considerable conflict will arise without either team's knowing quite why. On the contrary, if they *do* know quite why, a very intricate and dangerous situation may be resolved, as the result of each team's adopting the other's known conventions. Suppose for example that two major powers are locked in a diplomatic and quasi-military deadlock. Suppose that each side is dedicated to the use of science in decision-taking, and that this leads the set of advisers on each side to make use of the theory of games. As has been pointed out earlier, the theory of games is some-what restricted in the models it is able to deploy, and these limitations are very well known to scientists. In particular, the OR man is impelled, if he wishes to reach a clear-cut conclusion, to stretch a real-life problem of this sort on to the Procrustean bed of the two-person zero-sum game. Each side may know that the other side is likely to be doing this, and can verify its expectation by various tentative experiments which simulate the threat of actual war through diplomatic and military manœuvres. Suppose then that each side does come to this conclusion about the other; it will obviously be encouraged to use the same model itself. For although it knows full well that the model is grossly inadequate as accounting for the real pressures and complexities of the problem, these fade away in significance on the understanding that the opponent will behave (because he is limited by his model-building capability) *as if* the real situation were as simple as the only available model contends.

It follows that, although the genuine situation offers incomplete information to each side about the other, each is going to act *as if* it had complete information. Therefore the game which both sides are modelling has a saddle point—that is to say, an optimal solution which both sides can, and doubtless will, calculate. Therefore each side makes the following deduction: we cannot afford to play any other strategy than the minimax strategy which determines this saddle point—and of course the outcome of the game. Moreover, each side respects the intelligence of the opposing side and knows that the opponent will have come to the same conclusion. In such circumstances, each side will act *as if* the game were over. And the game *will* be over. In other words, the conflict is resolved.

An interaction of this kind between two major powers might well be called an 'inferred war'. It seems very likely that inferred wars may already have been fought. For example, the clash between America and Russia over Cuba in 1962 could at the least have involved this element. If so, the world stood momentarily on the brink of total disaster, but for a reason different from that normally proposed. For if both sides were using an inadequate game-theoretic model, there was not the slightest risk of nuclear war: no nuclear strategy could possibly be dominant in a game determined by these limits. No: the appalling risk was that one side or the other might have ceased to act scientifically, or that the other side would so fear this possibility that it would itself abandon the known-to-be-inadequate model. In either case, it could be expected to revert to an old-fashioned 'conquest' model instead, and set out to conduct its gaming experiments in real life. By this means, the inferred war would have become a real war. But neither of these things happened, and it seems that the peace of the world is a thousand times safer as a result. For the first test of nerve is always the worst; another time the two sides will be the more ready to assume scientific rather than emotional decision-taking by the other. Even if the state of science delimits the adequacy of the model, the conventions of conflict may see the world through.

Although the context of this argument is totally novel, its conclusions seem to bear the stamp of historicity. It ought to seem strange to the objective historian that for centuries opposing forces were willing to draw up on a particular battlefield, to encamp and to spend the night preparing for a formal clash at dawn. Why did the opposing commanders accept this convention? Why did they not arrange to outflank each other by night? Why did one side not simply go away? Such questions as these are unanswerable—except in the context of a language which both sides agree to speak. The case is then that a new language, just as inadequate perhaps, but based on a common understanding of what science can do, is being forged today. If so, it should be noted that military security, hitherto a primary virtue in a combatant nation, becomes a danger and not a requirement of war. In the inadequate game-theoretic model, neither side can exploit information about the other, because the game has a fixed saddle point; it is important, on the contrary, to each side that the other should have all its information. If so, and if the case of Cuba is a good example, the real risk was that the Russians might have thought that the Americans would not know that nuclear arms were being installed. Now no serious attempt appears to have been made to conceal those nuclear arms, so it is at least possible that the Russians thought it important that the Americans should know that the Russians did not think that the Americans might not know. In short, a circumstance which left political commentators gasping at the time, could easily have been a deliberate move to ensure that the conflict remained in simulated dimensions.

A consequence of this kind of argument is that the real threat to world peace does not lie with major powers who have tacitly accepted some set of scientific conventions for the resolution of conflict. If there is a nation which has nuclear capability, and is a lethal threat to the world at large, but which is not scientifically oriented towards potential conflict, then that nation is a menace to peace. Small wonder that the foreign policy pursued by both the world's major powers has been directed towards containing the spread of nuclear arms.

Such are the subtleties of governmental problems of control, both internal and external, to a given country. But when these problems are rightly seen as structural and informational, rather than as having to do with command and the issue of orders, progress can be made. The law, both national and international, is of this kind. And because international understanding of the point is, at least in official terms, non-existent, it is not surprising that a great divergence exists between what is written down as law (for example in conventions and undertakings, and in the resolutions of the Security Council of the United Nations) and what counts in practice as law, which is probably no more explicit than an accepted convention ever becomes. The great challenge to contemporary government is to acquire insights into how the control system of the nation and of the world is really working.

This leads to the final point of this introductory section. The practical concern of government must be above all to recognize its problems. Many ministers appear to believe that the acquirement of power is an end in itself; and they behave as if their job were to ornament the office they hold. The problems that arise can be handed to experts to resolve. But this ministerial posture assumes that the problems correctly identify themselves, whereas the whole lesson uncovered in this book is that they rarely do so. The result is that much brain-power is wasted in attempting to provide answers to problems which either do not exist, or which are so perverted in the setting that the answers are virtually meaningless. Lord Mountbatten has told a wartime story which convinced him of the truth of this argument. One of his advisers, Geoffrey Pyke, had transmitted an immense report to Lord Mountbatten. He found on the first page a quotation by G. K. Chesterton, extracted from one of his detective stories. 'Father Brown laid down his cigar and said carefully: "It isn't that they can't see the solution. It is that they can't see the problem." ' Mountbatten drew the correct lesson. He comments: 'Yet the habit in those days was for military planners to put problems to scientists for them to produce the solution. From now on, I said, scientists were to be associated with the planners in deciding what the problem was before they were asked to solve it. It is no good getting the right answer to the wrong questions: you've got to get the right question before the right answer can be of any use.' The point seems simple, but the lesson has by no means been learned.

2   The State and Polystability

As with industry, so *a fortiori* with government: it cannot pose the right problems, still less find their solutions, unless the system-in-context is understood. Therefore systemic models will be required, very much on the lines of those already discussed, within which to examine specific issues. Unfortunately, in national affairs there is an even bigger problem of data identification and collection than there is in industry. National statistics are often inadequate for our purposes; they contain many ambiguities, and a dangerously long lead time is involved for the decision-maker.

Accordingly, operational research ingenuity will have to be shown in devising models which are not too sensitive to these deficiencies; and this in turn requires that a new metric be devised in many cases. National decision-takers assume far too lightly that they require data in the form in which it is customary to present them, and that nothing can be done to improve the speed and accuracy of presentation. On the contrary, if science were confronted with the necessity to provide a more rapid response in the system, it could doubtless devise a metric in which this would be possible. To illustrate these points, and to contrast possible new methods with those currently accepted, an analysis will now be given of the situation facing the British government in 1961 in connection with the spread of technology. This is a typical case of a national policy requirement; many economic, industrial and educational policies depend on it. (The text of this section is an adaptation of an address published in the *Operational Research Quarterly*, Volume 13, in June 1962.)

A very competent example of the orthodox approach to the task of forecasting in national affairs appears in a government white paper entitled *The Long-Term Demand for Scientific Manpower*, which was laid before Parliament in 1961. The paper is set out as government papers normally are: as an analytic argument with parenthetical explanations. But it is reproduced at Figure 56 in diagrammatic form. This diagram, it must be clear, is the author's own version of what the white paper said; on the other hand, it was not denounced after publication as misleading.

The picture is projected (from 1959) to the year 1970. It will be seen that the various factors considered are expected to change their value in the next ten years by various amounts which are indicated. The distinguished committee which produced the study acknowledged the following facts. No standard questionnaire was used; the projection was based on 'informal views'; assumptions made about the state of affairs expected to exist in ten years time were not uniform across the study; and the growth of output from technical colleges was assumed to increase 'at a steady rate (a straight line growth)' [sic]. For all these reasons, the authors were suitably modest about the accuracy of their forecast; needless to say, however, little was said about possible errors or the effect of these assumptions when the paper was reported in the press. But we shall be concerned less with the adequacy of the statistics, than with the structure of the model. See how it works.

The left-hand side, which deals with the supply of technologists, is quantified numerically. There is a known planned increase in the provision of places for technical education, and it is assumed that all these places will be created and will be taken up. This implicitly assumes the willingness of potential students and teachers to co-operate; in the case of teachers it explicitly assumes that the ratio of university teachers to students will be maintained, and that there will be a 50 per cent increase in the intake to training colleges. Next, it is assumed (Sink 1) that the

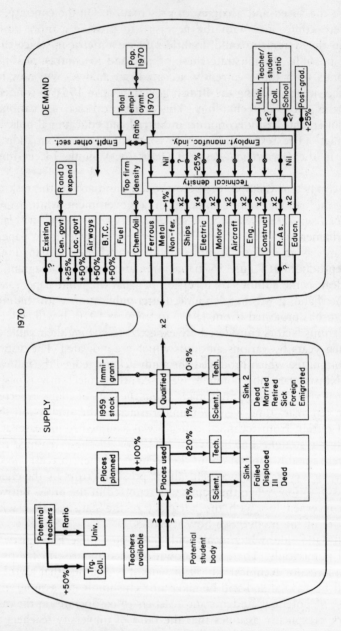

FIGURE 56. Model underlying white paper: Long-term demand for scientific manpower. Key: ● Change estimated, based on 'informal views'. ⊗ Assumption: 1959 rate unchanged in 1970.

wastage from these places will remain at the rates obtaining in 1959. The output of qualified persons joins with the existing (1959) stock, and is joined in turn by immigrants from abroad—who are assumed to arrive at the same rate as heretofore. The total pool of qualified people is then depleted (Sink 2) by a second form of wastage. The result of all these assumptions and careful statistical estimates on the supply side is remarkable. Whereas there were 173,000 qualified people at the last count in 1959, there will be 346,000 in 1970. So the supply of technologists is due to grow in the next ten years by a factor of *precisely* two.

The demand side of the model starts with the people who are already there, and goes on to estimate the changes in population in some detail, by public and private sectors, to avoid systematic errors. The process begins with the estimated population of the whole country in 1970. But the 1959 ratio of employment to population is assumed to hold; and so is the ratio between manufacturing industry and other sectors. This increased technological manpower is assumed, on the whole, to feed into each consuming industry by the 1959 ratios, although in the cases of iron and steel and construction work the 'informal views' result in a prediction that the manpower used will not change. In the case of shipbuilding, it is sadly held that technological employment will *drop* by 25 per cent. However, universities will maintain their student/teacher ratios, which will slightly improve in technical colleges and schools; even so, post-graduate research will absorb 25 per cent more people than before.

The estimated increases in demand from these preliminary assumptions are still determined by 'informal views'. There is an undisclosed change in usage by central government, deriving from another assumption, that the rate of expenditure on research and development will remain static. Local government usage will rise by 25 per cent; airways, railways and fuel and power will all take an increased number (50 per cent) of qualified people. The chemical and oil industries will increase their usage until the density of technical people in general equals that already to be found in the leading firms. What happens to the leading firms themselves is undisclosed. Most of the private industry, it will be seen, is due to increase its density of science and technology, and shipbuilding will do so by a factor of four—a differential improvement more than off-setting the drop in employment.

It is evident that the demand estimate made in such detail to avoid systematic bias, shows that exactly twice as many technically qualified people will be required in 1970 as were required in 1959, although there remain a few complacent quarters where the factor actually works out at 1·9. This conclusion also is remarkable in itself. But when we compare the two estimates, for supply and demand respectively, credulity is really strained.

It seems that by a remarkable serendipity the supply and the demand of technically qualified people will be exactly in balance at the target date, ten years ahead. The virtue attaching to this conclusion is surely much enhanced by the fact that the structure of the argument, as can be

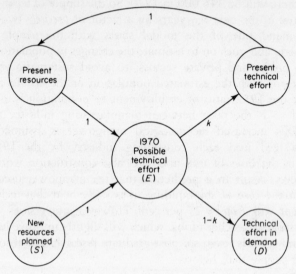

FIGURE 57. Amended white paper model conceived as a partially self-exciting system.

seen from the drawing, proposes no specific interaction between the supply and the demand halves of the diagram at all. Doubtless the committee realized that components of both halves would in fact communicate with each other; but the interaction is nowhere made explicit. To the OR scientist, it is precisely this interaction that matters; it is this interaction which will determine the balance that will doubtless occur. For that balance is in fact obtained by homeostasis. The trouble is that it may bear no relation to the nation's need. Secondly, the cybernetician in particular observes that the form of this interaction will (as is usual in the kind of system he studies) be interpenetrative as between the blocs of the system. Even so, the scientific model-building can begin from the simplified diagram offered in Figure 57.

The real-life system clearly includes a powerful self-exciting element: a feedback between existing demand and existing resources whose value is unity when these two things are held to be equivalent—as they were held to be in 1959. Science can propose various models of systems of this type. As drawn, Figure 57 is structurally identical to an economic model taken from Keynes, and this is in turn equivalent (as Tustin has pointed out) to a simple electrical system. An electrical generator that is partially self-exciting has the independent excitation of a dynamo, and a feedback from the self-exciting winding. An economic system of similar type has the independent excitation of investment, and a feedback from the self-exciting consumption of goods. Both the economic and the electrical models concern steady-state behaviour, in which circumstances the analogy between them is formally exact. The model of technical effort is isomorphic with them both, for the situation as conceived by the white paper is certainly not dynamic. Structurally, this system is indeed partially self-exciting. The possible technical effort for 1970 is exhaustively compounded of existing resources, taken as having unit value, and the provision of new resources which, being independent of the first component, was also taken as having unit value. The output of this effort, however, does not offer independent quantities. It consists of an element expressing the *existing* use of effort, which is assumed to continue and which may be called a proportion k of the total. Secondly, it consists of the new use of effort that is to be made by 1970—which is the complementary proportion $1-k$ of the total. This seems to be a fair account of the white paper's outlook, expressed in systemic terms.

By setting up the equations characteristic of this system, and taking the partial differentials, it was quickly shown that the feedback loop had an effect on the input called S (new resources planned). In fact that input, of unit value, becomes multiplied by a factor $1/(1-k)$. In Keynsian economics, this factor is precisely the investment multiplier. In the case of the generator, it is the value by which the self-exciting winding amplifies the separate excitation. In the present model, it is in turn the factor by which the provision of new resources is multiplied to create the technical effort possible in 1970. Hence, after applying the feedback, we obtain: $E = S(1/1-k)$, where E is the possible technical effort, and S is the supply of new resources. Transposing, this gives: $S = E(1-k)$, which means that the planned provision is equal to a proportion $1-k$ of the 1970 effort. But this is exactly the proportion said to be in *demand* on the right-hand side of the government schema, where $D = E(1-k)$ by very definition.

The argument is, then, that the government's analysis was based on a hidden model, not made explicit, under which the conclusion that supply and demand will be roughly in balance in the future is itself assumed in the structure of the enquiry. The investigation illustrates Lord Mountbatten's thesis. Questions are often begged in the no-man's-land between the knowledge that a question exists and the attempt to answer it. *Formulating* the question is itself a key task.

The fact is that the question with which the government ought to concern itself is not one of the *demand* for technologists at all. The real concern is surely for national survival in the face of foreign competition:

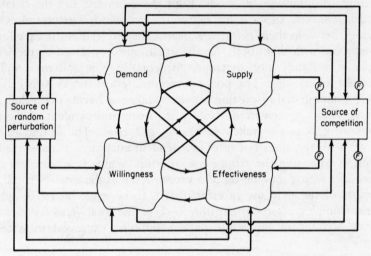

FIGURE 58. Homeostatic adaptation: a model of the technological
need to survive.

a problem of ecosystemic adaptation in which science and technology play commanding roles. Demand within our own system is not necessarily strongly coupled to survival: to say that it is would be to assume at least four things. First, that the demanders (namely management) are entirely aware of the problem; second and third, that both they and the educationalists are willing as well as able to face it; fourth, that management is competent to translate the supply that meets its demand into effective action. These unfulfilled conditions are the key to strategic model-building, which must take into account not only demand and supply, but willingness and effectiveness.

In short, the real question is not: is there more or less demand than supply? It is this: is *demand* sufficient to meet the *need*? Now the need cannot be entered into the systemic equation itself, because it is an expression of the response of the entire system to the challenge of its

ecological competition. The system meets the need in so far as it can
demonstrate a power of adaptation towards survival.

Thus it is that we derive a schematic diagram of characteristic form,
as shown in Figure 58. This schema describes a homeostatic model
which, by this time, we readily understand how to use. It offers, in
particular, the opportunity to discover by methods of simulation the
effects of interaction in the system, and through this knowledge to make
predictions about the effects of alternative policies for technological
development.

The particular difficulty encountered in the study of national ecosystems is, as was remarked earlier, the difficulty of defining a metric
appropriate to measuring such aspects of life as those nominated in
the boxes of Figure 58, and of obtaining actual measures which are up-
to-date. To find a practicable approach to the problem, we are going to
need a new idea: that of polystability. But first comes a recapitulation.
The self-vetoing homeostat itself is by now a familiar structure, and it
will be recalled that each of the boxes composing such a system represents a decision space in which the sub-system nominates (at any given
moment) a representative point. If the trajectory of the whole system
carries this representative point into a sub-set of preferred states, then
the particular sub-system which is so satisfied will distribute messages
that call for a cessation of adaptive experimentation. When all sub-
systems are so satisfied, the total system achieves its ultrastability.

There has been no need in earlier chapters to draw attention to the
undoubted fact that many systems contain sub-systems having *more than
one* sub-set of preferred states. Hitherto, we have gathered all satisfactory representative points into one location, drawn a ring round them,
and called them 'preferred'. But we shall now take advantage of the fact
that it is often more natural, especially in very large systems, to distinguish between groups of preferences—any one of which groups may
define an area of satisfaction roughly equivalent to any of the others.
That is to say, the systemic trajectories may carry the representative
point of a sub-system to one of several loci, each of which satisfies the
criterion for ultrastability as far as that sub-system is concerned. A
diagram illustrating such a polystable system is given in Figure 59.

This diagram shows how a sub-system of a homeostat may often be
divided into a collection of zones, each of which has an equilibrial point
—which now stands for a set of preferred states. Suppose that the representative point of this sub-system is at this moment somewhere in
zone *F*. Then the meaning of the arrows converging on the dot in zone *F*
is that the representative point must be carried to this position before the

behaviour of the sub-system is equilibrial. This means in turn, according to earlier arguments, that the entropies of the sub-system are such that if the state of the system is represented in zone *F* at all, then it will tend naturally to arrive at the equilibrial location. A zone structured by these lines of entropic drift is called a *confluent* (following Ashby's nomenclature as usual).

Consider the case where the representative point is in confluent *F*. Influences passing round the homeostat, of which this whole subsystem is a part, cause the point to be thrown out of equilibrium—but

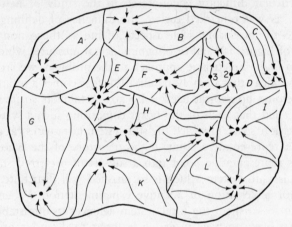

FIGURE 59. Diagram to illustrate nature of polystable system.

it remains within the confluent. Therefore it will tend to return to its own position: this is precisely the relaxation phenomenon familiar to control engineers. However, a sufficiently violent impetus from elsewhere in the total system may throw the representative point out of its confluent altogether. Then it becomes possible to specify a transformation; for example, $F \rightarrow K$. This means that the system's representative point has arrived in the new confluent *K*, where it will eventually settle to the *K* equilibrium point.

This structuring of the decision space of the sub-system means that a new kind of metric is available for describing reactions within it. For example, a particular policy applied to the total system might be described as having a serial effect specified by a chain of transformations, thus: $F \rightarrow K \rightarrow L \rightarrow A \rightarrow C$ and so on. The rules determining these transformations specify the conditions in which the system will change its stable state. In a practical study, it will be found that these transformations are not fully determined: we face a probabilistic system, as might be expected. Therefore the behaviour of the sub-system is to be described by a matrix of transition probabilities, in which some transformation chains of the kind just nominated are more likely than others.

There are three special types of transformation to which attention must be drawn. The first of these is the transformation $E \to E$. This, the identity transform, is the condition where the representative point of the system is trapped in a single confluent. That is a lethal state of affairs; the system can no longer adapt: however much it is stimulated, and however often the point leaves equilibrium in E, it always returns. This is the model of over-specialization, of obsolescence, leading to extinction and death. The second type of transformation is one of the form: $A \to B \to J \to A \to B \to J \to A \ldots$ Now the system has gone into a reverberatory oscillation; when this happens in the brain, the subject is called neurotic. Official policies, particularly in the field of economic affairs, seem to be given to such neuroses. Finally, there is a third peculiar transformation deriving from the equilibrial *cycle* shown in confluent D. In this case the point does not entirely settle at all; there are, as it were, a number of competing equilibria, and a stimulus greater than that confluent's threshold can contain will throw the representative point into one of several possible alternative confluents, depending upon the position of the point in the cycle at the time. Thus, the transformation from D is defined as $D_1 \to G; D_2 \to H; D_3 \to I$.

The phrase 'confluent threshold' is now all important. It is obvious that what matters in the behaviour of this sub-system is the sensitivity of its stability to input information from the rest of the total system, and there is first of all a marked distinction between (what may be called) a weak and a strong impetus. An input pattern constituting a weak stimulus will be defined as one which moves the representative point *within* its own confluent; a strong stimulus throws the point into some other confluent—according to a transition probability which may be established. What counts as a strong stimulus will depend entirely on the entropy contours of any given confluent; some equilibrial points are more unstable than others. Thus the strength of the stimulus that will throw a representative point out of any given confluent is a measure of the confluent threshold.

The idea is, then, that we should no longer seek to measure the characteristics of large sub-systems of the type under discussion by orthodox measuring rods, but by their expected systemic behaviour in response to stimuli. Suppose, for example, that the amount of technical education at present available defines a representative point for the sub-system of supply in confluent F. Local surges of demand, political lobbying, salary changes, and so on, are the weak stimuli which cause the point to move around its equilibrial position. To this locus it will, however, return unless a strong stimulus hits the system. For example, at the time of the white paper discussed earlier, Russia was spending just four times as much on education per inhabitant as Great Britain. Suppose that a real issue had been made of this fact in Parliament, and that the whole nation had been shocked. Certainly, this stimulus is sufficient to move the representative point; the question is, has it moved out of the confluent F or not? If the result of the Parliamentary debate is that the government announces an intention to build a dozen new technical colleges and five new universities, then doubtless a transformation will occur. The supply situation will radically alter, and it will be possible to say $F \rightarrow K$ (for example), where confluent K represents a different educational structure, of different capacity, and of different metabolism. The messages that go out from the supply system to the other three sub-systems will be strong impulses. The point of the research will be to determine what transformations are likely to obtain therein. Confluent thresholds have to be determined, and transition probability matrices set up.

The advantage of this metric now becomes clear. It is probably not possible, and almost certainly not worthwhile, to make elaborate differentiations among the very high variety states of the system. Society moves against massive inertia, and its behaviour patterns are so stable that subtle changes have little effect on results. It is reasonable to suggest that a simple five-point scale will usually offer sufficient discrimination in nominating systemic changes. Either things remain much as they are (the central point on the scale), or they are a little more or less profitable, or a lot more or less profitable. Profitability is here judged according to context; in the case under discussion, it is clear that movements conducing to a wider use of technology would be regarded as more profitable, and movements restrictive of technological advance as less profitable.

So the conclusion is that sub-systems of the kind that are now entered into homeostatic models to deal with problems at the national level can be structured as polystable fields, in which a metric is obtainable in terms of confluent thresholds measured on simple scales. If the scales are thus simple, then the obtaining of the actual measurements is not too daunting a problem. The techniques of the social sciences in investigating behaviour are relevant; so are the operational research techniques of simulation and gaming. Methodologically, the point is to wring the maximal information out of the minimum data, by ensuring that the way the system is structured and is interacting is properly taken into account. The great discovery of management cybernetics is perhaps that the outcomes of policies are determined more by the macrostructure of the total system, its sub-systemic interactions and the entropic infrastructure of the sub-systems themselves, than by the particular causal relationships which are activated by particular decisions. The research counterpart of this state of affairs is that very much more is learned about what ought to be done by inference from the system's cybernetics than from the analysis of enormous masses of data.

The importance of this conclusion cannot be over-emphasized. Almost the whole of government research is, quite typically, devoted to the collection and analysis of information about what has happened. Hardheaded people like to say that these data are the facts of the situation, and are therefore what most matters. On the contrary, they are so much flotsam, floating about on the entropic tides created by the systemic structures below the surface. Given a full understanding of those submarine structures and of the currents at depth, which are the more important facts about the system, it becomes possible to predict effects on the surface using very little data of the former kind.

3   Systemic Studies of National Problems

The stage has now been set for a discussion of the use of science in helping to determine national policy in any field one cares to specify. The methodological approach to these huge problems seems to be quite clear, and its comprehension leaves us poised to take a huge leap forward in the rational conduct of affairs. The argument runs as follows.

In every department of government, science has already made some advance. There is no need to disparage what has been done; there is certainly no reason to halt the forms of research with which we are already most familiar. A good deal of operational research has been undertaken into management problems involved in the administration of various government responsibilities, in various parts of the world, and the details will not be recounted here at any length. Typically, some troublesome issue is examined to see whether a better solution than that already used is available. It may be that a more effective deployment of resources will improve a refuse collection service. It may be that scientific research can show how an entire ministry ought to be reorganized. There have been many such studies of specific issues. This kind of attack is eroding the massive problem of government from the base, and will eventually make big inroads into it. Yet progress is slow. The reason seems apparent: it is twofold. In the first place, it is, as has been noted, extremely difficult to identify what really are the problems; in the second place, it is extremely difficult to relate sensible solutions to those problems to other issues in the same problem area. If the notion is once understood and accepted that the *whole* problem area can be mapped out in cybernetic terms, then not only will useful policies become quickly ascertained and verified, but the detailed research already going on will acquire a systemic framework. These points can be illustrated from a number of fields.

Consider the problem of running a health service. Now doctors have problems in organizing their practices, and some operational research has been done to find out how the work of the general practitioner may be facilitated. Yet this work is delimited, as is the doctor's own authority and responsibility, by the boundaries of general practice. What happens to the doctor's patients when they are referred to hospitals and to specialist consultants is notoriously hard to integrate with the general practice itself. How the pharmaceutical world supplies the doctor and his patient with their drugs and other necessities is a second sub-system virtually uncoupled. More operational research has been done in each of these two fields. Projects have been undertaken on the ward organization of hospitals, on the information flow within them, and on the organization of out-patient departments for example. But for the most part these studies are not even integrated within the macrosystem of the hospital—still less are they integrated within the total system of the health service.

Plenty of work that has not been started can quickly be imagined. For example, it would be possible to investigate prescribing habits and the dispensing of drugs and medicines; no doubt quite specific work in this restricted area could result in a vast reduction of the total national bill for these items. But again the study is necessarily incomplete; for the behaviour of the sub-systems constituting general practitioners on the one hand and pharmaceutical manufacturers on the other is implicitly bound up with the political policies that are being pursued. For example, the amount of medication specified through the use of one prescription will depend very much on who is paying for that prescription and by what methods. The doctor's first duty is to his patient; if a poor patient has to pay the full cost of his medication, the doctor will tend to prescribe small quantities. If, as has happened during a period of some years in Britain, the State pays for the medication leaving the patient to pay a nominal sum for each prescription, then clearly the doctor will tend to prescribe large quantities for poor patients.

It seems clear that the systemic structure of the entire health service ought to be studied *first*. An approximation to its systemic behaviour ought to be obtained by methods such as those advocated in the last section. Then it would become possible to see where to apply operational research to the infrastructure, and how to define the problems that have to be solved.

In Figure 60 a start is made in the creation of such an account of the health services. Even this simple diagram emphasizes at once that all the

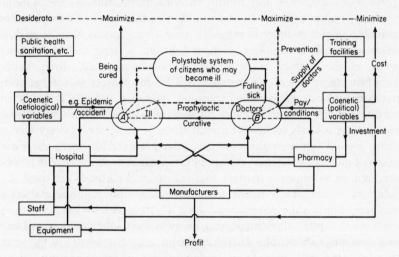

FIGURE 60. Health Service: an interactive system.

A = Citizens (ill) in preferred state of treatment.
B = Doctors in preferred state of successful activity.

sub-systems involved are entirely interdependent. By comparison with what is known of present practice, it suggests that the importance of properly organized information flows is paramount. It suggests that, since both cost and pay-off are functions of the whole diagram, questions as to who pays and who is paid what for what can be decided in terms of the system's total behaviour alone. Remember that pay and conditions on the one hand, and all manner of charges on the other, have effects on the metabolic rate of the system at large, on its efficiency, and on all other parts of the system through amplifiers and feedbacks of many sorts. Above all, it suggests that the desiderata of health are not to be influenced by direct action in any one direction ('pay nurses more'); they are maximal outputs of the total system. Simulation of this system is going to reveal what policies will produce what required effects, and also what side effects—both desirable and undesirable. It will reveal much about the optimal allocation of funds. Note that Figure 60 itself is the product of guesswork, not research. More detail and better analysis would have to be provided if this study were actually made, but sufficient is shown and said to indicate that we can learn more about health services by structural systemic study than by contemplating statistics. It is the same story as before.

As with education and health, so with transportation; the systemic totality is what matters. As long as each of the forms of transportation available in the country is regarded as distinct, and as long as each of them separately is required to show a profit, so long will the national good in the matter of transportation be overlooked. 'Rich' routes between major towns for instance will be the subject of intense competition between all forms of transport, whereas outlying districts will tend to get service from none of them. In fact, from the national point of view, there is likely to be an optimal mode of transport for every kind of thing moved between any two particular places. Also, from the viewpoint of national efficiency, it becomes important to discover which these are, and so to regulate matters that the optimal methods are used. It is futile to protest that a democratic country must not regulate matters in this way. For it is the government alone which specifies what permission, even what capital investment, can be awarded to the needs of railways and of roads for example. Therefore the government constrains the situation from the start. In so far as pricing policies for transportation services are a major factor in the national economy, a government can hardly disclaim any responsibility for influencing them. Where the services concerned are actually under national ownership, then the responsibility is absolute.

Again the situation is discovered where much use of operational research has been made to examine how traffic should flow on roads, how aeroplanes should be organized to arrive and depart from airports, how railways services should be grouped, and so on. But it seems that nowhere in the world has a systemic model of the overall transportation problem been created: the task simply appears to be too great. But, and this is a necessary repetition, the task appears too great simply because the methodology used is analytic; it is assumed that a detailed understanding of all the components of the system must be acquired before a proper account of the total system can possibly be built up as an aggregate of these elementary bits. Great efforts have already been made to show that this is a fallacy.

Exactly the same arguments apply to the national fuel policy. Operational research has been undertaken to a considerable extent in the coal industry, and to a lesser extent in the electricity industry. Very little has been done where gas is concerned, less still in the area where it is most required—that of atomic energy. A great deal of OR goes on in the oil industries of the world, and it is aimed very specifically at higher profits for that industry. Even less possibility exists that this fuel should be integrated with the others, because it is in private hands. Yet the nation's access to fuel is a prerequisite of every kind of progress; and it is of tremendous economic importance that the various fuels should be optimally used. Again the approach from the total system is terrifyingly absent.

When it comes to matters of security, an interesting fact emerges. In many countries, most notably Britain and the United States, the research undertaken into military policies and decisions was for many years devoted to individual arms. Only recently has the absurdity of this sub-systemic approach been realized, and both the countries mentioned have made large and traumatic efforts to integrate military security. But these efforts are by no means complete, nor is the research undertaken by any means integral. Of all the departments of government, however, it is the service departments which lead the way in the approach to cybernetic understanding. And this is not surprising, because it is very clear that in a fluid strategic situation as encountered in actual warfare, the vital necessity of understanding all arms of the service as part of an integral warlike capability is paramount.

Once the powerful ecological threat of extinction is removed, however, civilization typically collapses into its sub-systemic attitudes. The breakdown of a police force, which is also responsible for security, makes a startling contrast to military security. In most civilized countries police forces are compartmentalized by region and by function to a degree which makes a national optimum completely impossible. Occasionally, a national effort can be mounted and be successful—again under the stimulus of serious threat. Massive or otherwise serious crime may result in a mobilization of sub-systemic effort into a totality which is momentarily impressive. But in general, this does not happen. Moreover, even within the sub-systems of the constabulary, organization is looked upon more as a matter of command structure than as an informational interaction. Yet, given that all large complex systems are in-or-out of control and more-or-less successful by virtue of information alone, the point is nowhere more obvious than in the detection of crime.

The interaction of the sub-systems 'criminality' and 'law and order' can certainly be described as a self-vetoing homeostat. Suppose that every briefing meeting of a group of intending criminals were actually attended by a policeman. Then it is obvious that the police force would deploy themselves to catch the criminals in the act of committing their crime, and the chances of committing a successful crime would be precisely nil. This is one limiting case. If we then take the case where virtually no information about criminal intent reaches the police, then the chances of the culprits' being caught are a direct function of the search procedure used by the police to monitor the world in which crime is committed. Since this world is of extremely high variety, the police force is faced with a variety generation problem: a system of patrolling, a system of informing, a system of detection—all these are variety generators. But it is extremely difficult to attain to requisite variety, consequently the criminal's actual chance of success is remarkably high. This seems to be the position society is in today. Finally, however, if the police send messages to the criminal sub-system declaring exactly what *their* intentions are, the first case is reversed. The criminals are enabled to avoid police surveillance, since they will decide to move entirely within the complementary set of the set of police activity. In such cases no criminal could possibly be caught at all. This is the second limiting case.

It follows that a police strategy should seek to gain variety by every permissible means, and not to lose any variety by passing information to the criminal. In fact, any *regular* system of police activity, such as patrolling according to a time schedule, is at once seen to be an indefensible strategy. It will be recalled, for example, that most escapes from prisons and prisoner-of-war camps have in fact been based on this subtraction from the jailer's variety. Even in some such matters as the detection of road offences, deductions can be drawn from the requisite variety law. There is, after all, a class of known bad drivers—those who have previously been found guilty of some offence, or those who failed to pass certain tests which could be set up. Yet this large group of people, who are potentially causes of accidents, intermingle with the law-abiding motorists. The result is that a low variety police surveillance has to detect the law-breaking motorist in a high variety situation—and normally fails. That is, most offences against road discipline go unpunished, because they are not observed. There are only two basic methods of meeting the provisions of the requisite variety law in these circumstances. One is to increase the amount of police surveillance until *no* motoring act is unwatched; and this appears impracticable. The other is to decrease the variety of the field to be surveyed; and this could be done by compelling the potential offender to advertise his presence.

For example, if every motorist convicted of any road offence were required (let us say) to transmit a special signal from his car which the police could receive, then police patrols would have a feasible control task. Moreover, selection tests could be administered (at the time of driving tests) which would detect a potentially dangerous driver. The reason why such tests are not encouraged and are certainly not acted upon at present, is the basic legal requirement that until a man has actually *done* something wrong he must not be penalized. Indeed this seems reasonable in the present case, since no infallible selection test can be envisaged. But it would not be a particular hardship on some suspected driver to advertise his presence on the road so that he could come under special surveillance.

It is not the function of this chapter to make actual proposals about the way in which government departments and the services they control should be organized and administered. Scientists believe in undertaking competent research before reaching conclusions which they can put forward as the basis for recommended action and decision-taking. But it has somehow to be conveyed what is meant by the notion of engineering with uncertainty, and constructing control systems out of information circuits. Above all, it has to be made clear that there are laws of cybernetics which, disobeyed, result in an inefficient set of strategies. As was said at the outset, government is an informational process of complex systems, more than a question of mandatory law, simply because there is no variety generator capable of enforcing the latter. There seems to be but one exception to this rule. In the case where society at large is prepared to regard a particular action as reprehensible—immoral, perhaps, as well as illegal—then the offence may become very hard to commit. The reason is quite specific: requisite variety is being supplied by the entire population, since any one citizen may turn out to be an informer on any other citizen. Reticence or cowardice may in fact prevent that citizen from intervening in practice; but the palpable risk that he might do so is an inhibition on the criminal.

It seems as though any sphere of government can be treated in this fashion. The most obvious example has been left until last. If all branches of government are really dependent upon informational processes, then perhaps the most important branch of government is that which supplies the channels of communication. This is the branch of government responsible for posts and telegraphs, for the press (in so far as it may be influenced by government) and for broadcasting. There is certainly a

trivial sense in which the importance of these services to national government may be viewed. No would-be conqueror would fail to make the
conquest of the seats of these services a primary target of his invasion.
But the more important sense in which this branch of government matters
is that it supervises the only means by which *other* branches of government are made possible.

Therefore it is a mistake to think of the national means of communication as a primarily commercial and social requirement; it is fundamentally
an economic requirement. This is the modern position; the historical
position was quite the reverse, because the means of communication
were created by the powerful to serve the ends of power. So it pays to
reflect on the way in which the managerial approach to these matters is
influenced by history, with the result that the public is treated as the
master of the system, whereas the national economic need tends to be
neglected. At present, Britain seems to fall between the two stools. The
public is not in fact a master of the system, despite letters signed by
Civil Servants as 'obedient', for the individual citizen feels powerless in
the face of a bureaucracy. But the deployment of government by no
means exploits this unavoidable situation for the national good, since it
continues to accept fruitless gestures of mastery from the public. For
example, the citizen is permitted to send through the post any kind of
letter or packet, almost regardless of the way in which it is addressed or
the security of its fastenings. The result is that the government spends
an enormous amount of money in dealing with this noisy input.

There is great scope, in the national good, for change in the whole
structure and method of communication. It must begin from an enquiry
into the multifarious reasons for having communication at all, and work
out the systemic optimum which meets these reasons. The result would
take account of modern technology alone; it would ignore the vestigial
'methods now in use, because they are no more than glamorous versions
of outdated technologies. This is why no off-the-cuff attempt to draw a
diagram of the optimal system involved can possibly be attempted here.
It is by no means clear that it ought to incorporate the obvious boxes of
'posts' and 'telephones' at all. A new start is required; a new solution
ought to be obtained; a new plan for converting the existing system to
the new one would be essential.

Finally, it will be wondered why the departments of government dealing with the economy itself have been omitted from this list. Although
the list is partial, it would surely have been appropriate to dwell on the
role of the Treasury or of the Ministry for Economic Planning. The
answer to this question summarizes the entire argument. It looks very

much as if the economic planning and control function ought not to be regarded as a department of government at all. How the economy responds to everything that is going on is an output of the total system that is the State. That output can be effectively changed by structural intervention as between departments alone. There is a vital but not very interesting book-keeping job to be done by the Treasury, it is true. But the control function it exercises is vestigial, too; it persists as a relic of the idea that monetary policies ought to determine socio-economic policies, instead of acting merely as constraints on what the nation undertakes in total at any moment. The reason why the British economy oscillates so seriously is that feedback is applied to change the metabolism of the sub-systems of socio-economic behaviour, as a transfer function of departmental cash balances. But these are the crudest possible measures of ecological interaction that man has yet devised, and they take no notice at all of systemic interaction.

4   Control of a Decision

However much light may be shed on government policy by the approaches so far discussed, it remains a fact that decisions have to be taken. Moreover, the decision-taking machine is itself a complicated and disseminated organization of people. While this is also true in some measure of an industry, there is very often an autocrat at the head of the business who will mould the decision-taking process and eventually take the decision himself. But in the Civil Service this is no longer the case. Perhaps the minister will adopt the autocratic way in given cases; but he will on the whole dictate the broad lines of policy, and leave the process of reaching the correct decision within this framework to his staff. The kind of decision which is most important, furthermore, is not of the binary variety.

For example, it may appear to be a binary decision to say whether the nation needs a new steelworks or not. But any decision that it does involves the determination of a number of issues. For we must know what we are talking about: 'a steelworks' is nothing at all specific. It will be necessary to say that we are speaking of a steelworks of (say) between 300,000 and 500,000 ingot tons per annum capacity; that the works is located in this region rather than that; that it is or it is not integrated with an ironworks; that its major processes will be of one kind or another; that its raw materials and power will come from certain sources; that its products will range over various broad lines. It is only when this much has been determined about the subject of the decision that a decision can at all be taken. So the kind of decision to be discussed is one which *specifies a goal*. Given a specified goal, it will be a matter for detailed planning and perhaps research and development to elaborate the intentions. Now the process of the decision which specifies a goal is an elaborate informational process, and we may investigate its efficiency.

The starting point of a search for a goal is the present state of knowledge as it bears on all the factors involved. It may be noted that this knowledge constitutes a very large amount of information, but normally much of it is uncodified, and most of it is widely disseminated among many institutions. Hence the starting point of the search is an inefficiently connected, inadequately referenced, high-variety, store. The search for a decision is in part a task of retrieving and assembling *existing* information. The decision to erect a particular steelworks might possibly be uniquely determined by what is already known. If not, the rest of the search involves research into unknowns, and the assembling of results.

Both kinds of search are aimed at a goal, which is really the specification of a feasible outcome. No-one specifies an infeasible outcome if he can recognize the infeasibility. Now it is relatively easy to make a feasible decision when all the threads come into the hands of one autocrat. But if the decision is being taken in parts and in sequences, the men concerned often tend as a group to specify between them an infeasible outcome—which not one of them is in a position to recognize as such. For the characteristics underwritten from time to time by different authorities interact, producing directly or indirectly inconsistent demands. Thus it is best to view the searching process not as something that builds up to the goal, but as something that eliminates inconsistency and indeterminacy until the goal is laid bare. Given the feasible outcome, the decision itself is simply to say whether what has been specified is worth the money, or otherwise sufficiently profitable, in comparison with other goals which could be met within the budget available.

So the problem is this. The goal specifications, which those who devise and produce it regard as very complicated, is from the decision-maker's standpoint the simplest entity of all. It is a unit package of information. The starting point of the search is a disorganized, high-variety source sufficiently rich in information to specify thousands of unit packages. Once searching begins, there is a high-variety and more organized informational input, also sufficient to specify thousands of unit packages. The task is to destroy variety in this process until one unit package is left: the feasible outcome. The goal has to be identified.

What concerns the decision-taker is the efficiency of this informational process. The first scientific statement that can be made about it is this. The overriding determinant of efficiency is the use made of the initial degree of knowledge as to what the goal is. What *is* the outcome that the search must make feasible? It is possible to know the goal (in this sense) from the beginning; it is possible not to know anything about the goal until the search hits *and* recognizes it. The initial position on the continuous scale linking full knowledge to total ignorance about the goal largely determines the length of the search. The *use made* of that initial position largely determines the efficiency of the process.

The reason is that a competent search will use variety generators constructed from an understanding of what the goal really is. When the notion of a variety generator was first introduced, in Section 4 of Chapter 12, an illustration was drawn from the need to search a map. That argument was used again in Chapter 17. To reiterate: there is a decision space, regarded as a square array, containing 1,000,000 small squares. The unknown goal lies in one of these small squares, and there is no reason why an heuristic procedure for finding it should stumble on the answer early rather than late in the hunt. Then the expectation is that the goal will be discovered after 500,000 steps (on the average) from square to square. If, however, the goal is known in the sense that the co-ordinate system of the square array is known, the search is made much easier. It is now necessary to hunt for 1 row out of 1,000, and for 1 column out of 1,000. When the values on the two co-ordinates are known, the goal is uniquely specified. This procedure involves a search over twice the square root of the original number of small squares (2,000 instead of 1,000,000), and the expectation is that the answer will be found in 1,000 steps instead of 500,000. This means that to use a generalized heuristic procedure when the goal is, or could be, known in terms of the structure of the decision space is inefficient. The decision efficiency in this case is, as we saw before, a fifth of 1 per cent.

This measurement is startling. The more complicated the decision the more startling it is, because the efficiency is dropping as the square of the complexity of the decision. So this time through the explanation let us generalize. The sort of decision in which we are interested is n dimensional, where n is a sizable number. Hence if the *variety* of the decision (the number of distinguishable possibilities which could be chosen) is V, the total space for search is as large in general as the nth root of V. So the expected length of search is in general $\frac{1}{2}nV^{1/n}$. These statements about decision procedures accord well with intuition. To illustrate: to delimit the possible types of iron ore to be used in the ironworks of the integrated plant automatically delimits the possibilities of many of the processes that can be followed later.

In order to exploit the efficiency of a properly conducted search for a goal specification, it is necessary to analyse the dimensionality of the decision involved. From experience in the analysis of large-scale decisions, it seems that no algorithm exists by which to set about the task of stating the goal. Anyone involved in the process sits down to write from his own viewpoint, mentioning whatever seems to him to be important, building in what may be noise, and omitting whole areas of vital facts. It thus becomes difficult to collate statements from different sources, or to be sure that the information we have, we use—and this is the criterion of efficiency. The rigorous approach to the problem is to undertake research directed to setting out all the characteristics and considerations involved in terms of a logical formula. Now the use of symbolic logic at this point has an advantage: one can detect which variables are completely determined by other variables in the system. Such variables are variables no longer, for decisions about them are subsumed within decisions of higher order. In this way, unnecessary embroidery is kept out of the formulation of a problem, and unnecessary sub-decisions are not taken too early.

What this formula has to do is to take the completely unstructured idea of the goal (again, say, a steelworks), and to give it structure. The logical variables involved are all listed by some notation, and connected together by means of logical notation—conjunction and disjunction, implication and inclusion. If decisions can be reached about all these logical variables, we say, then the steelworks that is wanted is fully specified as a goal for the planners and those conducting research and development. The management decision process at this stage, then, is one which will settle the state of all the variables, cutting down the total variety V to a variety of one. By giving this structure (or dimensionality) to the problem, we set up the necessary conditions for an efficient decision-taking procedure.

In the first place, it will no longer be possible to indulge in a politically motivated or prestige-seeking search across the whole decision space V, as so often happens in real-life cases. In the second place, it will not be possible to have subsidiary issues (which are in fact consequential decisions of lower logical order) entertained and discussed. The real co-ordinates of the decision have been marked out. Thirdly, we have eliminated the risk that people insert meaningless statements into the goal outcome: an interesting aspect of the matter. In general, it can be said that the negation of a logical variable ought to constitute a meaningful possibility. Thus 'open hearth furnaces', when negated, gives 'non open hearth furnaces'—a perfectly sensible outcome. But official papers seeking to define a goal often bristle with bogus logical variables that do not meet this test. For example, it is often said that a product should be 'lowest cost'. But it is simply vacuous to ask for the product that does *not* have minimum cost: this would be a positive plea for inefficiency. What the cost will be is a function of all the procedures laid down to create a product sale. These procedures may of course be examined in order to *reduce* cost; but they are entirely consequential upon the decisions which determine the framework within which cost will be computed. Bogus statements of this kind must be kept out of the logical formulation.

Assuming then that a logical formula about the goal specification has been set up, and that we know the number n of logical variables, the remaining question is to specify a control procedure for the decision-takers. Their job is to propose logical values for the logical variables, which is a process that will take time. Now if the efficiency of the process is to be controlled, a measure of some kind is required. It is precisely a measure of the uncertainty that exists in the system. Variety V of the decision space includes all possible outcomes, therefore the initial uncertainty is very large. The uncertainty remaining at the end of the decision process is precisely nil, because the variety will be one: a specified unit package as the goal. Hence we want to measure the uncertainty and track it over the months of decision-taking until there is none left. Obviously, the process ought to be monotonic decreasing: that is, there should always be less uncertainty left now than before, and never more. If there were more, the sub-decisions already taken would have been abrogated. The management would need to know about this. Moreover, it is likely that the process of removing uncertainty normally follows a certain curve, or at least belongs to a family of curves. If so, a normative control system could be created to monitor the process of this decision taking against some criterion (which could now be measured) of *good* decision taking.

The measure of uncertainty required is an entropy. Measures of entropy were introduced in Section 3 of Chapter 14. Consider one of the logical variables: say, for example, the existence of an ironworks in the context of the steelworks. This offers a binary alternative, and the decision-takers must say either yes or no to this possibility at some stage of the argument. If there is a pair of alternatives between which to decide, and neither is more likely than the other, then the entropy equation is: $H = -(0 \cdot 5 \log_2 0 \cdot 5) - (0 \cdot 5 \log_2 0 \cdot 5) = 1$. When a decision has been taken, one of the brackets will go to $(1 \log_2 1) = 0$, and the other will cease to exist. This means that the entropy has completely disappeared and that the decision has been taken.

If one outcome has a prior probability greater than the other, the uncertainty is somewhat less. For instance, if there is an 80 per cent likelihood of selecting one alternative, we get: $H = -(0\cdot8 \log_2 0\cdot8) + (0\cdot2 \log_2 0\cdot2) = 0\cdot3$. A committee of ten, divided initially in favour of and against a particular outcome in the proportion eight to two, presents this much uncertainty that is left to resolve. If there are several alternatives of equal likelihood (say four) then we get: $H = -4(0\cdot25 \log_2 0\cdot25) = 2$.

Now there are many issues to be decided, specified by the totality of logical variables, according to the logical formula; the selection entropies of these have to be summed to measure the total uncertainty of the decision. Thus we reach the classical formulation of an entropy, in general: $H = -\Sigma\,(p_i \log_2 p_i)$. This is the measure of uncertainty that will be applied to the decision process. When $H = 0$ there is no uncertainty left and the goal is specified.

Now the way in which this measure is applied in a particular case is a matter of research and experience in using this tool, but it should be clear that if the alternative specifications for each variable can be listed, then the uncertainty introduced by this range of choices can be measured. Adhering to the simplest case in which all the choices are equally likely, we get a simplification of the measuring technique. Suppose that there are m choices. Then the entropy equation gives:

$$H = -m\left(\frac{1}{m} \log_2 \frac{1}{m}\right) = \log_2 m$$

This, it will be remembered, is precisely the version of entropy found in classical thermodynamics. It is also a measure very easy to apply. And when it has been applied to all of the logical variables, the sum of the entropies so measured will measure the uncertainty of the decision.

This is another way of saying that the total number of possible outcomes is a permutation of all the outcomes for each variable in turn. In a particular case which has been studied, the entropy of the decision was 43. As explained in Chapter 14, the reason for using logarithms to the base 2 is that it creates a measure expressed in terms of binary digits—or bits. Now 43 bits is a measure of variety $V = 2^{43}$. This number is in fact the total possible number of outcomes which our procedure has allowed us to entertain. Lest it be thought that any logical formula is bound to be unduly restrictive, or that not much effort is required to remove an uncertainty of 43 bits, it may be advisable to state what this number of alternatives actually is. 43 bits, then, specify a variety of 2^{43}, which equals 8,796,093,022,208 possible alternatives.

The analysis, argument, formalization and metric involved generate a control procedure for decision-taking. Put briefly, it is this. The first objective is to specify the goal. If an OR scientist (appropriately qualified) sits in at initial discussions, or otherwise acquaints himself with the nature of the goal under review, he will be able to prepare a logical model of the nature of the decision space. This means that the dimensionality of that decision space is specified from the start. He should next investigate the logical structure of the choice system attached to each logical variable, and create a measure of selection entropy. According to the argument that the task is not to build up a complicated requirement from elementals, but on the contrary to *reduce* a large number of initial possibilities to one (the unit package), the following course is undertaken.

A datal graph is set up, showing the initial variety which must be reduced to zero. This is the measure of the unspecified goal. A tabulation of the logical model must then be prepared. This means that all the logical variables are listed, together with the choice structure that applies to each. This is circulated among all decision-takers for their views on the choices that ought to be made. Where unanimity is obtained, the decision may be said to have been taken. This of course reduces the total entropy by the amount of entropy appropriate to that logical variable. But the fact that one of the logical variables has now been fixed begins to reduce available variety in other dimensions. This is analogous to fixing on one row of a square array: only the column is left to choose. In the steelworks illustration, it meant that once an iron ore input pattern was agreed, various other processes would be delimited. Now it is possible for the OR scientist to ensure that the entropy of each remaining choice is appropriately reduced as the consequence of each choice already made. For he has the tool of the logical notation of the general formula, and can work out consequential delimitations of choice from choices that have been taken. This is a technical matter; but it can be said in round terms that any decision made about a logical variable is likely to affect the range of choice remaining for all other logical variables which follow it and which are preceded by an implication sign ($\supset$). For this reason, entropy remaining falls faster than the decision taken itself expects. That is: more uncertainty is eliminated in making a choice than the choice itself eliminates. To repeat the earlier rigorous statement of this saving, the variety generating system reduces the length of search for the goal by the factor $\frac{1}{2}V - \frac{1}{2}nV^{\frac{1}{n}}$, where V is the decision variety, and n is the number of logical dimensions. We now have a control procedure for monitoring the progress of the reduction of uncertainty down this exceedingly concave curve.

As far as the decision-taker is concerned, a fairly simple rule can be stated. An attempt should be made to withhold any choice which could be considered arbitrary until later; for, strangely, the object is to take decisions not as quickly but as slowly as possible. For example, if the decision-takers were to go through the tabulation and immediately take a decision on *every* choice, they would reduce the variety to one at their first meeting. The goal would be fully determined, and almost certainly it would be unfeasible. This is because contradictory viewpoints would express themselves in incompatible sub-decisions. If, on the contrary, *no* choice is specified, the goal remains totally unknown— and the planning and research effort required to discover it goes back to the kind of inefficiency earlier discussed. So the rule is: determine those choices which are certainly known and unanimously agreed; give general rather than specific choices unless the latter are really essential; provide other comments in the form of notes. This simple rule ensures that the goal specification itself reduces the initial uncertainty of the logical formula very substantially. The new entropy can be marked on the datal graph, and another round of decision-taking can begin.

We have spoken in earlier sections of this chapter about how decision-taking is to be organized and informed through the medium of cybernetic models of informational processes. We are now talking about the *control* of the decision-taking. A criterion by which optimal efficiency is obtainable, and a measure by which progress can be monitored, has been stated. All that remains to be said about this procedure is that the curve plotting the expected form of entropy against time has a normative form against which the actual decay curve can be measured. We at once have a fiduciary measure for 'management by exception', and it is thought that this has never been available to a disseminated decision-taking group before. The normative curve itself may be one of three types.

It may be a 'theoretically expected' curve, derived from an exponential decay function. Secondly, it may be an empirical curve derived from accumulating experience of what the entropy curves of 'good' decisions turn out to be like in similar circumstances. Thirdly, it may be a curve measuring the consequences of a decision-taking programme evolved by such a technique as network analysis, which was described in Part II. In all three cases, fiducial limits can be set around the curve as a guide to management intervention, giving exactly the same effect as that obtained by statistical quality control on the shop floor.

Some rules about the control of entropy-decay against an expected curve can be stated in principle. As was remarked earlier, the elimination of uncertainty ought to be monotonic decreasing. It seems, then, a fair inference that if the curve suddenly *rises,* meaning that new uncertainty has been imported to the system, the objectives of the decision have in fact been changed. The logical model and the entropy progress chart offer precise analytical tools to discover exactly what has happened, what the consequences are in terms of the entailed delay, and what ought to be done about it. In general, if the objective has changed, and if this is approved, a new model should be made specifying the changed goal, and the progress made to date should be re-evaluated against it.

This combined operational research and cybernetic technique has been evolved to deal with the kind of large-scale decision discussed here. It ought to be appropriate to most governmental decision-taking, and it ought to reduce the (sometimes) many years of discussion and cross-reference by the square root factor explained before. Of course, those who seek to measure what has not been measured before always encounter objections. This approach tries to make a start in measuring the 'amount of decision' left to take from first to last in specifying a goal. The undoubted fact that the measures are somewhat arbitrary should not be regarded as fatal to their work. All measurements include a tacit assumption of certain conventions. For instance: 'The height of this tower is 200 feet' assumes that all agree with the convention whereby a ruler is placed *against* the object measured. We could have a convention that rulers were held at a distance of 100 yards from the measured object; then no-one would be surprised if tower heights were quoted at around 10 inches.

What matters about measurement is the ability of a metric to generate comparative data, given that certain conventions apply. The real difficulty in comprehending and accepting the approach to large-scale decision-taking given in this section is not that the measures do not measure quantities with which people are familiar, nor that they are more or less exact. The problem is that the conventions under which the measures are taken and quoted are not the tacit assumptions of us all.

19

THE OUTCOME FOR MANAGEMENT SCIENCE

Ceux qui s'appliquent trop aux petites choses
deviennent ordinairement incapables des grandes.

Those who stick too much to small things normally
become incapable of great things.

LA ROCHEFOUCAULD in *Maxims* (1665)

1   The Organization of Management Science

The future value of science to management depends only in part on
managers themselves; the major responsibility rests with the scientists.
It is to them that La Rochefoucauld's maxim is addressed, as well as to
the managers who are listening. There can be no doubt that the operational research profession as a whole, and even an occasional eminent
practitioner as an individual, displays an ambivalent attitude to the
point and utility of OR. For, after a quarter of a century of successful
development, many people have lost sight of the *raison d'être* of the
subject.

Here is a summary of an attitude towards a potential OR job which
one increasingly hears taken up by senior OR men, as well as by the
managers they serve. There is a well-defined problem; the facts appertain-
ing to this problem are readily available, well documented, accurate;
there is an established measure by which to quantify the facts; there
are known techniques which have proved reliable for solving similar
problems; there seems to be no particular difficulty in making another
application here; it follows that the outcome of the study will be of this
certain form; there is a simple way of implementing the conclusions in
practice. When all of this can be affirmed it is sensible to embark on
some work; if any one of these propositions is falsified then really we

496

ought not to tackle the job. This outlook is anathema. It is a straight-forward denial of the historical origins of the subject, as expounded in Part I, and has nothing at all to say about the future potentiality of science in management.

Now it is not denied that there is a place in the team of management advisers for people applying this set of criteria. After all, had operational research been unable, in its quarter of a century, to identify a large number of recurrent management problems and to propose formal solutions for them, then it would have failed. We do have groups of acknowledged problems; we do have groups of well investigated techniques. The backlog of successful approaches ought to be steadily assimilated into normal management practice. But if the consensus of opinion among OR men is that to offer *this* service to management constitutes operational research then the minority will wish to abandon their use of this term.

There remain hosts of problems which are ill defined, the precise questions which ought to be answered being unknown either to the manager or to the scientists. They are characterized by an absence of facts, by inadequate recording of data, by unsatisfactory mensuration concepts, and perhaps by the absence of any relevant metric whatsoever. No-one has the faintest idea what would count as a solution. It is these problems which keep managers awake at night, and which some group of scientists ought to attack in collaboration with the management concerned. If, in the consensus of OR opinion, to do this is not to do operational research, then we shall simply have to find a new term to describe the activity. This would not be a matter for regret, still less for recrimination; it is important only that the forces deployed in the service of management should sail under recognizable flags.

It is as a matter of fact not possible to operate both approaches under the same flag. There are so many differences in orientation, organization, training and development between the two that they ought to be separated. In particular, the kinds of application made will vary tremendously. Under the prudential policy that OR does only what it knows how to do, the profession becomes stuck with the relatively small things it has already mastered. Managers become used to these little activities and begin to draw boundaries to the scope of an OR group. The most creative and adventurous scientists depart, and the group that is left 'becomes incapable of great things'. This de-naturing of what was originally operational research has been observed in many individual groups, and a process looking very like it seems to be occurring within the profession as a whole. Prudence, caution and respectability have

widely taken the place of adventure, hard work and the motive to get
things done. It is so very easy to offer plausible justification for this:
science is a serious business, and its fair name must not be compromised.
The situation whereby an enterprise might make a sensationally large
profit, as the result of some scientific research into its policies which
might not meet the exacting requirements of a doctoral thesis, is obscene
to a certain cast of academic mind. It is, however, what the manager
wants. It is what the country needs.

This book is concerned with one topic alone: competent management. If a manager guesses when he could use the knowledge accumulated by mankind in its search for an understanding of the world, then
he acts incompetently. That is all there is to it. Science in management
has to be organized to this end and no other. If that practical criterion
attracts *odium academica,* that need concern neither management nor the
scientists who work for it. The universities are entitled to define their
own role *vis-à-vis* society. That leaves the management scientist free to
define his own role for himself, which is the function of this chapter.

The head of a group that does successful management science is faced
with many professional problems. These days the raw graduate is often
a man of quite astonishing specialism of knowledge and narrowness of
outlook. (Whatever happened to the idea that the individual mind is
broadened in its progression through the *universitas magistrorum et
scholarium?*) The potential OR man is someone ready to forget that he
is what it has so recently cost him so much effort to become. Thus it is
that the good potential OR scientist is likely to be an interdisciplinarian
manqué, a man who has come to realize that perhaps no-one has ever
told God that there is a difference between physics and chemistry. But
this demand for breadth of outlook cannot be used to justify ignorance
or a slipshod approach to science: the man must 'know his stuff'. He
has, moreover, to achieve both these well-nigh incompatible outcomes
without being arrogant, and the attainment of a philosophic posture of
humility in the face of the universe becomes increasingly difficult for
young men faced with the relentless advance of science. Next, the
potential OR recruit has to know about the world of affairs; he needs,
above all, to understand people. It is not worth proceeding with this
alarming catalogue of virtues, for it is fast becoming clear that we are
defining a paragon; each one of us is no more than human.

Hence, the head of an OR group has to think very deeply about his
problems of organization and of operation. His object must be to create
a kind of activity which would have been undertaken by paragons were
they available, using men—himself included—who are not paragons.

And although this may be strictly impossible, it is certainly possible to get either nearer to the desideratum or further away from it. For example, if the scientists in an OR group are organized (as they would be in most kinds of scientific research) according to their disciplines, then the chances of simulating a team of paragons are remote. It does not do to have a mathematics section, a biological section and an economic section. Not only will interdisciplinary collaboration be made difficult, which is a methodological point, but the members of the group will be formally encouraged in the wrong direction, which is a psychological point. Any such group of specialists under its head specialist feeds internally on its own prerogatives, protects its outlook from dilution by other outlooks, and comes to behave as if it had a uniquely satisfactory understanding of the universe. So if the OR group is not to be sub-divided by disciplines, it must be sub-divided into interdisciplinary lots.

The most obvious basis for structuring the organization in this way is to select teams of men who look as though they can work together and who have a natural leader. For example, an OR organization might well begin with a biologist, a physicist, a psychologist and a mathematician. When these people had become used to working together, it would be a pity (some would say) to break them up; a further team of four people could be recruited, and so on. But this approach has serious demerits. In particular, by the time there are sixty scientists in the group, arranged in fifteen teams of four men each, it is most unlikely that their allocation to a collection of fifteen OR projects will be optimal. That is to say, any fixed allocation would fail to release the full potential of the total group to those projects.

This appeal to our own principles of systemic integrity, provides the clue as to how an OR group can best be organized. Suppose that there are *at this moment* sixty scientists representing between them all possible scientific disciplines in the group, and that fifteen projects are on hand. Then clearly a good OR management would be able to determine the optimal allocation of men to jobs—taking into account the mixture of disciplines, the mixture of personalities, the size of the jobs, their current state (for they will be at different states), and so on. Call this allocation the Now organization. In a few days' time, something changes. A breakthrough is made in one of the projects, and other skills are called for; a new job arrives; a new man arrives; and so on. The Now organization changes to meet this change. By all means, however, we must be realistic. In a going concern, one cannot make a completely fresh optimal allocation every day; in the limiting case, it might mean that everyone had to change places daily with someone else, and continuity would be lost. What can happen every day, or every week, or better still *continuously*, is a modification of the Now organization—to keep the Now updated. Given due attention to the momentum of hard work, there will not often be radical changes; but the system will not stray far from optimality. In short, we have a virtually self-organizing system before us.

Now it is an administrative if not a scientific necessity that one member of each team should be its leader: the man who takes responsibility for the research. These leaders must answer to someone more highly placed in the organization. Thus if the leader of each team, which exists because it has work to do on a project, be called a project manager, then he should report to a project director—a more experienced man who may simultaneously be responsible for a number of projects. Call this man a projects director, and allow that there will be several such projects directors in a large OR group. It will be noted that no projects director, despite his elevated status in the group, has any actual staff 'of his own', because any one man, a member of a team working on a project under his direction according to the Now organization, may tomorrow be removed to work on another project—the manager of which is reporting to *another* projects director. The adaptive optimality of the Now organization is guaranteed by this high level of fluidity, and the refusal to tie people to each other in permanent hierarchical chains. But fluidity must not degenerate into chaos; it is obvious that the movement of people must be a controlled movement that pays proper regard to the coherence, continuity and integrity of each project. To this end, it is necessary to insert horizontal bonds across the pyramidal Now structure. This is straightforwardly possible by creating a kind of cabinet out of all the project managers at one level, and another out of all the general managers at another level. These cabinets will, at their appropriate levels, determine the tactics to be followed in matching the group's potential to the work in hand.

Although it has been suggested that the essence of OR organization is a Now structure, some mode of permanent structure must also be embodied. For tactical dispositions are not the sole decision-making problems relating to OR. There are strategic questions too; and there are administrative decisions of many kinds. But the two cabinets which emerged for Now organization purposes are, by virtue of their professional rank, permanent. Thus they can well constitute the junior and senior management bodies in the normal sense.

The organization chart at Figure 61 looks very different from the orthodox family tree. The permanent organization is depicted by the

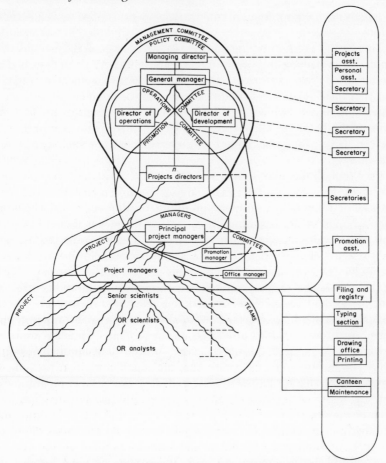

FIGURE 61. Fluid organization chart of an OR company. Curved lines enclose areas of permanent association and constant interaction; the wavy lines represent impermanent and variable groupings for operational purposes. The network of solid lines defines the ultimate chains of responsibility for discipline and administration only; broken lines the channels of administrative support.

steady lines; the Now organization is shown in wavering lines. Now there is nothing unique about this way of organizing a group: there are probably as many modes of organization as there are groups throughout the world. Indeed, it had better be admitted that the particular organization described here is that of the author's own group. At least, it works; and it does not offend or militate against the principles

DC—KK

of scientific methodology in the management context as elucidated before.

There is no point in giving an involved account of all the mechanisms employed in making this group into a viable entity. What matters is that the interdisciplinary nature of scientific work for management is fostered, and that there is sufficient fluidity for efficient deployment of resources. Any group, however placed, and of whatever size, ought to aim at these twin goals. In the small, institutional group there is no real problem; the very large group may adhere to these aims in some such way as that shown.

Easy though this may sound, few OR groups are organizationally successful by these two criteria. The large group often fails in this respect because of a failure in teamwork among the leading scientists. The horizontal bonds of the organization collapse. This means that sub-sets of staff cluster around individual seniors like disciples round a master: they resent being asked to work to any other master, and the seniors themselves become possessive. Once this process sets in, the results will be dangerous, for each self-contained pyramid grows more like itself as time passes, and begins to toe a party line. One kind of model begins to dominate its work, one set of techniques is regarded as superior, the operational research attack itself becomes stereotyped. Thus the group as a whole is denatured, losing the very spirit of collaborative enquiry which ought to unify its endeavours and exploit its interdisciplinary capacity. The disease has been observed in a variety of large groups in different parts of the world, and the work produced suffers gravely. Even in the small group, which has only one man of 'master' calibre, the interdisciplinary principle is commonly betrayed. The head appoints scientists of similar temperament and skills to himself, reinforcing his own ability in a supererogatory way and turning his own deficiencies into formal scientific lacunae.

It is such faulty organization which is basically responsible for the most dangerous OR disease of all: the preoccupation with small things mentioned at the start of this section. For the absence of horizontal bonds between disciplines, between projects, between masters at each level, leads to involution in each team. That isolated team, ill balanced, does even more work of the same kind as before, and receives positive feedback from management in this suicidal tendency. It takes more and more interest in the fine detail of the techniques it employs, and becomes more and more careless of the management's actual problems. It is not difficult to find groups of men who show immense skill in analysing situations that can be described as queueing systems or as linear programmes, but whose managerial employers would not think of posing to them a problem of immediate importance to the board. The scientists are happy in pursuing their self-perpetuating studies with ever more finesse. The managers hope all that work is useful, and continue to wrestle with their actual dilemmas as before. They are doubtless wise.

2   Education and Training for Management Science

A recent enquiry about the possibility of entering operational research came from a university scientist of considerable distinction in another field. Surprisingly, he turned out to have no bachelor's degree, although he had attended an ancient university as an undergraduate. He gave as his qualification: 'Sent down for speaking disrespectfully of Immanuel Kant.' The explanation, one may think, distorts the facts. However, the story somehow manages to convey the hopeless desperation with which some of the men most needed in operational research regard the academic training open to them. Some would—indeed do—contend that the organization, the teaching and even the research outlook of some universities is a positive discouragement to both creative and interdisciplinary thinking. However this may be, there is in fact no detectable supply of suitably qualified OR men emerging from the entire educational system of the United Kingdom. And the men who do enter the profession as a first post-graduate employment find that they have much to unlearn.

Many British universities, on the other hand, undertake some post-graduate teaching in OR according to a large variety of plans. These range from one-day seminars to full-year courses terminating in a master's degree; and of course it is possible in some cases to read for a doctorate in this field. The very clear difficulty about all this effort is that operational research is not usually envisaged by the university itself as an interdisciplinary subject. Its organization within the university is therefore not discussed in these terms, the courses are neither administered nor taught in these terms, and the examinations are neither set nor adjudicated in these terms. The inevitable consequence is that people who have undergone these courses do not have an operational research outlook when they have completed them. This is not to say that the courses are valueless; it is to say that they are not as good as they should be, and that the potential employer has a lot more training to impart and a reorientation to undertake.

Because British universities are organized in the way that they are, the operational research course must be founded in and sponsored by a particular department. Such courses are sponsored in some places by mathematics, in others by economics, in others by engineering; one new university uniquely has an operational research department as such. But wherever these courses are to be found, they tend to suffer from a defect which, on reflection, would seem to be almost inevitable in present academic circumstances. This is that the courses are at root technique-oriented, and not problem-oriented; and that far from being *inter-*disciplinary, they acknowledge one discipline alone—mathematics. Those responsible defend themselves against this charge by pointing to the case study method of teaching which, in one form or another, they all use. But often these case studies are in a way bogus, in that they usually turn out to be chosen to illustrate the application of a standard mathematical technique. The OR man in real life, on the contrary, finds that problems do not on the whole yield to these particular—almost proprietary—methods of solution. Arguments on this point will have been encountered *passim* throughout this book.

Clearly an OR man must know the techniques that are available in the many mathematical cookery books which masquerade as useful OR texts. But if a man is a graduate, and is more or less literate and numerate as he should be, the task of mastering the basic technical apparatus of his work is almost trivial. He will need enough mathematics to be able to read these texts, it is true; but if 10 per cent of an OR group is actually expert in manipulating the techniques, this is surely enough. What an OR man is really supposed to do is to think hard about a problem, to bring to it scientific discipline and methodology (which is other than an algebraic skill), and above all to penetrate a system according to his particular insight into the way that nature works. The courses that have been criticized produce instead applied mathematicians in the industrial context: a most useful breed, indeed, but not necessarily the kind of person sought for all OR purposes.

Since the basic problem of operational research is to understand what is going on in a situation, to recognize what exactly is worrying a manager, and to formulate a model of the system involved in such a way that it can be quantified and can provide conclusions which the manager finds helpful, it would seem that the basic discipline to be taught is the philosophy of science. What the world is really like, what counts as a problem, and what counts as a solution—these are the sorts of question the neophyte must be taught to discuss. Because the OR man must try to advance the frontiers of the measurable against the opposition of the thought blocks which exist amongst managers and scientists alike, it is vital that this instruction in philosophy of science should include a course on the history of science. People have to become aware, not only of the infra-structure of the methodology which advances a scientific process, but of general methodological tendencies in the development of the competent thought of mankind.

The OR man faces psychological problems of his own; he also faces the psychological problems of the manager. It is not an exaggeration to say that some component of the problem which the manager faces is usually a projection of his own personality difficulties. Thus some special kind of teaching in psychology should grow out of the instruction in the philosophy and history of science. In indicating these needs it is assumed that the candidate is already a graduate, and that he already knows one subject well. If he has been properly taught in his undergraduate years, he may already have acquired some of the understanding to be imparted by the courses mentioned, but it is unhappily a common experience to find that he has no knowledge of these things at all.

The advantage of this orientation and grounding is that the student can now be introduced the more readily to sciences of which he as yet knows nothing. He must acquire a sense of balance between the physical sciences, the biological sciences and the social sciences; he ought to know in a descriptive way the vision of the world to which each has so far attained; he should understand in what frontier posts they are now working, and why, and what sorts of outcome can be expected to be forthcoming. The academic work which has been so painfully done in areas intersecting established scientific fields is his great object lesson in the interdisciplinary approach. For example, some biologists have used engineering concepts to further the understanding of control systems in nature: these texts would make excellent study books for an OR course. At present, biological departments seem unaware of them because they usually cannot face the mathematical content, while engineering departments think more in terms of constructing bridges and computers than of cytology.

Some basic knowledge of economics, and especially of econometrics, is important to anyone working in the managerial field. He will need to know about the theory of the firm, and such important procedures as marginal analysis and demand analysis. At the operational level, the approaches of both financial and cost accountancy must be understood. The techniques of costing to pre-determined standards and of budgetary control, for example, form part of the management alphabet, while the ability to assess investment policies in terms of discounted cash flows is part of the OR alphabet too. There are things to learn at the operational level of industry, also, of other than economic kinds. There are relevant aspects of company law and of the structure and behaviour of organized labour. There are basic engineering concepts to be assimilated, particularly in regard to production engineering and to control engineering. There are the fundamentals of computer technology to be studied.

As far as the rigorous languages of science are concerned, mathematics and statistics are generally studied by the potential OR man. But unaccountably the study of formal logic is mostly neglected. Every sizable OR group should have a logician—if it can find one. But for some other members of the group, a knowledge of the basic principles of ratiocination and of mathematical logic in its elementary forms, should be regarded as essential. The three formal languages may be compared in the following way. An OR man should be able to read a text which uses the differential calculus or difference equations, or writes what it has to say in the language of set theory, although only a proportion of OR men needs to be skilled in manipulating these tools. In statistics, a deep comprehension of the nature of variation and of the ways in which it is handled through probability distributions is essential to all; the notions of significance testing are vital, and everyone should be able to undertake correlation and regression, and the analysis of variance. But again, it is not necessary that all members of a group should be able to handle such tools as stochastic processes, matrices and determinants, or factor analysis —although all should know what they are. As in mathematics and statistics, so in logic; people who depend so profoundly on cogent thought processes ought to understand syllogistic reasoning, and particularly the fallacies which this otherwise barren method of argument lays bare; and in modern logic they should be able to read Boolean algebra, to know how truth value analysis works, and to read a text which incorporates statements in the predicate calculus.

There are several thousand men engaged professionally in operational research throughout the world; few of them indeed would match up to this unexacting specification. Many would object that it is much too much to ask: here, after all, are three whole subjects, each of which is very difficult and can be studied at the level of the honours degree. But the difficulty is an artefact of university organization, given that we are not demanding experts, but people with a special sort of literacy in the various modes of calculus which quantify human thought. The urgent need is that these subjects should be taught to OR men by people who know what OR is and does. Such teachers are not yet generally available —except in the ranks of OR practitioners themselves.

Beyond all this, a demand for some understanding of the arts and humanities may sound a ridiculous aim, but really it is not. In fact, creative scientific workers are, almost invariably, men of sensibility and not inconsiderable culture. They are more often than not devotees of literature, painting and music—not indeed because they have attended formal classes on these topics, but because this is the stuff of civilization. It is a common myth that scientists are ignorant of the arts, Philistine even; it seems to arise because they are observed entering the wrong building within the university cloisters. We should have no hesitation in sending them into the right building from time to time.

Beware now of thought blocks of the most disastrous kind. It is easy to review the demands that have been made, and to say that a good OR man apparently needs a university degree in every subject there is. This is manifest nonsense. What is required is a course which takes all these subjects to a certain point, inter-relating them on the way; and this kind of course is terribly hard to contemplate, simply because there seems to be no academic organization which could currently contain it. This does not mean to say that no organization could be constructed to contain it: it assuredly could. But universities are not really constituted in this way, especially in Europe. Once this basic yet inter-related knowledge had been assimilated, however, a series of (what might be called) 'leap' courses could be arranged. By this is meant the study of advanced topics in some of the subjects discussed, which can in fact be understood *precisely because* of the inter-related background already assimilated. Now advanced topics in any one subject are normally taught on the understanding that their comprehension can be reached only by a ladder passing through intermediary topics of increasing difficulty. This is because the individual subjects are inevitably, and very properly, taught in this fashion. But in practice it is perfectly possible to explain the theory of relativity to a brilliant post-graduate student whose knowledge of intermediate physics is nil. This same man can learn about the coding problems encountered in the DNA molecule, without having an intimate acquaintance with Drosophila on the genetic hand or the ability to tabulate enzymes and their chemistries on the biochemical hand.

Yet this notion of a 'leap' course could well be anathema to any true academic. There is no quarrel with him: he is dedicated to his subject. But I am dedicated to mine. If we need to reorganize the hallowed structure of university teaching for the purposes of management science, there seems to be no reason why we should be debarred. A university taking the still relatively novel course of creating a department in operational research, or cybernetics, or management science, should have the equivalent courage when it comes to curricula. This would not imply an intention or even a desire to undermine the established order of teaching in existing subjects. But it may be suspected that a course of the kind described would attract very many students who had no intention of embarking upon a professional career in OR at all. The 'general degree' might become the unattainable target of the many, to be vanquished by the few. At present the very word 'general' seems to be a pejorative term in academic circles—which indicates the intensity of the thought blocks to be overcome.

Short of the ideal of a new kind of department, which is attainable only with much understanding and goodwill in any given university, it would be magnificent to see courses in OR springing from philosophy departments as well as from those already running them. If management science has perforce to be viewed through one of the departments already established in a college, then this might well be the one. For management science is a kind of applied philosophy, philosophy of the sort which investigates rigorous ways of argument rather than undertakes metaphysical debate. But there are thought blocks even here. For 2,000 years philosophy has been a 'pure' subject; many philosophers are perversely proud of the irrelevance of their enquiries to everyday affairs. Therefore the notion of an applied philosophy, having a profit-making potentiality in industry and commerce, will give many philosophers apoplexy. But how often apoplexy is the price of progress.

I do not know whether these proposals could be made to work: university teaching is not my job. They are composed from the point of view of an employer of graduates who finds recruitment his biggest headache. Another approach has therefore been invented, which can be and is being tested; it is now the subject of a preliminary trial. The argument goes like this. The good OR man blends three kinds of experience. He needs genuine academic discipline to make him intellectually tough; he requires a thorough grasp of the technology which he will manipulate; and he must understand what the world of affairs is really like. Accordingly, a senior lectureship in OR and two research fellowships have been set up in a leading college of technology wherein the central experience of these three can be gained. The research is actually done in this technological context, where the senior lecturer can direct it. But the Fellows are organizing their work in a form which makes it suitable for submission as a doctoral thesis in a university. Having been accepted as post-graduate students there, they receive the benefits of a pure academic discipline, and of a university tutor to supervise this aspect of their work. In the part of the year which is not occupied by academic terms, all three of these men work in the operational research firm which sponsors the arrangement—on paid consultancy. This three-year undertaking seems to provide what might be called an inter-experiential, if not strictly an interdisciplinary, training. It remains to be seen whether the results give a notable improvement over the orthodox training arrangements which this section has criticized.

Something, whatever it is, must be done. The education and training available for future management scientists is grossly inadequate from any point of view. Therefore the profession relies on the 'sorcerer's apprentice' method of development in the great majority of cases. Scientists are put into OR teams which are doing research; they are made to undertake the more menial tasks, such as sorting and collating data (and perhaps making tea), and the pious hope is that the abilities of their seniors will in some way rub off on to them. After a quarter of a century of operational research, this state of affairs is pathetic.

3   The Place of Management Science in the Enterprise

When the management of a large company decides to embark on operational research within the institution, it customarily feels a little self-conscious. It does not want to make a fool of itself; it does not want to spend a great deal of money which may not produce a return, it does not want to upset the existing senior staff. It is for all these reasons exceedingly cautious.

A common management tactic that is often observed is the following. An advertisement is inserted in the press, or letters are written to university appointment boards, asking for a newly graduated mathematician. Having mistaken the language of operational research for its substance, the management believes that it is about to embark on some applied mathematics. The interview selects a personable, but not too aggressive, candidate. He is a young mathematician, who declares that he has attended some evening lectures in OR techniques (he mentions queue theory, linear programming, and the rest); in the course of his degree work he has actually programmed an electronic computer, which impresses the interviewing panel no end. This man is appointed as an operational research officer at a salary of perhaps £850 per annum.

But where should he be installed? The answer this question usually receives depends on the state of management services in the company in general. If there is a flourishing work study department, he may go in there. Perhaps the only group in the company which knows anything at all about science is the research and development department, so he is put into that. Or he may find himself in production, or in sales, or on the office side. He is told that the company intends to do important work in the field of operational research, but that the activity must grow organically from small beginnings. This seems reasonable enough. Unfortunately, no manager knows quite what to do about this recruit. His boss in one of these departments may feel compelled to give him some work; he is after all a mathematician. Therefore he is just the man to analyse the results of a piecework study, and to plot some figures on a scatter diagram; or he may be invited to extrapolate the demand curve for a specimen product; or, if the founders of this movement in the company have really done their homework, he may be dispatched into the works to study the stocks. It has been known to happen that some time later the managing director remembers that he once founded an operational research group, and he asks after its progress. After some enquiry, it is discovered that the man has left the company's service. His acrimonious letter of resignation has, very sensibly, been lost.

More usually, of course, the enterprise does rather better than this. But the small group, which has extended itself to four, five or six people, gets completely immersed in one study (perhaps the stock control study); after some time has elapsed, the feeling begins to become current that the recommendations will never emerge. And of course if the firm makes 20,000 products, and the team is encouraged to believe that the orthodox inventory control theory written about in textbooks can be applied, the proper estimate of the time required to complete the job is perhaps 100 years. This group has a leader, in the shape of the original young man, but no director in the shape of a senior person sufficiently knowledgeable to stop the group from undertaking the absurd. The two really bright people in the team eventually become disenchanted and depart; they are replaced by less bright people who are glad to have the billet. In this way the overall capability of the team gradually sinks. Some senior person in the company then attends a lecture describing the influence of operational research on board policy in a number of particular instances, and he goes home to enquire what on earth his own OR group is doing. He has a look at them, and decides that anyone who allowed these poor chaps to influence board policy must be out of his mind. Various predictable outcomes typically follow this discovery.

Another approach used by management is to perceive these difficulties in advance, and to advertise at a more senior level. Now the leading operational research man whom this company wishes to attract may already be earning something in excess of £5,000 per annum; certainly no suitable candidate exists at less than £3,500. Without making the enquiries which would establish this, the board advertises the post at

£1,750, rising by £25 per annum. A strange selection of people applies for the job, and no decision is reached. The board then decides to appoint one of its own staff. After all, they all know George: a reliable man who already knows the company *mores*. He is in something of a dead-end job anyway. So George is told that he is to head up an important new company activity, and is given a salary rise. He is told to find out about operational research, and arrives at a one-day appreciation course laid on by a management institute or the local chamber of commerce. Several actual cases which conform to this specification have been studied; neither the writer nor the reader could possibly bear a protracted account of what happened next.

Clearly all three of these approaches are managerially incompetent, but they are often used. Equally clearly, there can be no completely general answer to the question: how do we start? It seems to follow that the right course is to approach an authority in the subject for advice on how this given company in its given circumstances should make use of management science, how create and administer the facility. This conclusion may be special pleading (please remember: it is a consultant who writes). But in all sincerity there seems to be no better course; if there is, it ought to be adopted. Assuming that the advice is valid, however, it is important to know what to expect from the authoritative report. Firstly, there should be an appraisal of what OR is likely to be able to do for the firm in question. How much of this work is there, what size of team could be committed and for how long? What is the cost of this possible outlay, and what are the minimum and maximum returns that can be expected? Are appropriate staff available, if so, how can they be obtained and under what conditions; if not, what longer term plans must be made to obtain and train suitable recruits? Where should the group be placed in the organization, and what are its channels of reporting and in general communicating with the company? The report considered by the board at this point should be extensive and thorough; it will take a number of weeks to prepare, and (depending on the size of the company) might cost up to £1,000 or £2,000.

But the board that has decided it is worth investigating the possible value of science to its management will have done a sensible thing in making its first step along the road scientific. The directors are now looking at the problem as a whole, and in context; they are asking that the relevant factors be quantified, if only by orders of magnitude and under some notion of probability; they are preparing themselves to take a properly informed decision. Certainly, nothing should be left to chance. Unless satisfactory answers are obtained and adopted to all these questions, the venture will probably fail. Consider the case of communications, which is often ignored on the basis that, after all, the people concerned will be on the staff and they only have to speak in order to communicate. This naive viewpoint takes little account of human nature. It is *very common* to find an apparently flourishing OR group which is in fact isolated and insulated from the rest of the firm. Some of these groups are in being simply for prestige; to own a small and perhaps distinguished OR group is a (relatively) cheap form of public relations. In other cases, the board genuinely intends that the operation should be effective; but the senior staff have not been carried along with the exercise, and have no intention that any of their own plans should risk criticism. Sometimes the trouble is that the OR group reports to a man who quite genuinely and sincerely has no idea what it is all about. Thus the creation of a powerful, and above all redundant, communication network between the OR group and everyone else is of primary importance.

It is against this background that the reputation of institutional OR groups has made little headway over the last ten years. Managements owe it to themselves to investigate carefully why this is so. It is a very easy self-deception to create conditions in which OR cannot possibly flourish, and then to refer to the group as a disappointment. Put the matter this way. The chances are that any well-intentioned board responsible for an existing OR group in Great Britain today, which commissioned an independent enquiry into the effectiveness of the group, would receive a series of very unpleasant shocks. And allowing that the group itself had to accept some responsibility for the criticisms implied by this prediction, the overriding responsibility would be the company's. For the questions posed earlier will turn out not to have been answered at the beginning, nor to have evolved answers in the course of time.

A cautious approach may be made towards some general statements on this question of organization. One generalization, at least, seems to be valid: the OR group cannot operate in a research and development department. This is no criticism of R and D which, it must be remembered, is concerned (at any rate by normal definitions) with products and processes; OR is concerned with the company's policies, and R and D as such has nothing to do with this matter at all. Another generalization is that the work will probably be effective in proportion to its level of reporting. Now it is true that practically everyone can and usually does make out a case for being responsible to the head of the enterprise—to the minister or to the managing director himself. If the principles of delegation are to be followed, then these cases cannot all be accepted. But looking at the problem strictly from the point of view of the enterprise, and not from the OR standpoint at all, it is clear that an operational research group deals only with that system which is exposed to it. If its level of responsibility is low, then the managing director simply must not expect that its recommendations will be optimal for the enterprise itself. This leaves the managing director with the task of working out how the recommendations made for that piece of the enterprise with which OR has dealt relate to and affect other pieces of the enterprise. But this kind of evaluation is precisely the sort of study which the OR activity was created to handle.

As a matter of fact, all the senior officials of the firm have considerable staffs. The sales director may command a number of sales managers; he may have a market research department, an economic adviser, a marketing director, advertising specialists, and so on. The production director commands a staff of works managers and of engineers, a work study department, a production engineering unit, and so on. The financial director has a chief financial accountant and a chief cost accountant and their subordinate staffs, various machine departments and an O and M group. These considerable staffs are, or ought to be, dedicated to the service of their own director; they feed him with information and ideas, they brief him for meetings and, above all, they see to it that the policies he is advocating are well-informed and foolproof from his own point of view. But the managing director himself has no such staff. All he has to command are these very directors. And although in theory they are a consolidated team which supports him in turn, the political facts of life do not often support this theoretical expectation. Thus the decisions of the company usually result from a tussle between the top men in it. There is therefore much to be said, from the managing director's point of view, for appointing an OR group as his personal servants. One of their routine jobs will be to evaluate company policies that are a source of dissension among the directors.

To create an OR unit at this level and for this reason will of course result in animosities, and the situation needs to be handled very carefully. That it can be done was demonstrated many years ago by the armed forces, in which the heads of operational research have general staff rank. Industry has yet to emulate this example, in Britain at least. It would be interesting to observe the progress of an important company in which the head of OR had a seat on the board in that very capacity. Several times two of those three conditions have been fulfilled, with valuable consequences. The first company to fulfil all three conditions (leading practitioner, board member, director of OR) should undergo a particularly impressive phase of development.

To end this discussion of the problems involved in placing a management science group, an actual case history will be quoted which tells more about the situation than any amount of moralizing. Some people find this story incredible; others have said that it is exactly what they would expect. At any rate, it happened.

A leading company in its field had a works organization as shown in Figure 62. Four departmental managers were responsible to a works manager, and the managers ran departments which had a definite order in the production process. This is indicated by the double arrows which represent the flow of material. The company's plan was to replace the

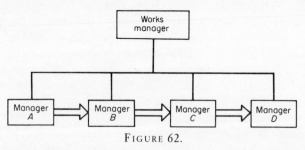

FIGURE 62.

entire plant in department *C* with the largest and most modern equipment in the world. An OR organization was asked to prepare a control system for department *C*, and advised that this should be done within the context of the whole figure. Now department *C* had a manager and also a manager designate who was due to take over on the completion of the new plant. It was he who wanted the control system, and he rejected the advice that the system as a whole should be investigated. The *enquiry* had to be confined strictly within the limits of his intended department, although it was understood that an OR group could make whatever *recommendations* it liked.

Notwithstanding the limitation on the enquiries that could be made, it was quite evident to the OR group that what happened in department *C* was very largely conditioned by the input arriving from *B* (which could be measured) which was in turn influenced by what arrived at department *B* from department *A* (which could not be investigated). The situation was also profoundly influenced by the demands made on department *C* by department *D* (and these too could be measured). Thus, despite the attempted limitation, enough information emerged to demonstrate clearly that an integrated control system for *A–B–C–D* was

essential, and one was designed. This was a very advanced plan, involving a good deal of automation, together with routine decision-taking by
computer. There would have to be a central control embracing all four
production areas, so that decision-taking in any one area would be consonant with the general situation. Secondly, it was advised that this
central control would be too cumbersome to accept information directly

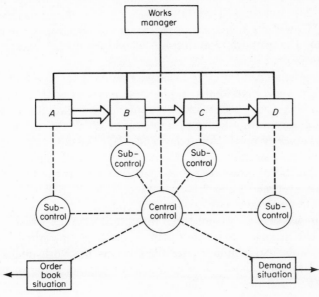

FIGURE 63.

from the four areas and to disseminate decisions to the four areas, bearing in mind that it would have to accept a great deal of background information about the state of the order book and the state of other works
within the firm as well. It could not (economically) have requisite variety.
Thus a series of sub-control centres would have to be set up. These
would be variety absorbers on the route to the central control, and
variety generators in the other direction. The recommended arrangement is shown in Figure 63. A closely argued and very full exposition of
the appropriateness of the solution was put forward to the manager
designate. It will be noted that the arrangement would constrain his
authority as manager of department *C*.

Over a series of meetings the manager designate refuted this recommendation. He contended that there was no need for any sub-control
system as one central control would suffice. This should be responsible

to the manager of department C; it would acquaint itself with the situation in the other three areas by telephone. The OR team strongly disagreed with this view, which was so clearly biased. It also considered that an analysis of the alternative proposal by information-theoretic means would make it possible to demonstrate scientifically that the idea would not work. There would be insufficient channel capacity in such a system to cope with the decision mechanisms, and the arrangement was hierarchically unsound. Thus OR undertook to make an analysis of the manager's own alternative proposal, which he agreed to write down in full detail. This was a formal decision which was minuted and passed to higher authority.

Nothing happened for more than two months. One Saturday morning the written version of the new plan was received, with the comment that it had already been formally approved by three different committees of increasing seniority, and would be finally ratified by the ultimate authority on the following Thursday. The OR team very hastily marshalled its objections, and dispatched them with the request that they should be allowed to represent their views at the final meeting. There was no time to undertake the scientific analysis that had been intended. Despite many enquiries and telephone calls, this institutional OR group was held at bay until after the critical meeting, which of course adopted the manager designate's plan. The OR group retired hurt.

Little more than a month after these events the works manager was promoted to another job. The manager designate of department C was promoted to the vacant position.

He immediately sent for the head of the institutional OR group, and said that a plan existed, and had indeed been formally approved, whereby the control of the new plant in department C would be vested in its own manager. This clearly would lead to a sub-optimal method of production control for the A–B–C–D complex. Furthermore the plan appeared to give undue authority to the manager of department C. Surely, he argued, there should be a central control directly responsible to the works manager; this would have sub-control centres in the four areas for which he would be responsible, thereby ensuring an integrated production flow and optimal decisions for the entire works.

The OR team thought this a good suggestion, and was able to specify a suitable scheme rather quickly. Indeed it is doubtful whether a manager's question, involving so many and complex problems, has ever been answered in less than a day before. The scheme has since been implemented.

4   Training the Manager to Use Management Science

Just as there are grave problems facing us if we wish to train operational research men properly, so there are massive difficulties to be faced in management training. A great debate centres these days on this issue, and discussion of various courses, institutions and business schools is heard everywhere. One major school of thought contends that 'management cannot be taught'; management is one of the gentle arts. Now the kind of argument that has been going on is largely irrelevant once it is recognized that a competent manager ought to be in a position to *use* the kinds of method described in this book. This point is very far from being recognized; many of the public figures who discuss these issues do not even know that these methods exist. Given that they do exist, however, and given that managers ought to use them, the argument about management training takes on a different complexion.

The first point to agree is that existing managers do not themselves aspire to expertise in operational research and management cybernetics. The existing manager is not expected to convert himself into a scientist, nor to embark on OR studies. But he does need a second-order knowledge. He ought to know what science can do for him, how to commission the work, how to control it, and how to make use of the results. It might be hoped that a manager who had read and understood the present book, for example, would be in this position. 'Understood' is the correct word to use, surely, and not the word 'mastered'. But the manager who gets through these many pages is a comparative rarity; he must be a determined man, intent on acquiring an insight into management science. Almost by definition, he does not need the special residential facilities that are available. These are required by people who cannot be persuaded to undertake private study.

There are of course various facilities available already in Britain, and more are being created. But the basic ideas on which these facilities, both existing and planned, are founded are open to severe criticism by the management scientist. The established doctrine seems to be that the benefits of attending some sort of management school are twofold. First, the manager who attends will meet managers from other industries; his mind will therefore be broadened, and he will appreciate that the world is a larger place than that contained within the boundaries of his own firm. Secondly, the method of training is the 'advanced' case study method, in which syndicates of managers tackle an actual problem and try to resolve it. Thereafter they may be given the school's official answer, or they may have explained to them the conclusions that actually emerged in real life. All this may achieve useful objects and succeed in making the manager a better manager than he was before. But of course these approaches by themselves do nothing to *instruct* the manager in the tools of management. So the courses are interlarded with lectures on particular topics such as budgetary control and cost control, labour relations and market research. It is within the compass of this subsidiary heading that it is just possible to find a fleeting reference to management science.

The facts, as they are known to management scientists themselves when they collaborate in courses of this kind, must be unambiguously stated. Again, this refers to Britain. In the first place, it is probable that one session lasting one hour will be devoted to the topic of operational research—out of a course lasting anything from a few weeks to several months. The briefing that the OR man typically receives is of the following kind. 'We are trying to nurse these chaps along a bit, and to open their eyes to some of the new things that are going on. However, you ought to bear in mind that people like this are very suspicious of people like you; they think you are going to blind them with science. I know you will not do that: words of one syllable if you please; the great thing is to give a whole lot of actual examples, with all the details worked out, so that they can see your stuff is thoroughly practical. Try not to criticize them, they are easily hurt. Most of them have agreed to come on the understanding that what they are really doing here is reporting to their companies on the value of the course.' This is all most encouraging news to the OR scientist, who has an hour to meet these exacting requirements. When he mounts the platform, the chairman may well introduce him as follows: '. . . who is an eminent authority. Now of course nobody really knows what these long-haired chaps are up to with their computers and so forth; between ourselves they probably are not quite sure themselves (titters). Certainly I often wonder how we ever managed to get any goods out of our works, or to make any profit at all, the way these fellows talk. But we can't let you go away from here without having heard the magic words "operational research". I now hand over to the speaker, then, without more ado; and I would remind you, sir, that if you cut into our drinking time, we shall all draw the proper conclusions about your subject.'

It does not do to get upset about this kind of situation, but those responsible for management training really ought to take a long hard look at the effectiveness of such an exercise as this. It is possible to argue that the manager who attends (say) a month's course really needs a week of this time on management science. The material must be put forward fairly simply, it is true. But if the instruction is to be at all useful, the psychological setting must be rather more favourable than that normally encountered. Exceptionally, the OR man may get a vigorous and stimulating introduction. Equally, he may receive far worse treatment than that recorded above. A tough struggle lies ahead in the attempt to improve the quality of decision-taking, policy-making and management control. Many honeyed words are spoken which mislead the public into thinking that management is quite generally full of self-improving intentions. Some managements are. But there are others who, it seems, are not merely behind-hand or conservative, but who are grimly determined to adhere to the prerogatives of their forefathers.

It is a strange and comforting fact, however, that if one talks privately and individually to the *members* of a typical management course, they will complain vigorously that the organizers are not taking matters seriously enough. In short, the middle manager is underrated (as we have had occasion to remark before) by his directors and management educators alike. Given the chance, then, a thoroughly good job could be done of instructing managers in modern approaches to management, in a way they would find exciting and acceptable, and to a useful end. This is defined as the readiness of the manager, when he is back at his desk, to tackle by scientific method some of the problems which have lain in his tray for long enough. But at this point a second difficulty arises, and this again is quoted from the mouths of many course-attending managers. When they ask for the assistance of operational research, they find there is no means of getting it. Because of this they often say to the OR lecturer: can you possibly find a way of enrolling my managing director on the next course—*he* is the man who should have been there. But there is no way. Management training may be defined in practice as an improving process which a man applies to his subordinates.

There is no more to say on this topic because the answers are so clear. The really senior people who are responsible for management schools, their organization, curricula, staffs and course membership must be provoked into thinking again. But they are not dishonest men, and many have already thought very hard about these topics. The real difficulty is that they simply do not know what management science is about, nor what it has to offer.

In all the talk of management training as a means of improving the quality of existing managers, the problem of training *new* ones is rarely mentioned. It seems to be tacitly assumed that a young man, say a graduate, must begin his industrial, commercial or Civil Service life 'on the job'. Here he finds out what it is all about through some more or less formal management apprenticeship, and samples responsibility at a rather low level in various capacities. By the time people think of sending him away for training, he has become one of the existing managers whose dilemma has already been discussed. It is in the case of such a young man, that the question of 'whether management can be taught' suddenly becomes relevant again. The question must not be balked. Surely it is common to all human experience that *anything* understood can be taught, if one is prepared to make the proper arrangements. To say that management cannot be taught, is simply to admit that one has not been able to analyse the manager's job or the qualities of a man that make him a manager. Were these things understood, it would be possible to devise a training scheme which would at the least bring out the latent managerial capacities in a man, and might at the best seem to create in him managerial capacities which he might never otherwise attain. Let us briefly consider this problem.

In several branches of affairs a kind of pendulum has been swinging in regard to management succession in Britain. It begins with the confirmed conviction that 'managers are born and not made'. Likely material is selected, and put through 'the hard school of experience'. At some point, probably in the nineteen-twenties or the nineteen-thirties, the opinion gained ground that management is a teachable subject. Graduates have been engaged, and non-graduates have been exposed to intellectual disciplines. Although in some cases (perhaps the police force makes an example) the people trained under this dispensation have been markedly successful and reached the highest rank, the pendulum has in the meantime swung the other way. It looks suspiciously as though we are faced with another false dichotomy. *Of course* it is true that human qualities and experience of the world are important to managers; and *of course* it is true that some component of the manager's job depends upon teachable technique. Why then plump for just one of these approaches, treating the two together as mutually exclusive? The organization which seems to have seen most clearly that both courses must be pursued at once is the Army. An officer cadet undergoes a mixed species of training. The Army acknowledges the indefinable capability called leadership; it tries very hard and with considerable success to foster this quality whenever it is apparent. But the Army is not so stupid as to imagine that officers can lead their men by panache alone. The ordinary soldier has very good sense in this matter: he will follow a leader, true; but should this leader turn out to be professionally incompetent, the private soldier will leave him to win his medals alone. There is an important lesson here for management training.

A selection system for intending managers can be envisaged in which candidates would have to achieve acceptable standards in academic work, in physical condition and in their mental attributes as measured by a battery of psychological tests. The 'profile' of a successful manager could be written down in these terms, after sufficient research, just as the profile of a potential officer was successfully defined in just this way during the war. Success at a national selection board would admit the managerial candidate to a training school. Before it is objected too strongly that the adaptation of the military system to the civilian requirement was attempted in Britain at the end of the Second World War with notably weak results, it should be emphasized that this adaptation is itself a matter for competent operational research. The post-war experiments were based on committee-generated modifications of the military scheme; but the civilian requirement may be totally different. The topic has never been properly studied. The primary object of scientific selection for trainable managers would be to find men fitted to do a predictable sort of job in the future. It would not be to find duplicates of the managers who do today's job without benefit of professional skills. Present methods of selection carry out the latter task, and result—in the main—in a perpetuation of the amateur approach. There should be an end to the system whereby the quality of future management is largely determined by the quality of existing management.

Assuming then that a suitable intake can be scientifically selected for a management training unit on the basis of good research, the next question is: what activities are to be undertaken by the trainee? This again is a matter for proper research, but some of the principles seem clear enough. These young men would actually be taught management science. They are, remember, managers of the future, not modifications of existing managers who already have a job to do and on whom time presses. In the management training unit youngsters will be collected who have the time to spare to be properly trained for a genuine profession of leadership in a technological age. They would therefore receive instruction in many obvious subjects, such as commerce, law, accounting and economics; they would be taught about the technological world in which they were due to operate. But they would also be taught a substantial corpus of knowledge in management science. Unlike their colleagues (see Section 2) who are training to *be* management scientists, they would not become deeply involved in the disciplines of the subject. But they would be taught much more than the 'appreciation' allocated to existing managers.

As in the military model, these men would spend about half their time 'in the field'; that is to say, they would actually work in industry, commerce and government. They would do so as members of teams assisting and working with existing managers; but they would be associated with men training for operational research work itself. Thus their course would integrate theory (at the school) and practice (in actual managerial situations); it would also integrate management itself (their future) with the undertaking of management science (the future of their OR colleagues). Their first steps in the leadership of men would be taken under properly supervised conditions, probably as managers of development projects. It would be as likely for them to fail their courses on the count of inadequate leadership, as of inadequate knowledge of the theory and practice of management science. Thus would end the absurd situation, obtaining today, whereby some men having academic qualifications in management topics could quite clearly not *manage* a staff of two others—because of personality deficiencies.

Surely a scheme of this kind would meet a desperate need. The newly graduated manager would have a huge advantage over the old-fashioned type of manager, over the OR man and over the straightforward scientist: he would be something of them all. His managerial assignments would incorporate the historical wisdom of the existing manager's experience with the scientific know-how of operational research, and the experience of blending the two. This is exactly what is needed. Special arrangements would have to be made to receive these graduates in management into the world of business, industry and government, and to demonstrate their capability. If a national school were set up for training purposes, there would have to be an induction scheme for (say) the first five to ten years of the manager's life whereby his progress could be monitored. Perhaps his entire career should be followed as it would be in the Army. The present fortuitous methods by which young managers are moved from job to job, or (more likely) remain stuck in one job, would be outmoded. They would of course retain their freedom to seek alternative employment, but the national training scheme would be entitled to know about this, and to try to learn from the reasons given. If some large companies operating management apprentice schemes had had the wit to make proper enquiries of this kind, their schemes would by now be vastly improved. Instead, they have either assumed that they knew the reasons why so large a proportion of their trainees was leaving them, or have adopted a condescending attitude towards the foolhardiness of the young men who had the audacity to find them wanting.

According to the system advocated here, even the small output of one management training unit would begin to influence national affairs within five years of the end of the first course. For, it is submitted, these people would be a superior breed of manager hitherto unknown. We have to be careful that the objections to this plan are not simply rationalized jealousies. Admittedly, it is very hard on other young men who have not had the advantage of this kind of education, and who must compete with its products. They will probably lose the race. But if every advance in the education of individuals has to be delayed until equal opportunities are available to all, no progress in any field of any kind will ever be possible. If the new managers were as successful as is here predicted, then a demand for equal opportunity would arise. So much the better. A fairly small number of really high-powered managers is required in the various spheres of national activity. This number would determine the cut-off point in the distribution of measured ability, below which men would fail the selection tests. Typically, this might be the top 5 per cent ('top' as measured by these criteria) of the university output each year. The task of supplying facilities of the kind advocated for this number of people, to provide equal opportunity across the nation, would not be very great. The financial investment would be trivial compared with the national pay-off. Such a scheme would have to be led by a man of immense drive and determination, and the programme treated by government as a priority scheme.

The outcome for management science in the training of managers, as in the use of OR by the enterprise, as in the training of management scientists, as in the organization of the group, to work backwards through this chapter, depends upon the intention of all who hold the relevant responsibilities. They may be pusillanimous or bold. They may be far-sighted or temporizers. Above all, they may be knowledgeable or ignorant. The country is running down; its metabolism has failed. The simplest, cheapest, most effective way of reversing this terribly dangerous trend is to provide a variety generator and intelligence amplifier in the line of supply to top management positions. Thus we should obtain a massive increase in managerial effectiveness, as opposed to the waste and frustration which abound in management circles today. It can be done, however, only by imaginative and courageous thinking and planning.

At present in Britain, the country is preoccupied with make-do-and-mend. We want scientific method in the shape of OR groups, but refuse to face the consequent problems in organizational structure—and therefore mismanage them. We want OR men for these groups, but refuse to accommodate their needs in our universities. We want a new sort of manager who can lead men and tackle problems scientifically at the same time, but refuse to think out his adequate training. Plans for all this are trivial and petty. It is as La Rochefoucauld said at the head of the chapter: 'In being too much concerned with small things we become incapable of great things.'

20

ON PRACTICABILITY

I define the practical man as the man who has no idea
what to do in practice.

BERTRAND RUSSELL, *Impromptu* (1958)

1   *Quis Custodiet Custodes?*

The management scientist may wistfully regard himself as the custodian
of the manager's good conscience. Certainly the manager may regard
himself as the custodian of 'common sense' and 'sound practice', in the
face of the hare-brained schemes of science. It is fruitless to protest that
the future success of enterprises depends fundamentally on the collaboration of management and science, until each party to the alliance understands his own weaknesses and achieves the right kind of humility. To
the layman, the scientist often appears arrogant. It is because the layman
knows that the scientist understands certain matters which he himself
does not understand, and he tends to assume that the scientist believes
that he understands everything and the layman nothing. In fact, the
scientist is terribly aware of the frailty of his models of the universe. It
may help to say that most scientists do not imagine that they know
what the universe is really like. For his part, the manager ought to
abandon the comforting belief that he knows what the answers really
are. The 'practical man' probably thinks of himself as humble, because
he does not pretend to sophistication. To the scientist, his self-assurance
in the face of the mystery of the universe appears arrogance indeed.
Both allies are trapped within their own conventions and ways of saying
things; each reaches out into a world of greater complexity than his
brain can really assimilate.

For me personally the outlook of the 'practical man' will always be
typified by the British ironmakers I knew in the nineteen-fifties. It is
easy to sit in an ironworks and to regard the blast furnace like a woman:

525

potent, demanding, satisfying, temperamental, unrequiting—a captivating mystery. It is far more difficult to set about a description of this amazing beast, and to specify ways in which it may be controlled in an operational environment. When the account that the scientist is able to give falls short of completeness, it is very easy to say that what is left over must for ever remain mysterious. The practical man sees (and has even described) himself as the king of the ironworks. Perhaps it is because he alone has the experience to woo and to beguile the blast furnace into acceptable behaviour. Rejection of the new aids of modern science springs from this posture. It is as if an unknown rival could suddenly seduce the object of affection who had resisted the courtship of a lifetime. This seemed in those days a possible explanation for the entrenched attitude associated with managers who insecurely boast of practicality while rejecting help from anyone else. At any rate, and whatever the reason, the outcome is sufficiently clear. By 1964, the International Conference on Iron and Steelmaking had devoted a whole session to the automation of the blast furnace. Papers were presented about experience with this problem, using all the scientific techniques available, in ironmaking companies from five different countries: Germany, France, Japan, Holland and Italy. Not surprisingly, there was no communication from Great Britain.

Just how practical, in short, is the practical man? And just how impracticable is the management scientist? It is fashionable to say in the wartime phrase that the scientist 'must be on tap but not on top'; that he is really rather dangerous; that he thinks science can supply the answer to every question whatsoever; that his work is all right for everyone else, but not for us (who are special); that he is twenty years ahead of his time; and above all that 'it just won't work'. But the charge of impracticability rebounds. Consider these examples.

An OR report was written indicating how the uncertainty of the order book could be offset against the vicissitudes of a difficult production process in a particular works. The recommended production control system was to be a tool for juxtaposing the two sets of probabilities so that the variety generated by each was absorbed by the other. This was a piece of operational research using a model from cybernetics. The commercial director of the firm concerned countered all this work with its demonstration of reduced cost and better service to the customer with the words: 'There is no place for probability in industry.' How inappropriate a model must lie behind that impracticable statement. Another report is recalled recommending an automated monitoring system on a highly complicated and expensive process, which would have given the manager of the works a warning as soon as any aspect of the process appeared to be moving out of control. The process was such that the labour force operating the plant could not themselves piece together all the information which would make such a conclusion possible; therefore it was proposed to telemeter the relevant factors, and to compute the answers directly on to the manager's desk. Both the labour force and the manager were delighted. But the scheme was stopped by the production director who wrote on the report: 'This is undemocratic.' It becomes a pity if the practicability of an idea has to be determined by the capability of a manager to break through an elementary thought block, as illustrated by both these stories; but it is the common fact.

Consider this further example. The head of a famous motor-car manufacturing company was tackled on the question of the availability of spare parts for the motor-car in service. It was demonstrated that difficulty was experienced in keeping the motor-car he manufactured on the road, because the lead time on a spare part tended to be longer than the frequency with which parts failed. Here is the written comment of this leading industrialist, who enjoys a particular reputation as a practical man—again, *ipsissima verba*: 'I am of the opinion that our system is efficient and that it only fails to maintain availability due to manufacturing conditions or outside deficiencies.'

Now this is not simply a series of jibes. It is important to understand why these three men turned out to be so grossly impractical. The commercial director in the first story was evidently living with a false notion of what counts as good management: he wanted to organize an uncertain world into a guaranteed pattern of behaviour. The production director in the second example must have been motivated by an altruistic attitude to his employees which is laudable; but he had clearly not thought out what really constitutes fair play. Thirdly, however, it is the attitude of the chairman of the motor company which is most revealing. For him, the system of spare parts provisioning was evidently isolated from its task. We must believe him when he says that the system *itself* looked all right. But of course the whole point of supplying spare parts to the customer is to see that a driver whose car breaks down receives the most rapid possible replacement service. The spare parts provisioning system, then, exists precisely to counteract manufacturing difficulties, and it must do so despite the inadequacies of distributors. To say that the system is efficient when these two factors are ignored is academic to the point of being meaningless. The precise fallacy is that the manager is looking at the part and not at the whole.

Now it has been shown throughout this book that an approach to totality is vital, and that it can be attained (perhaps for the first time) through scientific models and scientific methods of handling them. Admittedly, the approach is different from that entertained by pure science, and it is important to see why. The pure scientist works from particular examples towards generality: he is looking always for the ultimate generalization. This means that he shores away the constraints that happen to attach to particularities, in the search for generalities which are valid regardless of the special circumstances which happen to attach to any one instance. In operational research work, however, the management scientist is conducting an enquiry in almost the other direction. He argues that any real situation in which the manager finds himself is, as a matter of fact, constrained by many particular circumstances. Therefore the range of possible solutions is reduced; and if all the inferences from these circumstances can be followed through, it is quite possible that a unique solution will result.

This is to say that the world of mathematics is a boundless continuum: the optima to be recognized are infinitely small points in an infinitely large and multidimensional phase space. But decision-takers and policy-makers have a finitely small number of alternatives, as a result of the many constraints which an actual set of circumstances imposes, from which one alternative has to be selected. Thus it is that the problem the OR man solves is more difficult than the manager thinks and less difficult than the pure scientist would imagine.

One of the tools available to the OR man is the notion which he may borrow from psychology of the Just Noticeable Difference. The pure scientist, with his zest for precise quantification, thinks little of this rather crude mensuration device. But it ought to delight the manager. Suppose that the psychologist is attempting to invent a scale for some mode of perception. Take colour, for example. Here is a whole range of greens, beginning with a very light green and ending with a very dark green. With the aid of spectroscopy, it is possible to distinguish a huge number of different shades. But the human apparatus of perception cannot distinguish between all the shades: in fact, it can distinguish between very few. If we want to *make use* of different colours for human purposes, such as marketing a number of green dresses, it is impractical to talk of producing (say) 200 gradations of green. The production, distribution and marketing apparatus will be ruinously expensive to create and to run, and the customers will be none the wiser. What we must do to invent a reasonable metric in the circumstances, is to investigate how many shades of green the ordinary person can contra-distinguish. Given a certain shade of green, then, we shall increase the intensity of the colour until someone can detect that it is now a different colour from what it was before. This is the Just Noticeable Difference (JND).

Why this psychological model turns out to be so important in the management context is this. It is wasteful and indeed silly to attempt the calibration of any scale to a criterion of fineness which exceeds the JND of those who will be concerned with the measure. Many management decisions are concerned with money, and money is measurable on a scale of very fine calibration. It is possible to quote the amount of capital tied up in stock to the nearest penny; and this has actually been done by financial accountants in a case where the capital sum involved was more than £20,000,000. It should be quite apparent to anyone that, although a calibrated scale to the nearest penny exists, a figure of this magnitude quoted to that accuracy is ridiculous. Moreover, a sensible degree of fineness in calibration depends on the purpose to which any figures quoted will be put. In comparing stock investments with turnover, for example, and with that ratio for other companies, it may well be sufficient to talk about 'the nearest million pounds'. The JND, then, is determined by the resolving power of the perceiving subject, but it may be modified (in one direction alone) by that subject's purposes. The whole point was exemplified by the example in Section 2 of Chapter 18, where no more than five metabolic levels for educational progress were admitted for these very reasons.

A common example of the way in which management science can use this tool concerns quotations for complicated one-off products. Suppose that an engineering company wishes to manufacture a machine which, quite obviously, cannot cost less than £10,000, and certainly ought not to cost more than £13,500, then the question arises as to how accurately the scale between 10 and $13\frac{1}{2}$ needs to be calibrated. Many companies employ exceedingly elaborate pricing systems intended to arrive at 'the right answer'. But a possible OR approach to this matter is to ask what the Just Noticeable Difference in money is to the customer. Surely this contract will not be awarded to a competitor on the basis that his price is £10 less than ours? Will he really be influenced by a difference of £100? It may be possible to establish that the reputation of the supplying company for quoting short delivery dates, adhering to delivery dates, producing a good job, servicing the resulting machine, and so on, will mask any monetary difference up to (say) £500. If the JND, then, is £500 the task of quoting for the machine consists in a decision between eight alternatives: namely, all multiples of £500 between £10,000 and £13,500 inclusive. This is no more than a three-bit decision. In a particular case, it was possible to pick on the 'right' answer by means of a

simple algorithm which made a crude measure of the complexity of the
job under scrutiny, more often than could an exceedingly complicated
quotation system based on detailed costings. The OR-based quotation
could be made in about an hour; the system it set out to replace took
about six weeks to produce a result.

The practicability of a managerial technique must depend on its context. We must try to understand why a decision stands to be successful,
otherwise it is impossible to judge whether a more economical decision-
taking procedure can be evolved. Very often, people do not understand
why their decisions are successful, nor even whether they are successful
or not. For if the outcome of the decision is gratifying, it will be concluded that the decision was right; if the outcome is not gratifying,
reasons will be found to explain why matters did not work out as
planned. In either case, there is no feedback to the decision-making
procedure—which rarely comes under critical examination. To illustrate
once more the way in which we may be deluded on this score, an
example is taken from the behaviour of scientists instead of managers.
For, as has been reiterated, scientists are just people too.

The following experiment was conducted on the west coast of
America. An apparatus was displayed which flashed one-digit numbers
every so-many seconds. A scientist subject was told to watch these
numbers, and to guess the next number in the sequence every time. The
subject was told that he would be rewarded for a successful performance
every so often. Each scientist who undertook this test found that he was
being rewarded at a steadily increasing rate. When the test was over,
each scientist was asked if he had discovered any pattern in the numbers.
Typically, the subject said he had; he put forward elaborate rules for
guessing the next number in the sequence. In fact, the test was bogus.
The machine was producing numbers entirely at random, and the guesses
of the subject had no influence on the machine at all. The machine rewarded the subject at a steadily increasing rate *regardless* of the correct-
ness of the guesses he made. Hence the typical subject had built up an
impression of a mastery over the situation which was a delusion. For
although he could actually observe that the answers he was giving were
wrong for the most part, he came to the conclusion (presumably) that
they were right—otherwise he would not have ventured to propose his
system of guessing. The reason is perfectly clear: since the rewards were
steadily increasing, he was being conditioned to the belief that he was
making progress.

There is an even more interesting sequel. *Every* subject was 'uniformly
indignant' when told the truth. This indignation arose, not because he

had been hood-winked, but because he thought the experimenter was wrong. Each subject insisted that he had actually discovered the true sequence of numbers. It took some time to convince these people, by displaying the construction of the equipment to them in detail, that the problem had not been solved. Some of them were not convinced even then. As a result, a committee was actually formed to test the randomness of the numbers which emerged. Scientific objectivity died such a death in one subject, that the report of this experiment sadly declares that he physically assaulted the experimenter.

Perhaps the best way of thinking about management science, as we tried to indicate in Part I, is as a means of bridging the undoubted gap between theory and practice. The scientists in the experiment just described were unable to do that very job. The impracticability of the practical manager shows him, very often, unable to do the job either. For when a manager comes to the kind of conclusion quoted at the start of this section, he is allowing a theory about the way the world works to dominate and to overcome what practical experience really has to say. The alliance of scientist and manager, with their two quite different models of reality, is above all intended to create a viable bond between both sorts of theory and both sorts of practice. The manager is not the custodian of sound common sense, of which he has no monopoly. The scientist is not the custodian of all genuine insight, since he does not monopolize this commodity either. Each of them has a large component of truth, and each is humanly vulnerable to the thought blocks with which his upbringing, education and experience have surrounded him. The most valuable thing which each of these men can do for the other is to dismantle the thought blocks on the other side. The kindest and most humble approach to this task is, for each of them, to recognize his own need.

2   Finding a Metric

One of the basic operational problems of practicability is to determine how relevant measurements are to be obtained. People talk about 'imponderables' as if they were small demons lurking in their offices. And indeed, if one says: 'I must know what is going to happen on the 13th of June next year', then there is no means of knowing, and that is that. But there is no point in asking absurd questions which, in the nature of things, cannot be answered, and then setting up a wail about imponderables. A better approach, better because it works, is to invite the scientist to examine the problem situation from every possible slant, re-shuffling it as it were, in search for a commensurable approach. The scientist will look for some critical feature of the situation that is on the face of it measurable, and he will try to find a metric which fits it. Here is an actual example, which brings out both the ingenuity of the scientist and the thought block by which people deny the possibility of measuring anything which *they* regard as imponderable.

There is a narrow channel between Denmark and Sweden which provides the only entrance to the Baltic. The narrowest crossing is between Helsingor (which lovers of Shakespeare usually call Elsinore) in Denmark, and Hälsingborg in Sweden. The Scandinavians, a particularly civilized people, transport themselves and their goods freely across the Sound. The journey by ferry-boat takes less than half an hour and little fuss is made about such formalities as passports. Now the cross-channel traffic is steadily increasing, and so is the sea-going traffic between the Baltic and the outside world. Thus there is an increasing congestion in this channel and obviously an increasing risk of collision.

The Governments of Denmark and Sweden set up a joint commission to investigate this situation. In particular, there could well be a bridge between the two countries. Consider, said the Commission, the state of affairs when the traffic in both directions has doubled. Needless to say, it is not very difficult to make a statistical forecast of the date when this will occur, nor is it difficult to support the statistical extrapolation by arguments from the plans and intentions of all concerned. Clearly, the risk of collision will be increased, compared with the risk today. The layman might very well imagine that when the traffic is doubled the risk of collision is doubled; on the other hand, he might very well wonder whether this would be true. In any case, it is very likely that the layman will suppose that no conceivable way of computing this risk could be obtained—short of running an experiment, whether in the water or by computer simulation, in which a doubled traffic was allowed to run. But an experiment in the water is clearly impracticable, for it would take an enormous amount of organization and money even if it could be done. And a simulation may well be impracticable too, for the very good reason that collisions depend in the last resort on the failure of human beings standing on ships' bridges to avert them. It is very difficult indeed to say what role will be played by the human element in a situation which no-one has yet experienced.

In these circumstances, the commission very properly sought operational research advice. Professor Arne Jensen, now of the Technical University of Copenhagen, and incidentally the holder of the first so-named Chair of Operational Research in the whole of Europe, was asked to measure the increased risk for a doubled traffic flow. Many people said it could not be done: the research is impracticable; the risk is imponderable.

Jensen had in fact no more idea than anyone else, at the start, of how to set about the task of making this measurement. He talked with the captains of both ferry-boats and ocean-going ships about the problem, and everybody agreed that the risk of collision would be higher, and wagged their heads. This did not take the problem much further. Now Jensen knew that, given a knowledge of the stochastic processes governing the movement of ships, he could in fact calculate the likely number of incidents in which two ships could enter the same arbitrarily sized area of water at the same time. But no-one could tell him how near to each other the ships had to be before they could be said to have embarked irrevocably on a collision course. The practical men, very naturally, said that if the ships missed each other—even by a hair's breadth—then there was no collision; whereas if they did not, there was. But it is quite clear that to compute the probability that two ships simultaneously arrive on an area of water having the size of one ship, would seriously under-estimate the chance of a collision. Such a computation would be based on a model in which ships suddenly appeared at a point, whereas in reality we are obviously dealing with an interacting system of some complexity.

So Jensen, still entirely puzzled about the key problem of establishing a metric, decided that as an empirical OR scientist he should at least try to obtain some facts. People were free with opinions, beliefs and prognostications; but the first step should be to make some kind of measure of some kind of event which actually occurred. Accordingly, Jensen made a film of the traffic actually moving about on the Sound. What he filmed was a radar screen on which the movement of ships appeared as it would familiarly appear to ships' masters. The camera recorded the state of the screen at discrete time intervals and not continuously. The resulting film was a correct record of movements except that everything appeared to be happening at about 250 times the proper speed.

Having obtained some basic facts, Jensen did not know what to do next. He did of course study the film, and he observed certain areas in which congestion was characteristically high. But neither he nor experienced colleagues could yet find a means of defining a collision risk. The Professor's next move was therefore to mount his film in a theatre, and to show it to a group of very experienced men. These included six who had been ships' masters themselves, and now held posts in administration on behalf of responsible authorities. One had become an accident inspector, another was the chief of the harbour authority, another was running the ferry-boat service, and there was a representative of the Navy. These experts were asked to collaborate by watching the film, and trying to detect dangerous situations. How near would two boats have to approach each other before a genuine collision risk was involved? In particular, thought Jensen, a conglomeration of six, seven or eight boats, even if they were not right on top of each other, must surely take some sorting out. If the captains, having watched the film, could apply their own experience to it, they might help to suggest the approach to devising the 'risk metric' which was wanted. But unfortunately they could not.

The cybernetic computer in the cranium, however, often tells its owner things which he *cannot* analyse and report about to professors of operational research. Jensen noticed that there were moments of tension among his audience. The experts would catch their breath in unison: there would be a straining forward in the seat; there would occur curtailed exclamations. When he noticed that these incidents were occurring, Jensen had their times recorded. It is emphasized that this was not part of the plan: it was opportunism. For here were some more facts—if only one could make some use of them. In all, forty incidents of this kind were noted down, with the time at which they occurred from the start of the film. After the experts had gone home, Jensen made a careful analysis of the tape recording carrying this fluctuating level of noise, and of the frames on the film corresponding to the forty noisy incidents. It was here that he found his answer.

In sixteen cases everyone agreed that the audience reaction was due to especially high velocities. Since the film was an accelerated version of real life, unusually fast craft looked incredibly dangerous. This left twenty-four incidents for further study. Jensen was looking for a pair of ships which had become dangerously close, in the hope that the threshold of danger could be measured. He was looking for conglomerations of many ships, which might have looked threatening to experienced sailors. He found neither of these things. What he did find, in twenty out of the twenty-four cases, was a clear group of *three* ships: not appallingly close to each other, but still three. He recalled the experts and demonstrated this to them.

The situation suddenly became very clear. The codes of seamanship by which captains navigate their craft are based on a binary logic. If the captain of ship A sights ship B, then he has a set of rules which enable him to decide how to steer in relation to ship B. Since ship B has the same set of rules, it takes complementary action which is consistent, and the ships pass each other safely. It is cybernetically interesting to note that the only information which passes between the two captains is knowledge of what the other man has done, after he has done it, and after a suitable time lag has passed during which his orders take effect. Thus the feedback implicit in the situation is very slow and very lagged. The master of ship *A* makes a move, and can confirm its suitability only after he has observed the effect his action has had on the other man's action. In practice, however, this far too sluggish control mechanism is much accelerated by the ability of each master to project himself into the shoes of the other. Given a very firm navigational code, each master knows how his own situation will appear to the other master, and how the other master will reply. In other words, both captains are effectively simulating the entire affair in their heads in advance.

Now the situation that arises when a third ship appears on the scene is evidently dangerous. The master of ship *A*, who is conducting a simulated dialogue with the master of ship *B*, suddenly has to enter into a similar discourse with the master of ship *C*. Moreover, the action which the navigational code requires ship *A* to take in relation to ship *B* may not be consistent with the action it is supposed to take in relation to ship *C*. While the master of ship *A* is worrying about this, the masters of ships *B* and *C* are also faced with their versions of the dilemma, and the simulations may well become intolerably difficult. In fact, the difficulty of treating a triadic relationship in terms of a binary logic is notorious among logicians, never mind ships' masters. In practical terms, the human brain boggles at the difficulty of analysing a dynamic triadic situation—even when there is a capability to pass direct information. This is the reason why the search for incidents involving a considerable number of ships went unfulfilled. The mind trained in seamanship, and working to a binary logic, simply cannot encompass the further area of sea and the larger number of ships.

Here then we see the OR scientist grappling with a problem of measurement which appears impracticable, without knowing in advance what he really intends to do, and carrying in his mind ideas which he thinks must be right, but which will actively mislead him unless he keeps his wits about him. Here also, we find the experienced practical man, precluded by that very experience and that very practicality, from understanding precisely what is the difficulty in a situation with which he is trained by long experience to cope in practice. The captains agreed with the analysis when they saw it, but were incapable of making it themselves. Nor, incidentally, is there any obvious solution to the problem now defined. One cannot readily legislate for three-way radio conversations between ferry-boats and ocean-going ships of different nationalities which are within distance of each other for so very short a time. Nor is an OR man likely to propose a solution to a local problem of this kind by demanding that international shipping codes be radically changed. But this was not Jensen's problem. His problem was to calculate the increased risk in a doubled traffic flow.

The answer is now terribly simple. According to empirical analysis of the data, the distribution of ship interactions on the water is Poissonian. That is to say, it has as might be expected a structure characteristic of chance interactions. If the traffic flow doubles, *and the triadic relationship of vessels is the dangerous one*, then the rise in the risk of collision, because of the applicability of Poisson's laws, is $2^3 = 8$. So the risk of collision does not double, but is eightfold in the circumstances proposed. Professor Jensen is a sophisticated mathematician, and he struggled hard to obtain a more refined conclusion from these facts. But despite much effort, he found the robustness of this straightforward eightfold answer impregnable.

His report was put before the Bilateral Commission, and caused a furore. Jensen was denounced by people—practical men—who believed that the rules at sea were foolproof. Provided they were obeyed, people said, there could be no accident. Here is the thought block of the man who believes that a high variety system can be controlled by low variety regulations—provided they are obeyed. It is an incompetent notion, as was seen in Part III, unless a variety amplifier is present—and it is not in this case. But some of those concerned had seen the force of the argument and the sense of the measurement. They carried the day; perhaps because in the middle of the debate a collision actually occurred outside in the Sound. Fortunately, it was not a serious accident. But it is a sobering thought that men often wait for the inevitable tragedy before deciding that it can possibly occur.

For those who are wondering about the potential bridge across the Sound, it should be added that there were collision risks with the bridge itself to take into account, and also quite other considerations about the advisability of setting up the international link elsewhere. The crossing from Copenhagen to Malmø, though much longer, has economic attractions. This gives rise to the thought that if there were *two* bridges, a kind of inland sea would have been created between them. So there are many other issues involved, and there remains scope for more OR. But the point of the story remains. It is impracticable in the practical man to decide for himself what is practicable science.

3   The Measure of Value Judgment

The story just told does no more than reiterate that it is the job of the scientist to discover appropriate measures. We last saw him doing this at the end of the last chapter, when he set out to create a measure of the 'amount of decision' left to take in order to determine an outcome. But we saw it in the early passages of the book too. In particular, the wartime origins of OR stress the importance of discovering how to create measures which have had no conceptual existence, never mind usable measuring-rods, before. In most of the cases quoted, people may not have believed that a measure could be devised, but they would not necessarily have said that what had to be measured was not at all susceptible to measurement. Yet cases of this kind do occur. It has already been pointed out that the history of science discloses many examples of actual persecution based on the belief that certain things were strictly incommensurable.

Today the frontiers of measurement are commonly drawn this side of value judgments. Truth, beauty and goodness are notions that have always formed the cynosure of mankind's idealism, but assertions about them are strictly non-parametric to this day. The concept of truth has to some extent yielded to various forms of rigorous treatment: on the denary scales of arithmetical computation, on the binary scales of logical analysis, on the relative because tautologous scales of the mathematician, in the testing arguments of philosophers, and in the rules and evidence of law. Goodness, again, begins to yield to measurement in the sphere of social ethics if not that of private morals. This has come about because of a growing acceptance, in some form, of the proposition that the greatest good of the greatest number should be assured. Such a formulation of what is the good lends itself to mathematical treatment, and we have seen the emergence of cost-benefit analysis, in which an attempt is made to measure the advantage to the aggregate of citizens made available by public expenditure.

But of the trio of values which are the most admired, the concept of beauty remains altogether unmeasured. The notion is so pure, so subjective, so untainted with considerations of profit and loss, that most people will have nothing to do with the inclusion of aesthetic judgments in a scientific equation. Yet it is impossible to operate very long as a manager in the public or private sector of industry, or in government, without encountering a decision or a policy which involves aesthetic judgment. This may happen in one of two ways. Either the management of something intrinsically beautiful may be concerned, or the management of something prosaic may impinge on the beautiful. Consider an example of each case from the point of view of management science.

The management of an art gallery or a museum has an interesting function to perform. It owns, or has charge of, a vast number of beautiful things. These it exhibits to the public—because it has either a legal obligation or a public-spirited desire to do so. It is characteristic of such institutions to be impecunious; they rely for a perilous existence on public monies and private bequests. When in grave difficulty, they may decide to sell one of the treasures in their collection in order to raise funds—and a notorious case of this occurred in Britain in recent years. Now the professional manager has no *locus standi* with a board of trustees who may themselves be artists; still less has the scientist any acknowledged right to intervene. Art is for artists, and defies all kinds of logic. This view, interestingly, would probably be supported by the majority of people, and is not simply the delusion of the few concerned. Let us break through this thought block that surrounds aesthetics, and see what can be said about a problem of this kind without doing violence to artistic integrity.

In considering the matter objectively, the first point to note is that the art gallery or museum contains a priceless collection of objects. In the terms appropriate to a world of monetary measures, then, its assets are vast. Any other kind of institution with vast assets is almost automatically profitable, because its wealth is made to do useful work. Yet the art gallery, uniquely, finds itself in financial difficulties which it proposes to solve by selling off an asset. This would be patently mad management in any other context. The fact is, that the vast assets concerned constitute idle capital. This capital is set up to be admired in its aesthetic dimension, while its financial dimension is disdainfully treated as beneath the consideration of the artist. Nevertheless, the artist acknowledges a duty to enlighten the public when he displays the collection, and the public—in principle at least—regards this as a social good. Does this excuse the artist from doing the job incompetently?

Consider the typical gallery or museum. It has no entrance fee, which is laudable; we may admire the artists' altruism in granting free access to the world's most beautiful things, while noting, in passing, that this is the basic cause of his inability to produce revenue with which to enhance his activities. Next we note the forbidding character of the buildings that house the collection. There can surely be no doubt that many decent citizens have never been exposed to the joys of art because it would not occur to them to enter the mausoleum which houses the treasure. If they do go in, they are surrounded by an awesome silence, a clinical aesthetic considerations are a matter for subjective judgment. The Authority would not agree that a scientific approach to the matter had any bearing on the problem—nor would the lawyers involved in the legal enquiry. The legal mind will tell a jury that it must decide whether a man accused of a crime on the basis of circumstantial evidence is guilty or not 'according to the balance of probabilities'. But when it comes to a case of this kind, to account for the major causes of the citizen's objections is not enough. Either one must account for the whole of these objections, which is of course impossible because of the idiosyncratic nature of some small part of them, or one must rely upon guesswork and the bureaucratic machine. That people feel threatened when science begins to talk about value judgment was splendidly illustrated on this occasion by the words of learned counsel. He told the tribunal that to accept the method outlined above 'would reduce public enquiries to an absolute farce'.

And so it would. Indeed, there would be no need for public enquiries if people would adopt a rational approach to problems. The head of the electricity authority declared that people would resent the proposed method. But the people whose rights were affected in the sample case were already resentful; resentful in particular of the fact that a rational approach to the problem had never been made. Rationality ought always to begin with those who have the responsibility in any situation, and it is part of their responsibility to persuade the public that their rational approach is indeed rational. In this case history, however, the reply to the enquiry made by the head of the Authority explicitly eschewed rationality. He said of the OR technique employed: 'The end product would never be more than an elaborate way of stating what must always remain a matter of individual judgment.' But with whose individual judgment ought we to be concerned?—that of bureaucrats and experts in landscape gardening, or of the people whose rights are affected? If the latter, then an elaborate way of stating them so that all are taken into account is just what is required.

It was said earlier that a computer programme would be able to discover optimal routes very quickly, and indeed the example quoted had taken exactly a week to solve from first to last. But the head of the Authority said: 'The studies would be very time consuming.' In fact, the established processes by which this case was actually decided (and decided contrarily, incidentally, to the wishes of the objectors) took a total of four and a half years from the time when the original intention was published to the time when the minister gave his verdict. By the use of operational research, it would be possible to evaluate the opportunity cost to the nation of all this delay, of all this argument and of tribunals supported by a battery of counsel and other legal and professional gentlemen and witnesses. But people are not ready to admit that a delay of this magnitude actually costs anything, and doubtless the OR methods used to evaluate that would be stigmatized as invading the field of value judgment.

The point of this chapter bears repeating: the future of the scientific approach to management depends in the long run on the practicability of the practical man.

4   A Philosophical Model

The concluding remarks of this long book sum up the issues that have been before us in terms of practicability for one clear reason. Management of every kind of enterprise, from the smallest firm to national and international government, is for the most part in the hands of people who do not know what science has accomplished in the management field—and who would not believe it if they did. Still less have these people made any attempt to evaluate the meaning and the potential of such a discipline as operational research, or such a science as cybernetics. They find it easy to shrug off the demonstrations and the arguments of scientists by declaring them, *ex cathedra,* to be impracticable. This leaves the scientist with a moral duty to return the charge. For there are whole firms and whole countries that are slowly but steadily collapsing under the ineptitude of their impracticable policies; and it is hard not to think that the same may be true of mankind itself. It is of course a predictable thought block, and a major cause of this very impracticability, that people should say there is no evidence of this.

Some preliminary explanations have already been given as to why, in certain circumstances, management decisions 'cannot be wrong'. The reason turned out to be the conceptual isolation of a system which is in reality interacting with other systems—whose existence the management implicitly denies. The same mechanism can be observed in certain matters of government. In the first half of the decade 1960–1970, there was a growth of affluence in Great Britain which made it easy for most citizens to believe that everything was satisfactory. This is because they were not ready to look outside the national system, and to observe it as a sub-system of an international system. The external trading deficit of some £40,000,000 in 1963 became one of £800,000,000 in 1964. Yet the outgoing government at the end of the latter year solemnly declared that the economic situation had never been better. When mankind as a whole is concerned, there is a conspicuous lack of a world government atmosphere, which is daunting in the extreme. It is also engagingly different from the atmosphere which most of the artists who produced the treasures are at all likely to have approved. Most important of all, however, the citizen who does enter is confronted with such a wealth of riches that he is quite unable to assimilate them. By the time he passes through the third gallery, he will not bat an eyelid on being confronted by Rembrandt. Hence although the trustees accept a duty to give the public free access to the treasure house, and even go to some lengths to educate the public by means of lectures and catalogues, they do not go so far as to consider how the public enlightenment should most competently be done. Or, if they do consider this question, their solutions are deplorable.

This is no more than the old problem of considering part of a system instead of the whole. The holistic approach must take into account the effect of laudable policies *towards* the public *on* the public: it is at this point that these policies dismally fail. If the object is to communicate art to people, then it is competent to begin by asking what the target people are like. If this is not done, then what is apparently altruistic becomes the most nauseating arrogance. People at large do not understand art, nor can they cope with abstract statements about it. This is a scientific observation: it is open to test and experiment and to the formulation of hypotheses by psychologists. What people can understand about a particular work of art, the psychologist might well say, begins with the progenitor artist. Who he was, how he lived, what led him to do what he did, how he did it, and so forth, are topics which capture the interest of people. We are now on the track of the kind of investigation which a management scientist could make on behalf of the trustees of a gallery or museum. Let us fill out the picture.

The starting point is a psychological model of a stratified public in their relationship to aesthetic stimulation. The target population consists of those people who do not visit galleries, or those who, if they do, go there because the place is a tourist attraction. We shall not be concerned with the small minority of people who visit the gallery because they already love its treasures. Some art administrators would at once complain: why bother with this vast crowd of Philistines? Apart from ethical imperatives, which are severe, the answer is entirely practical. These same men who take a condescending attitude to the general public will next be complaining that the modern world is ugly, that buildings, furniture and decorations have no style and are in execrable taste. They cannot have it both ways. So the target population has been identified and a psychological model of its way of approaching art is being devised. Next there ought to be a model of social peregrination. By this is meant the typical pattern of movement undertaken by these people during their spare time. An art gallery that is ten miles from that part of town in which these people move will never attract them inside.

Pass then to the idea that space could be taken by the art institution where people actually are: in the midst of a shopping centre, or theatre-land, or for that matter an amusement park. And here comes the first economic point. If people are psychologically overwhelmed by many exhibits, and if one single exhibit is really 'worth' the huge sum of money for which it would change hands in the open market, then there is no need to show more than one masterpiece at a time. Using the psychological model, it becomes possible to work out how the exhibit should be displayed. First of all, the citizen passing this arcade will be beckoned by its external advertising. This will *not* declare: 'The trustees of the Flötsenheim Collection in collaboration with the Worshipful Company of Lapidary Masons and the archaeological department of the University of Thrace present an exhibition of statuary of the Sixteenth Olympiad.' It will say: 'Come inside and see the Thrace Venus: a world masterpiece.' Within, there will be a lengthy and carefully organized presentation, based on what the psychological model discovers that people can understand and enjoy. There might well be an account of the place and the time, of the artist and his tools, of the mode of discovery, and so on indefinitely. The visitor will be brought to a high pitch of excitement, and will finally be confronted with the masterpiece, set in perfect conditions; if a statue, then possibly revolving under a pro-gramme of lights. When this is properly done, these people will not for-get what they have seen. The associations will be correct, as well. They will remember the context of excitement and gaiety, of noise and colour. (Perhaps the first thing that these specimen administrators should under-stand is that the ordinary man's notion of enjoyment cannot be recon-ciled with a funereal atmosphere.)

The operation envisaged will cost a great deal. The money will be subscribed in entrance fees—which people will gladly pay. By all means permit schoolchildren and old-age pensioners free entrance; but make the general public pay a high price. Again, this is an economic point: people are conditioned to the almost universal fact that very valuable things and experience are very costly; therefore what is not costly is not valuable. Nor is this policy a betrayal of altruism. For this masterpiece will be back in its accustomed place in the gallery in a month's time, to be replaced by another. The people who really want to see it for nothing can do so then. Now, please note, the assets are beginning to work for the administration. A few exhibitions of this kind, running simultaneously and touring the country (another duty resting on the trustees which is seldom discharged), would make all the money required by the administrators. It could be used to rehouse the main collection properly; to provide adequate security; to make aesthetic appreciation a joy.

Surely no terrible violence is done to art by this policy. Equally surely, the policy would not pay off unless the job were competently done. It is not a matter, any longer, for art experts to decide how the policy should be implemented; it is a matter for management science, for the model-building faculty which knows how to deal with a communication system. Nor does that assertion detract from the prestige of the artist, rather the reverse. He is the man who creates the masterpiece and who conserves it; he is the man who knows enough to display its merit to the public. His prestige and recognition are enhanced by the project. But these are simply the thoughts provoked by the absurdities of the situation which exists and was rehearsed at the beginning. If responsible people really cared about sharing their private joy with the public ignorance, if they really wanted standards of art and design to improve, they would embark on research that could lead to a viable answer. And yet, that remark is naïve. The artist, the art administrator tells the scientist, knows best. There must not be any collaboration between them. Leonardo is dead these 500 years; and the artists who gain control of collections are not those who think it fun to design sewers, submarines and aeroplanes.

Turn now to the parallel problem: the management decision about some other matter which becomes ensnared in aesthetic considerations and is abandoned to subjective judgment. As an example, consider the problem of installing a new power-line carrying cables on pylons across the countryside. Economically, the optimal route is the shortest practical route; but aesthetic considerations arise which turn the optimal route into something longer than the most economic route.

An operational research enquiry into an actual case of a 5-mile stretch of line revealed the following facts. The authority concerned had routed the line between *A* and *B* in an economic fashion, and had then taken specialist advice on the aesthetic disturbance it created. No doubt they took an honest opinion. By law, the proposed route must be advertised in a newspaper column, to await objections. In the case reviewed, these were forthcoming. The householders in the area objected to the route and refused to grant way-leave. They objected that it was insufficient to consider the effect of the power-line on the general beauty of the countryside; they were the owners of the land concerned, and their individual viewpoints should be taken into account. The effect of the line on the view from all individual habitations should be considered, said the owners. But the Authority did not even know where these now were—it was discovered that they had been using maps more than forty years old. A deadlock developed and the legal machinery of public enquiries, to be followed by a ministerial decision, was set in motion.

So the question arises whether it is practicable to devise a measure of the aesthetic disturbance of any proposed route to the individuals who have rights in the matter. If so, it should be possible by scientific method to determine that route which would minimize the aggregate disturbance to them all. It is necessary to begin, not with the arbitrary judgments of an expert about what spoils the view, but with an analysis of the particular attitudes of people whose rights are to be protected. In the history being quoted, only a short stretch of line was involved for illustrative purposes; therefore not many householders and landowners were concerned. But pilot research indicated that, for these people at any rate, what was offensive about a power-line was its protrusion above the horizon. If the pylons and the lines were set against a background of countryside, they were not obtrusive; if they were visible against the sky then they were. This simple criterion accounted for most of the aesthetic disturbance caused to those who were affected. There were indications of other factors too, of course. By taking account of various kinds of background and the direction of the sun, of viewpoints other than habitations (such as beauty spots)—weighted if necessary by the number of people visiting them—nearly all the variation in judgment could have been accounted for. But, for this pilot project, the argument about horizons was considered alone.

The OR team took its model from the science of optics. Detailed maps of the countryside indicate all the habitations involved, and supply an automatic coding system for describing their location through a map reference; moreover, the convolutions of the terrain are also coded by the contour lines on the map. Using this quantified account of the terrain as a topographic model, together with the model from optics, to generalize lines of sight to the horizon, it obviously becomes possible to find a line which minimizes aesthetic disturbance (by this measure) for each house separately; and a little mathematical technique enables the identification of the optimal route for the aggregate of those concerned. The use of these two models, complicated or constrained as necessary by further factors such as those suggested, inside an electronic computer, would make the task of discovering the optimal line for long distances perfectly feasible.

But now the thought blocks come into play. It is well known that aesthetic considerations are a matter for subjective judgment. The Authority would not agree that a scientific approach to the matter had any bearing on the problem—nor would the lawyers involved in the legal enquiry. The legal mind will tell a jury that it must decide whether a man accused of a crime on the basis of circumstantial evidence is guilty or not 'according to the balance of probabilities'. But when it comes to a case of this kind, to account for the major causes of the citizen's objections is not enough. Either one must account for the whole of these objections, which is of course impossible because of the idiosyncratic nature of some small part of them, or one must rely upon guesswork and the bureaucratic machine. That people feel threatened when science begins to talk about value judgment was splendidly illustrated on this occasion by the words of learned counsel. He told the tribunal that to accept the method outlined above 'would reduce public enquiries to an absolute farce'.

And so it would. Indeed, there would be no need for public enquiries if people would adopt a rational approach to problems. The head of the electricity authority declared that people would resent the proposed method. But the people whose rights were affected in the sample case were already resentful; resentful in particular of the fact that a rational approach to the problem had never been made. Rationality ought always to begin with those who have the responsibility in any situation, and it is part of their responsibility to persuade the public that their rational approach is indeed rational. In this case history, however, the reply to the enquiry made by the head of the Authority explicitly eschewed rationality. He said of the OR technique employed: 'The end product would never be more than an elaborate way of stating what must always remain a matter of individual judgment.' But with whose individual judgment ought we to be concerned?—that of bureaucrats and experts in landscape gardening, or of the people whose rights are affected? If the latter, then an elaborate way of stating them so that all are taken into account is just what is required.

It was said earlier that a computer programme would be able to discover optimal routes very quickly, and indeed the example quoted had taken exactly a week to solve from first to last. But the head of the Authority said: 'The studies would be very time consuming.' In fact, the established processes by which this case was actually decided (and decided contrarily, incidentally, to the wishes of the objectors) took a total of four and a half years from the time when the original intention was published to the time when the minister gave his verdict. By the use of operational research, it would be possible to evaluate the opportunity cost to the nation of all this delay, of all this argument and of tribunals supported by a battery of counsel and other legal and professional gentlemen and witnesses. But people are not ready to admit that a delay of this magnitude actually costs anything, and doubtless the OR methods used to evaluate that would be stigmatized as invading the field of value judgment.

The point of this chapter bears repeating: the future of the scientific approach to management depends in the long run on the practicability of the practical man.

4   A Philosophical Model

The concluding remarks of this long book sum up the issues that have been before us in terms of practicability for one clear reason. Management of every kind of enterprise, from the smallest firm to national and international government, is for the most part in the hands of people who do not know what science has accomplished in the management field—and who would not believe it if they did. Still less have these people made any attempt to evaluate the meaning and the potential of such a discipline as operational research, or such a science as cybernetics. They find it easy to shrug off the demonstrations and the arguments of scientists by declaring them, *ex cathedra,* to be impracticable. This leaves the scientist with a moral duty to return the charge. For there are whole firms and whole countries that are slowly but steadily collapsing under the ineptitude of their impracticable policies; and it is hard not to think that the same may be true of mankind itself. It is of course a predictable thought block, and a major cause of this very impracticability, that people should say there is no evidence of this.

Some preliminary explanations have already been given as to why, in certain circumstances, management decisions 'cannot be wrong'. The reason turned out to be the conceptual isolation of a system which is in reality interacting with other systems—whose existence the management implicitly denies. The same mechanism can be observed in certain matters of government. In the first half of the decade 1960–1970, there was a growth of affluence in Great Britain which made it easy for most citizens to believe that everything was satisfactory. This is because they were not ready to look outside the national system, and to observe it as a sub-system of an international system. The external trading deficit of some £40,000,000 in 1963 became one of £800,000,000 in 1964. Yet the outgoing government at the end of the latter year solemnly declared that the economic situation had never been better. When mankind as a whole is concerned, there is a conspicuous lack of a world government which could possibly consider the systemic whole. The international institutions we have so far been able to evolve look at the totality through sectarian eyes. Therefore national blocs are able to pretend that problems of the total system which are indeed terrifyingly intractable will never result in their inevitable outcomes—because, presumably, some other bloc will give way, or will otherwise resolve them. Individuals endowed with much foresight, such as succeeding Secretaries-General of the United Nations, have been aware of the truth and have dedicated their lives to its dissemination. But the leaders of the sub-systemic elements seem content to hurtle towards the edge of the cliff like a pack of Gadarene swine. Quite apart from the capability of the scientific method, the international communion of scientists has perhaps a clearer view of this scene than most sub-sets of people. But so long as these scientists are regarded as impracticable, mankind may yet settle for a sort of practicability which will mean death and disaster.

A possible model that would reflect this dilemma, and might illuminate the reasons for it and the resolution of it, is drawn from philosophy. It may be remembered that one of the false dichotomies (and this is the penultimate that will be quoted here) which attended the development of man's serious thinking for thousands of years was the dichotomy of mind and matter. Savants could be either materialists, who believed in a physical universe and regarded mental events as some kind of excrescence; or they could be idealists, who believed that the totality of existence was mental, and that all matter was a projection of mental states. Some, such as Leibnitz, tried to resolve the dilemma in the notion of psychophysical parallelism. They could not encompass the unnatural idea that either mind or matter must be delusory, but, like everyone else, they were unable to show how the two modes of existence might interact. Therefore Leibnitz spoke of a pre-established harmony, a mutual correspondence, between soul and body. These seventeenth-century stirrings began a movement which triumphs in modern science in the rejection of the false dichotomy itself. Even now, however, some learned people who considered themselves to be faced with an apparent choice would adopt the subjective idealist viewpoint. According to this, mind alone exists; and the justification for this belief rests in the fact that on careful analysis the individual thinker finds that he has no evidence of anything other than his own mental states. He does not, after all, know *things*; he knows his perceptions of things. So although there is evidence of perceptions, the existence of the things perceived has been inferred—and may be mistaken.

Now those who adopted the subjective idealist viewpoint found themselves driven by the logic of their own theory towards the startling conclusion known as solipsism. If there is no evidence that *things* exist for the reason given, then equally there is no evidence that other people exist; the only existence of which the perceiving 'I' has any real evidence is its own. 'Therefore', says the solipsist, 'I alone exist and the entire universe is a projection of my imagination.' It can be argued, or at any rate used to be said, that the solipsist position was impregnable. If someone chose to adopt it, there was no way of dissuading him. If for example one were to beat the solipsist over the head with his own textbook, he would say that in 'creating' you he must (in his other role as God) have endowed you with free will. There is a logical attraction about the whole argument, and it says much for the good sense of philosophers that no serious school of solipsism ever emerged. The position was regarded, instead, as a theoretical possibility worth discussion. And this was just as well, for there seems to be no objective test whereby one could distinguish a genuinely convinced solipsist from a raving psychotic.

The posture of solipsism provides the model of bad management that is proposed. The mapping is this. When someone declares that everything is a projection of his own mind, he means that everything he knows about maps on to the model in his mind of the world as he knows it. The kind of management, and the kind of government, against which these concluding remarks object is precisely of this form. It is the scientist who knows that the real world cannot possibly map on to his model of the world, because the laws of communication theory prove conclusively that his brain has not requisite variety. But the bad manager is one who acts as if he believed that his conceptual model of the world really did encompass the real world. This is how it happens that the very taking of a decision can *mean* that the decision is right. For any evidence generated in the real world that the decision is in fact wrong does not belong to the model of the world which the manager entertains, and can therefore not be mapped on to his brain. He himself would say that he might be wrong; and he would agree with the scientist that, if he is, the rest of experience will show that his policy has failed. The interesting thing is that this never happens. One of the reasons for this is that the sub-group of people to which this man belongs shares the same model, which is fixed by the conventions of the social group. Therefore if *A* does something which he believes to be right, *B* will believe it to be right as well; the model they share says it is right. If the real world is meanwhile protesting that the decision is wrong, there may be no means of registering the fact with either the manager or his peers.

For example, a man believes that capital punishment is a deterrent to murderers, and he believes it because he acts as if he were a solipsist. The murderer is none other than himself; he knows that murder is wicked; if he commits murder then he has violated his own principles to a degree where death may be the only escape from guilt, and where the fear of death may be the only deterrent. It is useless to protest to such a man that murderers are not like him or they would not be committing murders. It is useless to say that there is scientific evidence to show that capital punishment is not a deterrent. In the limiting case, for instance, a murderer may not consider any consequences at all, so consumed is he with the notion of disposing of his victim. But our friend knows that people *do* consider consequences; it is useless to tell him that they do not. He himself considers consequences, and if he were going to commit a murder no doubt the threat of capital punishment would deter him. But he is not going to commit a murder. The intellectual position is impenetrable in exactly the same way that the solipsist position is impenetrable: one can do nothing about it. Moreover, in appealing to his peers, this man can be sure that they will reflect his judgment—for they suffer from the same kind of solipsist blindness. The whole group consists of people assuring each other that this view is right, and the positive feedback imparts a gain to the system which may well end, and has been seen to end, in hysteria. The lynching party is such a group of solipsist opinion-holders that has, however, turned to horrifying action.

The game of solipsist management is unreal; it is fought out 'in the mind'. And it is unassailable in an isolated system. Thus a firm consisting of a collection of subsidiary companies may opt for solipsism; an industry, likewise; a nation, certainly. Occasionally, sub-systems outside these sub-systems may impinge on the workings of the solipsist group. This happens when what they are doing maps on to what the group is doing so precisely that their influence breaks through the solipsist circularity. We call this state of affairs *competition*. Now it is characteristic of a healthy firm or nation to evaluate competition for what it is: another firm or nation that is threatening us because it bids fair to do the job we are doing more effectively. The healthy response is to improve what we are doing to the point where the competition is beaten. On the contrary, however, it is characteristic of solipsist management to categorize any such competition as 'unfair'. This is simply a way of saying that the competition does not count, a way of maintaining the solipsist attitude. Whole industries sometimes do this. It is, perhaps, no accident that the British shipbuilders, at the time when their output was being surpassed by the German shipbuilders, claimed that the latter had an unfair advantage, because all their shipyards had been dismantled as a result of the Second World War—they were in the extremely fortunate position of having to start all over again. Japanese shipbuilders, said some British shipbuilders, offered unfair competition because everyone knows that Japanese labour costs virtually nothing: they live on rice. In fact labour costs are high in Japan, and the conditions of shipworkers are excellent; but facts are not allowed to count. Arguments of this kind are insane in exactly the way that the solipsist is insane.

We may change the model at this point to another, drawn from the theory of games. Under certain conditions, it is true to say that a game with complete information has a unique and discoverable optimal strategy. Intuiting this, the solipsist management group pretends to itself that the game it plays is a game of complete information (when it clearly is not). To an observer who is mapping this game of quasi-complete information into the genuine game that is actually going on, the decisions of the solipsist management must appear absurd, for they do not react to real-life threats, which solipsism of course ignores. The result is that one should not accuse this kind of management of being irrational, but of being arational. That is to say, its decisions are not contrary to reason but devoid of it.

Solipsist management is the ultimate kind of impracticability. Some people would say that the protagonists of science in management have oversold their approach and the value of their work. Such people will certainly put this book into that category. No doubt, because I speak from conviction and alarm, I am culpable. But the shortcomings of an author do not necessarily detract from the value of his arguments, and the people who react against them are much more interesting. There is a tired, I-have-seen-it-all-before attitude displayed by many who are confronted with the facts of management science, its achievements and potentialities. The people who take this attitude are sometimes good scientists who cannot sell their ability; sometimes they are managers who have not really understood the point. For in fact there is nothing to oversell.

Why have I not laboured to expound the limitations of the scientific approach? It is not because there are no limitations, but because the question is irrelevant. The claim is not that science can do anything, or offers the answer to everything. The claim is simply that it is competent in managers to use the knowledge which mankind has systematically accrued (which it calls science) wherever this knowledge is needed, and not to resort to guesswork through ignorance of what that knowledge is. Certainly there are decisions to be taken and policies to be formulated to which science can contribute little or nothing. But there is no need to try and classify them. Management stands in no need of a system for categorizing problems into those with which science can help and those which it must face alone. For the object of this work is a collaborative object. The manager who seeks to be competent will keep his various advisers informed of the state of affairs and of his policies, and listen to their observations. If he wishes to employ an astrologer for the purpose, that is a matter for him. Personally, I would as soon consult the entrails of a chicken as try to work within the solipsist model of my own insights. If the scientist is lucky enough to be included among the manager's advisers, he will speak when there is something to say. The manager may accept or reject his advice, but it is sheer incompetence to ignore it or to pretend that it does not exist. The claim, therefore, is in reality modest. The idea that management must either hand over its responsibilities to science or else throw the scientist downstairs is the very last of the false dichotomies.

In particular, it is impracticable in the manager to demand from science a level of performance that is unattainable in a real world, and which laughably exceeds the possibilities open to management as things are. It is a common experience for operational research men to be told that the model they have been expounding is no use because some of the data needed to quantify it will perforce be inaccurate. Yet the management is already taking decisions and formulating policies; it is doing so despite the inaccuracy—and in the absence of much other information which the OR study makes available. The use of science can hardly make these matters worse. On the contrary, its use will ensure that the utmost value is wrung out of whatever knowledge the management has. Competence is the best one can do. To do less than this best is incompetent.

The genuinely practical man, then, is he who sees himself and his enterprise in the context of the total system. He is not a solipsist manager; he is not a solipsist scientist. The genuinely practical man today is one who sees a world made small by the speed and availability of every kind of communication as it really is, and who knows what part he has to play within it. He is one who sees, and does not fail to register, that half the population of this world is undernourished; who sees, and does not ignore, the fact that the world population will double by the end of this century. The policies of the world do not see these things; the decisions of nations ignore them. Given an iota of practicability, and that includes a glimmer of understanding of what science has to say, a man has only to look ahead to the future of his own grand-children to see a vastly congested globe, racked with psychological tensions, short of room, short of food, grown stale and incipiently poisoned in a sea of its own effluent.

The practical man will want to take practical action. The scientist stands ready to help him.

INDEX

551